COMPLETE
National Parks
OF THE UNITED STATES

COMPLETE
National Parks
OF THE UNITED STATES

*Featuring 400+ Parks, Monuments, Battlefields, Historic Sites,
Scenic Trails, Recreation Areas, and Seashores*

MEL WHITE

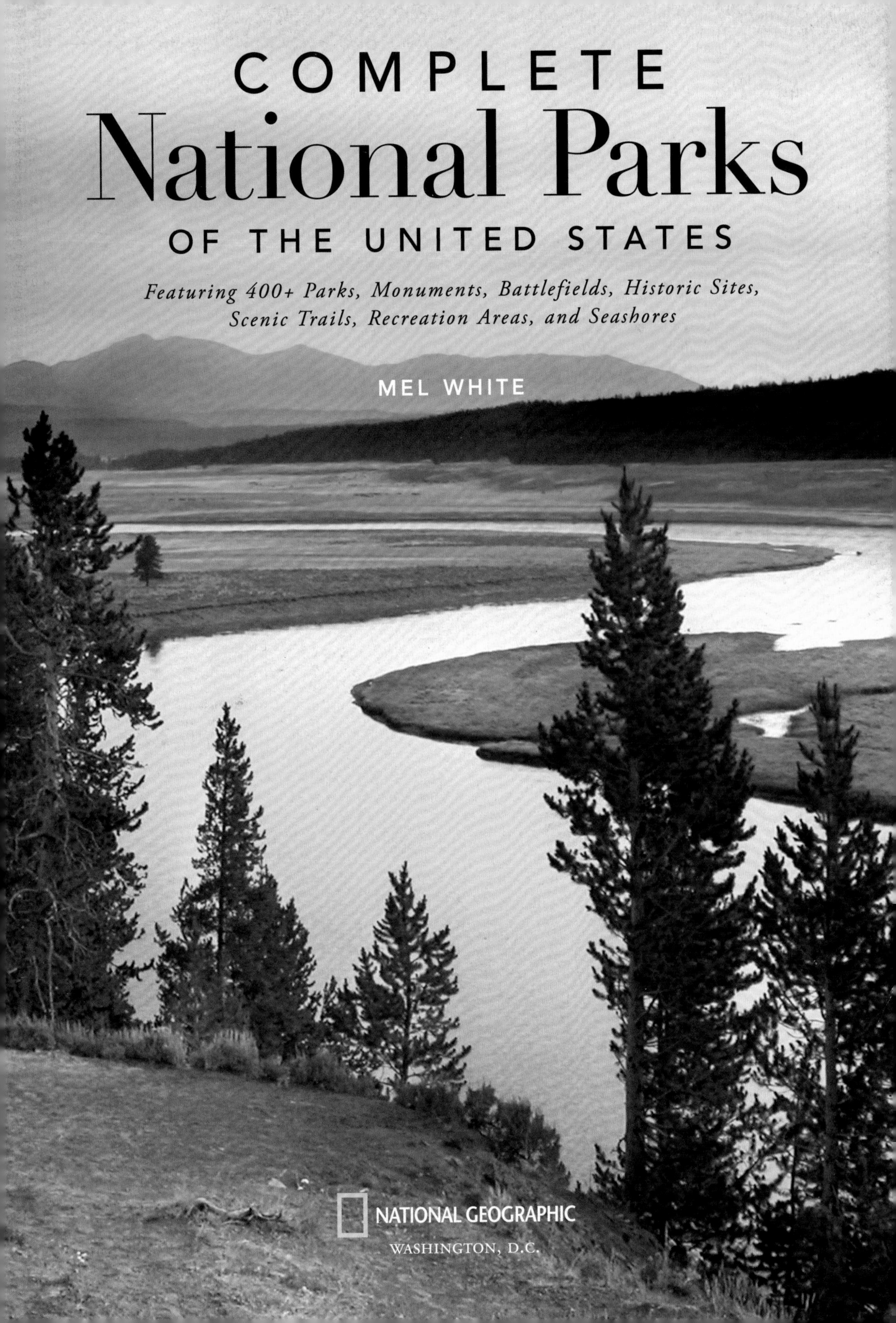

NATIONAL GEOGRAPHIC

WASHINGTON, D.C.

CONTENTS

Nauset Beach Light,
Cape Cod National Seashore, MA

NORTHEAST   12

MIDDLE ATLANTIC   78

SOUTHEAST   130

GREAT LAKES   200

Common loon, Apostle Islands
National Lakeshore, WI

Evergreen at twilight,
Voyageurs National Park, MN

Brook saxifrage,
Gates of the Arctic National Park, AK

PAGES 2–3: *Bison grazing along the Yellowstone River, Yellowstone National Park, WY*
FOLLOWING PAGE: *Cannon on autumn battlefield at Pea Ridge National Military Park, Garfield, AR*

FIND YOUR PARK

I love Zion National Park. So while reading this book I began nodding in vigorous agreement when author Mel White stated that the trek to the summit of Zion's 5,790-foot Angels Landing "is not for the faint of heart."

That trail can be terrifying. The footing is slippery and sheer thousand-foot plunges are often only inches away. The final half-mile follows a spine of rock so narrow that the Park Service has thoughtfully anchored support chains there. I reached for them with grateful if trembling hands. How quickly fear becomes exhilaration. Emerging onto the summit I came upon that sublime panorama of red cliffs and deep gorges that, engraved in my memory, quite literally remains one of the peak experiences of my life.

I also love the Grand Canyon. I'll never forget a "rim-to-rim" hike I once made with five of my best friends. As we wound down and then up the steep rocky paths every turn of the trail brought its own stupendous vista of butte and spire and mesa stretching to the horizon. Even more memorably, I later camped for three nights on the canyon floor, accompanied only by my two sons and the unceasing murmur of a Colorado River still at the same task it began some 17 million years ago.

Because I treasure such experiences I think of Zion and Grand Canyon as my national parks, mine in the sense that they are places that have touched me profoundly. No doubt millions of other people might make the same claim. Yet millions more might long for equally meaningful encounters in spots charged with natural or historical significance. That's why the National Park Service today is urging everyone to go out and "Find Your Park."

Be it biking in Rock Creek Park in the nation's capital, or discovering history at the *Brown* v. *Board of Education* National Historic Site in Kansas, or boating across the Lake Roosevelt National Recreation Area in Washington, the National Park Service has more than 400 units to discover.

I can't think of a better place to start your quest to find your park than with this second edition of National Geographic's *Complete National Parks of the United States*. It remains National Geographic's most comprehensive compendium to every single property administered as part of our far-flung national park system. And that's saying something, for not only have we published more than 500 books, articles, and maps on the parks—not to mention our new app as well as film and television efforts—but we have also enjoyed a remarkable partnership with the Park Service itself, one forged a century ago.

It was 1915 when our pioneering editor, Gilbert H. Grosvenor, having gazed awestruck at giant sequoia trees during a pack trip into California's Sierra Nevada, first enlisted this Society in the crusade to preserve such marvels. He dedicated an entire issue of *National Geographic* magazine—April 1916's "Land of the Best," enhanced with a two-foot long pictorial supplement of a sequoia—to showcasing America's scenic wonders. Tellingly, he placed a copy in the hand of each senator and representative in Washington. Few, apparently, could resist those pages, for only a few months later, on August 25, 1916, President Woodrow Wilson signed the act creating the National Park Service.

Over the succeeding decades National Geographic funding helped preserve key components of Sequoia National Park. Our lobbying was instrumental in the creation of Redwood National Park. And it was one of our expeditions that discovered Alaska's spectacular Valley of Ten Thousand Smokes, today enshrined in Katmai National Park.

Visit the famous Mesa Verde National Park, where the incredible cliff dwellings you'll see at Wetherill Mesa were first surveyed, restored, and opened to the public thanks to a Geographic grant. Or drop by Russell Cave National Monument in Alabama, site of some of the earliest evidence of human occupation in the eastern U.S., and take in the Gilbert H. Grosvenor Visitor Center, a fitting tribute to that long partnership.

Yes, even National Geographic has its special parks. And with this guide in hand, there is no reason why you can't find one, too.

—John M. Fahey, Jr.

Chairman of the Board, National Geographic Society
Commissioner, National Parks Second Century Commission

North Cascades

Olympic

PACIFIC

OCEAN

Glacier

Canada
U.S.

Mount Rainier

WASHINGTON

MONTANA

Theodore
Roosevelt

NORTH DAKOTA

N O R T H W E S T
pp. 448–499

MIDWES
pp. 228–257

O R E G O N

Crater Lake

I D A H O

Yellowstone

Grand Teton

SOUTH
DAKOTA

Redwood

W Y O M I N G

Wind Cave

Badlands

Lassen Volcanic

FAR WEST & PACIFIC
pp. 384–447

N E V A D A

U T A H

Rocky
Mountain

N E B R A S K A

Yosemite

Great Basin

Capitol Reef

Arches

Black Canyon
of the Gunnison

K A N S A S

Bryce Canyon

Kings Canyon

Pinnacles

Canyonlands

COLO.

Death Valley

Zion

Sequoia

Mesa
Verde

Great Sand Dunes

SOUTH
CENTRAL
pp. 258–297

Grand
Canyon

Channel
Islands

OKLAH

Joshua Tree

A R I Z O N A

Petrified
Forest

N E W   M E X I C O

U.S.
Mexico

Saguaro

SOUTHWEST
pp. 298–383

Carlsbad
Caverns

T E X A S

Guadalupe
Mountains

Big Bend

U.S.
Mexico

A R C T I C   O C E A N

0   mi   200
0   km   200

Russia

Bering Strait

Gates
of the
Arctic

Canada
U.S.

Kobuk
Valley

A L A S K A

Denali

Lake Clark

Wrangell-St. Elias

ALASKA
pp. 500–535

Bering Sea

Kenai Fjords

Glacier Bay

Katmai

Gulf of Alaska

PACIFIC   OCEAN

THE NATIONAL PARK SYSTEM

Voyageurs

Isle Royale

Lake Superior

MINNESOTA

WISCONSIN

M
I
C
H
I
G
A
N

Lake Michigan

Lake Huron

MAINE

Acadia

Canada
U.S.

VT.

N.H.

Gulf of
Maine

IOWA

ILLINOIS

IND.

OHIO

Cuyahoga
Valley

Lake Erie

Lake Ontario

NEW YORK

MASS.

CONN.

R.I.

NORTHEAST
pp. 12–77

N.J.

DEL.

**MIDDLE
ATLANTIC**
pp. 78–129

MD.

**GREAT
LAKES**
pp. 200–227

MISSOURI

ARKANSAS

MISS.

Mammoth
Cave

KENTUCKY

W.VA.
Shenandoah

VA.

PENNSYLVANIA

ATLANTIC

OCEAN

Hot
Springs

TENNESSEE

ALABAMA

Great
Smoky
Mts.

NORTH CAROLINA

Congaree

S.C.

GEORGIA

OMA

OT

T

LOUISIANA

F
L
O
R
I
D
A

SOUTHEAST
pp. 130–199

MAP KEY

■ National Park System

▪ Affiliated area

*A map of the National
Trails System appears on
pages 536 and 537.*

Gulf of Mexico

Everglades

Dry Tortugas

Biscayne

PUERTO RICO
and the U.S. VIRGIN IS.   pp. 194–199

*Atlantic
Ocean*

Virgin Islands

U.K.
Virgin Is.

U.S.

Isla
Mona
(P.R.)

Puerto
Rico
(U.S.)

Caribbean Sea

*Park Service units in
Puerto Rico and the
U.S. Virgin Islands are
included in the
Southeast chapter.*

HAWAI'I   pp. 428–438

Kaua'i

Ni'ihau

O'ahu

Pearl Harbor

Moloka'i

Lāna'i

Kaho'olawe

Maui

Haleakalā

PACIFIC OCEAN

Hawai'i

Hawai'i Volcanoes

*Hawai'i and Park
Service units in the
Pacific are included in
the Far West chapter.*

miles

0 100 200 300

kilometers

0 100 200 300

MAP KEYS

REGIONAL MAP KEY

National Park System

Affiliated area

UNESCO World Heritage site

Country capital

State capital

Other city

PARK MAP KEY and ABBREVIATIONS

National Park (N.P.)
National Park and Preserve (N.P. & Pres.)
National Preserve (Nat. Pres.)
National Conservation Area (N.C.A.)
National Historical Park (N.H.P.)
National Historic Site (N.H.S.)
National Lakeshore (N.L.)
National Memorial (Nat. Mem.)
National Monument (Nat. Mon.)
National Natural Landmark (N.N.L.)
National Recreation Area (N.R.A.)
National Seashore (N.S.)

National Grassland (N.G.)

National Forest (N.F.)
National Recreation Area (N.R.A.)
National Volcanic Monument (N.V.M.)
State Forest (S.F.)

National Wildlife Refuge (N.W.R.)
National Wildlife Range
State Game Refuge
State Game Sanctuary (S.G.S.)
State Wildlife Area
Habitat Area
Wildlife Management Area (W.M.A.)

Bureau of Land Management (B.L.M.)
National Monument (Nat. Mon.)
National Recreation Area (N.R.A.)

State Park (S.P.)
State Historic Site (S.H.S.)
State Primitive Park
State Recreation Area (S.R.A.)
State Wilderness Park (S.W.P.)
Provincial Park (P.P.)
County Park

Indian Reservation (I.R.)
Reserve (Canada)

Built-up Area

U.S. Interstate

U.S. Federal, State or Provincial Highway

Other road

Unpaved road

Trail

Ferry

Railroad / Tram

Continental Divide

Fault line

Park boundary over water

National Marine Sanctuary

National Wild & Scenic River

Military reservation

National boundary

State boundary

State capital
Provincial capital

Ranger station
Visitor center
Park headquarters

Point of interest

Elevation

Pass

Tunnel

Dam

Intermittent river

Intermittent lake

Dry lake

Sand dunes

Falls

Spring

Geyser

Glacier

Swamp

Reef

Shipwreck

OTHER ABBREVIATIONS

Admin.	Administrative	L.	Lake	P.P.	Provincial Park
AVE.	Avenue	M.	Middle	PRES.	Preserve
BLVD.	Boulevard	Mem.	Memorial	Pt.	Point
Cr.	Creek	Mt.-s.	Mountain-s	R.	River
Dep.	Department	Mus.	Museum	Ra.	Range
DR.	Drive	N.	North	RD.	Road
E.	East	NAT.	National	Rec.	Recreation
Eco.	Ecological	N.H.C.	National Heritage Corridor	Res.	Reservoir
Fk.	Fork	N.M.S.	National Marine Sanctuary	S.	South
ft.	feet	N.S.R.	National Science Reserve	ST.	Street
Gl.	Glacier	N.S.T.	National Scenic Trail	Str.	Stream
Hdqrs.	Headquarters	N.W. & S.R.	National Wild and Scenic River	TERR.	Territory
HWY.	Highway	Pk.	Peak	TR.	Trail
I.-s.	Island-s	PKWY.	Parkway	U.S.F.S.	United States Forest Service
Intl.	International			W.	West

USING THIS BOOK

National Geographic's *Complete National Parks of the United States* is designed to be a concise, practical, and easy-to-use compendium of all properties within the National Park System. The book can serve as both a travel planner and a resource guide to our national parks.

For ease in planning your trip, you'll find a national map at the front of the book with chapter breakdowns; as well as a regional map, with all sites listed at the beginning of each chapter. In addition, you can find the states listed in the table of contents.

The book is divided by region, and within each region by state. The national park sites are then listed alphabetically. In the case of properties located within two or more states, check the index for their locations.

Each site entry contains a number of features. The title is followed by an icon demonstrating the site's classification as designated by the National Park Service (see below), including historic sites, battlefields, wild and scenic rivers, and 16 other types of properties. This is followed by a detailed site description. At the end of the entry you'll find the address for the primary park entrance, as well as a contact phone number and website address. Should there be multiple entrances or no specific entrance, a main visitor center or park headquarters may instead be listed, with its phone number and website address. Finally, "At a Glance" is a quick reference box of the park's general location, its size, its opening hours, and activities available for the visitor.

Please use this book with a detailed map to plan your next visit to a national park property. Two points as you plan: Most parks charge admission fees; and, given today's emphasis on safety, some sites may require additional security procedures and identification. Please consult the park websites or contact the individual sites for additional information.

Finally, enjoy learning about and discovering all of the parks in our National Park System!

PARK DESIGNATION ICONS

National Park National Park & Preserve	National Preserve National Reserve	National Seashore National Lakeshore
National Memorial	National Parkway Memorial Parkway	National Scenic River National River National Wild & Scenic River and Riverway
National Monument	National Recreation Area	National Historic Trail National Scenic Trail
National Battlefield National Battlefield Park National Battlefield Site National Military Park	National Historical Park National Historical Reserve National Historic Site International Historic Site	Other Designations Affiliated Areas

Northeast

Birthplace of the United States, the Northeast is home to some of the country's most hallowed historic sites, from the church where the Boston Tea Party was planned to Philadelphia's Liberty Bell to the spot in New York City where George Washington took the oath of office as the first President. Names from Paul Revere to John F. Kennedy echo through the past. Even in this urbanized region, though, natural areas provide escape at places such as Acadia National Park, Cape Cod National Seashore, and New Jersey's Pinelands. Few regions offer such diversity of history and recreation.

Boston Lighthouse, built 1716

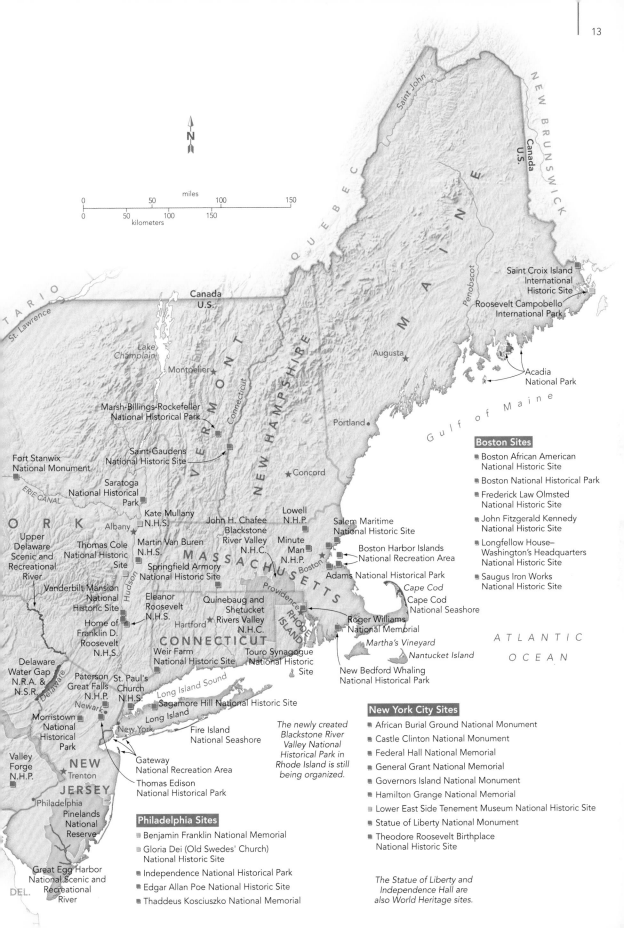

N

miles
0   50   100   150
0   50   100   150
kilometers

St. Lawrence

O N T A R I O

Canada
U.S.

ERIE CANAL

Lake
Champlain

Montpelier

V E R M O N T

Connecticut

Q U E B E C

Saint John

N E W   B R U N S W I C K

Canada
U.S.

M A I N E

Penobscot

Saint Croix Island
International
Historic Site

Roosevelt Campobello
International Park

Augusta

Acadia
National Park

Gulf of Maine

Portland

N E W   H A M P S H I R E

Marsh-Billings-Rockefeller
National Historical Park

Saint-Gaudens
National Historic Site

Concord

Fort Stanwix
National Monument

Saratoga
National Historical
Park

Kate Mullany
N.H.S.

Albany

John H. Chafee
Blackstone
River Valley
N.H.C.

Lowell
N.H.P.

Minute
Man
N.H.P.

Salem Maritime
National Historic Site

Boston Harbor Islands
National Recreation Area

Boston

Adams National Historical Park

Cape Cod

Cape Cod
National Seashore

N E W
Y O R K

Upper
Delaware
Scenic and
Recreational
River

Thomas Cole
National Historic
Site

Martin Van Buren
N.H.S.

Springfield Armory
National Historic Site

M A S S A C H U S E T T S

Hudson

Vanderbilt Mansion
National
Historic Site

Eleanor
Roosevelt
N.H.S.

Home of
Franklin D.
Roosevelt
N.H.S.

Quinebaug and
Shetucket
Rivers Valley
N.H.C.

Hartford

C O N N E C T I C U T

Providence

R H O D E
I S L A N D

Roger Williams
National Memorial

Martha's Vineyard

Nantucket Island

A T L A N T I C
O C E A N

Weir Farm
National Historic Site

Touro Synagogue
National Historic
Site

New Bedford Whaling
National Historical Park

Delaware
Water Gap
N.R.A. &
N.S.R.

Paterson
Great Falls
N.H.P.

St. Paul's
Church
N.H.S.

Newark

Sagamore Hill National Historic Site

Long Island

Long Island Sound

New York

Fire Island
National Seashore

N E W

Trenton

J E R S E Y

Philadelphia

Pinelands
National
Reserve

Valley
Forge
N.H.P.

Morristown
National
Historical
Park

Delaware

Gateway
National Recreation Area

Thomas Edison
National Historical Park

The newly created
Blackstone River
Valley National
Historical Park in
Rhode Island is still
being organized.

Great Egg Harbor
National Scenic and
Recreational
River

DEL.

Boston Sites
- Boston African American
  National Historic Site
- Boston National Historical Park
- Frederick Law Olmsted
  National Historic Site
- John Fitzgerald Kennedy
  National Historic Site
- Longfellow House–
  Washington's Headquarters
  National Historic Site
- Saugus Iron Works
  National Historic Site

New York City Sites
- African Burial Ground National Monument
- Castle Clinton National Monument
- Federal Hall National Memorial
- General Grant National Memorial
- Governors Island National Monument
- Hamilton Grange National Memorial
- Lower East Side Tenement Museum National Historic Site
- Statue of Liberty National Monument
- Theodore Roosevelt Birthplace
  National Historic Site

Philadelphia Sites
- Benjamin Franklin National Memorial
- Gloria Dei (Old Swedes' Church)
  National Historic Site
- Independence National Historical Park
- Edgar Allan Poe National Historic Site
- Thaddeus Kosciuszko National Memorial

The Statue of Liberty and
Independence Hall are
also World Heritage sites.

CONNECTICUT

The Connecticut River divides America's third smallest state from north to south, and this fertile valley attracted the first European settlers in the area. Later, industries grew up along the state's other rivers and fertile farmlands. Inventors such as Eli Whitney (mass production of muskets), Samuel Colt (revolvers), and Igor Sikorsky (aircraft) are among those who worked here. The state's coastline has been an economic asset as well, with fishing, shipping, and shipbuilding contributing to the economy. Although heavily urbanized, in large part with commuters to New York City, Connecticut maintains attractive green spaces around many of its cities and towns.

Quinebaug & Shetucket Rivers Valley N.H.C.

Pastoral scenes amid the urbanized Northeast

Though 25 million people live within 2.5 hours of this region, the area surrounding the Quinebaug and Shetucket Rivers remains surprisingly green, rural, and peaceful. Forest and farmland comprise more than 70 percent of the 695,000 acres within the Quinebaug & Shetucket Rivers Valley National Heritage Corridor (also known as "The Last Green Valley"), and many villages retain the atmosphere of a simpler, bygone time.

Though sanctioned by the National Park Service, the heritage corridor is a partnership of local and state governments, environmental and cultural organizations, and businesses working together to preserve and celebrate the region's cultural, historical, and natural heritage. The park's main partner is the nonprofit group called The Last Green Valley (*203B Main St., Danielson, CT, 860-774-3300, www.thelastgreenvalley.org*); its website lists activities, parks, museums, and special events such as Walktober (during the month of October), when dozens of guided walks are offered at historic, natural, and cultural areas throughout the 35 towns in the valley.

These rivers are actually cleaner today than they were in the 19th and 20th centuries, when industry poured pollutants into their waters. Boating and swimming are popular activities within the corridor, along with hiking in the many state parks, state forests, and nature centers in the area, such as Capen Hill Nature Sanctuary in Charlton, Massachusetts; and the Connecticut Audubon Center in Pomfret.

Historic sites within the heritage corridor include the Clara Barton Birthplace Museum in Oxford, Massachusetts; Old Sturbridge Village in Sturbridge, Massachusetts; and the Governor Jonathan Trumbull House in Lebanon, Connecticut.

www.nps.gov/qush

AT A GLANCE

Eastern Connecticut and south-central Massachusetts, 50 miles southwest of Boston ▪ 695,000 acres ▪ Spring through fall best ▪ Hiking, biking, boating, horseback riding, cross-country skiing

Weir Farm National Historic Site

A quiet retreat that inspired an influential American painter

Born to an artistic family in West Point, New York, in 1852, J. Alden Weir studied painting in Paris, where he rejected the growing Impressionism movement. Upon his return to the United States, he moved to New York City, and in 1882 he acquired a farm in rural Connecticut near Ridgefield. Until his death in

J. Alden Weir drew inspiration from the rural surroundings of his farm, painting much of his artwork at this studio.

1919, the farm served as his summer home; he built a studio here, where he hosted artist friends such as Childe Hassam and Albert Pinkham Ryder. As he painted scenes from the landscape around him, he gradually developed his own impressionistic style.

Weir became an influential figure in American art, serving as president of the Society of American Artists (he later resigned in protest of its policies)

and sitting on the Board of Directors of the Metropolitan Museum of Art. He was also a member of "the Ten," a group of painters that became the core of American impressionism. Weir's works hang in museums such as the Metropolitan Museum of Art, the National Museum of American Art, and the Phillips Collection.

Weir Farm National Historic Site preserves the house, barn, and studios

that inspired Weir and other artists, as well as personal items and paintings. The site is still a favorite of painters, who are welcome to roam the grounds and work.

A private, nonprofit arts organization on the farm, Weir Farm Art Center, cooperates with the site to administer the park's Artist in Residence program, which gives artists a month to live and work at Weir Farm.

735 Nod Hill Rd.
Wilton, CT
203-834-1896
www.nps.gov/wefa

AT A GLANCE

Southwestern Connecticut, 16 miles northwest of Bridgeport ▪ 60 acres (plus 50-acre adjacent Weir Preserve) ▪ Year-round ▪ Taking guided tours of historic buildings and grounds, hiking, painting

MAINE

Ninety percent forested, Maine is the least densely populated state east of the Mississippi, with most residents just a short drive from one of the most beautiful coastlines in the country. Maine's rugged shore is a "drowned coast," where rising sea level after the last ice age flooded coastal valleys and made islands out of mountaintops. This striking landscape is on display at Acadia National Park, which also has Somes Sound, the Eastern seaboard's only fjord. The northern half of Maine is a remote land of lakes, rivers, and woodland, home to abundant wildlife. Mount Katahdin, at 5,268 feet the state's highest point, is the northern terminus of the famed Appalachian National Scenic Trail.

Acadia National Park

Mountains, forests, and ponds on the rugged and spectacular Maine coast

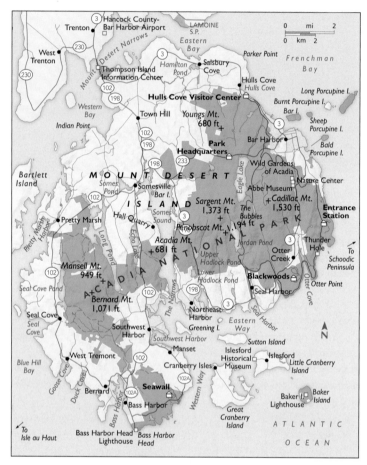

The iconic Atlantic coastline of Maine is familiar to nearly every American, from scenic calendar photographs if not from in-person visits. The rugged, rocky shore; the crashing waves; the lighthouses rising above dark coniferous forests; the colorful lobster buoys floating offshore—all form part of the beauty and mystique of coastal Maine, inviting travelers to explore its many facets.

Some of the very best of the coastal landscape is protected within Acadia National Park, a place whose history is just as fascinating as its mountains, streams, ponds, woods, shore, and wildlife. Added to the National Park System in 1916—a time when national parks were thought of as vast, untouched tracts in the West—this first eastern national park was assembled not from public land with public funds but with private donations, one tract at a time, on an island that was already an important tourist destination.

Human History

When Mount Desert was first discovered by Europeans, the Wabanaki, American Indians who had lived there for thousands of years, called the island Pemetic, or "range of mountains." But French explorer Samuel Champlain, who saw Mount Desert Island from his ship on September 5, 1604, wrote in his journal, "The mountain summits are all bare and rocky. . . . I name it Isles des Monts Desert," and the name took hold. (The French word *desert* means "barren," and did not indicate a dry, sandy place as does the English word. The island's name is usually pronounced like "dessert.")

Nineteenth-century landscape painters also "discovered" Mount Desert Island, sharing its beauty through their art. East Coast residents soon followed, looking for a peaceful summer retreat. By 1880, Mount Desert had 30 hotels; in 1887, the opulent *Boston and Mt. Desert Limited Express* train began transporting New England's elite. Soon, anyone with any pretension to the social register had a summer house on the island. Vanderbilts, Astors, Carnegies, Morgans, Fords, and—most significantly, as it turned out—Rockefellers built mansions

they called "cottages" along the shore, until the northeastern coast of Mount Desert was known as Millionaire's Row.

As development threatened the very tranquillity and scenery that had attracted them in the first place, some of these part-time residents lobbied for national park status for parts of Mount Desert Island. Gifts of private land made the park possible, with the largest amount—some 11,000 acres—donated by John D. Rockefeller, Jr. The federal government declared the land a national monument in 1916 and a national park three years later—though its original name was Lafayette National Park. (It became Acadia in 1929.)

Visiting the Park

In season, the park operates two visitor centers. The first one that visitors will encounter is the Thompson Island Information Center *(mid-May–mid-Oct.)*, which is located where Me. 3 crosses from the mainland to Mount Desert Island; however, the best first stop for travelers is the principal Hulls Cove Visitor Center *(mid-April–Oct.)*, north of Bar Harbor on Me. 3. It offers a 15-minute audiovisual program about the park and a three-dimensional map of the island to help in trip planning, as well as an information desk and exhibits. In winter the park headquarters provides visitor information; it is 2.5 miles west of Bar Harbor on Me. 233.

Park rangers lead an array of walks, programs, and tours around Acadia. Subjects include bird-watching, astronomy, wildflowers, trees, aquatic invertebrates, carriage roads and bridges, and mosses and ferns. In addition, the park offers four different guided boat cruises, focusing on topics such as history, ocean wildlife, and undersea life. Check with the park for a schedule of activities; they vary by season.

Those with an interest in the Mount Desert flora and fauna should stop at the Sieur de Monts Spring area, south of Bar Harbor, and tour the Nature Center *(May–early Oct.)*. The adjacent Wild Gardens of Acadia offers a microcosm of island habitats along a level, easy trail. Twelve of Acadia's plant communities are represented here: mixed woods, roadside, meadow, mountain, heath, seaside, brookside, bird thicket, coniferous woods, bog, marsh, and pond. The nearby, privately operated Abbe Museum *(207-288-3519, www*

.abbemuseum.org) explores Maine's Native American heritage from 12,000 years ago to the present.

Park Loop Road

Driving the scenic 27-mile Park Loop Road is arguably the most popular activity in Acadia National Park. The route begins at Hulls Cove Visitor Center and passes attractions such as Sand Beach (where people who can tolerate 55-degree water swim in summer), Thunder Hole (where heavy surf compresses air in a hole in the rocks, causing a low boom like distant thunder), and Otter Cliffs (one of the most picturesque sections of rocky coast). In an effort to ease traffic problems, a section of the road has been made one-way, but it can still be very crowded at peak times. Consider a visit early or late in the day. Or in summer, use the Island Explorer buses, which provide

One of the park's 17 stone bridges, each different from the others
FOLLOWING PAGES: *Bass Harbor Head Lighthouse, Mount Desert Island*

service to park destinations and local communities, stopping at sites such as campgrounds, carriage road entrances, and many trailheads.

Park Loop Road also provides access to the winding, narrow, 3.5-mile road up Cadillac Mountain. At 1,530 feet, Cadillac is the tallest mountain along the U.S. Eastern seaboard. The summit, with its expanses of pink granite, offers great views at sunrise and of the town of Bar Harbor and, beyond, the green stepping-stones of the Porcupine Islands that point northeast toward the mainland across Frenchman Bay.

Most of Park Loop Road is closed in winter, though a section south of Sand Beach stays open all year. The road up Cadillac Mountain also closes in winter.

Carriage Roads & Hiking Trails

After getting the lay of the land on Park Loop Road, visitors should explore the park's justly renowned carriage roads, courtesy of John D. Rockefeller, Jr., whose generous donation of land helped create the park. Beginning in 1913 he oversaw construction of a network of what he called "carriage roads" through some of the island's most beautiful areas. He took a very hands-on approach, personally siting the roads to follow the contours of the land and to take advantage of scenic views. His workers graded the roads so they weren't too steep or too sharply curved for horse-drawn carriages. Eventually 57 miles of these broad, smooth gravel roads were built; 45 are inside the park boundary today. Seventeen imposing stone bridges are scattered along the routes, each one designed for its particular setting.

In Rockefeller's time, walkers, horseback riders, bicycles, and carriages were welcome; automobiles were, and still are, banned. Intersections are well signed to guide travelers. In other words, they're perfect for leisurely walking as well as for biking and, in winter, cross-country skiing. A park concessionaire provides carriage tours *(mid-June–early Oct.)* for those who'd rather let horses do the work.

Separate from the carriage roads are Acadia's 125 miles of historic hiking trails. Many date from well before the national park, having been blazed by local village improvement societies in the late 1800s and early 1900s. Today many historic features such as the stonework are still visible. The walks range from the flat, easy 0.4-mile loop atop Cadillac Mountain to the strenuous 2.5-mile round-trip up Acadia Mountain, which offers views of glacier-carved Somes Sound, the only fjord on the Atlantic coast of the United States. Some trails, such as the 2-mile round-trip Perpendicular Trail up Mansell Mountain, use stairs and iron rungs in steep sections.

Mount Desert's Western Side

Though many park activities are concentrated on the eastern side of Mount Desert Island, the western side of the island—known as the "quiet side"—has its own special attractions. It encompasses Echo Lake (with a swimming beach where the water is warmer than at Sand Beach), the towns of Northeast Harbor and Southwest Harbor, Seawall Campground, and the 19th-century Bass Harbor Head Lighthouse, as well as many trails that are less crowded than those around Bar Harbor. The Ship Harbor and Wonderland coastal areas are excellent for tide-pooling: exploring pools left when the tide goes out, looking for creatures such as barnacles, mussels, sea stars, anemones, crabs, and young lobsters.

Schoodic Peninsula

The only part of Acadia National Park on the mainland is Schoodic Peninsula, an hour north of Bar Harbor. A 6-mile, one-way road loops south to Schoodic Point from the park entrance. Great views along the way include looks back at Mount Desert Island. An unpaved road leads to the top of 440-foot Schoodic Head, for even better panoramas. At the southern end of the peninsula, dark diabase dikes show where magma welled up between pink granite ledges.

Isle au Haut

Located 20 miles (as the gull flies) south of Mount Desert Island, Isle au Haut ("high island") was also named by Samuel Champlain in 1604. About half the island (about 2,700 acres) belongs to the national park; the rest is private property, including a small year-round community. The island is accessed via a mail boat leaving from the town of Stonington; the boat takes passengers on a first-come, first-served basis. Limited seasonal camping is allowed by prior reservation only, and the number of day-trippers is also limited. Despite all this, a visit here is definitely worthwhile. Eighteen miles of hiking trails meander across the southern part of the island, where hikers usually find complete solitude as well as views of beautiful rocky coastline.

Appalachian National Scenic Trail
America's most celebrated long-distance backcountry path

Its name is synonymous with adventure and challenge; books have been written and films made about it; it symbolizes freedom and wilderness to the millions of people who walk sections of it each year; it was designated the country's first national scenic trail; it may be the world's most famous hiking route—all these distinctions apply to the renowned Appalachian National Scenic Trail.

Beginning atop Springer Mountain in Georgia, its southern end, the trail crosses 14 states and covers about 2,185 miles to reach its northern terminus at Mount Katahdin in Maine. (That's an estimated five million footsteps.) Along the way it passes through six national parks, eight national forests, and dozens of state and local parks and similar protected areas.

An estimated two to three million people walk on the trail each year. Most make only relatively short day hikes on sections of the trail near parks and roads, but between 2,000 and 2,500 try to walk the entire length of the route in one hiking season, an effort that takes most people five to six months. About a quarter of these become successful "through-hikers." Others return over the years to tackle new sections until they have completed the entire length; more than 15,000 people can boast they've conquered the trail.

Appalachian Trail Conservancy

The Appalachian Trail (sometimes called the "A.T.") was conceived in 1921 by Benton MacKaye, a Massachusetts native and former Forest Service employee who was a strong advocate of wilderness as a retreat from urban life. Others—private citizens,

The Appalachian Trail crosses numerous creeks along its 2,185-mile length.

government agency personnel, and politicians—quickly took up the idea. A group called the Appalachian Trail Conference was formed by MacKaye in 1925, and by 1937 a route had been blazed roughly following the crests of the Appalachian Mountains along the eastern United States.

Located within a day's drive of two-thirds of the nation's population, the Appalachian Trail benefits from a dedicated group of advocates and volunteer workers. While the Appalachian National Scenic Trail is a unit of the National Park System, most of the management responsibility is held by the Appalachian Trail Conservancy (ATC) (renamed from Conference in 2005). The group's website and publications are the best sources of information about the trail, and an essential first step for anyone planning a long-distance hike along the trail *(304-535-6331, www.appalachiantrail.org)*.

In addition, 31 affiliated hiking and trail clubs under conservancy coordination work on sections of the trail.

More than 6,000 volunteers contribute more than 200,000 hours each year toward the protection, upkeep, and promotion of the Appalachian Trail. This includes maintaining approximately 260 trail shelters and 165,000 blazes (rectangles of white paint) that mark the route, as well as monitoring segments of the trail to provide advice and assistance to hikers.

Hiking the Trail

Today more than 99 percent of the trail runs through public land. The exact route continues to evolve to provide a better hiking experience and to protect resources. Some parts of the trail traverse remote wilderness, while others temporarily touch on the modern world. (The trail crosses the Delaware River between Pennsylvania and New Jersey on a pedestrian bridge alongside I-80.)

It's quite easy to access short sections of the Appalachian Trail for day hikes at places such as Great Smoky Mountains National Park in North

Carolina and Tennessee (see p. 187), along the Blue Ridge Parkway and in Shenandoah National Park in Virginia (see p. 103), in High Point State Park in New Jersey, in Mount Greylock State Reservation in Massachusetts, and at scores of other spots. Studying maps and trail guides will help hikers choose a section appropriate for their time and ability.

Elevation makes a huge difference in weather conditions: A high-elevation site in the south may at certain times of the year be much colder than a low-elevation spot hundreds of miles to the north. Elevations along the trail range from 6,643 feet on Clingmans Dome in Great Smoky Mountains National Park to 124 feet along the Hudson River in New York's Bear Mountain State Park.

While most would-be through-hikers start in Georgia in March or April and head north, they face logistical issues such as crowding (more than 30 people a day start north along the trail in March and early April), wintry weather on mountaintops for the first few weeks, and finishing the arduous hike along some of its most difficult sections in New Hampshire and Maine with winter approaching. Fewer people through-hike from north to south, but such a plan also has issues, including swollen streams, swarms of insects, and finishing the hike during hunting season in the south.

More and more hikers are starting somewhere in the middle of the trail, walking to one terminus, then returning and completing the other half in what's known as a "flip-flop" or "leapfrog" hike. The ATC encourages this kind of approach as a way to even out the flow of hikers and minimize resource damage to the trail.

Trail Prep

Whether setting out for a months-long trek or a weekend hike, travelers on the trail need to know the rules, options, and etiquette of overnighting along the route. Shelters (roofed and floored three-sided structures) are available in many places, but they may be occupied when a hiker arrives; a tent is mandatory even for those planning to use shelters. Designated tent sites must be used in some areas, while hikers are free to choose their own sites in some national forests. In several places, options include huts, cabins, or hostels operated by local trail clubs, private individuals, or parks. Some towns near the trail feature hotels or inns that cater to Appalachian Trail hikers.

On any hike on the trail, travelers should follow "leave no trace" practices, from avoiding campfires to choosing tent sites carefully to cleaning up shelters and campsites. Hikers should also read advice about safety listed on the ATC website on issues including weather, Lyme disease, poison ivy, and hunting seasons. Hiking the Appalachian Trail can be a pleasant afternoon's walk or a life-changing wilderness experience—in any case, the most successful hikers are those best prepared mentally as well as physically.

Saint Croix Island International Historic Site
The beginning of permanent French settlement in North America

In 1604, a 79-member French expedition led by Pierre Dugua, Sieur de Mons, settled on a small island in what is now called the Saint Croix River. The men (including famed navigator Samuel Champlain) hoped to claim the region for France and profit from trade with Indian tribes. During the severe winter of 1604–05, 35 men died and

Statue commemorating Pierre Dugua, Sieur de Mons

were buried in a small cemetery on today's Saint Croix Island.

When spring came, the survivors abandoned the island and founded the settlement of Port Royal, in today's Nova Scotia, Canada. Three years later, Champlain founded Quebec City. A link thus exists between Saint Croix Island and the enduring French presence in North America.

Saint Croix Island disappeared from public notice until the late 18th century, when ruins of the original settlement were found, positively identifying its location and helping resolve a boundary dispute between the United States and British North America (today's Canada).

In 1984 the island was designated an international historic site. Visitor facilities are on the mainland, not the island, and include an outdoor interpretive shelter; picnic tables; and a short, accessible interpretive trail with bronze figures of French settlers and Passamaquoddy Indians. There are also displays that discuss historical events and the interaction of the two cultures.

A visitor center, located in the ranger station, is open mid-May through mid-October. Short ranger-guided programs are available most days. Visits to the island itself are not encouraged because of its fragile nature.

Parks Canada administers an interpretive site on the river's opposite shore, in Bayside, New Brunswick.

U.S. 1, 8 miles south of Calais, ME
207-454-3871
www.nps.gov/sacr

AT A GLANCE

Eastern Maine, 90 miles east of Bangor ▪ 28 acres ▪ Spring through fall ▪ Walking short interpretive trail, viewing historic island, indoor exhibits

NEW BRUNSWICK (CANADA)

Roosevelt Campobello International Park

The grand "cottage" of America's 32nd President

This unique park is administered by a commission made up of members from both the United States and Canada and is owned, funded, and staffed by people from both countries. Though it occupies part of a Canadian island, the only bridge to the island connects it with the U.S. The explanation for this extraordinary circumstance can be traced to the history of one special family.

In the late 19th century, New Brunswick's Campobello Island became a favored summer retreat for prominent families from the U.S.'s Northeast. Many built houses they called "cottages"—though some were large and, for the day, luxurious. James and Sara Roosevelt bought land and built a cottage here, and their son Franklin Delano Roosevelt grew up spending summers on the island. Later Eleanor and Franklin had their own cottage:

Mulholland Point Lighthouse

an 1897 structure that he enlarged to 34 rooms to accommodate his growing family. It was here in 1921 that he was stricken with the disease polio, which left him partially paralyzed. After he was elected President in 1932, he

returned only three more times before his death in 1945, but Campobello remained his "beloved island."

Roosevelt Campobello International Park serves as a memorial to Franklin D. Roosevelt and a symbol of the close relations between the peoples of Canada and the United States. The park visitor center features historical exhibits and a video interpreting the Roosevelt story. Visitors can tour FDR's cottage, restored to its 1920s appearance, and walk through the adjacent flower gardens. Other activities include hiking the park's 10 miles of trails, taking self-guided tours of natural areas, listening to presentations by park interpreters, picnicking, and visiting the 1885 Mulholland Point Lighthouse.

Visitors should remember that they must pass through Canadian and U.S. customs as they travel to and from Campobello Island.

FDR Memorial Bridge from Lubec, ME, leads to island
506-752-2922
www.nps.gov/roca
www.fdr.net

AT A GLANCE

On Campobello Island in southwestern New Brunswick, Canada, 120 miles east of Bangor, Maine ▪ 2,800 acres ▪ Memorial Day weekend through Columbus Day ▪ Visiting Roosevelt summer home, scenic driving, hiking

MASSACHUSETTS

From the Pilgrims' landing at Plymouth in 1620, Massachusetts played a key role in England's American Colonies and the birth of the United States. For a time in the 18th century, Boston was the largest city in North America and a hotbed of patriotic fervor; today, it still possesses major industry and a busy seaport. Salem and New Bedford became major maritime centers in sailing days, and immigrants swelled industrial towns to work in textile and other factories. Harvard, founded in Cambridge in 1636, was the country's first college, and education remains a major state asset. Urbanites find nature in Cape Cod, the Berkshire Hills, and elsewhere.

Adams National Historical Park

The birthplaces and homes of two Presidents and their noted descendants

Among the most influential families in American history, the Adamses of Massachusetts produced two Presidents, international diplomats, and notable historian-writers. Adams National Historical Park preserves the grounds, homes, and personal property of five generations of the Adams family, who lived here from 1720 to 1927.

The park includes the two houses, just 75 feet apart, that were the birthplaces of John Adams, second U.S. President, and his son John Quincy Adams, sixth President. The nearby Old House, built in 1731, was home to John Adams and John Quincy Adams; Charles Francis Adams, minister to Great Britain during the Civil War; and Henry Adams and Brooks Adams, both literary historians. The Old House grounds include a historic orchard and a formal garden. The adjacent 1870s Stone Library, built at the request of John Quincy Adams, houses more than 12,000 volumes.

The buildings contain a great number of personal items, including furniture, fine art, and decorative art, all once belonging to various members of the Adams family. A prominent family member was Abigail Adams, wife of John Adams, a strong figure in her own right and one of the most intellectually capable and influential First Ladies of the United States.

These structures can be visited by guided tour *(fee)*. Tours leave from the visitor center, with visitors riding a trolley to the Presidential Birthplaces and the Old House and Stone Library.

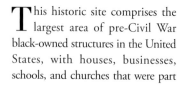

1250 Hancock St.
Quincy, MA
617-770-1175
www.nps.gov/adam

AT A GLANCE

Eastern Massachusetts, 7 miles southeast of Boston ▪ 11 acres ▪ Spring through fall ▪ Touring historic houses

Boston African American National Historic Site

A center of 19th-century African-American life on Beacon Hill

This historic site comprises the largest area of pre-Civil War black-owned structures in the United States, with houses, businesses, schools, and churches that were part of a thriving black community on the north side of Beacon Hill. Here, generations of African Americans struggled for equal rights both locally and nationally.

The Museum of African-American History, the site's primary partner, operates the Abiel Smith School and the African Meeting House. The Smith School served as a segregated public school for black children from 1835-1855 and now houses the museum's exhibitions. The African Meeting House hosted speakers such as Frederick Douglass and William Lloyd Garrison. Park Rangers lead talks at the African Meeting House and tours of Black Heritage Trail, a 1.5-hour, 1.6-mile walking tour. Visitors can take a self-guided tour at any time, while guided tours are offered seasonally.

In addition to the Abiel Smith School, sites along the trail include the Robert Gould Shaw and Massachusetts 54th Regiment Memorial, honoring a group of men who were among the first African Americans to fight in the Civil War; the Charles Street Meeting House, an early center of the fight for equal rights; and the Phillips School, one of the first integrated schools in Boston and also thought to be the first to hire an African-American teacher.

Most of the buildings on the Black Heritage Trail are privately owned and not open for public visitation.

Museum of African-American History, 46 Joy St. Boston, MA 617-742-5415 www.nps.gov/boaf

AT A GLANCE

Downtown Boston ▪ Less than 1 acre (nonfederal land) ▪ Year-round ▪ Touring historic buildings

Boston Harbor Islands National Recreation Area

A diverse array of recreational opportunities minutes from an urban center

A multifaceted partnership among federal, state, and local government agencies and private businesses, Boston Harbor Islands National Recreation Area, established in 1996, comprises 34 separate sites—islands and mainland peninsulas—offering a broad range of activities.

Some of these diversions are water-related, such as swimming, boating, taking narrated cruises of historic Boston Harbor, or simply strolling along a beach. Other activities include hiking, camping, and touring historic sites such as 19th-century Fort Warren on Georges Island, which served as an active military post until 1947 and is now a national historic landmark.

Spectacle Island encompasses the highest point within the park (157 feet above the harbor), as well

In good weather, sailboats crowd Boston Harbor.

as 5 miles of hiking trails and great views of the Boston skyline; a visitor center features exhibits on island history and nature. Worlds End is a 244-acre peninsula with hiking trails along rocky beaches, cliffs, and saltwater and freshwater marshes. The country's oldest light station sits on Little Brewster Island. Some islands, such as Shag Rocks, are so small or difficult of access that they are rarely visited.

Worlds End is one of four peninsula areas within the park that are accessible by vehicle; the park's other 30 sites can be reached only by boat. Ferries to various islands leave from Boston Harbor, Hingham, Quincy, and Hull.

To learn more about all the different destinations and activities within the national recreation area as well as ways to access the islands, check the websites for the National Park Service and the Boston Harbor Islands Partnership (*www.bostonislands.com*), which includes the Coast Guard, the City of Boston, and the Massachusetts Department of Conservation and Recreation (*www.mass.gov/dcr/parks/metroboston/harbor.htm*). (Some of the islands compose Boston Harbor Islands State Park.)

Boston Harbor Islands 617-223-8666 www.nps.gov/boha

AT A GLANCE

Boston Harbor ▪ 1,483 to 3,067 acres, depending on the tide ▪ Year-round, spring through fall best for boating ▪ Hiking, camping, swimming, picnicking, visiting historic structures, taking guided boat tours

Boston National Historical Park

The "cradle of liberty" during the American Revolution

Some of the most important events of the American independence movement and the Revolutionary War took place in and near the historic city of Boston, including the Boston Tea Party, the "midnight ride of Paul Revere," and the Battle of Bunker Hill. Visitors can relive those patriotic days at Boston National Historical Park, which encompasses eight sites pivotal in making Boston the cradle of independence for the country.

Visiting the Park

All the sites save Dorchester Heights are linked by the 2.5-mile Freedom Trail; this walking tour runs from Boston Common, a downtown city park; through the North End, the oldest part of Boston; to Bunker Hill, in the Charlestown area north of the Charles River. A redbrick path guides visitors along the trail, which was inaugurated in 1958 as part of the city's historic-preservation movement. Costumed interpreters are often present along the Freedom Trail, acting the roles of historical figures. (Some sites are privately owned and operated, with a fee charged for admission.)

Boston National Historical Park has two visitor centers: one on the first floor of Faneuil Hall *(617-242-5642)* and the other on the Boston Inner Harbor next to the historic U.S.S. *Constitution* in Charlestown *(Constitution Rd., 617-242-5601),* just inside Gate 1 of the Navy Yard. Both offer maps, brochures, and audiovisual presentations; park staff is available to

The 115-foot-tall monument at Dorchester Heights

answer questions and provide advice.

For much of the year, interpretive rangers lead 60-minute walking tours along the Freedom Trail *(mid-April–Oct.).* These popular tours begin at the Faneuil Hall visitor center; group size is limited to 30 participants and reservations are not accepted, so arrive early to secure a place. Self-guided tours are available anytime, and park rangers are also stationed daily at Bunker Hill Monument, giving regularly scheduled historical lectures.

Old South Meeting House

This 1729 building *(fee)* was a gathering spot where American patriots debated issues of British rule and independence. It was from here that Samuel Adams and other "sons of liberty," disguised as Native Americans, left to dump 342 chests of

tea into Boston Harbor. The Old South Association owns the site.

Old State House

Built in 1713, the Old State House *(fee)* is the oldest surviving public building in Boston. The 1770 Boston Massacre, in which British soldiers fired into a crowd of civilians, occurred in front of this building; this event added fuel to the fire of the independence movement. The Bostonian Society administers the site.

Faneuil Hall

A marketplace since its original construction in 1742, this building was gutted by fire in 1761. It was rebuilt and elevated vertically with the same walls in 1763 and enlarged in 1805–06. Its second-floor meeting room was the scene of public gatherings and speeches during the pre-Revolutionary period.

Paul Revere House

Dating from 1680, this house *(fee)* is the oldest remaining structure in downtown Boston. Silversmith Revere famously rode on horseback on the night of April 18, 1775, from Boston to Lexington to warn John Hancock and Samuel Adams that British military forces were moving to capture patriots and seize supplies. The Paul Revere Memorial Association owns the site.

Old North Church

Sexton Robert Newman hung two lanterns in the steeple of this 1723 church *(donation requested, fee for behind-the-scenes tour, offered seasonally)* to warn Charlestown patriots of the advance of British soldiers on the night of April 18, 1775. Still an active place of worship, the Old North Church welcomes visitors on the Freedom Trail.

Old Ironsides

Located in the Charlestown Navy Yard, this 1797 wooden-hulled frigate gained the nickname "Old Ironsides" in the War of 1812. Still a commissioned warship—the oldest in the world—in the U.S. Navy, *Constitution* has a crew of Navy sailors and officers.

The ship is in dry dock undergoing restoration until 2018, but the U.S.S. Constitution Museum, which interprets the ship's role in American history, remains open.

Bunker Hill Monument

This 221-foot granite obelisk marks the site of the first major battle of the Revolutionary War. The monument actually sits on Breed's Hill, where the clash known as the Battle of Bunker Hill took place on June 17, 1775. Inaugurated in 2007, the Battle of Bunker Hill Museum, located across the street from the monument, tells

the story of the battle, the building of the monument, and the history of Charlestown.

Dorchester Heights

The final site in the national historical park is Dorchester Heights in South Boston about 2 miles away from the Freedom Trail sites. A white marble tower here commemorates the events of early March 1776, when patriot forces built fortifications and installed cannon on high ground, giving the forces a tactical advantage and causing British troops to withdraw from Boston. The grounds are open daily.

AT A GLANCE

Boston Common
Boston, MA
www.nps.gov/bost

Downtown Boston ▪ 43 acres federally owned ▪ Year-round ▪ Touring historic sites

---

Cape Cod National Seashore

A sandy "arm" offering rewards for beachgoers and nature lovers

Serving as an oasis of still wild lands at the edge of urbanized eastern Massachusetts, Cape Cod National Seashore protects about 40 miles of beautiful beaches as well as salt marshes, freshwater wetlands, and scattered woodlands. While many visitors are simply intent on enjoying sunny summer days along the Atlantic and Cape Cod Bay beaches, there's much more to do here than swimming and sunbathing—from bicycling along paved trails to exploring historic lighthouses to enjoying flocks of seabirds skimming the waves.

Visitors can still find "lonely" spots on Cape Cod.

Natural History

The shape of the Cape Cod peninsula has often been compared with that of a bent arm, culminating in

a clenched fist, stretching out in the Atlantic Ocean from the mainland of southeastern Massachusetts. Cape Cod owes its geographic form to the advance and retreat of glaciers. The most recent continental ice sheet reached its maximum extent about 23,000 years ago, its edge near today's

Nantucket and Martha's Vineyard islands. By 18,000 years ago, it had retreated from the Cape Cod area.

Glacial features such as moraines and outwash plains compose most of the Cape Cod terrain. Large boulders called glacial erratics, picked up by moving ice and dropped when it melted, dot the landscape. Wind-deposited sand, silt, and clay from later periods cover glacier-shaped underlying material.

The relentless Atlantic Ocean continues to sculpt Cape Cod. In the late 1990s several historic structures within the park had to be moved inland, away from coastal areas eroded by wave action, including the historic Highland Light and the Nauset Light.

Coastal erosion is an important factor in Cape Cod's beautiful, wide, sandy beaches, such as Sandy Neck Beach.

Eastham Area

Cape Cod National Seashore's main visitor facility is the Salt Pond Visitor Center, located at the corner of Nauset Road and U.S. 6 in the village of Eastham. In addition to an information desk and bookstore, the center has a theater showing five different films and a museum covering several aspects of Cape Cod cultural history, including an exhibit on the Wampanoag people. Ask about the park's cell phone interpretation program, by which visitors can use cell phones to access two-minute messages about seashore history, resources, and activities at various Cape Cod locations.

Several popular park features can be found near the visitor center, including the 1.3-mile Nauset Marsh Trail (one of 12 self-guided nature trails in the park) and the Nauset Bicycle Trail.

Also nearby are two popular beaches, Coast Guard and Nauset Light. On summer days the parking lots for these and other beaches can fill by midmorning, so visitors should either arrive early or be prepared to try other beaches.

Two of the national seashore's most interesting sites lie farther north, off U.S. 6. The 1.25-mile Atlantic White Cedar Swamp Trail winds through a pine-oak forest into a woodland of white cedar, a coniferous tree that grows in wetlands. The trailhead is located at the site where Guglielmo Marconi transmitted transatlantic radio signals from a massive antenna array in the early 20th century. Little remains of the Marconi station, which closed in 1917, but display panels tell the story of this historic undertaking.

Provincetown Area

Near the popular resort town of Provincetown is the national seashore's Province Lands Visitor Center *(open May–Oct.)*. The rewarding 1-mile Beech Forest Trail starts here and passes through attractive woodland and onto the dunes. On the beach nearby is the Old Harbor Life-Saving Station, originally located in Chatham and operational from 1897 to 1944. In summer, rescue reenactments are conducted on the grounds on Thursday evenings.

AT A GLANCE	
Visitor center U.S. 6 near Eastham, MA 508-255-3421 www.nps.gov/caco	Eastern Massachusetts, 90 miles southeast of Boston (55 miles by ferry) ▪ 44,600 acres ▪ Year-round, spring through fall best seasons ▪ Hiking, surfing, bicycling, swimming, driving scenic route, visiting historic sites, bird-watching

---

Frederick Law Olmsted National Historic Site
The site where much of America's landscape design was created

Born in Hartford, Connecticut, in 1822, Frederick Law Olmsted, Sr., is honored as the founder of American landscape architecture, and he remains the most influential figure in the profession's history. Although Olmsted lacked formal training, and his early careers included journalism and public service, he was partially or completely responsible for the design of notable sites such as New York's Central Park and Prospect Park, the campus of Stanford University, the Biltmore Estate in North Carolina, the U.S. Capitol grounds and the National Zoo in Washington, D.C., as well as park complexes in Boston, Buffalo, and Milwaukee and the preservation of scenic reservations in Yosemite Valley and at Niagara Falls.

In 1883 Olmsted moved to the Boston suburb of Brookline, where he founded one of the world's first offices dedicated to landscape design. Employing up to 70 people, the office was responsible for hundreds of projects in the United States and other countries.

Visitors can tour Olmsted's home (called Fairsted) and office, see the grounds, and view design documents and other historic materials related to more than 5,000 landscape-design projects. New self-guided exhibits and a short biographical film are available on the first floor of the house. Regular programs are offered on Olmsted's legacy and rangers also occasionally lead tours of Olmsted-designed landscapes in the Boston metropolitan area.

AT A GLANCE	
99 Warren St. Brookline, MA 617-566-1689 www.nps.gov/frla	Eastern Massachusetts in Brookline, a western suburb of Boston ▪ 7 acres ▪ Year-round ▪ Visiting Olmsted's office and grounds

John Fitzgerald Kennedy National Historic Site
Birthplace of the 35th President

John Fitzgerald Kennedy, one-time United States representative and senator and the 35th American President, elected in 1960, was born in 1917 in a second-floor bedroom of this house in the Boston suburb of Brookline. In 1967, four years after he was assassinated, his mother, Rose Kennedy, restored the house to reflect her memory of its appearance at the time of his birth. The Kennedy family then donated the house to the National Park Service as a gift to the American people.

Visitors to John Fitzgerald Kennedy National Historic Site can take a ranger-led tour to see household furnishings, photographs, and mementos, including the bed in which JFK was born, the bassinet from the nursery, and the piano on which he took lessons as a boy. Self-guided audio tours are also available, during which visitors listen to a recording in which Mrs. Kennedy relates memories of life in the house.

Visitors may also take self-guided or ranger-led walking tours of the Coolidge Corner neighborhood where the future President, called Jack as a boy, grew up through the age of ten. (The family moved in 1920, but just three blocks away.)

83 Beals St.
Brookline, MA
617-566-7937
www.nps.gov/jofi

AT A GLANCE

Eastern Massachusetts, in Brookline, a western suburb of Boston ▪ 1 acre ▪ Late May through October ▪ Touring historic home and neighborhood, viewing family memorabilia

Longfellow House–Washington's Headquarters N.H.S.
A poet's home that was once headquarters for George Washington

Henry Wadsworth Longfellow, born in Maine in 1807, wrote celebrated poems such as "The Song of Hiawatha," "Paul Revere's Ride," "The Courtship of Miles Standish," and "Evangeline." He taught for a time at Harvard College, and moved into rented rooms in a Georgian-style mansion on Brattle Street in Cambridge, Massachusetts. In 1843, when Longfellow married Fanny Appleton, the house was purchased and given to the couple by her father. Longfellow lived here the rest of his life, during which time he was one of the best known literary figures in America and the world. Guests to his home included Nathaniel Hawthorne,

Longfellow House, built in 1759

Ralph Waldo Emerson, Charles Dickens, and Oscar Wilde.

The Brattle Street house had gained a measure of fame even before the poet's residence, though, for its supporting role in the Revolutionary War. When George Washington assumed command of the Continental Army in Cambridge on July 3, 1775, the house served as his headquarters for the next nine months. The owner, a Loyalist, had fled to England.

House tours are offered seasonally, Wednesday through Sunday. There is a limit of 15 persons per tour, and admission is on a first-come, first-served basis. Some tours focus on Longfellow's poetry, while others might discuss Washington's residency or the art and furnishings of the home. Visitors can see the formal gardens adjacent to the house year-round.

105 Brattle St.
Cambridge, MA
617-876-4491
www.nps.gov/long

AT A GLANCE

Eastern Massachusetts, in Cambridge, just west of Boston ▪ 2 acres ▪ Spring through fall; gardens open year-round ▪ Touring historic house, viewing garden

Lowell National Historical Park

The city that began America's great wave of industrialization

Lowell, Massachusetts, was developed in the early 19th century by businessmen as a planned industrial city focusing on textile manufacturing—a place that would be more efficient and attractive to workers than the gloomy mill towns of England. Water was the driving force behind the site selection: The Merrimack River provided ample flow for the waterwheels that powered the mills' machinery.

The population of Lowell rose from about 2,500 in 1826 to more than 33,000 in 1850, when it was the second largest city in Massachusetts. The technological advances made here, along with the growth of an urban working class drawn by the prospect of work, marked the start of the industrial transformation of America. In 1850 Lowell mills were producing enough cloth each year to circle the globe twice.

In the 20th century, though, Lowell underwent an inexorable decline. Many mill owners moved their operations to the South, where land and labor were cheaper, taxes were lower, and unions were less powerful. By the 1950s, nearly all the old mills had closed, and in succeeding years the great redbrick structures fell into ruin.

Lowell National Historical Park was born from local ambition to revitalize the city by creating museums in some of the old mills that would recall the area's historic importance in American economic

Pawtucket Canal, an old power canal

growth. Restoration efforts included renovation of 5.6 miles of canals, a canalway trail system, lock chambers, gatehouses, and many of downtown Lowell's historic buildings.

Visiting the Park

The park visitor center is located in the former Lowell Manufacturing Company mill complex, one of the city's original textile mills. Here visitors can make reservations for tours, view historical exhibits, and see audiovisual programs—including one called "Lowell Blues," on beat-generation writer Jack Kerouac, a Lowell native. The visitor center also has a bookstore.

The park offers a variety of guided tours and special events, most of which vary by season. There are boat tours on some of the park's

old power canals and the Merrimack River, including passages through restored locks. March through November, a reproduction trolley transports visitors among many of the park sites. Costumed interpreters, occasionally present at various locations within the park, add authenticity to historical presentations. The park's signature annual event, the Lowell Folk Festival, featuring traditional music, dance, crafts, and food, takes place during the last weekend of July

Boott Cotton Mills Museum

The Boott Cotton Mills Museum (*115 John St., fee*) features a 1920s-era weave room with operating power looms as well as interactive exhibits and video programs about the industrial revolution; labor; and the rise, fall, and rebirth of Lowell. Visitors can learn from hands-on experience how raw cotton was turned into finished cloth.

Patrick J. Mogan Cultural Center

The Patrick J. Mogan Cultural Center (*40 French St.*) is operated in partnership with the University of Massachusetts–Lowell. Its mission is to "tell the human story of Lowell" through a variety of programs. The "Mill Girls and Immigrants" exhibit tells the story of young single women from the farming communities of northern New England and immigrant workers in a Boott Mill boardinghouse.

246 Market St.
Lowell, MA
978-970-5000
www.nps.gov/lowe

AT A GLANCE

Northeastern Massachusetts, 25 miles northwest of Boston ▪ 140 acres ▪ Year-round ▪ Visiting restored mills, taking guided canal tours

Minute Man National Historical Park

Where "the shot heard round the world" was fired

History was forever altered outside Boston on April 19, 1775, when, for the first time, American patriot militiamen were ordered to fire back at British soldiers—thus committing treason and escalating long-simmering pro-independence tensions into the Revolutionary War. By law, elite units of the militia—formed of the best trained men and known as minute companies—had to keep their weapons ready at all times, and were required to march "on a minute's notice," hence the nickname "minute men."

Minute Man National Historical Park preserves sites along "Battle Road," the route followed by British troops marching from Boston to seize and destroy munitions stored by the colonial militia in the town of Concord. The first shots of the day, and the first patriot casualties, had happened in Lexington hours before; that battle site is a national historic landmark owned by the city of Lexington.

Visiting the Park

The national park's Minute Man Visitor Center *(250 N. Great Rd.)*, near the eastern entrance of the park, is a must-see for first-time visitors. A multimedia presentation called "The Road to Revolution" interprets the events of the first day of the Revolutionary War. The program depicts Paul Revere's Ride (he and other "alarm riders" set out from Boston on horseback on the night of April 18 to warn of the British advance) and the battles at Lexington Green, at North Bridge, and along the Battle Road back to Boston. Exhibits include a 40-foot mural that portrays the fighting between patriots and British forces.

Many park attractions and interpretive programs are offered only seasonally. Check the visitor centers or the park website for dates and times. Each year in mid-April, Minute Man National Historical Park and other groups host the Patriot's Day celebration, which includes parades, historical

weaponry demonstrations, and other commemorative events.

Battle Road Trail

Five-mile Battle Road Trail connects historic sites from Lexington to Concord. While the main theme of exhibits along the trail is the fighting on April 19, 1775, the trail also tells stories of the people whose lives were changed by the events of the day. Much of the trail follows original remnants of the Battle Road. One of the sites along the trail is the Paul Revere Capture Site, where British officers apprehended Revere during his midnight ride (later the subject of a famous poem by Henry Wadsworth Longfellow).

A short distance west of the Revere Capture Site is Hartwell Tavern, a restored home and tavern from the colonial era, once a noted landmark on the road between Lexington and Concord. Park rangers offer daily programs, including musket-firing demonstrations, here seasonally *(check park website for hours)*.

North Bridge

Among the many other sites within the park, the most illustrious is North Bridge in Concord, location of the April 19 battle in which the colonial militia was ordered to fire back at British troops. The clash is the subject of "The Concord Hymn," written by Ralph Waldo Emerson, which includes the often quoted lines, "Here once the embattled farmers stood, and fired the shot heard round the world." Nearby stands the famous statue by Daniel Chester French of a minute man: a patriot holding his musket, with his left hand on his plow, ready to answer

Colonial militiamen first fired upon British troops at North Bridge, Concord.

the call to arms. A second park visitor center, located in the 1911 Buttrick House *(174 Liberty St.)*, stands on the hill overlooking North Bridge.

The park also preserves the striking Wayside historic residence. During the colonial era, the house was the home of Samuel Whitney, muster-master of the Concord militia. In the 19th century it was home to authors Louisa May Alcott, Nathaniel Hawthorne, and Margaret Sidney.

North Bridge Visitor Center
174 Liberty St.
Concord, MA
978-318-7810
www.nps.gov/mima

AT A GLANCE

Eastern Massachusetts, 15 miles northwest of Boston ▪ 1,038 acres ▪ Spring through fall ▪ Viewing historic sites, historical exhibits, interpretive films

New Bedford Whaling National Historical Park
The enduring heritage of the 19th-century whaling capital of the world

In the 19th century whale oil was a lucrative commodity used in lamps to light homes and businesses around the world. In the mid-19th century, New Bedford, Massachusetts, was the world's whaling capital: In 1850, more whaling voyages—which lasted months or even years—set out from New Bedford than from all the rest of the world's ports combined.

New Bedford Whaling National Historical Park preserves and interprets America's 19th-century whaling story and the rich legacy of New Bedford. One of the sailors who embarked from the town in 1841 was Herman Melville, who later used his experience to write the classic novel *Moby-Dick.* In it Melville describes New Bedford as "perhaps the dearest place to live in, in all New England," and evidence of that heritage can still be seen in the 13-block Waterfront Historic District and elsewhere around the town.

The park is a partnership involving the National Park Service and several other organizations, which own and operate various historical attractions. The first stop in exploration should be the park visitor center, located in

New Bedford visitor center

an 1853 Greek Revival building, formerly a bank and courthouse. Nearby is the historic Seamen's Bethel, a mariners' house of worship since 1832. Herman Melville attended services here and later wrote about the chapel's marble memorials to sailors lost at sea. The pulpit in the shape of a ship's bow was added in 1959, based on Melville's description of a pulpit in *Moby-Dick.*

Across the street from the chapel is the New Bedford Whaling Museum *(www.whalingmuseum.org, fee)*, the largest museum in the United States devoted to the history of the American whaling industry. Among its many exhibits are *Lagoda*, a half-scale model of a whaling bark (it's the world's largest model ship); a full-size model of a whaling ship's forecastle; whale

skeletons; and many works of art, including paintings and scrimshaw (engravings on whalebone).

The 1836 U.S. Custom House is the oldest such facility in continuous operation, and was designed by Robert Mills, architect of the Washington Monument. Often docked on the New Bedford waterfront, the schooner *Ernestina* (launched as *Effie Morrissey* in 1894) has been a Grand Banks fishing ship, an Arctic exploration vessel, and a passenger ship.

A few blocks from the Waterfront Historic District is the Rotch-Jones-Duff House and Garden Museum, an 1834 Greek Revival mansion built for one of the city's wealthy whaling merchants. Furnished rooms and exhibits recount the city's history through the three families who lived here over a span of 150 years. The property includes a historic wooden pergola, a formal boxwood rose parterre garden, and an orchard. A couple blocks north, the Johnson House at 21 Seventh Street preserves the home of free black abolitionists Nathan and Polly Johnson who gave safe harbor to Frederick Douglass and others who fled slavery.

33 William St.
New Bedford, MA
508-996-4095
www.nps.gov/nebe

AT A GLANCE

Southeastern Massachusetts, 30 miles east of Providence, Rhode Island ▪ 34 acres ▪ Year-round ▪ Visiting museums and historic sites

Salem Maritime National Historic Site

Where ships embarked for "the farthest ports of the rich East"

In the first few decades after the United States gained independence from Britain, the Massachusetts town of Salem was one of the new nation's most important ports. Ships left Salem on trading voyages that took them around the world, and the goods that were loaded and unloaded along its docks created one of America's first millionaires, Elias Hasket Derby.

During the Revolutionary War, Salem was America's most successful privateering port, with its 158 privateers capturing 445 English ships. (Privateering was a government-sanctioned activity in which a merchant or captain could capture vessels and cargo belonging to a country with which his nation was at war.) American privateering ended in 1783, after which Salem's trade with the East Indies remained dominant until the War of 1812. Among the many items that were part of Salem's international trade were porcelains and silks from China; cotton cloth from India; ceramics made in England, Germany, and France; furniture; spices such as cinnamon and pepper; and indigo dye.

Salem Maritime National Historic Site (it became the first National Historic Site in the country in 1938) encompasses historic buildings, wharves, and a reproduction of a tall

An 1871 lighthouse sits at the tip of Derby Wharf.

ship, which preserve the heritage of the sailors, Revolutionary War privateers, and merchants who brought the riches of the Far East to America.

The national historic site's orientation center is in a former warehouse built in the 1770s; it stood on Front Street in Salem until it was moved to its site at Central Wharf in 1976. The film "To the Farthest Ports of the Rich East" is shown here, and visitors can make free reservations to see the historic buildings and ship *Friendship*.

The three wharves that extend into Salem Harbor at the national

historic site are the best surviving examples of the more than 50 wharves that once lined the harbor. Central Wharf dates from 1791; and Hatch's Wharf, the shortest wharf, from 1819. Derby Wharf, the longest of the three, was begun in 1762 by Richard Derby, Sr., a wealthy Salem merchant (his son, Elias Hasket Derby, was one of America's wealthiest citizens).

Docked at Salem Harbor is a modern, full-size model of the East India vessel *Friendship,* which was launched in 1797 and made voyages to India, China, South America, England, Germany, the Mediterranean, and Russia. The ship was captured by the British in the War of 1812. Guided tours of *Friendship* and other park sites are offered year-round, though the schedule varies so check with the park or visit the website for schedules.

Other structures within the national historic site include the Narbonne House, built in 1675 for butcher Thomas Ives; the Derby House, built in 1762 as a wedding present for Elias Hasket Derby and his wife, Elizabeth; the 1819 Custom House, where famed author (and Salem native) Nathaniel Hawthorne worked from 1846 to 1848; and the West India Goods Store, built about 1804 and used as a warehouse and shop for items from all over the world.

160 Derby St.
Salem, MA
978-740-1650
www.nps.gov/sama

AT A GLANCE Northeastern Massachusetts, 15 miles northeast of Boston ▪ 9 acres ▪ Spring through fall ▪ Visiting reproduction sailing ship and historic buildings

Saugus Iron Works National Historic Site

Where America's iron and steel industry was born

The 17th-century settlers of the Massachusetts Bay Colony needed a variety of manufactured goods as they built houses, farmed, and raised families in what was then the wilderness of North America. They brought some tools and other supplies with them from Europe, but a local source was a necessity.

From 1646 until 1668, an enterprise called the Saugus Iron Works produced the wrought iron bars that were used to manufacture goods, including axes, saws, hoes, nails, pots, skillets, firebacks, and hinges, using skilled workmen brought to the New World from England. Set along the Saugus River in eastern Massachusetts, just off the road between Boston and Salem, it was the first integrated

Carbon was removed from the pig iron at the forge.

ironmaking plant in colonial America.

Saugus Iron Works eventually went out of business, a victim of poor management, high production costs, and competition from imported iron. Nonetheless, because some of its workers moved to different regions of New England and continued to work in the iron industry, Saugus can be said to have helped provide a start

to the United States iron and steel industry.

The Saugus Iron Works National Historic Site features a blast furnace, forge, rolling mill, warehouse, working waterwheels, and dock area, all of which have been reconstructed on their original sites with designs based on extensive archaeological excavations. The park also includes the Iron Works House, a timber-framed 1680s mansion, still standing on its original location. It contains exhibits and period furnishings.

The park museum is set in a former chicken coop and blacksmith shop. It houses some of the thousands of artifacts found on the old iron works site. Visitors may also watch the 12-minute video entitled "Iron Works on the Saugus."

244 Central St.
Saugus, MA
781-233-0050
www.nps.gov/sair

AT A GLANCE Eastern Massachusetts, 9 miles northeast of Boston ▪ 9 acres ▪ Spring through fall ▪ Visiting reconstructed iron works

Springfield Armory National Historic Site

The source of weapons that fought America's wars

In 1777, in the midst of the Revolutionary War, an arsenal was established at Springfield, Massachusetts, near the Connecticut River, to manufacture ammunition, repair and store weapons, and maintain artillery. In 1794, after the United States had won its independence, President George Washington ordered that the site be used to manufacture flintlock muskets so the new nation wouldn't

be dependent on foreign weapons.

For the next 174 years, until the Springfield Armory closed in 1968, it developed and manufactured America's military weapons. Among these were many of the most famous arms in history, including the muzzle-loading Springfield rifle of the Civil War, the bolt-action Springfield Model 1903 of World War I, and the powerful Springfield M-1 Garand rifle of World

War II. The manufacturing methods developed at the armory, such as the use of interchangeable parts, formed the basis for the precision-metals industry in the United States, making possible mass production of many industrial items.

The museum at Springfield Armory National Historic Site is located in the main Arsenal Building, dating from around 1848.

In addition to showing an 18-minute orientation film and providing several video kiosks, the museum contains the largest collection of historic American military shoulder arms in the world. Along with muskets and rifles (the bulk of the collection), the museum also displays pistols, machine guns, edged weapons (swords and bayonets), and production machinery. Call the park for information on weekend ranger-led programs.

One Armory Sq.
Springfield, MA
413-734-8551
www.nps.gov/spar

AT A GLANCE

Southwestern Massachusetts, in the city of Springfield ▪ 55 acres ▪ Year-round ▪ Visiting museum collections of historic military weapons

NEW HAMPSHIRE

More than three-quarters of New Hampshire's residents live in the south, while the north is sparsely inhabited, heavily forested, and dominated by timber and paper production and outdoor recreational activities. Some residents work in the Boston metropolitan area, opting to live in slower-paced New Hampshire. The technology sector and tourism have replaced textile and small manufacturing as chief income producers. New Hampshire's (and New England's) highest peak, 6,288-foot Mount Washington, is notorious for having some of the world's worst winter weather. The state's coastline is the shortest of any state—just 18 miles long. The U.S. Navy maintains a shipyard in Portsmouth.

Saint-Gaudens National Historic Site
The home and works of one of America's most honored sculptors

Augustus Saint-Gaudens named his home (right) Aspet, after the village of his father's birthplace in the Pyrenees.

Augustus Saint-Gaudens—born in Dublin, Ireland, in 1848 to a French father and an Irish mother—went on to win acclaim as one of the finest sculptors in American history, as well as the designer of a double-eagle gold coin that many consider the most beautiful ever minted in the country.

Having come to New York City with his parents when he was six months old, Saint-Gaudens studied in Europe before returning to the

United States. In his thirties he began creating a series of public sculptures that brought him fame, including "Standing Lincoln" (Abraham Lincoln) in Chicago, the Adams Memorial in Washington, D.C., the Robert Gould Shaw Memorial in Boston, and a statue of Gen. William T. Sherman in New York's Central Park. His design for the 1907 $20 gold piece ranks at the top of American numismatic achievements.

Saint-Gaudens lived near Cornish, New Hampshire, where he worked, created gardens, and inspired an artists' colony. His homesite is now Saint-Gaudens National Historic Site, where more than a hundred of his works are exhibited in the galleries and on the grounds. From Memorial Day weekend through October, visitors can tour the sculptor's home, Aspet, and take guided tours of the gardens and exhibit galleries. The grounds remain open in winter, though snow can make touring the property difficult.

Several films on Saint-Gaudens and the process of creating sculptures are offered in the park visitor center, and in summer a sculptor-in-residence works in a studio on the grounds, allowing visitors to watch the creative process and ask questions. Concerts of classical music are held on Sunday afternoons in July and August.

The park is located on a west-facing slope with fine views of Mount Ascutney and the Green Mountains of Vermont. Two miles of hiking trails wind through more than 100 acres of woodlands, fields, and wetlands within the park. White-tailed deer, eastern chipmunks, gray squirrels, beavers, and mink might be seen along the trails, as well as more than 60 species of breeding birds.

---

139 Saint-Gaudens Rd.
(off N.H. 12A)
Cornish, NH
603-675-2175
www.nps.gov/saga

AT A GLANCE

Western New Hampshire, 60 miles northwest of Concord ▪ 150 acres ▪ Memorial Day weekend through October ▪ Touring Saint-Gaudens's home, viewing sculptures, hiking

---

NEW JERSEY

The most densely populated state, New Jersey lies in the middle of the great metropolitan corridor stretching from Boston to Washington, D.C., with numerous residents commuting to work in New York or Philadelphia. Manufacturing and transportation are big business. A surprising amount of land is still devoted to agriculture, though expanding suburbs eat up more farmland each year. The Pinelands, a unique ecosystem of sandy soil, swamps, and meandering rivers, covers a large area in the south. Famed Atlantic City sits on the southeastern shore, while the resort town of Cape May occupies the southern tip, where bird-watchers flock to see the spring and fall migrations.

Gateway National Recreation Area

Endless recreational opportunities near America's largest urban area

In 1972, the concept of an expansive National Park Service–administered recreation area in the heart of a major urban center was somewhat revolutionary. National parks and recreation areas were usually seen as wild places far from cities, with horizons bounded by mountains and forests. Gateway National Recreation Area represented a change in thinking when it was created that year, making the Park Service a large-scale landowner and neighbor to millions of people in the United States' most populous metropolitan area. Nowadays, an estimated ten million visitors enjoy Gateway's many park sites each year, and in most places the skyscrapers of Manhattan loom in the distance.

Covering more than 26,000 acres

Fort Wadsworth, beneath the Verrazano-Narrows Bridge, is one of the oldest military sites in New York Harbor.

in New York and New Jersey, the park comprises 11 separate sites in three main units clustered around the entrance to New York Harbor. Some are oriented toward beach recreation, others toward wildlife, history, participatory sports, or an array of other activities, from golf to educational programs to model-airplane flying. So diverse are the recreational possibilities here that it's nearly impossible to briefly characterize Gateway's opportunities—except to say that there truly is something for everybody.

Sandy Hook Unit

The Sandy Hook Unit *(732-872-5970)* encompasses 2,044 acres on a barrier beach peninsula at the northern tip of the Jersey shore. Thousands of visitors come in the summer to swim, sunbathe, windsurf, fish, or otherwise enjoy its beautiful beaches. (Gunnison Beach is a popular quasi-official "clothing optional" beach.) Walkers, bicyclists, and in-line skaters also share the 5-mile-long Multi-Use Pathway.

Now an inactive military base, Fort Hancock provided coastal defense for New York Harbor from 1895 until 1974. Tours of various parts of the fort are offered seasonally. Visitors can see the historic 1764 Sandy Hook Lighthouse, America's oldest continuously operated lighthouse, which is open seven days a week for tours (group reservations must be made in advance). The Keeper's Quarters is located adjacent to the lighthouse.

The salt marshes, ponds, fields, and a holly forest at the Sandy Hook Unit also attract a wide variety of bird species, making it an excellent place for bird-watching.

Staten Island Unit

A Gateway unit *(718-354-4500)* on New York's Staten Island includes Great Kills Park, a 580-acre tract with hiking trails, recreational fields, a multi-use pathway, and a popular marina. Tours are offered of 19th-century Fort Wadsworth, beside the Verrazano-Narrows Bridge at the entrance to New York's Inner Harbor. Miller Field, a former Army Air Corps base, is a hub of sports activities and has a white-oak forest that's good for bird-watching.

Jamaica Bay Unit

Jamaica Bay Wildlife Refuge in Queens is the only wildlife refuge in the National Park System. Its 9,155 acres comprise marsh, fields, woods, freshwater and brackish ponds, and an open expanse of bay. New York–area bird-watchers flock to Jamaica Bay in hopes of seeing one of the numerous rarities that have appeared here over the years. Programs and tours are offered throughout the year; information is available at the refuge visitor contact station.

Also in Queens, Breezy Point includes the Breezy Point Tip, an isolated peninsula beach with more than 200 acres of sand dunes, marshes, and coastal grasslands, an important nesting area for the threatened piping plover; Jacob Riis Park, a popular beach with a restored 1932 art deco bathhouse; and Fort Tilden, a decommissioned military base with attractive beaches, where several buildings have been adapted into a center for the arts.

Floyd Bennett Field, in Brooklyn, opened in 1931 as New York's first municipal airport, and served as a naval air station in World War II. It now offers visitors the chance to learn about the history of aviation; basic information on the entire Jamaica Bay Unit *(718-318-4340)* is also available.

The former runways are popular with model-airplane enthusiasts. Not far away, anglers cast for bluefish and fluke off Canarsie Pier, which stretches 600 feet into Jamaica Bay.

---

www.nps.gov/gate
www.nyharborparks.org
/visit/gana.html

AT A GLANCE Eastern New Jersey and Southeastern New York, in the vicinity of New York Harbor ▪ 26,600 acres ▪ Year-round ▪ Swimming, hiking, bird-watching, bicycling, camping, picnicking, boating, fishing

---

Great Egg Harbor N.S. & R.R.

A still natural river winding through New Jersey's Pinelands

In 1992, the Great Egg Harbor River was added to the National Wild and Scenic Rivers System in recognition of its natural, scenic, and recreational attributes. Beginning near the New Jersey town of Berlin, it flows for 59 miles to reach the Atlantic Ocean a few miles south of the bustling resort of Atlantic City.

The Great Egg (as locals call it) flows through Pinelands National Reserve (see p. 41), which encompasses more than one million acres of the area known as the Pinelands, or Pine Barrens, with sandy soil and woodlands dominated by pitch pine and scrub oak. Its lower reaches are wide and popular with boaters and anglers, while upstream the river is narrower, less visited, and quieter, with banks vegetated with red maple, blueberry, sweet bay, and swamp azalea.

Great Egg Harbor National Scenic and Recreational River is a National Park Service partnership area, with local management coordinated by a nonprofit organization called the Great Egg Harbor Watershed Association *(www.gehwa.org)*. The group has information on field trips and programs.

Canoeing and kayaking are popular, especially on the 22-mile stretch downstream from the town of Penny Pot, New Jersey. Boat rentals are available from outfitters in Mays Landing, where a dam on the river forms Lake Lenape.

215-597-5823
www.nps.gov/greg

AT A GLANCE Southern New Jersey, 25 miles northwest of Atlantic City ▪ 129 river miles ▪ Spring through fall ▪ Canoeing, kayaking, bird-watching

---

Morristown National Historical Park

Encampment sites of George Washington's Continental Army

Twice during the height of the Revolutionary War, Gen. George Washington chose Morristown, New Jersey, as his headquarters and encampment sites for forces of the Continental Army. The town had a strategic location with good access to roads and resources, and, while close to the British stronghold of New York City, was not vulnerable to

Wick House, Jockey Hollow

surprise attack because of the intervening terrain.

Morristown National Historical Park preserves sites associated with the two winter encampments of the Continental Army, and interprets the historical significance of those periods—one of which, winter 1779–1780, is considered by historians to have been the worst winter of the 18th century. Authorized in 1933, Morristown was America's first national historical park.

Washington Headquarters Unit

The Washington Headquarters Unit includes the Ford Mansion, a Georgian-style house that served as George Washington's command center during winter 1779–1780. Visited by guided tours only, the house includes furnishings that were present during Washington's stay. The tour begins in an adjacent museum, which has exhibits and offers an interpretive film.

Fort Nonsense Unit

The Fort Nonsense Unit preserves the site of a fortification constructed on Washington's orders in May 1777. The hill site (which may have received its name from the mistaken belief after the Revolution that the construction was simply a "keep busy" project for soldiers) had a good view of roads leading into town and was also planned as a place of retreat in case of British attack on Morristown (such an attack never occurred). Interpretive signs and reproduction cannon here assist visitors in understanding the site's significance.

Jockey Hollow Unit

Southwest of town is the park's expansive Jockey Hollow Unit, where soldiers camped during winter 1779–1780. The visitor center *(973-543-4030)* here shows a film and features exhibits and a full-size model hut of the type used by soldiers during their encampment.

An interpretive road through the Jockey Hollow area passes additional rebuilt huts, and there are 27 miles of trails for hiking, horseback riding, and cross-country skiing. These trails link to a Morris County project called the Patriots' Path, a trail system that will link many historical and recreational sites in the area. In addition, the circa 1750 Wick House, in Jockey Hollow, which quartered Maj. Gen. Arthur St. Clair during that winter, has been restored as a typical farm of the Revolutionary War period.

AT A GLANCE

30 Washington Pl.
Morristown, NJ
973-539-2016
www.nps.gov/morr

Northern New Jersey, 20 miles west of Newark ▪ 1,700 acres ▪ Spring through fall ▪ Visiting museums, touring Revolutionary War sites, hiking

---

Paterson Great Falls National Historical Park
One of America's most important early industrial centers

Designated a national historical park in 2011, Paterson Great Falls commemorates one of the country's earliest manufacturing cities. Alexander Hamilton, American statesman and Treasury secretary, saw the 77-foot-high Great Falls on the Passaic River as a force that could be harnessed to power nearby factories. Determined to make America economically independent of foreign powers, Hamilton was among those who founded the Society for Establishing Useful Manufacturers (S.U.M.) to encourage businesses that would compete with the products being imported from England's thriving industries.

Beginning in 1792, factories here turned out textiles, locomotives, guns, and other goods. Silk production was so important that Paterson gained the nickname "Silk City." Like many industrial areas, Paterson suffered economic decline in the 20th century, with its associated urban problems.

Today, visitors can view the spectacular Great Falls from viewpoints on both banks of the Passaic River, as well as the raceways that channeled river water to power machinery. National Park Service rangers conduct tours interpreting the city's history, including several still-standing factories from the height of the manufacturing era. The nearby Paterson Museum displays remnants of the city's industrial past, including textile machines, locomotives, and a prototype of the first modern submarine. As the new park is developed, additional facilities, tours, and interpretive programs will be added, including a focus on Paterson's important role in America's labor movement for better pay and conditions for factory workers.

AT A GLANCE

72 McBride Ave.
Paterson, NJ
973-523-5295
www.nps.gov/pagr

Northern New Jersey, 14 miles northwest of New York City ▪ 40 acres ▪ Year-round ▪ Walking tour centered on historic and scenic waterfall

Pinelands National Reserve

America's first national reserve offering countless recreational choices

Established in 1978 as the country's first national reserve, Pinelands encompasses more than 1.1 million acres of communities, farms, woodlands, streams, and marshes—all told, the reserve covers 22 percent of New Jersey. The area is often called the Pine Barrens area, though its ecological diversity makes it anything but barren—in fact, UNESCO designated Pinelands as an international biosphere reserve. The reserve constitutes the largest area of open space on the mid-Atlantic coast.

The reserve is a unique partnership between the Park Service and the state of New Jersey. About two-thirds of the area is privately owned. Land use is regulated by the New Jersey Pinelands Commission *(www.nj.gov/pinelands)* in cooperation with state agencies and local governments.

A small sampling of the sites within the reserve includes Belleplain State Forest; Island Beach State Park; Edwin B. Forsythe National Wildlife Refuge; Pine Barrens Byway;

Lily pads on Bordens Mill Branch in Pinelands

and 50-mile Batona Trail, which links Brendan T. Byrne, Wharton, and Bass River State Forests. Also within the reserve are many waterways including the Mullica River and its tributaries and both Great Egg Harbor (see p. 39) and Maurice National Scenic and Recreational River. These waterways are popular canoeing and kayaking destinations.

The high-quality water, sandy soil, and prevalent fire history of the Pinelands lead to a variety of plant communities, including upland forests of pitch pine and oak, some of it "pygmy forest" with mature trees less than seven feet high. Swamps and wetland bogs are home to hardwoods and Atlantic white cedar. Notable flora and fauna include rare amphibians, reptiles, orchids, and carnivious plants.

609-894-7300
www.nps.gov/pine
www.nj.gov/pinelands

AT A GLANCE Vast area of Southern New Jersey, north and west of Atlantic City ▪ 1.1 million acres ▪ Spring through fall best ▪ Hiking, camping, boating, fishing, wildlife-watching

---

Thomas Edison National Historical Park

The home and laboratory of a legendary inventor

The most famous and prolific inventor in United States history, Thomas Alva Edison created, developed, or significantly improved technology such as the lightbulb, the electric power system, the phonograph, the stock ticker, the telegraph, storage

batteries, and motion pictures. Edison was granted 1,093 U.S. patents, still a record number for a single person.

Born in Milan, Ohio, in 1847, Edison later moved to New Jersey, where he did much of his early work at Menlo Park (he was popularly

known as the wizard of Menlo Park). In 1886 he and his second wife moved to West Orange, New Jersey. He bought a 29-room Queen Anne–style mansion called Glenmont and built a laboratory nearby that was ten times larger than the one in Menlo Park.

"I will have the best equipped & largest laboratory extant and the facilities superior to any other for rapid and cheap development of an invention," Edison wrote. He lived and worked here until his death in 1931.

Thomas Edison National Historical Park preserves the laboratory complex and the entire Glenmont estate including the house filled with his belongings, inventions, and photographs. The park visitor center, located at the laboratory complex, offers an introductory film on Edison's life and work; there are also exhibit spaces covering historic photographs and documents, libraries, machine shops, inventions, products, and related subjects. Visitors can take a self-guided audio tour of the laboratory buildings and the garage at the Glenmont estate with several of his cars, including an early electric model.

211 Main St.
West Orange, NJ
973-736-0550
www.nps.gov/edis

AT A GLANCE

Northeastern New Jersey, 5 miles northwest of Newark ■ 21 acres ■ Year-round ■ Touring Edison's home, laboratory, and associated buildings

NEW YORK

To many people New York is synonymous with New York City, the metropolis that—along with its nightlife, shopping, and high finance—contains many historic sites. The U.S. capital from 1785 to 1790, the city remains a place of global significance and influence. Yet beyond it lies a big state with attractions such as the beaches of Fire Island, the glacially sculpted Finger Lakes, and Niagara Falls. Farms and wineries in the upstate area produce goods shipped throughout the Northeast and beyond. The vital transportation waterways of the St. Lawrence and Hudson Rivers, Erie Canal, and Great Lakes have been instrumental in the growth of the country.

African Burial Ground National Monument
Earliest known African cemetery excavated in North America

The outdoor memorial at African Burial Ground National Monument

From the 1690s until the 1790s, thousands of captive and freed Africans and their descendants were buried at a site in today's Lower Manhattan in New York City. Burial of Africans was not allowed within the city walls of the Dutch city of New Amsterdam (later New York City), and consequently as many as 15,000 bodies were interred at the site. Closed in 1794 and nearly forgotten to history, buried under urban growth over the ensuing decades, the grounds were rediscovered in 1991 during the construction of a federal office building.

Preservation efforts and public outcry against the desecration of the burial ground prompted a redesign, which allowed a portion of the cemetery to be saved. The burial ground was declared a national monument in 2006.

A visitor center within the federal building contains exhibits and interpretive displays. Ancestral remains of 419 individuals were ceremonially reinterred at the site in 2003, and copies of some artifacts found in the location are displayed, as are commemorative artworks specially commissioned for the national monument. In October 2007 a granite memorial was dedicated, incorporating a symbolic "Door of Return" and a world map centered on a West African slave port.

Ranger-led walking tours are conducted from the site, focusing on African-American heritage in New York City. Check with the park website or visitor center for a schedule.

290 Broadway
New York, NY
212-637-2019
www.nps.gov/afbg

AT A GLANCE

Lower Manhattan, New York City ▪ 0.3 acre ▪ Year-round ▪ Walking tours, Viewing outdoor memorial and exhibits in visitor center

Castle Clinton National Monument

A 19th-century fort that became a gateway for millions of immigrants

Southwest Battery was one of more than a dozen fortifications built to defend New York Harbor against possible British attack at the time of the War of 1812. The circular sandstone structure, located off the tip of Manhattan Island, was renamed in 1817 in honor of Mayor DeWitt Clinton. The military abandoned the coastal defense in 1821 and the fort was deeded to New York City in 1823, having never fired on an enemy force.

In succeeding years landfill extended the Battery area of Manhattan to encompass Castle Clinton, which was used as a restaurant, concert hall, and theater. In 1855 it was converted to an immigration station, and over the next 34 years more than eight million people entered the United States here. It later housed the New York City Aquarium and became one of the city's most popular attractions until it closed in 1941. Saved from demolition in 1946, Castle Clinton was restored to its original condition as an early 19th-century fort and given official designation as a national monument. It now serves as a museum as well as the ticket office for those who take the ferries to Ellis Island and the Statue of Liberty (see p. 55).

Park rangers guide thrice-daily tours of the site, interpreting the varied history of Castle Clinton and its many lives as fort, entertainment center, immigration depot, and aquarium. The museum's exhibits detail the site and interpret its role as the gateway to America for millions of immigrants.

"The Immigrants" celebrates diversity and fortitude.

Battery Park
New York, NY
212-344-7220
www.nps.gov/cacl

AT A GLANCE

Lower Manhattan, New York City ▪ 1 acre ▪ Year-round ▪ Touring historic fort, attending ranger programs

Eleanor Roosevelt National Historic Site

The home of the "First Lady of the World"

One of the most influential women of the 20th century, Eleanor Roosevelt, wife of Franklin D. Roosevelt, 32nd President of the United States, was a formidable advocate for human rights, equality for women, and world peace.

The Roosevelts owned a property near Hyde Park, New York, called Val-Kill that they considered a favorite retreat and picnic spot. In the 1920s, Eleanor and two associates set up a business there, employing local people in making furniture and other items. When that endeavor ended in 1936, Eleanor Roosevelt converted the factory building into a cottage (it is known as Val-Kill Cottage today), and after her husband's death, she made it her principal home, and lived there until her death in 1962. Her advocacy for

Stone Cottage was built as a retreat, on the suggestion of Franklin D. Roosevelt.

human rights issues caused President Harry Truman to call her "First Lady of the World."

Eleanor Roosevelt National Historic Site was the first National Park Service site dedicated to an American First Lady. Guided tours lead visitors through Val-Kill Cottage; and

a short film, "Close to Home," provides an overview in her own words.

Another building on the grounds, called Stone Cottage, was built in 1925 and was used as a retreat and "political think tank" by Eleanor Roosevelt and her friends. The building now houses an exhibit on them.

N.Y. 9G
Hyde Park, NY
800-337-8474
www.nps.gov/elro

AT A GLANCE

Southeastern New York, 90 miles north of New York City ▪ 181 acres ▪ Spring through fall ▪ Touring cottage and grounds

Federal Hall National Memorial

A site of crucial events in the earliest years of the United States

Several momentous acts in U.S. history took place at this site on Manhattan's famed Wall Street, including the inauguration of George Washington in 1789 as the first President of the United States and the first meeting of America's Congress and its passage of the Bill of Rights.

Historic events had occurred here even before the Revolutionary War. The building that stood here

in the 18th century was New York's original City Hall. It was the site of the libel trial of printer John Peter Zenger, whose acquittal was a milestone for the concept of freedom of the press. The Stamp Act Congress met here to protest "taxation without representation."

When New York was the national capital (1785–1790), the original Federal Hall was the seat of government.

When the capital moved to Philadelphia in 1790, the building housed city government until it was demolished in 1812. The current building, an impressive columned structure in the Greek Revival style, was completed in 1842 as the U.S. Customs House.

At Federal Hall National Memorial, the George Washington Inaugural Gallery features exhibits about the nation's first Inauguration, models of the original City Hall and Federal Hall, pieces of the original building, and the Bible that Washington used to take the oath of office. The New York Harbor Visitor Information Center can help visitors learn about things to do in Lower Manhattan and opportunities provided at the 23 destinations of the ten national parks of New York Harbor.

Park rangers lead three tours daily of the building on weekdays. In addition, rangers guide historical walks through the Wall Street neighborhood; check with the park office for details and schedules.

Each year in April costumed interpreters hold a reenactment of George Washington's 1789 Inauguration. A statue of Washington stands in front of the national memorial building.

---

26 Wall St.
New York, NY
212-825-6888
www.nps.gov/feha

AT A GLANCE

Lower Manhattan, New York City ▪ 0.4 acre ▪ Year-round (closed weekends) ▪ Viewing museum exhibits, taking ranger-led programs

---

Fire Island National Seashore
A quiet island escape from city congestion and traffic

Less than three hours from Manhattan, this mostly undeveloped, quiet, almost vehicle-free expanse of beach, sand dunes, forest, and wetlands offers a near-total contrast to the noise and bustle of metropolitan life. A unique mix of wilderness, recreation, and private communities, Fire Island has long symbolized escape for city dwellers seeking a quiet place to relax, as well as serving as a rewarding destination for nature enthusiasts eager to explore its varied habitats.

Fire Island is a 32-mile-long barrier island paralleling the southern coast of New York's Long Island. Averaging less than a mile in width, it's bounded on the north by bays, on the south by the Atlantic Ocean, and on the east and west by inlets separating it from other islands. The island can be reached only by car at its eastern and western ends; the island's road network is limited to small sections of the island, with no public roads through the main part, and even bicycle use is restricted in many areas. Ferries, water taxis, and private boats provide alternative means of transportation.

Fire Island National Seashore, established in 1964, stretches along 26 miles of the island. (It also includes the William Floyd Estate, a 613-acre historical site on the mainland of Long Island, donated to the park in 1965.)

The national seashore's most unusual attribute may be the 17 communities encompassed within its boundaries. The legislation that created it specified that these communities and preexisting commercial uses would be allowed to remain as long as development was consistent with zoning ordinances established by the secretary of the Interior. This means that the national seashore's lonely, windswept beaches, centuries-old forest, and wilderness exist not far from marinas, restaurants, hotels, businesses, and small towns. While some communities feature tourist facilities, others treasure their privacy and do little or nothing to encourage or even accommodate visitors.

The logistical issues involved in visiting Fire Island National Seashore make planning a priority—studying ferry schedules and hours of operation of various facilities is a must—but for those who prepare well, a visit here can be rewarding on many levels, from a sunny day at the beach to a wilderness camping experience. The national seashore has four visitor centers spaced along the island.

Fire Island Wilderness

The Fire Island Wilderness Visitor Center, located at the eastern end of the National Park Service property adjacent to Smith Point County Park, offers an interpretive film, a second-floor viewing area and exhibit space, ranger-led interpretive programs, and boardwalk access to the wilderness. Just west is the 1,363-acre Otis Pike Fire Island High Dune Wilderness, the only federally designated wilderness area in New York. Backcountry camping behind the dunes and salt marsh is allowed in the wilderness. Reservations are required and campers can access the wilderness via Watch Hill.

Fire Island Lighthouse

The Fire Island Lighthouse stands at the western end of the national seashore (though not of Fire Island: Robert Moses State Park is composed of the western part of the island).

FOLLOWING PAGES: *A bridge spans Fire Island Inlet to reach the distant western end of Fire Island, a barrier island.*

The original lighthouse here was built in 1826; the current 167-foot structure was completed in 1858. Its still operational light can be seen more than 20 miles away. The Fire Island Lighthouse is operated by a nonprofit preservation society under a cooperative agreement with the Park Service. It has exhibits, a nature trail, interpretive programs, and a gift shop. Birders come here September through mid-November to watch the fall migration of hawks.

The lighthouse site offers a lesson in the changing nature of barrier islands' geography: The first Fire Island Lighthouse was built at the end of Fire Island in 1826. Today, the Fire Island Inlet is more than 5 miles west of this foundation, as ocean currents have altered the landscape.

Watch Hill & Sailors Haven Visitor Centers

Watch Hill and Sailors Haven Visitor Centers are located in the middle of the island, accessible only by boat (or by a very long walk from the nearest road). Watch Hill Visitor Center *(open seasonally)* shows the Fire Island National Seashore orientation film and has an aquarium, bookstore, and adjacent nature trail. Guided canoe tours are offered during the summer. Watch Hill is located at the western edge of the High Dune Wilderness, and permits are available for backcountry camping *(www.recreation.gov)*. Watch Hill also has a family campground with restrooms.

The Sailors Haven Visitor Center offers similar features as Watch Hill, as well as interpretive exhibits specific to the nearby Sunken Forest. A 1.5-mile boardwalk trail leads through this rare example of maritime holly forest. The 40-acre woodland is dominated by American holly, with some trees estimated to be as much as 300 years old. Other trees in this forest include sassafras, serviceberry, black and post oaks, black cherry, and pitch pine. The forest is not really "sunken"; it appears so because it is protected by a dune behind which its canopy is "sunken."

Watch Hill and Sailors Haven both offer marinas, dining, and stores, as well as lifeguarded swimming beaches. An estimated 2.2 million people spend time on Fire Island each year, and a high percentage of those visits involve beaches on weekends in July and August. Even so, visitors willing to arrive on a weekday and walk away from developed areas can find uncrowded beaches for swimming, sunbathing, and picnicking.

Wildlife-watching

Fire Island's mix of forest, dune, and marsh habitats makes it an excellent place for bird-watching. More than 330 species have been sighted at the

Still operational, the Fire Island Lighthouse serves as a navigation aid to those at sea and on Great South Bay.

island, from small songbirds to loons, ducks, gulls, and other waterbirds. Two threatened and endangered birds that nest within Fire Island National Seashore are the piping plover and the roseate tern. Sections of beach are closed temporarily each spring and summer to protect nesting birds.

More than 30 mammal types can be seen within the seashore boundaries, including white-tailed deer, cottontail rabbits, red foxes, and mink. Whales occasionally pass near enough to be spotted from shore, and harbor seals are sometimes seen in winter.

| Park headquarters 120 Laurel St. Patchogue, NY 631-687-4750 www.nps.gov/fiis | AT A GLANCE | Southeastern New York, off Long Island ▪ 19,579 acres (6,241 federally owned); about 15,000 acres are bay and ocean ▪ Year-round, spring through fall best ▪ Swimming, hiking, camping, beachcombing, boating, fishing, taking historical tours |

Fort Stanwix National Monument

On a vital transportation route that played a role in two wars

American Indians of the Six Nations (Cayuga, Mohawk, Oneida, Onondaga, Seneca, and Tuscarora) used a portage path to travel between the Mohawk River and Wood Creek, a 1- to 6-mile trip, depending on the season and water levels. The portage took on major importance during the fur-trading years, when it was part of the route between New York and the Great Lakes.

The British called the route the Oneida Carrying Place and built a series of trading posts and forts along it in the early and middle 18th century. The largest of them, built in 1758, was Fort Stanwix. It was active in the French and Indian War (1754–1763), but it was later abandoned. Patriot forces rebuilt the fort during the American Revolution and renamed it Fort Schuyler. British troops laid siege to the fort for 21 days in 1777, but they withdrew to Canada because of fierce resistance and the arrival of American reinforcements. The defense of the fort stymied a British effort to move down the Mohawk Valley and conquer the northern Colonies, and led to the American victories at Saratoga, a turning point of the Revolutionary War.

Fort Stanwix National Monument centers on a reconstruction of the fort, now located in downtown Rome, New York, near the Erie Canal. Visitors should begin their experience at the Willett Center, housing museum exhibits, a historical time line, a bookstore, and an introductory film. The national monument has three short trails that circle the fort. One follows a portion of the Oneida Carrying Place; the other two interpret the events of the siege of 1777. Ranger-led programs and living-history demonstrations are offered seasonally.

| 100 N. James St. Rome, NY 315-338-7730 www.nps.gov/fost | AT A GLANCE | Central New York, 40 miles east of Syracuse ▪ 16 acres ▪ Spring through fall ▪ Touring museum and reconstructed fort, taking ranger-led tours |

General Grant National Memorial

A grand monument to "the defender of the Union"

Victorious in many important Civil War battles, Ulysses S. Grant became the first four-star general of the Army and was elected President of the United States in 1868, serving two terms. On his 1885 death, about 90,000 people from around the world donated more than $600,000 toward construction of his tomb, which was dedicated on April 27, 1897. Grant had asked to be buried in New York City, his residence for the last five years of his life. His wife, Julia Dent Grant, is buried beside him.

The marble and granite rotunda (commonly called Grant's Tomb) sits on a bluff overlooking the Hudson River in the Morningside Heights area of Manhattan. More than 150 feet tall, it is the largest mausoleum in North America. The rotunda interior is decorated with mosaics depicting scenes from the Civil War, as well as busts of other Civil War generals. Over the entrance are words from Grant's letter accepting the Republican nomination for President in 1868: "Let us have peace."

Ranger-led talks and tours are offered daily at General Grant National Memorial, and many special events take place on the grounds, from living-history demonstrations to music concerts. A new Overlook Pavilon near the memorial now functions as a visitor center and has public rest rooms—a practical feature the site previously lacked. (According to oral tradition, Mrs. Grant asked that there never be a public rest room in her tomb.)

122nd St. & Riverside Dr.
New York, NY
212-666-1640
www.nps.gov/gegr

AT A GLANCE

Upper Manhattan, New York City ▪ 1 acre ▪ Year-round ▪ Viewing tomb and exhibits, attending special events

Governors Island National Monument

A former military post that preserves important early fortifications

With its location off the tip of New York City's Manhattan Island, 172-acre Governors Island has always played a significant role in the city's life: For centuries it was valued for its strategic military importance, and in the future it will assume a new role culturally and environmentally.

After occupation by American Indians and Dutch settlers, the New York colonial assembly set aside the island for the benefit of their royal governors, leading to its present name. A young United States built forts as part of the federal system of coastal defense. Fort Jay and Castle Williams kept the British from entering New York Harbor in the War of 1812. The U.S. Army turned the post over to the U.S. Coast Guard in 1966; it served for 30 years as its largest base. The Trust for Governors Island *(www.govisland.com)*, an instrumentality of the City of New York, and the National Park Service acquired the island in 2003; the former administers 150 acres, the latter the 22 acres

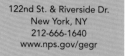

Strategically located, Governors Island was home to many military installations.

designated as a national monument.

The national monument offers seasonal ranger-led and self-guided tours of the historic forts and the later military buildings. Picnicking is allowed on the grounds, which provide excellent views of the Manhattan skyline. Access to the island is via ferry, departing from the Battery Maritime Building *(South & Whitehall Sts.)* in Lower Manhattan. Brooklyn service is available on weekends from Brooklyn Bridge Park Pier 6.

Along with the opening of the Trust's new 34-acre park, plans for the rest of the island call for the development of parkland and the preservation and reuse of more than 50 historic buildings for cultural and educational purposes.

10 South St.
New York, NY
212-825-3045
www.nps.gov/gois

AT A GLANCE

New York City Harbor, between Manhattan and Brooklyn ▪ 22 acres ▪ Memorial Day through September; tour schedule varies by season ▪ Touring forts and national historic landmark district, picnicking

Hamilton Grange National Memorial
The 1802 home of an American Founding Father

Alexander Hamilton, a trusted aide to George Washington during the Revolutionary War, was one of the most influential of the Founding Fathers of the United States. Serving in the Continental Congress, as a delegate to the Constitutional Convention, as co-author of *The Federalist Papers* (which greatly influenced adoption and interpretation of the U.S. Constitution), and as the first secretary of the Treasury, he as much as any other person helped shape what the United States would become.

After he retired from formal public service, Hamilton—who had been born in the West Indies but moved to New York City at age 17—commissioned prominent New York architect John McComb, Jr., to design a house on his 32-acre estate in Upper Manhattan. The house was completed in 1802 and named the Grange after the Hamilton family's ancestral home in Scotland. Hamilton lived there only two years before he was fatally wounded in a duel with political rival Aaron Burr on July 11, 1804.

The Grange was moved in 1889, and for decades it stood between an apartment house and a church. In 2008 it was moved to St. Nicholas Park. Here the Federal-style structure has been restored to its original appearance, and in its open location is visible from all sides, as it was on its original site. (It still sits on land that was part of Hamilton's 32-acre estate.) Recently reopened, the house has exhibits that interpret Alexander Hamilton's life and career as well as the significance and history of the Grange and its New York City neighborhood.

St. Nicholas Park
W. 141st St.
New York, NY
212-666-1640
www.nps.gov/hagr

AT A GLANCE

Hamilton Heights neighborhood, New York City ▪ 1 acre ▪ Spring through fall ▪ Touring house, viewing historical exhibits

Home of Franklin D. Roosevelt National Historic Site
The birthplace and lifelong home of America's 32nd President

Franklin Delano Roosevelt was born in 1882 at Springwood, his family's estate in the Hudson River Valley town of Hyde Park, New York. The boy who would become the 32nd President grew up riding horses, fishing, sailing, and enjoying other outdoor activities on the property. In 1905, five years after his father, James, had died, Franklin married Eleanor Roosevelt (the two were distantly related; she was the niece of President Theodore Roosevelt), and the couple joined his mother, Sara, at Springwood.

Roosevelt considered the Hyde Park estate his home, and lived there at least part-time the rest of his life, even when his official residence was

the White House. He entertained many foreign dignitaries and other notable visitors, including England's King George VI and Winston Churchill. At his request, Roosevelt was buried on the property at his death in 1945. Eleanor was buried at Springwood as well, after her death in 1962. (Fala, the Roosevelts' celebrated Scottish terrier, is buried in Springwood's rose garden with them.)

Visiting the Estate

A visit to the Home of Franklin D. Roosevelt National Historic Site begins at the Henry A. Wallace Visitor and Education Center. Tickets are sold here for visits to the house *(guided tour only)*. Tickets include

admission to the Franklin D. Roosevelt Presidential Library and Museum, located on the grounds. A 22-minute film at the center, "A Rendezvous With History," interprets Roosevelt's life and career as well as his relationship with Springwood.

A quarter-mile walk from the center leads to the Roosevelt House, where visitors can see some of Roosevelt's extensive collections of books, art, birds, naval prints, and political cartoons. Living areas and bedrooms are included on the tour, and visitors can observe changes made to accommodate Roosevelt's partial paralysis, which confined him to a wheelchair.

Self-guided tours are available at the Franklin D. Roosevelt Presidential

Library and Museum *(www .fdrlibrary.marist.edu),* which displays objects such as Roosevelt's desk from the Oval Office in the White House, shown just as he left it on his last day of work; his car, equipped with special hand controls to allow him to drive without the use of his legs; and exhibits on how Roosevelt dealt with the Great Depression and World War II. Roosevelt helped design the presidential library—the first of its kind—and it includes the study where he worked and from which he delivered some of his famous "fireside chat" radio addresses to the American people.

A period re-creation at Springwood

Park visitors can also take a shuttle bus to Roosevelt's Top Cottage *(May–Oct.),* the home he built in 1938 to "escape the mob" at Springwood. Designed by Roosevelt in the Dutch colonial architectural style found throughout the Hudson River Valley, the structure was planned with accessibility in mind to accommodate his wheelchair and give him greater independence.

The 2-mile Farm Lane links Springwood with Val-Kill (see p. 44), allowing visitors to walk the road that FDR once drove between the two estates.

The grounds, gardens, and trails within the national historic site are free and are open from dawn until dusk.

N.Y. 9
Hyde Park, NY
800-337-8474
www.nps.gov/hofr

AT A GLANCE Southeastern New York, 90 miles north of New York City ▪ 645 acres ▪ Spring through fall best ▪ Visiting FDR's home, presidential library and museum, and Top Cottage; touring gardens and grounds

Kate Mullany National Historic Site
Home of influential labor-union leader

In the mid-19th century, Troy, New York, was the manufacturing center for detachable collars and cuffs, which could be washed separately from men's shirts. Thousands of women worked 12 or more hours a day in difficult conditions for $2 a week, washing, starching, and ironing new collars before they were sold.

In 1864, a 25-year-old Irish immigrant named Kate Mullany led a successful strike by her fellow workers, resulting in a 25 percent pay increase and the founding of the Collar Laundry Union, the first women's labor union in the United States.

This was a landmark event in the history of the nation's labor movement, leading to increased cooperation between male and female workers. In 1868, Mullany was named assistant secretary of the National Labor Union, becoming the first woman to hold office in a national labor organization. The National Labor Union head called Mullany "one of the smartest and most energetic women in America."

The three-story house where Kate Mullany lived with her widowed mother and other family members was designated as a national historic site in 2004, in part because of the support of then Sen. Hillary Clinton. At present the house serves as the home of the American Labor Studies Center and does not offer regular visitation. Plans are under way to remodel the top-floor apartment using period furnishings to reflect its appearance when the Mullany family lived there.

350 8th St.
Troy, NY
518-331-4474
www.katemullanynhs.org

AT A GLANCE Central New York, seven miles north of Albany ▪ 0.1 acre ▪ Not yet open for visitation ▪ Future tours of residence with period items

Lower East Side Tenement Museum N.H.S.

Telling the story of New York City immigrants

Many of the millions of immigrants who entered the United States in the 19th and 20th centuries settled in New York City, often in neighborhoods that took on specific national character, such as Chinatown and Little Italy. The Lower East Side of Manhattan was a popular destination for many newcomers, offering affordable (though often cramped) housing. For decades it was a center of the city's Jewish community, though many other national and cultural groups settled in the area as well.

The Tenement Museum recalls the experiences of immigrants in an 1863 tenement building on Orchard Street, in the Lower East Side. An estimated 7,000 people from more than 20 countries lived in this building between 1863 and 1935, many working at various occupations or starting their own businesses in their small rooms.

Guided tours of the tenement focus on themes such as Shop Life (stories of butchers, saloonkeepers, and others), Sweatshop Workers, and Hard Times (survival during the Great Depression and other economic difficulties). Some tours feature costumed interpreters playing the parts of immigrants dealing with life in a new world.

The museum also offers guided tours of the Lower East Side, examining how immigrants created a thriving neighborhood with businesses and traditions that have endured over time. Walking tours are offered on a limited schedule January through mid-March.

103 Orchard St.
New York, NY
212-982-8420; 877-975-3786
www.nps.gov/loea
www.tenement.org

AT A GLANCE Lower Manhattan in New York City ▪ 0.2 acre ▪ Year-round ▪ Guided tours of tenement building and surrounding neighborhood

---

Martin Van Buren National Historic Site

The home of the President called the "red fox of Kinderhook"

The eighth President and the first born in the United States of America (previous Presidents were born under British colonial rule), Martin Van Buren served as U.S. senator, governor of New York, secretary of state, and Vice President before reaching the White House in the election of 1836. He organized the Democratic Party, and his renowned political skills can be inferred from nicknames such as the "little magician" and the "red fox of Kinderhook." The latter refers to the New York town where he was born and where in 1839 he bought an estate he called his "sweet Lindenwald."

In part because of a severe economic depression, Van Buren was defeated for reelection in 1840. He returned to Lindenwald and established a thriving 220-acre farm, from where he ran two more presidential campaigns, in 1844 and 1848. He entertained many politicians, businessmen, celebrities, and other notable guests at Lindenwald during his unsuccessful bids to return to Washington.

Visitors to the site should stop at the visitor center to buy tickets for a guided tour of Van Buren's 36-room Gothic Revival mansion.

Park rangers lead visitors through the main hall, with a banquet table and French wallpaper; the Green Room, a place for socializing, with musical instruments at the ready; the "Best Bedroom," with its canopy bed and carpet reproduced based on fragments found trapped under tacks; other bedrooms; the breakfast room; the library; the kitchen; and the laundry room.

Rangers conduct special programs and events through the park's season *(spring–fall)*. A three-quarter-mile wayside loop trail includes interpretive displays about Van Buren and his farm.

1013 Old Post Rd. (N.Y. 9H)
Kinderhook, NY
518-758-9689
www.nps.gov/mava

AT A GLANCE Eastern New York, 25 miles south of Albany ▪ 300 acres ▪ Mid-May through October ▪ Touring Van Buren's house and farm

Sagamore Hill National Historic Site
Theodore Roosevelt's beloved Long Island home

Theodore Roosevelt looms as large in American popular culture as any U.S. President in history: husband, father, rancher, adventurer, soldier, writer, hunter, nature lover, all-around colorful character, and advocate of "the strenuous life."

Roosevelt's father established a summer home on New York's Long Island when T.R. was 15, and ten years later the young man, then engaged, bought 155 acres in the vicinity. In 1884 he had a house built on the property. His wife, Alice, died that same year, but Roosevelt remarried, and he and his second wife, Edith, moved into the house in 1887.

He named it Sagamore Hill, from an Algonquin word for "a chief." Roosevelt would call this place home until his death in 1919; Edith continued to live at Sagamore Hill until her death in 1948. During his years as President, 1901–09, Roosevelt used Sagamore Hill as the summer White House, where he conducted the nation's business.

Sagamore Hill National Historic Site offers guided tours of the rambling, 23-room shingle-style house, which is full of original Roosevelt family furnishings and personal items. Tours see the library, dining room, kitchen, drawing rooms, bedrooms,

gun room, staff quarters, and piazza.

A Georgian house on the Sagamore Hill property, built in 1937 for Theodore Roosevelt, Jr., houses the Theodore Roosevelt Museum (at Old Orchard), which features exhibits and films on the elder Roosevelt's life and career.

The Sagamore Hill Nature Trail is an easy walk through a forest of oaks and tulip trees and over a boardwalk to Cold Spring Harbor. It's the same path T.R. and his family took on many swimming and camping excursions. Park rangers lead seasonal nature walks around the Sagamore Hill grounds.

20 Sagamore Hill Rd.
Oyster Bay, NY
516-922-4788
www.nps.gov/sahi

AT A GLANCE Southeastern New York, on Long Island, 35 miles east of New York City ▪ 83 acres ▪ Year-round ▪ Touring Roosevelt home; taking summer nature walks

Saint Paul's Church National Historic Site
A church with important ties to the American Revolution

Dating from 1665, the Mount Vernon parish established on this spot, just north of present-day New York, was one of the city's oldest. In the early 18th century, the parish church stood beside the village green of the community of Eastchester, site of the "great election of 1733." In this contest, a local popular candidate defeated the British governor's favorite despite the latter's deceptive actions. Journalist John Peter Zenger published

an account of the election that led to a libel trial establishing important issues of freedom of the press.

The Revolutionary War Battle of Pell's Point occurred nearby in 1776, and the present church, built in 1764, was used as a hospital for wounded soldiers. The bell in the tower was cast in 1758 at the same foundry that produced Philadelphia's famed Liberty Bell. The adjacent 5-acre cemetery contains gravestones dating back to 1704.

Declining attendance at worship services, coupled with the site's historical importance, led to the transfer of the property from the Episcopal Diocese of New York to the National Park Service in 1980. Ranger-guided tours are offered of the restored church on weekdays, including visits to the bell tower and a demonstration of the 1833 pipe organ, one of the oldest functioning organs in the United States.

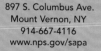
897 S. Columbus Ave.
Mount Vernon, NY
914-667-4116
www.nps.gov/sapa

AT A GLANCE Just north of New York City ▪ 6 acres ▪ Year-round ▪ Taking guided tours of church; visiting historic cemetery

Saratoga National Historical Park
Commemorating the turning point of the American Revolution

In 1777 British troops marched south through New York's Hudson River Valley with a plan to link forces with British-occupied New York City. The hope was to isolate New England from the rest of the states and bring an end to the American struggle for independence. The plan failed.

Battles on September 19 and October 7 south of Saratoga, New York, resulted in an American victory and the surrender of more than 6,000 British forces. The crucial American triumph convinced France to become an American ally and go to war with England, forcing the British to divide their military efforts throughout the world—a major factor leading to the independence of the United States. The Battles of Saratoga have been called "the turning point of

the American Revolution," and truly changed the course of world history.

Saratoga National Historical Park is made up of four noncontiguous locations. The major section comprises the battlefield site, where the visitor center offers an interpretive film, historical displays, and artifacts from the Revolutionary period. Using a brochure and roadside informational displays, visitors can then drive the 9-mile auto tour route, passing important locations such as Neilson Farm, used as a headquarters for patriot forces; Breymann's Redoubt, the site where Gen. Benedict Arnold received a serious leg wound in the October battle (because he later joined the British cause, a monument to him here does not bear his name); and the burial site of British Gen. Simon Fraser, mortally

wounded in the October battle.

Official Saratoga battlefield guides, trained by park personnel, can be hired for personalized tours of the site. In addition, visitors can download audio tours of the battlefield or use mobile phones to listen to interpretive audio programs as they drive the tour route.

Seven miles north of the battlefield, in Schuylerville, the restored 1777 house of American Gen. Philip Schuyler can be visited on free guided tours *(open seasonally)*. The Saratoga Monument, a 155-foot obelisk that commemorates the American victory, stands a short distance away. It is open for visitation on the same schedule as the Schuyler House. A walking path loops through nearby Victory Woods, which marks the final British campsite before the surrender.

AT A GLANCE

U.S. 4, north of Stillwater, NY
518-664-9821
www.nps.gov/sara

Eastern New York, 27 miles north of Albany ▪ 3,392 acres ▪ Year-round ▪ Touring historic battlefield and restored Schuyler House; viewing Saratoga Monument; hiking

---

Statue of Liberty National Monument
Symbol of America to the world

Standing tall over New York Harbor, the Statue of Liberty has welcomed millions of people to the United States, whether Americans returning from abroad, foreign tourists, or immigrants seeking a new life. For additional millions around the globe who have never been to America, Lady Liberty is an instantly recognizable symbol of the United States.

Lady Liberty, one of America's most recognizable icons

The statue—its proper name, "Liberty Enlightening the World"—was a gift from the people of France to the United States. Recognizing the bond established between the two countries during the American Revolution, the statue was originally scheduled to be dedicated in 1876, to commemorate the centennial of the American Declaration of Independence. French

Lady Liberty—more properly, "Liberty Enlightening the World"—has served as a beacon of hope for more than 120 years.

sculptor Frédéric-Auguste Bartholdi was commissioned to design the work, to be paid for by the people of France, while Americans were to build the pedestal. Fund-raising was a problem in both countries, though, and Liberty was dedicated October 28, 1886—ten years late. The statue was installed on an island in New York Harbor inside the walls of Fort Wood, a U.S. military post built around the time of the War of 1812.

Constructed with a shell of copper, the massive statue needed a strong interior skeletal framework for support; the firm of Gustave Eiffel, creator of Paris's Eiffel Tower, designed the iron framework. The statue depicts a robed woman (her face is said to have been modeled on Bartholdi's mother) holding a torch in one hand and a tablet in the other. The torch is a symbol of enlightenment, lighting the path to freedom. The tablet is inscribed in Roman numerals with the date of American Independence: July IV, MDCCLXXVI (July 4, 1776). Lady Liberty wears a crown with seven spikes representing the seven seas and continents of the world.

The Statue of Liberty has seen many changes over the years. It was closed to the public in 1984 for extensive renovation, including replacing parts of the interior support structure, which had deteriorated. The original torch was removed and replaced with a new copper flame covered in 24-karat gold. The gold reflects the sun during the day and is lighted by floodlights at night, truly making Lady Liberty a shining beacon to all those who see it. Visitors have not been allowed to climb to the torch since 1916.

Visiting Lady Liberty

Visits to the Statue of Liberty are made by ferry *(Statue Cruises, www .statuecruises.com, fee)* from either Battery Park in Lower Manhattan or Liberty State Park in New Jersey. Passengers must go through airport-style security screening before boarding a ferry. All those who arrive at Liberty Island are free to roam the 12-acre grounds, but those who want to ascend to the Pedestal or Crown (which includes access to the Liberty exhibit), should secure a reservation ahead of their visit. Reservations for weekends, holidays, and the months of May through September are often full months in advance.

Access to the crown, which was closed following the terrorist attacks of September 11, 2001, reopened to the public on July 4, 2009. Because of the narrow stairway and other concerns, the park limits the number of people who may go up at any one time. There is an extra fee to climb to the crown. Crown tickets need to be purchased at the same time as your ferry ticket. See Statue Cruises' website for more information.

The museum displays exhibits on the statue's history and construction, the original 1886 torch, full-size models of Liberty's face and foot, and a bronze plaque displaying Emma Lazarus's famous poem "The New Colossus" with the iconic lines "Give me your tired, your poor, / Your huddled masses yearning to breathe free, …" The pedestal observation level offers a close-up view of the statue and a spectacular panorama of New York Harbor. Ranger-guided tours of Liberty Island are offered at regularly scheduled times each day.

Ellis Island

Also encompassed within the administration of Statue of Liberty National Monument, and accessed by the same ferry system, is the historic harbor site called Ellis Island. Between 1892 and 1954 this island was the nation's most important federal immigration station, processing more than 12 million immigrant steamship passengers. More than 40 percent of America's population can trace ancestry through Ellis Island. Third-class and steerage immigrants made up the largest group processed at Ellis Island. First- and second-class immigrants were processed aboard steamships.

Abandoned for decades, some structures on the island have been restored. The main attraction for many visitors is the Ellis Island Immigration Museum, which contains three floors of interpretive displays, including an exhibit called "The Peopling of America," examining more than 400 years of immigration history. The film "Island of Hope, Island of Tears" imparts immigrants' experiences. A statue depicts Annie Moore, a 17-year-old Irish girl from County Cork, who on January 1, 1892, became the first immigrant to be processed at Ellis Island. Visitors can see the museum on a self-guided tour or join a ranger-led tour. Special programs are offered at various times, including re-creations of actual immigrant interviews and the events of processing.

Opened in 2001, the American Family Immigration History Center *(www.ellisisland.org)* at Ellis Island holds the more than 22 million passenger records (manifests) for those who arrived at the Port of New York between 1892 and 1924.

Liberty Island
New York, NY
212-363-3200
www.nps.gov/stli
www.nps.gov/elis

AT A GLANCE

New York Harbor ▪ 40 acres ▪ Year-round ▪ Visiting statue, touring museum of immigration on Ellis Island

Theodore Roosevelt Birthplace National Historic Site

The boyhood home of "the conservationist President"

Theodore Roosevelt was born to a wealthy New York City family in 1858, and lived for the first 14 years of his life in a brownstone on East 20th Street in Manhattan. The family home in the fashionable Gramercy neighborhood was also his school, for he was too sickly as a boy to attend regular classes. To help young "Teedie" improve his health, his father built an outdoor gymnasium, the beginning step in Roosevelt's dedication to "the strenuous life," which would lead to adventures as a rancher,

hunter, naturalist, and soldier. His interest in the outdoors and resource protection led to his being called "the conservationist President."

Roosevelt served as President from 1901 to 1909 and died in 1919. His childhood home had been demolished in 1916, but soon after his death an organization of prominent friends and supporters bought the property and reconstructed his early home as a memorial.

Visitors to Theodore Roosevelt Birthplace National Historic Site

take ranger-guided tours through five rooms furnished to recall the gilded age of the 1860s that immediately followed the Civil War, including the parlor, library, dining room, master bedroom, and nursery. Many of the furnishings and other items belonged to T.R. or other Roosevelts, and the house has been decorated according to family members' memories of the original. The site also includes galleries containing hundreds of original items from Roosevelt's life.

28 E. 20th St.
New York, NY
212-260-1616
www.nps.gov/thrb

AT A GLANCE

Manhattan, New York City ▪ 0.1 acre ▪ Year-round ▪ Touring reconstructed Roosevelt childhood home

Theodore Roosevelt Inaugural National Historic Site

The home where T.R. took the oath of office as President

On September 6, 1901, President William McKinley was attending a festival called the Pan-American Exposition in Buffalo, New York, when he was shot by anarchist Leon Czolgosz. Although his condition initially led to hopes of recovery, McKinley took a sudden turn for the worse and died on September 14.

Vice President Theodore Roosevelt, who had traveled to Buffalo but had departed when assured that McKinley would survive, rushed back to the city. Roosevelt went to the house where the late President's body lay and was urged to take the oath of office. He felt that site was

Site of Theodore Roosevelt's swearing-in as President

inappropriate, so instead, he went to the house of his friend Ansley Wilcox, a prominent local lawyer with whom Roosevelt had worked in various capacities. A Buffalo federal judge administered the oath in a brief, improvised ceremony, with

several Cabinet members and other public officials present.

The Wilcox house was originally built as the officers' headquarters for a short-lived U.S. Army post called Poinsett Barracks or Buffalo Barracks, established in 1837 because of a minor insurrection across the border in Canada. The structure eventually became a private residence, and the home of Ansley Wilcox in 1901. In the 1930s it was sold and later turned into a restaurant. In 1966, following a successful effort to save the building from the wrecking ball, the Department of the Interior declared the Wilcox House a national historic site.

Theodore Roosevelt Inaugural National Historic Site offers guided tours of the Wilcox home, with rooms restored based on photographs taken soon after Roosevelt's swearing-in. Exhibits interpret the events of September 1901 and the Roosevelt Presidency. The historic site has state-of-the-art interactives, audio, and lighting techniques that add to the visitor's experience.

Special events at the site include a yearly reenactment of Theodore Roosevelt's 1901 Inauguration on September 14.

641 Delaware Ave.
Buffalo, NY
716-884-0095
www.nps.gov/thri

AT A GLANCE Western New York, in Buffalo ■ 1 acre ■ Year-round ■ Touring restored mansion, viewing historical exhibits

Thomas Cole National Historic Site

Home of the artist who founded the Hudson River school of painting

Born in England in 1801, Thomas Cole moved to the United States in 1818, and within a decade his paintings had made him a notable figure in the American art scene. He first worked in the Catskill Mountains of New York's Hudson River Valley in 1825, and after a period studying in Europe he established a studio at a farm called Cedar Grove. In 1836 he married a niece of Cedar Grove's owner and moved into the house on the property. Nearby he then built a separate studio, which has since been demolished and rebuilt.

Thomas Cole is regarded as the founder of the Hudson River school, an artistic movement that demonstrated awe for the majesty of the American landscapes. It was to become the longest-running art movement in American history. Artists and writers such as James Fenimore Cooper visited Cedar Grove, and Cole took as a student Frederic Church, who would go on to become a prominent figure of the Hudson River school.

Thomas Cole National Historic Site is an affiliated site of the National Park Service. Visitors can take guided tours *(Wed.–Sun., first Sat. in May–last Sun. in Oct., fee)* of the restored 1815 Federal-style Main House, the 1839 Old Studio, and the rebuilt New Studio. A film about Thomas Cole can be seen in the visitor center. "Sunday Salons," a monthly lecture series, is offered in the winter, and guided hikes are offered in the summer months.

218 Spring St.
Catskill, NY
518-943-7465
www.nps.gov/hurv
www.thomascole.org

AT A GLANCE Southeastern New York, 30 miles south of Albany ■ 5 acres ■ Early May through late October ■ Touring Cole's home and studio, hiking nearby Catskill landscape

Upper Delaware Scenic & Recreational River

The Northeast's longest free-flowing river

Forming part of the boundary between New York and Pennsylvania, the Upper Delaware is the longest free-flowing stream in the Northeast. Seventy-three miles of the river are designated as the Upper Delaware Scenic and Recreational River, but the National Park Service owns only a small amount of land in the area. Like many similarly administered rivers throughout the country, the Upper Delaware is a partnership of federal, state, and local agencies, various organizations, and private businesses.

Winding through mountain scenery from Hancock, New York, to Matamoras, Pennsylvania, the Upper Delaware is a popular river for canoeing, rafting, and tubing. With Class I and II rapids, it's suitable for inexperienced boaters, with many stretches of flat-water pools. Public river-access spots are located on both the Pennsylvania and New York shorelines, and many outfitters offer canoe rentals and shuttle services. (Recreationists should always wear a properly fitted life jacket and stay aware of the possibility for severe floods.)

Anglers know the Upper Delaware as excellent for smallmouth bass, trout, walleye, and other species. The watershed hosts the largest population of wintering bald eagles in the Northeast, and a growing number of the birds remain in the area year-round.

Famed Western novelist Zane Grey lived in Lackawaxen, Pennsylvania, from 1905 to 1918. The Zane Grey Museum *(Scenic Dr.)* there displays his books, photographs, and personal items. Park rangers and volunteers can provide information about Zane Grey and recreation opportunities.

AT A GLANCE

274 River Rd.
Beach Lake, PA
570-685-4871
www.nps.gov/upde

Southeastern New York and northeastern Pennsylvania, 70 miles northwest of New York City ▪ 55,575 acres (30 acres federally owned); 73 river miles ▪ Spring through fall ▪ Canoeing, rafting, fishing

Vanderbilt Mansion National Historic Site
A look at Gilded Age opulence

Frederick W. Vanderbilt was born in 1856, a grandson of the railroad tycoon Cornelius Vanderbilt and an heir to one of America's great 19th-century family fortunes. In 1898 he added a new residence to the list of those he already owned: a 54-room mansion at Hyde Park, in New York's Hudson River Valley. Sited on a 600-acre estate with tremendous views of the Hudson River and Catskill Mountains, it today epitomizes the privileged Gilded Age way of life, one modeled on English country houses.

Vanderbilt's mansion was designated a national historic site in part

The Vanderbilt Mansion is representative of an age.

to examine the lives of immensely wealthy individuals and to provide insight into the philosophy of the American country house, the lives of its domestic staff, and its relationship to the surrounding community.

The house was designed in the beaux arts style by the famed architectural firm of McKim, Mead, and White. With furnishings, it cost the then astronomical sum of $2,250,000. It was the first house in Hyde Park to have electricity, generated by an on-site hydroelectric plant.

The well-preserved interior can be visited only on guided one-hour tours *(fee)*, but the grounds are open to the public daily, and visitors may stroll along the estate's carriage roads, wander through the beautiful Italian gardens *(www.vanderbiltgarden.org)*, or picnic at the overlook.

AT A GLANCE

N.Y. 9
Hyde Park, NY
845-229-7770
www.nps.gov/vama

Eastern New York, 90 miles north of New York City ▪ 211 acres ▪ Spring through fall ▪ Touring mansion, viewing grounds and formal gardens

Women's Rights National Historical Park
The place where five women changed the world

On July 19–20, 1848, a history-changing event took place in the village of Seneca Falls, New York. About 300 people gathered for the first women's rights convention, and at its conclusion many signed a Declaration of Sentiments stating, in part, "that all men and women are created equal." With this, a major step was taken toward gaining voting and property rights, access to education, and workplace equality for women.

Local arrangements for the convention began at a July 9 social gathering of five women: Elizabeth Cady Stanton, Lucretia Mott, Martha Wright, Mary Ann M'Clintock, and Jane Hunt. The effort was prompted, in part, by the 1840 World Anti-Slavery Convention in London, which focused many activists on the broader issues of human equality.

A visit to the Women's Rights National Historical Park should begin at the visitor center in downtown Seneca Falls, which offers an introductory film entitled "Dreams of Equality"; a sculpture depicting the five women who organized the convention standing with supporters; and exhibits describing true womanhood, the cult of domesticity, and progress in the demands of the Declaration of Sentiments. Ranger programs often touch on the connections among the abolitionist movement, the Underground Railroad, the Quaker faith, and the women's rights movement.

Nearby stands the restored 1843 Wesleyan Chapel, where the convention was held. Park visitors can also see the Elizabeth Cady Stanton home in Seneca Falls and, in nearby Waterloo, the restored home of Thomas and Mary Ann M'Clintock, where the convention was planned and the Declaration of Sentiments drafted. The home of Richard and Jane Hunt in Waterloo is also part of the historical park, but it is open to the public only on special occasions.

Visitor center
136 Fall St.
Seneca Falls, NY
315-568-0024
www.nps.gov/wori

AT A GLANCE
Central New York, 50 miles west of Syracuse ▪ 7 acres ▪ Year-round
▪ Viewing exhibits at visitor center, touring sites associated with the women's rights movement

PENNSYLVANIA

Bookended east and west by Philadelphia and Pittsburgh, Pennsylvania is in large part a state of dense forests, home to thriving populations of black bears, white-tailed deer, and other wildlife. The Appalachians along with rivers, lakes, and rugged woodlands provide a wide array of outdoor recreational opportunities. History lovers find a virtual treasure-house in Philadelphia, where the Declaration of Independence was signed and the Constitutional Convention convened; while the battlefield of the bloody 1863 Gettysburg engagement draws countless visitors. Discoveries of petroleum and coal helped drive the state's economic development in the late 19th and early 20th centuries.

Allegheny Portage Railroad National Historic Site

Where technological innovations conquered a mountain range

In the 1820s the young United States was moving westward, but transportation methods hindered the nation's growth. Mountains such as the Alleghenies of Pennsylvania presented major problems for railroads, as locomotives of the time couldn't ascend steep grades. To cross these highlands and link Philadelphia and Pittsburgh, the Pennsylvania Main Line of Public Works built the Allegheny Portage Railroad, which used ten inclined planes equipped with rollers and stationary engines to pull freight and passengers up and down slopes. From 1834 to 1854, this system was the best way to cross the Alleghenies, until improved locomotives were able to traverse the mountains on their own.

Allegheny Portage Railroad National Historic Site lets visitors see the remains of this system. The historic site's Summit Level Visitor Center has exhibits on the Allegheny Portage operation, and a model engine house shows how steam engines, pulleys, and ropes were used to move goods and people.

The Lemon House, once a tavern for travelers on the portage railroad, has been restored to its period appearance. The park also includes a nature trail and a path that traces part of the old portage route. The park's Skew Arch Bridge (a bridge built at an angle other than a right angle) showcases the skill of stonemasons of the early 19th century.

The portage's 900-foot-long Staple Bend Tunnel can be seen in a separate park unit, 4 miles east of Johnstown, Pennsylvania. Staple Bend was the United States' first railroad tunnel.

110 Federal Park Rd.
Gallitzin, PA
814-886-6150
www.nps.gov/alpo

AT A GLANCE Western Pennsylvania, 80 miles east of Pittsburgh ▪ 1,249 acres ▪ Year-round ▪ Visiting engine house, tavern, historic railroad tunnel, and bridge; hiking

Benjamin Franklin National Memorial

A massive statue honoring an iconic figure of American history

Among the most fascinating and influential figures in United States history, Benjamin Franklin was an 18th-century writer, newspaper publisher, inventor, advocate for national independence from Britain, signatory to both the Declaration of Independence and the Constitution, statesman, and diplomat. His instantly recognizable face is printed on the front of the $100 bill, among countless other ways in which he remains part of American culture.

The focal point of the Benjamin Franklin National Memorial is a 20-foot-high, 30-ton statue of a seated Franklin, located in Philadelphia, the city to which he moved as a young man, with which he was connected for the rest of his life, and in which he is buried. The statue, sculpted by James Earle Fraser and completed in 1911, sits in the rotunda of the Franklin Institute Science Museum, an institution inspired by and named for him.

The Franklin Memorial Hall, designed by John T. Windrim, is 82 feet in length, width, and height, with marble walls, ceilings, and columns. It contains exhibits on Franklin and his many inventions. In 2008 it underwent a substantial renovation, with upgrades to lighting, audiovisual systems, and interpretive programs. Every hour a four-minute multimedia program presents Franklin's public career.

Benjamin Franklin National Memorial is an affiliated site of the National Park Service, which provides funding for maintenance and improvements.

222 N. 20th St.
Philadelphia, PA
215-448-1200
www.nps.gov/inde

AT A GLANCE Downtown Philadelphia ▪ Less than 1 acre ▪ Year-round ▪ Viewing statue and Franklin-related exhibits

Delaware & Lehigh National Heritage Corridor

A legacy of mining and innovation in transportation

The abundance of anthracite coal in eastern Pennsylvania attracted thousands of immigrants to work the mines, swelling the population of the region in the early 19th century. At the same time, efficient ways were needed to move the coal to the important port of Philadelphia. Three modes of transport—the Delaware Division of the Pennsylvania Canal System, the Lehigh Navigation System, and the Lehigh Valley Railroad—were most important in meeting this need.

Delaware & Lehigh National Heritage Corridor stretches about 165 miles from Bristol, on the Delaware River just northeast of Philadelphia, to Wilkes-Barre in the Pocono Mountains, generally tracing the routes of the canals and rail line. A nonprofit partnership *(www.delawareandlehigh .org)* of the National Park Service, state and local governments, and organizations and businesses, it offers a way for travelers to explore the history of coal mining, groundbreaking innovations in transportation, and the multifaceted ethnic heritage. It comprises more than 50 different ethnic groups, including people of Irish, Czech, German, Italian, African, and Welsh descent.

A good first stop is the visitor information center at Two Rivers Landing (two blocks south of U.S. 22) in the city of Easton, located near the confluence of the Lehigh and Delaware Rivers. From here the range of attractions is nearly endless, from hiking along preserved sections of the old canal towpaths to white-water rafting through the Lehigh River Gorge near Jim Thorpe to touring the home of noted author Pearl S. Buck in Perkasie. Several state and local parks in the five-county area provide camping and other recreational opportunities.

Two Rivers Landing
Centre Sq.
Easton, PA
610-923-3548
www.nps.gov/dele

AT A GLANCE

Eastern Pennsylvania, north of Philadelphia ▪ 165-mile corridor through five counties ▪ Spring through fall ▪ Hiking, boating, taking scenic drives, camping, visiting museums

---

Delaware Water Gap National Recreation Area

A river offering a bounty of recreational opportunities

Along the Pennsylvania–New Jersey border, the Delaware River flows through a low point in a long, high ridge of the Appalachian Mountains. Geologists still can't quite explain the origin of this "water gap," but it has long been a landmark, and has served as a transportation corridor and even a 19th-century resort destination. Today this striking natural feature marks the southern end of Delaware Water Gap National Recreation Area, which protects 40 miles of one of the last free-flowing rivers in the eastern United States.

This natural and recreational resource was almost lost in the 1960s, when a proposed dam would have created a reservoir inundating 37 miles of the Delaware River and 18,000 acres of its valley. Conservationists rallied to defeat the dam, marking a milestone in the environmental movement. The 40-mile stretch of the river within the national recreation area is also designated as Middle Delaware National Scenic River.

For many visitors, the river is the central attraction of the area, offering canoeing, kayaking, rafting, swimming, and fishing. Several

Numerous waterfalls cascade off the mountains in Delaware Water Gap.

park-authorized outfitters rent canoes, kayaks, rafts, and tubes and can arrange shuttles. The water in the Delaware is noted for being exceptionally clean; the park is managed with the aim of maintaining that high quality.

There are more than 100 miles of hiking trails within the park, including 27 miles of the famed Appalachian National Scenic Trail (see p. 21). Backcountry camping is allowed only for hikers along this route. Limited riverside primitive camping is allowed

for boaters, and there is one developed campground within the park. Hikers and campers need to be aware that black bears are fairly common in the area, and to take precautions about proper food storage.

Other popular outdoor activities in the area include biking, rock climbing, and bird-watching. Good numbers of bald eagles winter along the Delaware River, and are likely to be seen from sites such as Smithfield Beach, Bushkill Access, and Milford

Beach in Pennsylvania and Kittatinny Point in New Jersey.

Kittatinny Point and Dingmans Falls (on the Pennsylvania side) have national recreation area visitor centers, open daily from Memorial Day weekend through Labor Day weekend and varying hours in fall (check ahead); both centers are closed in winter. Park headquarters in Bushkill, Pennsylvania, is open weekdays all year. Adjacent to the Dingmans Falls center is a trail to 80-foot-high Silver Thread Falls and 130-foot-high Dingmans Falls.

There are a number of historic sites within the area, including the small communities of Walpack Center and Millbrook Village in New Jersey; the latter features craft demonstrations and house tours on weekends in summer.

Park headquarters
1978 River Rd.
Bushkill, PA
570-426-2452
www.nps.gov/dewa

AT A GLANCE

Eastern Pennsylvania, 75 miles north of Philadelphia ▪ 69,269 acres; 40 river miles ▪ Year-round ▪ Canoeing, kayaking, boating, swimming, hiking, biking, cross-country skiing, horseback riding, rock climbing, picnicking, scenic driving

---

Edgar Allan Poe National Historic Site
The home of a master of the macabre

Though he died young, Edgar Allan Poe (1808–1849) authored a body of literary work that makes him one of the greatest names in horror and the macabre. Short stories such as "The Tell-Tale Heart," "The Black Cat," "The Masque of the Red Death," and "The Murders in the Rue Morgue" still bring chills to readers, and cause many to credit Poe as being the inventor of the detective story.

Poe wrote some of his most famous stories, and enjoyed his greatest stability and success, while living in Philadelphia. For about a year, beginning in early 1843, he lived in

A symbolic raven greets visitors.

the house now preserved as Edgar Allan Poe National Historic Site. It is the only one of his Philadelphia residences still surviving.

Visitors are greeted by a sculpture of a raven, a reminder of Poe's renowned poem "The Raven" (in which the bird utters the ominous word "nevermore"). Visitors can take self-guided or ranger-led tours of the site, seeing among other things a reading room (not original to the house) patterned after Poe's essay "The Philosophy of Furniture." Exhibits with the theme "Many Sides of Genius" examine the inspiration for and influences on his works. The site offers an audiovisual presentation on Poe's life, and recordings of Poe's works narrated by actors such as Vincent Price and Christopher Walken.

532 N. 7th St.
Philadelphia, PA
215-597-8780
www.nps.gov/edal

AT A GLANCE

Philadelphia ▪ Less than 1 acre ▪ Year-round ▪ Touring Poe house, viewing exhibits

---

Eisenhower National Historic Site
A peaceful retreat for a Cold War–era President

After a long military career that culminated in his World War II appointment as Supreme Commander of Allied Expeditionary Forces in Europe, Dwight D. Eisenhower and his wife, Mamie, bought a farm in Pennsylvania, near the Civil War battlefield of Gettysburg. His two-term Presidency (1953–1961) and the 1950s are sometimes recalled as uneventful, but in fact Eisenhower dealt with many major national and international issues, from civil rights to critical situations in Korea, Formosa (Taiwan), the Suez Canal, Hungary, and Berlin. Eisenhower used the farm as a retreat from the pressures of Washington, D.C., though he had daily staff briefings there, and after his 1955 heart attack the farm became the temporary White House.

The Eisenhowers retired to the farm in 1961. Eisenhower died in 1969 at the age of 78. Mrs. Eisenhower continued to live on the farm until her death in 1979. The National Park Service opened the farm to visitation in 1980 as Eisenhower National Historic Site. The farm is maintained as it was during the Eisenhowers' occupancy, with local farmers growing the same crops and raising Angus cattle as Eisenhower did.

Because of limited parking, visitors must board shuttle buses at the nearby Gettysburg National Military Park visitor center to reach the farm. Visits begin with a 15-minute orientation tour of the grounds. The reception center contains exhibits on Eisenhower's life, military career, and Presidency, and a biographical film is shown regularly throughout the day. House tours reveal a residence little changed from the Eisenhowers' time, with many personal items on display. Ranger-led, self-guided, and audio tours are available of the grounds, farm operation, putting green (Eisenhower was an enthusiastic golfer), gardens, and skeet range.

AT A GLANCE

Shuttle bus from Gettysburg visitor center 1195 Baltimore Pike (Pa. 97) 717-338-9114 www.nps.gov/eise

South-central Pennsylvania, 40 miles southwest of Harrisburg ▪ 690 acres ▪ Year-round ▪ Touring Eisenhower home, walking tours of grounds and farm

Flight 93 National Memorial

A site honoring heroes of September 11, 2001

During the terrorist attacks of September 11, 2001, in which nearly 3,000 people died in the United States, hijackers took control of four commercial airliners and used them as weapons. Two of the airplanes were crashed into New York's World Trade Center and one into the Pentagon in Virginia. The fourth, United Flight 93 from Newark to San Francisco, was being hijacked toward Washington, D.C., when the passengers aboard learned of the other attacks and tried to overcome the hijackers. During the struggle to regain control of the plane, the airliner crashed in rural Somerset County, in southwestern Pennsylvania, killing all aboard.

The Flight 93 National Memorial,

The Wall of Names follows Flight 93's final flight path.

dedicated in 2011, protects the 40-acre crash site of fields and woods that is the final resting place of the passengers and crew. The crash site itself is open only to family members of the victims, but a Memorial Plaza bordering the northern edge of the site can be accessed from the visitor center on a path that leads through 40 groves of trees, symbolic of the 40 passengers and crew of Flight 93. A Wall of Names, built of 40 white inscribed marble panels, honors the victims. The wall and a black granite walkway along it mark part of the final flight path. At its end, visitors can look through a wooden gate to the point of impact, marked by a large boulder near the treeline.

The visitor center, located on a ridge over the Memorial Plaza, has a bookstore, exhibits, and an overlook, and a learning center hosts a rotation of exhibits. Check ahead with the park for a schedule of interpretive programs and events.

AT A GLANCE

6424 Lincoln Highway Stoystown, PA 814-893-6322 www.nps.gov/flni

Southwestern Pennsylvania, 80 miles southeast of Pittsburgh ▪ 2,321 acres ▪ Year-round ▪ Viewing crash site of Flight 93 and memorial

Fort Necessity National Battlefield
The spot where a world war began

In 1754 22-year-old George Washington was in charge of British troops sent to build a military road in western Pennsylvania in response to French incursions into British territory. Washington made camp in a spot called Great Meadows, and soon engaged French troops in a skirmish. He returned later that year to Great Meadows and built a fortification he called Fort Necessity. Later attacked by a force of French soldiers and Indian allies, he was compelled to surrender and withdraw from the area.

From these incidents began the conflict that in the United States would be called the French and Indian War and in Europe the Seven Years' War. The lengthy conflict ended in 1763 with the French losing some of their territory in North America. Subsequent events gave impetus to the American Colonies' push for independence from England.

Fort Necessity National Battlefield preserves the Great Meadows site and features a reconstruction of Washington's fort and defensive earthworks. A film interpreting the site's significance is shown at the visitor center, and a path leads to the fort. Ranger-guided programs and demonstrations are offered here June through August. Also within the park is Mount Washington Tavern, which was built on land once owned by Washington and operated as a stage stop from the 1830s to 1850s. It now houses a museum dedicated to the National Road, the first federally funded road, which stretched from Maryland to Illinois.

Separate units of the park comprise Jumonville Glen, the site of Washington's first encounter with the French, and a monument marking the grave of British Gen. Edward Braddock, killed in 1755 in an ill-fated expedition (of which George Washington was a part) to attack the French at Fort Duquesne (at present-day Pittsburgh) on the Ohio River.

U.S. 40, 1 mile west of Farmington, PA 724-329-5512 www.nps.gov/fone	**AT A GLANCE** Southwestern Pennsylvania, 60 miles southeast of Pittsburgh ▪ 903 acres ▪ Year-round ▪ Viewing battle sites and reconstructed fort

Friendship Hill National Historic Site
The Allegheny home of an influential political leader and diplomat

A native of Geneva, Switzerland, Albert Gallatin immigrated to America in 1780 at the age of 19. Land speculation eventually brought Gallatin to southwestern Pennsylvania, where he bought land and built a house he called Friendship Hill in honor of his business-partner friends.

Gallatin soon entered the local political arena for the sake of his businesses. After serving in the Pennsylvania state legislature, he was elected to the U.S. Senate but was removed from office for failure to meet citizenship

Gallatin began building Friendship Hill in 1789.

requirements. He was then elected to the House of Representatives, where he became a party leader and helped bring about the election of Thomas Jefferson as President in 1800. Appointed secretary of the Treasury, he served 13 years, the longest anyone has held the post. He was involved in financing the Louisiana Purchase, the National Road, and the Lewis and Clark expedition. (When the explorers found the three upper forks that are the source of the Missouri River, they named one for Gallatin, the others for Jefferson and James Madison.) After his Treasury stint he served as U.S. minister to both France and England, and he later helped found New York University.

Friendship Hill National Historic Site preserves the home of this remarkably accomplished man. Parts of the house date from the 1780s, though additions were made into the early 20th century. Visitors can take a self-guided or ranger-led tour of the house *(open daily April–Oct. & weekends rest of the year)*, which features period furnishings and exhibits on Gallatin's life. A cell phone tour is available for the house and grounds.

Outside, more than 10 miles of trails wind through the 661-acre property amid the forests and fields of the Allegheny Plateau. The grounds are open daily throughout the year.

Pa. 166, 3 miles north of Point Marion, PA
724-329-2501
www.nps.gov/frhi

AT A GLANCE

Southwestern Pennsylvania, 55 miles southeast of Pittsburgh ▪ 661 acres ▪ Spring through fall ▪ Touring historic home, hiking

Gettysburg National Military Park
The bloody turning point of the Civil War

After his Civil War victory at Chancellorsville, Virginia, in May 1863, Confederate Gen. Robert E. Lee led his forces into Pennsylvania, hoping additional triumphs would demoralize the North and force it to grant independence to the South to avoid protracted bloodshed.

Lee's Army of Northern Virginia met the Army of the Potomac, commanded by Maj. Gen. George Gordon Meade, near the town of Gettysburg on July 1, 1863. The ensuing three days of fighting involved more than 160,000 soldiers and resulted in 51,000 casualties, making it the bloodiest battle of the entire Civil War. After a final futile assault on July 3 (the famed Pickett's Charge), Lee was forced to retreat. Never again did the Confederacy reach so far into the North or come so close to winning the war.

The Union victory was of tremendous psychological importance to the North, and plans for various memorials were soon developed, as was a cemetery for the Union dead. (Confederate dead, originally buried on the battlefield, were reinterred in southern cemeteries years after the war.) For the dedication of the Soldiers' National Cemetery in November 1863, President Abraham Lincoln—not the

Poignant reminders of a bloody battle

event's main speaker—was asked to provide "a few appropriate remarks." His short speech, the Gettysburg Address, has become one of the most famous speeches in U.S. history.

Gettysburg National Military Park was established in 1895. The park's telling of the momentous clash benefits from eyewitness accounts of participants, many of whom returned to the battleground in succeeding years to describe events and mark where they occurred. Veterans' organizations placed memorial structures around the battlefield denoting significant locations, and today the park encompasses more than 1,300 monuments, markers, and memorials.

Visiting the Park

A new museum and visitor center *(fee)* was completed in 2008, and tours of the park should begin here. The museum contains extensive exhibits and audiovisual presentations on the Civil War and the Battle of Gettysburg, helping visitors understand troop movements and other aspects of the battle. A film entitled "A New Birth of Freedom" (the title is from Lincoln's Gettysburg Address) provides additional background.

The visitor center's historic Gettysburg Cyclorama, a 360-degree painting by French artist Paul Philippoteaux, depicts Pickett's Charge, the climactic event of the battle. Completed in 1884 and measuring 377 feet by 42 feet, the painting underwent extensive restoration before being returned to public view in 2008.

Visitors can take a 24-mile self-guided tour of the Gettysburg battlefield, incorporating 16 stops at locations that include the Wheatfield, site of more than 4,000 casualties; the sites of Pickett's Charge; the Eternal Light Peace Memorial, dedicated 75 years after the battle by veterans to "Peace Eternal in a Nation United"; and the National Cemetery, setting for Lincoln's Gettysburg Address of November 19, 1863. The Gettysburg railway station, arrival destination for Lincoln's train, has also recently been added to the National Military Park.

The park offers licensed guides *(fee)* who will ride with visitors and give accounts of the battle; guides must be reserved at least three days in advance of a visit. Other tour options include commercial bus tours *(fee)* of the battlefield, some of which are hosted by licensed guides.

In spring, summer, and fall the park offers a variety of ranger-led activities, including guided battlefield hikes that bring the action to life, programs on Civil War medical practices, the life of a soldier, and other topics.

David Wills House

Located in downtown Gettysburg, the David Wills House is a museum operated by Gettysburg National Military Park. Here, at the home of a prominent local lawyer, the townspeople planned much of the cleanup of the battlefield and town. Lincoln also stayed here the night before his address, making the final edits to the now famous text. The house is on the National Register of Historic Places.

Gloria Dei (Old Swedes' Church) N.H.S.

Pennsylvania's oldest church, dating from 1698

S wedish immigrants in the mid-17th century founded a colony they called New Sweden in the vicinity of present-day Philadelphia. Their first church, in a log cabin, was established in 1677. A more permanent structure was begun in 1698, which endures as Gloria Dei, also known as the Old Swedes' Church. Additions and renovations were made later, but the church has changed little since 1846. The brick building shows various architectural styles, including Gothic,

Georgian, and traditional Swedish.

Gloria Dei (Old Swedes' Church) National Historic Site is an affiliated site of the National Park Service, and it remains an active church *(215-389-1513, www.old-swedes.org)* with regular services. Those who wish to view the interior should call the church for information. It is normally open daily in summer and closed on Mondays the rest of the year.

The church contains models of the ships that brought the original

colonists, a baptismal font from the 1731, a bronze bell cast in 1801 using metal from a 1643 bell, and a carving of the angel Gabriel similar to those found in churches throughout Sweden.

Those buried in the cemetery, which is one of the oldest in Philadelphia, include renowned ornithologist and artist Alexander Wilson, often called the father of American ornithology; as well as eight Revolutionary War officers.

Hopewell Furnace National Historic Site

A look at the origins of the American iron and steel industry

B eginning as early as 1716, Pennsylvania charcoal-fired furnaces and forges were producing iron for various manufactured products. In 1771 a man named Mark Bird established

an ironmaking operation about 50 miles northwest of Philadelphia, taking advantage of local ore; a water source; and abundant chestnut, oak, hickory, and maple trees to provide charcoal

fuel. Hopewell Furnace operated until 1883, when steel production and other industrial advances made it obsolete.

Hopewell was more than just an ironmaking site: It was a self-contained community with workers' houses, a store, a church, an orchard, and other facilities—hence the term "iron plantation" for its similarities to a plantation growing crops. It made items such as stoves and grates, but during the Revolutionary War it also produced cannon, shot, and shells for the Continental Navy.

Hopewell Furnace National Historic Site offers a visitor center with a 15-minute video on the history of the Hopewell Furnace community, as well as exhibits and a bookstore. A self-guided walking tour leads visitors to restored structures such as the "cold blast" iron furnace (one in which the air was not preheated before being blown into the furnace), the ironmaster's house, workers' houses, a store, a blacksmith's shop, and the 1782 Bethesda Church.

From late June through Labor Day, living-history programs explain how ironmaking operations were conducted, and re-create the lives of Hopewell's residents.

Apple trees near the visitor center represent an orchard that grew at Hopewell Furnace as early as the 1780s. They include more than 30 varieties of apples, many of which are no longer found in modern orchards. In September and October, visitors are allowed to pick apples for a fee per pound.

The site's 12 miles of hiking trails connect with trails in adjacent French Creek State Park.

Pa. 345
7 miles northeast of Elverson, PA
610-582-8773
www.nps.gov/hofu

AT A GLANCE

Southeastern Pennsylvania, 15 miles southeast of Reading ▪ 848 acres ▪ Late June through Labor Day ▪ Visiting restored "iron plantation," watching living-history demonstrations, hiking, picking apples

Independence National Historical Park

The most important shrine to American liberty

Many of the most important historic events of the American Revolution and the early years of the United States took place in Philadelphia, many of them in buildings clustered in a relatively small area. Here the First and Second Continental Congresses met, the Declaration of Independence was signed and read in public for the first time, the Articles of Confederation and the Constitution of the United States of America were debated and signed, the U.S. Congress met for a decade, and the Liberty Bell rang.

In the late 18th century, Philadelphia was the most populous, prosperous, and culturally advanced city in colonial America. No wonder, then, that it became the center of activities for those advocating independence from Britain, as people such

The Liberty Bell irreparably cracked in 1846.

as John Adams, George Washington, Patrick Henry, Benjamin Franklin, Thomas Jefferson, and John Hancock met to debate the issues, communicate with the British government, and plot the course toward liberty.

Independence National Historical Park encompasses numerous locations that played a role in the Colonies' quest for independence. More than two dozen sites within or associated with the park are open for the public to visit. Travelers should make their first stop at the Independence Visitor Center, a partnership of the National Park Service and various tourism-related groups, where information is available on places to go, operating hours of attractions, guided tours, and other activities. Films that interpret the American Revolution are shown here. Tickets are available at the visitor center for tours of Independence Hall. Free tickets that specify a certain time for a visit are required to see this site, except during the months of January and February.

A reenactment of the first public reading of the Declaration of Independence in front of Independence Hall

Independence Hall & Surroundings

Among the most iconic structures in United States history, Independence Hall was built between 1732 and 1756 as the State House of the Province of Pennsylvania. It was the meeting place for the Second Continental Congress, which acted as the governing body for the 13 Colonies in the Revolutionary War and adopted the Declaration of Independence on July 4, 1776. Other noteworthy events that occurred here include the selection of the American flag design in 1777, the adoption of the Articles of Confederation in 1781, and the drafting of the U.S. Constitution in 1787. Visitors can see the "rising sun" chair used by George Washington as he presided over the Constitutional Convention in 1787.

The West Wing of Independence Hall houses the "Great Essentials" exhibit, displaying copies of the Declaration of Independence, the Articles of Confederation, and the U.S. Constitution, as well as the silver inkstand that is believed to have been used during the signing of the Declaration of Independence and the Constitution.

Across the street, the Liberty Bell Center houses the historic bell that hung in the steeple of the Pennsylvania State House (now Independence Hall) and rang on many historic occasions, including the death of Alexander Hamilton, one of the Founding Fathers of the U.S., in 1804. With its famous crack (the origin of which is uncertain), the bell is now a symbol of freedom for Americans and others around the world.

Those wishing to tour Independence Hall and the Liberty Bell Center must pass through security screening, and visitors are urged to carry only small bags and bring as few items as possible to the sites.

Just west of Independence Hall, Congress Hall served as home to the U.S. Congress during the ten-year period before 1800, when the national government moved permanently to Washington, D.C. Among the historic events at the site was the adoption of the Bill of Rights in 1791. Now restored, Congress Hall can be seen on ranger-guided tours.

Other Important Sites

Franklin Court preserves the site of Benjamin Franklin's home, where he died in 1790. The house was demolished in the early 19th century; the spot now is home to a museum on Franklin's life and legacy, an 18th-century printing office, and a U.S. post office with special cancellation privileges.

Market Street's Carpenters' Hall—completed in 1774 by the Carpenters' Company of the City and County of Philadelphia, the oldest trade guild in America (which still owns it)—was the meeting place for the First Continental Congress in 1774.

The National Constitution Center is a historical museum dedicated to the U.S. Constitution. A permanent exhibit entitled "The Story of We the People" is offered, as is a theatrical presentation called "Freedom Rising."

Additional sites of note include the Second Bank of the United States, now housing a portrait gallery depicting many important figures in American history; Declaration House, a reconstruction of the house where Thomas Jefferson rented rooms and wrote the Declaration of Independence; Old City Hall, which housed the Supreme Court from 1791 to 1800; and New Hall Military Museum, which interprets the role of the military in the early history of the United States.

Visiting times for these and other sites within the park vary throughout the year; check with the park website or visitor center for schedules.

Independence Visitor Center
525 Market St.
Philadelphia, PA
800-537-7676
www.nps.gov/inde

AT A GLANCE | Downtown Philadelphia, Old City ▪ 55 acres ▪ Year-round ▪ Touring historic sites

---

Johnstown Flood National Memorial

Remembering the deadliest flood in American history

The southwestern Pennsylvania community of Johnstown was used to occasional flooding, seeing as it was set at the confluence of the Little Conemaugh and Stonycreek Rivers, but it was unprepared for the event of May 31, 1889. It all began when heavy rains on May 30 caused streams to overflow into the streets, and the downpour continued the next day.

Fourteen miles upstream on the Little Conemaugh, the South Fork Dam formed a 450-acre reservoir called Lake Conemaugh. Originally built to supply water for a canal, the dam and lake were owned by the South Fork Fishing and Hunting Club, whose membership included famous businessmen such as Andrew Carnegie, Andrew Mellon, and Henry Clay Frick. The earthen dam had received some maintenance but had also been modified in ways that made it less able to withstand flooding.

Shortly after 3 p.m. on May 31, as workers tried frantically to strengthen it and relieve the pressure of rapidly rising lake water, the dam gave way, and an estimated 20 million tons of water surged downstream in a wall up to 40 feet high. Several smaller towns were destroyed before the flood hit Johnstown at 4:07 p.m., 57 minutes after the dam failed.

In minutes, 4 square miles of the town were obliterated, and in the end more than 2,200 people died, including 99 entire families and 396 children under the age of ten. The disaster brought help from around the United States and foreign countries, including doctors, undertakers, food supplies, and construction materials for rebuilding. The American Red Cross, founded by Clara Barton just eight years earlier, arrived on June 5 to aid recovery, with Barton herself helping supervise.

Public opinion blamed the wealthy members of the South Fork Fishing and Hunting Club for neglecting the Lake Conemaugh dam and causing the disaster, but the club was never found legally responsible. Some of its members gave substantial amounts of money for relief efforts, and Andrew Carnegie built a new public library for the town. (The building now houses the Johnstown Flood Museum, operated by a local nonprofit group.)

Johnstown Flood National Memorial is located at the site of the former South Fork Dam. It includes a visitor center with exhibits on the flood and a 35-minute film, "Black Friday." Visitors can walk two short trails to the remains of the dam and look out over the old lake bed, maintained today as a wet meadow. One trail leads down into the lake bed and through the ruins of the dam. Nearby is the restored home of Elias J. Unger, caretaker of the dam, who organized workers to try to save the structure in the hours before it failed. In the nearby community of Saint Michael, along Pa. 869, visitors can view some of the original buildings of the South Fork Fishing and Hunting Club.

Each year on May 31, the park is the scene of a memorial service in which 2,209 luminaria candles are lit to honor those who died in the Johnstown tragedy.

733 Lake Rd. (off Pa. 869)
South Fork, PA
814-495-4643
www.nps.gov/jofl

AT A GLANCE

Southwestern Pennsylvania, 70 miles east of Pittsburgh (10 miles northeast of Johnstown) ▪ 164 acres ▪ Year-round ▪ Viewing exhibits and film; touring old dam site and structure

Steamtown National Historic Site
Reliving the era of steam railroading

For decades, steam-powered locomotives moved Americans and the country's products across the continent. In 1918, there were more than a quarter million miles of track and 65,000 steam locomotives in the United States. The popularity of automobiles and trucks and the development of the diesel-electric locomotive, however, doomed steam power, which had largely disappeared by the 1950s.

Steamtown National Historic Site was established to preserve the history of steam railroading in America, concentrating on the years 1850–1950. Located within the Scranton railroad yard of the Delaware, Lackawanna,

Canadian Pacific 2317

and Western Railroad, it showcases a collection of steam locomotives and passenger and freight cars assembled by a private enthusiast in the 1950s and 1960s and later acquired by the National Park Service. Locomotives include an impressive "Big Boy" built in 1941 for the Union Pacific, as well as a 1903 freight engine (the park's oldest locomotive) built for the Chicago Union Transfer Railway Company.

Other attractions at Steamtown include a visitor center; a theater showing an 18-minute interpretive film called "Steel and Steam"; a history museum with a time line of railroading; a technology museum with a sectioned steam locomotive, a caboose, and a boxcar; and a roundhouse where maintenance is performed regularly on the park's rail equipment.

Living-history programs are conducted at various times during the year, as are rides on steam-powered trains. The schedule for train trips varies depending on season and staff and equipment availability.

| 350 Cliff St. Scranton, PA 570-340-5200 www.nps.gov/stea | AT A GLANCE | Northeastern Pennsylvania, in downtown Scranton ▪ 40 acres ▪ Year-round ▪ Touring rail yard; viewing historic locomotives and rail cars; riding trains (seasonally) |

Thaddeus Kosciuszko National Memorial

Remembering a national hero of two countries' fights for liberty

In a life dedicated to the cause of freedom, filled with adventures, triumphs, and disappointments, Thaddeus Kosciuszko became a national hero in both the United States and his native Poland. Inspired to come to America in 1776 by the ideals of the Colonies' struggle for independence from Britain, he met and became a close friend of Thomas Jefferson's. While serving in the Continental Army, he put his skills to use in engineering tasks, fortifying locations throughout the Colonies. By 1783 he had been made a general.

After Kosciuszko went back home, he was wounded in battle and imprisoned while trying to help Poland resist Russian domination. Later exiled from his homeland, he returned to America

Kosciuszko's home in Philadelphia

in 1797, where he lived in a boardinghouse in downtown Philadelphia that is now Thaddeus Kosciuszko National Memorial. Suffering from his wounds, he mostly stayed at home, reading, painting, and entertaining visitors. Kosciuszko remained in Philadelphia less than a year before returning to Europe. He died in Switzerland in 1817. Thomas Jefferson once said of him that he was "as pure a son of liberty, as I have ever known."

Visitors to the memorial can view newly updated exhibits on Kosciuszko's life and dedication to the cause of freedom and see a short audiovisual program. Also on display are artifacts related to Kosciuszko on loan from Poland, and photographs of the scores of monuments to Kosciuszko that have been erected in the United States, Poland, and other countries around the world.

| 301 Pine St. Philadelphia, PA 215-597-7130 www.nps.gov/thko | AT A GLANCE | Downtown Philadelphia ▪ Less than 1 acre ▪ Spring through fall ▪ Viewing exhibits and audiovisual programs on Kosciuszko's life |

Valley Forge National Historical Park

Revolutionary War quarters that became a vital training ground

In December 1777, as winter approached, George Washington's Continental Army needed a place to camp, rest from fighting, and prepare for coming military campaigns of the Revolutionary War. The British had occupied the patriot capital of Philadelphia, but neither side wanted to engage in large-scale fighting during difficult winter conditions.

Washington chose to camp at a site called Valley Forge, named for an iron-manufacturing forge along Valley Creek, near the Schuylkill River about 20 miles from Philadelphia. The terrain gave the location good defensive capabilities, and it was far enough from the British to prevent surprise attacks. The generals occupied nearby farmhouses, while the soldiers set about building log huts. Cold weather, lack of adequate food and clothing, and disease made the next few months difficult.

During this time, though, the Continental Army actually made itself into a better organized and more highly trained force. A former Prussian army officer named Baron Friedrich Wilhelm Augustus von Steuben arrived in camp in February 1778 and set about personally drilling the troops and teaching them discipline. By the time the Continental Army left Valley Forge in June, the troops were better able to fight Britain's army of professional soldiers on equal terms. Five years later, America defeated the British, and the United States gained true independence.

Visiting the Site

Valley Forge National Historical Park preserves the site of George Washington's 1777–78 winter encampment, and offers many experiences to help visitors understand its significance in the American Revolution. The park theater shows an 18-minute film called "Valley Forge: A Winter Encampment," which provides an introduction to the events. The visitor center also displays authentic artifacts recovered at the site and a variety of historical exhibits.

The park offers several ways to tour the actual encampment site. Using a park brochure, visitors can take a 10-mile, self-guided auto tour. There are cell phone icons at many locations, where visitors can call a number and hear an audio presentation. Guided trolley tours are also offered seasonally *(fee)*, with interpreters providing historical information at stops along the way.

Notable locations within the historical park include the Muhlenberg Brigade Encampment, with huts depicting those constructed by soldiers; an equestrian statue of Gen. "Mad" Anthony Wayne, who was born in nearby Chester County; George Washington's headquarters at the Isaac Potts House; and traces of trenches dug to help defend against a British attack (which never came).

In the southern part of the park, the impressive National Memorial Arch—built along the lines of the Triumphal Arch of Titus in Rome, Italy—was dedicated in 1917 to honor the soldiers who camped here. An inscription quotes words of praise from George Washington on the "incomparable patience and fidelity" of his men.

Depending on the season, the park offers various ranger-led programs and walks and living-history demonstrations on subjects ranging from 18th-century medicine to archaeology. The park also has more than 20 miles of trails, including sections of paved multipurpose trail, for hiking, horseback riding, and biking.

1400 North Outer Line Drive
King of Prussia, PA
610-783-1099
www.nps.gov/vafo

AT A GLANCE

Southeastern Pennsylvania, 20 miles northwest of Philadelphia ▪ 3,500 acres ▪ Spring through fall ▪ Taking auto, trolley, and walking tours to soldiers' huts, viewing gallery and interpretive film, biking, enjoying nature walks

---

RHODE ISLAND

Rhode Island may be the smallest of the 50 states, but it has the longest official name: Rhode Island and Providence Plantations. The moniker dates from the 17th century, when Roger Williams was banished from Massachusetts for religious reasons and founded a colony based on freedom of belief. The major city, Providence, was named by Williams for "God's merciful providence" to him in his difficulties. Soon after the American Revolution, industrialization attracted new residents; today Rhode Island has large numbers of people of Italian, Portuguese, Irish, and Hispanic descent, among others. Though hardly representative of the state as a whole, Newport is also known as the place where wealthy 19th-century families built luxurious seaside "cottages."

John H. Chafee Blackstone River Valley N.H.C.

Preserving the historic landscape where American industry was born

Slater Mill, a cotton-spinning factory, was powered by the Blackstone River.

Called the birthplace of the American industrial revolution, the Blackstone River Valley of Massachusetts and Rhode Island is where English immigrant Samuel Slater took over a failed mill in Pawtucket, Rhode Island, and made it the first successful water-powered cotton-spinning factory in the United States. More mills followed in the area, setting off a wave of industrialization and immigration that changed the face of the country.

John H. Chafee Blackstone River Valley National Heritage Corridor does not own or manage any of the land within its boundaries. Instead, it is a partnership *(www.tourblackstone .com)* of governmental agencies, nonprofits, and businesses to help protect a landscape comprising hundreds of

natural, cultural, and historic sites, of which Slater Mill Historic Site is one.

There are heritage corridor visitor centers in Providence, Pawtucket, Lincoln, and Woonsocket, Rhode Island; and in Uxbridge and in Worcester, Massachusetts. The Park Service website offers advice on places to go and things to do within the region. There are trails along the Blackstone River and Canal, and several access points allow launching of canoes or kayaks.

Recreational sites include Blackstone River and Canal Heritage State Park, a tract of more than 1,000 acres in Uxbridge, Massachusetts. In Rhode Island, Blackstone River State Park includes 3.5 miles of bikeway along the preserved Blackstone Canal towpath; eventually the current 14-mile

bikeway will expand to 48 miles, running from Worcester, Massachusetts, to Providence, Rhode Island. Dozens more nature-oriented sites lie within the national heritage corridor. Visit the heritage corridor website *(www .blackstonevalleycorridor.org)*, or check with a visitor center for more information, including brochures on a series of self-guided walking and driving tours of sites across the Blackstone River Valley.

Among the recent changes to the National Park Service was the naming of the Blackstone River Valley National Historical Park *(www .nps.gov/blac)*. When fully established, it will include some facilities of the Corridor as well as additions in both Rhode Island and Massachusetts.

Visitor center
One Depot Sq.
Woonsocket, RI
401-762-0250
www.nps.gov/blac

AT A GLANCE

Central Massachusetts and northern Rhode Island ▪ 400,000 acres ▪ Year-round ▪ Hiking, bicycling, canoeing, kayaking, touring historic and cultural sites

Roger Williams National Memorial

Honoring a champion of religious freedom

Born in London in 1603, Roger Williams dedicated his life to the belief that there should be a "wall of separation" between government and religion, and that persons of all faiths should be allowed to practice their beliefs without government interference. His convictions led him to leave England in 1630 and, in 1636, to found a new community that would eventually become the state of Rhode Island.

The charter document creating Rhode Island in 1663 reflected Williams's ideas on liberty and religious

Rhododendrons in bloom at the memorial

freedom, and helped inspire Thomas Jefferson and James Madison to include similar language in the Declaration of Independence and the U.S. Constitution.

Roger Williams National Memorial includes the site of the freshwater spring and common area of Williams's original colony in Providence. Exhibits and a video presentation in the visitor center examine Williams's life and his contributions to the concept of religious freedom. Outside, trails wind through a landscaped park with exhibits further interpreting Williams's legacy. Various guided walking tours and ranger-led programs are offered seasonally.

282 N. Main St.
Providence, RI
401-521-7266
www.nps.gov/rowi

AT A GLANCE

Downtown Providence ▪ 4.5 acres ▪ Year-round ▪ Viewing museum exhibits and film; walking park trails

Touro Synagogue National Historic Site

A Colonial-era New England synagogue

Dedicated in 1763, Touro is the oldest synagogue in the United States and the only synagogue dating from the Colonial period. Designed by noted Newport architect Peter Harrison in the Palladian style, it continues to serve an active local congregation dating back to 1658. The original congregation was composed of families who had fled the Spanish Inquisition, first settling in the Caribbean and later moving to Rhode Island to seek religious freedom.

Among the congregation's historical highlights is its receipt of a letter from President George Washington in 1790 assuring them that the government of the United States "gives to bigotry no sanction and to persecution no assistance." The congregation holds an annual ceremony during which the letter is recited. Writers Henry Wadsworth Longfellow and Emma Lazarus both visited the Colonial Jewish Burial Ground and wrote poems about the site.

The adjacent Loeb Visitor Center, which opened in 2009, features exhibits on subjects including synagogue history, Jews in American history, and religious freedom in the United States. Tours of the Touro Synagogue are offered, with tickets sold at the Loeb Visitor Center. Tours, which last a half hour, are not offered on Saturdays or Jewish holidays, and are conducted only on Sundays from November through April.

85 Touro St.
Newport, RI
401-847-4794
www.nps.gov/tosy
www.tourosynagogue.org

AT A GLANCE

Rhode Island, in central Newport ▪ 0.2 acre ▪ Year-round (limited tours November through April) ▪ Viewing visitor center exhibits, touring synagogue

VERMONT

Only Wyoming has fewer residents than Vermont, the only landlocked New England state. The generally rocky soil limits most agriculture to dairy farming; in addition, Vermont produces more than a third of the nation's maple syrup. State laws protect its scenic and rural qualities, limiting excessive development. Vermont's beauty attracts scores of tourists, who hike and camp in the Green Mountains, enjoy fall foliage, and ski at the many winter resorts. Declining demand for wood products has hurt the forestry industry, but Vermont still yields important quantities of granite, marble, and slate.

Marsh-Billings-Rockefeller National Historical Park
A landmark site of the American environmental movement

This property at the foot of Mount Tom, outside the small town of Woodstock, Vermont, has had a succession of notable owners. George Perkins Marsh, a diplomat, writer, and early advocate of conservation, was born here in 1801. Then came Frederick Billings, a conservationist and pioneer in reforestation and scientific farm management, who continued the ideals espoused by Marsh. In the 20th century Laurance S. and Mary F. Rockefeller acquired the land and donated it to the American people as Marsh-Billings-Rockefeller National Historical Park.

This site is the only one in the National Park System dedicated to the history of conservation and the evolution of land stewardship in America. The 1895 carriage barn is now the park visitor center *(Mem. Day weekend–Oct.),* with exhibits on conservation history, a reading area, and a children's activity area.

The parlor of George Marsh's boyhood home near Woodstock

Seasonal tours are offered of the Marsh-Billings-Rockefeller Mansion, originally built in 1805 and later renovated in the Queen Anne style.

The park's 20 miles of carriage roads and trails crisscross the slopes of Mount Tom through one of the oldest sustainably managed forests in America. The trails are open year-round and are groomed for cross-country skiing *(fee)* in winter.

The park operates in partnership with the adjacent Billings Farm and Museum *(www.billingsfarm.org),* a working dairy farm and a museum of agricultural and rural life. Visitors to the national park should park at the Billings Farm and Museum.

Vt. 12 & River Rd.
Woodstock, VT
802-457-3368
www.nps.gov/mabi

AT A GLANCE

Eastern Vermont, 95 miles southeast of Burlington ▪ 555 acres ▪ Memorial Day weekend through October ▪ Hiking, touring mansion, attending ranger-led programs, cross-country skiing

Middle Atlantic

Two themes dominate parks in the Middle Atlantic region: the monuments and historic sites of Washington, D.C., and battlefields and associated locations of the Civil War. The Washington Monument, as one example, symbolizes the United States around the world, while the events of Harpers Ferry, Antietam, and Appomattox Court House changed the course of national history. Here, too, are sites as different as the spectacular New River Gorge in West Virginia, Wolf Trap (the only national park dedicated to the performing arts), and the windswept beaches of Assateague Island National Seashore.

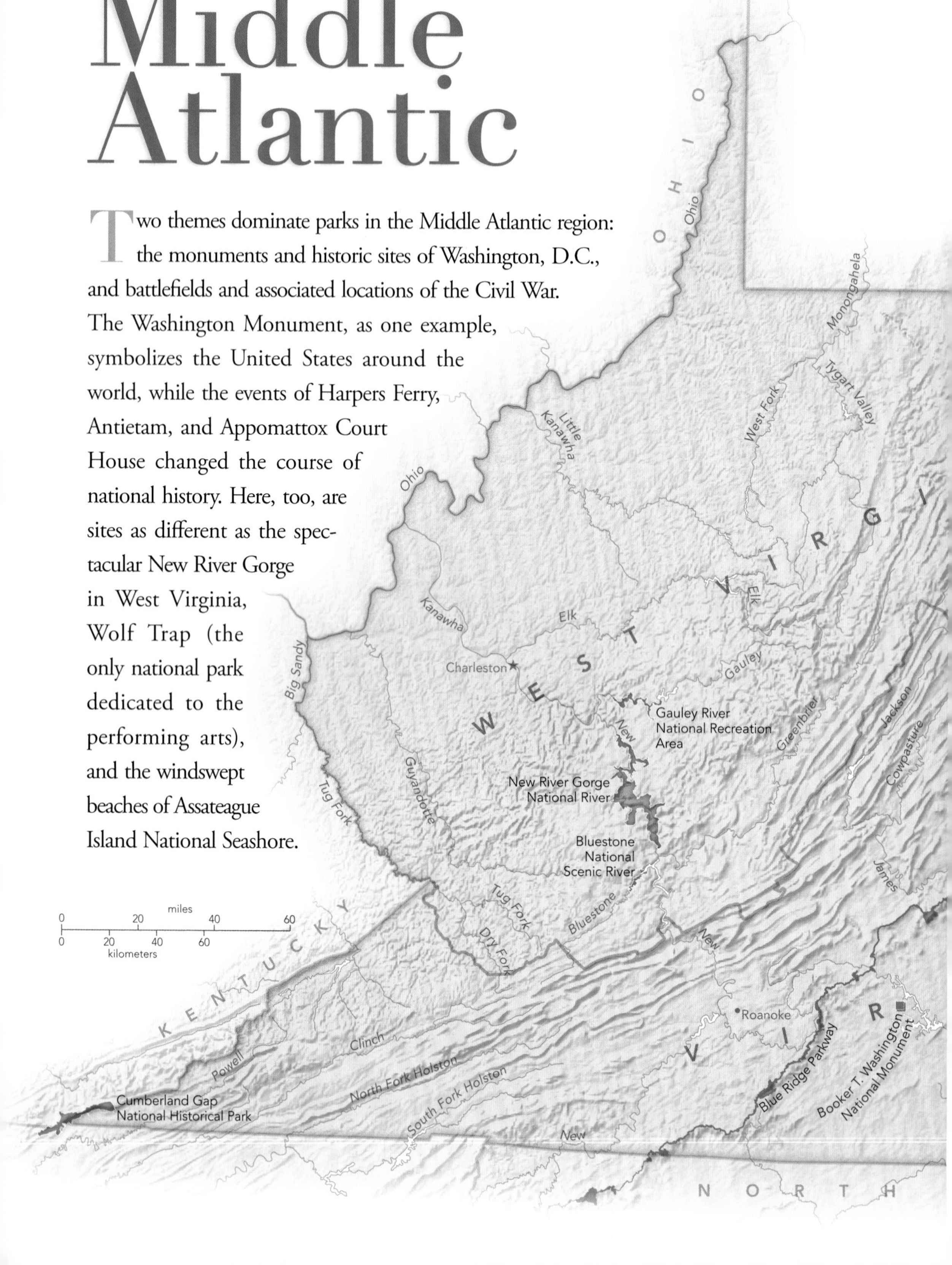

OHIO

Ohio

Monongahela

West Fork

Tygart Valley

Little Kanawha

Ohio

W E S T   V I R G I

Kanawha

Elk

Elk

Charleston ★

Gauley

Big Sandy

New

Gauley River
National Recreation
Area

Greenbrier

Jackson

Guyandotte

New River Gorge
National River

Cowpasture

Tug Fork

Bluestone
National
Scenic River

James

miles
0   20   40   60
0   20   40   60
kilometers

K E N T U C K Y

Tug Fork

Dry Fork

Bluestone

New

V I R

Roanoke

Clinch

Powell

North Fork Holston

South Fork Holston

New

Blue Ridge Parkway

Booker T. Washington
National Monument

Cumberland Gap
National Historical Park

N O R T H

Fort McHenry, Maryland, where Francis Scott Key was inspired to write "The Star-Spangled Banner" during the War of 1812

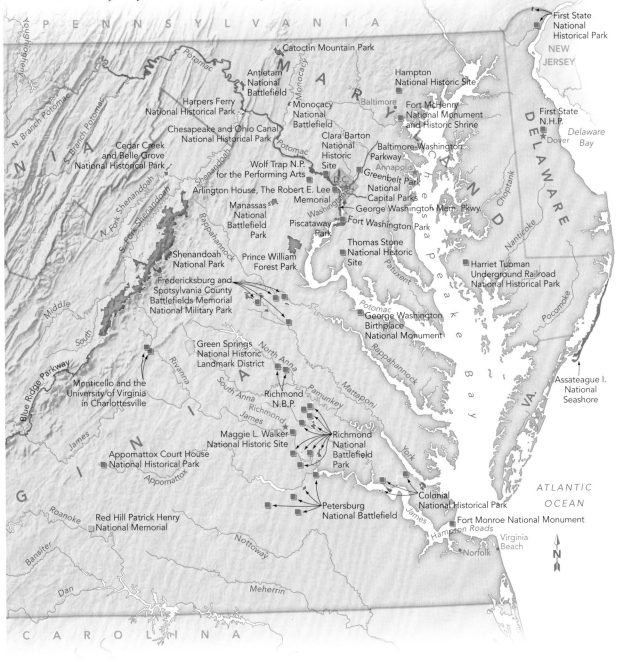

PENNSYLVANIA

NEW JERSEY

Youghiogheny

Potomac

Catoctin Mountain Park

Antietam
National
Battlefield

Monocacy

M A R Y L A N D

Hampton
National Historic Site

Baltimore

First State
National
Historical Park

N. Branch Potomac

Harpers Ferry
National Historical Park

Monocacy
National
Battlefield

Fort McHenry
National Monument
and Historic Shrine

First State
N.H.P.

DELAWARE

S. Branch Potomac

Chesapeake and Ohio Canal
National Historical Park

Clara Barton
National
Historic
Site

Baltimore-Washington
Parkway

Dover

Delaware
Bay

Cedar Creek
and Belle Grove
National Historical Park

Potomac

Annapolis

Choptank

Wolf Trap N.P.
for the Performing Arts

Greenbelt
National
Capital Parks

Nanticoke

V I R G I N I A

Shenandoah

Arlington House, The Robert E. Lee
Memorial

D.C.

George Washington Mem. Pkwy.

N. Fork Shenandoah

Manassas
National
Battlefield
Park

Washington

Fort Washington Park

Piscataway
Park

S. Fork Shenandoah

Shenandoah
National Park

Prince William
Forest Park

Thomas Stone
National Historic
Site

Patuxent

Harriet Tubman
Underground Railroad
National Historical Park

Rappahannock

Fredericksburg and
Spotsylvania County
Battlefields Memorial
National Military Park

Potomac

George Washington
Birthplace
National Monument

Pocomoke

Middle

Rappahannock

C h e s a p e a k e   B a y

South

Green Springs
National Historic
Landmark District

North Anna

Assateague I.
National
Seashore

Blue Ridge Parkway

Rivanna

Pamunkey

Mattaponi

Monticello and the
University of Virginia
in Charlottesville

South Anna

Richmond
N.B.P.

VA.

James

Richmond

York

G I N I A

Maggie L. Walker
National Historic Site

Richmond
National
Battlefield
Park

Appomattox Court House
National Historical Park

James

Colonial
National Historical Park

ATLANTIC
OCEAN

Appomattox

Petersburg
National Battlefield

James

Fort Monroe National Monument

Roanoke

Red Hill Patrick Henry
National Memorial

Nottoway

Hampton Roads

Virginia
Beach

Banister

Norfolk

N

Dan

Meherrin

C A R O L I N A

The Lincoln Memorial, Washington, D.C., honoring the 16th U.S. President

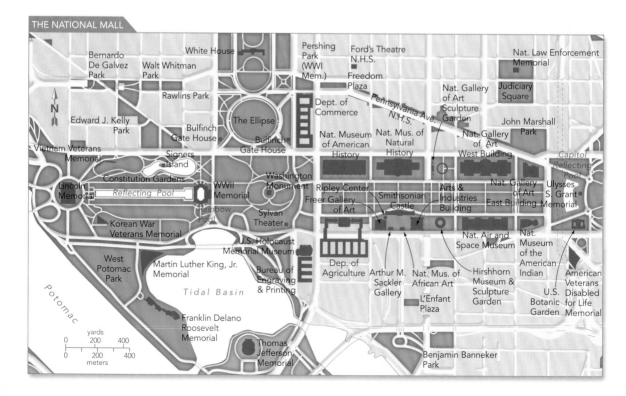

THE NATIONAL MALL

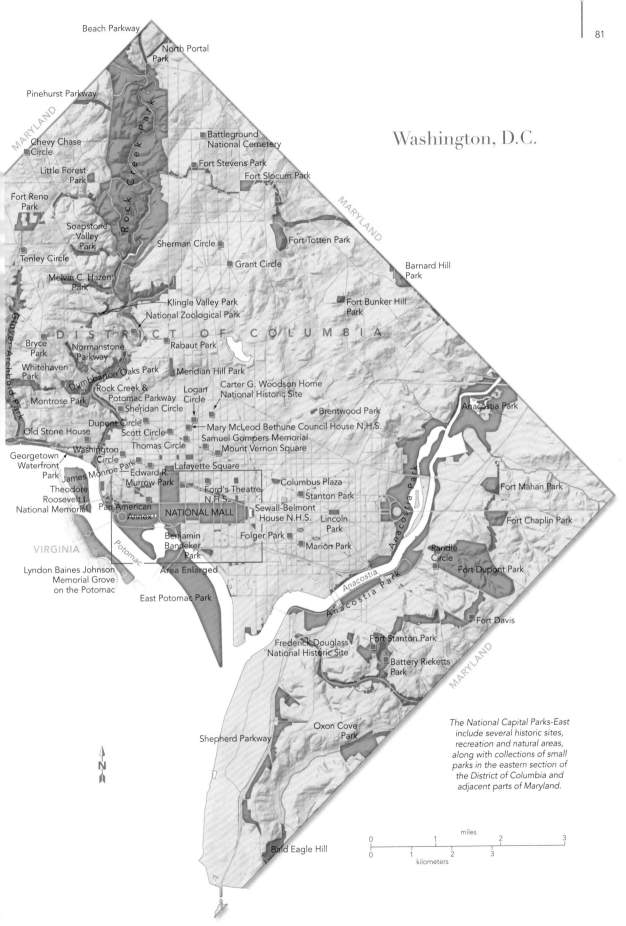

Beach Parkway

North Portal Park

Pinehurst Parkway

MARYLAND

Chevy Chase Circle

Little Forest Park

Fort Reno Park

Soapstone Valley Park

Tenley Circle

Melvin C. Hazen Park

Rock Creek Park

Battleground National Cemetery

Fort Stevens Park

Fort Slocum Park

Sherman Circle

Grant Circle

MARYLAND

Fort Totten Park

Barnard Hill Park

Washington, D.C.

Klingle Valley Park

National Zoological Park

D I S T R I C T   O F   C O L U M B I A

Fort Bunker Hill Park

Bryce Park

Whitehaven Park

Normanstone Parkway

Dumbbarton Oaks Park

Rabaut Park

Meridian Hill Park

Logan Circle

Carter G. Woodson Home National Historic Site

Brentwood Park

Anacostia Park

Glover-Archbold Park

Montrose Park

Rock Creek & Potomac Parkway

Sheridan Circle

Old Stone House

Dupont Circle

Scott Circle

Mary McLeod Bethune Council House N.H.S.

Samuel Gompers Memorial

Thomas Circle

Mount Vernon Square

Georgetown Waterfront Park

Washington Circle

James Monroe Park

Edward R. Murrow Park

Lafayette Square

Columbus Plaza

Fort Mahan Park

Theodore Roosevelt I. National Memorial

Ford's Theatre N.H.S.

Stanton Park

Anacostia Park

Pan American Annex

NATIONAL MALL

Sewall-Belmont House N.H.S.

Lincoln Park

Fort Chaplin Park

Potomac

Benjamin Banneker Park

Folger Park

Randle Circle

VIRGINIA

Area Enlarged

Marion Park

Fort Dupont Park

Lyndon Baines Johnson Memorial Grove on the Potomac

East Potomac Park

Anacostia

Anacostia Park

Fort Davis

Frederick Douglass National Historic Site

Fort Stanton Park

MARYLAND

Battery Ricketts Park

The National Capital Parks-East include several historic sites, recreation and natural areas, along with collections of small parks in the eastern section of the District of Columbia and adjacent parts of Maryland.

Shepherd Parkway

Oxon Cove Park

N

miles

0   1   2   3

0   1   2   3

kilometers

Bald Eagle Hill

DELAWARE

Besides becoming the nation's first state, Delaware now also has the distinction of being the last state to possess its own unique national park property. But the state also boasts a portion of the Captain John Smith Chesapeake National Historic Trail, honoring the discoveries made along the bay and its estuary.

First State National Historical Park

Historic sites recall the Revolutionary era

With the designation of First State National Monument in 2013, Delaware could boast its first unit within the National Park Service; it was the last of the states to gain one. The park's name honors Delaware's ratification of the new United States Constitution on December 7, 1787—the first of the United States to do so.

First State National Monument comprises four units scattered across 50 miles of Delaware, with one unit extending into southern Pennsylvania.

Dover Green, site of the tavern (no longer present) where Delaware voted to ratify the Constitution, is an open space in the heart of Delaware's capital city of Dover.

The New Castle Court House in New Castle, 35 miles north of Dover, was the first Delaware State House (1776–77). It is now a museum focusing on events of 1776 when three counties declared their independence from Pennsylvania and Great Britain, forming the State of Delaware.

The Sheriff's House, an 1858 brownstone building, is adjacent to the New Castle Court House.

The last unit, Woodlawn Tract, comprises more than 1,100 acres in northern Delaware and southern Pennsylvania. It was set aside for public enjoyment by a wealthy businessman more than a century ago and adjoins Brandywine State Park. The tract has trails for hiking and horseback riding, and historic Quaker houses.

The National Park Service is in the process of developing plans for public use and interpretation at this new national monument.

211 Delaware St.
New Castle, DE
302-544-6363
www.nps.gov/frst

AT A GLANCE

Four sites in Delaware and Pennsylvania ▪ 1,100 acres ▪ Year-round ▪ Visiting museum, hiking, horseback riding

MARYLAND

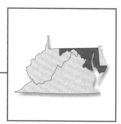

For a small state, Maryland offers great ecological diversity. Seashore fronts the Atlantic Ocean in the east; tidal salt marsh rings Chesapeake Bay, the largest estuary in the United States; and the forested foothills of the Allegheny Mountains mark the state's western border. There are even stands of bald cypress reminiscent of the South. Maryland was conflicted in its loyalties at the start of the Civil War, with slaves working in its extensive tobacco fields. Today most people live in the corridor between Washington, D.C., and Baltimore, many working for government agencies and high-technology firms. Western Maryland remains mostly rural, a world apart from the urban sprawl of the east.

Antietam National Battlefield
The bloodiest day of battle in U.S. history

The bloodiest day of fighting in the history of the United States occurred on the grassy knolls of Antietam.

In mid-September 1862, Confederate Gen. Robert E. Lee led his Army of Northern Virginia across the Potomac River into Maryland, part of the South's campaign to carry the Civil War into the North, take command of Union but slave-owning Maryland, and gain independence for the Confederacy. On September 17, Lee met the Army of the Potomac, led by Maj. Gen. George B. McClellan, near Antietam Creek.

A long day of bloody fighting involving nearly 100,000 soldiers resulted in more than 23,000 casualties, with both armies holding their positions. The following day, North and South cared for the wounded and buried the dead. That night Lee's army withdrew into Virginia, ending the Confederacy's first invasion of the North.

President Abraham Lincoln had been waiting for a Union victory before declaring freedom for enslaved people in the South. Soon after Antietam, on September 22, he issued the preliminary Emancipation Proclamation. From that point forward, the Civil War's aim was both to preserve the Union and to end slavery.

Visitors to Antietam National Battlefield can see exhibits on the battle and its aftermath and watch a 26-minute orientation film in the visitor center. A self-guided 8.5-mile auto tour makes 11 stops as it winds through the battlefield; a recorded audio commentary is available for sale or rent at the visitor center. Ranger talks are conducted daily.

A personalized tour can also be arranged with a park-authorized Antietam Battlefield guide *(301-432-4329, fee)*, who will accompany visitors in their vehicle around the park.

Rates depend upon the length of the tour and the size of the group.

The Pry House Field Hospital Museum *(301-416-2395, open daily in summer, donation)* is located in the house that served as General McClellan's headquarters during the battle. It features exhibits on military medical care in the Civil War era, with a re-creation of an operating theater. Abraham Lincoln visited the Pry House two weeks after the Battle of Antietam.

Antietam National Battlefield has been working to restore the battlefield to the way it appeared in 1862, undertaking projects such as replanting woodlots and orchards; reestablishing original fence lines, lanes, and trails; and maintaining the integrity of the historic farmsteads. The park has more than doubled in size since 1990.

5831 Dunker Church Rd. (off Md. 65), 1 mile north of Sharpsburg, MD
301-432-5124
www.nps.gov/anti

AT A GLANCE

Western Maryland, 60 miles northwest of Washington, D.C. ▪ 3,250 acres ▪ Year-round ▪ Visiting museum, touring battlefield

Assateague Island National Seashore

A beautiful barrier island for recreation and wildlife-watching

Horses and a foal on the beach at Assateague Island

Encompassing a 37-mile-long barrier island at the Maryland-Virginia state line, Assateague Island National Seashore welcomes those who enjoy beautiful beaches and the recreational opportunities they offer, as well as lovers of nature and wildlife. The seashore is a popular camping and beach destination in the warmer months; crowds decrease from fall through spring, when birds and other wild creatures are more visible.

Roads access the national seashore at its northern (Maryland) and southern (Virginia) ends but do not connect through the middle part of the island. The park offers two visitor centers, one in Maryland *(410-641-1441)*, on the mainland before crossing Sinepuxent Bay to the island; and Toms Cove *(757-336-6577)*, on the island in Virginia. Both feature exhibits, information desks, and seasonal ranger-guided walks and programs. Campers register at a ranger station in the Maryland section of the park; developed and backcountry sites are available. Several short

nature trails near the Maryland district entrance station interpret the plant and animal life of the dunes, the marsh, and the forest, providing an excellent introduction to barrier-island ecology.

The Assateague Island Alliance *(410-629-6095, www.assateagueisland alliance.org)* works in partnership with the park to provide interpretive programs for visitors to the seashore.

In summer, lifeguard-patrolled beaches in both the Maryland and Virginia districts invite swimmers. Some visitors launch canoes or kayaks to explore the bay and marshes, while others enjoy surf fishing, crabbing, clamming, or shell collecting. Several miles of biking trails are available as well. Travelers to the Maryland section of the national seashore pass through Assateague State Park, which also offers camping and swimming.

Visitors interested in natural history—and especially bird-watchers—spend most of their time at Assateague in Chincoteague National Wildlife Refuge *(757-336-6122, www.fws.gov*

/northeast/chinco), which is contained within the national seashore from the Virginia state line south. One of the best birding sites on the Atlantic, the 14,000-acre refuge comprises beaches, bays, mudflats, marshes, freshwater ponds, and pine forest, creating a mix of habitats that attracts a wide range of species, from flocks of wintering waterfowl to nesting herons, egrets, shorebirds, terns, and peregrine falcons.

The refuge's 3-mile loop is an excellent place to observe wildlife, especially waterfowl and wading birds. It is always open to walkers and bikers, but vehicles are permitted only from 3 p.m. until dusk.

The Famed Assateague Ponies

The most popular animal on Assateague isn't part of the native wildlife at all. The island's famed "ponies"—small horses, actually—inhabit both the national seashore and Chincoteague refuge, delighting visitors with their appealingly shaggy charm. The horses are descended from stock brought to the island in the 1600s by colonists; over the years, they've adapted well to the often harsh seaside environment. Their small size is thought to be an adaptation to a diet of salt marsh, cordgrass, salt meadow hay, and beach grass, and their chubby look comes from the amount of fresh water they must drink to offset the salt they take in. While the horses are undoubtedly delightful to look at, they are genuinely wild. Enjoy them from a distance to avoid bites and kicks.

Md. 611, 8 miles south of Ocean City, MD or Va. 175, 2 miles east of Chincoteague, VA www.nps.gov/asis

AT A GLANCE

Southeastern Maryland and eastern Virginia, 15 miles south of Ocean City, Maryland ▪ 48,000 acres ▪ Year-round ▪ Hiking, camping, swimming, wildlife-watching, bird-watching, beachcombing, fishing, crabbing, clamming, canoeing, kayaking

Captain John Smith Chesapeake N.H.T.

America's first water-based national historic trail

A unique area within the National Park System, Captain John Smith Chesapeake National Historic Trail was created in 2006 as America's first national historic trail following a water route. Located around the shoreline of Chesapeake Bay and along rivers leading into the bay, it is actually a network of trails that incorporates many separate boating trails, with more routes to be added in the future.

Existing boat trails include the 10-mile Eastern Neck Island Water Trail around Eastern Neck National Wildlife Refuge in Maryland, the James River Water Trail in Virginia, and the Susquehanna River Water Trail in Pennsylvania.

The trail is named for renowned English captain and adventurer John Smith, who arrived in Chesapeake Bay in 1607 in an attempt to found a colony in the New World. Smith played a major role in the settlement of Jamestown, the first successful English colony in North America. His (perhaps embellished) account of being saved from execution by Indians through the intervention of a chief's daughter

named Pocahontas has become a legendary incident in American history.

From 1607 to 1609 Smith sailed around Chesapeake Bay and up rivers on voyages of exploration. His books describing his discoveries and praising the region's natural resources helped encourage English settlement along the Atlantic coast. Captain John Smith Chesapeake National Historic Trail commemorates Smith's voyages and provides resources for modern boaters to follow in his wake. Smith explored some 3,000 miles of the bay and its tributaries, which can be accessed from locations in Virginia, Maryland, Delaware, Pennsylvania, New York, and the District of Columbia.

Chesapeake Bay is the largest estuary in the United States, encompassing 11,600 miles of shoreline, including tidal wetlands and islands. It has long been an important source of seafood, though pollution and other environmental degradation have harmed the resource and lowered harvests in recent decades. Federal, state, and local governments, as well as conservation groups, are working to reverse this

damage and to lessen effects of future developments. Captain John Smith Chesapeake National Historic Trail is also a partnership, linking the National Park Service with other government agencies, conservation groups, and private businesses to encourage travelers to explore and protect the bay.

The Park Service website is an excellent source of information on the trail's historical context and how one can explore the trail by boat, kayak, canoe, or by land. The website of the Chesapeake Conservancy *(www .chesapeakeconservancy.org),* a nonprofit group that supports the trail's development and conservation of the bay's significant landscapes, provides the public with information and tools to directly engage in and support the trail.

A fascinating feature of the trail is the implementation of "smart buoys" at various locations in the bay. These interactive buoys, accessible via telephone and Internet *(877-286-9229, www.buoybay.noaa.gov),* provide geographic and historical information while transmitting real-time meteorological and water-quality data.

Trail Office
410 Severn Ave., Suite 314
Annapolis, MD
410-260-2470
www.nps.gov/cajo

AT A GLANCE

Multiple sites in Maryland, eastern Virginia, western Delaware, southeastern Pennsylvania, and Washington, D.C. ▪ Hundreds of miles of water trails ▪ Year-round ▪ Boating, visiting historic sites, wildlife-watching

Catoctin Mountain Park

A mountain retreat born from the Great Depression

By the 1930s, the land that is now Catoctin Mountain Park had suffered from decades of industrial activity and unsustainable agricultural practices. During the Great

Depression, it was chosen for a federal demonstration program through which people would be given jobs rehabilitating the landscape while also creating a new recreation area.

Construction on the site was undertaken by both the Works Progress Administration and the Civilian Conservation Corps.

The southern part of the area

later became Maryland's Cunningham Falls State Park, while the northern section is now administered by the National Park Service. The Catoctin Mountain Park visitor center is located just off Md. 77, and offers advice about hiking, camping, and ranger-led programs.

More than 25 miles of hiking trails—from less than a mile round-trip to more than eight—wind through the park's mountain valleys and along ridges, some leading to spectacular lookout points. The trails on the western side of the park are more rugged and less used than those on the eastern. Six miles of trails are maintained for horseback riding. The park's Big Hunting Creek is a famed trout stream (fly-fishing only, catch and release). In addition to a developed campground, the park also offers rental cabins for families and groups.

A road runs through the center of the park, providing access to trailheads and picnic sites. Various spots offer

The tranquil woods of Catoctin Mountain blaze with color in autumn.

interpretive exhibits about its history of ironmaking, sawmilling, charcoal-making, and moonshining.

The famed presidential retreat called Camp David, named for Dwight D. Eisenhower's grandson, is located within Catoctin Mountain Park but is not open to the public and, for security reasons, is not shown on the park map.

	AT A GLANCE	
14707 Park Central Rd. (off Md. 77) Thurmont, MD 301-663-9388 www.nps.gov/cato		Central Maryland, 55 miles northwest of Baltimore ▪ 5,872 acres ▪ Year-round ▪ Hiking, camping, horseback riding, picnicking, scenic driving, cross-country skiing

Chesapeake and Ohio Canal National Historical Park

An early transportation corridor linking the coast with the Ohio Valley

In the mid-18th century, moving goods by water was discovered to be preferable to transporting them on overland routes, with their muddy roads and mountains to cross. George Washington was one of many who promoted rivers and canals as the best option for transporting goods. His work inspired the 1785 organization of the Patowmack Company, which intended to use navigation along the Potomac River and parallel canals to connect the East Coast with the Ohio Valley.

It wasn't until 1828, though, that the "great national project" to create the Chesapeake and Ohio Canal was initiated. For the next 22 years, around 35,000 laborers, many of them immigrants from Ireland and western Europe, dug the canal and built aqueducts, culverts, and locks. When the canal finally reached Cumberland, Maryland, in 1850, the business owners had given up on the original plan to extend the canal to the headwaters of the Ohio River.

In October 1850, the first five boats filled with coal traveled down the length of the canal, with lumber and farm crops among other products that moved to markets on the East Coast. At its peak of operation, the C & O Canal saw more than 540 boats in service, most of them carrying coal. The canal featured a brick-lined tunnel 3,118 feet long and 11 aqueducts, the longest of them 516 feet in length.

Visiting the Park

Flood damage and competition from railroads eventually put an end to commercial use of the canal, but today's Chesapeake and Ohio Canal National Historical Park allows hikers, bikers, boaters, and others to enjoy 184.5 miles of the old canal right-of-way, from the Washington, D.C., neighborhood of Georgetown upstream to Cumberland, Maryland. The towpath, once walked by mules pulling boats, has been restored, and portions of the old canal once again allow boating. (Read park rules and advice about safety and types of vessels allowed.)

Camping is permitted at many places along the canal, at five developed drive-in campgrounds, and at 30 hiker-biker sites.

Great Falls

One of the park's most popular areas is centered on Great Falls of the Potomac River, located about 14 miles upstream from Washington. Trails crisscross the site, and there are several loop hikes—the Billy Goat Trail is an especially popular one—as well as overlooks that provide views of the spectacular cascades of the Great Falls. The Great Falls Tavern Visitor Center is one of six visitor centers within Chesapeake and Ohio Canal National Historical Park. Others are located at Georgetown and in Maryland at Brunswick, Williamsport, Hancock, and Cumberland. Hours vary at the visitor centers, so be sure to check the opening times before visiting.

Canal Boat Tours

One of the park's most popular activities takes visitors back in time to the C & O Canal's height of activity. Park staff in period dress lead tours aboard reproduction 1870s-era canal boats pulled by mules. (Crosses between female horses and male donkeys, mules were preferred as boat haulers because they were more sure-footed and less prone to injury and had tougher skin than horses.)

Trips are offered seasonally at both Georgetown and Great Falls. Tours last about an hour and (except for group reservations) are first-come, first-served. Call for tour days and times. Park naturalists also offer seasonal nature walks, demonstrations of lock operations, and other programs.

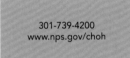

301-739-4200
www.nps.gov/choh

AT A GLANCE Along the Potomac River from Washington, D.C., to Cumberland, Maryland ▪ 19,236 acres, 184 river miles ▪ Year-round ▪ Hiking, biking, boating, horseback riding, camping, nature activities

---

Clara Barton National Historic Site
The home of the founder of the American Red Cross

Born in Massachusetts in 1821, Clara Barton devoted herself to caring for injured soldiers during the Civil War. Her dedication and accomplishments brought her national recognition and the nickname "angel of the battlefield." While in Europe after the war, she worked with the International Red Cross during the Franco-Prussian War, and was inspired to establish the American Red Cross in 1881.

Unlike the international group, which was originally founded for war relief, Barton's American Red Cross aimed to help those who suffered from natural disasters, such as fires and famines. Barton's skills and the American Red Cross's resources were put to good use in the Johnstown flood of 1889 and the massive hurricane that struck the southern Atlantic coast in 1893.

A structure built in 1891 in Glen Echo, Maryland, served as a warehouse for American Red Cross supplies. Barton moved into the building in 1897 and lived there until her death in 1912; her home was also the American Red Cross headquarters from 1897 to 1904. In 1975 it became the Clara Barton National Historic Site, the first National Park Service site dedicated to the accomplishments of an American woman. Guided tours of the home and the restored American Red Cross office are offered.

As of this writing, the site had closed for renovations expected to last well into 2016, so check the park website for updates before visiting.

5801 Oxford Rd.
Glen Echo, MD
301-320-1410
www.nps.gov/clba

AT A GLANCE Central Maryland, just west of Washington, D.C. ▪ 9 acres ▪ Year-round ▪ Guided tours of Barton's home and early American Red Cross headquarters

Fort McHenry N.M. and Historic Shrine

The birthplace of America's national anthem

The "Orpheus" statue honors poet Francis Scott Key.

Fort McHenry National Monument and Historic Shrine (the only National Park Service site so designated) features a visitor center where an orientation film, "The Battle of Fort McHenry," is shown regularly; exhibits include displays of British bombs and rockets.

Visitors can take a self-guided tour of Fort McHenry, which encompasses military artifacts, an electric battle map, barracks, commander's quarters, guardhouse, and powder magazine, or ranger-led walks in the summer.

Daily flag changes are held at 9:30 a.m. and 4:20 p.m., weather permitting. A volunteer group, the Fort McHenry Guard, conducts living-history programs and fires muskets and a cannon on summer weekends. Annual events include Flag Day in June and Defenders' Day in September, when celebrations feature music and fireworks.

The star-shaped fort on the shore of Baltimore Harbor was begun in 1799 to protect the city's port from attack. Completed in 1803, it was named for James McHenry, secretary of war from 1796 to 1800.

On September 13, 1814, during the War of 1812, the fort came under heavy bombardment from British ships. A lawyer and amateur poet named Francis Scott Key watched the attack while under British guard on an American truce ship. The next morning, when he saw the American flag flying over the fort "by the dawn's early light," he was inspired to write a poem that later became "The Star-Spangled Banner," America's national anthem.

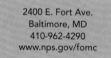

2400 E. Fort Ave.
Baltimore, MD
410-962-4290
www.nps.gov/fomc

AT A GLANCE Baltimore Harbor ▪ 42 acres ▪ Year-round ▪ Touring historic fort and museum

---

Hampton National Historic Site

An 18th-century mansion that was once America's largest private home

Established in 1745 by Col. Charles Ridgely, the Hampton estate grew into an industrial and agricultural empire. Ironworks owned by the Ridgely family supplied weapons for the Continental Army and provided the backbone of the family fortune. In 1783 Charles Ridgely, Jr., began construction of a mansion on the property. When

it was finished in 1790, Hampton was the largest private residence in the United States. The Hampton estate remained in the Ridgely family until 1948, at first growing to 25,000 acres on wealth generated by agriculture, mining, cattle, and other business interests (one Ridgely was elected governor of Maryland) and declining in prosperity in

the late 19th and 20th centuries.

Designated a national historic site in 1948, it was the first property to gain that honor for its architectural significance. Today, Hampton National Historic Site offers free guided tours of the beautifully restored mansion, as well as self-guided tours of farm buildings, gardens, and other areas of the estate.

The slave quarters are of particular interest, with emphasis given to the enslaved and indentured workers whose labor helped create the wealth on display in the mansion.

The site's collection includes more than 60,000 objects, from fine furniture to everyday tools and household items, providing a detailed and accurate look into the lives of the owners and workers over a long period of American history. The grounds encompass an extensive terraced garden and several state champion trees.

535 Hampton Ln.
Towson, MD
410-823-1309
www.nps.gov/hamp

AT A GLANCE Northern Maryland, 9 miles north of Baltimore ▪ 62 acres ▪ Year-round; buildings open Thurs. through Sun. ▪ Touring historic mansion and estate outbuildings and grounds

Harriet Tubman Underground Railroad N.H.P.

Sites commemorating the famed African-American abolitionist

A guide describes historic items inside the Bucktown store, where Harriet Tubman staged an act of defiance.

Established in 2013, this park honors the accomplishments of Harriet Tubman, born into slavery around 1820 in Maryland's Eastern Shore region. After escaping slavery herself, she became the best-known "conductor" on the Underground Railroad, the network of formerly enslaved people and abolitionists who helped enslaved African-Americans escape to freedom in northern states and Canada.

The national historical park encompasses a large expanse of public and private lands, centered at the federal Blackwater National Wildlife Refuge, with headquarters near the town of Church Creek, Maryland. An office at the refuge can provide information on the area. At present there are few attractions within the park, but more will be added in the future.

The National Park Service will partner with Harriet Tubman Underground Railroad State Park, a new Maryland park scheduled to open in early 2016. Located on a 17-acre site adjacent to Blackwater, the facility will include exhibits on Tubman's life and legacy in African-American rights, in aiding the Union Army in the Civil War, and in promoting women's suffrage.

Visitors can drive the 125-mile Harriet Tubman Underground Railroad Byway, which winds through the area where Tubman grew up. In many places the landscape is little changed from its 19th-century appearance. A self-guided byway tour passes more than 30 sites connected with Tubman's life.

Blackwater NWR
2145 Key Wallace Dr.
Cambridge, MD
267-838-2376
www.nps.gov/hatu

AT A GLANCE Eastern Shore of Maryland, about 60 miles southeast of Annapolis ▪ 25,000 acres ▪ Year-round ▪ Visiting museum, driving historic byway

Monocacy National Battlefield

The Civil War battle that saved Washington, D.C.

In the summer of 1864, events of the Civil War left the Confederacy with an opportunity to march through the Shenandoah Valley and capture Washington, D.C., with almost no opposition. Gen. Robert E. Lee ordered Lt. Gen. Jubal Early and a force of 15,000 soldiers to undertake the attack, which, if successful, would deal a devastating blow to the Union cause.

Learning of the Southerners' approach, Union Maj. Gen. Lew Wallace deployed 6,600 men at a strategic Maryland site called Monocacy Junction, where the Confederate and Union armies met on July 9. Although the battle ended with Wallace retreating and a Union defeat, the action had delayed Early's march to the capital by a day. This gave the North a chance to bring in reinforcements and thwart the Confederates' attempt to capture the city. The Union defeat had the effect of saving Washington.

The Monocacy National Battlefield visitor center offers interactive exhibits, including historic artifacts, interpretive displays, and electronic maps showing the course of the battle. A 6-mile self-guided auto tour winds through the battlefield site, with interpretive exhibits at important locations. In addition, there are several walking trails that focus on the battle, the history of the Monocacy River area, and the natural history of the region. The park offers a series of historical programs, including living-history demonstrations, depending on the season.

An interesting historical note: After the Civil War, Lew Wallace wrote the immensely popular novel *Ben Hur: A Tale of the Christ*, published in 1880 and several times made into a motion picture.

4632 Araby Church Rd.
Frederick, MD
301-662-3515
www.nps.gov/mono

AT A GLANCE

Central Maryland, 45 miles west of Baltimore ▪ 1,647 acres ▪ Year-round ▪ Viewing exhibits in visitor center, auto and walking tours

---

Thomas Stone National Historic Site

The home of a signer of the Declaration of Independence

A member of a family with a long history in government—one ancestor was a Maryland governor and two others served in the state assembly—Thomas Stone was a delegate to the colonial-era Continental Congress and one of the 56 signers of the Declaration of Independence. After the Revolutionary War he, along with other gentlemen, including George Washington, promoted the use of the Potomac River and canals to improve transportation to and from the Ohio Valley and other western areas. Stone met at Mount Vernon, Washington's home, in 1785 to make plans that eventually resulted in the construction of the Patowmack Canal.

In 1770 Stone bought a nearly century-old estate called Haber de Venture (later written as one word, Haberdeventure) and began building a house for his family. At his death in 1787, his plantation had grown to more than 1,000 acres. The estate remained in the Stone family until 1936.

In 1977 much of the main house burned. Haberdeventure (the name loosely means "dwelling place in or of the winds" in Latin) was sold to the National Park Service in 1981; the house was reconstructed and opened to the public in 1997. Visitors to Thomas Stone National Historic Site can take ranger-led tours of Haberdeventure and visit outbuildings of the farm, as well as Stone's grave. There are trails and old roads open to hiking. Interpretive exhibits focus on Stone's life and career and the Declaration of Independence.

6655 Rose Hill Rd.
(south off Md. 225)
Port Tobacco, MD
301-392-1776
www.nps.gov/thst

AT A GLANCE

Southern Maryland, 30 miles south of Washington, D.C. ▪ 322 acres ▪ Year-round ▪ Touring historic house and outbuildings, hiking

VIRGINIA

History is ever present in Virginia, especially from the turbulent Civil War era. With the Union capital of Washington on its border and the Confederate capital of Richmond at its center, Virginia saw many important battles, sites of which are now preserved as historical parks. Even earlier, Jamestown was the first permanent English settlement in North America, and patriots—including George Washington, Thomas Jefferson, and James Madison—were born in Virginia. From the Tidewater region of the east, Virginia rises westward to the Appalachian Mountains, with Shenandoah National Park and the Blue Ridge Parkway offering ways to enjoy the region's dense forests and wildlife.

Appomattox Court House National Historical Park

Site of the final events of the Civil War

As Union troops closed around his Army of Northern Virginia in early April 1865, Confederate Gen. Robert E. Lee desperately tried to lead his forces to safety and obtain supplies for the exhausted soldiers. Early on the morning of April 9, though, Lee realized that his men were outnumbered and surrounded, and concluded that surrender was his best option. He informed Union Lt. Gen. Ulysses S. Grant of his intention, and the two men met to discuss terms in the parlor of a private home in the town of Appomattox Court House, in south-central Virginia. This event essentially ended the long, bloody American Civil War, which had lasted four years and resulted in more than 630,000 killed.

Appomattox Court House National Historical Park offers visitors the chance to experience the setting of this momentous occasion, which was the first step in reuniting a

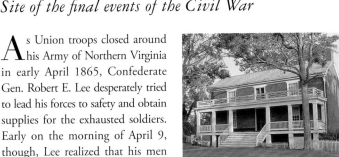

Lee surrendered at McLean House.

divided nation. The park's centerpiece is a reconstruction of the home of Wilmer and Virginia McLean, where the generals met. (Former owners had dismantled the house with the idea of moving it to Washington, D.C., and turning it into a Civil War museum.) The parlor is furnished with both original and reproduction items. (Many of the McLeans' parlor furnishings were purchased or taken as souvenirs by Union officers after the Grant-Lee meeting.) Original structures within the park include houses,

cabins, offices, stores, and the 1819 Clover Hill Tavern.

The park visitor center is located in a reconstruction of the county courthouse. Many original artifacts connected with the surrender are on display, including the pencil used by Lee to amend the terms of surrender; authentic military uniforms; and a doll that belonged to the McLeans' seven-year-old daughter, Lula. (In the room when the surrender was signed, the doll was taken by a Union officer; it was returned to the park in 1992.)

The park features a theater where audiovisual programs are presented, as well as a 4-mile History Trail that leads to several places associated with the surrender, including the site of Lee's headquarters. The park offers regular living-history programs *(Mem. Day–Labor Day)* with interpreters in period costume portraying historical figures.

Va. 24, 2 miles northeast of Appomattox, VA
434-352-8987
www.nps.gov/apco

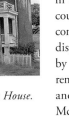

AT A GLANCE

South-central Virginia, 25 miles east of Lynchburg ▪ 1,743 acres ▪ Year-round ▪ Touring historic structures, viewing living-history programs, hiking

Arlington House, the Robert E. Lee Memorial

A house that has stood in witness to a diverse parade of history

Arlington House has been restored and furnished to its 1860s appearance.

Built by George Washington's adopted grandson, George Washington Parke Custis, between 1802 and 1818—in part as a memorial to America's first President—this grand Greek Revival mansion became the home of U.S. Army officer Robert E. Lee upon his 1831 marriage to Custis's daughter, Mary. Located across the Potomac from Washington, D.C., the house remained Lee's home (though it legally belonged to his wife) until the Civil War. Lee wrote a letter resigning from the U.S. Army at Arlington House on April 20, 1861, and left two days later to join the Confederate cause, never to return to the house.

As cemeteries in the area filled with dead from the Union Army in 1864, the Federals appropriated the Lee property as the site of a new cemetery, in part to assure that the Confederate general would not return to live there after the war. The new burial ground developed into today's Arlington National Cemetery, site of the Tomb of the Unknown Soldier and the grave of President John F. Kennedy, among many other significant memorials and monuments.

In 1925 Congress designated the mansion as a memorial to Lee. Visitors to Arlington House, the Robert E. Lee Memorial, may take a self-guided tour of the recently restored house, which displays many original furnishings of the Custis and Lee families, including paintings by George Washington Parke Custis and Lee's writing desk. More exhibits and artifacts can be seen in the adjacent Robert E. Lee Museum.

Arlington National Cemetery
(off G. W. Mem. Pkwy.)
Arlington, VA
703-235-1530
www.nps.gov/arho

AT A GLANCE

Northern Virginia, in Arlington ▪ 28 acres ▪ Year-round ▪ Touring Custis-Lee home and Robert E. Lee Museum

Booker T. Washington National Monument

The birthplace of the man known as the "great educator"

Born in 1856, Booker T. Washington overcame his slave origins to become one of the most influential African Americans of his era. A dedicated believer in the value and power of education, he was named at the age of 25 as the first president of Tuskegee Institute (now Tuskegee University) in Alabama. He recruited famed scientist George Washington Carver, among other faculty, and worked tirelessly to gain more educational opportunities for African Americans at a time of pervasive discrimination in the United States.

Booker T. Washington National Monument is located at the site of the Virginia tobacco plantation where Washington was born to an enslaved mother. The visitor center contains exhibits on the life, career, and legacy of the man who once wrote, "I had the feeling that to get into a schoolhouse … would be about the same as getting into paradise."

The quarter-mile Plantation Trail passes reconstructions of buildings like those that would have been on the farm in the 1850s, including a reproduction of the kitchen cabin where Washington lived as a

Reproduction of a slave cabin

boy. The 1.5-mile Jack-O-Lantern Branch Heritage Trail examines how natural resources were used on the plantation.

The park includes a garden and a farm area where sheep, pigs, horses, and chickens are raised. Park rangers and volunteers offer guided tours of the monument daily in summer (staff and weather permitting).

12130 Booker T. Washington
Hwy. (Va. 122)
Hardy, VA
540-721-2094
www.nps.gov/bowa

AT A GLANCE

Southern Virginia, 25 miles southeast of Roanoke ▪ 239 acres ▪ Year-round ▪ Touring visitor center, farm, and reproduction of the birth cabin; hiking

---

Cedar Creek & Belle Grove National Historical Park
Preserving the heritage of the Shenandoah Valley

Set in Virginia's Shenandoah Valley, this national historical park is in development. It currently features three sites operated by nonprofit historical groups *(www.ccbf.us* and *www.bellegrove.org)*.

Cedar Creek Battlefield preserves the site of an important 1864 Civil War battle in which Union troops, initially routed by a Confederate surprise attack, rallied to defeat the Southerners and take control of the valley. A visitor

contact station serves as an orientation center for the park and offers exhibits and a fiber-optic map program on the battle. Booklets are available for a driving tour of the battlefield. Each October, as many as 5,000 people participate in a reenactment of the battle.

Cedar Creek is but one Civil War battlefield in the Shenandoah Valley Battlefields Heritage Area, which comprises several other sites in the eight-county region. The Shenandoah

Valley Battlefields Foundation *(www.shenandoahatwar.org)* provides information on the heritage area.

The park also contains the nearby Belle Grove Plantation, with a 1797 limestone house owned by Isaac Hite, Jr., and his wife, Nelly, sister of future President James Madison. Visitors may take guided tours of the manor house *(April–Oct. and weekends in Nov. and Dec.)*, as well as a self-guided tour of the grounds and gardens.

7712 Main St.
Middletown, VA
540-869-3051
www.nps.gov/cebe

AT A GLANCE

Northern Virginia, 75 miles west of Washington, D.C. ▪ 3,593 acres ▪ Spring through fall ▪ Touring Civil War battlefield and 18th-century plantation

---

Colonial National Historical Park
The beginning and end of English colonial America

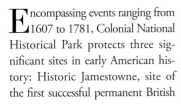

Encompassing events ranging from 1607 to 1781, Colonial National Historical Park protects three significant sites in early American history: Historic Jamestowne, site of the first successful permanent British

settlement in North America; Yorktown Battlefield, where George Washington defeated the British to end the Revolutionary War; and Cape Henry, which commemorates the first landing of the Jamestown settlers in Virginia.

Colonial Parkway

Historic Jamestowne and Yorktown Battlefield are linked by the 23-mile Colonial Parkway, which also provides access to Colonial Williamsburg *(www.history.org)*. This well-known attraction, operated by a nonprofit foundation, preserves buildings dating from 1699 to 1780, when Williamsburg served as the state capital. These three sites form a region referred to as the Historic Triangle. The parkway, completed in 1957, was designed to allow vehicular movement while protecting the environment and preserving the scenic landscape—as one early proponent described it, "as much as feasible giving the impression of an old-time road."

Historic Jamestowne

Historic Jamestowne allows visitors to experience the site of the 1607 settlement that became England's first successful colony in America. It was near here that one colony leader, Capt. John Smith, was saved from execution by Indians when the chief's daughter, Pocahontas, intervened (or so Smith wrote years later). Although the colony struggled at first, the cultivation of tobacco eventually helped it thrive. Jamestown served as the Virginia capital from 1616 until 1699, when the seat of government was transferred to what is now Williamsburg.

Extensive archaeological work has discovered the remains of the colonists' original fort from 1607 as well as sites of other structures, wells, and burial places *(www.historicjames towne.org)*. The site includes both Old Towne and New Towne locations: that is, the original fort and settlement location and the later town site of businesses, residences, and government offices. The Historic Jamestowne Visitor Center and the Archaearium museum display some of the hundreds of thousands of artifacts that have been recovered in the area, as well as exhibits on topics such as the role of Native Americans and Africans in the settlement's history.

The Susan Constant *brought colonists to Jamestowne.*

Trail loops offer walkers up to 5 miles of paths on which they can explore the site. Nearby is the Jamestown Glasshouse, where archaeologists discovered the remains of early glassmaking furnaces; demonstrations of 17th-century glassblowing are held in a reproduction of the facility. Park rangers and costumed interpreters offer a variety of historical programs seasonally.

Historic Jamestowne is jointly administered by the National Park Service and Preservation Virginia *(www.preservationvirginia.org).*

Yorktown Battlefield

The Yorktown Battlefield encompasses the site where on October 19, 1781, Gen. Charles Lord Cornwallis's British army was forced to surrender to Gen. George Washington's combined American and French army. This patriot victory forced England into negotiations with the rebellious Colonies, eventually granting the independence that made the United States a reality.

The siege that led to the British surrender destroyed much of the then thriving port town. An 1814 fire and events of the Civil War did further damage. The circa 1730 Nelson House *(open seasonally for tours)*—home of Thomas Nelson Jr., a signatory of the Declaration of Independence—still shows damage from siege bombardment. Nearby stand the remains of the factory of the once unknown "poor potter"—later discovered to be a man named William Rogers—who made pottery in technical violation of British laws. The 95-foot-high Yorktown Victory Monument, the centerpiece of the park, was dedicated in 1884 to commemorate the colonists' victory.

The Yorktown Battlefield Visitor Center shows an orientation film, "The Siege at Yorktown," and offers museum exhibits that feature Lord Cornwallis's campaign table and George Washington's tents. Two self-guided auto-tour routes pass through significant locations associated with the siege. Ranger-led tours are offered throughout the year.

Cape Henry

The Cape Henry Memorial unit of the park, just a quarter acre in size, marks the approximate landing place of the first Jamestown settlers in

1607. It includes a memorial cross, interpretive panels, and a statue of Admiral de Grasse, the French naval commander who aided colonists at the siege of Yorktown. This memorial is located at Virginia Beach, within Fort Story Military Reservation *(enter through Gate 1; there is a security inspection on arrival).*

Colonial Pkwy.
Williamsburg, VA
757-898-2410
www.nps.gov/colo

AT A GLANCE

Southeastern Virginia, 50 miles southeast of Richmond ▪ 8,677 acres ▪ Year-round ▪ Touring historic sites, hiking, biking, wildlife-watching

Fort Monroe National Monument
Preserving the history of America's largest stone fort

Completed in 1834 at a strategic location on Chesapeake Bay, Fort Monroe played a crucial role in America's coastal defense for decades. The country's largest stone fort, the moated structure was built in part under the supervision of Robert E. Lee, then a U.S. Army lieutenant and later commander of Confederate forces in the Civil War. It served as a haven for enslaved African-Americans escaping to freedom during the war, and afterward was the site where former Confederate President Jefferson Davis was imprisoned for treason.

Decommissioned in 2011, Fort Monroe was declared a national monument the same year. Plans for the property will combine federal, state, and local resources to emphasize historic preservation, recreation, and economic development.

Currently visitors can explore the grounds on foot, including the oak-bordered Parade Grounds, and can walk along the fort's ramparts. A brochure for a walking tour of the fort is available, and it points out important historic sites, including the 1819 Old Quarters, the oldest house inside the moat; Building 17, where Robert E. Lee and his family lived; and the 1858 Chapel of the Centurion. The Casemate Museum *(www.fmauthority .com)* has exhibits on the fort's history and the cell where Jefferson Davis was held. The 1803 Old Point Comfort Lighthouse is not open for tours but can be viewed from the grounds.

A three-mile boardwalk runs along Chesapeake Bay. Swimming is popular at Outlook Beach, where lifeguards are stationed in summer, and licensed anglers can fish from Engineer Wharf near Continental Park.

An aerial view of Fort Monroe and its surrounding moat

41 Bernard Rd.
Fort Monroe, VA
757-722-3678
www.nps.gov/fomr

AT A GLANCE

Southeastern Virginia, 65 miles southeast of Richmond ▪ 325 acres ▪ Year-round ▪ Touring museum and fort, walking, swimming, bird-watching, fishing

Fredericksburg and Spotsylvania County Battlefields Memorial National Military Park

The "bloodiest landscape" in North America

This military park in Northern Virginia focuses on four Civil War battlefields where clashes left more than 15,000 soldiers dead and 85,000 wounded. The park also encompasses other sites with connections to the Civil War, generally located in, west of, and south of Fredericksburg, Virginia.

Because the park includes sites scattered across a relatively large area, with different seasons and days of operation, visitors should stop first at one of the visitor centers at Fredericksburg Battlefield *(1013 Lafayette Blvd., 540-373-6122)* or Chancellorsville Battlefield *(Va. 3, 7 miles west of I-95, 540-786-2880)*. Park rangers and historians can provide an overview of the park and offer advice based on travelers' interests and available time.

Park rangers conduct a variety of guided tours, historical programs, and special events at park sites throughout the year; check at the visitor centers or visit the park website for a schedule.

Fredericksburg Battlefield

The Battle of Fredericksburg, in mid-December 1862, saw a Union attempt to cross the Rappahannock and advance south turned into a lopsided Confederate triumph that caused outrage in the North and jubilation in the South. Gen. Robert E. Lee's victory ended Union hopes of capturing the

Cannon at the Fredericksburg Battlefield, site of a Confederate victory

Confederate capital of Richmond until much later in the war.

The visitor center features exhibits and a 22-minute film on the battle. An auto tour links important sites such as Lee's Hill, the Sunken Road, and Marye's Heights. Chatham Manor, a Georgian mansion, served as Union headquarters and hospital during the battle; it is open for touring. Visitors to the house before and during the Civil War include George Washington, Thomas Jefferson, Abraham Lincoln, Clara Barton, and Walt Whitman.

Chancellorsville Battlefield

The May 1863 Battle of Chancellorsville is often called "Lee's greatest victory," a confrontation in which he used risky maneuvers to defeat a much larger Union force. The Confederates suffered a crucial loss, though, when legendary Lt. Gen. Thomas J. "Stonewall" Jackson was

mortally wounded by friendly fire. The spot where Jackson was shot can be visited, as well as the Stonewall Jackson Shrine, a plantation outbuilding where he died of pneumonia eight days later. Other notable places—including Salem Church, which was used as a hospital by both sides in the Battle of Chancellorsville—can be found along walking- and auto-tour routes.

Wilderness and Spotsylvania Battlefields

There are no visitor centers at Wilderness and Spotsylvania Battlefields, but there are interpretive displays, and historians are present during summer and on weekends in spring and early fall. These battles, fought in May 1864, were part of Union Gen. Ulysses S. Grant's efforts to pressure Lee and push his forces southward. Brochures are available for driving tours of both sites. Stonewall Jackson's amputated arm, lost at the Battle of Chancellorsville, was buried in a private cemetery at Ellwood Manor, now part of the Wilderness Battlefield site.

Union and Confederate Cemeteries

Casualties of the various battles are interred at Fredericksburg National Cemetery, Fredericksburg City Cemetery and adjoining Confederate Cemetery, and Spotsylvania Confederate Cemetery.

Fredericksburg, VA
Chancellorsville, VA
www.nps.gov/frsp

AT A GLANCE

Northern Virginia, 55 miles north of Richmond ▪ 8,374 acres ▪ Year-round ▪ Walking and driving tours of battlefields; touring visitor centers and historic buildings

George Washington Birthplace National Monument

The first home of America's first President

George Washington, hero of the Revolutionary War and the first President of the United States, was born in Virginia along Pope's Creek, near the Potomac River, in 1732, near land that had been settled by his great-grandfather in 1657. Washington lived here until age three, returning occasionally during his teenage years, when the property was owned by his half brother.

The house where Washington was born burned in 1779 and was never rebuilt; no one knows what it looked like. A "memorial house" of locally made bricks was built to honor Washington on the 200th anniversary of his birth, based on a design that would have been typical for a well-to-do Virginia family of the early 18th century. In 1931, the actual remains of Washington's birth home were discovered, and the outline of its foundation can be seen today.

The monument's visitor center features exhibits and a film on Washington's life, and tours are available

A "memorial house" of George Washington's birthplace

of the memorial house, which is furnished with period items. The Living Colonial Farm showcases heritage livestock and tobacco plants like those that the Washington family might have raised. During special events, costumed interpreters conduct activities typical of pioneer times. The Washington family burial ground includes graves of George Washington's father, grandfather, and great-grandfather, and a 1-mile nature trail winds through the property. A 50-foot-high scale model of the Washington Monument, originally erected in 1896 on what was erroneously thought to be the site of the house, now stands at the monument's entrance.

1732 Pope's Creek Rd.
(off Va. 3)
Washington's Birthplace, VA
804-224-1732
www.nps.gov/gewa

AT A GLANCE

Eastern Virginia, 70 miles south of Alexandria ▪ 550 acres ▪ Year-round ▪ Viewing memorial house, farm, and burial ground; hiking

George Washington Memorial Parkway

A scenic assemblage of parks, monuments, and historic sites

The George Washington Memorial Parkway entity encompasses more than 20 historic, recreation, and natural areas in the Washington, D.C., vicinity. Some of the locations are listed separately in this guidebook, including Arlington House, the Robert E. Lee Memorial (see p. 92); Clara Barton National Historic Site (see p. 87); Lyndon Baines Johnson Memorial (see p. 113); and Theodore Roosevelt Island (see p. 121).

Sites along the parkway appeal to a wide range of interests. Birders flock to Dyke Marsh Wildlife Preserve, 485 acres of tidal marsh and swamp forest on the Potomac River just south of Alexandria, Virginia. Hikers love the 15-mile trail network that threads through 730-acre Great Falls Park, 14 miles upstream from Washington on the Virginia side of the Potomac. And people interested in colonial America can get a sense of

life back then for a poor farm family at the Claude Moore Colonial Farm *(6310 Georgetown Pike, McLean, VA),* which offers seasonal living-history programs.

The parkway's headquarters are in Turkey Run Park, on the Potomac in McLean, Virginia, where 745 acres of mostly forested land attract hikers and nature lovers. The 18.5-mile Mount Vernon Trail runs alongside the Potomac River—from Theodore

Roosevelt Island to Mount Vernon—paralleling the George Washington Memorial Parkway, and is extremely popular with runners, walkers, skaters, and bikers.

The U.S. Marine Corps War Memorial, located near Arlington National Cemetery in Arlington, Virginia, depicts Marines raising the American flag on the island of Iwo Jima in World War II, based on a famous photograph of the event. Nearby stands the Netherlands Carillon, a gift from the Dutch people in gratitude for American aid received during and after World War II. Its 50 bells, in a tower 127 feet high, are played on special occasions and daily on the hour (10 a.m.–6 p.m.). Within Arlington National Cemetery, the Women in Military Service for America Memorial honors U.S. servicewomen of the past, present, and future, and features a reflecting pool, Court of Valor, and inscribed quotations from and about servicewomen.

The parkway includes several other small parks and natural areas, as well as three marinas for sailboats and powerboats.

The George Washington Memorial Parkway at dusk

Park headquarters
Turkey Run Park
G. W. Mem. Pkwy., McLean, VA
703-289-2500
www.nps.gov/gwmp

AT A GLANCE

South side of Potomac River, Washington, D.C. ▪ 7,374 acres ▪ Year-round ▪ Hiking, biking, picnicking, studying nature, touring historic sites

---

Green Springs National Historic Landmark District
A largely untouched rural landscape

Louisa County, Virginia, has retained much of its rural character over the years. Large estates with architecturally significant houses and outbuildings—many of which predate the Civil War—reflect more than 200 years of regional history. Around three dozen homes and other structures, preserved in their original context and little changed over the years, are listed on the National Register of Historic Places.

To preserve as much of the area's historic value as possible, local landowners have partnered with the National Park Service to create Green Springs National Historic Landmark District. Land within the area remains privately owned, but the National Park Service and other preservation entities have acquired easements on thousands of acres, preventing development that would harm historic aspects. The area, pastoral as much of it seems, has not been without controversy over the years, as mining and other developments have threatened parts of it.

For now, there are no public facilities and visitation is primarily limited to driving through the area to see the impressive estates and enjoy the rural scenery. The Green Springs National Historic Landmark District sits along U.S. 15 in central Virginia, between Charlottesville and Richmond.

U.S. 15
Louisa County, VA
540-371-0802
540-967-9671
www.nps.gov/grsp

AT A GLANCE

Central Virginia, 15 miles east of Charlottesville ▪ 14,000 acres ▪ Year-round ▪ Viewing historic structures from highway

Maggie L. Walker National Historic Site

The home of America's first African-American female bank president

Born in Richmond, Virginia, in 1864 to a mother who had been enslaved, Maggie L. Walker rose to prominence as the leader of an African-American fraternal and social organization. While serving as head of the Independent Order of St. Luke, Walker realized a dream in 1903 when she founded the St. Luke Penny Savings Bank, where depositors could "take the nickels and turn them into dollars." By doing so, she became the first African-American woman to charter and serve as president of a bank in the United States.

In 1904, the Walker family bought an 1883 house in the Jackson Ward neighborhood, the center of Richmond's African-American business and social life and a national historic landmark district. Walker lived there until her death in 1934, by which time she had achieved prominence in many local, state, and national organizations, including serving on the board of directors of the National Association for the Advancement of Colored People (NAACP).

Visitors to Maggie L. Walker National Historic Site can view exhibits and a film on Walker's life in the visitor center, and then take a guided tour of her home. Owned by the Walker family until 1979, the 28-room house contains many original personal family items and has been restored to its appearance in the 1930s. It includes an elevator added in 1928 to assist Walker who, by then, confined to a wheelchair, continued to be active professionally and socially.

600 N. 2nd St.
Richmond, VA
804-771-2017
www.nps.gov/mawa

AT A GLANCE Central Virginia, in Richmond ▪ 1 acre ▪ Year-round ▪ Touring home of groundbreaking entrepreneur

---

Manassas National Battlefield Park

The Civil War's bloody future revealed

At the beginning of the Civil War, many on both sides thought the conflict would be over in a matter of weeks. Northerners assumed a ragtag Confederate Army would be easily defeated. Southerners thought that the North would simply allow the South to secede rather than fight a costly war to preserve the Union.

The first major battle of the Civil War occurred on July 21, 1861, near a Northern Virginia creek named Bull Run and the important railroad junction at Manassas. Many soldiers were naively looking forward to the adventure of a fight, and some residents of Washington, D.C., drove out in their carriages to watch the battle, as if it were going to be an entertainment.

Although Union troops gained an early advantage, the arrival of Confederate reinforcements turned the battle into a rout, with Union soldiers fleeing back to Washington in near panic, impeded by the carriages of spectators. More than 800 combatants were killed and more than 2,500 wounded. Both sides then realized the war would be longer and bloodier than expected.

A much larger battle at the same location in late August 1862 also ended in a Confederate victory. The triumph by Gen. Robert E. Lee's Army of Northern Virginia marked the high-water mark of southern military success in the Civil War.

During the war, Northerners tended to name battles after rivers or other geographic features, while Southerners used names of towns or railroad junctions. Thus the names Manassas and Bull Run are both used for the battles that occurred here.

Manassas National Battlefield Park preserves the land on which these important events took place and offers many ways to learn of the battles and their significance. The park's Henry Hill Visitor Center features historical exhibits, artifacts and memorabilia, an interactive battle map, and a film entitled "Manassas: End of Innocence"; outside the center, a 1-mile self-guided trail focuses on the First Battle of Manassas. Several additional hiking trails of varying lengths wind through the park. A driving tour (with available audio interpretive program) includes stops at important locations of the Second Battle of Manassas.

The recently opened Brawner Farm Interpretive Center provides orientation to the Second Manassas battlefield and includes a fiber-optic battle map and exhibits on Second Manassas.

A popular feature of the park is the equestrian statue of Confederate Gen. Thomas "Stonewall" Jackson. Jackson got his nickname at the First Battle of Manassas when another Confederate general was said to have pointed out "Jackson standing like a stone wall" facing a Union attack.

The park offers various seasonal guided tours and living-history programs, including infantry and artillery demonstrations around the anniversaries of the battles.

6511 Sudley Rd. (Va. 234)
Manassas, VA
703-361-1339
www.nps.gov/mana

AT A GLANCE Northern Virginia, 25 miles west of Arlington ▪ 5,073 acres ▪ Year-round ▪ Viewing museum exhibits and film, driving auto-tour route, hiking, picnicking

Petersburg National Battlefield
The final chapters of the Civil War

In June 1864, Union Gen. Ulysses S. Grant changed tactics in his campaign against the forces of Confederate Gen. Robert E. Lee. Grant aimed to capture the Confederate capital of Richmond, Virginia, by taking control of Petersburg, 25 miles south, a vital transportation hub and link in the supply route to Richmond.

Grant's direct attack on Petersburg failed, so he repositioned his troops and began what would become the longest siege in American warfare. Constant attacks and bombardment caused Lee to abandon Petersburg in early April 1865, pursued by Union forces. The weakened Confederate Army couldn't hold out long; Lee was forced to surrender to Grant at Appomattox Court House on April 9, essentially ending the Civil War (see p. 91).

Petersburg National Battlefield comprises several units in and around Petersburg. The park's Eastern Front Visitor Center is the best first stop for visitors, offering interpretive exhibits and audiovisual programs telling the story of the siege and its significance

One of several memorials at Petersburg

in the Civil War. Beginning here, a 33-mile driving tour leads to more than a dozen sites associated with the battles around Petersburg. One nearby site is the "crater," where Union troops set off explosives under the Confederate lines, killing more than 200 soldiers.

In the town of Hopewell, City Point became Grant's headquarters during the siege, as well as the center of supply operations for the Union Army. Located at the confluence of the James and Appomattox Rivers, City Point saw supplies arrive by boat. A visitor center *(804-458-9504)* is located in the Appomattox plantation house, on the grounds where Grant was based.

The Five Forks Battlefield in Dinwiddie protects the site of a battle on April 1, 1865, that ended in a Union victory, leading directly to Lee's decision to abandon Richmond and Petersburg. A visitor contact station *(804-469-4093)* is located here.

Poplar Grove National Cemetery serves as the final resting spot for nearly 6,000 Union soldiers. In the summer, rangers man a visitor contact station *(804-861-2488)* in a historic lodge. Call ahead of visiting as restorations are expected to close the cemetery to visitors until 2017.

Park rangers give seasonal talks, guided tours, demonstrations, or special events at each of the park's units.

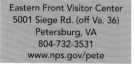

Eastern Front Visitor Center
5001 Siege Rd. (off Va. 36)
Petersburg, VA
804-732-3531
www.nps.gov/pete

AT A GLANCE South-central Virginia, 25 miles south of Richmond ▪ 2,738 acres ▪ Year-round ▪ Driving tour of siege and battlefield locations; guided tours and programs

Potomac Heritage National Scenic Trail

A recreational path linking Chesapeake Bay with the Alleghenies

A partnership between the National Park Service and several different government agencies and private organizations, the Potomac Heritage National Scenic Trail (PHNST) network connects many existing and planned trails between the mouth of the Potomac River and the Allegheny highlands of west-central Pennsylvania.

The PHNST includes more than 800 miles of trails, with additional trail mileage to come. Hiking is the main recreational activity afforded by the trail, but canoeing, kayaking, biking, horseback riding, cross-country skiing, camping, and backpacking are possible along some trail sections.

Some segments of the trail are covered elsewhere in this guide, such as the 184.5-mile-long towpath in the Chesapeake and Ohio Canal National Historical Park (see p. 86), the 18.5-mile-long Mount Vernon Trail in the George Washington Memorial Parkway (see p. 97), and routes in Prince William Forest Park (see below). Other trails include the Laurel Highlands Hiking Trail in western Pennsylvania; the Fort Circle Parks Trail in Washington, D.C.; and the Alexandria Heritage Trail in Alexandria, Virginia.

The trail office in Harpers Ferry, West Virginia, can provide maps, brochures, and information, as can the NPS website of the PHNST and that of the Potomac Heritage Trail Association (*www.potomactrail.org*), a partnership organization formed to support trail development and maintenance.

Trail office
Harpers Ferry, WV
304-535-4014
www.nps.gov/pohe

AT A GLANCE
Along the Potomac River in the District of Columbia, Maryland, Virginia, and Pennsylvania ▪ 830 trail miles ▪ Year-round ▪ Hiking, boating, biking, horseback riding, camping

---

Prince William Forest Park

The largest green space in the Washington, D.C., area

Prince William Forest Park owes its existence to the New Deal programs developed by President Franklin D. Roosevelt during the Great Depression of the 1930s. Creating new federal recreation areas was seen as a way to provide work for unemployed people while restoring land damaged by unsustainable farm, forestry, or industrial use. As one result of this history, the park preserves the largest inventory of Civilian Conservation Corps structures (153) in the National Park System. Many of these are rustic wood-and-stone cabins that are available for rent, providing overnight accommodations apart from developed campgrounds.

Prince William's beautiful forest straddles the line between the

South Fork Quantico Creek in the winter.

Appalachian Piedmont and the Atlantic coastal plain and comprises trees such as oak, hickory, beech, sycamore, butternut, black walnut, cottonwood, and even aspen and hemlock. The park is excellent for bird-watching and is home to black bear, beaver, and white-tailed deer.

The park encompasses 37 miles of hiking trails and 21 miles of bicycle-accessible roads and trails. Hikers may come across the remains of old farms, villages, and mining operations that existed before the park was established. Some trails parallel attractive Quantico Creek, noted for its high water quality. Anglers enjoy fishing for species such as bluegill, pumpkinseed, largemouth bass, and channel catfish.

The park visitor center offers an introductory film and information about ranger-led programs such as guided walks and summer campfire talks. The nonprofit Friends of Prince William Forest Park (*www.fpwfp.org*) supports the preservation of the forest and sponsors several activities throughout the year.

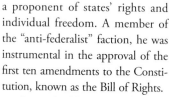

Red Hill Patrick Henry National Memorial
Final home of "the voice of the Revolution"

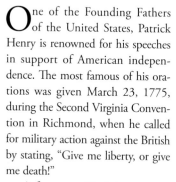

One of the Founding Fathers of the United States, Patrick Henry is renowned for his speeches in support of American independence. The most famous of his orations was given March 23, 1775, during the Second Virginia Convention in Richmond, when he called for military action against the British by stating, "Give me liberty, or give me death!"

A five-term Virginia governor who also served in the state legislature for 25 years, Henry was a proponent of states' rights and individual freedom. A member of the "anti-federalist" faction, he was instrumental in the approval of the first ten amendments to the Constitution, known as the Bill of Rights.

At age 57, Henry moved to Red Hill, a 2,920-acre tobacco plantation near the Staunton River, living there in a simple 1½-story frame house until his death in 1799.

A visit to the memorial site begins with a short video on Henry's life. Exhibits in the museum include the famous Peter F. Rothermel painting "Patrick Henry before the Virginia House of Burgesses," depicting Henry giving his "If this be treason, make the most of it!" speech against the Stamp Act of 1765.

Visitors can tour the reconstructed house and other buildings, including Henry's original law office, a detached kitchen, smokehouse, and cabin that was home to enslaved workers. Henry's grave site features a monument inscribed with the words "His Fame His Best Epitaph."

Richmond National Battlefield Park
Remembering the long struggle for control of the Confederate capital

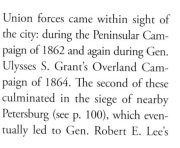

When war broke out between the North and South, the Confederates named Richmond, Virginia, their capital city; only 110 miles separated it from Washington, D.C., the Union capital. The land between the two cities saw many bloody battles as the North tried to capture Richmond and the South fought desperately to protect it.

Richmond was not only the Confederate capital but was also a major supply base for troops, a manufacturing and transportation hub, and the site of the largest Confederate military hospital. Twice during the Civil War, Union forces came within sight of the city: during the Peninsular Campaign of 1862 and again during Gen. Ulysses S. Grant's Overland Campaign of 1864. The second of these culminated in the siege of nearby Petersburg (see p. 100), which eventually led to Gen. Robert E. Lee's surrender at Appomattox (see p. 91) and the final Union victory.

Visiting the Battlefield

Richmond National Battlefield Park comprises 13 units with five visitor centers *(some open only seasonally)*. An 80-mile driving tour links the 13 park areas; the park provides a map with marked route and driving directions.

The first stop should be the Civil War Visitor Center at Tredegar Iron Works in downtown Richmond. Three floors of exhibits and an interpretive film give an overview of the many battles that were fought around the city. For more than a century this was the site of an iron-manufacturing facility, and during the Civil War the Tredegar Iron Works was the major source for Confederate artillery and ammunition. For example, it provided the South with nearly 1,100 cannon.

Fewer than 2 miles east is the park's Chimborazo Medical Museum, located on the site of a hospital that once contained more than a hundred wards and even had its own bakery. The hospital was later demolished; the museum here has exhibits on 19th-century medical procedures, original medical instruments, and a short film on Civil War medicine.

Traditionally fenced fields, where the North and South battled for Richmond

The Cold Harbor Battlefield Visitor Center *(5 miles southeast of Mechanicsville on Va. 156)* houses war-related exhibits and artifacts and lighted map programs that depict the 1862 Battle of Gaines' Mill and the 1864 Battle of Cold Harbor, both Confederate victories that saved Richmond from Union attack. Other visitor centers *(open seasonally)* are located at Fort Harrison, south of Richmond; and Glendale National Cemetery, southeast of the city.

Totopotomoy Battlefield, which includes the Rural Plains home (ca 1725), is located five miles north of Mechanicsville and features walking trails and earthworks.

Among other park locations are Drewry's Bluff on the James River, where a battle on May 15, 1862, ended the Union naval threat to Richmond; and Malvern Hill Battlefield, where a July 1, 1862, clash dealt the Confederates a defeat. Malvern Hill is the best preserved battlefield in the Richmond area. Cold Harbor, Gaines' Mill, Fort Harrison, Drewry's Bluff, and Malvern Hill Battlefields each feature interpretive walking trails.

Park rangers and volunteers offer seasonal guided tours and living-history programs, including artillery-firing demonstrations. Check at the visitor centers for schedules.

Civil War Visitor Center 470 Tredegar St. Richmond, VA 804-771-2145 www.nps.gov/rich	**AT A GLANCE**	East-central Virginia, in and around Richmond ▪ 2,100 acres ▪ Year-round ▪ Visiting battlefields, museums, and historic sites; hiking; attending ranger-led programs

Shenandoah National Park
Where fabulous mountain views and more than 500 miles of trails beckon

Occupying more than 300 square miles of ridgeline between the Appalachian Piedmont and the Shenandoah River Valley, Shenandoah National Park was created in the 1920s and '30s, when the development of national parks in the West spurred calls for similar recreation and natural areas in the East. Unlike the West, however, which possessed vast areas of unpopulated terrain, the East had seen centuries of settlement nearly throughout the region.

More than 400 families lived within the area that is now the park.

Sunrise kisses Shenandoah National Park's Welcome Center.

park's 513 miles of trails—including 101 miles of the famed Appalachian National Scenic Trail (see p. 21) and more than 200 miles where horse-back riding is allowed—are located off Skyline Drive.

Skyline Drive: Mile 0 to 44

Travelers beginning at Skyline Drive's mile zero in the north will quickly reach the Dickey Ridge Visitor Center, offering an interpretive film and exhibits on Blue Ridge natural history, as well as information on park facilities and ranger talks. Nearby are the Fox Hollow Trail, leading to old homesites and a cemetery; and the Snead Farm Trail, to an old orchard and barn.

Skyline Drive has one of its many crossings of the Appalachian Trail at Thornton Gap, around mile 31. Just to the south, Marys Rock Tunnel has a height limit of 12 feet, 8 inches—something for drivers of large vehicles to keep in mind. Just past mile 37 is the trail to Corbin Cabin in Nicholson Hollow. A small community of more than 20 homesteads once existed here. This area is the site of one of six primitive huts in the park maintained and rented by the Potomac Appalachian Trail Club *(703-242-0693, www .potomacappalachian.org).*

At mile 42 is the concessionaire-run Skyland. This resort dates from the 1890s and includes a dining room. *(Call 877-247-9261 for all park commercial lodging.)* Here, too, is an authorized park concessionaire for guided horseback rides. Skyland's Massanutten Lodge was the home of Addie Nairn Pollock. Rangers lead tours of the 1911 structure; the living room has been restored to its 1916 appearance. The lodge is home to an exhibit called "The Women of Skyland," which documents the lives

Some moved voluntarily, some went to Depression-era resettlement communities, and a few older people were given permission to live out their lives in the park. The remains of former communities or isolated cabins where mountaineers once lived and farmed still stand deep in the backcountry of Shenandoah.

Visiting the Park

Life was difficult for many of those residents, but today's travelers will find several lodging and dining opportunities in addition to countless ways to explore the park's backcountry by driving, hiking, backpacking, or horseback riding. Shenandoah National Park features a visitor center *(late March–Nov.).* There are four developed campgrounds and three concessionaire-operated lodging areas.

All park facilities close in winter (except Byrd Visitor Center, which stays open on weekends), though hiking and other outdoor activities are allowed year-round. The park's most crowded conditions occur in

the "leaf peeping" season of autumn, usually in mid-October, when the foliage of oaks, hickories, maples, and other hardwood trees turns yellow, orange, and red.

Skyline Drive

The park's centerpiece—and the only part that many visitors see—is 105-mile-long Skyline Drive, which runs from U.S. 340 at Front Royal, Virginia, south to Rockfish Gap at I-64. Skyline Drive and its historic districts are national historic landmarks. Dozens of overlooks along the drive provide splendid panoramas of the eastern Appalachian Blue Ridge landscape.

Skyline Drive reaches a high point of 3,680 feet at mile 42 (mileposts along the drive begin at zero at the northern terminus). The route is occasionally closed by winter snow or icy conditions.

There's a lot to see and do along Skyline Drive, but much more to be experienced for those who venture away from paved roads and developed areas. Several trailheads for the

FOLLOWING SPREAD: *The forest-cloaked Blue Ridge is one of several mountain ranges that make up the Appalachians.*

of several women who frequented the resort in the Roaring Twenties.

The 1.6-mile loop trail to Stony Man Mountain reaches the park's second highest point (4,011 feet) and offers great views. A bit farther south is the easy Limberlost Trail, one of the park's most beautiful areas in June when the mountain laurel is blooming. Limberlost Trail is accessible for persons with disabilities.

Skyline Drive: Mile 44 to 105

At mile 44 the Crescent Rock Overlook offers a view of the park's highest point, 4,051-foot Hawksbill Mountain. Around mile 50 is the popular but steep 1.4-mile round-trip hike to Dark Hollow Falls, a 70-foot-high waterfall once admired by Thomas Jefferson. This is the shortest walk to see a waterfall in the park; none are visible from Skyline Drive.

At mile 51 is the Byrd Visitor Center and the adjacent Big Meadows area, with a lodge, campground, and other facilities. Here hikers can access the Appalachian National Scenic Trail, and horseback riders can access the Skyland–Big Meadows horse trail.

Skyline Drive crosses the Appalachian Trail again at Milam Gap, where a trail leads to Rapidan Camp, which served as the summer White House from 1929 to 1932, during the Presidency of Herbert Hoover. Hoover wanted a getaway from Washington, D.C., that would offer trout fishing and be high enough in the mountains to be cooler than D.C. Hoover donated the camp to the new national park when he left office. His cabin has been restored to its 1930s appearance, and is listed as a national historic landmark. Rapidan Camp is open when staffing allows; check with the Byrd Visitor Center about its status and about ranger-led van tours to the site.

Continuing south, Skyline Drive reaches the Loft Mountain area, where

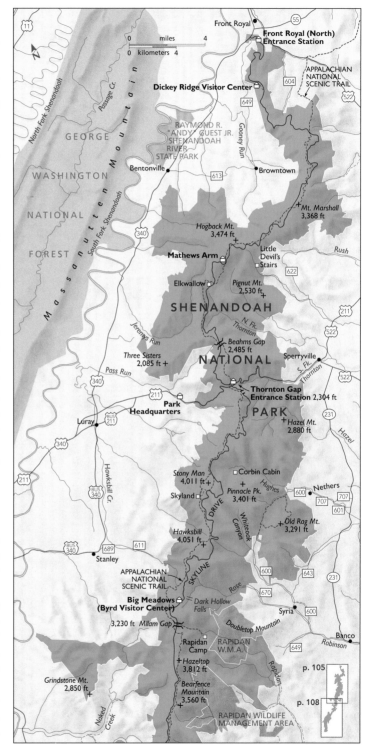

there's a campground. The Big Run Overlook here stands out for its truly exceptional views. Hiking trails in the area provide access to several waterfalls, including Jones Run Falls and the upper and lower falls on Doyles River.

Skyline Drive reaches Shenandoah National Park's southern boundary at Rockfish Gap, which is also the northern terminus of the Blue Ridge Parkway (see p. 171), a scenic 469-mile drive through Virginia and North Carolina to Great Smoky Mountains National Park (see p. 187).

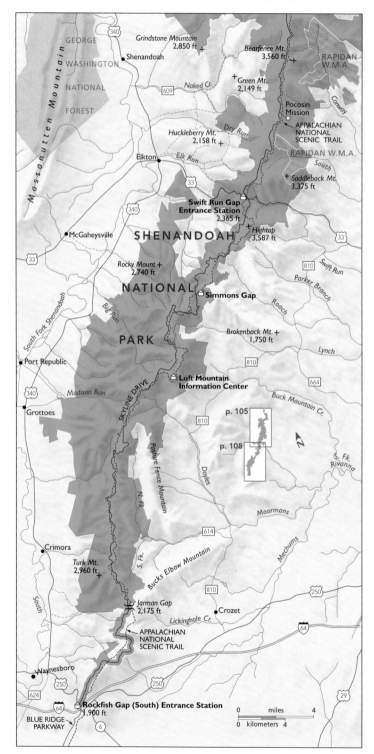

Flora

Nature lovers could spend years exploring Shenandoah National Park without exhausting its opportunities for discovery. With the elevation ranging from 561 feet to 4,050 feet, vegetation within the national park is highly diverse.

Though the area was timbered before establishment of the park, the forest is forever changing, as is its natural diversity. Forest covers some 95 percent of the park. The most common trees include pine, oak, hickory, maple, birch, ash, basswood, blackgum, and tulip tree (a type of magnolia). Only a few stands of eastern hemlock remain within the park: They have suffered greatly from an insect pest called the hemlock woolly adelgid, which has wiped out the species in many areas of the Appalachians. Balsam fir and red spruce grow in limited areas of high elevation.

The park is renowned for its wildflowers and flowering shrubs. The most famous of the latter is mountain laurel (usually blooming in June), with other shrubs such as flowering dogwood, serviceberry, viburnum, redbud, fringe tree, and witch hazel. Interestingly, though mountain laurel is native to the area, workers of the Civilian Conservation Corps planted in the 1930s much of the population seen along Skyline Drive. Wildflower season begins in early spring with bloodroot and hepatica; continues with violet, orchid, columbine, and trillium; and finishes in fall with composites, including sunflower, aster, and goldenrod.

Fauna

Thanks to its diverse vegetation, the park is equally diverse in its wildlife. From black bears (the park boasts a healthy population of 300 to 500 individuals) to salamanders (the Appalachian Mountains constitute a world center of diversity for these small amphibians), Shenandoah's wildlife offers abundant pleasures for the observant visitor. White-tailed deer are the most common large mammals seen in the park, with other mammalian resident species such as gray and red fox, bobcat, raccoon, woodchuck (groundhog), gray squirrel, and eastern chipmunk.

More than 200 species of birds have been observed within the park, and its mix of riparian hardwoods, moist coves, and high-elevation forest makes it highly rewarding for

The views from Skyline Drive stretch for miles.

bird-watchers. Among its more interesting breeding birds are common raven, brown creeper, veery, black-throated blue warbler, Blackburnian warbler, worm-eating warbler, scarlet tanager, and rose-breasted grosbeak. A program is trying to reintroduce the

peregrine falcon to the park after its extirpation, in part caused by the use of DDT in the 20th century.

Backcountry Camping

Most of Shenandoah National Park, including the 40 percent of the park that is officially designated federal wilderness area, is open for backcountry camping. Hiking and backpacking are the best ways to find solitude (something that can be nearly impossible in the eastern United States) and observe flora and fauna. A free permit is required for backcountry camping. Long-distance hikers on the Appalachian Trail can take advantage of several Appalachian Trail huts.

Skyline Drive between I-66 & I-64 Northern Virginia 540-999-3500 www.nps.gov/shen	**AT A GLANCE** Northern Virginia, 20 miles west of Charlottesville or 75 miles west of Washington, D.C. ▪ 197,439 acres ▪ Year-round; may close in winter ▪ Hiking, scenic driving, camping, backpacking, horseback riding, picnicking

Wolf Trap National Park for the Performing Arts

A green space for music, theater, dance, and opera

One of the National Park Service's most unusual sites, Wolf Trap owes it existence to the late Catherine Filene Shouse, who donated 118 acres of her Virginia farmland to the federal government, along with funds to build a performing-arts center. Congress accepted the donation in 1966, and the center's first performances were held in 1971.

The major venue at Wolf Trap is the Filene Center, which offers both covered seating and an outdoor area

where many people bring blankets or cushions on which to sit for concerts and other performances. (Many in the outdoor audience bring picnic baskets, too.) More than 90 performances are held here each year, late May to early September, ranging from opera to country music to Broadway musicals. Shows for children, including puppet shows, dance performances, concerts, and similar events, are presented in summer at Wolf Trap's Theatre-in-the-Woods, adjacent to the Filene Center.

The National Park Service operates Wolf Trap National Park for the Performing Arts in partnership with the Wolf Trap Foundation. The foundation also administers a smaller indoor performance space called The Barns at Wolf Trap, which is not part of the national park.

Guided backstage tours are offered on a regular schedule. The park is open for picnicking all year. Dining is available at the Filene Center restaurant on days of performances.

1551 Trap Rd. Vienna, VA 703-255-1800 www.nps.gov/wotr	**AT A GLANCE** Northeastern Virginia, west of Washington, D.C. ▪ 130 acres ▪ Late May to early September ▪ Attending performances, picnicking

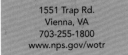

WASHINGTON, D.C.

Washington, D.C., capital of the United States and where thousands of people work for the federal government, is one of the nation's most popular tourist attractions. People come to see historic structures such as the Lincoln Memorial, the Washington Monument, and the Capitol, as well as to visit museums covering subjects from history to art to science. Located at a site chosen by George Washington, the city was designed by Frenchman Pierre Charles L'Enfant, using broad avenues and traffic circles. Building-height restrictions mean D.C. seems less urban than other cities, less hemmed in, and more inviting to exploration. Green spaces offer all sorts of recreational opportunities.

Constitution Gardens

Bicentennial tribute to the U.S. Constitution

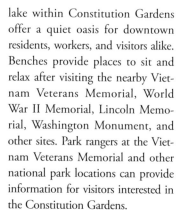

Located just north of the Reflecting Pool on Washington's National Mall, this site was for decades home to "temporary" buildings constructed for military agencies in World War I. After the buildings were demolished in the early 1970s, President Richard Nixon directed that a park be established here. Dedicated in the United States' Bicentennial, the park was created as a tribute to the American Revolution and its 200-year legacy.

An artificial lake was built within the park, and on July 2, 1984, a memorial was dedicated on a small island within the lake. It consists of 56 stones bearing the names of the signers of the Declaration of Independence. On September 17, 1986, in honor of the bicentennial of the U.S. Constitution, President Ronald Reagan issued a proclamation making Constitution Gardens a living-legacy tribute to that enduring and inspirational document.

The green expanse and peaceful lake within Constitution Gardens offer a quiet oasis for downtown residents, workers, and visitors alike. Benches provide places to sit and relax after visiting the nearby Vietnam Veterans Memorial, World War II Memorial, Lincoln Memorial, Washington Monument, and other sites. Park rangers at the Vietnam Veterans Memorial and other national park locations can provide information for visitors interested in the Constitution Gardens.

Constitution Ave.
& 17th St., NW
Washington, DC
202-426-6841
www.nps.gov/coga

AT A GLANCE

On the National Mall, between the Washington Monument and Lincoln Memorial ▪ 40 acres ▪ Year-round ▪ Viewing memorial to signers of the Declaration of Independence

Ford's Theatre National Historic Site

The tragic site of Abraham Lincoln's final evening

Just days after Confederate Gen. Robert E. Lee surrendered, ending America's bloody Civil War, President Abraham Lincoln and his wife, Mary, attended a play as a means to escape the pressures of the immediate postwar period. At Ford's Theatre, six blocks from the White House, Lincoln was shot by John Wilkes Booth, a Confederate sympathizer and actor whom Lincoln had watched perform previously at Ford's.

The mortally wounded Lincoln was taken across 10th Street to the house of William Peterson, where he died on the morning of April 15, 1865.

In succeeding years the theater building served as government offices and a warehouse. It was abandoned for a time before a restoration in the 1960s made it again a theater, as well as a museum of Lincoln and the assassination. After additional renovation, Ford's Theatre and the museum reopened in 2009, the 200th anniversary of Lincoln's birth.

Visitors can tour the theater, museum, and Peterson House, seeing the assassination site, historic artifacts, and exhibits on Lincoln and related events before and after his death. Free tickets for a specific time are required for tours. Tickets can be reserved in advance *(fee)*, and a limited number

are available each day on a first-come, first-served basis.

Ford's remains an active professional theater, and at times visitors are not allowed to enter the theater itself because of preparation for plays or similar activities. Call the theater or check the website for affected dates.

---

511 10th St., NW
Washington, DC
202-426-6924
www.nps.gov/foth
www.fords.org

AT A GLANCE

Northwest D.C. ▪ Less than 1 acre ▪ Year-round ▪ Visiting assassination site and museum; attending theater productions

---

Franklin Delano Roosevelt Memorial
Remembering FDR's long and eventful Presidency

Elected President in 1932 during the Great Depression, Franklin D. Roosevelt was reelected three times, dying in office in 1945. The only U.S. President to serve more than two terms, FDR not only led the nation during the Depression but also served as Commander in Chief during the world-shaking events of World War II. Despite coming from a wealthy background, he was a hero of the working people, dedicating himself to improving American lives through the economic programs of the New Deal.

Located on the southwestern side of Washington's Tidal Basin, Franklin Delano Roosevelt Memorial covers more than 7 acres. In its conception and design elements, the memorial is dedicated to FDR's era as well as to the man himself. The memorial comprises four open-air galleries, one for each of his four terms. Waterfalls and other water features make up a major component of the memorial,

The sculpture of Franklin Delano Roosevelt by artist Neil Estern

reflecting the importance of water in FDR's life, from his service as assistant secretary of the Navy during World War I to the dam-building projects of the Tennessee Valley Authority. One area within the gallery dedicated to FDR's third term includes scattered granite blocks and a waterfall crashing over jagged boulders that evokes the violence and

tumult of World War II.

Among the memorial's features are inscribed Roosevelt quotations—such as "The only thing we have to fear is fear itself," from his first Inaugural Address, and "We must be the great arsenal of democracy," from 1940. Sculptures include a depiction of FDR with his beloved Scottish terrier Fala, and a controversial sculpture of FDR in a wheelchair, realistically reflecting the paralysis he suffered from the age of 39. A sculpture by famed artist George Segal shows people standing in a Depression-era breadline; another Segal sculpture depicts a man listening to one of the famed "fireside chat" radio addresses. FDR's wife, Eleanor Roosevelt, is shown standing in front of the seal of the United Nations, in recognition of her service as a delegate to that body.

The memorial is open at all times, and rangers are present from 10 a.m. to 11:30 p.m. daily.

West Basin Drive, SW
Washington, DC
202-426-6841
www.nps.gov/frde

AT A GLANCE

West Potomac Park, near the Jefferson Memorial ▪ 8.1 acres ▪ Year-round ▪ Viewing sculptures, waterfalls, and exhibits on FDR's life

Frederick Douglass National Historic Site

The final home of a famed advocate for African-American rights

Born into slavery in 1818, Frederick Douglass learned to read despite his lack of formal schooling, escaped to the free North, and went on to become internationally known and respected for his dedication to the abolitionist movement and equal rights for African Americans. His 1845 autobiography, *Narrative of the Life of Frederick Douglass,* brought him fame, and his eloquence as a public speaker resulted in lecture tours across the United States and England. Douglass was also a newspaper publisher and served in various government positions, including U.S. minister to Haiti.

In 1877, Douglass bought a 9-acre estate in southeastern Washington, D.C., and named it Cedar Hill. He lived in the house, built between 1855 and 1859, until his death in 1895. At Frederick Douglass National Historic Site, visitors

Douglass lived at Cedar Hill for more than 35 years.

can learn of this extraordinary man and his accomplishments in the face of prejudice.

The park visitor center features exhibits on Douglass's life and a

17-minute film, "Frederick Douglass: Fighter for Freedom." Steps lead up a hill to the house, from which there are excellent views of the U.S. Capitol and the Washington Monument.

Because visiting the 14-room Anacostia house is by ranger-led tours only, tickets are required and advance reservations strongly encouraged. About 70 percent of the objects in the house are original, including personal belongings, furnishings, books, musical instruments, photographs, and gifts that Douglass received from friends, such as Abraham Lincoln.

With a self-guiding brochure, visitors can tour the grounds of Cedar Hill, where picnicking is allowed. On the grounds is a reconstruction of the Growlery, a small building that Douglass used as a retreat to be alone to read and write.

AT A GLANCE

1411 W St., SE
Washington, DC
202-426-5961
www.nps.gov/frdo

Anacostia neighborhood ▪ 9 acres ▪ Year-round ▪ Touring Douglass's home and grounds; viewing film and exhibits

Korean War Veterans Memorial

Remembering the "forgotten war"

When the Communist government of North Korea sent troops into South Korea in June 1950, it set off a bloody three-year conflict that involved the United States, the United Nations, and allied countries on one side and China and

the Soviet Union on the other. Coming only five years after the end of World War II and never an officially declared war—it was the Korean conflict, a police action—Korea has often been called the forgotten war.

Dedicated on the National Mall

in 1995, the Korean War Veterans Memorial honors the American men and women who served in the conflict: "sons and daughters who answered the call to defend a country they never knew and a people they never met," as an inscription states.

At the heart of the memorial are 19 realistic stainless-steel statutes depicting members of the armed services—Army, Navy, Marine Corps, and Air Force—each dressed to reflect the harsh climate. A polished granite wall reflects the troops on patrol, doubling their number. Also part of the memorial are photographic images of participants in the war, sandblasted into the granite; a United Nations wall listing the countries that aided the allied cause; and a Pool of Remembrance.

The Korean War Veterans Memorial is a unit of National Mall and Memorial Parks. National Park Service rangers are in the area daily to answer questions and provide advice.

Independence Ave., SW
Washington, DC
202-426-6841
www.nps.gov/kowa

AT A GLANCE

On the National Mall, near the Lincoln Memorial ▪ 2 acres ▪ Year-round ▪ Viewing statues and related monuments

---

Lincoln Memorial

A grand tribute to the memory of the Great Emancipator

One of the most recognizable memorials in a city filled with iconic structures, the Lincoln Memorial stands at the western end of the National Mall in Washington, facing the Washington Monument and the United States Capitol. It honors Abraham Lincoln, the 16th President, who served during the tumultuous years of the Civil War; emancipated enslaved people in the South; preserved the Union; and was assassinated only days after the surrender of the Confederacy in 1865.

Dedicated in 1922, the Lincoln Memorial takes its architectural inspiration from Greek temples, with 36 Doric columns around the exterior. Inside is a famed statue of a seated Lincoln by artist Daniel Chester French, as well as two large murals entitled "Unity" and "Emancipation," by artist Jules Guerin. Over the 19-foot-high statue are the words, "In this temple, as in the hearts of the people for whom he saved the Union, the memory of Abraham Lincoln is enshrined forever." On opposing walls are inscribed the texts of two of Lincoln's most famous speeches: his Gettysburg Address of 1863 and his 1865 Inaugural Address.

The builders of the memorial made an effort to use materials from different parts of the United States. The exterior, interior, and statue incorporate limestone from Indiana; granite from Massachusetts; and marble from Colorado, Tennessee, Georgia, and Alabama.

The memorial receives millions of visitors each year, and it has been the scene of many political and social events in American history. It was here that civil rights leader Martin Luther King, Jr., gave his influential "I Have a Dream" speech in 1963, one of the landmark moments of the African-American struggle for equality. Engraved words mark the spot where King stood to give his address.

In 2012, the National Park Service completed a renovation of the Reflecting Pool, including replacement of the pool's structure and installation of a sustainable circulation system that pulls the 6.75 million gallons of water that fill the pool from the nearby Tidal Basin.

23rd St. & Constitution Ave. NW
Washington, DC
202-426-6841
www.nps.gov/linc

AT A GLANCE

West end of the National Mall, overlooking the Potomac River ▪ 7.3 acres ▪ Year-round ▪ Viewing memorial statue, inscriptions, and paintings

---

Lyndon Baines Johnson Mem. Grove on the Potomac

A nature-oriented memorial to the 36th President

After former President Lyndon B. Johnson died in 1973, an idea for a memorial took shape, with a more natural remembrance envisioned. It recalls the link LBJ always had with the land in his native Texas and elsewhere, and was inspired by Theodore Roosevelt Island.

The resulting 17-acre site on an

island in the Potomac River, on the Virginia side, was landscaped in a way that promoted appreciation of the natural setting. At its heart is a 43-ton, 19-foot monolith of red Texas granite. Arrayed around it are hundreds of dogwoods, azaleas, and rhododendrons. Winding paths lead past picnic tables, benches, and granite markers inscribed with LBJ's words on subjects such as education and the environment.

LBJ's wife, Lady Bird, was known for her dedication to beautification projects and promotion and protection of wildflowers. The LBJ memorial is located within Lady Bird Johnson Park, renamed in her honor in 1968 for her efforts to improve the appearance of Washington, D.C. She admired Washington for, in her words, its "beautiful buildings that belong to all of us." Lady Bird Johnson Park includes trails; a marina; and the Navy and Marine Memorial, which honors U.S. Navy sailors and others who toil "upon the waters of the world."

Lady Bird Johnson Park
(off Arlington Memorial Bridge)
Washington, DC
703-289-2500
www.nps.gov/lyba

AT A GLANCE

Off George Washington Memorial Parkway, along the Potomac River, Virginia side ▪ 17 acres ▪ Year-round ▪ Walking, biking

Martin Luther King, Jr. Memorial
Sculpture honoring the famed civil-rights leader

OUT OF THE MOUNTAIN OF DESPAIR, A STONE OF HOPE

Martin Luther King, Jr. Memorial, carved from pink granite

During the turbulent years of the American civil rights movement, until his assassination in 1968, Dr. Martin Luther King, Jr., spoke with passion and eloquence in advocating equality and justice for all citizens. His stirring speeches inspired millions of African Americans working for equal access to education, voting rights, housing, and economic opportunity.

Dedicated in 2011, the Martin Luther King, Jr. Memorial stands on the National Mall in Washington, near the spot where King gave his famous "I have a dream" speech as part of the 1963 March on Washington for Jobs and Freedom. The granite sculpture, by Chinese artist Master Lei Yixin, depicts King as a "Stone of Hope" emerging from a "Mountain of Despair"—words taken from his "I have a dream" address. The 30-foot-tall figure of King is shown with arms crossed, looking hopefully toward the horizon. Visitors enter through the Mountain of Despair to reach the Stone of Hope, symbolic of the struggle for equal rights and the obstacles King overcame in his own life.

Located northwest of the Tidal Basin between the Lincoln and Jefferson Memorials, the King site also includes a wall inscribed with quotations from his speeches, such as "Injustice anywhere is a threat to justice everywhere," and "True peace is not just the absence of tension; it is the presence of justice."

900 Ohio Dr. SW
Washington, DC
202-426-6841
www.nps.gov/mlkm

AT A GLANCE

National Mall in Washington, D.C. ▪ 4 acres ▪ Year-round ▪ Viewing sculpture and inscriptions

Mary McLeod Bethune Council House N.H.S.

Where African-American women planned the journey to equality

Born in South Carolina in 1875 to parents who had been enslaved before Emancipation, Mary McLeod Bethune enthusiastically pursued her education and became one of the most influential African Americans in the mid-20th century. She believed that education was crucial to the empowerment of African-American women, and she fought to make it a priority and a reality.

While she was living in Daytona Beach, Florida, in 1904, she founded a school for poor black girls that eventually grew into the present Bethune-Cookman University, which

she served as president. In 1936, President Franklin D. Roosevelt appointed her director of the Office of Negro Affairs of the National Youth Administration, making her the first African-American woman to head a federal agency.

In 1935 in Washington, D.C., Bethune worked to establish the National Council of Negro Women (NCNW), which united more than two dozen organizations to work for better education and political and employment opportunities for African-American women. The group acquired a building in the Logan Circle area for

its headquarters in 1943; Bethune lived at the house until 1949. Because of a fire, the NCNW moved to nearby Dupont Circle in 1966.

Mary McLeod Bethune Council House National Historic Site preserves the original NCNW headquarters structure and serves as a memorial to Bethune, who died in 1955. Visitors can take guided tours of the house and view a film reviewing Bethune's life and legacy. The National Park Service has re-created its appearance during Bethune's residence through historic photographs and some of the original furnishings.

1318 Vermont Ave., NW
Washington, DC
202-673-2402
www.nps.gov/mamc

AT A GLANCE

Northwest Washington ▪ Less than 1 acre ▪ Year-round ▪ Touring historic home, viewing interpretive film and exhibits

National Capital Parks-East

A diverse collection of cultural, natural, and recreational opportunities

Grouped under the title National Capital Parks-East (NCP-E) are several historic sites, recreation and natural areas, and collections of small parks in the eastern section of Washington, D.C., and nearby Maryland. Some of them, such as Frederick Douglass (see p. 112) and Mary McLeod Bethune Council House (see above) National Historic Sites, are treated separately in this book.

The Carter G. Woodson Home National Historic Site *(1538 9th St., NW, Washington, D.C.)* was acquired by the National Park Service in 2005. The son of former slaves, Woodson was a historian and educator who is often called the father of

African-American history. Woodson lived in this ten-room house from 1915 until his death in 1950. The Park Service is performing a rehabilitation of the house before opening it to the public. The Mary McLeod Bethune Council House National Historic Site serves as the temporary visitor center.

Other areas include 1,100-acre Greenbelt Park in Maryland, with camping and four hiking trails (1 to 6 miles). Bisected by the Baltimore-Washington Parkway, Greenbelt Park is accessible off Greenbelt Road *(Md. 193)*. The NCP-E's Anacostia Park is excellent for bird-watching. The 1,200-acre site encompasses Kenilworth Park and Aquatic Gardens, displaying

cultivated aquatic plants. Located east of the National Arboretum along the Anacostia River, the park includes extensive wetland areas. Anacostia Park also features a roller-skating rink, 18-hole Langston Golf Course, marinas, and a public boat ramp.

Oxon Cove Park/Oxon Hill Farm in Maryland includes exhibits and living-history programs interpreting farm life of an earlier era. In the early 19th century, this land was a plantation known as Mount Welby. Later, it was a Civil War hospital and a facility where patients received therapy by doing farmwork. Ranger-led programs at the park cover topics such as the environment, multiculturalism,

19th-century history, and agriculture.

Some of the smaller parks and green spaces within NCP-E evolved from Pierre L'Enfant's original 1790 design for the capital city of Washington. They include traffic medians, circles, squares, and triangles that are attractive and provide spaces for relaxation on Capitol Hill. These parks encompass areas between Second Streets NE and SE and the Anacostia River. Included in this group are the Maryland Avenue Triangles, the Pennsylvania Avenue Medians, the Eastern Market Metro Station, the Potomac Avenue Metro Station, Seward Square, and Twining Square.

The four major parks on Capitol Hill are Folger, Lincoln, Marion, and Stanton. Lincoln Park includes a well-known statue of civil rights activist and educator Mary McLeod Bethune, as well as a somewhat controversial statue of Abraham Lincoln holding the Emancipation Proclamation before a kneeling African-American man.

Oxon Hill, a 19th-century farm at Oxon Cove Park

At 376 acres, Fort Dupont Park is one of the largest parks in Washington. Within it are the remains of Civil War earthworks, a skating rink, community gardens, and an outdoor summer theater that hosts free musical concerts in July and August. It is located in the southeastern part of the District of Columbia.

Fort Washington Park in Maryland preserves the remains of a 19th-century military post and an 1882 lighthouse. The park stages occasional Civil War artillery demonstrations, and a 3-mile trail follows the park perimeter. Fort Foote Park, north of Fort Washington, displays two massive Rodman guns, the largest in the United States arsenal during the Civil War.

Near Accokeek, Maryland, Piscataway Park was established to preserve the landscape across the Potomac River from Mount Vernon, George Washington's home in Virginia. With almost 5,000 acres, Piscataway Park encompasses the National Colonial Farm, a living-history museum that re-creates the life of a typical tobacco-planting family in the 1770s. The farm is operated by the nonprofit Accokeek Foundation (*www.accokeek. org*). Piscataway Park also features nature trails and boardwalks through wetlands.

Park headquarters
1900 Anacostia Dr., SE
Washington, DC
202-690-5185
www.nps.gov/nace

AT A GLANCE

Various locations in and around the District of Columbia ▪ More than 8,000 acres ▪ Year-round ▪ Hiking, camping, picnicking, wildlife-watching, touring museums and gardens

National Mall

The "grand avenue" at the heart of the nation's capital

Pierre L'Enfant's original 1791 design for the federal city of Washington called for a "grand avenue" that would run westward from the U.S. Capitol. While parts of L'Enfant's plan were realized early on, the proposed mile-long avenue was at first not developed. Troops were stationed on the site in the Civil War, and a train station was built at its eastern end.

In the early 20th century, a special commission recommended that the Mall be restored to its original concept as a long, broad, grassy open space. The train station was removed, and slowly the National Mall was developed to its present appearance, stretching two miles from the steps of the Capitol to the Lincoln Memorial, with the tall

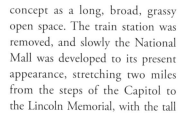

obelisk of the Washington Monument rising slightly to the west of the central point. The National Mall, as defined by the National Park Service, encompasses the original Mall, the Washington Monument grounds, the Tidal Basin area, and West Potomac Park, ending at the Potomac River behind the Lincoln Memorial.

It's estimated that 24 million people visit the National Mall annually, with more than 3,000 events held yearly. The National Mall has more than 26 miles of pedestrian sidewalks and 8 miles of bike trails.

Famous Sights on the Mall

Some of America's most famous museums line the original Mall, including the National Air and Space Museum, the National Museum of Natural History, and the National Museum of the American Indian.

At the western end of the National Mall are relatively recent additions such as the Vietnam Veterans Memorial (see p. 124) and the Korean War Veterans Memorial (see p. 112). The creation of the World War II Memorial (see p. 126), dedicated in 2004, sparked debate on the loss of open space within the Mall. In 2003, Congress passed the Reserve Act, which declared the National Mall a completed work of civic art and restricts further construction on it.

On the eastern end of the National Mall, just to the south of Independence Avenue, sits the American Veterans Disabled for Life Memorial (www.avdlm.org), dedicated in October 2014. This inspirational site is the first national memorial devoted to permanently disabled veterans of America's armed services. The memorial is located near Bartholdi Park, just southwest of the U.S. Capitol. At its center is a

star-shaped fountain of black granite where a ceremonial flame seems to float on the water. Surrounding glass panels display images of soldiers and veterans, along with quotations honoring their sacrifices. A grove of pond cypress and ginkgo trees signifies survival under difficult conditions.

A Gathering Place

Because of its location and symbolic importance, the National Mall has been the scene of many public events and demonstrations. Among the most famous is the 1963 March on Washington for Jobs and Freedom, at which Martin Luther King, Jr., gave his inspiring "I Have a Dream"

Bordered by museums of the Smithsonian Institution, the National Mall extends west from the U.S. Capitol steps.

speech, standing on the steps of the Lincoln Memorial (see p. 114 for the Martin Luther King, Jr. Memorial). The Mall also has seen large gatherings protesting the Vietnam and Iraq wars. More celebratory occasions—music concerts, Fourth of July fireworks shows, and the like—are attended by hundreds of thousands of people, as are presidential

Inaugurations: When Barack Obama was sworn in, crowds packed the length of the Mall.

The National Mall is an especially lively place during the National Cherry Blossom Festival *(late March–early April),* which celebrates the blooming of thousands of Japanese cherry trees around the Tidal Basin and elsewhere in Washington. A

variety of special programs are conducted during the two-week event.

National Park Service rangers are on duty daily at several sites around the National Mall, including the three war memorials and the Lincoln (see p. 113), Jefferson (see p. 121), and Franklin Delano Roosevelt (see p. 111) Memorials, where regular programs are presented.

Washington, DC
202-426-6841
www.nps.gov/mall
www.nationalmall.org

AT A GLANCE Area stretching from U.S. Capitol to Lincoln Memorial to Potomac River ▪ 155 acres ▪ Year-round ▪ Visiting museums, memorials, gardens; picnicking, jogging, biking, attending concerts

Pennsylvania Avenue National Historic Site
The nation's ceremonial thoroughfare

Pierre L'Enfant's original 1791 design for the federal city of Washington, District of Columbia, called for an important street to run from southeast to northwest between the U.S. Capitol and the White House. That street became Pennsylvania Avenue, site of many public events, and one of the most famous avenues in the nation—and even the world.

The avenue traditionally has been the route of presidential Inaugural parades. At Abraham Lincoln's 1861 Inauguration, emotions regarding the impending Civil War caused cannon to be placed at both ends of Pennsylvania Avenue to try to assure the President's safety.

Pennsylvania Avenue's location didn't prevent it from being overtaken by a degree of urban blight from the late 19th through mid-20th century. In 1965, Pennsylvania Avenue National Historic Site was

created, encompassing the avenue and areas around it. (Interestingly, the national historic site does not include the roadway of the avenue itself, though it does include the sidewalks on each side.)

Beginning in the 1960s, serious efforts were made to improve and beautify this major thoroughfare and the historic sites along it.

Significant Sites

Located at Pennsylvania Avenue's western end, between 15th and 14th Streets, Pershing Park features a statue of World War I Gen. John J. "Black Jack" Pershing. In 2014, Pershing Park was redesignated by Congress as the national World War I Memorial, with plans to have the new memorial built and dedicated in time for the 2018 centennial of the armistice that ended World War I. Across 14th Street is Freedom Plaza, with a scale model of

L'Enfant's street and park design for Washington's monumental core.

The avenue's most striking structure stands at the intersection with 12th Street: At 315 feet tall, the 1890s Old Post Office Tower is one of Washington's notable landmarks. Slated for demolition in the 1970s, it was saved after public protests. National Park Service rangers were stationed here so visitors could ascend to the 270-foot-high observation deck for a panoramic view of the city and surroundings, but the tower is closed until 2016 for renovation into a luxury hotel, so call ahead of visiting to check the site's status.

Farther east, between 9th and 7th Streets, the United States Navy Memorial includes the statue "The Lone Sailor," fountains, flags, a map of the world's oceans set into the plaza, and a wall inscribed with famous quotations from naval history.

Pennsylvania Ave., NW
Washington, DC
202-606-8691
www.nps.gov/paav
www.nps.gov/opot

AT A GLANCE Between the U.S. Capitol and the White House ▪ 18 acres ▪ Year-round ▪ Visiting parks and historical markers; viewing city from Old Post Office Tower

President's Park (White House)

A look at the President's home and the nation's "front yard"

President's Park includes open spaces, monuments, statues, and buildings around the White House in Washington, D.C., as well as the White House itself.

Information on things to do and see in the park is available at the White House Visitor Center, located in the northern end of the Department of Commerce Building at 1450 Pennsylvania Avenue, NW. The visitor center was renovated in 2014 and now contains interactive displays, and a new film called "The White House: Reflections From Within." New tactile exhibits allow visitors to touch significant White House artifacts, like stone that was used to construct the White House, and a doorknob from the North Portico.

The visitor center also has self-guiding brochures for exploring the area. Visitors can walk north and

The south facade of the White House faces the Ellipse.

south around the White House, seeing sites such as Lafayette Park, the First Division Monument, the Boy Scout Memorial, the Haupt Fountains, the Ellipse, the National Christmas Tree, and the Zero Milestone (the symbolic starting point for mileages from Washington). Statues dotting the routes include depictions of Civil War Gen. William T. Sherman, Gen. (later President) Andrew Jackson, and four Europeans who aided America in the

Revolutionary War: Marquis de Lafayette, Thaddeus Kosciuszko, Comte de Rochambeau, and Baron Friedrich Wilhelm von Steuben.

Tours of the White House are by advance reservation only (three weeks to six months ahead), and must be made through a prospective visitor's member of Congress *(switchboard: 202-224-3121)*. Public tours are scheduled Tuesday through Saturday.

The White House Visitor Center can also provide information on annual special events such as the Easter egg roll on the White House South Lawn, White House fall and spring garden tours, and the lighting of the National Christmas Tree.

Both Lafayette Park and the Ellipse are popular sites for political demonstrations, protests, and other activities in which citizens take advantage of their right to free speech.

Visitor center
1450 Pennsylvania Ave., NW
Washington, DC
202-208-1631
www.nps.gov/whho

AT A GLANCE

1600 Pennsylvania Avenue ▪ 82 acres ▪ Year-round ▪ Touring White House, viewing exhibits in visitor center

---

Rock Creek Park

The green heart of the nation's capital city

The legislation that created Rock Creek Park in 1890 declared that it would be "set apart as a public park or pleasure ground for the benefit and enjoyment of the people of the United States." For more than a century it has fulfilled that goal, providing enjoyment to residents of

the Washington, D.C., area as well as visitors to the nation's capital. One of the oldest federal parks, it stretches north more than 10 miles from the Potomac River along Rock Creek to the boundary line between the District of Columbia and Maryland. (Parkland contiguous to Rock

Creek Park extends the green space well into Maryland.)

Located in the figurative backyard of residents of Northwest Washington, Rock Creek is extremely popular with joggers, bicyclists, and skaters; in addition to its trails, some of its streets are closed to vehicles on weekends and holidays to make way for nonmotorized uses. It's also a popular location for picnics and sports activities such as golf, soccer, and tennis. An equestrian center within the park offers riding lessons and trail rides along the 13 miles of bridle trails in the northern section of the park. Thompson Boat Center near Rock Creek's confluence with the Potomac rents bicycles, kayaks, canoes, sailboats, and rowing shells.

A first-time visitor to Rock Creek Park should stop at the nature center *(5200 Glover Rd., NW, closed Mon.–Tues.)*, just south of Military Road, to learn about the park's natural and cultural history. Exhibits interpret the park's flora and fauna, and the Discovery Room offers hands-on activities for children and adults. Guided nature walks are held on a regular schedule. The nature center's planetarium (the only planetarium in the National Park System) offers free astronomy programs throughout the year. Evening stargazing programs are held monthly *(April–Nov.)* at nearby Military Field.

For hikers, Rock Creek Park encompasses about 25 miles of trails. A blue-blazed route follows the east side of the creek, a green-blazed trail follows the western ridge of the park, and tan-blazed trails connect the sides.

White-tailed deer are seen often in the park, while resident mammals such as beavers, raccoon, foxes, and coyotes are seen less frequently. Rock Creek is extremely popular with area bird-watchers, especially during spring and fall migrations when species such as warblers, thrushes, tanagers, and vireos pass through.

One notable bird-watcher who enjoyed Rock Creek was Theodore Roosevelt. A famous anecdote involves the time T.R. rushed in late to a Cabinet meeting, excitedly announcing that he had just seen a chestnut-sided warbler in the park.

Peirce Mill *(Tilden Dr., NW)*, built in the 1820s, operated as a commercial gristmill until 1897; it is open to visitors April through Nov., Wed.–Sun. Carter Barron Amphitheater *(17th St. & Colorado Ave., NW)* offers concerts and free Shakespearean theater during the summer months. The 18th-century Old Stone House in Georgetown *(3051 M St., NW)*, one of the oldest structures still standing in Washington, is now a museum dedicated to the daily lives of ordinary citizens in the colonial era.

Memorials within the park include statues of the Italian poet Dante Alighieri, French heroine Joan of Arc, and radio pioneer Guglielmo Marconi.

On the eastern side of the park are preserved the remains of Civil War–era Fort Stevens, where President Abraham Lincoln came under Confederate fire while observing a battle in 1864.

| Nature Center & Planetarium 5200 Glover Rd., NW Washington, DC 202-895-6070 www.nps.gov/rocr | AT A GLANCE | Green space along Rock Creek from Potomac River to Maryland state line ▪ 1,754 acres ▪ Year-round ▪ Hiking, biking, horseback riding, picnicking, bird-watching, astronomical observation |

Sewall–Belmont House N.H.S.

The home of a pioneer in the fight for women's rights

The Sewall-Belmont House and Museum, located a short distance northeast of the U.S. Capitol, tells the story of the struggle for the American woman's right to vote and achieve equal rights in all areas of society.

The museum is the headquarters of the historic National Woman's Party and was the Washington, D.C., home of the party's founder, Alice Paul, author of the equal rights amendment. Holder of a Ph.D. in economics, Paul was a leader in the effort to gain women the right to vote, a goal that was achieved in 1920 with ratification of the 19th Amendment to the U.S. Constitution. She pushed for an equal rights amendment for women, but the decades-long effort continues today. Paul also worked to incorporate language recognizing women's equality in the United Nations Charter and to establish a permanent U.N. Commission on the Status of Women.

The museum showcases a major collection of documents and artifacts of the suffrage and equal rights movements. There are suffrage banners used in picketing and parades, and the museum features paintings and sculptures of notable women, including Lucretia Mott, Elizabeth Cady Stanton, and Susan B. Anthony. The museum's Florence Bayard Hilles Library is the nation's first feminist library; its collection includes pamphlets, political cartoons, scrapbooks, photographs, records, newsletters, and similar items.

The historic Sewall-Belmont House is believed to date from around 1800, and has been the headquarters of the National Woman's Party since 1929. Docent-led hour-long tours are available *(check the website for schedule, www.sewallbelmont.org, fee)*.

---

144 Constitution Ave., NE
Washington, DC
202-546-1210
www.nps.gov/sebe

AT A GLANCE

Near the U.S. Capitol ▪ 1 acre ▪ Year-round ▪ Guided tours of house, viewing exhibits

---

Theodore Roosevelt Island
A living memorial to a conservationist President

Usually regarded as the most conservation-minded President, Theodore Roosevelt was responsible for the protection of such beautiful natural sites as Devils Tower in Wyoming (see p. 488), Muir Woods in California (see p. 409), and the Grand Canyon in Arizona (see p. 304). He established the U.S. Forest Service and set aside more than 230 million acres of land as national parks, forests, monuments, and wildlife refuges.

In 1932, 13 years after Roosevelt's death, the Theodore Roosevelt Memorial Association bought an 80-acre wooded island in the Potomac River in Washington, D.C., in his honor. Today the memorial features a statue of Roosevelt as well as fountains and

Theodore Roosevelt, 26th President

stone monuments inscribed with some of his quotations.

Roosevelt loved the outdoors and enjoyed watching wildlife, and he would approve of the 2.5 miles of hiking trails that crisscross the island, which offer the chance to see birds, mammals, reptiles, and amphibians.

The island was owned for a century by the Mason family of Virginia, who built a brick mansion on the property in the early 1800s. Only the foundation of the house remains. Union troops were stationed on the island in the Civil War.

Theodore Roosevelt Island can by reached by car only from the northbound lanes of the George Washington Memorial Parkway (see p. 97) on the Virginia side of the Potomac. From the parking area, a footbridge leads over a channel of the Potomac to the island.

Off George Washington Pkwy.
Arlington, VA
703-289-2500
www.nps.gov/this

AT A GLANCE

Island in Potomac River, off George Washington Memorial Parkway ▪ 88 acres ▪ Year-round ▪ Hiking, nature study

---

Thomas Jefferson Memorial
A Founding Father's image and words preserved in metal and stone

No one had a greater influence on the creation and development of the United States than Thomas Jefferson: chief author of the Declaration of Independence, third U.S. President, and force behind the Louisiana Purchase and the Lewis and Clark expedition. Jefferson's extraordinary range of knowledge and limitless curiosity led to accomplishments in architecture and to ingenious inventions; he experimented in agriculture and

FOLLOWING PAGES: *The Thomas Jefferson Memorial honors one of the most influential Founding Fathers of the U.S.*

founded the University of Virginia.

Though Jefferson had been revered by some contemporaries as one of the greatest of U.S. Presidents, it wasn't until the 1930s that serious preparations were made for a national memorial to honor him. A design competition was held and sites were debated, with noted architect John Russell Pope chosen to create the memorial at a location on the southeastern side of Washington's Tidal Basin—a site that had once been Potomac River wetlands until elevated with material dredged from the river. The memorial lies directly south of the White House.

The memorial was dedicated in 1943, although (in large part because of World War II) the Rudolph Evans 19-foot-high bronze statue of Jefferson was not ready for installation until 1947. With its Ionic columns and dome, the memorial bears resemblance to the Roman Pantheon and Jefferson's own architectural designs at the University of Virginia.

Surrounding the statue inside the memorial are marble panels inscribed with quotations from Jefferson's writings, including the Declaration of Independence and letters to James Madison, George Washington, and others. Themes include human rights, equality, and freedom of religion.

Thomas Jefferson Memorial is open at all times (it is especially striking when lighted at night), and park rangers are on duty daily. The memorial is a major site of events during Washington's annual two-week-long National Cherry Blossom Festival (late March–early April), when the Japanese cherry trees around the Tidal Basin are in full flower.

East Basin Dr., SW
Washington, DC
202-426-6841
www.nps.gov/thje

AT A GLANCE

On the National Mall, at the Tidal Basin ▪ 18 acres ▪ Year-round ▪ Viewing Jefferson statue and writings

Vietnam Veterans Memorial

A moving tribute to a controversial war

D i
viding the people of the United States as have few other events or issues, the Vietnam War of the 1960s and '70s saw more than 58,000 American military personnel killed while serving in the war zone. Emotions in support of or in opposition to the war ran deep, and endured after the conflict ended.

Based on ideas promulgated by a group called the Vietnam Veterans Memorial Fund, Congress authorized a memorial to those who served in Vietnam, to be placed in Constitution Gardens north of the National Mall in Washington. The "Wall" portion of the Vietnam Veterans Memorial was dedicated in 1982. A V-shape of polished black granite walls 246 feet long,

Tributes to those who fought

it displays the names of all those who died in the war or are listed as missing in action, and was designed by Maya Lin, at the time a student at Yale University, who said, "The names would become the memorial." Lin stated that

she kept the design simple to "allow everyone to respond and remember."

The abstract nature of the Wall caused controversy and led to a later addition to the memorial: a realistic sculpture by Frederick Hart of three soldiers who stand facing the Wall holding their weapons. It was placed at a distance from the Wall, with the intention of not intruding on the design of the original memorial.

Millions of people have visited the memorial to find names of friends or relatives or to contemplate the war's lessons and legacy. Many leave items in tribute, which are collected each day by National Park Service rangers and taken to the archive collection of the memorial.

21st St. &
Constitution Ave., NW
Washington, DC
202-426-6841
www.nps.gov/vive

AT A GLANCE

On the National Mall, near the Lincoln Memorial ▪ 2 acres ▪ Year-round ▪ Viewing the "Wall" and memorial sculptures

Washington Monument National Memorial

The capital's most famous icon honoring the first President

It was natural that the young United States would search for an architecturally distinctive way to honor George Washington, commander of the Continental Army and first President. In the 1830s the government held a design competition for a grand monument to be erected in Washington, D.C. Robert Mills's winning design called for a stone obelisk that would, on completion, be the tallest structure in the world. (It would hold that distinction only briefly: The taller Eiffel Tower was completed in 1889.)

Construction began in 1848, but lack of funding and the Civil War delayed completion of the 555-foot-five-and-one-eighth-inch-tall monument until 1884, with the official dedication taking place the next year.

When construction on the monument resumed in 1878 after a long hiatus, marble for the remainder of the monument was extracted from lower down in the same quarry, and this newer stone was slightly darker in color. The top two-thirds of the monument is therefore a different shade than the lower third, clearly delineating where construction was originally halted. The monument finally opened to the public in 1888.

An elevator takes visitors to the 500-foot viewing level in 70 seconds—a much easier trip than climbing the 896-step staircase that was open to the public until the 1970s. The panorama from the observation area can stretch 30 miles.

Fifty flags, one for each state, surround the Washington Monument.

Admission to the Washington Monument is free, but tickets are required, available at the Washington Monument Lodge on 15th Street, the eastern side of the site *(advance tickets: www.recreation.gov or 877-444-6777).*

15th St. & Madison Dr., NW
Washington, DC
202-426-6841
www.nps.gov/wamo

AT A GLANCE

Midpoint of the National Mall ▪ 106 acres ▪ Year-round ▪ Viewing monument; ascending to observation deck

World War II Memorial

A National Mall tribute to the "greatest generation"

Dedicated in 2004, the World War II Memorial honors the 16 million people who served in the United States military, the more than 400,000 who died, and those who supported the war effort on the home front: "Americans who took up the struggle during the Second World War," in the words of the memorial's inscription.

Located on the National Mall between the Washington Monument and the Lincoln Memorial, the World War II Memorial includes a large pool and fountains, two pavilions (labeled Atlantic and Pacific), a Field of Stars honoring those who died in the war as well as those listed as missing in action, and two semicircles of pillars denoting states and territories. Additional features are engraved quotes from wartime civilian and military leaders, including Gen. Dwight D. Eisenhower's remarks on the eve of D-Day in 1944; and bas-relief

The World War II Memorial, prominently located on the National Mall

sculptures depicting battle scenes, medics caring for wounded soldiers, and civilians listening to radio news reports, among other war-related experiences. The main design of the memorial is by Austrian-born architect Friedrich St. Florian, whose concept was chosen out of more than 400 entries in a national competition.

Park rangers are on duty in the area daily to provide information and interpretive programs.

National Mall at 17th St., NW
Washington, DC
202-426-6841
www.nps.gov/wwii

AT A GLANCE

On the National Mall between the Washington Monument and Lincoln Memorial ▪ 7 acres ▪ Year-round ▪ Viewing memorial

WEST VIRGINIA

Created in 1861 by residents of western Virginia who refused to secede from the Union, West Virginia had already witnessed John Brown's raid on the federal armory at Harpers Ferry in 1859, when he hoped to inspire an uprising that would end slavery. Ruggedly mountainous, with deep, river-cut gorges, the state for decades has been economically dependent on coal mining, often to the detriment of its environment and the health of its workers. West Virginia's white water attracts thousands of boaters annually, challenging rapids on streams such as the New and Gauley Rivers. Extensive forested areas of the Appalachian Mountains also are popular with hikers, rock climbers, and hunters.

Bluestone National Scenic River

A remote and beautiful section of an Appalachian river

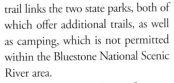

A tributary of West Virginia's better-known New River, the Bluestone River runs northward from Virginia to join with the New near the town of Hinton. Bluestone National Scenic River is administered by the same National Park Service office that oversees New River Gorge National River (see p. 129). Travelers should stop at the Sandstone Visitor Center (*W. Va. 20, just off I-64, 304-466-0417*) of the New River Gorge for information about the Bluestone.

The park protects 10.5 miles of the Bluestone River, which was named for the bluish limestone of the streambed in its upper reaches. Not accessible by vehicle, this segment of the river is best reached through either of two West Virginia state parks that adjoin it: Bluestone State Park on the north and Pipestem Resort State Park on the south. The Bluestone Turnpike Trail follows the path of an old riverbank road once used by settlers and loggers; it is popular with hikers, mountain bikers, and horseback riders. Spring through fall, park rangers lead guided walks along a portion of the Bluestone Turnpike Trail. The

trail links the two state parks, both of which offer additional trails, as well as camping, which is not permitted within the Bluestone National Scenic River area.

The Bluestone River features good fishing for smallmouth bass, rock bass, and bluegill. The river area is also popular with hunters; visitors are advised to wear safety-orange clothing during hunting seasons.

A limited amount of canoeing and kayaking is available on the Bluestone, which usually is high enough for boating only during spring.

W. Va. 20
15 miles south of I-64
www.nps.gov/blue

AT A GLANCE Southern West Virginia, 70 miles southeast of Charleston ▪ 10.5 river miles ▪ Spring through fall ▪ Hiking, biking, fishing, horseback riding, canoeing, kayaking

---

Gauley River National Recreation Area

A legendary white-water river for experienced kayakers and rafters

West Virginia's Gauley River is famed for its autumn white-water boating season, but the adventure and thrills here are not for everyone. With notorious chutes such as Pillow Rock and Sweet's Falls rated Class III–V+, a steep gradient (more than 668 feet through 28 miles), and formidable waves, the Gauley is for experienced and skilled kayakers only. Even those who take guided trips with white-water rafting companies should have some previous rafting experience, and the

minimum age for the upper Gauley is 16 years old. The lower Gauley, while still rated Class III–V, is not quite so demanding (minimum age is 12 to 14 years old).

The boating season on the upper Gauley begins the first weekend after Labor Day and continues for six weekends. (Flow on the river is determined by water releases from the upstream Summersville Dam.) Additional floating days may be possible depending on water levels. Tens of thousands of people visit

the Gauley during this period, making it the annual autumn center of American white-water activity. The lower Gauley is floatable for more of the year.

Gauley River National Recreation Area is administered by the same National Park Service office that oversees New River Gorge National River (see p. 129). Travelers should stop at the Canyon Rim Visitor Center of the New River Gorge (*162 Cty. Rd. 82, Lansing, 304-574-2115*) for information about the Gauley.

W. Va. 129
8 miles southwest of Summersville
www.nps.gov/gari

AT A GLANCE South-central West Virginia, 30 miles east of Charleston ▪ 31 river miles; 11,495 acres (4,092 acres owned by National Park Service) ▪ Peak boating season is early September through mid-October ▪ Rafting, kayaking, fishing

Harpers Ferry National Historical Park

A hub of history at the confluence of two rivers

Located at the confluence of the Potomac and Shenandoah Rivers, Harpers Ferry witnessed several notable historic events. Named for a landowner who operated a ferry in the 18th century, the site attracted the attention of George Washington (who saw the Potomac as a major transportation corridor) and Thomas Jefferson (who described the landscape as "placid and delightful . . . wild and tremendous"). Washington also pushed for the establishment of a federal armory and arsenal, using water power to run machinery to manufacture weapons.

Those weapons drew abolitionist John Brown, who with his followers seized the armory in 1859, hoping to arm enslaved African Americans and start a battle to end slavery in the United States. After thirty-six hours, U.S. troops captured Brown. He was put on trial, convicted of murder, treason, and inciting slave rebellion, and was hanged. When the Civil War started in 1861, Confederate and Union troops fought over the weapons and manufacturing equipment at Harpers Ferry, and in 1862, Maj. Gen. Thomas "Stonewall" Jackson's Confederates captured 12,700 Union troops here—the largest such Union surrender of the war.

In 1867, missionaries established Storer College, located in vacant armory buildings. An integrated school aimed primarily at educating former slaves, Storer included famed writer and orator Frederick Douglass as a trustee. Harpers Ferry became a place of pilgrimage for African Americans and played an important role in the early civil rights movement.

Visitors to Harpers Ferry National Historical Park will find a large number of history-related sites to explore. The Lower Town area of the park holds attractions such as a dry goods store, a tavern, a confectionery, a ready-made clothing store, and the fire engine house where John Brown made his last stand and was captured. Also located here are the John Brown Museum, an industry museum, and a nature museum examining wetlands of the Shenandoah River. The town's historic district encompasses dozens

Once home to an important Union armory, Harpers Ferry sits at the confluence of the Potomac and Shenandoah Rivers.

of 19th-century buildings, many now restored as homes or businesses.

Crossing the Potomac, visitors can reach the Maryland Heights section of the park, the old Chesapeake and Ohio Canal (see p. 86), and remains of military installations. Other park trails lead to Civil War battlefields and the sites of former factories and armsmaking industries. The Appalachian National Scenic Trail (see p. 21) passes through the park, offering additional hiking opportunities.

Park rangers and volunteers present seasonal guided tours and living-history programs on topics like "untold Civil War stories," the C & O Canal, John Brown's raid, and civil rights.

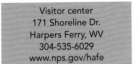

Visitor center
171 Shoreline Dr.
Harpers Ferry, WV
304-535-6029
www.nps.gov/hafe

AT A GLANCE

Eastern West Virginia, central Maryland, and northern Virginia, 55 miles northwest of Washington, D.C. ▪ 3,670 acres ▪ Year-round ▪ Visiting museums and historic sites, hiking

---

New River Gorge National River
An ancient river boasting world-class white-water rafting

Adventure, history, and beauty merge in West Virginia's New River Gorge, where the stream at the bottom (not new, and in fact possibly one of the oldest river systems on Earth) lies more than 1,000 feet below the plateau through which it runs. Most famous for its white-water boating opportunities, the New River offers a variety of paddling options.

The upper river or the southern section, as the New runs northward, features rapids rated Class I–III separated by long pools. Thus, it is suitable for canoeists and other boaters with medium experience level. However, the famed "lower gorge" below Thurmond includes rapids rated to Class V and is appropriate for skilled paddlers only. Many commercial outfitters offer guided river trips, which provide the less experienced an opportunity to enjoy the gorge. Five primitive campgrounds are located along the river; all are reachable by gravel roads. Meadow Creek Campground, located

New River Gorge Bridge stands 876 feet above the river.

one mile south of Sandstone Visitor Center, is a full service campground.

The hard sandstone cliffs of New River Gorge have made the park one of the most popular rock-climbing locations in the country. More than 1,600 climbing routes have been established, most rated 5.9 and higher. Certain cliffs may occasionally be closed to protect nesting areas of the peregrine falcon, a once endangered raptor making a comeback in the eastern United States. The park also offers hiking trails from easy quarter-mile walks to more strenuous hikes up to 7 miles in length.

New River Gorge National River features two year-round visitor centers: Sandstone *(304-466-0417)* in the southern part of the park and Canyon Rim *(304-574-2115)* in the northern section. Both offer exhibits, audiovisual programs, and information desks. Near Canyon Rim on U.S. 19 is the spectacular New River Gorge Bridge. The world's second longest single-arch steel span, it's also the second highest bridge in America, behind only Royal Gorge Bridge in Colorado.

The 1977 completion of the bridge is celebrated annually the third Saturday in October with Bridge Day *(www.officialbridgeday.com)*, the state's largest one-day festival. Daring BASE jumpers and rappelers descend from the bridge, which is closed for the day.

The headquarters for New River Gorge National River also administers nearby Gauley River National Recreation Area (see p. 127) and Bluestone National Scenic River (see p. 127).

U.S. 19, north of
Fayetteville, WV
& W. Va. 20 at I-64
www.nps.gov/neri

AT A GLANCE

South-central West Virginia, 40 miles southeast of Charleston ▪ 53 river miles, 72,189 acres ▪ Spring through fall peak boating ▪ White-water boating, hiking, rock climbing, mountain biking, primitive camping

Southeast

A parade of history is on display at the many National Park Service properties in the United States' Southeast. Native American sites such as Ocmulgee National Monument date back thousands of years, while Spanish forts on Florida's Atlantic coast preserve traces of some of the earliest European settlements in what is now the United States. Abraham Lincoln was born in this region, and later the Wright brothers conquered the air; more recently, Rev. Martin Luther King, Jr., worked for civil rights. All this took place in an unparalleled environment: The Everglades' "river of grass," the lush forests of Great Smoky Mountains National Park, and the beautiful beaches of Gulf Islands National Seashore are just a few of the region's rewarding natural areas.

Ohio

ILL.

MO.

KE

Fort Donelson
National
Battlefield

Tennessee

TEN N

Shiloh
National
Military Park

Memphis

ARKANSAS

Mississippi

Brices Cross Roads
National
Battlefield Site

Tennessee

Tupelo
National Battlefield

MISSISSIPPI

Natchez Trace
Parkway and National
Scenic Trail

Vicksburg
National
Military
Park

ALA

L.A.

Jackson

Alabama

Natchez
National
Historical Park

Pearl

Mobile

Mobile Bay

Gulf Islands
National Seashore

Gulf

The bald cypress, with its knobby knees, is a common sight in many Southeast wetlands.

INDIANA

OHIO

Frankfort
Louisville
Ohio

Abraham Lincoln
Birthplace
National
Historical Park

KENTUCKY

Mammoth Cave
National Park

Cumberland Gap
National
Historical Park

Big South Fork
National River and
Recreation Area

Cumberland

Nashville

Obed
Wild and
Scenic
River

Andrew Johnson
National
Historic
Site

Knoxville

Holston

VIRGINIA

Roanoke

Albemarle Sd.

Wright Brothers
National Memorial

Fort Raleigh
National Historic Site

Cape Hatteras
National Seashore

Stones River
National Battlefield

TENNESSEE

Russell Cave
National
Monument

Great Smoky Mountains
National Park

Blue Ridge Parkway

Asheville

Guilford Courthouse
National Military Park

Raleigh

NORTH CAROLINA

Carl Sandburg Home N.H.S.

Charlotte

Pamlico Sd.

Cape Hatteras

Raleigh Bay

Cape Lookout
National Seashore

Cape Lookout

Chattanooga

Little River
Canyon
National
Preserve

Chickamauga and
Chattanooga
National Military
Park

Cowpens
National
Battlefield

Kings
Mountain
National Military Park

Ninety Six
National
Historic Site

SOUTH

Columbia

Pee Dee

Moores Creek
National
Battlefield

Wilmington

Onslow Bay

Kennesaw Mountain
National Battlefield Park

Chattahoochee River
National Recreation Area

Atlanta

Martin Luther King, Jr.
National Historic Site

Congaree
National Park

CAROLINA

Santee

Long Bay

ALABAMA

Birmingham

Horseshoe Bend
National Military Park

GEORGIA

Macon

Ocmulgee

Ocmulgee
National Monument

Savannah

Charleston

Charles Pinckney
National Historic Site

Fort Sumter
National Monument

ATLANTIC

OCEAN

Montgomery

Tuskegee Airmen
National Historic Site

Columbus

Tuskegee
Institute
National
Historic
Site

Chattahoochee

Andersonville
National Historic Site

Jimmy Carter
National Historic Site

Savannah

Altamaha

Fort Pulaski
National Monument

Fort Frederica
National Monument

Alapaha

Fort Caroline
National
Memorial

Cumberland Island
National Seashore

Timucuan Ecological
and Historic Preserve

Apalachicola

Tallahassee

Suwannee

FLORIDA

Jacksonville

Castillo de
San Marcos
National
Monument

Fort Matanzas
National Monument

Apalachicola

Apalachee
Bay

Waccasassa Bay

Orlando

Canaveral
National
Seashore

Cape Canaveral
(Cape Kennedy)

of Mexico

Tampa

Tampa Bay

De Soto
National Memorial

PUERTO RICO and
the U.S. VIRGIN ISLANDS

Atlantic Ocean

San Juan
N.H.S.

Virgin Is.

St. Thomas

Virgin Is.
Coral Reef
Nat. Mon.

Virgin Is.
N.P.

Isla
Mona
U.S.

Puerto Rico

Buck I. Reef Nat. Mon.

U.S.

St. John

U.K.

Salt River Bay N.H.P. and Eco. Pres.

Christiansted N.H.S.

St.
Croix
U.S.

Caribbean Sea

Everglades N.P., Great
Smoky Mountains N.P.,
Mammoth Cave N.P., and
San Juan N.H.S. are also
World Heritage sites.

Fort Lauderdale

Big Cypress
National Preserve

Miami

Biscayne Bay

Biscayne
National Park

Everglades
National Park

Florida Bay

Dry Tortugas
National Park

Key West

Florida Keys

N

ALABAMA

Located in the heart of the Deep South, Alabama has a history entwined with that of the region, from an antebellum economy based on slavery to hard times during Reconstruction to a long struggle for civil rights in the mid-20th century. Cotton once drove the economy, especially in the state's central "black belt" of dark, rich soil. The crop's importance was later replaced in part by steel and aerospace development. The area around the port city of Mobile still hints at its 18th-century French heritage. The Alabama landscape varies from the white-sand beaches of the Gulf Coast to pinelands farther north to the southernmost reach of the Appalachians in the northeast.

Horseshoe Bend National Military Park

Site of a decisive battle in the Creek War

As white settlers moved into the Southeast in the early 19th century, conflicts increased between the new arrivals and resident Native Americans. Within the Creek (also known as Muscogee) people, the Red Stick faction violently opposed European ways and assimilation into the young United States.

On March 27, 1814, Gen. Andrew Jackson led a force of white and allied Indian soldiers against a Red Stick group who had camped within a horseshoe-shaped bend of the Tallapoosa River. The attackers suffered 49 dead and 154 wounded, while more than 800 Red Stick warriors lost their lives. This is the largest number of Native Americans killed in any single battle in American history. The Battle of Horseshoe Bend broke the power of the Creek Nation, which was forced to cede about 20 million acres (much of today's Alabama and Georgia) to the United States.

Horseshoe Bend National Military Park preserves and interprets the site of this significant battle. A film and exhibits at the visitor center provide an introduction to the event, and a 3-mile tour road edges the battlefield and winds along the Tallapoosa River. A 2.8-mile nature trail offers a more intimate experience of the battle site. In addition, the park is a popular launch area for canoeing on the Tallapoosa.

Check with park staff for information on special historical events at the park, including the Anniversary of the Battle of Horseshoe Bend, held on the weekend closest to March 27.

11288 Horseshoe Bend Rd.
Daviston, AL
256-234-7111
www.nps.gov/hobe

AT A GLANCE

East-central Alabama, 68 miles northeast of Montgomery ▪ 2,040 acres ▪ Year-round ▪ Auto touring, hiking, canoeing

Little River Canyon National Preserve

An unusual river-carved mountaintop canyon

Thanks to a quirk of geology, Little River flows for most of its length along the top of Lookout Mountain, an outlying part of the Appalachians located in northeastern Alabama. Over time, the river has cut a deep canyon into the mountaintop, creating cliffs hundreds of feet high in places.

The park's most popular attractions are located along the canyon south of Ala. 35. A scenic drive follows the canyon rim, passing lookout points with spectacular views, as well as fascinating formations such as Mushroom Rock. At the beginning of the drive, 45-foot-high Little River Falls ranks with the park's most beautiful spots. A steep and strenuous 0.75-mile trail at the Eberhart Point lookout descends to the canyon floor. The overlook at Grace's High Falls provides a view of the 133-foot-high waterfall that flows seasonally (it's usually dry in summer). The Canyon Mouth day-use area, off Ala. 273, offers picnicking, swimming, and a short nature trail.

The backcountry area north of Ala. 35 is popular with horseback riders, mountain bikers, and hikers, who can explore 23 miles of unpaved roads. Camping is allowed at three designated primitive campgrounds.

(More camping and other developed activities are available at adjacent DeSoto State Park.)

Experienced kayakers enjoy running Class III and IV rapids on Little River during high-water periods (winter and spring). Sheer sandstone cliffs up to 300 feet high provide plenty of challenge for rock climbers.

4322 Little River Trail NE
Fort Payne, AL
256-845-9605
www.nps.gov/liri

AT A GLANCE

Northeastern Alabama, 70 miles southeast of Huntsville ▪ 13,797 acres ▪ Year-round, though winter can bring occasional severe weather ▪ Scenic driving, hiking, swimming, kayaking, primitive camping, rock climbing, horseback riding

Russell Cave National Monument
A home for Native Americans for thousands of years

Carved by geologic forces into limestone that was once a seafloor, Russell Cave has yielded one of the most comprehensive records of habitation by Native Americans ever discovered in the Southeast. Artifacts found within the cave date back 10,000 years and continue up to recorded history—evidence of the attractiveness of the cave to Native Americans for its shelter and proximity to water and varied food sources.

The Gilbert H. Grosvenor Visitor Center (named for a former President of the National Geographic Society, which bought the cave and donated it to the American people) contains a museum displaying some of the thousands of artifacts that have been excavated here, including fishhooks, pottery, jewelry, and weapons. A short boardwalk leads to the cave entrance, where park rangers conduct guided tours and explain the lifestyles of ancient inhabitants,

Native Americans lived in Russell Cave as long as 10,000 years ago.

as well as the significance of the archaeological discoveries. Evidence suggests that many of the earliest people who lived in the cave depended on hunting and fishing for much of their food.

Though cave passages stretch for miles underground, venturing farther into the caverns is prohibited in order to safeguard the presence of rare bats, amphibians, fish, and other animals. A 1.2-mile hiking trail winds through a forest of hickory, beech, tulip poplar, white oak, and black cherry.

Rangers give regular demonstrations of prehistoric tools and weapons, while other special programs are offered throughout the year.

3729 Cty. Rd. 98
Bridgeport, AL
256-495-2672
www.nps.gov/ruca

AT A GLANCE

Northeastern Alabama, 60 miles northeast of Huntsville ▪ 310 acres ▪ Year-round ▪ Taking guided tours of cave shelter, hiking

Selma to Montgomery National Historic Trail
Commemorates a landmark moment in the civil rights movement

The Selma to Montgomery National Historic Trail memorializes the route taken by marchers during the Voting Rights March of March 21 through March 25, 1965. The march was a watershed event in the civil rights movement, eventually leading to passage of the 1965 Voting Rights Act, forever changing the social landscape in the United States by helping African Americans gain political representation.

Some 3,000 people assembled in Selma, Alabama, on March 21 and set off on foot for the State Capitol in Montgomery, 54 miles to the east. By the time they reached their goal, they numbered 25,000 people. Famed civil rights leader Dr. Martin Luther King, Jr., addressed the crowd at a concluding rally near the

Lowndes Interpretive Center

Capitol, giving his famed "How Long, Not Long" speech.

Events associated with the Voting Rights March and with "Blood Sunday"—March 7, 1965, when police on the outskirts of Selma stopped an earlier march attempt,

attacking peaceful marchers with clubs and tear gas—sent shock waves around the world, raised the nation's consciousness, and convinced political leaders that the time had come for voting rights legislation.

The national historic trail traces the route taken by the marchers. It begins at the Brown Chapel AME Church in Selma and ends at the Capitol in Montgomery. Travelers following the trail can visit a number of significant sites along the way, including the Martin Luther King, Jr., Walking Tour in Selma; the Lowndes County Interpretive Center, located midway between Selma and Montgomery; and the Dexter Avenue King Memorial Baptist Church and the Civil Rights Memorial in Montgomery.

7002 U.S. 80
Hayneville, AL
334-877-1984
www.nps.gov/semo

AT A GLANCE Central Alabama, Montgomery to Selma ▪ 54 miles ▪ Year-round ▪ Driving march route, visiting historic sites

Tuskegee Airmen National Historic Site
The birthplace of African-American military aviation

As World War II drew near, discrimination still held sway within the U.S. military. African Americans were generally relegated to noncombat roles and were not allowed to be pilots in the Army Air Corps (the precursor to today's Air Force). That changed when an experimental program was put into place to train fliers and aircraft support personnel at sites such as Tuskegee

Institute in eastern Alabama and nearby Moton Field airport.

Tuskegee Institute (now Tuskegee University) was chosen for its experience in aviation training, including existing programs in engineering. The famed school for African Americans had been profoundly influenced by noted educator Booker T. Washington, its first president when it was founded in the 1880s.

The hundreds of African Americans who eventually made up the group now called the Tuskegee Airmen included pilots, bombardiers, navigators, instructors, and maintenance staff. During wartime combat the unit distinguished itself for its skill and bravery, helping break down barriers to full integration within the nation's military.

At Tuskegee Airmen National

Historic Site, visitors tour museums in restored hangars, which contain historic aircraft, model airplanes, audiovisual presentations of personal recollections from airmen, and exhibits on the unit's accomplishments in and out of combat. Films tell the story of the Tuskegee Airmen.

Each year on Memorial Day weekend the site hosts a fly-in of historic aircraft and a reunion of surviving airmen.

1616 Chappie James Ave.
Tuskegee, AL
334-724-0922
www.nps.gov/tuai

AT A GLANCE

East-central Alabama, 50 miles east of Montgomery ■ 44 acres
■ Year-round ■ Visiting museum in historic aircraft hangar

Tuskegee Institute National Historic Site

A historic and influential African-American educational institution

Concerned about the lack of educational opportunities for formerly enslaved African Americans during the Reconstruction years after the Civil War, in 1880 a former slave and a former slave owner began working together to create a school in Alabama that would provide opportunities for people who had long been denied the chance to gain an education.

In a move that would have enormous effects, they hired as the school's first president a 25-year-old African American named Booker T. Washington. As one of his first moves, he bought a 1,000-acre abandoned plantation in eastern Alabama and set to work creating a school called Tuskegee Institute. "We began with farming because we wanted something to eat," Washington later wrote. He hired the finest teachers he could find, including famed botanist George Washington Carver, who conducted research here in making southern crops such as peanuts and sweet potatoes more productive.

Today the school is called Tuskegee University, and over the years it

Residence of Booker T. Washington

has produced graduates influential in business, politics, agriculture, entertainment, literature, athletics, and many other fields. A national historic landmark, the university also encompasses Tuskegee Institute National Historic Site. Here, visitors can take a guided tour of The Oaks, Booker T. Washington's house; and the George Washington Carver Museum, with exhibits on the renowned scientist's

life and career. Tours of the university campus are also available, visiting buildings designed by Robert R. Taylor, the first African-American graduate of the Massachusetts Institute of Technology.

At the start of World War II, Tuskegee Institute was selected to train African-American military pilots and aviation support staff, who went on to gain fame as the Tuskegee Airmen.

1212 W. Montgomery Rd.
Tuskegee, AL
334-727-3200
www.nps.gov/tuin

AT A GLANCE

East-central Alabama, 50 miles east of Montgomery ■ 58 acres (8 acres NPS)
■ Year-round ■ Touring historic university campus

FLORIDA

Known for its theme parks, world-class beaches, and glitzy Miami Beach, Florida has a quieter side that can be just as intriguing. Cowboys still ride on cattle ranches in the central part of the state, and black bears and a few panthers roam woods a short distance from major cities. A post–World War II population boom caused serious environmental disruptions, especially to the vast "river of grass" called the Everglades. But a project on the Kissimmee River aims to restore large areas of wetlands damaged by development. With its policy of acquiring public land for conservation, Florida has a good chance of maintaining a natural environment to complement its urban attractions.

Big Cypress National Preserve
Essential part of the Everglades ecosystem

This expansive tract of protected land is a continuation of similar habitats found in the far more famous Everglades National Park (see p. 145) to the south. Wet prairie, swampy sloughs, hardwood hammocks, and large stands of bald cypress are home to a great diversity of wildlife: black bear, bobcat, wood stork, alligator, river otter, snail kite, and many more species.

The preserve's most notable inhabitant, though, is the critically endangered Florida panther, a subspecies of cougar. There are believed to be only 120 to 180 left in the wild, with an estimated 40 living in Big Cypress National Preserve. The big cats are extensively studied, and protective measures have included building underpasses beneath highways to cut down on panther deaths caused by fast-moving vehicles.

The preserve's two visitor centers, on U.S. 41 (Tamiami Trail), each offer an introductory film and information on ranger-led walks and other activities.

Hiking is one way to see the preserve; the Florida National Scenic

A denizen of Big Cypress

Trail (see p. 149) traverses the area for about 43 miles. In the rainy season, though, hikers should be prepared for extensive wading.

Many people enjoy driving slowly along the preserve's two scenic drives, from which many species of wildlife are usually visible. The 27-mile Loop Road passes through a forest of dwarf bald cypress trees; while the 17-mile loop comprising Turner River, Wagonwheel, and Birdon Roads leads

mostly through open grassland and along waterways where flocks of wading birds can often be seen. In open areas, watch for the snail kite, a bird found in the United States only in southern Florida. This small hawk feeds almost exclusively on the large apple snails that can be seen on shrubs and trees.

The best chance to see large gatherings of alligators is from December to May, but good numbers may be seen at any time of year. The odds of seeing a black bear or panther are slim, though campers in the preserve should be sure to heed bear-country cautions.

By the way, extensive logging in the past has meant that there really aren't many tall cypress trees in the preserve. The "big" part of the preserve's name comes from the large size of the stands of bald cypress found in the area.

Because Big Cypress is a national preserve, not a national park, some activities are allowed here that would be prohibited in a park, including hunting and cattle grazing. The most controversial, though, is the use of off-road vehicles. Some visitors call for more trails to be opened to ATVs, while many scientists believe their use is damaging to the environment and disruptive to wildlife, and would therefore like them further restricted.

Far less developed and significantly less visited than Everglades National Park, Big Cypress offers visitors the chance to explore an ecosystem similar to the Everglades in relative solitude.

AT A GLANCE	
33100 Tamiami Trail East (U.S. 41) Ochopee, FL 239-695-2000 www.nps.gov/bicy	Southern Florida, 50 miles west of Miami ▪ 729,000 acres ▪ Year-round, though summers are hot, humid, and buggy ▪ Hiking, wildlife-watching, camping, scenic driving

Biscayne National Park

An undersea wilderness of coral reefs and colorful marine life

Every unit of the National Park System has its own attractions and natural features, of course, but Biscayne National Park stands apart in its unique qualities. Located next door to the metropolitan area of Miami, it's nonetheless an enigma to most Americans. Biscayne is teeming with colorful wildlife, though much of it remains invisible except to those who leave dry land—because 95 percent of the park area is made up of the waters of Biscayne Bay and the nearby Atlantic Ocean.

Biscayne National Park's Dante Fascell Visitor Center (named for a former congressman who was a dedicated supporter of the national park's creation) sits on the bay shore 9 miles east of the city of Homestead. This site, called Convoy Point, is the hub for park activities. Call the park ahead of your visit to ask about the availability of boat tours and kayak, canoe, and paddleboat rentals. A list of commercial entities authorized to operate tours in the park is also available on the park website (*www.nps.gov/bisc/planyour visit/guidedtours.htm*).

Videos at the visitor center and museum exhibits provide an introduction to the Biscayne environment, and a schedule of ranger programs is available.

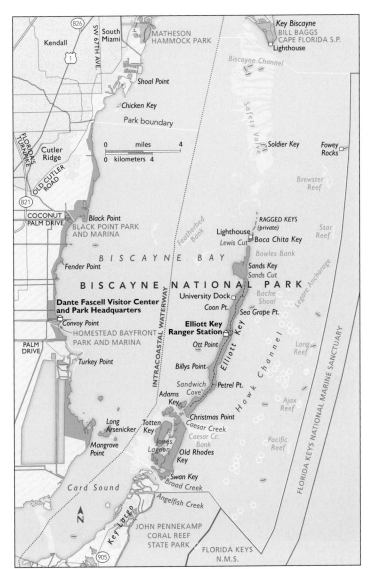

The reefs below the clear blue waters of Biscayne National Park, such as Elkhorn Reef, are a snorkeler's paradise.

Biscayne National Park encompasses four ecosystems: a narrow strip of mangrove trees bordering the shore of Biscayne Bay; part of the bay itself; the northernmost islands of the Florida Keys; and the northernmost section of the world's third largest coral reef, in the Atlantic Ocean just beyond the Keys. The quarter-mile Jetty Trail at Convoy Point offers a glimpse of the above-water world of Biscayne, but truly experiencing the park requires taking a boat trip.

Water Adventures

Boat tours and snorkeling and scuba diving excursions require a fee. One of the park's most popular activities is a trip on a glass-bottom boat, which crosses Biscayne Bay, passes the Keys (coral islands) that form its eastern edge, and continues to the reefs beyond the Keys. The trip is weather-dependent, but on calm days with good water visibility visitors can see some of the 512 species of fish that frequent the park, and possibly sea turtles, moray eels, and dolphins as well. On days when weather doesn't allow good underwater viewing, the boat takes visitors to the Keys, including Boca Chita Key with its distinctive lighthouse, symbol of the park (see below).

Those who would like to get into the water for a closer experience can take a snorkeling trip. These trips allow visitors to spend an hour either floating over the reef, looking down at masses of coral and the creatures that live in this fascinating habitat; or exploring the sea grasses in the calmer Biscayne Bay. Snorkeling equipment is provided. On weekends, certified scuba divers can take a boat trip out to the reef.

Among the wondrous creatures that might be seen around the coral reefs are spiny lobsters (which can be harvested in parts of the park during the legal season); sea cucumbers; Christmas tree worms; sponges; and fish, including colorful species such as angelfish, butterflyfish, damselfish, parrotfish, wrasses, and gobies. Occasionally a barracuda may appear, looking fiercer than its true behavior merits.

Visitors with their own canoes or kayaks have several options for exploring the park. The mainland's shoreline fringe of mangroves rewards explorers with wildlife such as the mangrove cuckoo and white-crowned pigeon (both much sought-after species by bird-watchers) and the manatee, the massive sea cow that floats peacefully, grazing on underwater vegetation. (Manatees are more common in winter than in summer.) But the park's real attraction is the maze of narrow waterways and shallow water around the Keys, especially south of the inlet called Caesar Creek.

Experienced paddlers can cross 7-mile-wide Biscayne Bay to camp on Elliott Key or Boca Chita Key (the trip can be difficult in windy conditions). Once there, boaters can paddle the areas around Jones Lagoon, Hurricane Creek, and nearby sites, possibly seeing sharks, rays, and a variety of birds.

In recent years, windsurfing has become popular. When windy conditions prevent most other water sports, windsurfers bring their own gear and take over the boat launch for an exhilarating experience.

The Keys

At 7 miles long, Elliott Key is the largest of the park's Keys, and well worth a visit whether by private boat (docking is available; overnight stays require a fee), kayak, or boat tour. In the late 19th century, the island was inhabited by a hardy group of pioneers who built a thriving pineapple plantation here. There was no fresh water on the island, so barrels were hauled in from the mainland or the springs in Biscayne Bay. Luckily for visitors, drinking water is available there today, and the island also has picnic tables, and cold-water showers. Primitive camping is allowed too, and Elliot Key has the park's longest hiking trail, which was the result of a conservation victory.

In the 1950s and '60s, when southern Florida was attracting more and more tourists and residents, developers planned a new city (to be called Islandia) in Biscayne Bay, as well as an industrial port and a deep channel to be dredged through the bay. Conservationists protested the destruction these activities would bring to the pristine environment of Biscayne Bay, and a coalition of anglers, environmentalists, writers, and politicians began promoting a plan to create a national park that would protect a long stretch of undeveloped shoreline, part of the bay, several Keys, and sections of coral reef. A bitter battle ensued, culminating in the creation in 1968 of Biscayne National Monument, later designated a national park.

In the meantime, though, angry would-be developers had bulldozed a wide roadway down the length of Elliott Key, trying to make the environment less appealing for protection. This "spite highway" has now recovered somewhat over the years through the regrowth of vegetation, and serves as a trail allowing hikers to explore the tropical hardwood forest of the island.

Boca Chita Key, though smaller than Elliott Key and lacking drinking water, is also a popular camping area. This island was once owned by wealthy businessman Mark Honeywell; he built several structures that still stand, including the 65-foot-high ornamental lighthouse in the

1930s. The lighthouse is open when park staff is on the island, and from the observation deck, visitors enjoy sweeping views of the islands and bay.

Both Elliott and Boca Chita can be accessed by private boat all year; call the park to ask about other options for campers without boats who wish to access the keys in winter and spring. Visitors with their own boats can also make a day trip to Adams Key, once the site of an exclusive fishing club that hosted several Presidents.

Visitors who take private boats into the park should read and be aware of regulations applying to both personal safety and protection of the environment. It's imperative to have nautical charts and to know tide schedules to avoid running aground in shallow water. Coral reefs and other areas of the seafloor are easily damaged by anchors and boat hulls. Boaters should use mooring buoys when they are available rather than anchoring among reefs.

Flora & Fauna

Among the fauna found within Biscayne National Park are five species of sea turtles; two of them, loggerhead and hawksbill, nest on sandy beaches in the park. Lucky visitors might spot some of the other endangered or threatened species found here, including the large, beautiful indigo snake and the very rare Schaus's swallowtail butterfly, the latter confined to just a few sites in the Florida Keys. Boaters occasionally see American crocodiles resting on the shore.

Unfortunately, the animal that you're certain to encounter within the park, in great numbers, is the mosquito, and its presence can lessen the fun of a visit, especially spring through fall. Insects are less bothersome in winter, making it the most pleasant and popular season.

Biscayne National Park lies adjacent to John Pennekamp Coral Reef State Park and Florida Keys National Marine Sanctuary, which offer additional protection for the marine species inhabiting these waters and the reef system, ranked as the third longest in the world, after Australia's Great Barrier Reef and the reef off the Central American nation of Belize. The sanctuary extends west to Dry Tortugas National Park (see p. 142), 70 miles west of Key West, Florida.

9700 SW 328th St.
Homestead, FL
305-230-7275
www.nps.gov/bisc

AT A GLANCE

Southern Florida, 20 miles south of Miami ▪ 173,000 acres ▪ Year-round ▪ Scuba diving, snorkeling, canoeing, kayaking, swimming, paddleboating, windsurfing, island camping, boat touring, hiking

Canaveral National Seashore
24 miles of undeveloped barrier island beach

Most of the million-plus visitors who enjoy Canaveral National Seashore each year are looking for nothing more than a beautiful beach where they can sunbathe, swim, surf, and generally relax on one of the most unspoiled stretches of America's Atlantic coast.

Those who venture from the ocean's edge, though, will discover this area has much more to offer than just its beaches. Abundant wildlife, fascinating plants, and history dating back thousands of years are all part of this area. Canaveral encompasses Merritt Island National Wildlife Refuge and adjoins the Kennedy Space Center, adding to its multifaceted appeal.

The national seashore includes a 24-mile-long barrier island, a thin strip of sand fronting the Atlantic Ocean. Just inland from the beach, dune, and vegetation of the island is Mosquito Lagoon, a wetland that's part mangrove forest and part salt marsh. Farther inland are oak scrub, slash pine flat woods, and hardwood and palm hammocks. Together, these habitats provide homes for a great diversity of flora and fauna.

For sun-and-surf seekers, the park's most popular area is the southern stretch of sand called Playalinda Beach. A road provides access to 13 parking areas from which the beach can be accessed. Apollo Beach, at the north end of the national seashore, is reached by road from the town of New Smyrna Beach. In between is Klondike Beach, little visited, not accessible by road, and offering solitude *(backcountry permit required)*. Parts of Playalinda may be closed when there are space shuttle launches from Kennedy Space Center.

Taking the Black Point Wildlife Drive or walking one of the trails in the national wildlife refuge will bring possible views of wading birds (including wood storks and roseate spoonbills), bald eagles (which nest in tall pines), and the threatened Florida scrub jay, among many other species. At Haulover Canal, a platform for manatee viewing often provides glimpses of the huge, peaceful aquatic mammals.

Ask about guided tours of the area by pontoon boat *(fee)*, leaving most Sundays from the national seashore visitor center in the northern part of the park. This short voyage is a great way to learn about the area's environment and history. Check at the seashore's visitor center or the Merritt Island National Wildlife Refuge Visitor Information Center *(on Fla. 402,*

on the way to Playalinda Beach) for other ranger-led programs.

Several Native American sites are found within the national seashore, the most famous of which is Turtle Mound, in the Apollo Beach area. At 35 feet tall, it's the highest spot in the national seashore. It consists of an estimated 1.5 million bushels of oyster shells discarded by Indians between 1,200 and 600 years ago. It may have been a ceremonial site or a lookout point; in any case, today it offers a

wonderful view of coast and marsh.

Backcountry camping is allowed within the national seashore *(permit and fee required)*, though not in the national wildlife refuge. There are two campsites on Apollo Beach, available November through mid-April. There are also campsites on islands scattered about Mosquito Lagoon for those who have their own boats, canoes, or kayaks. Reservations must be made for all campsites. Canoe rentals are available locally.

Fla. A1A
New Smyrna Beach, FL
321-267-1110
www.nps.gov/cana

AT A GLANCE

Northeastern Florida, off Cape Canaveral ▪ 58,000 acres ▪ Year-round ▪ Swimming, surfing, hiking, horseback riding, canoeing, kayaking, birdwatching, backcountry camping

Castillo de San Marcos National Monument
Survivor of wars to control North America

The only 17th-century military structure still existing in the United States, Castillo de San Marcos offers visitors a direct link to the days when Spain controlled the largest empire in history. Though the fort has changed hands repeatedly in the more than three centuries since its construction, it was never taken by force in battle.

Castillo de San Marcos National Monument is located in downtown St. Augustine, the oldest continuously occupied European-settled city in the United States (founded by Spanish colonists in 1565). Several wooden forts were built in the community, but in 1672 construction began on a more

The imposing walls of the Castillo de San Marcos

substantial masonry fort to help protect Spain's interests in North America. The *castillo* (castle) was built as a star-shaped bastion using material called coquina, a mixture of broken shells and sand bound by calcium carbonate. Coquina's compressibility causes

it to, in effect, absorb cannonballs rather than shatter—the major factor that allowed Castillo de San Marcos to survive bombardments during the period when Spain and England warred for possession of the region.

Visitors can tour the fort and enjoy living-history reenactments by costumed interpreters, including weapons demonstrations and presentations on life in Spanish and English colonial times. Rangers also offer a variety of programs each day. The view from the upper-level gun deck takes in historic downtown St. Augustine and the Matanzas River. The palm-shaded grounds of the fort are a pleasant place for a picnic.

1 S. Castillo Dr.
St. Augustine, FL
904-829-6506
www.nps.gov/casa

AT A GLANCE

Northeastern Florida, in St. Augustine ▪ 20 acres ▪ Year-round ▪ Touring historic Spanish fort, picnicking

De Soto National Memorial

Where a controversial conquistador began his final journey

In the 16th century, Spain sought ways to exploit the New World lands that Christopher Columbus had reached in 1492. Hernando de Soto, who had already gained fame for his part in Spanish explorations and occupation of Peru, mounted an expedition to La Florida, the area that is now the southeastern United States.

In May 1539, de Soto landed at Tampa Bay, his nine ships having brought more than 600 men, more than 200 horses, a herd of pigs, and weapons such as crossbows and muskets. His intention was to conquer territory; subjugate native peoples; and find riches, including gold. For three bloody years de Soto led his expedition on a wandering path through the Southeast, fighting Native Americans and failing to find wealth, before the conquistador died on May 21, 1542. Survivors, their numbers reduced by half—sick, wounded, and mostly without weapons—finally made their way to Mexico City months later, the expedition's grand plans having come to almost nothing. Though stories told by survivors added much to knowledge of the New World, the expedition had created suspicion and hatred among Native Americans, and European diseases wiped out entire villages throughout the region.

Located near the site where the expedition landed, De Soto National Memorial uses exhibits and artifacts to tell the story of the undertaking—its background, incidents from de Soto's journey, and its consequences. From December to April, costumed living-history guides give demonstrations on topics such as Native American crafts, period weapons, and historical tools and clothing, and rangers lead kayak tours from April to October. The park theater presents an excellent video on the expedition's four-year journey.

75th St. NW
Bradenton, FL
941-792-0458
www.nps.gov/deso

AT A GLANCE

West-central Florida, 15 miles south of St. Petersburg ▪ 26 acres ▪ Year-round ▪ Living-history demonstrations, hiking

Dry Tortugas National Park

Isolated islands where history and nature coexist

Combining nature, history, and a sense of pristine isolation in the vast Gulf of Mexico, Dry Tortugas National Park deserves its place among our most unusual and fascinating parks. Just getting there provides visitors with a feeling of accomplishment: The only way to reach the park is by boat or seaplane.

More than 99 percent of the park's 100 plus square miles is composed of waters of the Gulf of Mexico. Dry land consists of seven small islands of coral and sand, rising only a few feet above sea level. A visit to the Dry Tortugas centers on Garden Key, dominated by a massive 19th-century U.S. fortification. The surrounding

Fort Jefferson, built in the mid-19th century, dominates Garden Key.

Gulf is home to beautiful coral reefs where sea turtles, sharks, and hundreds of species of fish swim. Thousands of seabirds nest within the park, their breeding colony forming a stunning avian spectacle.

Sea turtles gave the islands their name, at least in part. Spanish explorer Juan Ponce de León came across these specks of land in the 16th century as he was sailing around Florida and named them *tortugas* (Spanish for "turtles") for the number of sea turtles of several species that frequented the beaches and Gulf. Sailors, including pirates, used the turtles as a food source, and they also took huge quantities of eggs from bird colonies. The word "dry" was later added as a descriptive, testament to the total lack of fresh water on the islands, and a warning to sailors hoping to replenish their ships' supplies.

The U.S. Takes Possession

After the United States acquired the islands from Spain, a lighthouse was built in 1825 on what is now Garden Key to guide ships through the reefs and shallow waters. After years of study and planning, in 1846 the Army began construction of a massive brick fort to help the country maintain control of the Gulf of Mexico. Plans called for Fort Jefferson to stand 50 feet high, have 2,000 arches housing 420 guns, and be home to 2,000 soldiers and other residents. Sixteen million bricks later, with walls a half mile in circumference, the fort took up the bulk of 16-acre Garden Key.

Construction of Fort Jefferson was far more complicated and costly than planners had envisioned, and it dragged on for decades. In the Civil War it became a military prison, its most famous inmate Dr. Samuel Mudd. The physician was convicted of conspiracy to assassinate President

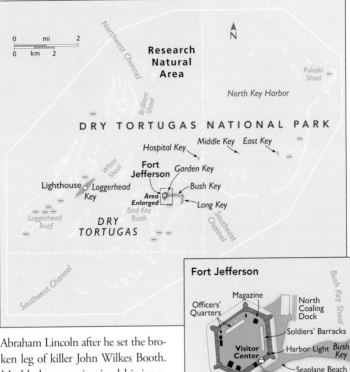

Abraham Lincoln after he set the broken leg of killer John Wilkes Booth. Mudd always maintained his innocence, and he was pardoned after four years because of his service during an 1867 yellow fever epidemic at the fort.

The Army abandoned still unfinished Fort Jefferson soon thereafter, in part because new types of cannon had been developed that could have demolished even its 8-foot-thick brick walls. In the 1880s and '90s it served as a naval station; coal docks from that steam era can still be seen. In 1908, Garden Key, six other Dry Tortugas keys, and the surrounding waters were declared a national wildlife refuge; in 1935 the Dry Tortugas were named a national monument, and in 1992 a national park. In 2007, 46 square miles of the Gulf of Mexico part of the park were declared a research natural area, providing even more protection for marine life.

Visiting Dry Tortugas

Except for those with their own boats, reaching Dry Tortugas requires reserving a spot on a seaplane (the flight takes about 40 minutes) or a ferry (three-hour ride). The waters of the Gulf of Mexico are often so clear that turtles, sharks, and other animals can be seen during the trip, especially with the bird's-eye view from an airplane. Visitors should be aware that facilities at Garden Key are extremely limited: There is no drinking water, no public rest room (except for campers; others use rest rooms on commercial ferries), and nowhere to buy food or drinks or other supplies. All trash must be taken out.

Garden Key

For most visitors, the priority is touring the imposing Fort Jefferson, with its casemates (gun rooms), arches, huge walls, and the cell where Samuel Mudd was imprisoned. Note how the fort's second tier was left unfinished. The weight of the bricks created subsidence of the sand and coral beneath, causing the structure to begin to sink.

A moat surrounds Fort Jefferson, and walking its wall (a 0.6-mile circuit) is not only a good way to experience the fort but it's also an excellent way to see coral, fish, and other marine creatures in the surrounding Gulf. An even better way is to go snorkeling in the designated area outside the moat and around the coal-dock piers. Snorkeling is not permitted inside the moat, and snorkelers and swimmers should be aware of jellyfish and sea urchins.

Bird-watching & Camping

Some of the most avid visitors to Dry Tortugas National Park are bird-watchers. From spring to fall, thousands of sooty terns and brown noddies (also a type of tern) nest on Bush Key, easily visible from Garden Key. (Landing on Bush Key is prohibited during the nesting season to protect the breeding colonies.) A few black noddies are occasionally seen mixed with the browns. Other seabirds seen with some regularity around Garden Key are the common magnificent frigatebird (which nests on Long Key, also visible from Garden Key), brown pelican, brown and masked booby, roseate tern, and the rare white-tailed tropicbird.

The most amazing experience at Garden Key, though, occurs in

![Some visitors take seaplanes to the Dry Tortugas.]

Some visitors take seaplanes to the Dry Tortugas.

spring, when millions of birds fly northward across the Gulf of Mexico on their way to nesting grounds throughout eastern North America. Tired from their long flight, thousands of these birds spot Garden Key and fly down to land and rest before resuming their journeys. Late March to mid-May the islands of the Dry Tortugas may almost literally swarm with migrating birds. The spectacle is so awe-inspiring that several nature tour companies offer special boat trips to the national park for bird-watchers.

While most visitors come to Garden Key on day trips to enjoy Fort Jefferson, snorkeling, and birds, the national park does allow camping in a primitive campground outside the fort walls. Sites have picnic tables and grills, but campers must bring their own water and food. (Note that seaplanes and ferries will not allow the transportation of propane or camp fuel; self-igniting charcoal is allowed.) Camping is on a first-come, first-served basis, but an overflow area is available if the regular campground is full. All trash must be packed up and removed from the park. Composting toilets

are available for campers but are open only between 3 p.m. and 10 a.m.; at other times, visitors should use the rest room facilities on the commercial ferries.

Visitors with their own boats or on a commercial tour can visit 30-acre Loggerhead Key, the largest of the Dry Tortugas. Located about 3 miles west of Garden Key, it's an important nesting ground for green and loggerhead sea turtles, as well as a stopover for migratory birds. A 150-foot-tall lighthouse built in 1856 still stands here in the center of the key.

Diving & Fishing

Over the years hundreds of ships have run aground in the shoals and reefs of the Dry Tortugas, and diving to explore shipwrecks is a popular park activity. Several commercial dive companies offer tours of the area. Visitors with private boats should be aware that all anchoring must be on sandy sea bottom (to protect coral and sea grass), and overnight anchoring must be within one nautical mile of the Garden Key light.

Noncommercial fishing is allowed within some parts of the national park, but interested anglers need to read and abide by the park's regulations.

Most visitors to the park embark from Key West, where a good preliminary stop is the Key West Eco-Discovery Center (*35 E. Quay Rd., 305-809-4750*), with 6,000 square feet of interactive exhibits interpreting the terrestrial and underwater habitats of the Florida Keys.

Visitor center
Garden Key, FL
305-242-7700
www.nps.gov/drto

AT A GLANCE

In the Gulf of Mexico, 68 miles west of Key West, Florida (accessible only by boat or seaplane) ▪ 64,700 acres ▪ Year-round; spring is most popular season for bird-watching ▪ Camping, snorkeling, bird-watching, swimming

Everglades National Park

A *wildlife-rich "river of grass"*

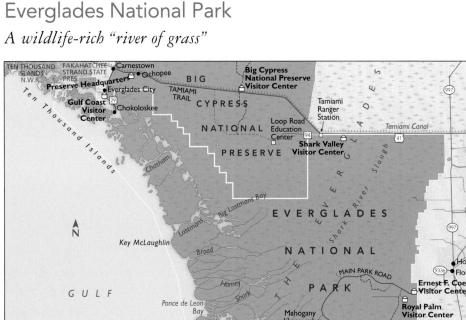

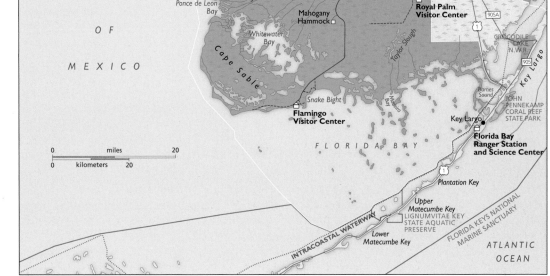

Unique in North America—indeed, in the world—for its combined geology, subtropical ecosystem, and specialized flora and fauna, Everglades National Park holds many distinctions within the National Park System.

It was the first large area of wilderness protected not for mountains, canyons, seacoasts, or other scenic features but rather to preserve its amazing ecological diversity. It was the first park in which controlled burning was used to restore ecosystems. It protects the largest wilderness area east of the Mississippi River. And, unfortunately, it ranks among the most threatened of our parks, an issue that gained fame back in 1947 with the publication of Marjory Stoneman Douglas's classic book *The Everglades: River of Grass*.

In recent years Everglades National Park has been the focal point of what may be the most extensive environmental-restoration project in history, though a report issued in late 2008 warned that the effort was not moving quickly enough to take the Everglades out of danger.

FOLLOWING PAGES: *One of the largest bodies of water in the Everglades, Florida Bay is home to manatees and sea turtles.*

A Unique Ecosystem

Even first-time visitors quickly sense that this is a different sort of national park. Superficially, the Everglades is as flat as it is vast, the elevation of its entire area within a few feet of sea level. Yet even without high peaks, cliffs, or waterfalls, the Everglades encompasses nine separate ecosystems, home to more than 700 species of plants, more than 360 species of birds, nearly 300 species of fish, more than 40 species of mammals, and more than 50 species of reptiles. Among them are such endangered or threatened species as the American crocodile, eastern indigo snake, West Indian manatee, Florida panther, and snail kite. The Everglades has been designated an international biosphere reserve, a World Heritage site, and a Wetland of International Importance.

Expansive as it is—it amounts to more than 2,350 square miles—Everglades National Park covers only about one-fifth of the original Everglades ecosystem. More of the ecosystem is protected by state and federal agencies and in other parks and preserves, but about half has been destroyed by development and changes in water flow.

In its original form, the Everglades comprised a low, primarily saw-grass-dominated wet prairie, across which a shallow sheet of water flowed slowly, fed by the Kissimmee River and Lake Okeechobee to the north, and by summer rains. The water level in this "river of grass" rose and fell seasonally, and plant and animal life had adapted to its rhythms. Agriculture, levees, urban development, and water diversion disrupted the pattern, leading to loss of wetlands and associated life. To give the most famous example: The enormous

Flamingos frequent the southern tip of Everglades.

flocks of egrets, herons, ibises, storks, and other wading birds that once filled the skies over the Everglades have been reduced an estimated 93 percent. Reduced flow of fresh water into Florida Bay has altered its environment as well, reducing populations of shrimp, lobsters, and game fish.

Regardless of past or present issues, though, Everglades National Park remains a natural treasure, with hiking and boating trails leading through its many habitats. Rangers at the park's four visitor centers—one in each main area of the park—will help travelers plan an enjoyable and educational visit.

Pinelands Area

Most people enter the park from Florida City on Fla. 9336, where the first stop is the Ernest F. Coe Visitor Center. Schedules for ranger-led tours and programs are available here. Just a few miles beyond is the turn to the Royal Palm area, where two of the park's most popular trails are located.

The half-mile, wheelchair-accessible Anhinga Trail winds through a marsh where sightings of alligators and wading birds are common. The readily seen long-necked, long-beaked, black bird—the anhinga—gave the trail its name. A relative of pelicans, it often sits on a limb with its wings spread to dry after diving for fish. The nearby half-mile Gumbo Limbo Trail, also wheelchair accessible, passes through a woodland of gumbo-limbo trees (look for bark peeling like skin after a sunburn) and tall royal palms.

The main park road continues 38 miles to dead-end just beyond the Flamingo Visitor Center. Along the way it crosses a sampling of Everglades habitats. Note the patches of slash pine and bald cypress trees; the latter will grow tall in wet areas and be stunted in the drier prairie, which has shallow, nutrient-poor soil. It's worth stopping at the next three interpretive trails along the road: Pineland, to see slash pines and saw palmettos; Pahayokee Overlook, to gaze over the "river of grass"; and Mahogany Hammock, to admire the largest mahogany tree in the United States. (In Florida, "hammock" means a dense woodland located on a slightly higher area of ground.)

Near the coast, saltwater-loving mangrove trees line the edges of ponds and other wetlands. Great and snowy egrets, great blue herons (look for the uncommon white form), and glossy and white ibises feed and rest all through this area. Among the park's other notable birds are the lovely roseate spoonbill, pink with a spatula-shaped bill; and the wood stork, which with its odd, naked head might best be described as striking rather than beautiful.

Flamingo Area

Flamingo, the village at the road's terminus, suffered great damage in recent hurricanes, and at this writing the lodge and other facilities were closed; picnic tables, grills, rest rooms, and dump stations are available. Plans are under way for a new lodge, restaurant, cabins, RV campground, marina developments, and resumption of commercial boat trips and other guided tours. Some of the biking and walking trails in the Flamingo area also suffered damage, but favorites such as the short Eco Pond Trail and the 1.6-mile (one-way) Snake Bight Trail are still open. The latter is one of the park's best bird-watching trails, especially for those who arrive at Florida Bay at high tide. (This is also a good trail for bicycling.)

Several short and relatively easy canoe trails offer the chance to see the Flamingo area environment from the water. Ask a ranger about canoeing the Nine Mile Pond or Noble Hammock loops. If it's a calm day, consider a trip out into Florida Bay, where the opportunities for exploration are limited only by time and stamina. On some of these routes, such as the West Lake Trail, paddlers have the chance to see the threatened crocodile. Canoe rentals are available at the Flamingo Marina.

Shark Valley Area

On the northern edge of the park, the Shark Valley Visitor Center is located on U.S. 41, also known as the Tamiami Trail. Named for the Shark River, this area is the gateway to the essence of the Everglades, the vast sawgrass marsh—the "river of grass"—that flows 100 miles from Lake Okeechobee to the Gulf of Mexico.

Two short trails are available here—Bobcat Boardwalk and Otter Cave Hammock Trail—but the real attraction is the Tram Road, a 15-mile loop that heads south, deep into the heart of the marsh. Closed to private vehicles, the route is open to bicyclists, hikers, and to guided tram tours narrated by park rangers or naturalists. During the two-hour tour, visitors may see alligators, wading birds, the endangered snail kite (a small hawk), and deer, among other wildlife. Halfway around the Tram Road, a 65-foot-high tower offers an unobstructed panorama of the Everglades.

Gulf Coast Area

The park's Gulf Coast Visitor Center is located 5 miles south of the Tamiami Trail in Everglades City. There are no hiking trails here; rather, the center is the main entry point to the maze of mangrove islands and waterways called the Ten Thousand Islands. Commercial boat tours are available in the area, and canoeists, kayakers, and powerboaters can explore nearby water routes such as Turner River, Halfway Creek, Sandfly Island, and East River. Boaters should use caution; getting lost is a real danger.

Adventurous boaters can set out along the challenging, 99-mile-long Wilderness Waterway, which follows the coastline to Flamingo. Canoeists should allow at least eight days to paddle the entire length, camping on elevated platforms called "chickees." Rangers highly recommend studying the park's guide to the Wilderness Waterway, which provides advice and warnings for the journey, along which it's possible to see dolphins, manatees, alligators, and a wide array of birds. Canoe rentals are available at the Gulf Coast Marina in Everglades City.

Although the future of Everglades National Park, and of the ecosystem of which it is a part, remains in doubt, restoration efforts continue. A coalition of conservationists, public officials, and politicians is working to balance development in southern Florida with protecting one of the world's environmental treasures.

Fla. 9336
Homestead, FL
305-242-7700
www.nps.gov/ever

AT A GLANCE

Southern Florida, 30 miles southwest of Miami ▪ 1,508,537 acres ▪ Year-round, though summers are hot, humid, and buggy ▪ Hiking, boating, wildlife-watching, taking boat and tram tours, biking

---

Florida National Scenic Trail

A 1,300-mile hiking route traversing the state of Florida

Begun as a hiker's dream more than 50 years ago, the Florida National Scenic Trail has grown over the years to stretch from Big Cypress National Preserve (see p. 136), on the northern edge of the Everglades, to Fort Pickens, at the western tip of Santa Rosa Island within Gulf Islands National Seashore (see p. 151). Side trails to and through scenic areas add 400 miles of hiking opportunities.

A cooperative effort involving private landowners and many agencies (including the National Park Service and the state of Florida), the trail is administered by the U.S. Forest Service and supported by the nonprofit Florida Trail Association.

Along its route, the path passes Lake Okeechobee; Ocala, Osceola, and Apalachicola National Forests; Suwanee River State Park; the Tallahassee–St. Marks Historic Railroad Trail; St. Marks National Wildlife Refuge; and several state conservation areas.

More than 1,000 miles of trail in the protected corridor are open for the public to enjoy. Additional land is still being purchased and easements acquired to provide a continuous corridor of protected trail; blazed and mapped road walks connect completed segments. A map of the trail can be found on the Forest Service website *(www.fs.usda.gov/fnst)*.

With its variety of terrain and great number of trailheads, Florida National Scenic Trail offers visitors opportunities for both short, easy day hikes and multiday backpacking trips, spanning ecological habitat ranging from subtropical forest to prairie to pinewoods.

Florida Trail Association
5415 SW 13th St.
Gainesville, FL
352-378-8823 or 877-445-3352
www.floridatrail.org

AT A GLANCE
From southern Florida to the Panhandle ▪ 1,400 linear miles ▪ Year-round ▪ Hiking, backpacking

Fort Matanzas National Monument
Where Spanish soldiers watched for invaders

In the early 18th century, St. Augustine was a vital part of Spain's control of the region that's now the state of Florida. The city was defended by the imposing fort called Castillo de San Marcos, built in 1672 (see p. 141). Spanish leaders knew, though, that rival English troops might reach the city by ship through Matanzas Inlet, 14 miles to the south. To guard against this, in 1740 the Spanish built a small stone watchtower armed with cannon that could fire on approaching ships and from which soldiers could return to St. Augustine to warn of invasion.

The new Fort Matanzas was built of coquina, a limestone-like mixture of shells and sand naturally cemented with calcium carbonate. The British tried to attack and stop construction but were repelled by Spanish ships. After the fort's completion it saw action only once, in 1742, when British ships sailed into the inlet but turned back in the face of cannon fire.

The national monument preserves the restored watchtower as well as 300 acres of barrier island salt marsh, forest, and dunes. Located on Rattlesnake Island, Fort Matanzas is reached via a free ferry from Anastasia Island, where a visitor center has exhibits and

The sentry box at Fort Matanzas

a half-mile nature trail winds through the maritime forest. At the fort, visitors receive an interpretive program and can tour the troops' quarters, sentry box, powder magazine, and cannon and observation decks.

8635 Fla. A1A S
St. Augustine, FL
904-471-0116
www.nps.gov/foma

AT A GLANCE
Northeastern Florida, 14 miles south of St. Augustine ▪ 300 acres ▪ Year-round ▪ Touring historic watchtower fort, hiking, beachcombing, nature viewing

Gulf Islands National Seashore

World-class beaches, historic forts, and pristine island wilderness

The waters of the Gulf of Mexico lap against Santa Rosa Island, a barrier island off the Florida Panhandle.

Several barrier islands within Gulf Islands National Seashore appear regularly on lists of the world's most beautiful beaches. One reason: their dazzling white sand, which originated as quartz in the Appalachian Mountains to the north and was eroded and washed down to the Gulf of Mexico by rivers over countless millennia.

Miles of these beaches constitute the major attraction within the national seashore, which encompasses 12 units stretching along the Gulf Coast of the Florida Panhandle and southern Mississippi. Great numbers of visitors arrive during the warmer months to enjoy sunbathing and swimming. But there's more to Gulf Islands than the beach life.

Harbors on the adjacent mainland have long been important militarily, from the days of early Spanish exploration through the Civil War and on to the World War II era. Visitors can tour several forts within the park for a look at days when nations contended for control of the Gulf Coast. Fort Barrancas served as a post for British, Spanish, and American troops; it was protected by the Advanced Redoubt, a 19th-century masonry fortification built to repel a land-based assault on the fort and the Pensacola Navy Yard. Fort Pickens, begun in 1829, was active into the 1940s. Little remains of the 1830s Fort McRee save artillery batteries from the 20th century.

Nature lovers can explore a variety of coastal habitats, from groves of live oaks to salt marshes to beach dunes, in which they may see a whole range of wildlife, including bottlenose dolphins, alligators, gopher tortoises, river otters, and remarkable birds such as ospreys, black skimmers, and piping plovers. Four species of sea turtles—loggerhead, green, leatherback, and Kemp's ridley—nest on beaches within the park.

Exploring the Park

Gulf Islands National Seashore contains four visitor centers: Naval Live Oaks in Gulf Breeze, Florida; Fort Barrancas, within Pensacola Naval Air Station, Pensacola, Florida; Fort Pickens, at the western end of Santa Rosa Island, Florida; and Davis Bayou, in Ocean Springs, Mississippi. Information is available at all centers on activities, including ranger-led tours, which may focus on the Civil War, wildlife of the marsh, or bird-watching.

A ferry *(March–Oct., fee)* takes passengers from Gulfport, Mississippi, to West Ship Island for swimming, hiking, and tours of Civil War–era Fort Massachusetts. Visitors with their own boats, or who hire a charter boat, can visit the undeveloped islands of Horn, Petit Bois, East Ship, and parts of Cat. The experience of camping on these barrier islands invokes a feeling of being in a world far removed from the mainland, though they're only about 12 miles offshore.

Popular trails within the park include the short, easy Perdido Key Discovery Trail, which crosses a salt marsh, maritime forest, and dunes; and the Brackenridge Nature Trail, with exhibits on ways live oaks were used in shipbuilding (both trails are in Florida). The Nature's Way Trail, at the Ocean Springs, Mississippi, visitor center, passes through varied habitats and offers the chance to see diverse wildlife.

1801 Gulf Breeze Pkwy.
Gulf Breeze, FL
850-934-2600
www.nps.gov/guis

AT A GLANCE Twelve units along Florida Panhandle and southern Mississippi coast ▪ 135,000 acres ▪ Year-round ▪ Swimming, hiking, touring historic sites, camping, fishing, bird-watching

Timucuan Ecological and Historic Preserve & Fort Caroline National Memorial
Natural and cultural diversity preserved in a metropolitan setting

This unusual park combines lands under the control of the National Park Service, the state of Florida, the city of Jacksonville, and private landowners to present a variety of ways to experience the history and environment of the St. Johns River region near Jacksonville, Florida.

The park's heart is the Timucuan Preserve Visitor Center, which focuses on the human interactions with the natural world here. Exhibits focus on the Timucua Indians (for whom the preserve is named) and the French settlers who tried to establish a community here in the 16th century, before being driven out by the Spanish. Adjacent to the visitor center are a one-third-scale exhibit of the French Fort Caroline and a Timucuan hut and shell mound.

The nearby Theodore Roosevelt Area offers miles of hiking trails through pine flat woods, hardwood hammocks (higher ground with groves of trees), and marshy wetlands. A 1.5-mile trail leads to an observation platform from which wading birds and waterfowl can often be seen in Round Marsh.

Other areas encompassed by the park are located north of the St. Johns River and include several Florida state parks as well as 1798 Kingsley Plantation, the oldest surviving plantation house in Florida. Here enslaved African Americans were used to grow and harvest Sea Island cotton. Visitors can tour the grounds, slave cabins, barn, kitchen, and garden. The main plantation house is open for tours on weekends, by reservation only.

12713 Fort Caroline Rd.
Jacksonville, FL
904-641-7155
www.nps.gov/timu

AT A GLANCE Northeastern Florida, in Jacksonville ▪ 46,000 acres (9,000 acres owned by National Park Service) ▪ Year-round ▪ Touring historic sites, hiking, kayaking, bird-watching

GEORGIA

The largest southern state east of the Mississippi River, Georgia is dominated culturally by the metropolis of Atlanta. Burned during the Civil War, Atlanta recovered to become a major financial and transportation hub of the South and one of the fastest growing cities in America during the late 20th century. Beyond the city, the state offers the high peaks of the Appalachians, the vast Okefenokee Swamp, and the beautiful coastal "sea islands." The famed Appalachian National Scenic Trail has its southern terminus in northern Georgia. Civil rights leader Martin Luther King, Jr., was born in Atlanta; and Jimmy Carter, 39th President, grew up on a farm in southwestern Georgia.

Andersonville National Historic Site
A Civil War prison site commemorating American POWs

In early 1864, at the height of the Civil War, the Confederacy built a prison in southwestern Georgia to hold captured Union soldiers. Officially called Camp Sumter but later commonly known as Andersonville Prison (for a nearby small town), the compound became infamous for the terrible conditions endured by the inmates, resulting in the deaths of nearly 13,000 men by the close of the Civil War.

Today's Andersonville National Historic Site encompasses the location of the prison as well as a national cemetery and the National Prisoner of War Museum, which commemorates the sacrifices of all American prisoners of war in conflicts such as World Wars I and II, Korea, Vietnam, and the Middle East.

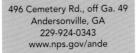

Nearly 13,000 Union soldiers died at Andersonville.

displays, and memorials from 16 states that were the homes of soldiers who died at Andersonville. Exhibits recount the horrors of conditions at the prison and the postwar investigation into causes and responsibility.

Andersonville National Cemetery began as the burial site of prisoners from Camp Sumter, and it later became the resting place for others who served in the United States military. Unlike other national cemeteries overseen by the Department of Veterans Affairs, Andersonville is one of two administered by the National Park Service. It is still in use and contains nearly 20,000 graves.

Prisoner of War Museum

The National Prisoner of War Museum opened in 1998 with a ceremony that also marked the anniversary of the fall of Bataan in World War II, an event that led to the cruelties of the Bataan Death March and the imprisonment of U.S. soldiers by Japanese forces. Museum exhibits on the hundreds of thousands of American men and women who have been POWs, dating back to the Revolutionary War, range from military dog tags to a reproduction of a cell in the "Hanoi Hilton" (a North Vietnamese prison where POWs were held during the Vietnam War).

Andersonville Prison

The original Camp Sumter was a 16.5-acre site surrounded by a wooden stockade. With a small creek flowing through its center, it was designed to house a maximum of 10,000 prisoners of war. A smaller fence was erected inside the tall stockade; any prisoner who crossed this "dead line" to approach the outer wall was shot by sentries stationed in guard posts around the stockade.

Crowded conditions quickly led to a 10-acre expansion of Camp Sumter.

In August 1864 Andersonville housed some 32,000 prisoners, all suffering from malnutrition, disease, and the heat of a Georgia summer. Prisoners likened conditions to "hell on Earth," and the death rate at times topped 100 men a day. After the Civil War the Confederate camp commander, Henry Wirz, was convicted of war crimes and hanged, despite his protests that he worked to get more food and better conditions for prisoners.

Today's site includes a reconstructed stockade wall, interpretive

496 Cemetery Rd., off Ga. 49
Andersonville, GA
229-924-0343
www.nps.gov/ande

AT A GLANCE Southwestern Georgia, 55 miles southwest of Macon ▪ 550 acres ▪ Year-round ▪ Exploring historic prison site, visiting National Prisoner of War Museum and national cemetery

Chattahoochee River National Recreation Area

A river retreat handy to metropolitan Atlanta

Chattahoochee River National Recreation Area owes its being to public officials and private citizens who, in the midst of Atlanta's 1970s growth boom, had the foresight to act to protect undeveloped sections of the scenic Chattahoochee River, stretching from just below Buford Dam (northeast of the city) downstream to the northern outskirts of the city. As a result of their hard work, more than three million visitors a year now enjoy a green linear oasis just a short distance from a major metropolitan area.

Activities possible in the national recreation area include hiking, canoeing, kayaking, rafting, picnicking, and wildlife-watching. Mountain biking and horseback riding are restricted to 2 of the area's 15 land units, which are located along 48 miles of the river. Motorized watercraft are allowed only on limited stretches of the river (check with park officials for details). Anglers will find the cold waters of the Chattahoochee, released from the Buford Dam at Lake Sidney Lanier, filled with trout and other species of fish.

The visitor contact station is located at the Island Ford unit, in Sandy Springs about 6 miles north of I-285. This unit features hiking trails (as do all the developed areas) as well as access for canoes, kayaks, and rafts. Within the Cochran Shoals unit, at Columns Drive there is access to a wetlands boardwalk and fitness trail, while at nearby Sope Creek there is an entrance to a challenging mountain bike trail. Other units offer various combinations of trails, picnic tables, boat ramps, and other attractions.

1978 Island Ford Pkwy.
Atlanta, GA
678-538-1200
www.nps.gov/chat

AT A GLANCE

Northern Georgia, just north of Atlanta ▪ 48 river miles; 9,200 acres ▪ Year-round (day use only) ▪ Boating, hiking, fishing, mountain biking, horseback riding, observing wildlife, picnicking

---

Chickamauga & Chattanooga National Military Park

The sites of pivotal Civil War battles for control of the South

America's first officially established national military park, Chickamauga and Chattanooga was dedicated in 1895 in recognition of the significance of the Civil War battles fought on these two major sites in September and November 1863.

Confederate and Union forces alike considered Chattanooga, Tennessee—with its railroads, roads, and position beside the Tennessee River—vital to their success. A fierce series of battles centered at Chickamauga, Georgia, on September 18–20 left the Southerners in control and Union troops isolated

and under siege. Union Gen. Ulysses S. Grant arrived on the scene in October with reinforcements and defeated the Confederates in November at Orchard Knob, Lookout Mountain, and Missionary Ridge, all in Tennessee. With control of Chattanooga, the Union held a strong position in the mid-South. In 1864 Maj. Gen. William T. Sherman used Chattanooga as a base for his decisive march through Georgia.

Visitor center displays, battlefield exhibits, trails, and monuments at both sites help visitors learn about the importance of the battles. Because the

park was established just 30 years after the war, the sites appear much the same as during the battles. Military historians and strategists have long studied the Chattanooga Campaign to better understand the way natural geographic features affected events. (Chickamauga Visitor Center is off U.S. 27 in Fort Oglethorpe, Georgia; Lookout Mountain Visitor Center is off Tenn. 148 in Chattanooga.)

Throughout the summer, ranger-guided programs and living-history demonstrations help visitors understand the lives of Civil War soldiers.

Fort Oglethorpe, GA, or
Chattanooga, TN
706-866-9241
www.nps.gov/chch

AT A GLANCE

Northwestern Georgia and southeastern Tennessee, just south and west of Chattanooga, Tennessee ▪ 9,000 acres ▪ Year-round ▪ Taking auto tour routes, hiking trails, watching living-history demonstrations, visiting exhibits

Cumberland Island National Seashore
Pristine beaches, expansive wilderness, and diverse human history

The largest of the barrier islands along Georgia's Atlantic coast, Cumberland boasts a long and varied history that chronicles Native Americans, 19th- and 20th-century landowners of great wealth, and most of the island's eventual acquisition by the National Park Service and later designation as a national seashore. Today Cumberland Island offers visitors solitude on miles of undeveloped beaches, within a wilderness area of maritime forest and salt marsh.

Most people travel to Cumberland Island by a regular ferry service *(fee)* from the small town of St. Marys, Georgia (the park visitor center is located dockside). Reservations for the ferry are recommended and can be made up to six months in advance *(www.cumberlandislandferry.com).* Private boats are also allowed, though dock space is limited and boats must be either anchored or beached overnight. (Adventurous visitors can also paddle kayaks to the island.) Day trips are popular, but to experience the best of the island—wildlife-watching, stargazing, beachcombing, and the greatest solitude—camping is recommended. Both developed and primitive campsites are available. There is also a private inn on Cumberland offering overnight accommodations.

Exploring the Island

One early island landowner was Revolutionary War Gen. Nathanael Greene, who acquired property here in 1783. He died in 1786, and his

Feral horses roam Cumberland Island.

widow later built Dungeness, a large house constructed of tabby (a mixture of oyster shells, sand, lime, and water). A century later, much of Cumberland Island was purchased by Thomas Carnegie (wealthy brother of businessman Andrew Carnegie); he and his wife, Lucy, started a mansion (also called Dungeness) on the foundation of the earlier structure in 1884, though Thomas died before its completion. This second Dungeness burned in 1959 and only ruins remain. Self-guided tours are available. Another Carnegie mansion, the 1898 Plum Orchard, survives and was donated to the National Park Service in 1972. It is open when volunteer caretakers are in residence; check at the visitor center for details. The northern end of the island was home to a small community of African-American workers in the 1890s;

the First African Baptist Church survives and is a popular destination.

Traveling around the island involves hiking or riding bicycles, which are restricted to the roads. Bikes are not allowed on the ferry, though they can be brought to the island by private or charter boats; rentals are available on the island. Some of the island's 50 miles of hiking trails lead through forests of live oaks and palmettos; others to marshes and ponds.

Bird-watching is the most popular form of wildlife observation on Cumberland Island, with pelicans, herons, shorebirds, gulls, and terns on beaches and wetlands; and turkeys, woodpeckers, and songbirds in forests. Other animals that might be seen include alligators, deer, armadillos, river otters, and feral horses, with the occasional dolphin surfacing in offshore waters. Beachcombing is popular on the island as well; check regulations for objects permissible to collect. Mornings after storms are usually best for finding a variety of seashells. Sharks' teeth are also frequently found, even in the material used to surface park roads.

Many people enjoy soaking up the sun and swimming off Cumberland's pristine beaches, but no lifeguards are present, so swim at your own risk.

Private property still exists on the island; visitors need to respect the No Trespassing signs. Much beach access is private; public paths across the dunes are marked with black-and-white striped poles.

113 St. Marys St.
St. Marys, GA
912-882-4336
www.nps.gov/cuis

AT A GLANCE

Coastal Georgia, 45 miles north of Jacksonville, Florida ▪ 36,400 acres ▪ Year-round ▪ Camping, hiking, swimming, beachcombing, wildlife-watching, touring historic structures

Fort Frederica National Monument

The British fort that kept Georgia out of Spanish hands

With British colonies established along the mid-Atlantic coast and Spanish settlements and forts in Florida, the intervening area (now the coastline of Georgia) was the focus of decades of conflict between the two nations. Called the "debatable" land, in 1736 it became the site of a fortified town established by James Oglethorpe, founder of the British colony of Georgia. Named for Frederick, Prince of Wales, its mission was to protect the southern boundary of the colony.

Set on the western edge of what is now called St. Simon's Island, Fort Frederica combined military, commercial, and residential functions. The area was fortified with a palisade and an earthen rampart, and its population reached 800 to 1,000 at its peak. During this period Frederica was briefly the home of visiting minister John Wesley, founder of the Methodist Church.

Spanish soldiers invaded St. Simon's Island in 1742 but were defeated by Oglethorpe-led British troops. The action ended Spanish hopes of expanding its colonies northward along the Atlantic coast, but it also meant the end for the settlement. With the fort abandoned, the town slowly withered away.

Today, Fort Frederica National Monument preserves remnants of the fort and town, including remains of barracks, a magazine, and a defensive bastion. Many buildings were constructed of tabby, a mixture of oyster shells, lime, sand, and water. The park's visitor center shows a 23-minute film called "History Uncovered."

The Bloody Marsh unit, located between six and seven miles south of Fort Frederica on Old Demere Road, commemorates the Battle of Bloody Marsh, one of the British-won skirmishes that convinced the Spaniards to leave Saint Simon's Island.

6515 Frederica Rd.
St. Simon's Island, GA
912-638-3639
www.nps.gov/fofr

AT A GLANCE

Southeastern Georgia, 75 miles south of Savannah ▪ 250 acres ▪ Year-round ▪ Touring archaeological site and museum, viewing interpretive film

Fort Pulaski National Monument

A turning point in the Civil War and military history

Today the beautiful city of Savannah, Georgia, is known as home to historic and architecturally significant buildings as well as to Old South traditions. In the 19th century, though, its importance as a port gave it great military significance.

In the 1820s, as in colonial times, Cockspur Island, in the Savannah River east of the city, was chosen as a fort site—part of a system of coastal defenses expected to protect the United States from attack by sea. The massive brick-and-masonry structure would be named in honor of Casimir Pulaski, the Polish-born hero of the Revolutionary War. A young West Pointer

Confederate cannon guard the main entrance of Fort Pulaski.

named Robert E. Lee helped supervise early construction work on the fort. He couldn't know that 30 years later he would return as a general in an army fighting for the Confederacy against the United States.

More than 25 million bricks were used to build Fort Pulaski. Because of its location on an island, any artillery used to bombard it would have to be located a mile or more away, and no cannon of the time was powerful enough to breach its 7-foot-thick walls from that distance.

Civil War Action

Soon after the start of the Civil War, Union military strategists determined that Fort Pulaski had to be taken in order for the North to seize and control the entrance to the Savannah River, thus crippling the South's ability to ship and receive goods at Savannah. Union forces began bombarding Fort Pulaski with cannon fire on April 10, 1862. For 30 hours, they concentrated their firepower on the corner wall using the new rifled cannon. This weapon, untested as yet in battle, had

shown it could fire shells accurately and powerfully across much greater distances than any previous artillery. Soon huge gaps had been opened in the fort's walls, forcing Confederate Col. Charles Olmstead to surrender because 40,000 pounds of ammunition were now exposed to the projectiles from the rifled cannon. In that moment, systems of fortifications all around the world became vulnerable to the new weapon and, in essence, obsolete.

Cockspur Island

Though Fort Pulaski was allowed to deteriorate after the Civil War, restoration efforts in the early and middle 20th century make today's Fort Pulaski National Monument a memorable reminder of a turning point in U.S. history and military technology. Visitors to Cockspur Island can tour the fort as well as the demilune (a crescent-shaped protective earthwork), dikes, ditches, and drawbridges.

The visitor center features exhibits on Casimir Pulaski, the construction of the fort, and the importance

of the 1862 battle. "The Battle for Fort Pulaski," a 20-minute film, is shown regularly. Scheduled interpretive programs include daily guided tours of the fort and musket-firing demonstrations.

Walking some of the trails on Cockspur Island and nearby will bring into view a variety of wildlife, including pelicans, oystercatchers, terns, painted buntings, alligators, raccoon, white-tailed deer, and occasional dolphins swimming in the channels around the island. About 90 percent of the national monument land area is classified as wetland, making it attractive to wading birds such as herons, egrets, and ibises. The North Pier Trail, Lighthouse Overlook Trail, and Historic Dike System are all fine walks for both historical significance and wildlife observation. The 0.75-mile Lighthouse Overlook Trail offers the best views of the historic Cockspur Island Lighthouse, set on a tiny islet just east of the main island. The 1856 lighthouse has survived war and storms for more than a century and a half.

Jimmy Carter National Historic Site

The rural environment that shaped America's 39th President

Jimmy Carter (1924–), who served as the United States' 39th President and in 2002 won the Nobel Peace Prize, grew up on a farm outside the small town of Plains, Georgia. His home lacked electricity until he was 14 years old. This rural background influenced Carter's life in many ways, including his respect for the land; his deep religious beliefs; his empathy for

the poor and oppressed; his business experience in farming; and, of course, his long marriage to Rosalynn Smith, valedictorian of the Plains High School class of 1944.

The Jimmy Carter National Historic Site encompasses Plains High School, now the park visitor center and museum, where exhibits include interpretation of the Carters'

lives in southwestern Georgia; the train depot, where displays focus on Jimmy Carter's state and presidential political campaigns and where his presidential victory celebration was held in 1976; and the Boyhood Farm, where Carter lived from the age of four until he left for college. The farm, 2 miles west of Plains, has been restored to its appearance during Carter's childhood; self-guided tours are available at all times, with ranger-guided tours offered on weekends.

At the visitor center, a 25-minute video includes interviews with family and Plains neighbors and friends to help review and interpret Carter's

accomplishments, both in the White House and after his Presidency, when he traveled the world to promote peace and human rights.

300 N. Bond St.
Plains, GA
229-824-4104
www.nps.gov/jica

AT A GLANCE

Southwestern Georgia, 90 miles southwest of Macon ▪ 72 acres ▪ Year-round ▪ Visiting Plains High School (visitor center), train depot (campaign memorabilia), boyhood farm home; watching interpretive video

Kennesaw Mountain National Battlefield Park
The scene of a key battle in the Atlanta Campaign

In late 1863 Union forces took control of Chattanooga, Tennessee, in one of the decisive moments of the Civil War (see p. 154). The next step for Maj. Gen. William T. Sherman was to advance toward Atlanta, Georgia, and capture that important Confederate city. Some of the bloodiest battles of Sherman's Atlanta Campaign took place on and around Kennesaw Mountain, northwest of the city, from June 19 through July 2, 1864.

Sherman's troops outnumbered those under the command of Confederate Gen. Joseph E. Johnston, 100,000 to 63,000. Southern forces had constructed trenches and other defensive fortifications, though, and they strongly resisted Union attempts to advance. During the entire Atlanta Campaign, leading to the eventual fall of the city, 67,000 soldiers were killed, wounded, or captured; more than 5,350 died in the fighting at Kennesaw Mountain.

Today's national battlefield park offers visitors an introductory film in the visitor center, a museum, and interpretive exhibits on a driving route and along 20 miles of hiking trails. Trenches and sites of gun emplacements are visible at sites such as Pigeon Hill and Cheatham Hill; at Kolb's Farm, visitors can view

the exterior of an 1836 log cabin. Private vehicles are allowed to drive up the mountain only on weekdays; visitors must take a park shuttle bus to the top on weekends and major holidays.

The Battle of Kennesaw Mountain was the bloodiest in the Atlanta Campaign.

Trails at Kennesaw Mountain National Battlefield Park are popular for general recreational use, including exercise and bird-watching, as well as for those interested in its Civil War history. Horseback riding is allowed on some of the trails, though bicycling is prohibited except on park roads.

900 Kennesaw Mountain Dr.
Kennesaw, GA
770-427-4686
www.nps.gov/kemo

AT A GLANCE

Northwestern Georgia, 20 miles northwest of Atlanta ▪ 2,923 acres ▪ Year-round ▪ Visiting museum, viewing interpretive film, taking auto tour route, hiking trails, wildlife-watching

Martin Luther King, Jr., National Historic Site

A *memorial to an influential leader of the civil rights movement*

With his commitment to nonviolent direct action, Dr. Martin Luther King, Jr., was the most prominent and influential leader of the American civil rights movement during the turbulent years of the 1960s. King's powerful and eloquent speeches inspired millions to continue their efforts to work toward social integration, voting rights, and economic power for all citizens of the United States. His lifework was ended by an assassin's bullet in Memphis in 1968, but his legacy lives on, even decades later.

The Martin Luther King, Jr., National Historic Site protects and interprets several locations connected with King's life and work. Located in Atlanta's Sweet Auburn neighborhood, the site is set within a larger preservation district that includes private houses and businesses, many of which are connected with King family history. Former Atlanta Mayor Maynard H. Jackson once described the Sweet Auburn area as having offered African Americans "the three Bs: bucks, ballots, and books."

Martin Luther King, Jr.'s tombstone

The historic site's visitor center provides orientation through advice from park rangers, varied exhibits, and audiovisual presentations on King and the American civil rights movement. The Ebenezer Baptist Church, built 1914–1922, is where King's father preached, where King was baptized and ordained as a minister, where King joined his father as co-pastor in 1960, where important meetings of civil rights leaders occurred, and where King's funeral was held after his assassination on April 4, 1968. (In another tragic event, King's mother, the church organist, was shot and killed here by a mentally disturbed man while playing for a service in June 1974.)

The King Center includes exhibits on King's life and work in Freedom Hall as well as his grave site, an eternal flame, and a reflecting pool that serves as a place for contemplation. The 1894 Fire Station #6, Atlanta's oldest surviving firehouse, contains displays on the desegregation of the city's fire department.

At 501 Auburn Avenue stands the King Birth Home, where Martin Luther King, Jr., was born in 1929 and where "M.L." (as he was sometimes called) lived until age 12. The house had been bought in 1909 by A. D. Williams, who was the father-in-law of Martin Luther King, Sr., as well as minister at Ebenezer Baptist Church previous to the father and son Kings. Furnished with items from the 1930s and '40s, the house can be visited only on ranger-led tours with a maximum of 15 participants. The popular tours fill on a first-come, first-served basis, and early arrival to secure a spot is highly recommended.

450 Auburn Ave., NE
Atlanta, GA
404-331-6922
www.nps.gov/malu

AT A GLANCE

Downtown Atlanta ▪ 34 acres ▪ Year-round ▪ Touring historic structures, viewing exhibits and films at visitor center

Ocmulgee National Monument

The ruins of important early Native American cultures

Located along the Ocmulgee River on the "fall line" (a strip of ancient ocean beach separating the Appalachian foothills from the coastal plain), the area within and surrounding Ocmulgee National Monument has seen a diverse succession of historic events dating back about 12,000 years. From Ice Age hunters of the Pleistocene epoch through European exploration, the Revolutionary War, the period of Indian "removal," and the Civil War, the park preserves traces of human culture and conflict.

A film at the striking art moderne Ocmulgee Visitor Center provides an introduction to the park, which encompasses ceremonial mounds (including the 50-foot-high Great Temple Mound, as well as other temple and funeral mounds), earth lodges, the site of a frontier-era trading post, and Civil War earthworks. More than 5 miles of trails meander through woods and fields to access sites. A museum in the visitor center houses artifacts from various periods of human occupancy of the area.

In addition to its historical importance, Ocmulgee is an excellent place for nature study and wildlife-watching. Riparian forest and wetlands along Walnut Creek and the Ocmulgee River are home to a notable diversity of plants and animals. The park's 800-foot-long boardwalk offers easy access to an emerging wetland environment.

Archaeological resources here have suffered significant damage over the years, from excavations for railroad beds to destruction of mounds for fill dirt and clay for brickmaking. In addition, I-16 cuts through the national monument. Nonetheless, it remains an important historical site and a rewarding place to visit. Special programs are offered at various times of year, such as the popular Ocmulgee Indian Celebration in September and ranger-led tours to the outlying Lamar Mounds and Village section of the park, which features a mound with an unusual spiral ramp to the top.

1207 Emery Hwy. (U.S. 80)
Macon, GA
478-752-8257
www.nps.gov/ocmu

AT A GLANCE

Central Georgia, on the eastern edge of Macon ▪ 702 acres ▪ Year-round ▪ Visiting archaeological sites, hiking, observing wildlife

Trail of Tears National Historic Trail

Tracing the tragic journey west for Cherokee forced from their homeland

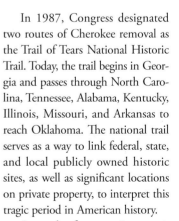

As the young United States grew in the early 19th century, conflicts increased between European-American settlers and the Native American tribes into whose traditional homelands the new nation was expanding. Dozens of treaties were signed between Indian tribes and the U.S. government, by which millions of acres of Indian land were given up. Nonetheless, pressure mounted to force Indians out of eastern North America entirely.

The discovery of gold in Georgia in 1828 exacerbated the conflict, as whites wanted access to Indian lands that might contain the precious metal.

In 1830, Congress passed the Indian Removal Act, which mandated the relocation of all eastern Indians to lands west of the Mississippi in Indian Territory (now Oklahoma). Over the next decade, the Choctaw, Seminole, Creek, Chickasaw, and Cherokee tribes were forced to travel westward, often under harsh conditions. Though many routes were followed, both on land and on rivers, the overall forced journey has come to be called the Trail of Tears for the hardship and death it brought. It is estimated that of the 15,000 Cherokee forced to move west, more than 1,000 died en route.

In 1987, Congress designated two routes of Cherokee removal as the Trail of Tears National Historic Trail. Today, the trail begins in Georgia and passes through North Carolina, Tennessee, Alabama, Kentucky, Illinois, Missouri, and Arkansas to reach Oklahoma. The national trail serves as a way to link federal, state, and local publicly owned historic sites, as well as significant locations on private property, to interpret this tragic period in American history.

A sample of current sites associated with the trail includes Chieftains Museum/Major Ridge Home in

Sunrise at Trail of Tears State Park, Missouri, a site where 11 groups of Cherokee crossed the Mississippi River

Rome, Georgia, once home to members of the noted Ridge family of Cherokee leaders; the Museum of the Cherokee Indian in Cherokee, North Carolina; The Hermitage, near Nashville, Tennessee, home of President Andrew Jackson, one of the foremost proponents of Indian removal; David Crockett State Park along Little Shoal Creek in Tennessee, with a museum depicting the life of the great frontiersman, who vehemently opposed the Indian Removal Act; Lake Dardanelle State Park at Russellville, Arkansas, beside the Arkansas River, the route followed by many Cherokee on their way west; and the Cherokee National Museum in Tahlequah, Oklahoma, with many exhibits and artifacts related to the Trail of Tears.

For a list of sites, maps, and other information, travelers should consult the trail website or contact the office of the National Trails Intermountain Region in Santa Fe, New Mexico. Roads, trails, and sites officially part of the national historic trail are marked with a blue-and-white triangular sign bearing the trail's logo.

National Trails Intermountain Region
Santa Fe, NM
505-988-6098
www.nps.gov/trte

AT A GLANCE The trail passes through nine states from Georgia to Oklahoma ▪ 5,045 miles of land and water routes ▪ Year-round ▪ Following auto routes, visiting historic sites, viewing exhibits in parks and museums

KENTUCKY

The Appalachian Mountains and Cumberland Plateau cover much of eastern Kentucky, where forests, rivers, and highlands invite exploration despite decades of logging and coal mining. In the central part of the state, a karst landscape overlays Mammoth Cave, the world's longest known cave system. In the north, the Bluegrass region's horse farms are renowned for producing Thoroughbreds. The Cumberland, Kentucky, Tennessee, Ohio, and Mississippi Rivers flow through or border the state. River commerce—by flatboat, steamboat, or barge—has long played a role in Kentucky's development; today recreational boating and fishing are popular on rivers and lakes.

Abraham Lincoln Birthplace National Historical Park
Interpreting Lincoln's boyhood in rural Kentucky

Abraham Lincoln, one of the United States' most influential and revered Presidents, was born in 1809 on a farm that his parents had bought a few months earlier in rural Kentucky. Two years later the family moved about 10 miles away to another farm, where they lived for five years until moving to Indiana.

Abraham Lincoln Birthplace National Historical Park encompasses both of these historic sites: the Birthplace Unit at Sinking Spring Farm (named for a spring that disappears into a sinkhole on the property) and the Boyhood Home Unit at Knob Creek Farm.

The Birthplace Unit centers on a symbolic one-room log cabin like the one in which Lincoln was born, which stands within the imposingly columned granite-and-marble Memorial Building. The visitor center offers a film called "Lincoln: The Kentucky Years" as well as exhibits that include a Lincoln family Bible and period furnishings and tools.

The Boyhood Home Unit was operated as a private tourist attraction for many years before being donated to the National Park Service and added to the historic site in 2001. A log cabin here, built to possibly resemble the Lincoln family home, was constructed in part with logs from a house owned by a neighbor and friend, and so provides a historic link to Abraham Lincoln's childhood. The Overlook Trail is a moderately strenuous hike through hardwood forest where Lincoln played as a child. Another walk passes alongside Knob Creek, where the young Lincoln almost drowned after falling from a log.

2995 Lincoln Farm Rd. Hodgenville, KY 270-358-3137 www.nps.gov/abli	**AT A GLANCE** Central Kentucky, 50 miles south of Louisville ▪ 344 acres ▪ Year-round, though winter weather can sometimes impede travel ▪ Visiting rebuilt cabins, hiking, picnicking

Cumberland Gap National Historical Park
A vital route through the Appalachian Mountains

As the population of eastern North America grew during the British colonial period of the 18th century, those in search of new lands to settle sought a route westward through the imposing barrier of the Appalachian Mountains. In 1750, a Virginian named Thomas Walker found a "gap" in the highlands, which he named for the Duke of Cumberland, son of King George II. Long used by Native Americans, Cumberland Gap became an important part of the famed Wilderness Road blazed by Daniel Boone. In the years between 1775 and 1820, as many as 300,000 people passed through the gap to start new lives in Kentucky and elsewhere in what was then the American West.

Fog rolls through the valleys below Pinnacle Overlook.

Cumberland Gap National Historical Park protects a beautiful area of the Appalachians at the meeting point of Kentucky, Virginia, and Tennessee. The park stretches along 20 mountaintop miles and varies from 1 to 4 miles in width. Forests, streams, mountains, and valleys look, in many places, much as they did when pioneers made their way westward on the primitive Wilderness Road. U.S. 25E once traversed the gap, but it was rerouted through a parallel tunnel in 1996, allowing the landscape to return to a more natural condition.

Exploring the Park

The park visitor center, near Middlesboro, Kentucky, offers two introductory films and a variety of exhibits on the natural and human history of the area. The nearby 4-mile Skyland Road winds up to Pinnacle Overlook (elevation 2,440 feet) for a grand panorama of the Cumberland Gap area.

Eighty-five miles of hiking trails offer the most intimate way to experience the park. Visitors can retrace original routes of Native Americans, pioneers, and Civil War soldiers and explore Civil War-era earthworks, a centuries-old iron furnace, and the infamous Indian Rock. Those visitors who are even more adventurous can (with a free permit) camp in backcountry sites as well as in the developed Wilderness Road campground. All campers should be aware that black bears are common in the park, and should take necessary precautions, especially regarding food storage. Horses and mountain bikes are allowed on some of the park trails.

Two special sites within the park offer additional opportunities for exploration. Rangers lead two-hour tours of Gap Cave, which features varied stalagmites and other formations along a moderately strenuous 1.5-mile trail (the cave is generally open spring through fall, but check with the park before visiting). Another guided tour visits the remote Hensley Settlement, occupied from 1903 to 1951. Homes, a blacksmith shop, a one-room schoolhouse, and a springhouse are among the historic buildings remaining atop Brush Mountain. The tour includes a bus ride from the park visitor center (*mid-May–Oct.*).

An area of more than 14,000 acres within the park is managed as wilderness, where hardwood and conifer forests, streams, and bogs are home to black bear, bobcat, white-tailed deer, wild turkey, and 16 species of salamander.

U.S. 25E
Middlesboro, KY
606-248-2817
www.nps.gov/cuga

AT A GLANCE Southeastern Kentucky, southwestern Virginia, and northeastern Tennessee, 125 miles south of Lexington, Kentucky ▪ 24,000 acres ▪ Year-round, though winter can bring occasional snowstorms ▪ Hiking, camping, backpacking, scenic driving, touring cave and historic settlement

Mammoth Cave National Park

The world's longest known cave

Without doubt one of the world's greatest natural wonders, Mammoth Cave lives up to its name in a variety of ways.

The word "mammoth" was first applied by awed visitors in the early 19th century to describe the size of the cave's underground chambers. Those who used the name had no way of knowing a distinction that geologists would later discover: They were in fact seeing the world's longest known cave. With more than 400 miles of passageways, it's so long that when the total lengths of the world's second and third largest caves are added together, Mammoth is still more than 100 miles longer. Geologists believe there could be hundreds more miles of passages yet to be found and explored.

"Mammoth" could apply, as well, to the national park's popularity; it hosts more than 640,000 visitors a year, about 400,000 of whom take an underground tour. Expansive, too, are the possibilities for exploring the park, with cave tours ranging from short, easy walks to belly-to-the-ground "wild cave" tours; and above-ground adventures such as hiking, camping, horseback riding, biking, canoeing, and kayaking, among others.

Natural History

The geologic conditions that created Mammoth Cave began 350 million years ago when sediments in a warm, shallow sea formed limestone, later overlaid by a cap of sandstone and shale. Water seeping down into and through the easily eroded limestone formed underground streams, which carved and dissolved rock to create caverns varying in size from narrow passageways to enormous rooms. The process endures today, hundreds of feet below the surface.

The water that continues to expand Mammoth Cave's passages

comes from rain that falls largely out-side the boundaries of the national park. Abundant sinkholes—typical of a karst landscape—allow more than pure rainwater into Mammoth Cave's underground rivers; any pol-lutants that occur in the drainage area can also wind up in the cave. Many species living below ground could be endangered by surface activities miles away from the park, and thus, biolo-gists and conservationists work with regional residents and businesses to try to protect the cave's entire watershed.

People & the Cave

Centuries before Europeans settled North America, early Indians were using torches to venture miles inside the cave to gather gypsum and other crystals—though no one knows for certain what the mineral was used for. The remains of their cane torches can still be found, preserved by the con-stant conditions of the cave. Then, 2,000 years ago, Native American uses of the cave changed, and studies sug-gest humans didn't frequent its deep passageways again until Europeans discovered it around 1798.

During the War of 1812, Mam-moth Cave's store of the mineral niter was intensively mined for making gun-powder. Later, the cave's fame as a tour-ist destination began to spread. Stephen Bishop, an enslaved African American belonging to the property owner, began guiding visitors to the cave in 1838. On his own initiative, he discov-ered many of the passages most com-monly toured today. Bishop famously described the cave as a "grand, gloomy and peculiar place," and modern visi-tors are sure to agree with at least the first and last adjectives.

In one of the cave's strangest episodes, a doctor bought the cave, believing that its atmosphere would cure consumption, now known as tuberculosis. He placed 16 patients

Snow and ice decorate the Historic Entrance to Mammoth Cave.

in the cave in the winter of 1842–43, turning parts of it into a sanitarium. (Tourism continued, though, with vis-itors passing the sickly patients along the passageways.) After the subjects of the experiment worsened and five died, the doctor called off his under-ground treatment and sent his patients back to the sunlight. The doctor's heirs owned the cave until the 1920s.

Private tourism continued into the 20th century, while public pres-sure grew to establish a national park at Mammoth Cave—a goal that was

fulfilled in 1941, 15 years after Con-gress passed the initial authorizing leg-islation. Since then, millions of people have visited the cave and come away marveling at its size and beauty.

Visiting the Park

Most people arrive first at the park headquarters area, location of the visitor center, which has exhibits and information on activities and ranger-led programs. Cave tours also begin here, with participants walking or taking buses to various entrances.

There is also a concessionaire-operated hotel in the area.

Exploring the Cave

Mammoth differs from many caves in that portions of it are quite dry. The sandstone cap prevents water from seeping directly downward in most places, which results in extensive dry passages lacking typical formations such as stalagmites and stalactites. In insolated areas, though, breaks in the overlying rock occur, and these formations and others such as draperies, helictites, and rim-stone dams are common. Some of Mammoth Cave's natural features have gained fame in keeping with their evocative names, including Fat Man's Misery (a narrow passageway), the Bottomless Pit (not really—it's 105 feet deep), the huge Rotunda and Mammoth Dome, the Snowball Room, the Ruins of Karnak, and Frozen Niagara.

The Frozen Niagara Tour ranks as the shortest and easiest way to see Mammoth Cave. A quarter-mile long, it's designed for those with limited mobility and people with young children. Nonetheless, it offers views of striking cave formations. The Discovery and Mammoth Passage Tours (both 0.75 mile long) require only moderate effort. For people able and willing to exert more effort, the strenuous Grand Avenue (4.5 hours) and Violet City Lantern (3 hours, conducted by lantern light in conditions such as those experienced by early cave explorers) tours will not disappoint.

The extremely strenuous Wild Cave Tour (up to 6.5 hours) is for those who want to climb cave walls, crawl through tight passages, and see parts of the cave inaccessible to most

visitors. Participants must be 16 years or older, and (to give an idea of the claustrophobia-inducing conditions) chest and hip measurements cannot exceed 42 inches.

For photographers, a special tour is offered in summer that visits notable formations such as Rainbow Dome, Crystal Lake, and the Frozen Niagara flowstone. Tripods, prohibited on other tours, are allowed on this 1.5-hour walk.

Talking with staff allows visitors to decide on the tour that matches their interests and available time. Some tours focus on history, others on geology, and some longer tours overlap trails followed by shorter tours. Tours also vary in availability by season. Check with the park for tour schedules and to reserve spots on tours (in summer and on spring and fall weekends). A fee is charged for all tours. The average temperature inside the cave is 54°F, so a sweater or jacket is recommended, as are long pants and sturdy walking shoes.

Aboveground Activities

There's much more to do at Mammoth Cave than go underground. More than 85 miles of hiking trails traverse the forests that cover much of the park's 82 square miles. In the front country, several short trails beckon hikers, including the 9-mile Mammoth Cave Railroad & Hike Trail. Most backcountry trails are open to horseback riders, too. Backcountry campsites (*free permit required*) offer the chance for solitude even in this popular park. Mammoth Cave has three developed campgrounds, including one for groups and horseback riders. Most trails are located in the backcountry

north of the Green River, which bisects the park. No bridges cross the river within the park and a ferry, the operation of which can be halted by water level and other conditions, operates at the center of the park.

One of the best ways to experience the park environment is from a canoe, kayak, or johnboat, paddling along the Green or Nolin River. Combined, these two rivers offer 31 miles of stream to explore. Though both rivers can flow rapidly at times, neither has white-water rapids, making them appropriate for people who are less than expert paddlers. Outfitters outside the park boundary can provide rental boats and arrange shuttles. With a free permit, camping is allowed on sandbars and in other areas of the river floodplain. Consult park officials for boating regulations; riverside campers should be aware that the streams can rise rapidly after heavy rain.

Mammoth's Flora & Fauna

Set in the transitional zone between many habitats, Mammoth Cave National Park supports an incredible number of species. Its forests are made up of oaks, hickories, American beeches, maples, tulip poplars, eastern red cedars, Virginia pines, and other tree species. Glades and patches of native grassland increase the natural diversity of the park. Wildlife includes white-tailed deer, bobcats, beavers, raccoon, mink, opossums, and birds such as wild turkeys, bobwhite quail, whippoor-wills, gray catbirds, and scarlet tanagers. More than 130 forms of life have been found living inside Mammoth Cave; some are only visitors, while others such as eyeless fish and crayfish are full-time residents.

1 Mammoth Cave Pkwy.
(Ky. 70/255)
Mammoth Cave, KY
270-758-2180
www.nps.gov/maca

AT A GLANCE

South-central Kentucky, 85 miles south of Louisville ▪ 52,830 acres
▪ Year-round ▪ Touring cave, hiking, camping, boating, fishing, horseback riding, bicycling

MISSISSIPPI

Music fans come to Mississippi to see the Tupelo boyhood home of Elvis Presley and to tour the delta area around Clarksdale, home to legendary African-American blues artists. Oxford attracts literary types in the footsteps of novelist William Faulkner. On the Mississippi River, Vicksburg was the site of one of the most important battles of the Civil War, and Natchez preserves antebellum mansions. Mississippi's hurricane-battered Gulf Coast serves up beaches and casinos; while the Natchez Trace Parkway, winding northward through rolling terrain from Natchez into Tennessee, offers greater solitude.

Brices Cross Roads National Battlefield Site

Where a Confederate Civil War victory helped the Union cause

In 1864, as Union Maj. Gen. William T. Sherman began his famed March to the Sea during the Civil War, he was dependent for supplies on the rail line between Nashville and Chattanooga, Tennessee. Sherman knew the line was vulnerable to attack by Confederate forces led by Maj. Gen. Nathan Bedford Forrest, moving through Alabama.

To keep Forrest away from the railroad, Sherman sent Federal troops commanded by Brig. Gen. Samuel D. Sturgis into northern Mississippi. As a result, Forrest was ordered to move his men to intercept Sturgis. A battle took place on June 10 at a site known as Brices Cross Roads, resulting in a victory for the southern side. Nonetheless, the outcome was positive for the greater Union cause: Sherman's supply line remained intact, and his capture of Atlanta and subsequent march through Georgia hastened the ultimate northern victory in the war.

The National Park Service controls only 1 acre at the site of this important battle, but a local battlefield commission owns 1,400 additional acres with the goal of preserving the site, and has constructed interpretive walking trails. Stop at the Mississippi's Last Stands Visitor and Interpretive Center (*www.finalstands.com, 662-365-3969; closed Mon.*) at the junction of Miss. 370 and U.S. 45 (*5 miles east of the battlefield*) for more information and to view exhibits. The Battle of Tupelo is also interpreted here. The NPS administers its acre from the visitor center of Natchez Trace Parkway (see p. 168) near Tupelo, Mississippi.

2680 Natchez Trace Pkwy.
Tupelo, MS
800-305-7417
www.nps.gov/brcr

AT A GLANCE

Northeastern Mississippi, 85 miles southeast of Memphis, Tennessee ▪ 1 acre (NPS); 1,400 (privately owned) ▪ Year-round ▪ Visiting Civil War battle site

Natchez National Historical Park

Two sides of life in the antebellum South

Thanks largely to cotton, Natchez, Mississippi, was once one of the wealthiest cities in the United States. Though its prosperity declined after the Civil War, this community on the Mississippi River still boasts many impressively restored houses from the antebellum period. Many privately owned homes can be visited on guided tours; two houses can be toured as part of Natchez National Historical Park, providing glimpses of the lives of two quite different families of the era.

Melrose, completed in the late 1840s, was the home of wealthy lawyer and plantation owner John McMurran and his family. The white-columned Greek Revival–style mansion had furnishings reflecting "fine taste and a full purse" and was considered one of the grandest houses in a region full of impressive estates. As many as 25 enslaved people cooked, cared for children, tended gardens, and performed other tasks for the McMurrans before the Civil War and emancipation.

Guided tours (*fee*) of Melrose are offered daily, during which park rangers discuss the lives of wealthy plantation owners and enslaved people and provide details of the house and its grounds and furnishings.

The other park property open to the public, the William Johnson House, was completed in 1841 in downtown Natchez. Johnson had been born into slavery but freed by his owner (who is presumed to have been his father). He went on to own three barbershops and a bathhouse in Natchez, and was prosperous enough to own slaves himself. Johnson and his family lived on the second floor of the structure he built on State Street, while the ground floor was rented as retail space.

Self-guided tours at the Johnson House focus on the lives of free African Americans in the pre–Civil War era. The upstairs living quarters area includes some family furnishings and personal items; a ranger is available to answer questions. Knowledge of William Johnson's life is greatly enhanced by the detailed diary he kept from 1835 until his death in 1851, offering a personal look into daily life in the city during that prosperous time.

1 Melrose Montebello Pkwy.
Natchez, MS
601-446-5790
www.nps.gov/natc

AT A GLANCE

Southwestern Mississippi, in the city of Natchez ▪ 80 acres ▪ Year-round, though summers are hot and humid ▪ Touring two restored antebellum homes

Natchez Trace National Scenic Trail
Following in the footsteps of Native Americans and pioneers

The 444-mile-long scenic drive called the Natchez Trace Parkway (see p. 168) runs from Natchez, Mississippi, to Nashville, Tennessee, following a corridor of trails once used by Native Americans, soldiers, and post riders as well as flatboatmen returning north after taking their boats to New Orleans. In the early 19th century, the Natchez Trace was one of the most important "highways" of the American frontier.

Natchez Trace National Scenic Trail allows hikers and horseback riders to recall the experience of travelers on the original Trace. Five unconnected segments of the trail have been

Original portions of the Natchez Trace still exist.

completed, totaling about 67 miles. The trail runs parallel to the parkway and never strays far from it. In several places, modern hikers and riders can travel the exact path of the old Trace, often along paths worn deeply into the earth by decades of boots and hooves. Hardwood and pine forests, creeks, and swamp wetlands make up some of the habitats traversed by the trail.

The five sections of the trail are Potkopinu (miles 17-20 of the parkway); the segment near the Rocky Springs campground in Mississippi (miles 52–60); just north of Jackson, Mississippi (miles 108–130); near Tupelo, Mississippi (miles 260–266); and near Leipers Fork, Tennessee (miles 408–427). Each segment has various access points with parking available.

The trail is administered in conjunction with the Natchez Trace Parkway, which has its visitor center at mile 266, just outside Tupelo.

Headquarters, Mile 266
2680 Natchez Trace Pkwy.
Tupelo, MS
800-305-7417
www.nps.gov/natt

AT A GLANCE

Four trail sections in Mississippi and one in Tennessee ▪ 67 miles of trail ▪ Year-round; spring and fall are most scenic ▪ Hiking, horseback riding

Natchez Trace Parkway

A beautiful modern drive that evolved from ancient paths

At the beginning of the 19th century, the road called the Natchez Trace served as part of the major thoroughfare between the United States' developing East and new settlements in the Southwest. Used by post riders, pioneers, military expeditions, and flatboatmen returning north from trips down the Ohio and Mississippi Rivers, the route followed Native American paths and game trails as it meandered from Natchez, Mississippi, to Nashville, Tennessee.

When the first steamboats appeared in 1812, travelers no longer needed to make this arduous and sometimes dangerous journey. The once busy Trace was almost abandoned, except for a brief period during the Civil War when some sections were used for troop movements. In the 1930s the idea arose to create a national motor road commemorating this venerable route.

Today the Natchez Trace Parkway stretches 444 miles, its length marked by mileposts numbered from south to north. Administered by the National Park Service, the parkway is dotted with campgrounds, picnic areas, exhibits, and trails. Much of the interpretive focus is on its human history, from the Native American tribes that roamed here to the first European explorers to later travelers and settlers. Natural history is well represented, too, on this scenic and relaxing drive, which prohibits commercial vehicles and limits vehicle speed to at most 50 miles an hour.

Natchez to Jackson

The southern end of the parkway, winding north from Natchez, passes through low hills of fine,

Traditional split-rail fences line portions of the Natchez Trace Parkway.

wind-deposited soil called loess, most visible at the Loess Bluff exhibit at mile 12, where the yellowish earth forms a high cliff. These hills, which were shaped by prevailing westerly winds during the last ice age, stretch from Louisiana all the way north to Tennessee, where they form the bluffs at Memphis.

You can walk along the original Natchez Trace in several places, including the Sunken Trace on the new Potkopinu segment of the trail which—at 3 miles long—is the longest stretch of sunken historic trace remaining. (Watch along the way for other sections of the old Trace, marked with arrowhead signs.)

At Owens Creek, mile 52, you'll find a section of the Natchez Trace National Scenic Trail (see p. 167), which comprises five disjunct units near the parkway and is administered by the same National Park Service office. Three other trail sections are found in Mississippi, with one in Tennessee.

Jackson to Tupelo

The Cypress Swamp exhibit, mile 122, features one of the prettiest roadside trails: A boardwalk crosses an old channel of the Pearl River, now shaded by tall water tupelos and bald cypresses. Water oaks, loblolly pines, red maples, American hornbeams, and red buckeyes line the oxbow's banks, and alligators sometimes appear in the backwaters of Ross Barnett Reservoir.

The parkway continues north into Mississippi's North Central Hills. At Jeff Busby campground, mile 193, a side road climbs to a lookout atop 603-foot Little Mountain, one of the highest points in this part of the state. A half-mile nature trail loops down into a rugged hollow where oak-leaf hydrangeas and young beeches grow under tall oaks.

At mile 233 the parkway enters a unit of the Tombigbee National Forest, where the Witch Dance trail network offers 15 miles of loop trails through mixed pine-hardwood forest, popular with hikers and horseback riders.

Exhibits at Chickasaw Village, on the outskirts of Tupelo at mile 261, interpret the history of the Native Americans who lived here. This spot ranks with the parkway's most interesting sites for natural history, too. Tree-clearing and prescribed burns are helping restore a parcel of blackland prairie, so named for its underlying dark soil, formed atop the limestone of an ancient seafloor. A trail here passes through an area of bottomland hardwoods.

Tupelo to the Tennessee State Line

At the visitor center (mile 266), you'll find exhibits, a bookstore, video programs, a short nature trail, and interpreters to answer your questions. At Dogwood Valley, mile 275, a very short trail loops into a hollow with many flowering dogwoods, including large mature specimens. Eight miles north, the short walk at Donivan Slough describes plants and shrubs that thrive in moist conditions. Look for bald cypresses, black willows, water tupelos, water and swamp chestnut oaks, and sweet leaf along the path. In early spring, an amazing concentration of trilliums brightens the understory.

At mile 286 you'll find the striking Pharr Mounds, considered the largest archaeological site in northern

Mississippi. Eight burial mounds more than 1,800 years old, the highest 18 feet tall, rise evocatively in a 90-acre clearing beside the road—a reminder that a complex civilization existed in these forests and prairies long before the first European explorers arrived.

There's a fine short walk at Rock Spring, at mile 330. (You're in Alabama now, along the 33-mile section of the parkway that cuts across the northwestern corner of the state.) The trail crosses Colbert Creek on stepping-stones and leads to a pretty spot where a year-round spring creates a small pond full of lush aquatic vegetation.

Tennessee State Line to Nashville

The route crosses into Tennessee, and at mile 376 you can leave the main parkway for a one-way road following the original Trace for 2.5 miles. This narrow ridgetop lane through the forest provides great views over valleys to the east, with pullouts to let you pause and enjoy the panoramas.

Over time, rustic inns—often called "stands"—sprang up along the Trace, providing food and shelter to travelers. Grinder's Inn, near today's mile 386, was the site of a tragic and still mysterious event: Meriwether Lewis, of the famed 1804–06 Lewis and Clark expedition, died at the inn

of two gunshot wounds one October night in 1809. Though it's probable that the troubled Lewis committed suicide, over nearly two centuries many have believed he met with foul play. A symbolically broken column rises over the explorer's grave in the Pioneer Cemetery here; only foundation stones remain of Grinder's Inn. A cabin built in period style houses interpretive exhibits on Lewis.

The cemetery and monument lie within the Meriwether Lewis Site, which also has one of three park-operated campgrounds located along the Natchez Trace Parkway. Here, too, you can walk an attractive section of the old Trace.

At mile 402 a tobacco barn exhibit illustrates the importance of this crop in the Tennessee uplands, an area too hilly and rocky for cotton. The parkway section through Tennessee is among the most natural-appearing along the entire drive, bordered by beautiful hillsides covered in oak and beech. At mile 426 is another spot where you can walk on the old Trace, following a woodland path under red and white oaks, sugar maples, beeches, and tulip magnolias. The walk here is popular with horseback riders, recalling the old Natchez Trace's use by both walkers and riders.

Visitor center, Mile 266
2680 Natchez Trace Pkwy.
Tupelo, MS
800-305-7417
www.nps.gov/natr

AT A GLANCE

Route stretches from Natchez, Mississippi, to Nashville, Tennessee
■ 444 miles; 52,000 acres ■ Year-round; spring and fall are most scenic
■ Scenic driving, camping, hiking, horseback riding

Tupelo National Battlefield

Where a Union victory aided Sherman's March to the Sea

After the Confederate victory at the 1864 Civil War Battle of Brices Cross Roads, in northeastern Mississippi, Union Maj. Gen. William T. Sherman knew that he had to keep

Confederate forces from disrupting his supply lines if he was to continue his march across Georgia. He ordered Maj. Gen. Andrew J. Smith to find and defeat the troops commanded

by Confederate Maj. Gen. Nathan Bedford Forrest, to keep Forrest from attacking the Union-controlled railroad in eastern Tennessee.

The opposing armies met in battle

July 14–15, 1864, in what became known as the Battle of Tupelo. Historians count the result as a victory for the North. Forrest was prevented from moving east to attack Sherman's supply lines, and he himself was wounded and kept out of action for three weeks.

Tupelo National Battlefield comprises a 1-acre site in Tupelo. The site is administered from the visitor center of Natchez Trace Parkway, at milepost 266 north of Tupelo. More information on the battle is available there and at the Mississippi's Last Stands Visitor and Interpretive Center (see p. 166).

Vicksburg National Military Park
A city under siege, and a turning point in the Civil War

With its commanding site atop bluffs overlooking the Mississippi River, the city of Vicksburg occupied a highly valued strategic position during the Civil War. President Abraham Lincoln famously called Vicksburg the "key" to the Confederate South, and stated that "the war can never be brought to a close until that key is in our pocket."

The Union campaign to take Vicksburg began in spring 1863 with Maj. Gen. Ulysses S. Grant leading his Army of the Tennessee toward the city. A series of battles allowed Union troops to approach the outskirts of Vicksburg, where geography played an important role in the coming clash. Bluffs formed of powderlike soil called loess allowed easy construction of trenches and other earthworks for defensive fortification—a vital factor in the Confederates' ability to resist two Union attacks in late May.

Following the failure of those direct assaults, Grant circled his forces around Vicksburg, cutting it off from communications and supplies. Southern troops and citizens of the city endured 47 days of artillery bombardment, increasing sickness, and decreasing food supplies before Confederate Gen. John C. Pemberton agreed to surrender terms on July 4.

Monument to the men of Illinois

When Lincoln received the news that the Union now controlled this Mississippi River port, he said, "The Father of Waters again goes unvexed to the sea." This, combined with the Union prevailing at Gettysburg, cinched an eventual victory for the North.

Exploring the Battlefield
Vicksburg National Military Park commemorates this turning point of the Civil War, encompassing a 16-mile auto-tour road winding through the battlefield *(fee)*, which is studded with 1,330 monuments and markers. States whose soldiers fought here have erected elaborate memorials across the park; plaques and tablets denote the sites of events of the fighting and siege. One such location is the site of the oak tree under which Grant and Pemberton met on July 3, 1863, to discuss terms of the Confederates' surrender.

Because many veterans of the actual battle helped mark locations of trenches and campaign actions, Vicksburg National Military Park ranks as one of the most accurately laid-out battlefield memorial sites in the nation. Visitors can stand where soldiers stood, and imagine the long, tense days of the siege, when opposing forces were so close they could call out to each other during lulls in the fighting.

Displayed in a museum within the park is the Union ironclad gunboat U.S.S. *Cairo*, sunk in the nearby Yazoo River in 1862. The first warship ever sunk by an electronically detonated mine, *Cairo* was located in 1956 and recovered in 1964. The museum is located near Vicksburg National Cemetery, where 17,000 Union troops are buried. About 5,000 Confederate graves are located in the "Soldiers' Rest" area of the Cedar Hill Cemetery outside the park.

Visitors can hire licensed professional guides for personalized tours of the battlefield. A long-standing tradition at Vicksburg, guides can provide details on all aspects of the Vicksburg Campaign, offering a rich historical experience beyond the facts presented on markers and interpretive exhibits. Tours last about two hours, and guides ride in the client's vehicle.

Information about guided tours *(reservations recommended)* and brochures, maps, and info about self-guided tours are available at the visitor center. The center offers a film on the Vicksburg Campaign and a model Confederate trench, a Union field officer's tent, and a cave representative of those used by Vicksburg citizens as protection from artillery shelling.

Some sites related to the Vicksburg Campaign are located outside the main area of the park, including Louisiana Circle, where Confederates placed cannon on a bluff beside the Mississippi River; and Grant's Canal, across the river in Louisiana, where the Union leader tried to bypass Vicksburg by digging a channel and diverting the Mississippi's flow.

3201 Clay St. Vicksburg, MS 601-636-0583 www.nps.gov/vick	**AT A GLANCE** West-central Mississippi, 45 miles west of Jackson ▪ 1,850 acres ▪ Year-round, though summers are hot and humid ▪ Following auto-tour road, hiking, visiting museum

NORTH CAROLINA

Stretching 500 miles east to west, from the Atlantic coast to the Appalachians, North Carolina contains three major geographic areas: the coastal plain, the Piedmont, and the mountains. The Piedmont is home to financial services and high-tech industries that have boosted a declining economy built on textile mills, furniture makers, and tobacco farms. The beaches and surf of the Outer Banks islands attract tourists; in 1903, the Wright brothers made the first successful powered airplane flight here. The Blue Ridge Parkway offers gateways to the Appalachians, where hiking, camping, and river running are the top recreational activities.

Blue Ridge Parkway
A historic highway through the scenic Appalachian Mountains

One of the most famous highways in the United States, the Blue Ridge Parkway winds 469 miles through the high country of the Blue Ridge and other mountains of the eastern Appalachians. With a top speed limit of 45 miles an hour, and with commercial vehicles and billboards banned, it offers motorists a chance to slow down and enjoy some of the finest scenery in the East. Short walking trails lead to even more panoramic views, and scattered along the parkway's length are a variety of historical and recreational attractions.

During the difficult economic times of the Great Depression, government officials conceived of the Blue Ridge Parkway as a way to create employment opportunities while constructing a recreational motor road linking two national parks: Great Smoky Mountains (see p. 187) on the Tennessee–North Carolina border and Shenandoah (see p. 103) in Virginia. At the time it was built, the parkway was the longest road ever planned as a single unit in the United States.

Though it was begun in 1935, the parkway was only about halfway built by World War II. The route wasn't fully finished until 1987, when the last section was completed around Grandfather Mountain in North Carolina. The Linn Cove Viaduct there, while visually striking, was designed primarily to cause as little damage to the environment as possible.

The Blue Ridge Parkway's northern terminus is located at Rockfish Gap, Virginia, where it meets Skyline Drive, a 105-mile scenic road through

Shenandoah National Park. As the parkway winds south, roadside mileposts ascend in number to the southern terminus near Cherokee, North Carolina. These mile markers make it easy for travelers to find trailheads, campgrounds, picnic areas, and other attractions along the way.

Parkway Attractions

Driving the parkway, seeing the scenery, is by far the biggest attraction: The roadway varies in elevation from 649 feet at the crossing of the James River in Virginia (mile 63) to 6,047 feet near Mount Pisgah in North Carolina (mile 431). A short side road at mile 356 leads to Mount Mitchell, at 6,684 feet, the highest point in the United States east of the Mississippi River.

The National Park Service's Blue Ridge Parkway Visitor Center in Asheville, North Carolina, at mile 384, offers exhibits on nature, cultural diversity, economic traditions, and

recreational opportunities. Nearby at mile 382 is the Folk Art Center, operated in partnership with the Southern Highland Craft Guild and featuring a craft shop, exhibition galleries of Appalachian arts and crafts, a library, and an auditorium. The North Carolina Minerals Museum, at mile 331 near Spruce Pine, North Carolina, focuses on regional geology and the economic role of North Carolina minerals. (All of the preceding attractions are open year-round; the park has other attractions open only spring through fall.)

Hiking trails along the parkway vary from easy strolls to longer treks. They afford the best way to experience the natural features of this part of the Appalachian Mountains. Habitats range from oak-pine forests in drier locations to hardwood cove forests typical of the moister Appalachian areas to spruce-fir forests at the highest elevations. The Blue Ridge Parkway is famed for its wildflowers,

and is also popular for bird-watching. Songbirds flood along the ridgetops in their northbound spring migration, while hawks and eagles soar along the mountains while heading south in fall.

Nine campgrounds are open seasonally along the parkway. Advance reservations can be made at three of them: Mount Pisgah, Price Park, and Linville Falls. During the summer, park rangers lead nature walks and give programs on a variety of topics at campgrounds and other developed areas.

Two lodges and three restaurants are located along the parkway; most are open late April through fall. The Peaks of Otter lodge and restaurant north of Roanoke, Virginia, is open all spring and summer and on weekends in the fall and winter.

Motorists pulling trailers or driving oversize vehicles should check the park's website in advance on maximum size for tunnels and for other restrictions along the parkway.

Visitor center
Mile 384, Blue Ridge Pkwy.
Asheville, NC
828-298-0398
www.nps.gov/blri

AT A GLANCE

Western North Carolina and western Virginia, from Rockfish Gap, Virginia, to Cherokee, North Carolina ▪ 469 miles, 83,000 acres ▪ Year-round ▪ Scenic driving, hiking, horseback riding, biking, visiting museums

---

Cape Hatteras National Seashore

An Outer Banks haven for recreation and nature study

Stretching for a length of 70 miles along North Carolina's Outer Banks, Cape Hatteras National Seashore, the United States' first national seashore, was established in 1953 to preserve parts of three unspoiled barrier islands. The islands—Bodie, Hatteras, and Ocracoke—form part of a chain of barrier islands that fringe the United States coastline from New York to

Cape Hatteras Lighthouse was moved inland in 1999.

Mexico. These long, narrow strips of land are built of sand carried seaward by rivers, then shaped by waves and wind.

Lighthouses

At Cape Hatteras, the southeastern point that forms the "elbow" of the Outer Banks, a lighthouse built in 1870 provides graphic proof of the islands' always changing nature. The beach that once stretched more than 1,500 feet east of the light gradually eroded until, by the 1990s, only about 100 feet remained. Without intervention, this historic structure inevitably would have toppled into the ocean. In 1999 the Cape Hatteras Lighthouse was placed on rollers and moved 2,900 feet inland. The black-and-white spiral-striped tower (at 208 feet, the tallest brick lighthouse in the country) still stands proudly as the focal point for visitors to the national seashore.

Visitors keen for a strenuous adventure can climb to the top of the lighthouse (*mid-April–Columbus Day, fee*). Its 248 steps are equivalent to walking the stairs of a 12-story building. The nearby keeper's quarters is now the Museum of the Sea, with exhibits on the human history and natural features of the Outer Banks. One of Cape Hatteras National Seashore's three visitor centers is adjacent to the museum and lighthouse.

Two other lighthouses are within the national seashore: the 1872 Bodie Island Light Station can be climbed (see park website for details), and the 1823 Ocracoke Light Station can be visited but not climbed. The Bodie lighthouse is one of a few that still retain their original first-order Fresnel lenses; the keeper's quarters has been restored and now serves as a ranger office and visitor center.

Ocracoke is the second oldest operating lighthouse in the nation. Nearby is the third of the park's visitor centers. Ocracoke Island can be reached only by free ferry from Hatteras Island or by toll ferries from Cedar Island or Swan Quarter on the North Carolina mainland.

Seashore Activities

The former U.S. Weather Bureau station in the village of Hatteras has been restored to its 1901 condition and operates as a welcome center by the Outer Banks Visitors Bureau through a partnership agreement with the National Park Service.

In the summer, Cape Hatteras is crowded with vacationers enjoying typical beach pastimes: swimming, sunbathing, picnicking, sightseeing, surfing, shell-collecting, and fishing.

For those interested in nature, other times of year provide greater opportunities for solitude and tranquil observation. Self-guiding nature trails include the Hammock Hills Nature Trail on Ocracoke Island and the Buxton Woods Nature Trail on Hatteras Island.

Many bird-watchers find autumn the best time on the Outer Banks. The great southbound migration of birds gets under way in September, bringing an array of species to beaches, thickets, and the marshes fronting Pamlico Sound, the shallow body of water between the islands and the mainland.

Contained within the national seashore, Pea Island National Wildlife Refuge has long been a favorite destination for birders. Thousands of waterfowl congregate in shallow wetlands here fall through spring, including tundra swans, Canada and snow geese, and two dozen or more species of ducks. Much of this variety can be easily seen from trails and from observation points a few miles south of Oregon Inlet near the refuge visitor center.

Five species of sea turtles can be found within Cape Hatteras National Seashore: leatherback, hawksbill (rare), Kemp's ridley, loggerhead, and green. Of these, loggerheads, greens, and sometimes leatherbacks nest on the beaches here, at the northern limits of their breeding range.

All along Cape Hatteras's beaches anglers cast into the surf for red drum, bluefish, flounder, speckled trout, croaker, and other species. There are several commercially operated fishing piers in the park.

AT A GLANCE

N.C. 12
south of Nags Head, NC
252-473-2111
www.nps.gov/caha

Eastern North Carolina, 85 miles south of Norfolk, Virginia ▪ 24,470 acres (5,880 acres in Pea Island National Wildlife Refuge) ▪ Year-round ▪ Swimming, hiking, camping, beachcombing, bird-watching, windsurfing, boating, fishing

Cape Lookout National Seashore
Undeveloped barrier islands that beckon adventurous travelers

Located across Ocracoke Inlet to the south of Cape Hatteras National Seashore (see opposite), Cape Lookout National Seashore offers much the same environment of beach and surf, only with greater solitude. Reached only by commercial ferries or private boats, this 56-mile-long section of the North Carolina Outer Banks comprises three main islands: North Core Banks, South Core Banks, and Shackleford Banks. The national seashore has two visitor centers, one located at Harkers Island and one within the town of Beaufort.

Except for small areas near the ferry landings, the islands are undeveloped, with no paved roads, concession stands, bathhouses, stores, or trash cans. Limited drinking water is available seasonally in a few spots. Camping is allowed almost anywhere, but campers must be prepared to be completely self-sufficient. Basic cabins are available for rental on North Core Banks and South Core Banks.

Many visitors enjoy seeing the 163-foot-high Cape Lookout Lighthouse, completed in 1859. The lighthouse is one of several areas where park rangers conduct regular programs in summer. (Diamond City, a community that once existed on the eastern end of Shackleford Banks, was named for the black-and-white diamond "day mark" design on the lighthouse.) Another popular activity involves viewing the wild horses that live on Shackleford Banks. Regular tours are also offered of historic Portsmouth Village, located at the northern tip of North Core Banks.

131 Charles St.
Harkers Island, NC
252-728-2250
www.nps.gov/calo

AT A GLANCE
Eastern North Carolina, 160 miles southeast of Raleigh ▪ 29,990 acres ▪ Spring through fall ▪ Swimming, beachcombing, primitive camping, touring historic village and lighthouse

Carl Sandburg Home National Historic Site
The final home of a quintessentially American writer

Born in Illinois to Swedish immigrant parents in 1878, Carl Sandburg dedicated himself to chronicling and celebrating American history and life. He won Pulitzer Prizes for both poetry and his biography of Abraham Lincoln; he also wrote children's books and novels and published a collection of folk songs.

In 1945 Sandburg and his wife, Paula (the sister of noted photographer Edward Steichen), bought a house and property in Flat Rock, North Carolina, primarily so she could have a place to raise her prizewinning dairy goats. Sandburg lived the final 22 years of his life here and died at his home in 1967 at the age of 89.

Visitors can take guided tours of the Sandburgs' house and see thousands of personal items collected by the poet and his family, including his very extensive library. The National Park Service maintains a small herd of goats, as well, and rangers demonstrate milking and cheesemaking seasonally.

The park includes more than 5 miles of trails winding through the woods, where Sandburg felt it was important "to go away by himself and experience loneliness; to sit on a rock in the forest and to ask himself, 'Who am I, and where have I been and where am I going?'" His wife and daughter were both bird-watchers and enjoyed taking binoculars and identifying birds on their walks.

In summer, live performances of some of Sandburg's works are presented at the park amphitheater.

81 Carl Sandburg Ln.
Flat Rock, NC
828-693-4178
www.nps.gov/carl

AT A GLANCE
Southwestern North Carolina, 25 miles southeast of Asheville ▪ 264 acres ▪ Year-round ▪ Touring Sandburg home and goat farm, hiking, bird-watching

Fort Raleigh National Historic Site
The home of the mysterious Lost Colony of Roanoke Island

The first two English attempts to colonize North America occurred in the late 16th century on Roanoke Island, in what is now North Carolina, both settlements organized by famed adventurer Sir Walter Raleigh. The first colony, in 1585, encountered difficulties and returned to England the following year. A second attempt in 1587 also met with immediate problems and quickly sent its leader, John White, back to England for help. Among the 117 colonists White left behind was his granddaughter, Virginia Dare, the first child of English parents born in the New World.

War with Spain delayed White's return to Roanoke Island for three years and, when he arrived in 1590, he found the settlement abandoned and the word "Croatoan" carved on a post at the site. The fate of the Lost Colony has been a mystery ever since.

Fort Raleigh National Historic Site protects the area of these early settlements. (The name Fort Raleigh was given by later residents to a raised earthwork, now partially restored.) The park visitor center offers exhibits as well as a 17-minute video presentation on the Roanoke colonies. Park rangers conduct interpretive programs in the summer. The park also features a short nature trail and a 1.25-mile hiking trail. (Roanoke Island became a destination for escaped slaves after the Union captured it from the Confederacy.)

Within the national historic site are two partner sites: The Elizabethan Gardens *(252-473-32334, www.eliza bethangardens.org)* comprises a variety of landscaped plantings, fountains, and statuary. A play entitled *The Lost Colony* has been performed since 1937 at the adjacent Waterside Theatre *(www.thelostcolony.org)*, dramatizing the story of the fate of the Roanoke Island settlement.

1500 Fort Raleigh Rd. (off U.S. 64/264) Manteo, NC 252-473-2111 www.nps.gov/fora	**AT A GLANCE** Eastern North Carolina, 90 miles south of Norfolk, Virginia ▪ 355 acres ▪ Year-round ▪ Touring site of early English colony; hiking

---

Guilford Courthouse National Military Park
A British "victory" that helped the cause of American independence

In 1778, British strategy in fighting its war against the American patriots changed direction. Troops were sent south with the aim of moving northward from Georgia and taking back control of the colonies. Years of give-and-take fighting led, in March 1781, to a decisive battle at the small North Carolina community of Guilford Courthouse.

British Gen. Lord Cornwallis led a force of 1,900 highly trained soldiers against 4,500 patriot soldiers commanded by Maj. Gen. Nathanael Greene. A brief but intense battle ended with Greene's army retreating. The patriots suffered only about 7 percent casualties, though, compared with 28 percent for the British. (When he learned of

Statue commemorating Gen. Nathanael Greene

the battle, British parliamentarian Charles James Fox said, "Another such victory would destroy the British Army.") Cornwallis marched his seriously weakened force north to Virginia, where seven months later he was forced to surrender to George Washington at Yorktown, granting victory to the cause of American independence.

Guilford Courthouse National Military Park lies now within the city of Greensboro, which was named for the American commander. The park visitor center features a 32-minute film called "Another Such Victory," an animated map depicting the tactics of the battle, and museum exhibits of original artifacts and weapons.

A battlefield tour road encompasses eight interpretive stops, including one at an equestrian statue of Nathanael Greene. The park also offers 2.5 miles of battlefield walking trails. Rangers and volunteers conduct a variety of living-history programs seasonally.

2332 New Garden Rd. Greensboro, NC 336-288-1776 www.nps.gov/guco	**AT A GLANCE** North-central North Carolina, in the city of Greensboro ▪ 220 acres ▪ Spring through fall ▪ Touring battlefield by vehicle, bicycle, or on foot

Moores Creek National Battlefield

A vital early patriot victory of the American Revolution

At the time of the American Revolution, by no means were all colonists in favor of war with England. The residents of North Carolina were divided in their loyalties, and British commanders relied on those loyal to the crown to help put down the patriot rebellion.

On February 27, 1776, a force of Loyalists tried to cross a bridge at "Widow Moore's Creek" on their way to meet British troops on the Atlantic coast. A patriot force was waiting, though, having dismantled the bridge planks and greased the support girders. When the first wave of Loyalists, armed with broadswords, crossed the bridge they were met by musket and artillery fire. Suffering devastating losses, they quickly retreated. In the aftermath, patriots soon captured Loyalist troops, weapons, and money. The victory inspired greater revolutionary spirit throughout the Colonies, discouraged Loyalist sentiment, and ended British hopes of a quick victory in the South.

Moores Creek National Battlefield visitor center offers interpretive exhibits, including a film, a battlefield map, period weapons, and a diorama depicting the clash at the bridge. Outside, a 0.7-mile history trail in part follows the original road used by Loyalist and patriot troops. Along the trail is a monument to the only patriot soldier to die in the battle. (The Loyalists suffered 30 to 40 casualties.) A 0.3-mile trail loops through a forested area of the park.

The battle is commemorated annually during the last full weekend in February, with living-history encampments, weapons demonstrations, colonial and military music, and a wreath-laying ceremony.

N.C. 210
Currie, NC
910-283-5591
www.nps.gov/mocr

AT A GLANCE Southeastern North Carolina, 20 miles northwest of Wilmington ▪ 88 acres ▪ Year-round ▪ Touring historic battlefield, hiking

Wright Brothers National Memorial

The site of the first powered flight

The Wright brothers made the first successful, sustained heavier-than-air flight at Kitty Hawk, on December 17, 1903.

In 1900 Wilbur and Orville Wright were two bicycle mechanics from Dayton, Ohio, who had a company manufacturing and repairing bikes, but they had been harboring ideas of trying to fly. They began looking for a place where they could experiment with their ideas for a flying machine, and they chose a site on North Carolina's Outer Banks where the winds were steady, there was little obstructing vegetation, tall dunes provided places from which to launch their glider, and sand promised soft landings. It was also a private place to conduct their early experiments in flight.

Three years later, the Wright brothers succeeded in the first sustained powered flights in a heavier-than-air machine, and an age-old dream of humankind was realized. The age of flight had begun.

Wright Brothers National Memorial commemorates this historic achievement. A 60-foot pylon stands atop Big Kill Devil Hill, from which the Wrights launched their gliders before moving on to powered airplanes. A monument indicates the location of the first takeoff spot and four markers show the landing locations. (The longest of the four flights on December 17, 1903, traveled 852 feet in 59 seconds.)

The park visitor center features interpretive exhibits and a functional reproduction of the 1903 *Flyer* (the original is in the Smithsonian National Air and Space Museum in Washington, D.C.) along with its original engine block, as well as a copy of the 1902 *Glider* and the Wrights' first wind tunnel.

Nearby stand reconstructions, based on photographs, of the hangar and living quarters used by the Wright brothers during their years at Kill Devil Hills.

Pilots are allowed to land small planes at the park on the 3,000-foot First Flight Airstrip.

1000 N. Croatan Hwy.
Kill Devil Hills, NC
252-473-2111
www.nps.gov/wrbr

AT A GLANCE

Northeastern North Carolina, 90 miles south of Norfolk, Virginia ▪ 431 acres ▪ Year-round ▪ Touring museum and exhibits, following paths of first flights

---

SOUTH CAROLINA

South Carolina grew wealthy during colonial and antebellum times. Most of the wealth came from rice and cotton fields, where enslaved African Americans toiled, a situation that led the state to push for secession as North-South tensions brought on the Civil War. The first shots were fired in Charleston Harbor in April 1861. Today Charleston ranks among America's most popular tourism destinations, having survived war, hurricanes, fires, and economic woes. Elsewhere on the coast, beach towns and upscale island resorts attract a range of visitors. Upcountry South Carolina rises through the Sandhills region to the Blue Ridge Mountains, bordered by a "textile belt" of mill towns.

Charles Pinckney National Historic Site
Memorial to a shaper of the United States Constitution

Charles Pinckney served in many influential positions in his long public life, though he is best known as a signatory to the United States Constitution in 1787, after having played an important role in the creation of the historic document. Pinckney's work in shaping the Constitution was recognized by his nickname: "Constitution Charlie."

Born into a wealthy family in South Carolina's Lowcountry in 1757, Pinckney fought in the Revolutionary War (he was captured by the British), and later was elected governor of South Carolina and to positions in both the U.S. Senate and the U.S. House of Representatives. President Thomas Jefferson appointed him ambassador to Spain, as well.

From his father, Pinckney inherited a 715-acre estate called Snee Farm outside Charleston, noted for having hosted George Washington for breakfast one morning in 1791. (Tradition says that Washington ate under an oak tree.) As many as 40 enslaved African Americans worked here at one time, in the household and in fields where rice, cotton, and other crops were grown. Pinckney was later forced to sell the farm to pay debts, and his original house there was demolished.

Today's Charles Pinckney National Historic Site occupies a 28-acre section of Snee Farm; the visitor center is located in a house built about 1828 (after Pinckney's death). Exhibits focus on Pinckney's career, 18th- and early 19th-century life in the Lowcountry, and the lives of enslaved people. In addition to the indoor interpretive displays, the site features a half-mile walking trail with exhibits on agriculture, archaeology, and the surrounding environment.

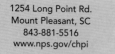

1254 Long Point Rd.
Mount Pleasant, SC
843-881-5516
www.nps.gov/chpi

AT A GLANCE

Eastern South Carolina, 6 miles northeast of Charleston ▪ 28 acres ▪ Year-round ▪ Exploring visitor center with historical exhibits, walking trail

Congaree National Park
Wilderness of magnificent old-growth bottomland forest

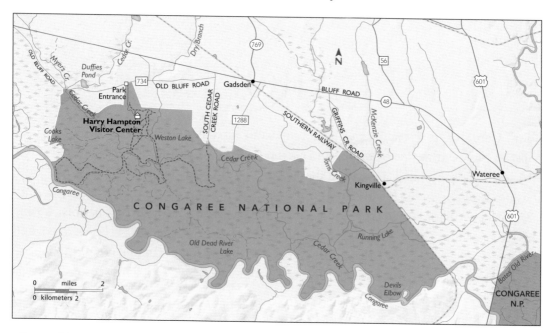

One of the wildest and most awe-inspiring forests in North America lies about a half hour from South Carolina's capital city of Columbia—and a good case could be made for extending that geographic distinction to "in the world."

Congaree National Park, a vast floodplain ecosystem, encompasses the largest remaining tract of southern old-growth bottomland forest still intact on this continent. The forest is among the tallest in the United States; broadly speaking, only the redwood forests on the West Coast are taller. Bald cypresses, oaks, hickories, tupelos, and loblolly pines are among the trees that grow to lofty heights here, forming a canopy that towers over hikers.

How was such a forest spared from the waves of logging that swept the South in the 19th and 20th centuries? How did it escape the "cut and run" timber companies that, in many cases, reduced virgin woods to nothing but stumps? The answer lies partly in the word "floodplain." Frequent flooding over a large area through much of the year made it difficult to float logs out of surrounding forest; this confined most logging to the vicinity of rivers, and that provided a kind of de facto protection for decades. When, in the late 1960s, timber companies again took a look at Congaree, conservationists pushed successfully for protection of this last great tract of southern bottomland forest.

Congress established Congaree Swamp National Monument in 1976, and in 2003 the area was redesignated Congaree National Park. "Swamp" was dropped from the name because Congaree is technically not a swamp: It is a floodplain.

The generally flat landscape within the park, lying along the north bank of the Congaree River, continues to flood ten times a year, on average. These events bring nutrients to the land in the form of silt that remains when floodwaters recede. While flooding sometimes makes access difficult or impossible, it's one of the factors contributing to the national park's diversity of both flora and fauna. (It's also the main reason that travelers should call the park before a visit to check on conditions.)

Hurricane Hugo struck this region in 1989, and the effects of the storm can still be seen in places within Congaree National Park. The park lost a national champion Shumard oak, for example, though it still is home to the nation's largest water hickory, loblolly pine, and swamp tupelo (a variety of black tupelo), as well as many state champion trees. Hugo opened up the forest canopy so that sunlight could reach the ground, stimulating new growth of shrubs and young trees—a natural process keeping the forest diverse and vigorous.

Exploring the Park

The Harry Hampton Visitor Center (named for a South Carolina newspaperman who advocated protection for the Congaree area as early as the 1950s) offers excellent exhibits on the local environment, and rangers are always available to answer questions and provide advice on ways to see the park appropriate to visitors' interests.

The most popular activity at Congaree is a walk on the wheelchair-accessible Boardwalk Loop Trail.

Together, elevated and low sections of the trail total 2.4 miles of easy walking. The elevated section of the loop sits 6 feet above the forest floor, allowing access even during times of flooding. This loop provides close looks at tall specimens of loblolly pine, tupelo, bald cypress, and various oak species. Numbered markers here correlate to an interpretive brochure available at the visitor center. The route passes Weston Lake, an oxbow lake, formed when a former bend of the Congaree River was isolated when the stream changed its course. There are many oxbow lakes within the park.

A few other trails thread through Congaree National Park. The 1.7-mile Bluff Trail, near the visitor center, offers a nice easy walk. The park's longest trails are the 10.4-mile River Trail and the 11.1 Kingsnake Trail; the former winds south to the Congaree River, where the forest shows the effects of decades-old logging, while the latter explores the remote eastern part of the park. Hikers should allow plenty of time to walk slowly and enjoy the sights and sounds of the forest, given an evocatively subtropical look by Spanish moss, dwarf palmetto, and the varied species of vines that drape trees.

Wildlife

Wildlife observation is best early and late in the day, but there's always something visible, or in the case of birdlife, audible. The *who-cooks-for-you?* call of the barred owl often rings out through the swamp, as does the scream of the red-shouldered hawk and the rapping hammer of seven woodpecker species. The huge pileated woodpecker is fairly common, and there are persistent rumors that the legendary ivory-billed woodpecker might still exist here. In spring and summer, brilliant yellow-gold prothonotary warblers sing *sweet, sweet, sweet.*

Lucky visitors may see river otters swimming in lakes or streams, or a bobcat stalking prey. Less welcome are the invasive feral hogs that are seen with some regularity and cause significant damage to the environment.

An eastern cottonmouth, the poisonous snake often called water moccasin, might be seen sunning itself on a log, and of course should be given a wide berth. More colorful is the Carolina anole, a lizard that can change hue from green to brown to better match whatever it is sitting on. Some people call this animal "chameleon," though it is not related to the true chameleons of the Old World.

Congaree's wetlands attract many waterfowl, including hooded mergansers.

A Watery Paradise

For many visitors, the best way to experience the watery world of Congaree is by canoe or kayak. A designated canoe trail follows Cedar Creek through the heart of the park, offering the chance to float silently under towering trees in a true wilderness experience. Wildlife is often more approachable from a canoe or kayak, so close views of white-tailed deer, river otters, or raccoon are possible.

Check with the park visitor center for information on guided canoe trips on Cedar Creek, offered throughout the year. The tours are free and canoes, life jackets, and paddles are provided to participants *(reservations are required)*. Park rangers identify wildlife and vegetation along the route, and they assure nobody gets lost, making these easy-paddling trips excellent for beginners.

Visitors who wish to paddle on their own must provide their own canoe. (The park does not rent canoes; rentals are available in Columbia.) Also, although the Cedar Creek canoe trail is marked, boaters are cautioned to watch closely for trail signs, especially on the upper parts of the creek, where losing the trail is more of a possibility. Canoeists should carry a compass, insect repellent, life jackets, a map, and water.

For experienced canoeists who are prepared to camp in the park's backcountry and can arrange a shuttle, the 20-mile trip from Cedar Creek Landing to the U.S. 601 bridge (outside the park) offers an enjoyable experience. Following Cedar Creek for 7 miles and the Congaree River for 13 miles, the route should be undertaken as an overnight trip. Visitors can get a free camping permit by self-registering at Longleaf Campground or calling the Harry Hampton Visitor Center.

Park rangers offer programs including "owl prowls" (dusk walks to hear and see owls and other nocturnal creatures) and guided tours to introduce visitors to the forest and wildlife of Congaree. Schedules are available at the visitor center for these and other programs.

Just a reminder, occasional flooding may close trails or make canoeing and kayaking difficult. It's wise to check with the park before visiting.

100 National Park Rd.
Hopkins, SC
803-776-4396
www.nps.gov/cong

AT A GLANCE

Central South Carolina, 20 miles southeast of Columbia ▪ 26,000 acres
▪ Year-round, though July and August are hot, humid, and buggy
▪ Hiking, canoeing, kayaking, backcountry camping, bird-watching

Cowpens National Battlefield
Where a one-hour battle changed the course of the Revolutionary War

More Revolutionary War battles and skirmishes were fought in South Carolina than in any other of the American Colonies. This is reflective of the fact that patriots and Tories (those who remained loyal to the King) both had strong support here and often lived side by side, making the Revolution a kind of civil war among colonists.

Throughout 1779–1780, the British won a series of victories in the South, giving them confidence that they would soon control the entire region—an important step in defeating the rebellious Americans. For this reason, British

Green River Road was the center line of the battle.

Lt. Col. Banastre Tarleton was full of confidence when he sent his travel-weary soldiers against a patriot force commanded by Gen. Daniel Morgan in early 1781.

On January 17, the two sides met at a site now called Cowpens (a local term for an open area where stock grazed). In what military historians now describe as a brilliant display of tactics, Morgan contained the initial charges by the more experienced British troops and eventually swept around both flanks of the foe (a move called double envelopment), leading to a clear victory for the patriots in a battle that lasted less than one hour.

The "devil of a whipping" (in Morgan's words) that the British suffered changed the momentum of the war and gave the patriots an enormous psychological boost. It also set in motion events that led to the British surrender at Yorktown, Virginia, in October 1781.

The Cowpens National Battlefield visitor center offers an 18-minute film depicting the events of the battle, as well as period artifacts and interpretive exhibits. Additional interpretive displays are found along the 3.8-mile auto-tour route and the 1.2-mile Battlefield Trail, which encompasses part of the historic Green River Road, the center line of the battle.

Each January the park hosts a celebration that includes events such as musket- and cannon-firings, guided walks, and cavalry demonstrations.

AT A GLANCE

4001 Chesnee Hwy. (S.C. 11)
Chesnee, SC
864-461-2828
www.nps.gov/cowp

North-central South Carolina, 15 miles northeast of Spartanburg ▪ 845 acres ▪ Year-round ▪ Following auto tour, hiking, horseback riding, picnicking

Fort Sumter National Monument

Where the Civil War began

In the early 19th century, Charleston, South Carolina, was a port city of great importance. It was home to plantation owners made wealthy by rice and cotton, crops grown and harvested by enslaved African Americans. It was also an urban center for the domestic slave trade.

As the United States moved slowly to restrict slavery in the middle decades of the century, South Carolina was among the southern states that felt the federal government was encroaching on the "reserved rights of the States," in effect threatening their traditional way of life. The election of Abraham Lincoln in 1860 further heightened North-South tensions, and in December, South Carolina become the first state to secede from the Union.

Of the four federal forts in the Charleston area (Castle Pinckney and Forts Johnson, Sumter, and Moultrie), only Moultrie, on nearby Sullivan's Island, had a Union military presence. Its commander, Maj. Robert Anderson, considered it indefensible in case of attack, and so moved his men to Fort Sumter on an island at the entrance of Charleston Harbor. Construction on Sumter had begun in the 1820s—on a sandbar that had been built up with 70,000 tons of

The interior of Fort Sumter

rock—but by late 1860 Sumter was only about 90 percent complete, with just a small part of its planned armament installed.

Confederate forces demanded the fort's surrender, but Anderson—despite his limited personnel and supplies—refused. As Union resupply ships approached, the Confederates made the decision to attack. At 4:30 a.m. on April 12, 1861, the explosion of a mortar shell gave the signal for the artillery bombardment of Fort Sumter, and the Civil War had begun.

Anderson surrendered the next afternoon, and Fort Sumter remained in Confederate hands until February 1865, when southern forces abandoned Charleston. By then Union bombardment had left Sumter in ruins.

After the Civil War, Fort Sumter was used as a lighthouse island, but during the Spanish-American War in 1898 a new concrete artillery battery was built. In 1947 historic Fort Sumter was deactivated, and today is administered by the National Park Service.

The monument's Fort Sumter Visitor Education Center near the Charleston waterfront presents an overview of the events leading up to the Civil War. Access to Fort Sumter is by ferry, operated by a private concessionaire *(800-789-3678, www.fortsumtertours.com, fee)*. The historical background of Charleston and Fort Sumter is narrated during the half-hour ride to the fort, where exhibits interpret the site's eventful past and park rangers stand ready to answer questions.

Fort Moultrie

Fort Moultrie is also a Park Service property. Fort Moultrie predates Fort Sumter. The brick fort seen today dates to 1809, but this is the third fort on Sullivan's Island, the first having been built of palmetto logs during the colonial period. Like Sumter, the Confederate-held Moultrie was mostly destroyed during the Civil War and reconstructed around 1898 for coastal defense. Today's park visitor center offers exhibits that tell the story of U.S. coastal defenses from 1776 to 1947, as well as a 20-minute orientation film. Like Sumter, Moultrie can be explored on a self-guided tour.

Visitor center
340 Concord St.
Charleston, SC
843-883-3123
www.nps.gov/fosu

AT A GLANCE

Southeastern South Carolina, in Charleston Harbor ▪ 230 acres (including Fort Moultrie) ▪ Year-round, though summers are hot and humid ▪ Touring historic forts, viewing exhibits at visitor centers

---

Historic Camden Revolutionary War Site
Outdoor museum recalling early days of South Carolina's oldest inland town

An affiliated area of the National Park Service, Historic Camden Revolutionary War Site recalls the history of a community important in the American colonial era and during the Revolutionary War.

The village got its start as part of a development plan ordered by King George II in 1730, and by 1768 was the most successful inland commercial center in South Carolina. Growth was due in part to Joseph Kershaw, a native of Yorkshire, England, who settled in the area and established a store for a Charleston mercantile firm.

After the British successfully took Charleston in May 1780—resulting in a lengthy occupation—military commander Lord Cornwallis moved troops to Camden and made it the major supply post for British activities in the southern region of the Colonies. The patriot forces suffered a terrible defeat nearby in August 1780, but after another clash in April 1781 the British were forced to evacuate Camden.

Visitors can take a self-guided tour of the 18th-century Camden town site and structures such as restored colonial-period houses and log cabins; reconstructed military fortifications; a blacksmith exhibit; and the reconstructed 1777 Joseph Kershaw house, which served as headquarters for Lord Cornwallis. The site also includes a 0.8-mile nature trail and the 3.5-mile Old Camden Trace walking trail. Guided tours *(fee)* are also available.

U.S. 521
Camden, SC
803-432-9841
www.historic-camden.net

AT A GLANCE

North-central South Carolina, 30 miles northeast of Columbia ▪ 107 acres ▪ Year-round ▪ Touring historic structures, hiking

---

Kings Mountain National Military Park
The battle that turned the tide for American independence

The situation for American patriots looked grim after the British captured Charleston, South Carolina, in May 1780. The citizens of the state were strongly divided between Loyalists to England and those who supported American independence. Part of British military strategy was to support Loyalists in their many clashes with patriots, in hopes of taking control of the South and then moving

A monument to the patriot victory

northward to crush the rebellion.

South Carolina was the site of more Revolutionary War battles than any other American Colony—most of them clashes involving not regular British troops but Loyalist and patriot factions of colonists, often pitting neighbor against neighbor and even brother against brother.

The battle that took place at Kings Mountain on October 7,

1780, saw patriot forces defeat Loyalists, providing some much needed good news to the independence struggle. The defeat was a serious setback to British Gen. Lord Charles Cornwallis's plans to move his forces northward. The Kings Mountain battle led directly to the resounding British defeat at Cowpens (see p. 180), and was part of the chain of events that resulted in the colonists' overall victory in October 1781. Thomas Jefferson called Kings Mountain "the turn of the tide of success."

The visitor center at Kings Mountain National Military Park offers a film on the battle and displays artifacts, including an original Ferguson rifle, one of very few in existence. Its inventor, British Maj. Patrick Ferguson, was killed and is buried at Kings Mountain. A 1.5-mile self-guided walking trail provides a close-up look at the battle site and passes by Ferguson's grave.

The national military park lies adjacent to 6,885-acre Kings Mountain State Park *(803-222-3209, www .southcarolinaparks.com)*, which offers camping, hiking, fishing, and a representation of a 19th-century farm.

2625 Park Rd.
Blacksburg, SC
864-936-7921
www.nps.gov/kimo

AT A GLANCE

North-central South Carolina, 35 miles southwest of Charlotte, North Carolina ▪ 3,945 acres ▪ Year-round ▪ Visiting museum; hiking, walking interpretive trail

Ninety Six National Historic Site

Where Revolutionary War patriots besieged a Loyalist town

A thriving town grew in western South Carolina in the early 18th century at a spot where frontier roads met. The spot was called Ninety Six because traders thought (mistakenly) that it was 96 miles from a Cherokee village called Keowee, in the hills to the west. Native Americans, Europeans, and enslaved African Americans lived here, and as the settlement grew from a simple trading post into a community, its buildings counted a courthouse, a jail, taverns, and shops, as well as houses.

In November 1775, in the earliest days of the Revolutionary War, a battle was fought here (the first land battle of the conflict south of New England), as pro- and anti-independence factions clashed. Ninety Six evolved into a stronghold of Loyalists: colonists who opposed separation from England and set themselves against independence-minded patriots.

British forces were determined to hold the town, and patriots were just as determined to capture it. In June 1781 Maj. Gen. Nathanael Greene led Continental Army troops against Ninety Six, where Loyalists had erected stockades and built an earthen stronghold now known as Star Fort. (Much of this work was performed by enslaved workers.) Patriot troops built trenches and a 30-foot tower from which they could fire into the fort. They also started digging a tunnel under the fort in which they hoped to set off explosives and blow an opening in the wall, but to no avail. Twenty-eight days into the siege, reports of advancing Loyalist reinforcements caused the patriots to withdraw, despite their superior numbers. Loyalists then burned and abandoned the fort.

At today's Ninety Six National Historic Site (2 miles south of the modern town of the same name), the visitor center features a short video on the site's history, exhibits, and period artifacts. A 1-mile interpretive walking trail leads past reconstructed trenches, the original Star Fort and a well dug by Loyalists, the old village site, a reconstructed stockade fort, and segments of the original pioneer roads dating from European settlement days. Near the visitor center, the Black Swan Tavern is an authentic log cabin set up in the style of an 18th-century tavern. A memorial honors James Birmingham, killed in the 1775 battle and the first South Carolinian to die in the patriot cause.

Historians credit the Ninety Six site with having one of the least altered landscapes of any Revolutionary War site. The park stages many special living-history events throughout the year, including musket- and cannon-firing, colonial-era music and games, and ranger-led tours. Check with the park for a schedule of events.

1103 S.C. 248
Ninety Six, SC
864-543-4068
www.nps.gov/nisi

AT A GLANCE

West-central South Carolina, 60 miles west of Columbia ▪ 1,022 acres ▪ Year-round ▪ Walking tour of historic town site and Revolutionary War fort

Overmountain Victory National Historic Trail

The path to victory in the Revolutionary War

A trail winds through Kings Mountain Military Park.

The situation looked bad for the patriot cause in 1780. The British had taken Charleston, South Carolina, and were continuing their strategy of pushing northward to defeat the rebellious colonists once and for all. In late September a group of patriots gathered near Abingdon, Virginia, and began marching southward to engage an army of Loyalists (anti-independence colonists still loyal to England). The patriot army, made up of private citizens, gathered strength as it crossed the Appalachians and entered South Carolina in early October.

On October 7 the patriot troops defeated a Loyalist force commanded by British Maj. Patrick Ferguson at Kings Mountain. The victory was an important boost to the cause of independence, and it set in motion events

that led to the British surrender at Yorktown, Virginia, in 1781.

Overmountain Victory National Historic Trail allows visitors to retrace the route of that patriot army, from southern Virginia across the Appalachians near Roan Mountain, Tennessee, into North Carolina to Kings Mountain. A partnership of the National Park Service with other governmental agencies and private landowners, the

trail has an officially designated length of around 330 miles, with about 87 miles currently available to the public for non-motorized use. Accessible segments include Hampton Creek Cove State Natural Area in Tennessee, Gillespie Gap on the Blue Ridge Parkway in North Carolina, and Kings Mountain National Military Park (see p. 182) in South Carolina. There is also a Commemorative Motor Route that follows the general path of the patriot march and in some spots follows the actual trail.

For maps, general advice, and information on the annual reenactment of the patriot journey, contact the headquarters of Overmountain Victory National Historic Trail.

The Overmountain Victory Trail Association *(www.ovta.org)* also provides information on the trail.

2635 Park Rd.
Blacksburg, SC
864-936-3477
www.nps.gov/ovvi

AT A GLANCE

Route through Virginia, Tennessee, North Carolina, and South Carolina ▪ 330 miles authorized ▪ Year-round, though winter weather can affect high-elevation travel ▪ Hiking, horseback riding, following auto-tour route

TENNESSEE

Three cities anchor Tennessee's three major geographic areas. Knoxville serves as a gateway to the Appalachian Mountains in the east. In the central area, Nashville is a legendary hub of country music, home to the famed Grand Ole Opry. Memphis, in the west, sits on bluffs overlooking the Mississippi River and its delta, home of blues music and cotton farms. Much of the state's outdoor recreation takes place in the east, not only at Great Smoky Mountains National Park but also on renowned white-water rivers and the Appalachian National Scenic Trail. Fishing is popular on the natural streams as well as on the expansive reservoirs created by hydroelectric dams.

Andrew Johnson National Historic Site

The homes, business, and burial place of a controversial President

Rising from humble beginnings to become President on the death of Abraham Lincoln, Andrew Johnson remains a controversial public figure. He never went to school yet became a wealthy businessman. He owned slaves yet opposed the secession of the Confederate states and, as Civil War military governor of Tennessee, emancipated that state's slaves. He was impeached, tried, and acquitted on charges of violating the Tenure of Office Act. (He had vetoed the act as unconstitutional, a position later affirmed by the Supreme Court.) Historians still argue about his influence on Reconstruction and civil rights.

Andrew Johnson National Historic Site, in Greeneville, the eastern Tennessee town where Johnson lived when he was boy and where he maintained homes the rest of his life, lets visitors consider Johnson's legacy as they learn about his life. The site encompasses the tailor shop that gave Johnson his start in business, two houses in which he and his family lived, and the cemetery in which he and members of his family are buried. The visitor center offers an orientation film and museum displays.

Guided tours are offered several times a day to the Johnson Homestead, which the family occupied for 24 years, both before and after the Civil War and Johnson's Presidency. During the war it was occupied by both Union and Confederate troops and was used in part as a hospital. The Johnson family renovated it after the war, and today it contains many original family furnishings.

101 N. College
Greeneville, TN
423-638-3551
www.nps.gov/anjo

AT A GLANCE Eastern Tennessee, 55 miles east of Knoxville ▪ 16 acres ▪ Year-round; winter conditions can sometimes affect travel ▪ Touring visitor center, homes, tailor shop, national cemetery

---

Big South Fork National River and Recreation Area

Pristine streams and beautiful gorges within the Cumberland Plateau

Crossing the Tennessee-Kentucky state line within the Cumberland Plateau, west of the Appalachian Mountains, is a 90-mile-long gorge cut by the Big South Fork of the Cumberland River. In the 1960s a dam was considered for this stream, a development that would have turned much of the gorge into a deep artificial reservoir. Instead, the federal government in 1974 designated nearly 200 square miles surrounding the river as Big South Fork National River and Recreation Area, protecting the area's free-flowing streams, tall bluffs, forests, and wildlife for public enjoyment.

With more than 400 miles of hiking trails and extensive horse and mountain-bike trails, Big South Fork

South Arch of the Twin Arches

offers near-endless opportunities for getting away from roads and developed areas to see the wilder parts of the area. Big South Fork River and its tributaries (Clear Fork, North White Oak, and New Rivers) are renowned among white-water enthusiasts, with rapids rated up to Class IV, providing an additional array of outdoor opportunities.

Park Attractions & Activities

Big South Fork has six visitor centers, and a stop at one of them is recommended for first-time visitors. In Tennessee, the Bandy Creek Visitor Center is located off Tenn. 297 between Oneida and Jamestown. Bandy Creek is also the site of one of the park's four developed campgrounds with water and electric hookups. The Stearns Visitor Center *(open summer–fall)* is located in Kentucky off Ky. 92. It is near the departure point for Big South Fork Scenic Railway *(800-462-5664, www.bsfsry.com, fee)*, a concessionaire-operated attraction that makes a stop at the Blue Heron community, a coal-mining town begun in 1937 and abandoned in 1962. Displays here recall life in an Appalachian mining town in the 1940s and '50s. Blue Heron Campground is nearby.

Not far from Blue Heron is Devil's Jump Overlook, one of several spots where visitors can stand on the edge of the Big South River gorge and enjoy the view. (The Devil's Jump rapids in the river below are among the park's most hazardous for boaters.) Another good vista point is East Rim Overlook, off Tenn. 297 east of Bandy Creek. Leatherwood Ford, where Tenn. 297 crosses Big South Fork River, is an easily accessible spot

from which to explore the river via an old low-water bridge and riverside boardwalks and trails.

Because of the easily erodible nature of the sandstone that makes up much of the landscape of Big Fork, the area encompasses not just the high bluffs of the Big South Fork gorge but also a significant number of rock arches—perhaps the largest concentration of natural rock arches in the eastern United States, totaling in the hundreds. Some of the arches are easily accessible, such as Wagon Arch, along Ky. 742 on the road to Blue Heron. Twin Arches, the largest double arches in Big South Fork and possibly in the East, are reached at the end of a 0.7-mile walk from the Twin Arches trailhead in the western part of the park, off Tenn. 154. Park rangers can provide information on finding many other arches.

Near Twin Arches is the concessionaire-operated Charit Creek Lodge *(865-696-5611, www.ccl-bsf .com)*, a remote spot accessible only by foot, mountain bike, or horse. Charit Creek offers lodging (without electricity; cabins have kerosene lanterns and fireplaces), meals, and horse stables.

Hikers should be aware that hunting is allowed in the area; the park recommends that hikers wear orange or other brightly colored clothing during hunting seasons. Hunting is not allowed near campgrounds and other developed areas.

Two popular special events, the Spring Planting Festival *(last Saturday in April)* and the fall "Haunting in the Hills" Storytelling Festival *(third Saturday in Sept.)*, offer a variety of free activities including traditional music and crafts demonstrations.

| Big South Fork Visitor Center 4564 Leatherwood Rd. Oneida, TN 423-569-9778 www.nps.gov/biso | AT A GLANCE | Northeastern Tennessee and southeastern Kentucky, 125 miles northeast of Nashville ▪ 125,000 acres ▪ Year-round; occasional winter snow can affect travel ▪ Hiking, canoeing, kayaking, horseback riding, camping, mountain biking |

Fort Donelson National Battlefield
Site of the first significant Union victory of the Civil War

At the beginning of the Civil War, both Union and Confederate forces understood the importance of the Tennessee and Cumberland Rivers. If the North controlled these waterways, it could use them to strike into the heart of the Confederacy, perhaps even capturing the important city of Nashville. The Confederates built Fort Henry on the Tennessee and Fort Donelson on the Cumberland to try to prevent a Union invasion of Tennessee.

Brig. Gen. Ulysses S. Grant, assisted by Flag Officer Andrew H. Foote, captured Fort Henry with little

difficulty on February 6, 1862. (Its site is now beneath the waters of Kentucky Lake.) The two then moved eastward to attack Fort Donelson. Here the Union forces met far greater resistance, in part because Donelson was better situated for defense than was Henry. The southerners, outnumbered and aware that even more Union troops were on the way, decided to try to escape to the southeast. They fought their way through the Union lines and probably could have fled successfully, but confusion and indecision among commanders led to an order to withdraw behind their previous battle lines.

Realizing his position was hopeless, Confederate Brig. Gen. Simon Buckner (an acquaintance of Grant's from their West Point days) asked for terms of surrender. Grant's reply: "No terms except an unconditional and immediate surrender can be accepted."

More than 12,000 Confederate troops were taken prisoner on February 16, and news of the Union triumph caused widespread celebration in northern states. It was the first significant Union victory, and after taking control of the Tennessee and Cumberland Rivers the North moved quickly to capitalize on its momentum. The city of Nashville was abandoned to Union forces later in February 1862, and became a strategic supply station for Union Army activities.

At the park visitor center, the orientation film "Fort Donelson: Gateway to the Confederate Heartland" provides background on the battle fought here, as well as on the events of the fight and its aftermath. A 6-mile self-guided driving tour leads to important battlefield sites, including the remains of the earthen-walled fort, the batteries from which Confederate cannon fired on Union gunboats, the spot where Union soldiers camped the night before the fort's surrender, and the road along which the Confederate forces almost escaped. The route continues into the small town of Dover to the 1851–53 Dover Hotel, where Grant and Buckner worked out details of the southern surrender. (The exterior of the hotel can be viewed anytime; an exhibit room on the first floor is open when the visitor center is.) Fort Donelson National Battlefield also encompasses Fort Donelson National Cemetery, where 670 Union soldiers number among those interred.

Later in the Civil War, Fort Donelson and nearby Fort Heiman, across the state line in Kentucky, were among the havens used by enslaved African Americans to escape to freedom in the North via the famed Underground Railroad.

U.S. 79
Dover, TN
931-232-5706
www.nps.gov/fodo

AT A GLANCE

North-central Tennessee, 80 miles northwest of Nashville ▪ 1,063 acres ▪ Year-round; wintry weather can occasionally affect driving ▪ Taking battlefield self-guided auto tour, hiking

Great Smoky Mountains National Park
Ancient mountains hosting unparalleled biodiversity

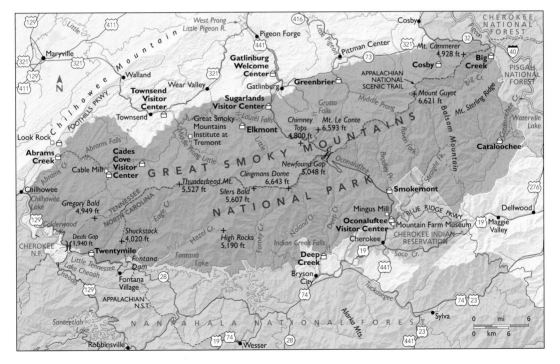

Many of the great national parks of the West have an iconic geographic feature: Carlsbad Caverns, its vast cave; Grand Canyon, its spectacular gorge; and Bryce Canyon, its colorful rock formations, to name a few. The East's Great Smoky Mountains National Park, while less immediately eye-catching, nonetheless has its own iconic feature: a biodiversity of global significance. Its 814 square miles offer nearly unlimited opportunities for exploration and discovery.

An Amazing Biodiversity

No other place of equal size on Earth outside the tropics can match the biodiversity of Great Smoky Mountains, which spans the southern Appalachians along the border between Tennessee and North Carolina. An ambitious project called the All Taxa Biodiversity Inventory aims to identify every plant and animal found in the park; so far more than 12,000 species are known to occur, and estimates of the potential total range from 50,000 to 100,000.

The factors behind the park's unparalleled diversity of flora and fauna are complex, and begin more than 200 million years ago—the estimated age of the Great Smoky Mountains, making them among the oldest mountains on Earth. The glaciers that spread over North America in recent ice ages, ending about 15,000 years ago, didn't reach as far south as the Smokies, although the regional climate at that time created alpine conditions on the peaks. These highlands have been relatively untouched by major geologic forces for more than a million years, giving life-forms time to diversify and sparing them certain conditions leading to local extirpation.

Elevations in the park range from 875 to 6,643 feet, providing a wide span of ecological niches and creating a broad array of habitats for species from mosses and trees to invertebrates, birds, and mammals. To drive or hike from the park's low valleys to its highest peaks is like traveling northward from Georgia to Canada. This means the park hosts eastern cottonwoods and Fraser firs, hooded warblers and golden-crowned kinglets, wisterias and catawba rhododendrons.

Some areas of the park receive 85 inches of rain a year, another factor adding to plant diversity. More than 100 species of trees grow in Great Smoky Mountains National Park (more than in any other national park); the number of species of flowering plants totals around 1,600. The United Nations has designated the park as an international biosphere reserve in recognition of its global importance as a center of biodiversity.

The focus on the park's biodiversity is well merited, but don't think that means that Great Smoky Mountains National Park falls short in terms of scenery. On the contrary, its mountain vistas, waterfalls, rocky streams, and cove forests of towering trees make it a place of striking beauty. The "smoke" that gave this part of the Appalachian Mountains its name—fog that commonly floats over the Smokies and originates from rain and evaporation from trees—helps create landscape views as picturesque and evocative as any in our park system.

Visiting the Park

The park's beauty, as well as its proximity to major population centers, is one of the reasons it's the country's most visited national park, with between eight and ten million people spending time here annually. This can lead to traffic problems that lessen the enjoyment of a trip. To avoid crowds, follow the park's tips, including visiting in the off-season (avoiding mid-June to mid-August and October), arriving early in the morning (crowding is at its worst between 10 a.m. and 6 p.m.), and visiting less popular areas of the park (Cades Cove and the main park road through Newfound Gap see the most traffic).

U.S. 441 provides access to the park's two main visitor centers: Sugarlands, 2 miles south of Gatlinburg,

Great Smoky Mountains National Park is 95 percent forested, sheltering more than a hundred species of trees.

Tennessee; and Oconaluftee, 2 miles north of Cherokee, North Carolina. Another visitor center is found along the loop road through the historic Cades Cove area, and others are located in the Tennessee towns of Gatlinburg, Sevierville, and Townsend. The park newspaper is available at all visitor centers, as is advice on road and trail conditions and other hints for a more pleasant and rewarding journey into the park.

The highway route between Gatlinburg and Cherokee is called Newfound Gap Road, a winding, highly scenic path that climbs to a high point of 5,048 feet at the gap (a local name for a mountain pass). Observation points and trailheads along the way provide far-reaching panoramas of Appalachian Mountains terrain. Other popular routes for auto tours include Roaring Fork (accessed from Gatlinburg) and Cades Cove.

Hiking Opportunities

The best way to avoid the crowds is to get away from the vicinity of roads—especially by hiking along some of the more than 800 miles of trails in the park. Whether a short, quiet stroll or an overnight long-distance hike, a walk through the forest offers a chance to experience the Great Smoky Mountains environment up close, see wildlife and wildflowers, hear birdsong, and smell the pungent scent of conifers.

Probably the most popular destinations for hikers are the park's scores of waterfalls, ranging from lovely and highly visited sites such as Laurel Falls, Mingo Falls, and Ramsey Cascades to countless unnamed cascades along the park's more than 2,100 miles of creeks and rivers.

Another of the park's best known trails leads to Clingmans Dome, at 6,643 feet the highest spot in the park

and the third highest mountain east of the Mississippi River. From Newfound Gap along the main road through the center of the park, a 7-mile road *(closed in winter)* winds westward to a parking area, from which a steep, half-mile foot trail leads through spruce-fir forest to an observation platform atop Clingmans Dome. Visibility here ranges from 100 miles on an exceptionally clear day down to mere yards when clouds close in.

The famed Appalachian National Scenic Trail passes along the ridgetops at Clingmans Dome and through Newfound Gap on its 2,185-mile path from Georgia to Maine. Following the trail northeast from the gap to the scenic spot called Charlies Bunion is another very popular hike, an out-and-back trip of 8.8 miles.

Horseback riding is allowed on most of the park's trails. Except in winter, concessionaires in the park offer guided trail rides, hayrides, and carriage rides; check with park rangers for contact information. The park also has five drive-in horse camps, which provide ready access to backcountry trails for those with their own horses.

A Bounty of Wildlife

Opportunities for wildlife observation abound within Great Smoky Mountains National Park. People willing to be out at dawn or dusk and to watch quietly and patiently at spots away from crowds will be especially fortunate. The most charismatic and popular animal is no doubt the black bear; around 1,500 individuals live in the park, so campers and hikers should understand precautions needed in bear country. Elk have been reintroduced into the park, and a self-sustaining herd numbers around 140. Other mammals that might be encountered along roads and trails are woodchucks,

raccoon, gray and red squirrels, eastern chipmunks, and red and gray foxes.

Bird-watchers find the park an extremely rewarding destination, as it offers the chance to see species usually associated with locations far to the north. The saw-whet owl, common raven, blue-headed vireo, winter wren, red-breasted nuthatch, veery, Canada and blackburnian warbler, and dark-eyed junco are just a few of the birds that extend their ranges southward along the tops of the Appalachians.

Far less conspicuous but no less interesting are the park's 30 species of salamanders. In terms of sheer numbers of individuals, salamanders are the most abundant animals in the park, aside from invertebrates such as insects and spiders. The southern Appalachian Mountains are noted for the diversity of salamander species, placing this region among the most important on Earth for this fascinating group of amphibians. Most park species are lungless salamanders, which breathe through the walls of blood vessels in their skin and linings of their mouths and throats.

Human History

The human history of Great Smoky Mountains National Park is worth exploring just as much as is the natural history. The most popular place to enjoy the park's historic past is the beautiful valley called Cades Cove, where more than 680 people lived before the Civil War. An 11-mile one-way loop road passes structures from the late 19th and early 20th centuries—several barns, three churches, and various log houses and outbuildings. At the Cades Cove Visitor Center, travelers can see a gristmill *(operating spring–fall),* a blacksmith shop, and other historic buildings. The park sometimes presents special

FOLLOWING PAGES: *White-tailed deer are commonly seen in Cades Cove, a lush, rural valley ringed by mountains.*

programs interpreting pioneer life; check with park rangers for the schedule.

At the Oconaluftee Visitor Center in North Carolina, the park has restored a number of buildings to depict rural life in the Appalachians. A farmhouse (built of logs from the now decimated chestnut tree), a barn, an apple house, a springhouse, and a blacksmith shop—most from the late 19th century—were moved here from various locations. As at Cades Cove, interpreters demonstrate pioneer life-styles at select times.

The most populous community within what is now the national park was located in Cataloochee Valley, now an isolated interpretive area in the eastern part of the park. Visitors willing to drive twisting gravel (but well-graded) roads to this pastoral valley will find a school, churches, cemeteries, a barn, and several houses. A self-guiding auto-tour brochure provides histories of the buildings. Cataloochee Valley is also the park area where elk are most likely to be found. Here, as elsewhere, feeding or otherwise approaching wildlife is prohibited. The easiest way to get to this site is to take exit 20 from I-40 in North Carolina and continue to Cataloochee for 11 miles on a partly gravel route.

Another of the park's "off the beaten path" driving routes explores the Balsam Mountain area along a 28-mile, partially unpaved road that begins by turning off the Blue Ridge Parkway 11 miles east of Cherokee, North Carolina. A paved road leads to a campground and picnic area (with many viewpoints along the way), then loops back to Cherokee along a road that is gravel for the first 18 miles.

Staying in the Park

In addition to developed and back-country campsites, the park is also home to Le Conte Lodge *(865-429-5704, www.lecontelodge.com)*, located on the 6,593-foot summit of Mount Le Conte and accessible only by hiking. The shortest trail to it is Alum Cave Trail, a steep 5-mile climb that has its trailhead on Newfound Gap Road.

Sugarlands Visitor Center
107 Park Headquarters Rd.
southwest of Gatlinburg, TN
865-436-1200
www.nps.gov/grsm

AT A GLANCE

Eastern Tennessee and western North Carolina, 30 miles southeast of Knoxville ▪ 521,455 acres ▪ Year-round; winter storms can affect travel in the mountains, where weather can be very different from that in lower parts of the park ▪ Hiking, camping, scenic driving, horseback riding, wildlife-watching

Obed Wild & Scenic River
A wild-river corridor within the Cumberland Plateau

Preserving segments of four free-flowing streams—Obed River, Emory River, Clear Creek, and Daddys Creek—Obed Wild and Scenic River provides a variety of ways to experience this scenic region of the Cumberland Plateau.

The Obed area is popular with white-water canoeists, kayakers, and rafters, who challenge Class II–IV rapids. The park provides six main put-in/take-out sites. There are no commercial outfitters in the immediate vicinity, so paddlers need to bring their own boats. The deep, beautiful gorges through which the streams in part flow can make access difficult in case of emergency, so paddling experience is a must—as is consulting with park staff on conditions and dangers. Boating is dependent on rainfall, and in an average year, the best months are between December and May; summer water levels are usually too low.

A premier sport-climbing destination in the Southeast, Obed's over-hanging sandstone cliffs boast more than 300 bolted routes ranging in difficulty from 5.7 to 5.13.

The 1.9-mile (one-way) Point Trail begins at an overlook of Clear Creek and runs to the confluence of the creek and the Obed River, passing Lilly Arch, a distinctive sandstone geologic feature. A 14-mile section of the Cumberland Trail runs from the Nemo access area to the rock formation called Devil's Breakfast Table, alongside Daddys Creek. A primitive campground adjacent to the Nemo area has 11 first-come, first-served sites.

The park visitor center in the town of Wartburg offers maps, exhibits, and advice on recreational opportunities.

Visitor center
208 N. Maiden St.
Wartburg, TN
423-346-6294
www.nps.gov/obed

AT A GLANCE

East-central Tennessee, 45 miles northwest of Knoxville ▪ 45 river miles ▪ Year-round; winter and spring best for paddling ▪ White-water paddling, hiking, rock climbing

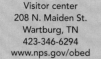

Shiloh National Military Park

The site of a bloody Civil War battle to control Confederate railroads

In 1862 Union forces, having taken control of Kentucky and the middle section of Tennessee, moved to attack an important rail crossroads at Corinth, Mississippi. Traveling southward, Union troops stopped at a log church called Shiloh Meeting House, near Pittsburg Landing, Tennessee. Southern forces marched north from Corinth to engage them. So vital was the Corinth rail site to both sides that a combined total of around 100,000 soldiers did battle here on April 6–7. Of that number, more than 23,000 were killed, wounded, captured, or listed as missing in two days of fighting.

The battle ended with no clear victor, though Confederate troops withdrew to Corinth and, faced with a larger Union force, soon abandoned the rail crossroads to the opposition. On October 3–4, Confederates tried and failed to recapture Corinth in a fierce battle that resulted in around 7,000 combined casualties for the northern and southern armies.

Shiloh National Military Park encompasses much of the April 1862 battlefield at Pittsburg Landing as well as an interpretive center 22 miles away at Corinth, near the site of some of the heaviest fighting of the October battle. At both sites, visitors can view exhibits and films on the battles. The Shiloh site offers a 12.7-mile auto-tour route with 20 stops at locations such as Bloody Pond, the Hornet's Nest, and the spot where Confederate Gen. Albert Sidney Johnston was killed. The park features more than 150 commemorative monuments, 600 troop position markers, and 229 authentic Civil War–era cannon. Both park locations offer living-history programs, the most important of which is the annual Battle of Shiloh anniversary.

The Shiloh park location also includes a national cemetery containing the graves of more than 4,000 military personnel and family members, and an assemblage of 800-year-old Native American mounds designated as a national historic landmark.

Tenn. 22, Shiloh, TN
731-689-5696
501 W. Linden St., Corinth, MS
662-287-9273
www.nps.gov/shil

AT A GLANCE Southwestern Tennessee and northeastern Mississippi, 110 miles east of Memphis ▪ 4,200 acres ▪ Year-round ▪ Visiting interpretive centers, attending ranger programs, following auto tour of battlefield

Stones River National Battlefield

Remembering one of the Civil War's bloodiest battles

On December 26, 1862, a Union force set out from Nashville, Tennessee, to attack Confederate troops camped at Murfreesboro, 30 miles southeast. The Union commander, Gen. William S. Rosecrans, knew the North needed a victory to boost morale after the important Confederate triumph at Fredericksburg, Virginia, less than two weeks earlier.

The battle that was to take place alongside Stones River, December 31–January 2, was one of the bloodiest of the Civil War, with 23,500

Civil War–era cannon dot Stones River N.B.

of the 80,700 participants either killed or wounded—the highest percentage of casualties of any major battle of the war. Names of locations such as Slaughter Pen and Hell's Half Acre evoke the terrible cost of the clash to both sides. The battle concluded with the Confederates withdrawing from the strategically important city of Murfreesboro. President Abraham Lincoln congratulated Rosecrans on "a hard earned victory, which had there been a defeat instead, the nation scarcely could have lived over."

The visitor center at Stones River National Battlefield offers museum exhibits and a short film on the battle, as well as access to important battle sites via road and hiking trails. Disjunct areas of the park include the site of Confederate Gen. Braxton Bragg's headquarters and a portion of the earthen wall of Fortress Rosecrans, a supply depot used by Union troops after they took control of Murfreesboro. The park's 7 miles of trails also connect to the 4.5 miles of trails within the city's greenways along Stones River and Lytle Creek.

3501 Old Nashville Hwy.
Murfreesboro, TN
615-893-9501
www.nps.gov/stri

AT A GLANCE

Central Tennessee, 25 miles southeast of Nashville ▪ 650 acres ▪ Year-round ▪ Touring battlefield sites, hiking

PUERTO RICO & U.S. VIRGIN ISLANDS

These Caribbean islands offer many opportunities to experience diverse cultures. Long a Spanish colony, Puerto Rico maintains strong Hispanic traditions, and Spanish is the primary language; influences from Africa and Latin American countries are strong as well. The Virgin Islands are primarily populated by descendants of enslaved Africans who were brought to work on sugar plantations during colonial times. At Christiansted National Historic Site on St. Croix, visitors can learn about Denmark's control of what are now the United States Virgin Islands (purchased in 1917). Diving, snorkeling, hiking, and historical tours are among the recreational activities on offer.

San Juan National Historic Site

The enduring heritage of the Spanish colonial era in Old San Juan

Founded by Spanish conquistador Juan Ponce de León in 1509 on the northern coast of the island of Puerto Rico, San Juan became an important military outpost for Spain. It was a port of call for ships transporting silver, gold, and other riches of the New World back to Europe, and it formed a vital link in the chain of fortress cities that helped Spain maintain its dominance in the Caribbean region.

In 1539 Spanish authorities in San Juan began building a fortification called Castillo San Felipe del Morro

The view from San Felipe del Morro, aka El Morro

(often shortened to El Morro) on a headland, or bluff *(morro,* in Spanish), on an island in San Juan Bay, an excellent natural harbor. Construction would continue on this massive fortification for more than two centuries. Another fortification, called Castillo San Cristóbal, was constructed to the east beginning in 1634; by the time it was completed in the late 18th century it was the largest citadel built by Spain in the New World, covering 27 acres. Construction of a third fortress, Fortín San Juan de la Cruz (also known as El Cañuelo), on a small island across the bay, began in 1610; built of wood, it later burned and was rebuilt with stone in the 1660s.

San Juan saw many battles as European rivals tried to take control of parts of Spain's New World empire. English privateer Sir Francis Drake attacked in 1595 at the request of Queen Elizabeth, but he was repulsed by the armaments and soldiers of El Morro. Three years later, another English privateer, Sir George Clifford, successfully captured El Morro after a 13-day siege. But Clifford abandoned the city after a few weeks because of disease and food shortages.

United States warships fired on El Morro during the 1898 Spanish-American War, the conflict that resulted in the United States taking possession of Puerto Rico and other Spanish colonial possessions. The lighthouse was destroyed in the attack but later reconstructed.

Today's San Juan National Historic Site encompasses Castillos San Cristóbal, San Felipe del Morro, and El Cañuelo plus bastions, powder houses, and three-fourths of the wall erected around the old city for

defensive purposes. Visitors can see these fortifications on their own or on one of the ranger-led tours offered on weekends. Views from the walls and sentry towers are spectacular, and many interior passages lead to chambers where soldiers lived and worked and prisoners were held.

The U.S. military maintained a presence in the San Juan forts until 1961, when the forts were turned over to the National Park Service. In 1983, UNESCO declared San Juan National Historic Site a World Heritage site.

501 Norzagaray St.
San Juan, PR
787-729-6777
www.nps.gov/saju

AT A GLANCE Within Old San Juan, Puerto Rico ▪ 75 acres ▪ Year-round; hurricane season runs June–November ▪ Touring historic fortifications

---

Buck Island Reef National Monument
Beautiful undersea "garden" of the Caribbean

A ccessible only by park-authorized concessionaire-operated boats or private boats with anchoring permits, Buck Island Reef National Monument offers the opportunity for a close-up look at a barrier reef ecosystem, with all the myriad shapes and colors of an underwater garden—so diverse it's sometimes called "the rain forest of the sea." Buck Island is located 1.5 miles offshore from St. Croix, one of the main islands in the United States Virgin Islands.

One of only a few sites within the National Park Service that are wholly marine, Buck Island is the only location within United States waters that's home to a reef composed primarily of elkhorn coral. Reefs are built by tiny animals called coral polyps, which

Denizens of Buck Island Reef

extract calcium carbonate from seawater. Coral polyps live in symbiotic partnership with algae called zooxanthellae, which provide nutrients through photosynthesis. Tropical fish, invertebrates such as shrimp and clams, and coral relatives called gorgonians are among the many colorful forms of life in and around the reef.

The most popular visitor activity is snorkeling within the lagoon, formed by barrier reefs off Buck Island's northern and eastern shores. A marked undersea trail features interpretive signs. Scuba diving is allowed at two mooring sites.

The island's terrestrial environment took a hit in the 18th century, when the lignum vitae tree was logged and vegetation-destroying goats were introduced, but it has since recovered. A hike across the island is an enjoyable experience, with good views of the blue green sea from lookout points. Bird-watchers can spot brown pelicans, magnificent frigatebirds, least terns, gray kingbirds, bananaquits, and pearly-eyed thrashers, among other species.

Park office
2100 Church St., #100
Christiansted, VI
340-773-1460
www.nps.gov/buis

AT A GLANCE Island 1.5 miles off the northeast coast of St. Croix, U.S. Virgin Islands ▪ 19,015 acres (including surrounding waters) ▪ Year-round ▪ Diving, snorkeling, swimming, hiking

Christiansted National Historic Site

A memorial to Denmark's heritage in the Caribbean

An enduring Danish legacy on an island that has belonged to the United States for nearly a century, Christiansted National Historic Site on St. Croix was established in 1952 to explain the Danish economy and way of life here between 1733 and 1917.

Denmark purchased St. Croix from France in 1733 and sold it and two other islands—St. Thomas and St. John—to the U.S. in 1917 for $25 million. The U.S. bought the islands in part for military and security reasons. While the Danes had possession, the cultivation of sugarcane (using enslaved workers until the mid-19th

Fort Christiansvaern, once a Danish stronghold

century) was the economic mainstay of the islands.

Christiansted National Historic Site on St. Croix preserves 7 acres centered on the Christiansted waterfront, as well as five historic buildings on the

grounds: Fort Christiansvaern (dating from 1749), Danish West India & Guinea Company Warehouse (1749), the Steeple Building (1753), Danish Custom House (1841), and the Scale House (1856).

Visitors can tour the fort and see the other buildings by using a self-guiding park brochure or by taking a ranger-led tour (ask at the park office for a schedule). Exhibits at the park examine the era of Denmark's sovereignty, including military aspects, the slave trade (Christiansted was the site of a thriving slave market), religious diversity, architecture, business, and crime and punishment.

Park office
2100 Church St., #100
Christiansted, VI
340-773-1460
www.nps.gov/chri

AT A GLANCE

Waterfront area of Christiansted, St. Croix, U.S. Virgin Islands ▪ 7 acres ▪ Year-round ▪ Touring historic buildings, picnicking

---

Salt River Bay N.H.P. & Ecological Preserve

An archaeological landmark and a Columbus landing site

Salt River Bay, a small natural harbor on the north coast of the island of St. Croix in the United States Virgin Islands, preserves important evidence of occupation by native Caribbean cultures as well as of the 17th-century colonial era when European countries vied for control of the region. It may be best known, though, as the only completely documented site of a landing by a Christopher Columbus expedition in what is now U.S. territory.

Salt River Bay was home to a succession of cultures in the era before

European contact, including the Taino and the Kalinago (Carib) Indians. They were living in the area when Columbus arrived on November 14, 1493, on his second voyage to the New World. A violent encounter, the first documented resistance to European encroachment by Native Americans, resulted in fatalities on each side.

England, the Netherlands, France, and even the French chapter of the Knights of Malta each possessed St. Croix at various times during the 17th century. The earthworks of a mid-17th-century Dutch-built fort

are the only extant structures from this era at Salt River Bay. The fortification is the only one of its type from this period that has survived in the West Indies, and possibly in North America. Later in the 17th century, the village that had grown up at Salt River was relocated to a site to the southeast that became the town of Christiansted.

Several archaeological excavations have been conducted at Salt River. One of the most significant discoveries was that of a Taino ball court or plaza, where a ritual game was played that had ceremonial importance and involved human sacrifice. Salt River is the only ball court known from the Lesser Antilles.

The ecological preserve aspect of the National Park Service property encompasses the single largest mangrove system in the Virgin Islands, and the waters of the bay and nearby are home to a wide variety of sea creatures, from corals to tropical fish.

Salt River Bay National Historical Park and Ecological Preserve, created in 1992 and co-managed by the Territory of the U.S. Virgin Islands, is still under development and has limited visitor facilities. It is administered by Christiansted National Historic Site (see opposite), and information is available there when there are no NPS personnel at the Salt River Bay contact station.

Park office
2100 Church St., #100
Christiansted, VI
340-773-1460
www.nps.gov/sari

AT A GLANCE
Five miles northwest of Christiansted, St. Croix, U.S. Virgin Islands
▪ 1,015 acres ▪ Year-round; contact station open mid-November–June
▪ Visiting historic site, snorkeling, kayaking, hiking

Virgin Islands Coral Reef National Monument

A pristine Caribbean coral reef ecosystem

Few sights on Earth offer such a colorful diversity of life as does a tropical coral reef. From multicolored fish to shrimp, worms, corals, and other invertebrates in an array of shapes and hues, a healthy reef is an undersea ecosystem of astounding complexity. Less common, but seen frequently, are larger creatures such as sea turtles and fish, including sharks and barracuda; while the space above is home to terns, pelicans, boobies, frigatebirds, and other birds attracted to the prey beneath the surface.

Created to protect some of the best reef systems in U.S.-controlled territory, Virgin Islands Coral Reef National Monument was established in 2001, encompassing nearly 20 square miles of Caribbean Sea off the island of St. John in the United States Virgin Islands. The national monument is administered by the staff of Virgin Islands National Park; information is available at that park's main office (see p. 198). There are no separate facilities for the national

Species of hard and soft corals form the reefs around the U.S. Virgin Islands.

monument, which can be enjoyed by scuba divers and snorkelers. No fishing or anchoring is permitted within the monument. Moorings are available for diving or day use in Hurricane Hole.

The only land access to the site is via the Hurricane Hole area on the eastern part of St. John, where the national monument extends eastward from Estate Hermitage to Haulover Bay along the southern coast of the eastern peninsula of the island. St. John itself is accessible only by ferry service from St. Thomas (U.S. Virgin Islands) and other islands.

Park administration
1300 Cruz Bay Creek
St. John, VI
340-776-6201
www.nps.gov/vicr

AT A GLANCE
Off the coast of St. John, U.S. Virgin Islands ▪ 12,708 acres ▪ Year-round
▪ Diving, snorkeling

Virgin Islands National Park

Tempting tropical beaches, forests, and crystalline Caribbean waters

The elements of a dream tropical vacation can be found on the island of St. John, one of the United States Virgin Islands, located east of Puerto Rico in the Caribbean Sea. Some of the world's most beautiful beaches invite sunbathing and swimming, while coral reefs and sea-grass beds located just offshore offer the beauty of diverse marine life to snorkelers and divers. Hiking trails wind through moist and dry tropical forests and cactus scrubland, allowing visitors to enjoy an array of birds and hundreds of species of plants.

The contemporary appeal of St. John contrasts with dark elements in the island's history. Christopher Columbus was the first European to reach the Virgin Islands, during his second exploration of the New World in 1493. In the early 18th century, when St. John was Danish territory,

there were more than a hundred sugarcane and cotton plantations on the island. The enterprises prospered from the forced labor of enslaved Africans, some of whom in 1733 staged a revolt and killed many of the plantation owners and their families, as well as soldiers stationed on the island. The insurrection was later quelled, and slavery continued on St. John until 1848. The United States bought the Virgin Islands—St. John, St. Thomas, and St. Croix—from Denmark in 1917 for $25 million, and the islands remain a U.S. territory.

By the middle of the 20th century, the beauty of St. John had attracted the attention of influential people who sought to make it a national park. Most prominent among this group was Laurance Rockefeller, who used some of his family fortune to acquire land on St. John that was then given

to the National Park Service in 1956. Since that time, the park has been expanded to include adjacent marine areas and most of Hassel Island, in Charlotte Amalie harbor (the island of St. Thomas, to the west of St. John).

Visiting the Park

St. John lacks an airport, so most visitors arrive by ferry from nearby islands St. Thomas and Tortola (part of the British Virgin Islands). The park's visitor center is located just a short walk from the ferry landing at Cruz Bay on the western end of the island. Exhibits here interpret the island's natural and cultural history, and maps and brochures are available. Visitors can check here for a schedule of ranger-led activities, including hikes and programs.

Many visitors get acquainted with St. John on a commercial guided tour via "safari bus," leaving from near the ferry dock and making a circuit of the island. These tours stop at roadside viewpoints and at some historic sites; most last two or three hours. Drivers recount stories of the island's history as they travel the winding roads, pausing at noteworthy locations.

North Shore Road leads to some of the main attractions on St. John, including renowned Trunk Bay, often hailed as one of the world's most beautiful beaches. Here, snorkelers will find a 225-yard-long underwater interpretive trail featuring signs identifying many elements of undersea life. The road also passes two other popular beaches at Hawksnest Bay and Cinnamon Bay; the park's only campground is located at the latter site. Rentals of snorkeling gear, kayaks, and windsurfing boards are available for visitors at Cinnamon Bay, as are lessons in water sports, including windsurfing and diving.

East of Cinnamon Bay stand the ruins of the sugar plantation called Annaberg, where travelers can see the remains of a windmill, sugar factory, and school. Regular living-history demonstrations are given here, including bread baking and gardening. The Catherineburg sugar plantation and factory, on Center-line Road above Cinnamon Bay, features the remains of a windmill and boiling house. The ruins of sugar estates at Reef Bay can be seen only by a 2.2-mile (one-way) hike. Ranger-led tours visit Reef Bay at least twice a week, but the schedule changes monthly and reservations must be made in advance, so call ahead.

The 20 trails located within Virgin Islands National Park range from easy strolls to fairly strenuous treks ascending hills to panoramic views of the Virgin Islands and the Caribbean. Some pass historic sites, while others focus on nature. The Petroglyph Trail, which branches off the Reef Bay Trail, leads to rock carvings thought to have been made by Taino Indians.

Flora & Fauna

There are many species of wildlife on St. John (some, such as mongooses, deer, and goats, were introduced), but birds are the most conspicuous. Brown pelicans, brown boobies, magnificent frigatebirds, and royal terns skim over the waters of the Caribbean, while mangrove cuckoos, zenaida doves, Antillean crested hummingbirds, gray kingbirds, pearly-eyed

thrashers, and bananaquits dwell inland. Lucky visitors might spot a sea turtle in the water near shore. (Trunk Bay was named for the leatherback sea turtle, which was once likened to a leather travel trunk.)

Early settlers destroyed around 50 percent of the island's native vegetation to plant sugarcane and other crops, but trees and shrubs are gradually reclaiming the land. Among them is one native palm species and the native tree that has been used for centuries to produce the famed bay rum, used in perfumes, medicines, and cooking.

Dry subtropical forest is a common habitat on the island, and stands of mangroves fringe the shoreline in places. The stiltlike roots of mangroves provide shelter for juvenile fish and other creatures, serving as a critical part of the cycle of life in near-shore waters.

Of course, the majority of visitors to Virgin Islands National Park are irresistibly drawn to the beach, whether to sunbathe, to swim, or to sightsee beneath the waves. One of the best beaches, publicly accessible and undeveloped Maho Bay has long been mistakenly considered to be within the park. Now a large portion is, or will be soon: After years spent tracking down the many owners, the land has been bought, assuring the preservation of sites representing the remarkable beauty and natural history of the Caribbean. The 415-acre tract (of which about 325 acres eventually will be transferred to the park) includes nearly a quarter mile of beachfront.

The crystal-clear waters of Trunk Bay, St. John

1300 Cruz Bay Creek
St. John, VI
340-776-6201
www.nps.gov/viis

AT A GLANCE

More than half of the island of St. John, as well as most of Hassel Island, U.S. Virgin Islands ▪ 13,000 acres ▪ Year-round ▪ Hiking, snorkeling, scuba diving, swimming, sailing, kayaking, windsurfing, camping

ONTARIO
Canada
U.S.
Isle Royale
National Park

L a k e   S u p e r i o r

Apostle Islands
National
Lakeshore

Keweenaw
National
Historical Park

Keweenaw Bay

Whitefish Bay

Pictured Rocks
National Lakeshore

ONTARIO

Sault Ste. Marie

MINNESOTA

Saint Croix
National Scenic
Riverway

Ice Age
N.S.R.

Ice Age National
Scientific Reserve

W I S C O N S I N

Wisconsin

M I C H I G A N

Father
Marquette
National
Memorial

Lake Huron

Green Bay

Green Bay

Ice Age
N.S.R.

Saginaw Bay

Sleeping
Bear Dunes
National
Lakeshore

La Crosse

Ice Age
N.S.R.

Lake
Winnebago

Ice Age
N.S.R.

Wisconsin

Madison

Milwaukee

Grand Rapids

Flint

Lansing

Lake
St. Clair

Detroit

U.S.
Canada

Mississippi

Rockford

IOWA

N

Chicago Portage
National Historic Site

Chicago

ONT.

River Raisin
National Battlefield Park

Illinois & Michigan Canal
National Heritage Corridor

Indiana Dunes
National Lakeshore

South Bend

Toledo

Perry's
Victory and
International
Peace
Memorial

Fallen Timbers Battlefield
and Fort Miamis
National Historic Site

Pullman National Monument

Illinois

Fort Wayne

O   H   I

Mississippi

Wabash

I L L I N O I S

I N D I A N A

Columbus

Charles Young
Buffalo Soldiers
National Monument

Springfield

Lincoln Home
National Historic Site

Indianapolis

Dayton
Aviation Heritage
National Historical Park

Dayton

MISSOURI

William Howard Taft
National Historic Site

Cincinnati

Cahokia Mounds
State Historic Site

Jefferson National
Expansion Memorial
National Memorial

George Rogers Clark
National Historical Park

Hopewell Culture
National Historical
Park

Ohio

Mississippi

Lincoln Boyhood
National Memorial

Evansville

K E N T U C K Y

Ohio

miles
0   50   100   150

0   50   100   150
kilometers

Great Lakes

Industry and agriculture dominate much of the landscape in the heart-land of the Great Lakes, the area into which the United States expanded as it grew beyond the states of the original 13 Colonies. Sites such as Cuyahoga Valley National Park and Keweenaw National Historical Park preserve aspects of the region's industrial past, while wilderness areas in Isle Royale National Park and Apostle Islands National Lakeshore offer solitude far from the sights and sounds of the modern world. In the Ohio River Valley, Hopewell Culture National Historical Park preserves one of the nation's most important archaeological sites, with Native American earthworks more than 2,000 years old.

A pair of moose walk along the shore of Hidden Lake, Isle Royale.

ILLINOIS

When most Americans think of Illinois, they think of Chicago, the great, ethnically and culturally diverse metropolis on Lake Michigan that is the country's third largest city. It was founded where a portage provided passage between the Great Lakes and the Mississippi River, and it grew to be the Midwest's center for industry, transportation, and financial services. Yet four-fifths of the state is farmland, producing a variety of agricultural products. In the extreme south, a hilly area is actually an extension of the Ozark Plateau, stretching west through Missouri into Arkansas and Oklahoma. Most industry and the majority of residents are found in the northeastern part of Illinois.

Chicago Portage National Historic Site/ Illinois & Michigan Canal National Heritage Corridor

The route that gave birth to the city of Chicago

When French-Canadian explorers Jacques Marquette and Louis Jolliet were returning north after their historic trip down the Mississippi River in 1673, they learned from Native Americans that by ascending the Illinois and Des Plaines Rivers they could reach Lake Michigan with only a short portage between waterways. Soon afterward, Jolliet suggested that a canal could connect the Great Lakes with the Mississippi, providing a transportation link of tremendous significance.

It wasn't until 1836 that construction began on Jolliet's envisioned canal, as the growing United States and the state of Illinois acted to join the two watersheds. Completed in 1848, the Illinois & Michigan Canal made the town of Chicago a nationally important transportation hub

A statue commemorating the Chicago Portage

and helped it become a major city.

This historic route is commemorated today at several related sites, including Illinois & Michigan Canal National Heritage Corridor (a National Park Service entity, although there are no Park Service facilities). The Lock 16 Visitor Center *(754 1st St., LaSalle, 815-223-1851)* is one contact point for learning about the canal. The Illinois & Michigan Canal State Trail

(815-942-0796) is administered by the state of Illinois and links a number of portage- and canal-related parks and other sites. A bike trail runs along the canal for 75 miles from Lockport to LaSalle.

Chicago Portage National Historic Site is located in Portage Woods and Ottawa Trail Woods, two adjacent forest preserves in the Chicago suburb of Lyons. At this site, which remains relatively undeveloped, visitors can experience the same environment as that traveled by Native Americans, Marquette and Jolliet, and countless fur traders and explorers before completion of the canal. Both preserves are located west of Harlem Avenue (Ill. 43), just north of I-55. A volunteer group, Friends of the Chicago Portage *(www.chicagoportage.org)*, holds free public tours *(May–Oct.)*.

Portage Woods Forest Preserve
4800 S. Harlem (Ill. 43)
Lyons, IL
www.iandmcanal.org

AT A GLANCE

Northeastern Illinois, on the southwestern edge of Chicago ▪ Canal 96 miles long ▪ Year-round, though winter can bring occasional severe weather ▪ Visiting site of historic transportation link, hiking

Lincoln Home National Historic Site

The home central to the life of America's 16th President

In 1844 Abraham and Mary Todd Lincoln bought a six-room cottage in Springfield, Illinois, where Lincoln was practicing law. The couple had one young son, Robert. Eleven years later, they doubled their home to 12 rooms. Lincoln was living here when he was elected to the U.S. House of Representatives, lost a race for the U.S. Senate, and in November 1860, was elected President. By then, Mary had given birth to three more sons.

The house at Eighth and Jackson Streets was the first and only house Lincoln owned, and today—restored to its 1860 appearance—it serves as the centerpiece for Lincoln Home National Historic Site. The park preserves 13 other historic houses in a surrounding four-block area, maintaining a 19th-century setting for the Lincoln Home neighborhood.

Tours begin at the visitor center, which offers an orientation film, exhibits, and a museum shop. The only access to the Lincoln Home is with a free ticket for a specific tour time. Visitors will see the Lincolns' formal parlor, dining room, sitting room, bedrooms, and other areas, furnished with personal family items. Robert Lincoln donated the house to the state of Illinois in 1887 with the stipulation that public admission would always be free and that the house always be kept in good repair.

Other exhibits in the neighborhood include "What a Pleasant Home Abe Lincoln Has" in the Dean House, which examines the Lincoln family's life in Springfield; and "If These Walls Could Talk" in the Arnold House, which focuses on historic preservation. Other interpretive displays are located throughout the park neighborhood.

413 S. Eighth St.
Springfield, IL
217-492-4241
www.nps.gov/liho

AT A GLANCE

Central Illinois, within the city of Springfield ▪ 12 acres ▪ Year-round ▪ Touring visitor center, Abraham Lincoln's Springfield home, and adjoining 19th-century structures

Pullman National Monument

An industrial town sparked gains for labor unions and civil rights

In the 1860s, when railroads were becoming the major mode of transportation in America, George Pullman built a factory on the south side of Chicago, Illinois, and began manufacturing the sleeping cars that made his name synonymous with luxury travel. His dream of a safe, healthy community for his workers came true in 1881, when the first residents moved into the planned town of Pullman. Architect Solon Spencer Beman designed the town's beautiful landscaping and parks, as well as high-quality housing.

Labor issues led to a workers' strike in 1894, and although the action failed, it was a catalyst in the American labor movement. In a related effort, the African-American porters, waiters, and maids who worked on Pullman cars founded the Brotherhood of Sleeping Car Porters in the 1920s, the first labor union led by African Americans to receive a charter in the American Federation of Labor.

Established in 2015 as Chicago's first unit of the National Park Service, Pullman National Monument comprises several remaining public buildings from the factory town and will interpret Pullman's role in industrial development and the labor movement. Visitors can tour historic neighborhoods and recreation areas such as Arcade Park and West Pullman Park. Some buildings are currently open for visitation during limited hours, and as the new park is developed, additional facilities and tours will become available.

11141 S. Cottage Grove Ave.
Chicago, IL
773-785-8901
www.nps.gov/pull

AT A GLANCE

Northern Illinois, in southern Chicago ▪ 203 acres ▪ Year-round ▪ Touring historic buildings and parks

INDIANA

Indiana surprises those who associate it only with cropland and the legendary Indianapolis 500 automobile race. Its southern hills are home to substantial deposits of coal, and the extreme northwest ranks as the nation's leading steel-producing area. Quarries in the south-central region have provided limestone for the Empire State Building, the Pentagon, and many state capitol buildings. Sand dunes, including 126-foot-high Mount Baldy, line the southern shore of Lake Michigan. Indiana Dunes National Lakeshore protects part of the expansive dune field and supports an extremely high diversity of plants. Indiana residents have long been known as Hoosiers, a word of uncertain origin.

George Rogers Clark National Historical Park
Honoring a pivotal event of the American Revolution

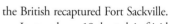

George Rogers Clark Memorial at sunset

While important battles of the American Revolutionary War were occurring in the original 13 Colonies, fighting was also taking place in Illinois country, the land to the west of the Appalachian Mountains, as patriots clashed with British troops, American Indians, and French-Canadian militiamen.

American Col. George Rogers Clark—brother of William Clark, who would later be co-leader of the Lewis and Clark expedition—fought with success against the British and their Indian allies, capturing forts along the Mississippi River near St. Louis. Americans also gained control of Fort Sackville, at Vincennes, Indiana, on the Wabash River. In December 1778, though, the British recaptured Fort Sackville.

In an arduous 18-day trek in frigid weather, Clark led 170 American and French militiamen to Vincennes, where they surrounded Fort Sackville and forced its surrender in February 1779. As a result of this and other campaigns, Clark prevented the British from achieving their goal of driving the Americans from the frontier. The British later ceded to the United States a vast area of land that now comprises the states of Ohio, Indiana, Illinois, Michigan, and Wisconsin and the eastern part of Minnesota.

George Rogers Clark National Historical Park, located on the site where historians believe Fort Sackville stood, honors the patriot military leader with a bronze statue inside an imposingly columned classical-style granite building. A 30-minute film, "Long Knives," explains Clark's military campaigns, and seven murals depict events of the time.

401 S. 2nd St.
Vincennes, IN
812-882-1776
www.nps.gov/gero

AT A GLANCE

Southwestern Indiana, 50 miles north of Evansville ▪ 26 acres ▪ Year-round ▪ Visiting memorial structure, viewing interpretive film

Indiana Dunes National Lakeshore
A lakefront playground and biological treasure

A peaceful retreat for centuries, the shore along the southern tip of Lake Michigan became a virtual battleground in the mid-20th century. Business interests envisioned more ports along the waterfront to facilitate shipping, as well as expansion of steel mills and other industry in the Chicago area. Vast sand dunes were viewed as raw material for glass factories. At the same time, conservationists recognized that the Indiana duneland was home to a notable diversity of flora and fauna, and many city dwellers valued the lakeshore as a place to relax in a natural setting.

Controversy and political fights continued for decades. A state park was formed as early as the 1920s, but it took until 1966 before the federal government established Indiana Dunes National Lakeshore to protect the area's beaches, high dunes, woodlands, and wetlands and their associated plants and animals.

Many visitors come to the lakeshore simply to sunbathe, swim, and picnic along 15 miles of shoreline. So many come, in fact, that in summer some parking lots at the park's eight beaches can fill up by mid-morning. Pollution is sometimes a problem, and officials monitor water quality and post warning signs when E. coli levels become too high. West Beach *(fee)* is the only beach with lifeguards and showers.

A trail leads across sand dunes to Lake Michigan.

There's much more to do at Indiana Dunes National Lakeshore than swim, though. First-time visitors should stop at the Indiana Dunes National Lakeshore Visitor Center *(Ind. 49, Porter),* where there's an introductory film, exhibits, and staff to answer questions. (The visitor center is shared with Indiana Dunes State Park, which protects 2,100 acres adjacent to the national lakeshore.)

The national lakeshore's many trails include Miller Woods Trail, an easy 1.5-mile trail through wetlands and forest; the 2-mile Heron Rookery Trail, good for bird-watching and spring wildflowers; and the Glenwood Dunes Trail, a series of loops through forested dune ridges, wetlands, and reclaimed prairie (this is the only trail in the park open to horseback riding). At Mount Baldy, a short trail leads to the top of the national lakeshore's largest moving dune, 126 feet tall,

for a fine view of Lake Michigan and its southern shore. (Mount Baldy moves 4 to 10 feet a year because of prevailing winds.) Pinhook Bog, Indiana's only true bog, can be visited only on ranger-guided tours along an easy 0.75-mile trail.

Botanists recognize Indiana Dunes National Lakeshore for its significant diversity of plants, a result of the area's encompassing several different habitats. Amazingly, the 15,000-acre park ranks seventh in plant diversity among all sites administered by the National Park Service, with more than 1,100 flowering plant and fern species. Habitats include dunes, oak savannas, swamps, bogs, marshes, prairies, streams, and forests, providing homes for abundant wildlife: 352 species of birds, 46 mammals, 18 amphibians, and 23 reptiles. Indiana Dunes' 60 species of butterflies include the endangered Karner blue.

Indiana Dunes also contains sites of historic interest, such as the Chellberg Farm, where three generations of a family of Swedish farmers lived. The house, restored to its appearance in the first decade of the 20th century, can be visited at certain times and on ranger-led tours; check with park personnel for details. Another historic property open for tours at limited times, the Bailly Homestead, began as a fur-trading post in 1822.

1100 N. Mineral Springs Rd.
Porter, IN
219-395-8914
www.nps.gov/indu

AT A GLANCE

Northern Indiana, 15 miles east of Gary ▪ 15,091 acres ▪ Year-round
▪ Swimming, hiking, camping, horseback riding, bird-watching,
cross-country skiing, taking historic property tours

Lincoln Boyhood National Memorial

The farm home that shaped a President

A scene of Lincoln's life

By the time Abraham Lincoln was seven years old, his father had lost two tracts of land in Kentucky to title disputes. In 1816 the family moved to southern Indiana, where Abraham's father, Thomas, could buy government land and where there was no slavery (which Thomas opposed). On this 160-acre tract, 16 miles north of the Ohio River, Abraham Lincoln would grow to manhood, shaped by family, education, work, and friends. In 1830, the Lincoln family moved to Illinois. By then, Thomas's wife, Nancy, had died, and he had remarried.

Lincoln Boyhood National Memorial preserves land associated with these early years in the life of America's 16th President. Encompassed within the park's 200 acres are a foundation display symbolizing the site of the Lincolns' cabin, the cemetery where Nancy Lincoln is buried, and the spring that was the family's water source. The informative Memorial Visitor Center offers exhibits on Lincoln's boyhood and family life, and a 15-minute interpretive film. On the center's exterior walls, large sculpture panels, carved from Indiana limestone, illustrate events in Lincoln's life, with accompanying quotations from his speeches and writings.

Mid-April through September, costumed interpreters depict life on a pioneer homestead of the early 19th century at the Living Historical Farm. An authentic period log cabin and outbuildings were moved to the park from other sites in Indiana. The farm also features split-rail fences, gardens, field crops, livestock, and an array of tools and furnishings typical of the era. Interpreters perform tasks such as feeding animals, quilting, harvesting crops, and making shingles, and they are available to answer questions from visitors.

Trails totaling about 2 miles loop through the woodland of the memorial site, offering visitors a chance to experience an environment similar to that in which Abraham Lincoln worked and played as a boy.

Ind. 162
Lincoln City, IN
812-937-4541
www.nps.gov/libo

AT A GLANCE Southern Indiana, 45 miles northeast of Evansville ▪ 200 acres ▪ Year-round ▪ Visiting museum and cabin site, touring Living Historical Farm (open mid-April through September and weekends in October), hiking

MICHIGAN

Michigan is the state with the second longest coastline in the country, behind Alaska, thanks to the fact that it comprises two peninsulas and is bordered by four of the five Great Lakes. The sparsely populated Upper Peninsula is a land where mines once produced substantial amounts of iron and copper. Its outdoor recreational opportunities make tourism a big business today. The mitten-shaped Lower Peninsula is dominated by Detroit, a city long known for its automobile industry. The upper half of lower Michigan is a place of lakes and forests, quite different from the industrial south. Isle Royale National Park lies isolated in Lake Superior, offering great rewards to intrepid visitors.

Father Marquette National Memorial
Honoring a 17th-century missionary and explorer

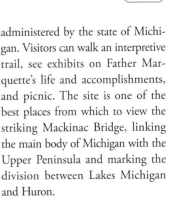

One of the most influential figures of North American history during the period of European settlement, Jacques Marquette was a French Jesuit missionary who traveled to Canada in 1666 to work among Native American tribes. He founded missions at sites that are now Michigan cities (Sault Ste. Marie and St. Ignace). With Louis Jolliet, in 1673 he made a pioneering voyage of exploration down the Mississippi River, providing the first accurate record of its path for European travelers. He died in 1675 along the shore of Lake Michigan at the mouth of the river now called Pere Marquette.

Father Marquette National Memorial, an affiliated site of the National Park Service, is located within Straits State Park *(www .michigan.gov/marquettememorial)*, administered by the state of Michigan. Visitors can walk an interpretive trail, see exhibits on Father Marquette's life and accomplishments, and picnic. The site is one of the best places from which to view the striking Mackinac Bridge, linking the main body of Michigan with the Upper Peninsula and marking the division between Lakes Michigan and Huron.

720 Church St.
St. Ignace, MI
906-643-8620
www.nps.gov/fama

AT A GLANCE — Northern Michigan, 50 miles south of Sault Ste. Marie ▪ 52 acres ▪ Memorial Day through mid-September ▪ Visiting memorial, walking interpretive trail, picnicking

Isle Royale National Park
Remote island wilderness in Lake Superior

There are no casual visitors to Isle Royale National Park. No one sees a road sign, changes plans on a whim, and cruises through on a quick scenic drive. This island rising above the waters of vast Lake Superior is accessible only by boat or seaplane, and, while a day trip is possible, most visitors spend at least a few days in the park to better experience its beauty, wildness, and natural and human history.

At 45 miles long and less than 10 miles wide, Isle Royale was declared a national park in 1940. The park encompasses the main island, about 400 smaller islands, and the waters of Lake Superior to a distance of 4.5 miles from any island's shoreline. Because of the park's ecological significance, it was declared an international biosphere reserve in 1981. In large part an official wilderness area, Isle Royale National Park offers visitors a chance to experience the environment as it was before humans altered the Great Lakes landscape. The park's remoteness, lack of land access, and harsh seasonal weather (including the notoriously rough waters of Lake Superior) mean that it's one of the few sites administered by the National Park Service to close completely in winter.

Isle Royale, like the surrounding region, was sculpted by the glaciers that covered the land during the most recent ice age, which ended about 10,000 years ago—just a moment in geologic time. Glaciers carved Lake Superior, gouged depressions that became smaller lakes, and scraped the land surface clean. The plants and animals that inhabit the island today are all relatively recent immigrants.

Getting to the Park

As might be expected, careful planning is imperative for the best experience at Isle Royale National Park. Most visitors arrive on one of four ferries that link the island with Copper Harbor, Houghton, and Grand Portage (the first two in Michigan, the third in Minnesota). Ferries dock at Windigo on the western end of the park's namesake island and at Rock Harbor on the eastern half. Ferry departures and arrivals vary depending on the day and season, so studying the schedules is a must—as are reservations made well in advance. In addition, some visitors use

FOLLOWING PAGES: *Traces of Native American occupation have been found at the mouth of McCargoe Cove on Isle Royale.*

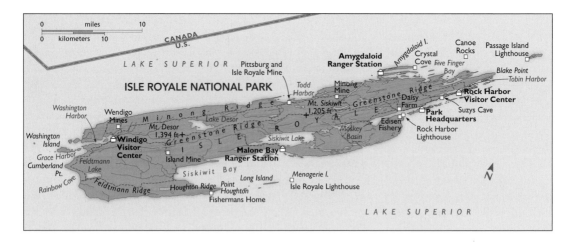

a seaplane to travel to the island via a half-hour flight.

One of the ferries, *Ranger III,* is notable as the largest single piece of moving equipment owned and operated by the National Park Service. It was specially built and outfitted to serve the transportation needs of Isle Royale National Park. The 165-foot-long ship replaced two previous *Rangers* that had successively become inadequate to carry sufficient numbers of passengers to the island. Because the *Ranger III* is a National Park Service ferry (the other ferries are operated by private companies), passengers can get park information, pay fees, arrange for backcountry camping permits, and hear presentations on nature and history while en route to Isle Royale. *Ranger III* can carry 128 passengers and has made more than 4,400 crossings of Lake Superior since being christened in 1958.

Ranger III makes a six-hour trip to Rock Harbor from Houghton, Michigan, remains for the night, and returns the next day, with two round-trips a week.

It is feasible to travel to Isle Royale and back in a single day, visiting either Rock Harbor or Windigo, but such a visit leaves only a few hours for exploration—time for a short nature walk at most. Camping or staying at the lodge in Rock Harbor allows venturing into the park backcountry along parts of the 165 miles of trails.

Rock Harbor and Windigo

Rock Harbor, at the eastern end of Isle Royale, is home to, among other facilities, a visitor center, concessionaire-operated lodge, and the only restaurant on Isle Royale *(www.isleroyaleresort .com; summer: 906-337-4993, winter: 866-644-2003).* Windigo, at the other end of the island, has an information station, two rustic cabins, camping sites, and a grocery store, though fewer facilities than at Rock Harbor. Park rangers lead programs at Windigo and Rock Harbor, including evening talks, nature walks, and history-oriented programs.

One of the most popular hiking routes, beginning at the Rock Harbor area, is the Scoville Point Trail, a 4.2-mile loop with dramatic views all along the rugged Lake Superior shoreline. Views from the point look out at some of the more than 400 islands that make up the Isle Royale Archipelago. At the western end of the island, the Windigo Nature Trail, a 1.2-mile loop, winds through a woodland of mixed conifers and hardwoods with good opportunities for wildlife observation. The park's longest trail, Greenstone Ridge, runs 40 miles—nearly the entire length of the island. Along the way it ascends Mount Desor, at 1,394 feet the highest point on Isle Royale.

A boat based at Rock Harbor offers tours *(fee)* to popular locations, including Raspberry Island, where a mile trail winds through boreal forest and traverses a spruce bog via a boardwalk. A second tour visits the Edisen Fishery, which belonged to one of the last commercial fishermen on the island; park rangers demonstrate mid-20th-century fishing techniques here for visitors. The tour also goes to the 1855 Rock Harbor lighthouse, the oldest on Isle Royale. Boat tours vary by day and season.

One ferry circumnavigates Isle Royale, providing a means to access campsites away from Windigo and Rock Harbor. (It can also shuttle hikers on the Greenstone Ridge Trail back to their starting point.) A water taxi based at Rock Harbor can transport campers to sites on the eastern part of the island.

Another popular method of camping is via canoe or kayak on the many lakes on Isle Royale (small craft can be brought to the island on the ferries, and can be rented at Windigo and Rock Harbor). There are also campsites on some of the smaller islands offshore from Isle Royale.

Isle Royale's Wildlife

The eerie calls of loons ring out in many places around Isle Royale, as do the loud "laughing" calls of pileated woodpeckers. Ospreys, yellow-bellied sapsuckers, tree swallows, gray jays, common ravens, hermit thrushes, Canada warblers, ovenbirds, and red crossbills also flit around the island.

Red fox, beaver, snowshoe hare, and red squirrel number among the species of mammals of Isle Royale, but the park's two most famous denizens are the gray wolf and the moose. These two species interact as predator and prey, their populations changing in response to many factors. The ongoing study of wolves and their relationship to the moose herd on Isle Royale, begun in 1958, is the longest running predator-prey study in the world.

It is long believed that moose swam across to Isle Royale from the adjacent mainland in the early 20th century, but recent genetic studies could possibly challenge that idea. Intensive browsing by moose greatly affects the vegetation of the island. (An area near Windigo that has been fenced to exclude moose dramatically demonstrates how the animal affects plants.) Wolves are thought to have arrived at Isle Royale in the late 1940s, walking across ice during a very cold winter. Research has shown that all wolves on Isle Royale have descended from a single female. Inbreeding has led to a 50 percent loss of genetic variability, a factor in the decline of the wolf population to just three animals in 2015.

Weather, disease, predation, and other factors have caused the populations of moose and wolves to rise and fall over the years—trends that are carefully watched by biologists. Because of its relative isolation, the island affords the biologists a unique and easily monitored environment in which to study the species' interactions.

Shipwrecks and Scuba Diving

One of the most specialized attractions for visitors at Isle Royale is scuba diving, to observe some of the scores of shipwrecks resting beneath the frigid waters of Lake Superior. Such trips are for experienced divers who are prepared for water that can be as cold as 34° to 37°F. All divers must register beforehand at either Windigo, Rock Harbor, or Houghton Visitor Center. All artifacts and other parts of shipwrecks are protected by federal law.

While private boats can access the wrecks around Isle Royale, many divers use one of the companies licensed by the National Park Service to guide trips in the park. Contact the park for a list. The park's most famous shipwreck is *America,* an 1898 freighter that sank in 1928. Located in shallow water near Washington Harbor, *America* can be seen by passengers on the ferry to and from Windigo.

The presence of so many shipwrecks around Isle Royale and elsewhere in Lake Superior should remind boaters of the frequency and severity of storms. Persons in canoes, kayaks, and other small craft are discouraged from leaving the safety of Isle Royale harbors for open lake water. In addition, lower levels of water in Lake Superior in recent years have meant that all boaters should use extra caution near shore and around docks.

Administrative office
800 E. Lakeshore Dr.
Houghton, MI
906-482-0984
www.nps.gov/isro

AT A GLANCE

Northwestern Lake Superior, 50 miles southeast of Thunder Bay, Ontario ▪ 133,782 land acres plus 438,008 acres of Lake Superior ▪ Mid-April through October ▪ Hiking, camping, kayaking, wildlife-watching, scuba diving

Keweenaw National Historical Park

Preserving communities built on the world's richest copper deposit

The heritage of the Keweenaw Peninsula, a finger of land sticking up into Lake Superior from Michigan's Upper Peninsula, is intimately tied to a remarkable mineral resource: The combined forces of tectonic activity, volcanism, and erosion, working over countless millennia, resulted in the accumulation of the world's richest known deposit of 97 percent pure copper.

Native American tribes knew of the metal's presence, excavating it and using it to make tools and other articles. These artifacts traveled along trade routes as far as present-day Alabama and Alberta, Canada. Early European settlers learned about the copper from the Ojibwa Indians and made some attempts to mine it.

In the 1840s, "copper fever" brought an influx of people seeking their fortunes in the mines, among them many from western England

and Finland (all told, people from 38 different ethnic groups participated in mining activities). By 1849, Michigan's Copper Country was producing 85 percent of the United States' copper output. By the time most copper mining ended in the late 1960s, Michigan's Keweenaw Peninsula had yielded 11 billion pounds of the metal.

The Calumet & Hecla company stored its mining machine patterns here.

Visiting the Park

Keweenaw National Historical Park was established to preserve the Copper Country heritage, both by protecting mine buildings and other structures and by interpreting the region's history. The presence of the National Park Service here is limited; to accomplish the park's goals, the National Park Service partners with entities called Keweenaw Heritage Sites. These sites are not owned or operated by the National Park Service, though park personnel cooperate with them to coordinate services and preservation efforts. Information and exhibits are available at the visitor center in Calumet *(year-round, call ahead for open days and hours)* and at a seasonally operated information desk in the Quincy Mine & Hoist building located north of Hancock on U.S. 41.

Keweenaw National Historical Park consists of two units: Quincy and Calumet, located at the sites of former large-scale copper mines about 12 miles apart.

There are presently 21 heritage sites associated with the park, and more may be added in the future. Most charge fees for admission or tours. They include the Calumet Theatre, an 1899 opera house in Calumet; the Finnish American Heritage Center, on the campus of Finlandia University in Hancock; and the Laurium Mansion in Laurium, a 1908 home built by a mining-company owner.

At the Quincy Mine, where the world's largest steam-driven hoist reached 9,260 feet down into the mine shaft; and other mine sites, such as the Delaware Copper Mine *(U.S. 41, 12 miles south of Copper Harbor)*, visitors can tour underground mine shafts.

Park headquarters 25970 Red Jacket Rd. Calumet, MI 906-337-3168 www.nps.gov/kewe	**AT A GLANCE** Northwestern Michigan (Upper Peninsula), 200 miles east of Duluth, Minnesota ■ 1,870 acres (140 acres federally owned) ■ Mid-April through October ■ Touring historic mining operations, visiting restored 19th- and 20th-century buildings

---

Pictured Rocks National Lakeshore
A colorful Great Lakes landscape—America's first national lakeshore

A shallow sea once—more than 500 million years ago—covered part of the area that is today Michigan's Upper Peninsula. Over time, sediments were washed into river deltas and near-shore areas, eventually becoming compressed into sandstone. In most places that ancient rock is covered by younger materials, but along 15 miles of the Lake Superior shore the sandstone is visible on the surface—to spectacular effect.

In places cliffs rise 200 feet high from the water, displaying bands of color reflecting the minerals present in the sandstone. Where copper is present, layers are tinted green and blue shades; iron creates red, orange, and yellow shades; manganese makes rock look black; and lime (calcium carbonate) shows as white.

Pictured Rocks National Lakeshore was established in 1966 to protect this scenic landscape, as well as the recreational values of miles of cliffs and sandy beaches along the southern Lake Superior shore. The country's first national lakeshore, it was placed under the administration of the National Park Service. The park encompasses more than 42 miles of shoreline as well as attractions such as lighthouses, waterfalls, campgrounds, and more than 100 miles of hiking trails.

Visiting the Park

Before exploring the area, travelers

are encouraged to stop at the Inter-agency Visitor Center in the town of Munising at the western end of the national lakeshore. The center (closed Sun. & holidays mid-Sept.–Mem. Day weekend) is so named because it serves both Pictured Rocks National Lakeshore and nearby Hiawatha National Forest. Maps, information, exhibits, and backcountry permits are available here.

At the eastern end of the national lakeshore is the Grand Sable Visitor Center (on Cty. Rd. H-58, 1 mile west of Grand Marais, open season-ally). Nearby are the 5 square miles of Grand Sable Dunes, perched atop the 300-foot-high Grand Sable Banks, a landscape created by glacial action, wind, and the rise and fall of water levels in Lake Superior. Also nearby is 75-foot-high Sable Falls, one of several beautiful waterfalls within the national lakeshore.

Of course, viewing the Pictured Rocks ranks as the highest priority for many visitors. The most popular spot from which to enjoy the cliffs is from the overlook at Miners Castle, named for a rock formation jutting out into Lake Superior. One "tur-ret" of the castle fell in 2006, but it's still a striking sight. A portion of the North Country National Scenic Trail (see p. 226) runs the length of the

park, with many viewpoints along the way for hikers.

The best way to see the Pictured Rocks, though, is from the water. Commercial tour companies offer boat trips from Munising (check with the park for contact information; cruises operate late May–mid-Oct.). Some visi-tors take sea kayaks along the cliffs for close-up views. Paddlers should be aware that Lake Superior is known for its frigid water and frequent storms; it's a good idea to get advice from park rangers on safety issues.

Day-hiking trails lead to many appealing sites, including the his-toric 1874 Au Sable Light Station, reached by a 1.5-mile hike along the shore from the Hurricane River

campground. From a trailhead in the central part of the park, hikers can visit Mosquito Falls and Chapel Falls, and from the latter cascade they can continue to the lakeside formation called Chapel Rock.

The park contains three camp-grounds accessible by vehicle and 14 backcountry camping areas. All backpackers must obtain a permit, as must kayakers camping overnight. Permits must be obtained in person the day of the trip or one day prior. Permits are available at the Inter-agency Visitor Center in Munising year-round. From Memorial Day to Labor Day, permits are available at the Grand Sable Visitor Center in Grand Marais.

Snags poke up through the Grand Sable Dunes of Pictured Rocks N.L.

Interagency Visitor Center 400 E. Munising Ave. Munising, MI 906-387-3700 www.nps.gov/piro	AT A GLANCE	Northern Michigan (Upper Peninsula), 130 miles west of Sault Ste. Marie ▪ 73,325 acres ▪ Year-round ▪ Hiking, camping, kayaking, boat tours, cross-country skiing, snowshoeing, ice climbing

River Raisin National Battlefield Park

Site of one of the bloodiest battles of the War of 1812

The War of 1812 saw United States troops contending with combined British and American Indian forces for control of the western

Great Lakes region. The British army conquered Detroit early in the war, a major blow to the United States. In January, 1813, an American army of

nearly 1,000, heading north to try to recapture Detroit, suffered a terrible defeat on the bank of the River Rai-sin in southeastern Michigan; only 33

U.S. troops escaped death or capture.

"Remember the Raisin!" became an inspirational battle cry for American troops, who counterattacked and took control of the region in October 1813 (though the war continued on other fronts for more than a year).

Previously operated as a local historic site, River Raisin National Battlefield Park officially opened in May 2011. It's the only such park dedicated to a conflict from the War of 1812. A fine visitor center includes weapons and other artifacts, dioramas of battle scenes, and costumed models of American, British, and Indian soldiers. An innovative lighted map depicts the ebb and flow of fighting in the area during the war.

Outside, walking trails lead to interpretive displays scattered across the battlefield alongside the River Raisin. One trail connects River Raisin to nearby Sterling State Park and the Ford Marsh Unit of the Detroit River International Wildlife Preserve, on the shore of Lake Erie.

1403 E. Elm Ave.
Monroe, MI
734-243-7136
www.nps.gov/rira

AT A GLANCE

Southeastern Michigan, 30 miles south of Detroit ▪ 42 acres ▪ Year-round ▪ Museum with historical exhibits, interpretive walking trails

---

Sleeping Bear Dunes National Lakeshore
A Lake Michigan park combining striking scenery and fascinating history

Few National Park Service sites in the Midwest have so many varied attractions as does Sleeping Bear Dunes National Lakeshore. With 31 miles of shoreline on the Michigan mainland plus 34 more shore miles on two wilderness islands, the park offers endless opportunity to explore the nexus of land and water. The park encompasses massive sand dunes, 32,000 acres of designated wilderness, 26 inland lakes and more than 80 ponds, eight sites on the National Register of Historic Places, a scenic drive, a lighthouse, and more than 100 miles of trails (including the Sleeping Bear Heritage Trail), among many other natural and historic features.

The national lakeshore takes its name from an Indian legend of a mother bear and two cubs forced to swim across Lake Michigan to escape a forest fire on the lake's western shore. The cubs, too young for such an undertaking, drowned. The Great Spirit Manitou created two islands (North and South Manitou Islands)

Boardwalk to the sandy shoreline of Lake Michigan

to represent the cubs and a perched dune on the eastern shore to honor the faithful mother bear.

The extensive high dunes within the park are "perched" dunes, sand that has accumulated atop bluffs that are actually glacial moraines (hills of rock, sand, silt, and clay deposited by continental glaciers) from the most recent ice age. One of the park's most popular activities is the Dune Climb, a sandy scramble up—followed by a slide or tumble down—a more than 100-foot-high sandy hill with a fine panoramic view at the top. Sledding is permitted on the Dune Climb when enough winter snow covers the sand.

The Philip A. Hart Visitor Center, the lakeshore's main contact station with exhibits, maps, and more, is in the town of Empire. North of the center, the Pierce Stocking Scenic Drive is a 7.4-mile auto tour featuring spectacular overlooks of inland lakes, coastal dunes, and Lake Michigan. The drive is open from late April into November, and it becomes a cross-country ski trail when the snows fall.

Commercial ferries leave from the town of Leland to reach North and South Manitou Islands, the former popular with backpackers. The 1871 South Manitou Island Lighthouse is open for tours, staff permitting.

Other historic sites within the park include Port Oneida Rural Historic District with farms typical of the late 19th and early 20th centuries; the Glen Haven Village Historic District with a general store, a working blacksmithy, and a cannery now converted into a museum with the largest public exhibit of Great Lakes small watercraft; and Sleeping Bear Point Coast Guard Station Maritime Museum with exhibits covering the U.S. Life-Saving Service, the U.S. Coast Guard, and Great Lakes maritime history. Ranger programs at Sleeping Bear include wildflower walks, guided winter snowshoe tours, and bird-watching walks. Check with the park for program schedules.

Visitor center
9922 Front St.
Empire, MI
231-326-4700
www.nps.gov/slbe

AT A GLANCE Northwestern lower Michigan, 25 miles west of Traverse City ▪ 71,213 acres ▪ Year-round; weather is best May through October ▪ Hiking, camping, biking, swimming, dune climbing, cross-country skiing, snowshoeing, kayaking, canoeing, touring historic sites, fishing

OHIO

Bordered north and south by two major early transportation corridors—Lake Erie and the Ohio River—the state of Ohio grew rapidly in population and economic importance in the 19th century, with industry centering in Cleveland, Toledo, Akron, Youngstown, and elsewhere. Industrial development severely polluted the environment; however, cleanup efforts have largely succeeded, with the Cuyahoga River a shining example. The hilly, forested southeastern section of Ohio is part of the Appalachian region. The Ohio River Valley is studded with important earthworks built by Native Americans, especially well preserved at Hopewell Culture National Historical Park.

Charles Young Buffalo Soldiers National Monument
Home of groundbreaking African-American military leader

Born in 1864 to enslaved parents, Charles Young in 1889 became only the third African American to graduate from the United States Military Academy at West Point and be commissioned as an army officer.

Young served with distinction in a variety of posts during his military career, both in the United States and abroad. He was a noted leader of African-American infantry in the West, where black troops were called "buffalo soldiers" because of their dark, curly hair resembling a buffalo's coat and because of their fierce nature of fighting. Young eventually became the highest-ranking African-American officer in the U.S. Army. He was also the first African American to serve as a superintendent of a national park, when in 1903 he commanded troops overseeing Sequoia and General Grant (now part of Kings Canyon) national parks in California.

Young taught military science at Wilberforce University in Ohio, and in 1907 he bought a nearby house, which he named "Youngsholm." The house was built in 1839 and may have been used as a stop on the Underground Railroad. Young died in 1922 while on assignment in Liberia and was honored with a funeral service at Arlington Memorial Amphitheater. He is buried in Arlington National Cemetery.

In 2013, Young's home was declared a national monument, celebrating both his career and the history of the Army's "buffalo soldiers." The site offers occasional special programs and tours while permanent exhibits are being prepared.

1120 U.S. 42 East
Wilberforce, OH
513-607-0315
www.nps.gov/chyo

AT A GLANCE Southwestern Ohio, 20 miles east of Dayton (60 miles southwest of Columbus) ▪ 60 acres ▪ Not yet open for regular visitation ▪ Touring home of noted Army officer and educator

Cuyahoga Valley National Park

A green corridor connecting bustling urban centers

All national parks have their unique attractions, but Cuyahoga Valley boasts several features that make it a special place for visitors and set it apart from most other national parks.

It's one of America's newest national parks—its status was changed from national recreation area in 2000—and that fact explains some of Cuyahoga Valley's distinctiveness.

Unlike older parks that were designated by drawing map lines around vast wild areas, this area was established in a predominantly urban and suburban setting between the cities of Cleveland and Akron. It encompasses a variety of landscape types: wild places, yes, but also villages, businesses, roads, a music center, skiing centers, golf courses, and a segment of railroad track, among other developments. As a result, the park offers a peaceful retreat with a broad array of recreational opportunities.

At the heart of the park is the river called Cuyahoga, a Native American word that means "crooked." The waterway runs for 22 miles through the national park area. Once notorious for its level of pollution, the Cuyahoga is much cleaner today, though park personnel still advise against swimming.

In the 1820s a canal was constructed parallel to the river, allowing commercial boat traffic between Lake Erie and the interior of Ohio. In the late 19th century, scenic carriage rides and boat trips marked the start of an era of recreational use of the Cuyahoga Valley.

As the 20th century progressed, local residents and public officials worked for parks to be set aside in the area to protect it from development, and pressure eventually grew for federal involvement. Such efforts culminated in the establishment of Cuyahoga Valley National Recreation Area in 1974. That action led to renovation of many historic structures and creation of various recreational facilities.

Foremost among those attractions is the Ohio & Erie Canal Towpath

Brandywine Falls cascades over layers of shale.

Trail. Once the path used by mules and horses to pull watercraft along the canal, it's now a route immensely popular with walkers, runners, and bicyclists as well as nature lovers who use it for easy access to forests, fields, and wetlands, home to a notable diversity of plants and wildlife. Traversing the national park for nearly 20 miles, the trail continues both north and south beyond the park boundary and will eventually cover 101 miles.

The Ohio & Erie Canalway Scenic Byway, a 110-mile-long scenic drive that follows the general route of the canal from Cleveland to Dover, runs through the center of the park, primarily along Canal, Chaffee, and Riverview Roads. Many other roads offer access to various parts of the national park, so a good map is essential for exploration.

Canal Exploration Center Area

The Canal Exploration Center in the northern part of the park is a good first stop for travelers. Exhibits provide in-depth information on canal history and the importance of canals to the region and nation. Made obsolete by railroads in the late 1800s, the canal was largely abandoned for decades. Near the Canal Exploration Center is Lock 38, the last working canal lock within the national park. It was one of a series of locks that allowed boats to change elevation by nearly 400 feet as they traveled between Lake Erie and Akron. Rangers demonstrate the lock's function on summer and fall weekends.

Another of the area's major attractions, the Cuyahoga Valley Scenic Railroad *(800-468-4070, www.cvsr .com, fee)* runs through the park on its route linking the Akron and Cleveland metropolitan areas. In addition to standard journeys, the rail line (operated by a nonprofit

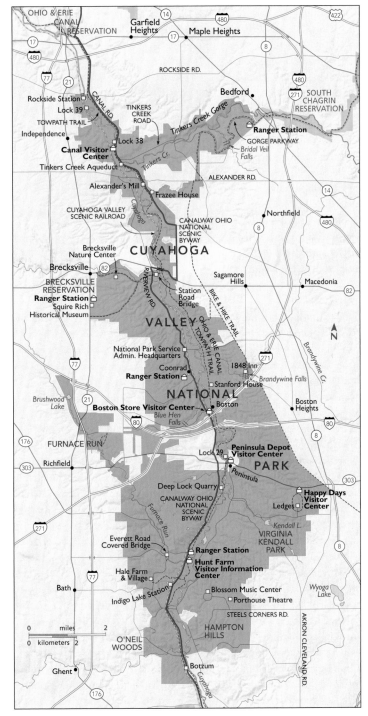

group) offers special themed trips at various times throughout the year. The train allows hikers and bikers to travel along the Towpath Trail in one direction and ride back to their starting points; bikes are permitted on the train, which makes seven stops within the park.

A little ways from the Canal Exploration Center, Tinkers Creek

Road (which eventually turns into Gorge Parkway) heads east into beautiful Tinkers Creek Gorge, a national natural landmark. An overlook along the parkway allows a view 200 feet down through the wooded valley to the creek. Not far away is the trailhead for the short walk to pretty Bridal Veil Falls, where, in a steep-sided valley, a tributary of Tinkers Creek cascades over a series of sandstone ledges. The gorge is wooded with hemlocks, beeches, maples, oaks, and birches.

Around Boston

The national park's most famous natural feature is found in the central part of the park, east of the Cuyahoga River. Brandywine Falls can be viewed from platforms alongside Brandywine Creek; the site is a popular subject for photographers. Brandywine is one of nearly 70 waterfalls, large and small, in the park. Another striking cascade, Blue Hen Falls, is found west of the river off Boston Mills Road.

Also located on Boston Mills Road, the Boston Store Visitor Center is an 1836 building where rangers can provide information on the park and nearby attractions; its exhibits tell the story of building canal boats in the valley. Peninsula, the village just to the south, was, like Boston, a center for boatbuilding in the 19th century, and the craft produced here were regarded as the best of any produced in the Cuyahoga Valley. Peninsula today is a charming place of shops, cafés, art galleries, and bike rentals. The Peninsula Depot sells train tickets and is one of the places to catch a ride on the Cuyahoga Valley Scenic Railroad.

The Ledges & Kendall Lake

Southeast of Peninsula, off Kendall

The Frazee-Hynton House, site of archaeological digs

Park Road, is one of the most popular areas within the park: the Ledges. The main trail here curves around a plateau beneath sandstone bluffs, leading to spots such as Ice Box Cave, a rock formation with narrow passageways; and the Ledges Overlook, a locally famous viewpoint for fine sunset views over wooded ridges to the west.

When winter snows cover the park landscape, cross-country skiers and snowshoe enthusiasts hit the trails. The Winter Sports Center at Kendall Lake Shelter, built from native chestnut and sandstone by the Civilian Conservation Corps in the 1930s, offers ski and snowshoe rentals, hot drinks, a warm place to relax, and information about park activities. Sledding is also popular with kids and adults, and the park is home to a downhill ski center as well.

The South End of the Park

In the southwestern part of the park, Hale Farm and Village *(Mem. Day–Oct.)* is a living-history attraction that re-creates 19th-century farm life in the Cuyahoga Valley. Visitors can watch artisans spinning, weaving, making candles, weaving baskets, blowing glass, and throwing pottery, amid a collection of structures centered on the 1826 Hale family farmhouse. It's

well worth a side trip north of Hale Farm to see the Everett Covered Bridge, a reconstruction of an 1870s structure that was destroyed in a 1975 flood.

Birds, wildflowers, and mammals such as deer, squirrels, woodchucks, and coyotes can be seen all along the park's 186 miles of trails. One particularly good nature path is the segment of the Towpath Trail north of the Ira Road trailhead. The marsh here is home to beaver, which returned to the Cuyahoga Valley in the late 1970s after being extirpated a century earlier. Wetland birds such as great blue herons, belted kingfishers, red-winged blackbirds, and prothonotary warblers nest nearby.

The Blossom Music Center, a unique Cuyahoga Valley National Park attraction, serves as the summer home of the Cleveland Orchestra, one of the world's finest music ensembles. Located off Steels Corners Road, the center was built in the 1960s and renovated in 2003. Listeners sit on the lawn in a natural bowl to hear concerts. Nearby is the home of the Porthouse Theatre Company, a professional regional repertory company affiliated with Kent State University.

Park Activities

Cuyahoga Valley has a small campgrounds, and overnight accommodation is available at Stanford House in the Village of Boston *(see park website for info)*. Additionally, the privately operated Inn at Brandywine Falls, an 1848 structure now serving as a bed-and-breakfast *(330-467-1812, www.innatbrandywinefalls.com)*, offers accommodations within the park.

With so many varied activities, from hiking along a nature trail to watching a blacksmith work to hearing Mozart, Cuyahoga Valley National Park ranks among the most diverse and rewarding sites administered by the National Park Service.

Here, even more than at many parks, it's important to take time to seek advice from park staffers on available activities and obtain a schedule

of ranger-led programs. Being aware of the list of possibilities will help you get the most from a visit, and not miss any of the park's highlights.

15610 Vaughn Rd.
Brecksville, OH
330-657-2752
800-257-9477
www.nps.gov/cuva

AT A GLANCE — Northeastern Ohio, just south of Cleveland ▪ 33,000 acres authorized; 20,000 acres in National Park Service ownership ▪ Year-round ▪ Hiking, bicycling, horseback riding, snowshoeing, cross-country skiing, traveling scenic railroad

David Berger National Memorial
Remembering an Olympic tragedy

A sculpture on the grounds of the Mandel Jewish Community Center in Beachwood, a suburb of Cleveland, honors the memory of David Berger, an American citizen who was one of 11 Israeli athletes killed at the 1972 Olympic Games in Munich, Germany. The event, often called the Munich Massacre, was followed on live television by an estimated one billion people, adding to the emotional effect of the tragedy.

David Berger, a native of Shaker Heights, Ohio, was a weight lifter who

The commemorative sculpture by David E. Davis

earned a law degree in the United States before immigrating to Israel. He earned a place on the 1972 Israeli Olympic team, and in September of that year was among those taken hostage and

killed by members of a group called Black September.

The sculpture, by the late artist David E. Davis and completed in 1975, features five broken rings, symbolizing the interrupted Olympic Games; and 11 supporting elements, one each for the 11 athletes who lost their lives in the terrorist attack. The upward motion of the rings suggests the peaceful intent of the games, a search for understanding, and hope for the future. Plantings and a plaque are also part of the site, which was designated a national memorial in 1980.

26001 S. Woodland Rd.
Beachwood, OH
216-831-0700
www.nps.gov/dabe

AT A GLANCE — Northeastern Ohio, in the eastern suburbs of Cleveland ▪ 1 acre ▪ Year-round ▪ Viewing memorial sculpture

Dayton Aviation Heritage National Historical Park
The enduring legacy of three extraordinary local men

This multifaceted park honors three men with ties to the Dayton, Ohio, area: brothers Orville and Wilbur Wright, aviation pioneers who built the world's first practical airplane; and influential African-American writer Paul Laurence Dunbar. Four

national historic landmarks and two National Register historic districts are encompassed within the park.

The National Park Service operates the Wright-Dunbar Interpretive Center and Aviation Trail Visitor Center and Museum in downtown

Dayton, and the Huffman Prairie Flying Field Interpretive Center on the grounds of Wright-Patterson Air Force Base (AFB), about 7 miles northeast of the city center. Both facilities provide an orientation to all park units and exhibits on the Wright brothers and Dunbar.

Highlights in and near the downtown interpretive center include an orientation movie, a restored Wright brothers' print shop, and exhibits. Ranger-guided tours of the restored Wright Cycle Company building, where the brothers began brainstorming aviation experiments, are available.

The Wrights' 1905 *Flyer III,* flown at Huffman Prairie, is on exhibit at

Wright Brothers Aviation Center in Carillon Park *(1000 Carillon Blvd., 937-293-2841).* Dunbar House *(219 Paul Laurence Dunbar St., 937-313-2010)* is where the writer worked in the two years before his 1906 death.

Exhibits at Huffman Prairie Flying Field Interpretive Center *(2380 Memorial Rd., Wright-Patterson AFB, 937-425-0008)* focus on the Wright brothers' development of the world's

first practical airplane, their flying school, and the accomplishments of Wright-Patterson Air Force Base. Huffman Prairie Flying Field *(Gate 16A, Wright-Patterson AFB)* is the 84-acre pasture where the Wright brothers taught themselves to fly during 1904 and 1905. Orville Wright lived the last 34 years of his life in his success mansion at Hawthorn Hill *(901 Harman Ave., Oakwood, 937-293-2841),*

Wright Cycle Co. Complex 16 S. Williams St. Dayton, OH 937-225-7705 www.nps.gov/daav	**AT A GLANCE**	Downtown Dayton and at Wright-Patterson Air Force Base, northeast of the city ▪ 86 acres ▪ Year-round ▪ Touring interpretive center, site of Wright brothers early flight tests, and Dunbar House

Fallen Timbers Battlefield and Fort Miamis N.H.S.

The site of the last battle of the Revolutionary War

On August 20, 1794, a United States military force commanded by Gen. "Mad" Anthony Wayne defeated an army of Native American warriors led by Miami chief Little Turtle at a site near the Maumee River marked by trees blown down by strong winds. Called one of the three most important battles in the development of the United States, the Fallen Timbers victory opened the Northwest Territory for westward expansion, paving the way for eventual statehood

for Ohio, Michigan, Indiana, Illinois, and Wisconsin. With a different outcome of the battle, areas north of the Ohio River might have become part of British-controlled Canada.

Fallen Timbers Battlefield and Fort Miamis National Historic Site is an affiliated area of the National Park System that is managed by Metroparks of the Toledo Area. The park consists of three units: Fallen Timbers Battlefield; Fallen Timbers State Monument; and Fort Miamis, a British post ceded

to the United States in the War of 1812. Work on these areas is continuing, with new archaeological evidence being uncovered and plans being developed to protect the resources. The site became affiliated with the Park Service in 2000. A bicycle/pedestrian bridge over U.S. 24 links the monument and the battlefield.

The battlefield is an Ohio Historical Society site, whose website *(www.ohiohistory.org)* is a good source of information.

Off U.S. 24, southwest of Maumee, OH 419-407-9700 www.metroparkstoledo.com www.nps.gov/fati	**AT A GLANCE**	Southwest of Toledo ▪ 251 acres ▪ Year-round ▪ Visiting site of 18th-century battle

First Ladies National Historic Site

Examining the varied roles of presidential spouses

At the heart of this relatively new (authorized in 2000) national historic site is the childhood home of Ida Saxton, who later

became the wife of President William McKinley. The 1841 brick Victorian mansion, remodeled in 1865, was also home to William and Ida Saxton

McKinley from 1878 to 1891, the era when he served as a congressman and before he become the 25th President in 1897.

Authentically restored with period furnishings, the Saxton-McKinley House now displays images and personal items of First Ladies, examining their supporting roles in the lives of United States Presidents. Costumed guides give regularly scheduled tours of the home. Throughout the house, wallpaper and curtains have been reproduced to match those of the McKinleys' residency, often based on photographs of the time.

One block north is the seven-story 1895 City National Bank Building, now home to the National First Ladies' Library Education and Research Center. Visitors should begin their orientation to the national historic site here, viewing exhibits on the first floor or watching a movie in the 91-seat Victorian theater in the building's lower level. Among the center's goals is to collect current and out-of-print books by and about First Ladies, as well as films, documentaries, and similar materials, and to gather copies of First Ladies' letters, speeches, and manuscripts.

This site is operated by the National First Ladies' Library (www.firstladies.org) in partnership with the National Park Service through a cooperative agreement allowing the nonprofit group to conduct daily management duties.

---

205 S. Market Ave.
Canton, OH
330-452-0876
www.nps.gov/fila

AT A GLANCE

Northeastern Ohio in downtown Canton ▪ 2 acres ▪ Year-round ▪ Touring restored house, viewing exhibits

---

Hopewell Culture National Historical Park
The imposing earthworks of a vanished Native American society

Between 200 B.C. and A.D. 500 a social and ceremonial phenomenon known as the Hopewell culture flourished among Native American groups living in the woodlands of eastern North America. The term "Hopewell" is used to describe a shared cultural tradition marked by a distinctive burial ceremonialism, the construction of earthen monuments, and a production in craft arts made from exotic materials.

The Hopewell built earthen mounds for burial of their dead and constructed large earthen enclosures where community rituals were held. Hopewell-related groups had social and trade contacts ranging from the Atlantic coast to the Rocky Mountains, from the Gulf Coast to present-day Canada,

The earthwork complexes of the Scioto River region

exchanging items such as mica, shark's teeth, obsidian, copper, and shells, which were fashioned into ornate craft items.

Some of the most spectacular earthworks—constructed in geometric patterns of circles, squares, and other shapes—are found in the Scioto River region of southern Ohio. Some earthwork complexes had walls up to 12 feet high, while others enclosed areas in excess of 100 acres.

Visiting the Park
Hopewell Culture National Historical Park preserves six earthwork complexes near the town of Chillicothe in the Scioto Valley: Spruce Hill Works, High Bank Works, Hopeton Earthworks, Hopewell Mound Group (the type of site or place for which the entire cultural tradition

was named), Mound City Group, and Seip Earthworks.

The Mound City Group Visitor Center offers a 20-minute orientation film and a museum housing some of the thousands of artifacts found buried at Mound City, including effigy pipes, copper ornaments, pottery, and stone tools.

The Mound City Group, Seip Earthworks, and Hopewell Mound Group have self-guided walking trails for visitors. In addition, a short section of a 34-mile bike trail runs through the Hopewell Mound Group.

The Hopeton site is open with limited facilities. The High Bank site is not yet open to the public.

AT A GLANCE 16062 Ohio 104, Chillicothe, OH, 740-774-1126, www.nps.gov/hocu — South-central Ohio, 40 miles south of Columbus • 1,828 acres • Year-round, though winter storms can interfere with visits • Touring Indian-built structures, viewing museum exhibits

James A. Garfield National Historic Site

The site of the first successful "front porch" presidential campaign

In 1876, when James A. Garfield was serving in the U.S. House of Representatives, he bought a farmhouse in northeastern Ohio for his large family (wife Lucretia and six children). Originally built in 1832, the house would be remodeled by the Garfields, who added a porch and enlarged it to two and a half stories.

Garfield campaigned from the front porch of his home.

Garfield unexpectedly gained the Republican nomination for President in 1880, and he conducted his campaign largely from his home, where he met visitors and gave interviews. It was during this "front porch" campaign that reporters gave the property the nickname "Lawnfield." Winning the election, Garfield moved to the White House in 1881. He would never return to Lawnfield. Shot by an assassin, he died in September of that year, having served the second shortest presidential term in history.

Today Lawnfield is the center of the James A. Garfield National Historic Site. The National Park Service has carefully restored it to its Garfield-era appearance. About 80 percent of the furnishings in the house are from the Garfield family, and 11 wallpapers have been re-created.

The Carriage House, added in 1893, now serves as the park visitor center *(May–Oct.),* with exhibits on President Garfield's life and career. An 18-minute film is shown on request. Ranger-guided tours of the Garfield home last about 45 minutes.

AT A GLANCE 8095 Mentor Ave. (U.S. 20), Mentor, OH, 440-255-8722, www.nps.gov/jaga — Northeastern Ohio, 25 miles east of Cleveland • 7.8 acres • Year-round • Viewing exhibits in visitor center, touring historic home

Perry's Victory and International Peace Memorial

A monument to both wartime victory and a long-lasting peace

On September 10, 1813, U.S. ships under the direction of Master Commandant Oliver Hazard Perry defeated British naval forces on Lake Erie in one of the most important military victories in U.S. history. Reporting the result, Perry famously wrote, "We have met the enemy and they are ours." The battle changed the course of the War of 1812 and helped give the United States a much better position during peace negotiations with England in late 1814.

The battle took place near a spot called Put-in-Bay on what is now known as South Bass Island. In 1912, construction began here on a 352-foot-tall Doric column to commemorate not only Perry's victory but also the peaceful relationships shared by the United States, Great Britain, and Canada, including the existence of the longest undefended international border in the world, between the U.S. and Canada.

Access to South Bass Island from the Ohio mainland is by ferry, airplane, or private boat. Visitors can take an elevator to the 317-foot top level of the memorial column (*small fee*) for a view that, on a clear day, reaches across Lake Erie to Cleveland, Toledo, and Detroit. The remains of the three American and three British soldiers who died during the battle are interred beneath the floor of the rotunda. Interpretive and living-history programs are conducted in the summer season, including firing demonstrations of reproduction muskets. The Perry's Victory Heritage Festival takes place every September.

South Bass Island in Lake Erie
Put-in-Bay, OH
419-285-2184
www.nps.gov/pevi

AT A GLANCE

On South Bass Island in Lake Erie, northwestern Ohio, 50 miles east of Toledo ▪ 25 acres ▪ May through October ▪ Viewing exhibits, ascending monument for vista of Lake Erie

William Howard Taft National Historic Site
The first home of one of America's most influential political leaders

Born here in 1857, William Howard Taft would become the only person ever to serve as both President and Chief Justice of the United States. His father served as both Secretary of War and U.S. Attorney General, and the Taft family has remained active in politics ever since.

William Howard Taft lived at the family home in Cincinnati's Mount Auburn neighborhood until he left for Yale in 1874. His widowed mother sold the house in 1899, and the structure was later greatly altered by a succession of owners. Under National Park Service ownership it has been restored to its appearance in the mid-19th century, when the future 27th President and 10th Chief Justice was growing up.

Visitors should stop first at the adjacent Taft Education Center, which serves as the park visitor

William Howard Taft spent his childhood in this Cincinnati house.

center. Exhibits and a film interpret the legacy of the Taft family. A life-size animatronic figure of Charles P. Taft II, son of William Howard Taft, "talks" to visitors about what he calls "quite a family."

Ranger-guided tours of the circa 1840 Taft home visit four rooms on the first floor, all furnished with period items, many of them Taft family possessions. The second floor of the house holds exhibits offering information on William Howard Taft's life and career and glimpses into the lives of his parents, siblings, wife, and children.

2038 Auburn Ave.
Cincinnati, OH
513-684-3262
www.nps.gov/wiho

AT A GLANCE

Cincinnati ▪ 3 acres ▪ Year-round ▪ Visiting education center and historic Taft home

WISCONSIN

Abundant lakes (including two of the Great Lakes), expansive forests, and areas of rugged hills make Wisconsin a popular vacation destination for travelers in the Midwest. Tourism competes with manufacturing and agriculture in the state's economic picture. Dairy products and cheese have long been important in Wisconsin, in part a legacy of early Swiss immigrants. Milwaukee, the state's largest city, is part of the Chicago metropolitan area stretching along Lake Michigan, but its residents can easily escape the urban scene for outdoor activities from fishing to boating to hiking to winter sports.

Apostle Islands National Lakeshore

A spectacular group of Lake Superior islands with historic lighthouses

The rugged beauty of the Lake Superior shore attracts visitors to this park on the northern tip of Wisconsin. Apostle Islands National Lakeshore encompasses 12 miles of shoreline on the mainland, but when the park's 21 islands are included, the total rises to 156 miles. With miles of beaches, more than 50 miles of trails, and 42 square miles of Lake Superior, it is best explored on foot or by boat.

The main visitor center in Bayfield (in the old county courthouse) is constructed of Apostle Islands brownstone (sandstone), rock that was extensively quarried to build countless houses and other structures in the Midwest. Here, visitors can see audiovisual programs and view exhibits about the park's history, natural history, and recreational opportunities. Other visitor centers *(open in summer only)* are located at Little Sand Bay *(13 miles north of Bayfield, 32260 Little Sand Bay Rd., 715-779-7007)* and on Stockton Island.

Bayfield is also home to Apostle Islands Cruises *(715-779-3925 or 800-323-7619, www.apostleisland .com),* authorized by the National Park Service to offer seasonal sightseeing excursions and shuttles that carry hikers and campers to several islands. The most popular trip is a 55-mile tour that travels through the heart of the Apostle Islands archipelago, offered daily late May to mid-October.

Apostle Islands National Lakeshore is known for its historic lighthouses, some of which can be explored on guided tours in summer, led by park rangers or volunteers.

Camping is allowed on 19 of the islands and one mainland site; a permit *(fee)* is required. Black bears are present (they are especially common on Sand, Oak, and Stockton Islands), so campers and hikers need to follow rules for safety in bear country.

Many visitors enjoy exploring the mainland shoreline and islands by sea kayak. (The park can provide a list of rental outfitters.) Kayaks allow paddlers

close looks at sea caves and the tall sandstone cliffs around the mainland and islands, but park staffers caution boaters about the notoriously changeable and often severe Lake Superior weather. It's strongly recommended that kayakers use wet suits or dry suits, especially in spring and fall when the risk of hypothermia is high. Public docks are available to boaters on a first-come, first-served basis on 13 of the islands *(fee for overnight docking).*

On years when Lake Superior freezes in late winter, visitors can walk across the surface to ice-covered sea caves and cliffs on the park's mainland unit. The park has an "Ice Line" *(715-779-3397 ext. 499)* for information about ice conditions and fees.

In 2004, 80 percent of the land area of Apostle Islands National Lakeshore was designated as federally protected wilderness. It was named for the late Gaylord Nelson, former Wisconsin governor and U.S. senator and a longtime advocate of wilderness areas.

Headquarters & visitor center
415 Washington Ave.
Bayfield, WI
715-779-3397
www.nps.gov/apis

AT A GLANCE

Northwestern Wisconsin, 75 miles east of Duluth, Minnesota ▪ 69,372 acres (including 27,232 acres of water) ▪ Year-round ▪ Hiking, kayaking, camping, fishing, boating cruises, visiting lighthouses

The waters of Lake Superior crash against the terraces and wave-cut benches of Apostle Islands National Lakeshore.

Ice Age National Scenic Trail/Ice Age Scientific Reserve

A long-distance geology lesson through Wisconsin wild areas

About 15,000 years ago, during the peak of the most recent ice age, a vast sheet of ice covered northern North America, in places extending into what is now the central United States. The southern edge of this huge glacier followed a curving line across today's Wisconsin, leaving behind countless geologic features: moraines (ridges of debris deposited at the outer edge of a glacier), erratics (large boulders moved and "dropped" by a glacier), drumlins (elongated, teardrop-shaped hills), kettles (crater-like depressions), and many others.

The Ice Age National Scenic Trail, one of only 11 trails with that designation in the country, will eventually wind for 1,200 miles across Wisconsin, generally following the

terminus of the last glacier, which retreated from the area about 10,000 years ago. About 650 miles of the trail have been completed, with temporary routes (often on roads or sidewalks) connecting finished segments.

The Ice Age Trail is intended for low-impact activities—hiking, backpacking, and snowshoeing. The National Park Service administers the trail in cooperation with local and state agencies and private groups. Land through which the trail runs includes both public and private property.

There are hundreds of trailheads and access points located along the trail. Access points are generally located every few miles; in remote areas, though, they can be more than 10 miles apart. Some parts of

the trail pass through state or local parks with rest rooms, campgrounds, and other amenities, while wilder segments lack any facilities. Hiking on the trail can include easy strolls of less than an hour or multiday treks through national forest.

The National Park Service has purchased 157 acres for use as an interpretive site for the Ice Age National Scenic Trail. The property is located in the town of Cross Plains, several miles from the Ice Age Trail Alliance *(2110 Main St., Cross Plains, WI, 608-798-4453, www .iceagetrail.org)*, a nonprofit group that partners in trail management. Contact the park service or the Alliance for more information, including maps of the trail segments and restrictions on activities.

Trail office
700 Rayovac Dr., Suite 100
Madison, WI
608-441-5610
www.nps.gov/iatr

AT A GLANCE   Winds through much of Wisconsin ▪ 1,200 miles (proposed) ▪ Year-round ▪ Hiking, camping, backpacking, snowshoeing, cross-country skiing

---

North Country National Scenic Trail

The nation's longest off-road hiking trail, spanning seven states

One of the most ambitious outdoor-recreation projects in the United States, the North Country National Scenic Trail is projected to someday run for as much as 4,600 miles across seven northern states—a distance that would make it the nation's longest trail dedicated to nonmotorized travel. It is one of 11 trails authorized by Congress to be national scenic trails (the most famous is the Appalachian Trail, 2,185 miles long).

The North Country National Scenic Trail will extend from the vicinity of Crown Point, New York, on Lake Champlain, to Lake Sakakawea State Park, on the Missouri River, in central North Dakota. 2,030 miles of off-road trail have been built, with more than 1,800 noncontiguous miles certified as meeting trail criteria by the National Park Service. Though the Park Service administers the trail, the land through which the route runs is owned by many different entities, from local and

state governments to national parks and forests to private landowners. As a result, regulations about trail use vary, with some segments allowing horseback riding or bicycling and others prohibiting those activities.

Landscapes and ecosystems vary greatly along the length of the trail. At the moment one hiker on the route is flushing up a greater prairie-chicken in North Dakota's Sheyenne National Grassland, another might catch a glimpse of a gray wolf in Minnesota's

Superior National Forest, while yet another might be landing a lake trout on Seneca Lake in New York. A short list of trail highlights would include the beautiful bluffs bordering Lake Superior in Pictured Rocks National Lakeshore (see p. 212), on Michigan's Upper Peninsula; Itasca State Park in Minnesota, source of the Mississippi River; the deep gorges and spectacular waterfalls of Wisconsin's Copper Falls State Park; rugged Ohio River Valley hardwood forests of Wayne National Forest in Ohio; and old-growth woodland of beech, hemlock, and sugar maple in the Tionesta Scenic Area of Pennsylvania's Allegheny National Forest. Of course there are scores more notable sites along the trail, from tallgrass prairie to coniferous forest to canoe rivers.

A nonprofit group, the North Country Trail Association *(229 E. Main St., Lowell, MI, 866-445-3628, www.northcountrytrail.org)*, partners with the park in developing the trail and is a good source of maps and up-to-date information on current conditions and recent additions to the route. Many affiliated trail organizations help with trail construction and maintenance, including the Finger Lakes Trail Conference in New York, the Keystone Trail Association in Pennsylvania, the Buckeye Trail Association in Ohio, and the Superior Hiking Trail Association in Minnesota. The Park Service website for the North Country National Scenic Trail lists contact information for many local, state, and federal partner agencies, such as national wildlife refuges and state parks departments.

Trail office
219 E. Main Street
Lowell, MI
616-430-3495
www.nps.gov/noco

AT A GLANCE

Traverses states from North Dakota to New York ▪ 4,600 miles ▪ Spring through fall ▪ Hiking; in some places cross-country skiing, snowshoeing, horseback riding, bicycling

St. Croix National Scenic Riverway
Two still natural rivers offering an array of recreational opportunities

Once a trade route for Indians and early European fur traders, and a river of pine during 19th-century log drives, the St. Croix River and a tributary, the Namekagon, today offer visitors recreation, from quiet canoe float trips to hikes through lush forests to fishing for trout and smallmouth bass.

St. Croix National Scenic Riverway encompasses 155 miles of the St. Croix above its confluence with the Mississippi River and the entire 99-mile length of the Namekagon, including land on each side for an average total width of a half mile. Property within the riverway boundaries is owned by the National Park Service, private citizens and businesses, the states of Minnesota and Wisconsin, counties, and communities, so

Enjoying a sail on the St. Croix

the range of permitted activities varies along the rivers' paths. As an example, the riverway has been divided into three sections with different camping regulations, which visitors need to know before beginning a trip.

Canoeing and kayaking are probably the most popular and intimate way to enjoy these rivers. The upper St. Croix and the entire Namekagon are quiet canoe streams with gentle rapids suitable for paddlers with little experience. The park can provide a list of outfitters for rentals. The lower St. Croix is deep and wide enough for motorboats and houseboats, and there are many marinas offering services to boaters and anglers.

The Park Service maintains seven hiking trails along the riverway, and several more are available in adjacent state parks and state forests. In winter, some of these are suitable for snowshoeing or cross-country skiing.

The riverway's main visitor center is located in St. Croix Falls, Wisconsin. Another visitor center (open in summer only) is in Trego, Wisconsin, on the Namekagon.

Visitor center
401 N. Hamilton St.
St. Croix Falls, WI
715-483-2274
www.nps.gov/sacn/

AT A GLANCE

Western Wisconsin and eastern Minnesota ▪ 255 river miles ▪ Spring through fall best for boating ▪ Canoeing, kayaking, boating, camping, hiking, swimming, tubing, wildlife viewing

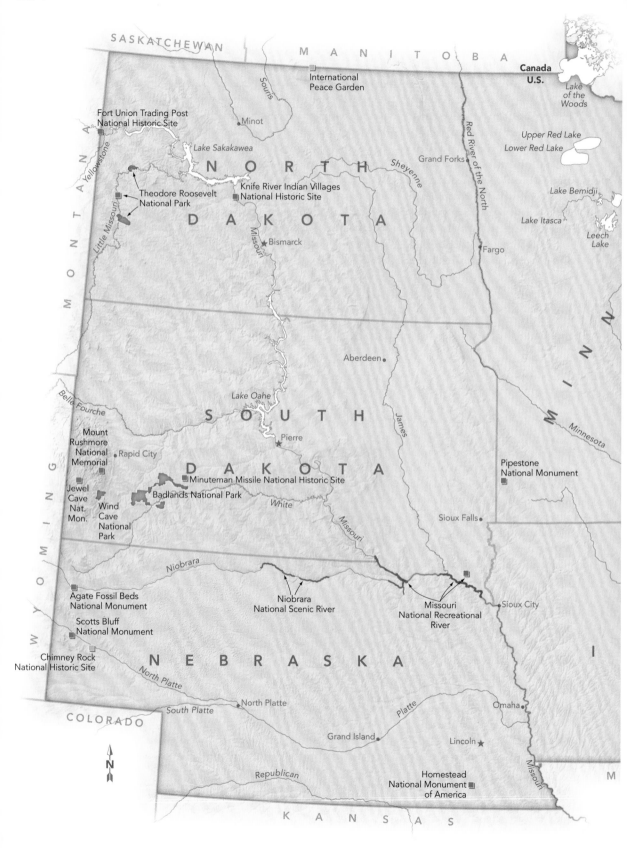

SASKATCHEWAN

MANITOBA

International
Peace Garden

Canada
U.S.

Lake
of the
Woods

Souris

Minot

Fort Union Trading Post
National Historic Site

Lake Sakakawea

Upper Red Lake

Lower Red Lake

N O R T H

Sheyenne

Grand Forks

Red River of the North

Yellowstone

Theodore Roosevelt
National Park

Knife River Indian Villages
National Historic Site

Lake Bemidji

Lake Itasca

D A K O T A

M O N T A N A

Little Missouri

Missouri

Bismarck

Fargo

Leech
Lake

M I N N

Aberdeen

S O U T H

Belle Fourche

Lake Oahe

James

Mount
Rushmore
National
Memorial

Rapid City

Pierre

D A K O T A

Pipestone
National Monument

Jewel
Cave
Nat.
Mon.

Wind
Cave
National
Park

Minuteman Missile National Historic Site

Badlands National Park

White

Missouri

Sioux Falls

Minnesota

W Y O M I N G

Niobrara

Agate Fossil Beds
National Monument

Niobrara
National Scenic River

Missouri
National Recreational
River

Sioux City

I

Scotts Bluff
National Monument

Chimney Rock
National Historic Site

N E B R A S K A

North Platte

North Platte

South Platte

Platte

Omaha

COLORADO

N

Grand Island

Lincoln

Missouri

M

Republican

Homestead
National Monument
of America

K A N S A S

Midwest

Those people who think of the Midwest as simply an expanse of wheat, corn, and grazing land are overlooking an intriguing array of parks, both natural and historical. Mount Rushmore is the most famous, an American icon set in the spectacular Black Hills of South Dakota. Equally impressive in its own way is Theodore Roosevelt National Park in North Dakota, a wild place of colorful rocks and diverse wildlife. Knife River Indian Villages National Historic Site is one of many places where travelers can walk in the footsteps of Lewis and Clark, while Nebraska's Platte River was the route of thousands of pioneers along the Oregon and California Trails.

Eroded sandstone butte, Theodore Roosevelt National Park

IOWA

Possibly the quintessential midwestern state, Iowa is a place of endless fields of corn, soybeans, and oats, interspersed with hog and cattle farms, small towns, and cities where manufacturing and financial services diversify the economy. Most of the landscape is gently rolling, with rugged terrain in the northeast along the Mississippi River and hills of wind-deposited loess soil in the west, along the Missouri River. Small patches of tallgrass prairie offer a glimpse of the native environment before the coming of the plow. Lakes and wetlands provide important breeding habitat for waterfowl, and hardwood forests in the southeast abound with species typical of the Mississippi bottomlands farther south.

Effigy Mounds National Monument

One of the nation's largest concentrations of Native American effigy mounds

From about 1,400 to 850 years ago, the Native Americans living along the upper Mississippi River built hundreds of effigy mounds, low-relief earthen structures seemingly in the shape of birds, turtles, lizards, bison, and, most commonly, bears. Native American peoples built mounds at various times and places across America, but only in the upper Midwest did they build effigy mounds.

Effigy Mounds National Monument, located along a scenic stretch of the upper Mississippi in an area of tall limestone bluffs, preserves more than 200 burial and ceremonial mounds, including conical and linear mounds; 31 are effigy mounds, one of the largest concentrations of such earthworks in existence. Most of the effigy mounds in the park represent bears and birds. The monument is recognized as a Native American sacred site.

The park visitor center, set at the base of 400-foot-tall bluffs near the

The monument protects 31 effigy mounds, most representing bears and birds.

Mississippi River, offers a 15-minute film, "Earthshapers," describing the mounds and the people who built them. In summer, rangers lead walks of varying lengths. Some burial and effigy mounds can be viewed along accessible paths near the visitor center, but most lie to the north and south, reached only by walking fairly strenuous trails. Out of respect for the site's sacredness and ecological fragility,

picnicking and camping are prohibited, and bicycles are not allowed.

Nature enthusiasts find Effigy Mounds especially rewarding to visit. The park's 14 miles of trails lead to beautiful views of the Mississippi River, and they wind through forests of oak, maple, hickory, aspen, and basswood, as well as through wetlands along the Yellow River and 81 acres of restored and native tallgrass prairie.

151 Iowa 76
Harpers Ferry, IA
563-873-3491
www.nps.gov/efmo

AT A GLANCE

Northeastern Iowa, 65 miles north of Dubuque ▪ 2,526 acres ▪ Year-round
▪ Viewing exhibits in visitor center, walking trails to see Indian mounds

Herbert Hoover National Historic Site
The small-town places that shaped the nation's 31st President

A native of the small town of West Branch, Iowa, Herbert Hoover was the first American President born west of the Mississippi River. Though he went to live with relatives in Oregon at age 11 (his father, a blacksmith, had died in 1880, and his mother four years later), Hoover was greatly influenced by the early years in his hometown; the family's Quaker religion; and the values of education, hard work, and community.

Herbert Hoover and his wife, Lou Henry, helped plan what is now

Herbert Hoover National Historic Site with the intent of providing an understanding of the life and work of the 31st President (inaugurated 1929). A Stanford graduate who had a successful career in mining, a humanitarian who worked to feed hungry people around the world, a President whose legacy was shaped by the Great Depression— Hoover lived a long life (to the age of 90) with enduring influence in American politics and public service.

The site includes a visitor center, with an exhibit and a short film on

Hoover's childhood in West Branch; the restored two-room cottage where he was born; a blacksmith shop representative of the one his father ran; the 1853 one-room school and the 1857 Society of Friends (Quaker) Meetinghouse he attended; the grave site of Herbert and Lou Henry Hoover; and a restored 81-acre tallgrass prairie. Visitors can take self-guided tours of the grounds and prairie. The nearby Herbert Hoover Presidential Library and Museum has many exhibits on his life and career.

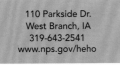

110 Parkside Dr.
West Branch, IA
319-643-2541
www.nps.gov/heho

AT A GLANCE East-central Iowa, 35 miles southeast of Cedar Rapids ▪ 186 acres ▪ Spring through fall best for outdoor locations ▪ Visiting birthplace cottage, presidential grave site, presidential library, and related sites

MINNESOTA

Traveling far up the Mississippi River in the North Woods, early explorers found Saint Anthony Falls, which later powered mills that ground grain and sawed logs, industries that helped neighboring settlements grow along the river. Today, well over half of Minnesota's residents live in the Twin Cities area of Minneapolis and St. Paul. Elsewhere, Minnesota encompasses iron-ore production in the northeast, extensive timberlands, and fertile croplands. Remnant prairies endure in the west, while thousands of lakes dot the landscape (much recreation in the state centers on water). Forests, grasslands, and wetlands are home to abundant wildlife, including a healthy population of gray wolves.

Grand Portage National Monument
Terminus of a strategic travel route to the fur-rich Northwest

The Pigeon River was vital to the commercial interests of the 18th century, allowing fur traders to travel from Lake Superior northwest

into the hunting grounds of what is today Canada. The 21 miles of its lower reaches, though, had many rapids difficult or impossible for a canoe

to navigate. From the local Ojibwa, traders learned of a portage (an overland route between waterways) called Kitchi Onigaming (Great Carrying

Place), which allowed them to bypass the rapids and join the Pigeon at a navigable point upstream.

In the 1780s, the North West Company, a prominent fur-trading enterprise, developed seasonal settlements at each end of the 8.5-mile Grand Portage. Little trace remains of Fort Charlotte, on the Pigeon River, but the summer headquarters on the shore of Lake Superior is now Grand Portage National Monument, located within the boundaries of Grand Portage Reservation of the Grand Portage Band of the Ojibwa.

Visitors can see a reconstruction of the trading post, including a stockade, great hall, kitchen, Ojibwa village, canoe warehouse, and dock. Living-history demonstrations are held on the grounds in summer, including canoe building, bread baking, weapons firing, gardening; and programs explaining the natural history of the beaver, the animal whose fur was so valuable in the early days of European trade in the Northwest.

The park's historic gardens are notable for growing "heirloom" varieties of crops whose seeds have been passed down through generations of Ojibwa, dating back to the 18th century or earlier. The Three Sisters Garden grows the three crops especially important to the Ojibwa: corn, beans, and squash. The historic depot area of the park is closed in winter.

Completed in 2007, the Grand Portage Heritage Center houses an information desk, exhibit galleries about Ojibwa culture and the fur trade, a bookstore, spaces for multimedia programs, offices, archives, and displays of works by Ojibwa artists. The park movie, "Rendezvous with History: A Grand Portage Story," is narrated in the Ojibwe language with English subtitles. The Heritage Center, the best first stop for those visiting the park, is open throughout the year.

Hikers will enjoy the half-mile trail up Mount Rose for a fine view of the stockade area and Lake Superior. A self-guiding brochure explains local geology and flora. Adventurous hikers can walk the 8.5-mile route of the historic Grand Portage all the way to the site of Fort Charlotte. A backcountry permit is required.

The park's popular Rendezvous Days and Pow Wow is held the second full weekend of August annually. Costumed reenactors from across the country and Canada gather to camp and challenge each other in games and frontier skills in a historical celebration that includes music, dancing, craft demonstrations, and hands-on workshops.

170 Mile Creek Rd.
Grand Portage, MN
218-475-0123
www.nps.gov/grpo

AT A GLANCE

Northeastern Minnesota, 150 miles northeast of Duluth ▪ 710 acres ▪ Late spring though fall best ▪ Hiking, visiting reconstructed fur-trading post and Indian village

Mississippi National River & Recreation Area
An incomparably diverse stretch of America's greatest river

Flowing 2,320 miles from Minnesota's Lake Itasca to the Gulf of Mexico, the Mississippi River has served as an important transportation corridor, an endlessly varied recreational resource, and an inspiration for an array of art, from Mark Twain's novels to musical theater to folk songs—and continues to do so. Over the past two centuries this fabled waterway has been dammed, channeled, leveed, diverted, polluted, and altered in countless other ways.

The upper Mississippi has a rich and diverse ecosystem.

Nowhere along its length does the river change more than along a 72-mile stretch north and south of Minneapolis–St. Paul, transforming from a relatively undeveloped and quiet prairie stream to a major commercial waterway. (St. Paul began as the Mississippi's historic head of navigation, the bookend to New Orleans.) In recognition of this uniqueness and the need to maintain the river's resources for all citizens, Congress designated this stretch the Mississippi National River and Recreation Area in 1988 in order to provide it with special protection.

Within Mississippi National River and Recreation Area, the National Park Service works with other agencies (federal, state, regional, county, and municipal) to protect, enhance, and provide access to special places along the river. The Park Service owns only 35 of the approximately 54,000 acres within the recreation area boundary; the rest is owned and managed by partner agencies. The recreation area encompasses nature parks, wildlife refuges, historic sites, scenic areas, and museums.

Several visitor centers can be found along the length of the national river area, all of which can provide information about the many recreational opportunities available. The Park Service visitor center is located in the lobby of the Science Museum of Minnesota *(120 West Kellogg Blvd.)* in St. Paul. The Carl W. Kroening Interpretive Center is located in North Mississippi Park *(4900 Mississippi Ct.)* in Minneapolis. Another visitor center is the 1906 Longfellow House, southeast of downtown Minneapolis in Minnehaha Park, famed for 53-foot-tall Minnehaha Falls, mentioned in Longfellow's poem "Song of Hiawatha."

At these and other information centers, visitors can learn of the attractions in Mississippi National River and Recreation Area, including, in the central cities, St. Anthony Falls—the Mississippi's only major waterfall; and the nearby Stone Arch Bridge—a national engineering landmark.

The federal recreation area offers places to exercise, play, and educate oneself. The Minnesota Valley National Wildlife Refuge in Bloomington has eight marsh units along the Minnesota River, forming an inviting urban greenbelt. Coldwater Spring has a trail to the fresh water spring where soliders camped in 1825 while Fort Snelling was being built. Indian Mounds Park, atop Dayton's Bluff east of downtown St. Paul, served as a burial site for at least two American Indian cultures. Mississippi Gorge Regional Park, where sandstone and limestone bluffs rise above the Mississippi, creates an oasis of solitude in the metropolitan area.

Mississippi River Visitor Center
120 W. Kellogg Blvd.
St. Paul, MN
651-293-0200
www.nps.gov/miss

AT A GLANCE

Along the Mississippi River, north and south of the Minneapolis–St. Paul metropolitan area ▪ 72 river miles; 54,000 acres (35 acres NPS) ▪ Year-round ▪ Hiking, biking, cross-country skiing, bird-watching, wildlife-watching, boating, fishing, viewing historic sites

---

Pipestone National Monument
Centuries-old quarries sacred to Plains Indians

For centuries, American Indians have been visiting this site in the tallgrass prairie to quarry a soft reddish rock—pipestone—using it to carve pipes for sacred smoking ceremonies as well as effigies. According to tradition, the quarry itself, as well as the pipestone, is sacred—a place where different tribes can come in peace to collect the stone.

Pipestone was formed more than a billion years ago, when a sea covered this region. Sand and clay collected on the seafloor in layers and was covered by other sedimentary material. The clay was transformed into pipestone, which exists today between layers of quartzite, formed from compressed sand. Pipestone is sometimes also called catlinite for the renowned frontier painter George Catlin, who collected a sample in the 1830s and sent it to a geologist for study. Indians may still extract pipestone from the quarries today, though there's a waiting list of several years for the necessary National Park Service permit.

Visitors to Pipestone National Monument can see exhibits and a short interpretive film in the visitor center, as well as watch Native American craft workers demonstrate the art of pipemaking *(April–mid-Oct.)* in the monument's visitor center. Outside, the paved, 0.75-mile Circle Trail winds through native tallgrass prairie, leading visitors to the pipestone quarries and historical markers. The trail passes the spot where Pipestone Creek drops over the edge of a quartzite cliff, forming beautiful Winnewissa Falls. Visible from the trail is Nicollet Rock, on which members of a mapmaking expedition carved their names during a stopover at the quarries in 1838.

---

36 Reservation Ave.
(off U.S. 75)
Pipestone, MN
507-825-5464
www.nps.gov/pipe

AT A GLANCE

Southwestern Minnesota, 35 miles northeast of Sioux Falls, South Dakota ▪ 300 acres ▪ Year-round ▪ Nature walking, viewing active quarries, observing seasonal cultural demonstrations

Voyageurs National Park

A boater's paradise in a North Woods water landscape

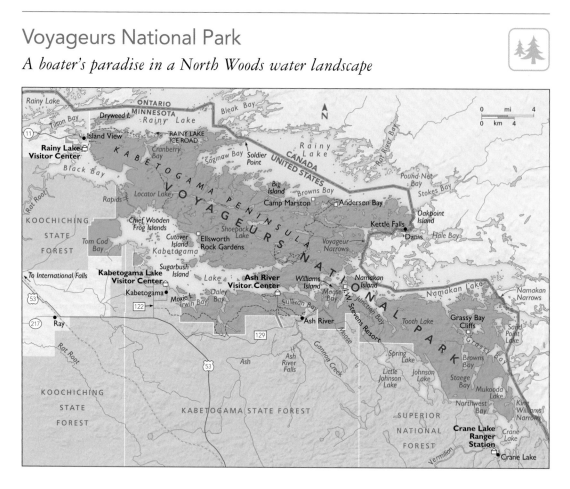

V ast forests of pine, spruce, fir, aspen, and birch; dozens of lakes and more than 500 islands; the crazy laughter of a loon's call and the howl of wolves—all these are essential elements of Voyageurs National Park, set in the heart of Minnesota's North Woods. The park is a watery wonderland: With more than a third of its area composed of lakes, and with all of its 200-plus campsites accessible only by boat, Voyageurs most rewards those who explore it by canoe, kayak, or houseboat.

Voyageurs & Native Americans

To the voyageurs for whom the park is named, this water wilderness was essentially a commercial route. Beginning in the late 17th century, these men of legendary strength and endurance paddled birch-bark canoes laden with goods between northwestern Canada and Montreal. Trade primarily involved exchanging manufactured goods for beaver pelts, which were shipped to Europe to meet the huge demand for fur.

The voyageurs moved westward as the supply of furs in the eastern part of North America diminished; as a result, they were the first Europeans to explore the territory to the northwest and to engage the indigenous peoples in commercial-scale fur trading. "Montreal men" paddled large canoes from Montreal to a rendezvous site at Grand Portage (see p. 231) on the western edge of Lake Superior. There they met "winterers,"

who shuttled goods and furs between Grand Portage and areas farther west and north.

Of course, Native American peoples—chiefly the Cree, Monsoni, and Assiniboin tribes—had lived in this area for centuries, paddling their own canoes on its lakes and rivers; by the time of the voyageurs, however, the Ojibwa were the main inhabitants. They soon became important players in the fur trade, suppling canoes and serving as guides for the voyageurs, among other things.

The 55-mile-long national park in part marks the boundary between the United States and Canada. The route of the voyageurs, whose trading journeys largely ceased by the 1820s, was used to describe a segment of the international border in the treaty that ended the American Revolution.

The beauty and wildness of this area, and the need to protect those qualities, were recognized as early as 1891, when the first proposal was made to establish a national park. In 1975, the idea became a reality, by which point activities such as mining, logging, and dam building had left their marks on the land.

Exploring the Park

There are three visitor centers in Voyageurs National Park: Rainy Lake *(year-round)* and Kabetogama Lake and Ash River *(both late May–Sept.).* All three centers show the park orientation film and have information desks and exhibits. Hiking trails at or near all the visitor centers can provide a sample of the Voyageurs environment, but to really see the park, a trip on one or more of the lakes is mandatory.

A variety of cruises are offered in summer, led by park rangers and allowing visitors without their own boats to experience the beauty and wildlife of the park lakes. The North Canoe voyage—offered at each visitor center—lets participants travel in a 26-foot canoe for a taste of what life was like for the original voyageurs. The *Voyageur* cruise boat, run out of the Rainy Lake center, offers trips such as a tour to Little American Island for a visit to a historic gold mine; and the Bald Eagle Watch trip to observe active eagle nests.

At the Kabetogama Lake visitor center, the *Amik* cruise boat takes visitors to Ellsworth Rock Gardens, where a former landowner created a scenic grotto of rock statuary, terraces, and plantings on a large granite outcrop. Another cruise visits historic Kettle Falls, where a 1913 hotel is still in operation, now run by a concessionaire. Voyageurs portaged their birchbark canoes and traded goods across

Voyageurs used to paddle across the tannin-stained waters of Namakan Lake.

this narrow strip of land between Rainy and Namakan Lakes. (The Kettle Falls Hotel is the only noncamping accommodation in the park.)

Boat ramps are located at several places along the shores of Rainy, Kabetogama, Namakan, Sand Point, and Crane Lakes and their various arms. Rentals of canoes, kayaks, and houseboats are also available from private outfitters in the area. Exploring the national park by boat is the best way to see the backcountry in

solitude, and the only way to reach the park's various campsites

All visitors should observe park regulations concerning safety and protection of resources, including rules to prevent the spread of exotic plants and animals. For example, no private watercraft are allowed on the park's interior lakes in order to protect them from invasive pests, such as the spiny water flea. The Park Service provides canoes and rowboats on several interior lakes on the Kabetogama

Peninsula *(reservation required, fee)*; boaters must make their own way to the peninsula (such as via water taxi).

Voyageurs in Winter

Winters are long and conditions can be harsh in the Voyageurs area, but the park by no means shuts down for the season. Although many activities are suspended, the Rainy Lake Visitor Center remains open *(Tues.–Sat.)*, offering a gathering place for those who want to experience the snowy landscape. The center provides the free loan of snowshoes, as well as cross-country ski rentals. Snowmobiling is allowed—and popular—on some park trails.

A winter trip to Voyageurs also affords visitors a unique experience: a drive along Rainy Lake Ice Road, which runs from the boat ramp at Rainy Lake Visitor Center to as far as ice conditions will allow on the north side of the Kabetogama Peninsula. Two ice roads (the other, Kabetogama Lake Ice Road, runs from Kabetogama Lake Visitor Center to Ash River Visitor Center) are open to vehicles of less than 7,000 pounds gross weight. Ice on the park lakes can be up to 2 feet thick, but the ice road may be closed or shortened when thin ice or other unsafe conditions are present.

The Glory of Voyageurs

The park's living landscape is relatively young: The last glaciers of the most recent ice age disappeared only about 10,000 years ago, and trees and other vegetation grow on a thin layer of soil that has accumulated since that time. Continental glaciers scraped the land bare, exposing ancient Precambrian rocks of the Canadian Shield that formed more than two billion years ago.

Voyageurs National Park is located in an ecosystem called the southern biome of the northern boreal forest, where northern coniferous forest and southern hardwood forest intermingle. In addition to woodland, the park encompasses peat lands, fens, marshes, rocky outcrops, and lakeshore environments.

Wildlife in the park includes more than 240 species of birds, 10 species of reptiles and amphibians, 53 species of fish, and 42 species of mammals. Black bear, white-tailed deer, moose, beaver, coyote, porcupine, pine marten, river otter, woodchuck, and red fox number among the larger mammalian species. The park's healthy bear population means that campers should learn and put into practice recommendations for food storage around campsites, using park-provided containers where they are present or hanging food well away from the ground and tree limbs.

Most notable for many visitors, though, is the presence of several packs of gray wolves. Though seldom seen, these predators might be heard at night—their howls can be quite haunting—or their tracks seen in snow. In recent years there has been evidence of the rare, secretive Canada lynx in Voyageurs National Park, making it the only national park east of the Rocky Mountains to host this cat. Researchers are working to determine how many lynx might be in the park and what kind of management practices might encourage the population's health.

The park's birds, which range in size from the long-legged great blue heron to the tiny ruby-throated hummingbird, tend to be more obvious than the mammals. Breeding species include many associated with the North Woods, such as common loon, spruce grouse, great gray owl, sawwhet owl, black-backed woodpecker, boreal chickadee, gray jay, common raven, Connecticut warbler, evening grosbeak, pine grosbeak, and white-winged crossbill. Bald eagles may be the park's most popular breeding birds, building their huge nests along lakeshores. Ospreys, too, build large, conspicuous nests, and feed their young with fish caught in the lakes' cold waters. Taking a ranger-led nature walk is an excellent way to see and learn about the park's wildlife.

Park managers deal with many issues affecting the Voyageurs environment, not all of which are under their control. Dams built in the early 20th century determine the water level in Rainy and Namakan Lakes. Recent decisions by the International Joint Commission affecting lake levels may improve environmental conditions in the park regarding factors such as fish communities, aquatic vegetation, and loon-hatching success. Prescribed fire is a valuable tool in creating desired environmental conditions in the park. In the past, fire suppression greatly changed the composition of the forest; today, controlled burning helps restore a more natural species composition.

Summer or winter, on land or on the water, Voyageurs offers visitors a chance to experience the life and times of adventurous boatmen following rivers into the Northwest, blazing trails for the pioneer settlers who followed.

Rainy Lake Visitor Center Minn. 11, 11 miles east of International Falls, MN 218-286-5258 www.nps.gov/voya

AT A GLANCE

Northern Minnesota, 190 miles northwest of Duluth ▪ 218,054 acres (134,265 land, 83,789 water) ▪ Late spring through fall for boating; winter for cross-country skiing and snowshoeing ▪ Canoeing, kayaking, houseboating, hiking, camping, fishing, snowmobiling, cross-country skiing, snowshoeing

NEBRASKA

Tens of thousands of pioneers passed through Nebraska in the mid-19th century, following the Platte River along the California, Oregon, and Mormon Trails; features such as Chimney Rock and Scotts Bluff became well-known landmarks along the way. Parts of Nebraska remain little changed from those frontier days, with vast cattle ranches covering much of the western part of the state and very sparse human population. The Sandhills (grass-covered dunes) and the Pine Ridge country provide landscape diversity in the western part of the state, while croplands blanket the east. Parts of the Niobrara River in the north have been protected and offer canoeing, tubing, and kayaking.

Agate Fossil Beds National Monument

A globally important site for the study of ancient mammals

Twenty million years ago, the Agate Fossil Beds National Monument region was savanna grassland, home to mammals such as a predatory bear-dog, a land-dwelling beaver, a small rhinoceros, a small camel-like animal, and a 10-foot-long piglike omnivore.

Set in a mostly undeveloped section of the Niobrara River Valley, Agate Fossil Beds National Monument was established to preserve a rich deposit of fossils of these and other Miocene-epoch animals. (There are no dinosaur fossils here; the dinosaurs had died out 40 million years before the Miocene.) It's believed that during a period of drought, animals concentrated around the few available water holes, where many of them died, became covered in mud, and were preserved as fossils.

The mixed-grass prairie land of Agate Fossil Beds N.M.

The park visitor center displays life-size model skeletons of many of the Miocene mammals whose fossilized bones have been found here, as well as actual fossils. Also exhibited are casts of the odd, spiral burrows excavated by the early beaver

Paleocastor. The fossil burrows, which long mystified scientists, are called Daemonelix ("devil's corkscrew").

The visitor center also features a notable collection of Native American artifacts acquired from the rancher who once owned the land here. Included in the collection are beaded and quilled moccasins, a painted hide of the Battle of Little Bighorn, guns, decorated clubs, pipe bags, and ceremonial clothing.

The 2.7-mile interpretive Fossil Hills Trail crosses the Niobrara River and loops around University and Carnegie Hills, where fossil beds were discovered in 1904. The 1-mile Daemonelix Trail leads past exhibits of fossils to the north rim of the Niobrara River Valley for a fine panoramic view of the surrounding landscape.

Neb. 29
22 miles south of
Harrison, NE
308-668-2211
www.nps.gov/agfo

AT A GLANCE

Northwestern Nebraska, 47 miles north of Scottsbluff ▪ 3,050 acres (2,270 federally managed) ▪ Late spring through fall best ▪ Viewing fossils of ancient mammals and Indian artifacts, hiking

Chimney Rock National Historic Site

A legendary landmark for westbound pioneers

Nineteenth-century pioneers heading west on the Oregon and California Trails, alongside the North Platte River, noted a tall rock formation atop a conical hill—a distinctive shape that had long served as a landmark for American Indians. Over time, Chimney Rock became the most famous milestone for travelers along these historic routes. Highways paralleling the North Platte follow the approximate path of the wagon trails, and modern travelers remain impressed by the 326-foot-tall rock, an eroded remnant of what was once a more substantial butte.

Pioneers could see Chimney Rock from miles away.

Chimney Rock National Historic Site, an affiliated site of the National Park Service, is owned and operated by the Nebraska State Historical Society *(www.nebraskahistory .org/sites/rock)*. The society's Ethel and Christopher J. Abbot Visitor Center features interpretive exhibits on the great American westward migration and the significance of Chimney Rock in the experiences of the nearly half million travelers who passed it during that era.

The same erosive forces that gave the formation its current shape inevitably will destroy it. Basing their ideas on early drawings and photographs, observers debate just how much Chimney Rock has changed since pioneer days, by lightning strikes and other environmental factors. Chimney Rock is featured on the Nebraska state quarter, issued in 2006.

Neb. 92, 3 miles south of
Bayard, NE
308-586-2581
www.nps.gov/chro

AT A GLANCE

Western Nebraska, 22 miles southeast of Scottsbluff ▪ 83 acres ▪ Year-round ▪ Viewing historic rock formation and exhibits in visitor center

Homestead National Monument of America

Commemorating the changes wrought by the Homestead Act of 1862

The Homestead Act of 1862, passed by Congress and signed into law by President Abraham Lincoln, had a tremendous effect on the westward expansion of the United States. The legislation effectively transferred vast areas of land from the public domain to private ownership. Over the decades that the act was in effect, about 270 million acres, or 10 percent of the area of the United States, was legally claimed and settled.

The opportunity to acquire land was open to nearly anyone, including newly arrived immigrants, single women, and former slaves, expanding the diversity of western landowners. (Women were allowed to homestead land 58 years before being granted the right to vote in federal elections.) To claim land, potential settlers had to choose a 160-acre plot (a quarter section, or one-fourth of a square mile), apply and pay a fee at a land office; they then had to build a home and begin farming at least 10 acres within five years, a process that was called "proving up" the land. The Homestead Act remained technically in effect until 1976, though it was little used after the 1930s. A special law allowed homesteading in Alaska to continue until 1986.

Homestead National Monument of America was established in 1936 to commemorate this influential legislation and the pioneer settlers who, under the act, began new lives in states from Florida to Michigan, from California to Alaska. The park is located on land west of Beatrice, Nebraska, that was claimed by Daniel Freeman early on January 1, 1863—the very first day the Homestead Act was in effect. His descendants sold the land to the Department of the Interior in the

1930s for the purpose of creating a national monument to homesteading and the Homestead Act.

The Homestead Heritage Center presents exhibits on subjects such as immigration, agriculture, industrialization, Native Americans, the tallgrass prairie ecosystem, and federal land policies. The center's roof was designed to represent a single-bottom plow moving through the sod. The parking lot is exactly 1 acre in area, helping visitors visualize

how much land homesteaders were required to plant in crops to "prove up" their claim. The Living Wall at the entrance to the center represents the percentage of land that was successfully homesteaded in each state included in the act.

The Homestead Education Center is an institution of lifetime learning that focuses on the effects of the Homestead Act and offers arts and crafts demonstrations, science exhibits, and special exhibits. On display

is the Palmer-Epard Cabin, built in 1867; and tools and farm equipment used by pioneers. Nearby is the one-room 1872 Freeman School.

The national monument encompasses a 100-acre tract of restored tallgrass prairie and 40 acres of mesic bur-oak forest, a rare community type in Nebraska. Hiking trails traverse both the tallgrass prairie and the forest, providing visitors the opportunity to experience the diverse ecosystems.

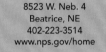

8523 W. Neb. 4
Beatrice, NE
402-223-3514
www.nps.gov/home

AT A GLANCE

Southeastern Nebraska, 40 miles south of Lincoln ▪ 210 acres ▪ Year-round ▪ Viewing pioneer buildings, hiking

Lewis and Clark National Historic Trail

A long-distance route tracing a historic transcontinental expedition

When the United States acquired the vast lands of the Louisiana Purchase from France in 1803, President Thomas Jefferson was determined to complete a plan he had worked toward for many years: sending an expedition to explore western North America and find a feasible water route to the Pacific Ocean.

Jefferson named the expeditionary group the Corps of Discovery, with Meriwether Lewis and William Clark as co-leaders. The undertaking—known today as the Lewis and Clark expedition—which officially started in May 1804 and ended in September 1806, holds a high place among the greatest exploratory expeditions in history.

Following the Missouri River upstream, crossing the Rocky Mountains, and making their way via the Columbia River to the Pacific Ocean, the Corps suffered only one fatality —a death near the beginning of the

Lewis and Clark followed the Missouri all the way to its Montana headwaters.

trip, thought to have been caused by appendicitis. Through encounters with hostile Native American tribes, wild-animal attacks, bitter winter conditions, near starvation, and raging river rapids, their resourcefulness and courage saved the explorers time and again. They were aided, too, by

fortunate encounters with friendly Indians, including a young Lemhi Shoshone woman named Sacagawea. Her presence helped in several ways, not the least of which was demonstrating that the Corps of Discovery was not a war party.

Today's Lewis and Clark National

Historic Trail invites travelers to follow the general path of the adventurers and to visit many of the exact sites that they explored and where they camped. Though the trail's headquarters is in Omaha, Nebraska, interpretive centers are scattered across the Midwest and Northwest, as well as sites related to the expedition in five states east of the Mississippi.

The North Dakota Lewis & Clark Interpretive Center in Washburn; the Lewis & Clark National Historic Trail Interpretive Center in Great Falls, Montana; and the Lewis & Clark Interpretive Center in Ilwaco, Washington, to give three examples,

are excellent local resources for learning about the Corps and events related to it in the regions. At Pompeys Pillar National Monument in southern Montana, visitors can view an actual carving in the rock done by William Clark on July 25, 1806, while on the expedition's return trip from the Pacific. (This remains the only visible, authenticated physical evidence of the Corps's journey.) The Sgt. Floyd Monument in Sioux City, Iowa, memorializes the nearby burial site of the only fatality suffered among Corps members. There are dozens of similar locations marking significant events of the expedition.

The more than one hundred sites along the national historic trail include those administered by local, state, and federal governments as well as Native American tribes and private organizations. Using a map of the trail, travelers may experience much of the same landscape viewed by members of the expeditionary Corps, from the broad lower Missouri River to Rocky Mountain forests—scenes "of visionary inchantment [sic]," as Lewis wrote.

Distinctive signs identify highways segments designated as part of the Lewis and Clark National Historic Trail's auto route, as well as official trail sites.

Trail headquarters 601 Riverfront Dr. Omaha, NE 402-661-1804 www.nps.lecl	AT A GLANCE	Passes through 11 states; related sites in 5 eastern states ▪ 3,700 miles ▪ Year-round; spring through fall best ▪ Discovering parks and historic sites along trail

Missouri National Recreational River
A glimpse of the wild Missouri River of Lewis and Clark days

The nutrient-rich bottomlands of the Missouri River are important feeding grounds for migratory birds in the fall.

Few rivers anywhere in the world have been so important to a nation's heritage as has the Missouri to the growth and development of the United States. If history had played out a little differently, the upper Mississippi would have been considered a tributary of the Missouri, not the other way around.

The Missouri was important to Native Americans, and it served as a major transportation route for early European explorers and fur trappers. Its greatest moment in American history, of course, was as the most significant part of Lewis and Clark's path on their expedition to the Pacific Ocean in 1804–06. The Corps of Discovery followed the river for its entire length, with countless adventures and scientific advances along the way.

Exploring the River

The National Park Service's Missouri National Recreational River oversees 98 miles of the Missouri on the Nebraska–South Dakota border, as well as the lower part of the Niobrara River and its tributary Verdigre Creek. The recreational river corridor ties together many parks, boat ramps, picnic spots, and other related sites, helping visitors find ways to explore and enjoy the Missouri.

Missouri National Recreational River comprises two noncontiguous segments. The 39-mile-long western section stretches from Fort Randall Dam, near Pickstown, South Dakota, downstream to the community of Running Water, South Dakota. Below this point, the next 29 miles, known as the Lewis and Clark Lake, are administered by the U.S. Army Corps of Engineers. The recreational river corridor begins again below Gavins Point Dam

and continues 59 miles to Nebraska's Ponca State Park.

On the upper, 39-mile reach, the river valley is generally less than 2 miles wide, and in some areas it is defined by limestone cliffs and loess bluffs towering more than 250 feet above the river. The floodplain is much wider in the lower, 59-mile reach—up to 12 miles across. The Nebraska side of the river is characterized by colorful chalk and shale bluffs. Both segments feature many sandbars, islands, backwaters, and side channels, with extensive areas covered in willows and cottonwoods. The Missouri has been greatly altered along its entire length by dams and dredging, but there are places within the recreational river corridor where visitors can enjoy scenes not too different from those encountered by Lewis and Clark.

Canoeing and kayaking are excellent ways to experience the Missouri, but such an adventure is not for inexperienced paddlers. Confusing channels, underwater hazards, strong winds, and occasional long distances

between put-in and take-out points are just a few of the factors that make careful preparation and caution necessary. Boaters need to be aware of and respect private property along the riverbanks as well.

Three good sources of information on the river's offerings are the Lewis and Clark Visitor Center near Gavins Point Dam in Crofton *(Neb. 121, west of U.S. 81)*, the Missouri National Recreational River Education and Resource Center *(402-755-2284)* in Nebraska's Ponca State Park, about 3 miles north of Neb. 12 and the town of Ponca, and the Missouri National Recreational and Scenic River headquarters in Yankton, South Dakota *(605-665-0209)*.

While the Park Service doesn't administer any campgrounds or hiking trails, these recreational offerings can be found at state parks, Corps of Engineers sites, and other parks adjacent to the river. Contact the national recreational river office, or visit the website for a map showing boat ramps and riverside parks.

Lewis and Clark Visitor Center
55245 Neb. 121
Crofton, NE
402-667-2550
www.nps.gov/mnrr

AT A GLANCE
Northeastern Nebraska and southeastern South Dakota ▪ 34,128 acres (300 acres managed by National Park Service); 98 miles of the Missouri River, plus 20 miles of the lower Niobrara River and 8 miles of Verdigre Creek ▪ Late spring through fall best ▪ Boating, canoeing, fishing, bird-watching

Niobrara National Scenic River

A surprisingly picturesque river through the Great Plains

A true gem of the Great Plains, the Niobrara River begins in Wyoming and winds more than 500 miles across northern Nebraska to its confluence with the Missouri River. A long battle to preserve it as a free-flowing recreational stream culminated in 1991 when 76 miles of the Niobrara were designated as a national scenic river.

Few might associate the Great Plains with waterfalls, bluffs, and rocky rapids,

but the Niobrara ranks with the region's most picturesque (and popular) natural resources. With most rivers in the area either dammed or flat and sluggish, the Niobrara attracts thousands of visitors on summer weekends to canoe, kayak, tube, or raft its most popular section just east of the town of Valentine, Nebraska.

The National Park Service manages the scenic river through partnerships with various agencies and

organizations, and with the cooperation of private landowners. Most land along the river is privately owned, and there are limited points for public access and camping; the majority of floaters arrange trips with private outfitters and campgrounds. (Check the website or request a list from the park office.) Public camping and river access are available at Smith Falls State Park *(402-376-1306)*, which also features Nebraska's highest waterfall, with a drop of 63 feet. Other sites adjacent to the river offer hiking trails, excellent wildlife-viewing, horseback riding, and mountain biking.

The Niobrara receives drainage from the huge Sandhills area to the south, and springs help maintain a constant flow even in drier months. Nonetheless, it's good to check river levels before making a trip in July or August. In winter, tall ice cliffs form on the river's sandstone bluffs, occasionally attracting ice climbers.

Park headquarters
146 S. Hall St.
Valentine, NE
402-376-1901
www.nps.gov/niob

AT A GLANCE

Northern Nebraska, 300 miles northwest of Omaha ▪ 76 river miles ▪ Spring through fall for floating, winter for ice climbing ▪ Canoeing, kayaking, tubing, ice climbing

Scotts Bluff National Monument
A towering geologic feature along the Oregon Trail

Nineteenth-century pioneers on the Oregon Trail followed the North Platte River when possible, but in western Nebraska they were forced to find a pass through bluffs that rose more than 800 feet above the river. A narrow passage allowed horses but not wagons to pass until 1851, when it was widened and the trail improved. Later called Mitchell Pass, it saw hundreds of thousands of travelers pass on the Oregon, California, and Mormon Trails, as well as riders of the Pony Express and U.S. Army soldiers.

The striking geologic formation called Scotts Bluff became a famed landmark for these travelers. Its historical significance was so great that in 1919 it became a national monument under the administration of the National Park Service.

The Oregon Trail Museum and Visitor Center offers an audiovisual presentation on the trail and displays historic paintings and drawings by 19th-century artist William Henry Jackson. Nearby is an actual segment of the Oregon Trail at Mitchell Pass on which visitors can walk, following

For the pioneers, Scotts Bluff signaled the start of their crossing of the Rockies.

a swale worn into the earth by wagon wheels, feet, and hooves.

The top of the bluff can be reached on the 1.6-mile Saddle Rock Trail or by the Summit Road, which passes through three tunnels on its way up *(size limits on vehicles)*. In summer, and other times depending on staffing, the park also operates a shuttle vehicle to the top. Once at the summit, visitors can walk to lookout

points, where views extend over the North Platte River Valley; the town of Scottsbluff; the Oregon Trail; and the surrounding prairie, badlands, and farms and ranches.

Geologists study Scotts Bluff because it features 740 feet of continuous rock strata covering a time period from 33 to 22 million years before the present, including layers of sandstone, siltstone, volcanic ash, and limestone.

190276 Old Oregon Trail
Gering, NE
308-436-9700
www.nps.gov/scbl

AT A GLANCE

Western Nebraska, 7 miles southwest of Scottsbluff ▪ 3,003 acres ▪ Year-round ▪ Hiking, driving the Summit Road, viewing museum exhibits

NORTH DAKOTA

The geographic center of North America is a point near the town of Rugby, North Dakota. Far from the moderating influence of oceans, the state experiences very hot summers and very cold winters, one reason it's the fourth least populous state. Only eight cities have populations above 20,000. Most people live in the east, where the fertile soils of the Red River Valley were once the bottom of glacial Lake Agassiz. "Prairie pothole" lakes host a significant number of nesting waterbirds, and North Dakota has more national wildlife refuges than any other state. Theodore Roosevelt National Park protects the badlands around the Little Missouri River in the southwestern part.

International Peace Garden

A living monument to an untroubled international border

In 1930 a nonprofit group was established to create a garden "as a memorial to the peace that has existed between the United States and the Dominion of Canada." After a search along the international boundary, a site was selected near Turtle Mountain, on the North Dakota and Manitoba border.

The International Peace Garden was dedicated at a ceremony in 1932, at which representatives from the U.S. and Canada unveiled a plaque on which was inscribed a pledge "that as long as man shall live we will not take up arms against one another."

Despite the hardships of the Great Depression, a construction team from the Civilian Conservation Corps, under the supervision of the National Park Service, cleared land and built lakes, roads, a lodge, and other infrastructure. Over time, gardens were planted and an arboretum was established, along with many attractions, such as a floral clock incorporating as many as 5,000 plants, a bell tower housing a copy of London's Westminster Chimes cast by Gillette and Jonston

of Croydn, England, floral re-creations of the American and Canadian flags, a Peace Tower, seven Peace Poles presented by the Japanese government, and a 9/11 Memorial Contemplative Garden with steel girders taken from the ruins of the World Trade Center. Each year more than 150,000 flowers are planted in varied displays.

Visitors must pass through U.S. or Canadian customs on leaving the International Peace Garden. Check the garden's website for information about required documents.

10939 U.S. 281 **Dunseith, ND** 701-263-4390 or 888-432-6733 www.peacegarden.com	**AT A GLANCE** North-central North Dakota, 110 miles northeast of Minot ▪ 2,339 acres (888 in the United States, 1,451 in Canada) ▪ Year-round ▪ Visiting gardens, driving auto-tour route, picnicking, camping, cross-country skiing

Knife River Indian Villages National Historic Site

An Indian earth lodge like those seen by Lewis and Clark

At the beginning of the 19th century a thriving community of about 4,500 Hidatsa and Mandan Indians existed at the confluence of the Knife and Missouri Rivers in what

is now North Dakota. The Lewis and Clark expedition encountered these people in October 1804, as they traveled up the Missouri on their way to the Pacific Ocean. Warmly welcomed

by the Indians, the expedition decided to build a fort and spend the winter nearby. In November, Lewis and Clark hired Toussaint Charbonneau, a French-Canadian fur trapper living with the Hidatsa, as an interpreter. His wife, Sacagawea, would gain fame for the ways in which she aided the expedition during the next two years. The expedition stopped again at the villages on their return from the Pacific, in August 1806.

Later the villages were ravaged by smallpox, a disease brought by Europeans and from which the Indians had no immunity. The Mandan population was reduced by 90 percent and the Hidatsa by half. In 1845 they left their Knife River villages and moved upriver along the Missouri.

Knife River Indian Villages National Historic Site provides visitors with a look into the lives of these Northern Plains Indians, with exhibits and an interpretive film in the visitor center, a reconstructed earth lodge, and walking trails. The Village Trail (1.3 miles) takes visitors past the remains of the Awatixa Xi'e Village and Awatixa Village, where depressions of the lodges can be seen. The second village is situated on the banks of the Knife River and was formed by people fleeing a smallpox epidemic at Awatixa Xi'e. A Sioux raid later burned Awatixa to the ground.

Hiking trails of up to 7 miles also wind through prairie and riverside forests, making the park an excellent place for bird-watching and other nature activities.

Cty. Rd. 37
(off N. Dak. 200)
Stanton, ND
701-745-3300
www.nps.gov/knri

AT A GLANCE Central North Dakota, 60 miles northwest of Bismarck ▪ 1,758 acres ▪ Year-round ▪ Touring reconstructed Indian earth lodge, observing cultural demonstrations, hiking, picnicking

---

Theodore Roosevelt National Park
The badlands landscape that shaped Theodore Roosevelt's character

It is fitting that a ruggedly spectacular national park be named for Theodore Roosevelt, arguably the most influential conservationist in the history of the United States. As the 26th President, Roosevelt established the U.S. Forest Service (under the Department of Agriculture) and backed legislation to create wildlife refuges, national forests, national parks, and national monuments. All told, Roosevelt placed approximately 230 million acres of the United States under public protection.

Much of Roosevelt's dedication to conservation can be traced to his experiences in North Dakota. He arrived as a 24-year-old in 1883, eager to hunt bison. Enchanted by the wild country known as the badlands, he became a partner in one cattle ranch and bought another, residing off and on for several years in the area of today's national park.

A male bison can weigh as much as 2,000 pounds.

He suffered hardships and performed ranch chores that built his character; he later wrote, "I never would have been President if it had not been for my experiences in North Dakota."

Roosevelt also saw, even in those late 19th-century times, how the human presence was affecting land and wildlife. The vast herds of bison that had once roamed the plains were almost gone, and many other species were greatly reduced in numbers. "[I]t is also vandalism wantonly to destroy or to permit the destruction of what is beautiful in nature, whether it be a cliff, a forest, or a species of mammal or bird," he once wrote—a sentiment that has its roots in what he learned in the badlands.

The Lay of the Land
Considering its many attractions, Theodore Roosevelt National Park is undoubtedly underappreciated. This may be because of the name "badlands" attached to the terrain here. Though the word might indicate a barren and uninviting place, in reality this is a colorful, strikingly shaped landscape, home to an array of fascinating wildlife. Roosevelt once called this region "the so-called Bad Lands," and also wrote that in part they are "so fantastically broken in form and so bizarre in color as to seem hardly properly to belong to this earth."

The land owes its shape and color to many factors. Beginning about 60

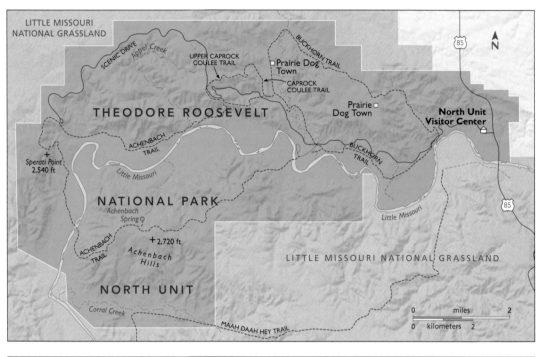

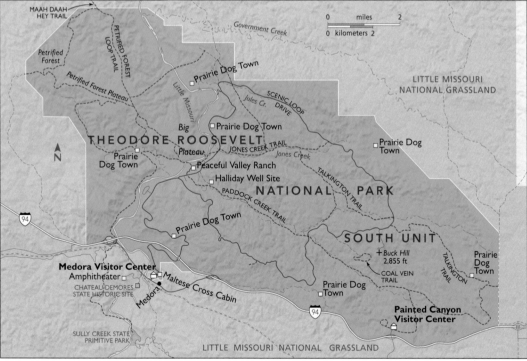

million years ago, material eroding from the young Rocky Mountains was brought here by streams. Later, vegetation in swampy areas was buried and turned into lignite, a form of coal. Volcanic ash weathered into a blue-gray clay called bentonite. Much later, the Little Missouri River and other streams cut down into the layers of rock, exposing multicolored strata and carving buttes, ravines, and other landforms.

Exploring the Park

The park comprises three units that

are not connected geographically. Most visited is the South Unit, just off I-94. The North Unit lies about 68 miles north, along U.S. 85. Both these areas have visitor centers *(the North Unit Visitor Center is generally closed in fall and winter, but check the park website for exact dates and hours),* scenic drives, campgrounds, and, in combination, more than 100 miles of hiking trails. In between is the Elkhorn Ranch Unit, site of one of Theodore Roosevelt's ranches. None of the ranch buildings remain today, and access can be difficult. Travelers should check at a visitor center before making the trip.

A quick overview of the national park can be seen from the Painted Canyon Visitor Center *(closed Nov.– April, although the overlook remains open to walk-in visitors),* 6 miles east of the town of Medora. The next stop should be the South Unit Visitor Center in Medora, with an orientation film, information desk, and museum. Behind the visitor center is Roosevelt's Maltese Cross Cabin, moved from its original location 7 miles south. Built of ponderosa pine railroad ties, it contains a few of Roosevelt's personal items. Guided tours are available in summer.

Regardless of preferred activities or interests, every visitor to this beautiful, lightly publicized national park will come to appreciate Roosevelt's love for the badlands, and what he called "the attraction of its lonely freedom."

Scenic Drives

The South Unit is home to what is arguably the park's most popular feature: the paved, 36-mile Scenic Loop Drive, featuring many pullouts and interpretive signs explaining historical and natural features, as well as trailheads for walks both easy and challenging. Visible from the Scoria Point Overlook is a site where a coal seam caught fire and baked adjacent clay and sand into a reddish, brick-like substance locally called scoria (though the term is properly applied to material of volcanic origin). Farther along is the fairly strenuous Ridgeline Nature Trail, along which grow plants such as juniper, sage, prickly pear cactus, and yucca. A side road off the scenic loop leads to Coal Vein Trail, with views of a spot where a lignite bed burned from 1951 to 1977.

The loop continues past other trails and overlooks to the Little Missouri River Valley. The short trail at Wind Canyon leads up a ridge to one of the most dramatic views in the South Unit: a bend in the Little Missouri River and a site where windblown sand has shaped the canyon walls.

The North Unit's 14-mile scenic drive is an out-and-back route, not a loop; it leads to the Oxbow Overlook. Interesting pullouts are located along the drive, including the River

Bend Overlook, with dramatic views of the Missouri River and a historic shelter built by the Civilian Conservation Corps.

Hiking & Canoeing

While the scenic drives lead to beautiful views and informative exhibits, leaving roads and walking some of the national park's trails offers a more intimate experience. Whether you take the very short walk to the River Bend Overlook, with its panoramic view of the badlands and the Little Missouri River; or the 16-mile Achenbach Trail loop (both in the North Unit), you'll have a better chance to smell sagebrush, hear birdsong, and feel the wind and sun away from a vehicle.

Backcountry camping is allowed in the park with a free permit; hiking into the backcountry and camping provide the best way of all to experience the badlands environment. Backpackers (and horseback riders camping in the backcountry) should be adequately prepared with maps. There are no sources of safe drinking water in the backcountry, so all water must be boiled or otherwise treated.

When water levels are adequate (May and June are best), it is possible to make a canoe or kayak trip along the Little Missouri River, a wild and solitary journey for those who are properly prepared. A three- or four-day trip can be made from Medora to the Long-X Bridge adjacent to the North Unit, passing through the national park and the Little Missouri National Grassland. Paddlers should be aware and respect the fact that private property does front lengths of the river, and that emergency help might be difficult to summon in this remote region.

The Park's Wildlife

Wildlife might be seen from any road or trail in the park. Most visitors are especially eager to see bison (also called buffalo), which were extirpated in the area in the late 19th century but reintroduced in 1956. The size of the park's herds varies, but ranges from 200 to 400 individuals in the South Unit and from 100 to 300 in the North Unit. Though it's tempting to try to get close for photographs, bison (despite weighing up to a ton or more) can run surprisingly fast and when provoked can be extremely dangerous. Persons on foot should stay at least 100 yards away, and vehicles should give them plenty of room to move.

Elk, also extirpated from this region, were reintroduced to the South Unit in 1985. They are less easily seen than bison, and are best spotted at dawn or dusk, as they

The Little Missouri River flows through the badlands of Theodore Roosevelt National Park.

rest in wooded areas during the day. Another favorite of visitors are the park's wild (feral) horses. The park maintains a herd of 70 to 110 animals as part of the historical setting. Theodore Roosevelt National Park is one of the few areas in the West where free-roaming horses can be observed. Bighorn sheep have also been reintroduced and are resident in the North Unit of the park.

Much smaller but just as charismatic are the park's prairie dogs. These social rodents live in "towns" that can be seen at several places along the loop drive in the South Unit. Visitors can see for themselves whether Theodore Roosevelt was accurate in calling them "the most noisy and inquisitive animals imaginable." At the least, they make themselves difficult to miss.

Other mammals that might be seen around the park include mule and white-tailed deer (the former in rough country and uplands, the latter in riverside woods), pronghorn, porcupines, beavers, coyotes, and badgers. A small herd of longhorn steers resides in the North Unit, kept to commemorate the historic Long X Trail, a cattle-drive route running from Texas to a ranch north of the current national park.

The golden eagle is among the park's most notable breeding birds, preying on prairie dogs, rabbits, and other small mammals. Bird-watchers also frequent the area to spot species such as sharp-tailed grouse, wild turkey, upland sandpiper, burrowing owl (which is found around prairie-dog towns), Say's phoebe, black-billed magpie, mountain bluebird, and black-headed grosbeak.

AT A GLANCE

South Unit, off I-94
North Unit, off U.S. 85
Medora, ND
701-623-4466 or 701-623-4730
www.nps.gov/thro

Western North Dakota, 135 miles west of Bismarck ▪ 70,466 acres ▪ Year-round; portions closed in winter ▪ Scenic drives, hiking, camping, backpacking, canoeing, kayaking, observing wildlife

SOUTH DAKOTA

To many people, the face of South Dakota is really four faces: the presidential granite visages on Mount Rushmore, in the Black Hills. There's more to see in the Black Hills, though, including the abundant wildlife at Wind Cave National Park and the historic mining town of Deadwood. Elsewhere, Badlands National Park is a geologic wonderland as well as home to important fossil deposits and an extensive prairie ecosystem. The Missouri River divides the state into ranching country to the west and farmland to the east, where higher rainfall levels allow cultivation of corn, soybeans, and wheat. About 90 percent of the state's land is devoted to ranches and farms.

Badlands National Park
Rugged backcountry, expansive prairie, and a historic deposit of fossils

Many visitors to Badlands National Park simply drive the length of S. Dak. 240 (also known as Badlands Loop Road) as it loops south and back to I-90. While this 36-mile odyssey through the park provides a sense of place and some beautiful views, there's much more to see and do here for those who take a little more time.

The word "badlands" appears often on maps throughout the American West, indicating rugged terrain, usually with limited or no water, that was difficult—or even dangerous—to traverse. Ironically, many of those "bad" places are today among our most treasured wild areas, spared from development by their terrain and isolation and now offering great rewards to lovers of nature and solitude.

When a park was originally proposed for this area in 1928, the

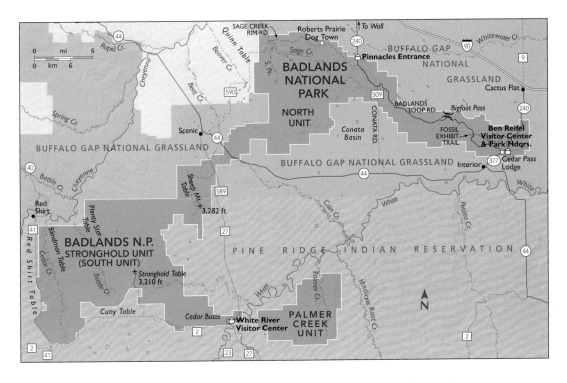

suggested name was "Teton National Park"—an attempt to avoid discouraging those who might be kept away by the word "badlands." If potential visitors dismiss Badlands National Park today for the same reason, they're missing out on one of the most scenic and interesting parks, with the largest expanse of protected prairie ecosystem in the National Park System and one of the world's richest mammal fossil beds.

A Geologic Wonderland

From the park's overlooks, views take in a remarkable inventory of canyons, cliffs, tall spires, flattop buttes, and infinite variations on those shapes. The story of the park's geology begins with shale that was deposited during the Cretaceous period about 70 million years ago and is visible as a blackish layer at the bottom of some formations. Above that are strata of sandstone, volcanic ash, ancient soils, and siltstone, in shades of yellow, gray, brown, and red.

The erosion that sculpted Badlands National Park began only 500,000 years before the present—geologically speaking, a very short time ago. The process continues today at a relatively rapid pace, with formations being worn away at an average of an inch a year. If conditions remain essentially unchanged, visitors 500,000 years from now will be looking at a flat plain.

The best place to get an overview of the park's geology and other resources is the Ben Reifel Visitor Center, located at Cedar Pass on the park loop road (S. Dak. 240), in the eastern part of the North Unit of Badlands National Park. The film shown here, "Land of Stone and Light," offers an excellent introduction to the badlands. Interactive exhibits cover prairie ecology, paleontology, and the human history of the area. Many ranger-led programs are offered here in the summer. Nearby is Cedar Pass Lodge *(605-433-5460, www.cedarpasslodge.com, closed in winter)*, a concessionaire-operated lodge and restaurant.

Exploring the Park

From the Ben Reifel Visitor Center area, the park's scenic loop road heads northwest, ascending through Bigfoot Pass and offering many spectacular overlooks, including Yellow Mounds and Pinnacles. The road roughly follows the Badlands Wall, a 60-mile-long line of buttes that dominates the surrounding terrain. The erosive forces of wind, rain, and freezing and thawing have worn away at badlands sediments, creating this geologic feature. The town of Wall, South Dakota, takes its name from this imposing line of buttes.

Where S. Dak. 240 heads north to I-90 and Wall, the unpaved Sage

FOLLOWING PAGES: *At sunset, the sandstone buttes of Badlands National Park offer a kaleidoscope of changing colors.*

Creek Rim Road heads west, offering the chance to see wildlife such as bison and pronghorn, as well as prairie dogs. This road, which may close temporarily after storms, leads out of the park and continues to the town of Scenic, gateway to the park's Stronghold Unit (see below).

For a rewarding closer look at the park's geologic features, hike some of the park's trails, concentrated in the eastern section near the visitor center. Some are very short and easy, such as the Door Trail, named for a break in the Badlands Wall; and the Window Trail, with a view of an intricately eroded canyon. The 10-mile Castle Trail is the park's longest developed route; it connects with other trails, offering varying loop trips.

The half-mile, moderately strenuous Cliff Shelf Trail follows boardwalks and climbs stairs through a juniper forest perched along the Badlands Wall. A huge block of stone fell from a nearby cliff, creating a flat "shelf." Water sometimes collects here, creating an oasis-like small pond. The availability of water attracts mule deer and, occasionally, bighorn sheep.

Wildlife: Then & Now

The badlands have yielded extremely important deposits of fossils, revealing that a long time ago—some 26 million to 37 million years ago—prehistoric mammals such as a hornless rhinoceros, a three-toed horse, a tiny deerlike creature, and a small saber-toothed cat roamed the area. The exhibits at the visitor center provide an introduction to the park's fossil riches, as does the short, easy Fossil Exhibit Trail, which has interpretive panels and casts of fossil bones of now extinct animals.

Today Badlands National Park is populated by animals typical of the Great Plains: mule and white-tailed deer, coyotes, pronghorn, black-tailed prairie dogs, thirteen-lined ground squirrels, golden eagles, black-billed magpies, and mountain bluebirds.

Not so typical, at least in modern times, are four threatened or endangered mammal species that have been reintroduced into the park: bison, bighorn sheep, swift fox, and black-footed ferret. The latter species, one of the world's rarest mammals, depends largely on prairie-dog towns for its survival and was on the verge of extinction in the 1980s. It has made an encouraging comeback thanks to reintroduction programs and strict protection; however, the ferret, nocturnal like the little swift fox, is unlikely to be spotted by most visitors to the park.

Badlands National Park encompasses more than 64,000 acres of wilderness, partly comprising the largest area of mixed-grass prairie in the National Park System. This expanse supports the recovering populations of bison and black-footed ferrets, as well as many other species, from prairie rattlesnakes to sharp-tailed grouse. Visitors thrill to the sight of bison roaming the grasslands (they occasionally appear in or near the Sage Creek campground, at the western end of the North Unit).

Pine Ridge Indian Reservation & Stronghold Unit

Half of Badlands National Park lies within the Pine Ridge Indian Reservation and is co-managed with the Oglala Lakota Nation. The White River Visitor Center

(605-455-2878), located off Hwy. 27, is open in summer and features exhibits on the Oglala Lakota. The Stronghold Unit, as the southern part of the park is called, is almost totally undeveloped; roads are rough (and sometimes impassable) and often lead through private property. In addition, there's the possibility of coming across unexploded bombs and other ordnance from the period when the U.S. military used this area as a bombing range. All visitors who plan to leave the main roads should check first with a ranger at the visitor center for advice.

One of the few accessible sites in the Stronghold Unit is the Sheep Mountain Table Road, 4 miles south of the town of Scenic. At the road's end is a wonderful panoramic view of cliffs and pinnacles. The Oglala Lakota consider this area sacred ground, and visitors should not touch or remove objects tied to trees and shrubs. Sheep Mountain Table Road is passable under dry conditions, but it is often impassable when wet or snow covered; high-clearance vehicles are recommended.

Camping

The park offers two developed campgrounds and also allows relatively unrestricted backcountry camping. Though no permit is required for backpacking, it's recommended that visitors check with a park ranger and sign a trail register before setting out through the backcountry. There is essentially no water available, and hikers should be aware of dangers such as rattlesnakes, sudden severe storms, and unstable rock that can give way along bluff edges.

S. Dak. 240, off I-90
Interior, SD
605-433-5361
www.nps.gov/badl

AT A GLANCE

Southwestern South Dakota, 75 miles east of Rapid City ▪ 244,000 acres ▪ Year-round; may be inaccessible in winter ▪ Hiking, scenic drives, camping, backpacking, horseback riding, observing wildlife

Jewel Cave National Monument
Striking formations within the world's third longest cave

When it was discovered in 1900, Jewel Cave was thought to be a pretty but very small cave. Over time, however, explorers mapped more than 175 miles of passages, earning Jewel the distinction of being the world's third longest cave. (The longest cave is Kentucky's Mammoth Cave; see p. 163.) As recently as 1959, only 2 miles of passageway were known, but in the 1960s vast new scenic areas were discovered, and a new visitor center, elevator, and tour trails were completed in 1972.

All tours through the cave *(fee)* are ranger-guided. The moderately strenuous Scenic Tour (1.5 hours) is offered daily, spring through fall. The Historic Lantern Tour, following an unpaved trail using only lantern light, is offered in summer, as is the Wild Caving Tour, on which visitors don hard hats and squeeze through tight passageways. The Discovery Talk is a 20-minute introduction to Jewel Cave's natural and cultural history during which visitors view one large room of the cave; it is offered year-round.

The "jewels" of the cave's name are sparkling calcite crystals, just one form of the many speleothems (cave formations) seen on tours. Other types include stalactites, stalagmites, flowstone, draperies, and popcorn.

Two hiking trails in the national monument and another in the adjacent Black Hills National Forest wind through ponderosa pine forest. The Jasper Fire of August 2000 burned 83,500 acres here, including around 95 percent of the land within the national monument. While scenic values were certainly affected, visitors today have a chance to watch the fascinating process of regrowth and natural vegetative succession. Hikers may spot elk, white-tailed and mule deer, and birds such as the wild turkey, black-backed woodpecker, piñon jay, and red crossbill.

U.S. 16
13 miles west of
Custer, SD
605-673-8300
www.nps.gov/jeca

AT A GLANCE   Southwestern South Dakota, 50 miles southwest of Rapid City ▪ 1,275 acres ▪ Year-round (closed weekends in winter), though winter weather can affect travel to the cave ▪ Cave tours, hiking, interpretive programs

Minuteman Missile National Historic Site
A once lethal legacy of the Cold War

During the Cold War period from World War II to the early 1990s, the arms race between the United States and the Soviet Union led to weapons that could have destroyed both nations as well as civilization itself. The policy of "mutually assured destruction"—or MAD—made their actual use in a "hot" or "shooting" war almost unthinkable. The weapons were themselves seen as a deterrent to war.

South Dakota was one of several states on the Great Plains that together hosted a force of a thousand Minuteman missiles. Each missile was stored underground in

Minuteman II, at Delta-09

a concrete "silo" and armed with a nuclear warhead. Crews stationed in remote underground launch-control centers stood ready around the clock for decades in the event that an Emergency Action Order arrived with a launch command.

Touring Missile Facilities
At Minuteman Missile National Historic Site, visitors can tour both the aboveground Launch Control Facility Delta-01 and the underground launch-control center it supported. Eleven miles away, visitors can also see Launch Facility Delta-09 (a missile silo), with an inoperative Minuteman

inside. At this site, cell-phone tours are available, by which visitors can call a number and listen to a recorded interpretive tour.

Tours for Delta-01 begin at the visitor center *(open year-round, closed weekends in winter),* which also has an orientation film and museum exhibits. Space on tours is limited and tickets are available on a first-come, first served basis. Check the park website or call ahead for the most current hours for the visitor center and the tour schedule, which changes seasonally.

24545 Cottonwood Rd,
Philip, SD
605-433-5552
www.nps.gov/mimi

AT A GLANCE Southwestern South Dakota, 75 miles east of Rapid City ■ 15 acres ■ Year-round ■ Touring missile launch facility and launch-control center

Mount Rushmore National Memorial
Icon of America carved in South Dakota granite

One of the best known and most enduring symbols of the United States was born as a tourist attraction to bring visitors to the scenic Black Hills of South Dakota. In 1924 South Dakota historian Doane Robinson contacted sculptor Gutzon Borglum with the idea of creating a mammoth carving on a mountaintop in the area. After scouting trips, Borglum chose Mount Rushmore, a peak that had been named in 1885, almost on a whim, for a New York lawyer who happened to be in the Black Hills on business.

Getting congressional approval and funding, however, did not always go smoothly—partly because of Borglum's fractious personality (though that same forceful personality also was effective in raising money for the project). Work began in 1927 and ended in 1941, shortly after Borglum died and the work had been taken over by his son Lincoln. Amazingly, none of the ambitious project's 400 workers were killed over those 14 years, despite laboring on a cliff face and using heavy equipment and dynamite.

The four Presidents portrayed on Mount Rushmore—George Washington, Thomas Jefferson, Abraham Lincoln, and Theodore Roosevelt—represent the first 150 years of American history. Their heads are about 60 feet high. Original plans for the memorial called for the figures to be shown from the waist up, but the carvings were declared complete with only the heads finished when the sculptor realized the rock below was not granite and couldn't be carved.

Gutzon Borglum chose Mount Rushmore in part because it is an outcrop of fine-grained granite, a mineral that provides an excellent medium for carving. The granite originated as molten rock deep beneath Earth's surface about 1.6 billion years ago, later cooling and rising to the surface. The hardness of granite assures that Mount Rushmore will endure: Erosion is estimated at about 1 inch every 10,000 years.

Mount Rushmore was placed under the administration of the National Park Service in 1933. About three million people a year visit Mount Rushmore, walking down the Avenue of Flags and approaching the huge faces on the mountainside. (Morning light is best for photography of the carvings.) The Lincoln Borglum Museum offers an excellent interpretive film and a variety of exhibits on the

From left to right: Washington, Jefferson, Theodore Roosevelt, and Lincoln

creation of the memorial. The Sculptor's Studio *(closed in winter)* displays scale models and tools.

From late May through September, a special lighting program is held each evening, complete with music, narration, and a patriotic film. Ranger-led tours offered in summer include a walk along the Presidential Trail to the base of the mountain, and a talk in the Sculptor's Studio. Visitors can also rent an audio-tour program that tells the story of Mount Rushmore through music, narration, interviews, historic recordings, and sound effects while the listener walks a scenic route around the park.

S. Dak. 244
Keystone, SD
605-574-2523
www.nps.gov/moru

AT A GLANCE Southwestern South Dakota, 24 miles southwest of Rapid City ▪ 1,278 acres ▪ Year-round ▪ Viewing memorial, taking ranger-guided tours, attending evening programs (Memorial Day through September)

Wind Cave National Park

A picturesque prairie landscape atop the world's sixth longest cave

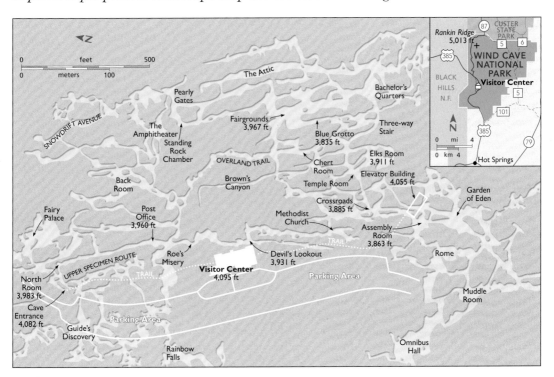

Humans have long noted this underground marvel as a distinctive feature of the Black Hills. American Indians told stories of a "hole that breathes cool air"; they regarded the site as sacred. In 1881 brothers Jesse and Tom Bingham heard a loud whistling noise and traced it to the cave's only natural opening, where a strong wind blew Tom's hat off. That wind, which gave the cave its name, results from the difference in atmospheric pressure between the cave and the surface.

After a period of commercial tourism (the "Wonderful Wind Cave Improvement Company"), the site in 1903 was designated Wind Cave National Park—the eighth United States national park and the first park in the world created to protect a cave. At first the cave was noted primarily for its outstanding display of boxwork, an unusual formation composed of thin calcite fins resembling honeycombs. As time passed and explorers ventured farther into its passages, Wind Cave came to be recognized as the world's sixth largest cave. Cavers continue their explorations, and the length of known passageways grows each year.

As intriguing as the cave is, though, it's only part of what makes a visit here so rewarding. The park also protects a globally important tract of mixed-grass prairie, an ecosystem that has largely disappeared elsewhere in North America in the face of agriculture, ranching, and other development. Ponderosa pine forest makes up part of the park landscape as well, adding to its ecological diversity and making it an excellent place to observe a variety of wildlife, from massive bison to diminutive songbirds.

Wind Cave's visitor center is located off U.S. 385 in the southern part of the park. Three rooms house exhibits on cave geology, wildlife, Wind Cave history, and related subjects. An 18-minute film entitled "Wind Cave: One Park, Two Worlds" is shown regularly.

The Underground World

Visitors may enter Wind Cave only on one of the many ranger-guided tours. The tours all leave from the visitor center, and admission is first come, first served (except for Candlelight and Wild Cave Tours), so an early arrival helps ensure a place on a tour, especially in the busy summer months. From late September through May, a smaller variety of tours is offered.

The one-hour, 0.25-mile Garden of Eden tour is Wind Cave's least strenuous walk and is suitable for people with physical limitations. After entering by elevator, visitors see a sample of the cave's formations such as boxwork, cave popcorn, and flowstone. The 1.5-hour, 0.5-mile Fairgrounds Cave Tour is the park's most strenuous cave walk. It explores both the upper and middle levels of the cave, passing abundant popcorn and frostwork in the Temple Room, the Bachelor's Quarters, and the Chert Room, among other areas.

Even in winter, Wind Cave's prairie lands support a wealth of wildlife.

The 1.25-hour, 0.5-mile Natural Entrance Cave Tour is regarded as moderately strenuous. On this tour participants visit the natural entrance of Wind Cave, then enter the cave through a constructed entrance and walk through the cave's middle level. The tour winds through the Post Office (named for the abundant boxwork on the walls) and Devil's Lookout before exiting via the elevator.

In summer, rangers offer a Candlelight Tour of Wind Cave. The two-hour tour is conducted using only the light from candlelit lanterns, similar to those used by tour guides when Wind Cave was a commercial tourist attraction in the 1890s. Passing through areas such as Blue Grotto and the Pearly Gates, the tour lets participants step back in history and imagine the challenges faced by the earliest explorers. Even more adventurous is the four-hour Wild Caving Tour *(summer only)*, which involves crawling through narrow passageways—only people in good physical condition who are willing to get dirty should sign up for this outing.

Aboveground Wonders

Visitors who exit the cave after even the longest tour have seen only half of Wind Cave National Park. A 30-mile network of hiking trails spreads across the park's aboveground 28,295 acres, offering a sea of prairie vegetation, the invigorating scent of a ponderosa pine forest, and the chance to see an array of wildlife. Much can be seen from park roads, too—and while hiking affords a more intimate communion with nature, vehicles can serve as blinds from which wildlife can sometimes be seen fairly closely. This is especially true at pullouts along U.S. 85 near prairie-dog towns, where it's often better to observe the prairie dogs' antics from a car than to get out and risk disturbing them.

Wind Cave's most famous denizen—and arguably its most popular—is the bison (commonly called buffalo). Once abundant beyond comprehension on the Great Plains, the species *Bison bison* came close to extinction in the late 19th century. Fourteen bison were reintroduced to Wind Cave National Park in 1913, and six more were added in 1916, all believed to have descended from true wild bison, with no cattle genes intermingled from crossbreeding. Disease free, and with good genetic makeup, Wind Cave's bison population plays an important role in the survival of this iconic American mammal.

Bison are commonly seen from park roads, though they wander constantly as they graze. These huge animals look placid and sluggish, but they can accelerate quickly to 35 miles an hour (faster than humans can run) and can be extremely dangerous when angered. Though it's tempting to approach them for a photograph, approaching within 100 yards is prohibited.

The same holds true for other park wildlife, such as elk and pronghorn—both extirpated from the Wind Cave area and reintroduced in 1914. A good rule is that when an animal reacts to your presence, you're too near. Binoculars and telephoto lenses are the best ways to get up close.

Park managers deal with many factors to maintain healthy populations of once widespread species such as bison, elk, and pronghorn. Lacking predators, elk can overgraze habitat, hindering the regeneration of trees such as aspen, willow, oak, and birch. Pronghorn numbers are greatly affected by the population of coyotes. Bison numbers must be limited to prevent overgrazing. Even with its 44 square miles of land, Wind Cave is a tiny area compared to the vast prairies over which herds of mammals were once able to roam.

Much can be learned about the local environment on Wind Cave's three nature trails, each about a mile long. Interpretive signs and brochures help hikers understand the ecology of the southern Black Hills. The Prairie Vista Nature Trail starts at the visitor center and explores the mixed-grass prairie. This ecotone (a zone where two habitats meet) blends species of the eastern tallgrass prairie, which need more moisture to survive, with the shorter grass species of the western High Plains, which are more tolerant of drought. The amount of rain and snow received in any given year determines which species dominate that year. The Rankin Ridge Nature Trail, in the northern part of Wind Cave National Park, leads to a fire lookout tower at the highest point in the park, with excellent views of hills and prairie. The Elk Mountain Nature Trail, near the park's developed campground, passes through both grassland and ponderosa pine forest.

Other park trails include the easy, 1.8-mile Wind Cave Canyon Trail, recommended as a good route for bird-watching (look for red-headed and Lewis's woodpeckers in dead trees); and the moderately strenuous, 3.6-mile Sanctuary Trail, which passes a prairie-dog town. In 2007 Wind Cave reintroduced the endangered black-footed ferret, a member of the weasel family, to the park. The ferret's chief prey is the prairie dog, and as a result the species was nearly wiped out as a side effect of persecution of these colonial rodents. Hikers should be aware that prairie rattlesnakes also frequent prairie-dog towns, as well as rocky hillsides.

Unpaved roads winding through the eastern part of the park allow more leisurely driving and good chances to stop and enjoy views of bison and pronghorn.

Apart from the main Elk Mountain campground, a mile north of the visitor center, Wind Cave allows backcountry camping in the northwestern section of the park with a free permit.

Custer State Park

Adjoining park on the north, Custer State Park *(U.S. 16A)* encompasses 71,000 acres of woods and prairie, home to bison (at 1,500 animals, one of the largest herds in the world, often seen along the 18-mile Wildlife Loop Road), pronghorn, elk, bighorn sheep, mountain goats, and feral burros. Lodging and restaurants are located within the park, along with commercial tour companies.

U.S. 385
Hot Springs, SD
605-745-4600
www.nps.gov/wica

AT A GLANCE

Southwestern South Dakota, 50 miles south of Rapid City ▪ 28,295 acres ▪ Late spring through fall best ▪ Taking cave tours, driving scenic route, observing wildlife, hiking, horseback riding

South Central

Traversing this region east to west means seeing an ecological transition from the swampy forests of the Mississippi River Valley to the dry, rocky Chihuahuan Desert of West Texas. From south to north, the area encompasses the subtropical Rio Grande Valley and the nearly treeless High Plains of western Kansas. Nature lovers will enjoy highlights as diverse as Buffalo National River in Arkansas, Tallgrass Prairie National Preserve in Kansas, and Big Bend National Park in Texas. New Orleans, arguably the most culturally distinctive city in America, is home to two national park units where visitors can experience unique history and learn how jazz was born.

Native American life on the Plains, Washita Battlefield N.H.S.

NEBRASKA

IOWA

Oakley

Nicodemus
National Historic Site

KANSAS

Salina

Topeka

Fort Larned
National Historic Site

Tallgrass Prairie
National Preserve

Dodge
City

Arkansas

Wichita

Cimarron

Brown v. Board of Education
National Historic Site

Independence

St. Joseph

Harry S Truman
National Historic Site

Jefferson City

MISSOURI

Missouri

Jefferson National
Expansion Memorial

St. Louis

ILLINOIS

Ulysses S. Grant
National Historic
Site

Fort Scott
National Historic Site

George Washington Carver
National Monument

Springfield

Wilson's Creek
National
Battlefield

Ohio

KY.

Ozark
National
Scenic Riverways

Pea Ridge
National Military Park

Buffalo
National River

White

TENNESSEE

Neosho

OKLAHOMA

Tulsa

Washita
Battlefield
National
Historic Site

Canadian

Oklahoma City

Oklahoma
City
National
Memorial

Chickasaw
National Recreation Area

Fort Smith
Fort Smith
National Historic Site

ARKANSAS

Little Rock Central High School
National Historic Site

Little Rock

Hot Springs
National Park

Arkansas Post
National Memorial

Mississippi

Wichita Falls

Red

President William Jefferson
Clinton Birthplace Home
National Historic Site

Brazos

Fort
Worth

Dallas

Shreveport

LOUISIANA

Poverty Point
National
Monument

Mississippi

MISS.

Waco Mammoth
National Monument

Colorado

Waco

Red

Cane River Creole
National Historical Park
and National Heritage Area

TEXAS

Austin

Jean Lafitte
National Historical
Park and Preserve

New Orleans Jazz
National
Historical
Park

Lyndon B. Johnson
National Historical Park

Big Thicket
National Preserve

Baton
Rouge

Houston

New Orleans

San Antonio

Galveston

San Antonio Missions
National Historical Park

Jean Lafitte
National Historical
Park and Preserve

U.S.
Mexico

Corpus Christi

Gulf of Mexico

*The Monumental Earthworks
of Poverty Point Nat. Mon. in
Louisiana and San Antonio
Missions N.H.P. in Texas are
both World Heritage sites.*

Laredo

Padre Island
National Seashore

miles

0   50   100   150

0   50   100   150

kilometers

Palo Alto Battlefield
National Historical Park

Brownsville

ARKANSAS

A line from the southwestern corner to the northeastern corner divides Arkansas into two topographic regions, which might be described briefly as highlands in the west and lowlands in the east. The Ozark Plateau and Ouachita Mountains contain some of the most rugged terrain in the central United States, while the Mississippi River Plain in the east is dominated by cropland. National forests comprise more than 2.5 million acres in Arkansas, providing excellent hiking and camping, while rivers offer challenging white-water canoeing. The most famous float stream is Buffalo National River, winding more than 130 miles through the Ozarks.

Arkansas Post National Memorial

The site of an important 17th-century French settlement

French explorer Henri de Tonti established a trading post in the flatlands along the Arkansas River in 1686—the first permanent French settlement in the entire lower Mississippi River region. Set near the location of a Quapaw Indian village, the so-called Poste de Arkansea served as a center of business and government for nearly two centuries, as well as the site of occasional military clashes as French, Spanish, British, American, and Confederate forces fought for control of the lower Mississippi Valley. Famed naturalists Thomas Nuttall and John James Audubon also visited the community on their travels.

By the early 1800s Arkansas Post had become an important river port and the largest town in the region, so much so that it was named capital of the newly designated Arkansas Territory in 1819. Two years later, though, the seat of territorial government was relocated to higher ground upstream

A 10-pound Parrott rifle stands ready at the Arkansas Post.

at Little Rock, beginning the flood-prone post's decline into near oblivion. During the Civil War, in 1863, Union forces attacked a Confederate fort established here; the artillery bombardment devastated what was left of the community.

Today visitors can see a film recounting the historic site's past, and

walk through the town site, of which almost nothing remains. Interpretive signs along the 2 miles of trails tell the story of significant local places and events. Forest and wetlands around the area offer excellent wildlife-watching, with alligators, white-tailed deer, bald eagles, moorhens, herons, orioles, and many other animals often seen.

Ark. 169
south of Gilette, AR
870-548-2207
www.nps.gov/arpo

AT A GLANCE

Southeastern Arkansas, 80 miles southeast of Little Rock ▪ 758 acres ▪ Year-round ▪ Studying history, wildlife-watching

Buffalo National River

A beautiful Ozark mountain canoe stream

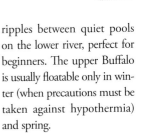

In the rugged hollows of the Boston Mountains, a small stream flows east for a few miles through an Ozark National Forest wilderness area, soon taking on a new status as the Buffalo National River—one of the wildest, most beautiful, and most rewarding natural areas in mid-America. Celebrated as a canoe stream, the Buffalo winds through a region of splendid scenery, abundant wildlife, and intriguing human history.

The placid Buffalo's top rapids are usually only Class II.

Smallmouth bass, catfish, bluegills, sunfish, and an array of other species flit through the Buffalo's astoundingly clear water. Countless spots along the river make perfect summer swimming holes. Limestone and sandstone bluffs rise more than 400 feet straight from the riverside, dwarfing canoeists who pause in their paddling to look up in awe. Black bears, elk, white-tailed deer, mink, bobcats, and beavers live in the Buffalo River country, along with dozens of kinds of nesting birds and more than 1,500 species of plants.

Enjoying the River

Buffalo National River Visitor Center is located at Tyler Bend (off U.S. 65, 10 miles north of Marshall). Ranger stations are located at Steel Creek *(on Ark. 74, 12 miles west of Jasper)* and Buffalo Point *(off Ark. 14, 14 miles south of Yellville)*. Speak to a ranger at one of these offices about current conditions, especially if you're planning to canoe or go for a lengthy hike. Unlike in many units in the National Park System, hunting is permitted in Buffalo National River; hikers should exercise caution at certain times of the year.

Eleven campgrounds are spaced along nearly the entire 135-mile length of the river, and at Buffalo Point you can stay in historic cabins built by the Civilian Conservation Corps in the 1930s. The national river encompasses three official wilderness areas: the Upper Buffalo, above Boxley Valley; the Ponca, on the river's most popular canoeing segment; and the Lower Buffalo, a remote area located where the Buffalo flows into the White River.

For many people, "floating the Buffalo" is the most exciting and satisfying experience in the Ozark Mountains. Although the Buffalo is usually placid, its superb scenery and wilderness qualities make it a memorable destination. There's something here for all abilities, too: thrilling rapids on the famed Ponca-to-Pruitt stretch of the upper river, for the daring; and gentle ripples between quiet pools on the lower river, perfect for beginners. The upper Buffalo is usually floatable only in winter (when precautions must be taken against hypothermia) and spring.

Hiking & More

More than 100 miles of trails offer everything from short day hikes to long, strenuous treks. Among the most popular trails are Lost Valley and Indian Rockhouse. The latter, at Buffalo Point, follows a 3.5-mile loop to a bluff shelter used by Native Americans. Another popular, and strenuous, hike leads to Hemmed-in Hollow, in spring a 200-foot-waterfall that's one of the Buffalo's most unforgettable sights. All these hikes wander through beautiful woodland dominated by oaks, hickories, and maples, with sweet gums, beeches, dogwoods, shortleaf pines, and many other trees interspersed. Sycamores, willows, and river birches line the river itself. In spring and summer a bloom of wildflowers, from violets to sunflowers, carpets the Buffalo River forest.

Take time, too, to visit historic Rush, where a boom in zinc mining in the late 19th century created a boomtown. Now a ghost town, Rush, located off Ark. 14 north of Buffalo Point, features a short interpretive trail passing several abandoned buildings and the remains of an ore-processing site, including an 1886 smelter.

U.S. 65
Marshall, AR
870-439-2502
www.nps.gov/buff

AT A GLANCE

North-central Arkansas, 90 miles northwest of Little Rock ▪ 94,294 acres; 135 river miles ▪ Year-round; white-water canoeing is best in spring ▪ Canoeing, hiking, wildlife-watching

Fort Smith National Historic Site

A center of frontier law and order

In 1817 the U.S. Army established Fort Smith at Belle Point, at the confluence of the Arkansas and Poteau Rivers. The post was abandoned in 1824, but a new fort was constructed in 1838 on higher ground nearby. In 1872 the barracks building was converted into a federal courthouse at a time when near-lawless conditions prevailed on what was then the border of Indian Territory (now Oklahoma).

Visitors today can see the foundations of the original fort (discovered in 1963) as well as the commissary and barracks from the second fort. The courtroom in the old barracks has been restored to reflect its appearance during the period 1875–1896, when federal Judge Isaac C. Parker presided. He was renowned as the "hanging judge" because of the 160 people he sentenced to death; 79 were actually hanged. Parker asserted that he was "the most misunderstood and misrepresented of men," and in fact his legacy is of a fair-minded jurist who had evenhanded justice as his highest ideal. (In those days the death sentence was mandatory for murder and rape, and Parker had no choice in his sentencing once a defendant was found guilty.) A reconstructed gallows reminds visitors of the fate of so many Wild West outlaws. Below the courthouse is the old jail, where conditions for prisoners were so bad that it earned the nickname "hell on the border."

Thousands of American Indians passed through Fort Smith in the 1830s during the forced relocation now called the Trail of Tears, and a self-guided trail along the Arkansas River leads to exhibits on the period.

> 301 Parker Ave.
> Fort Smith, AR
> 479-783-3961
> www.nps.gov/fosm

AT A GLANCE

West-central Arkansas, within the city of Fort Smith ▪ 37 acres ▪ Year-round ▪ Touring historic structures

---

Hot Springs National Park

A historic reminder of the glory days of American spas

The hot springs of this Ouachita Mountains valley, heated by geologic forces deep underground, have been used for therapeutic bathing for hundreds of years. American Indians, traders, and pioneer settlers likely used them to soothe tired bodies and as a cure for various illnesses.

In 1804, President Thomas Jefferson sent a scientific team to investigate "the hot springs on the Washita," by then already well known. In 1832, Congress designated the area as the Hot Springs Reservation to protect these "healing" springs, making what is now Hot Springs National Park the oldest unit in the National Park System. (It was not designated a national park until 1921.) A ragtag

The Fordyce Bathhouse's Hubbard Tub Room was used for physical therapy.

community had already grown up around the hot springs. The conjunction of city and park has continued to this day, so that the present national park area surrounds the north end of the modern city of Hot Springs.

A Thriving Spa Town

In the late 19th century and the first decades of the 20th, when the popularity of therapeutic bathing was at its height, Hot Springs developed into a thriving spa, visited by sports heroes, politicians, the wealthy, and organized-crime figures; even indigents in need of the healing waters, as ordered by physicians, were welcome, though only at the government-owned free bathhouse. Nearly all the natural springs were capped, and their water was piped to local hotels and to Bathhouse Row, a series of eight lavish establishments built between 1892 and 1923. A slow decline in public bathing eventually caused most of the bathhouses to go out of business.

Today the beautiful 1915 Fordyce Bathhouse has been restored and now houses both the park visitor center and a museum detailing the glory days of spas. A tour of the grand building ranks at the top of the park's must-do list. The 1912 Buckstaff Bathhouse is the only establishment on Bathhouse Row to have remained in continuous operation, and today visitors can enjoy an old-fashioned bathing experience, from thermal water soaks to hydrotherapy sessions to massages. The 1922 Quapaw Bathhouse, closed for many years, was renovated and reopened in 2008 as a modern spa. The Ozark Bathhouse is the park's cultural center, and the Superior Bathhouse now houses a brewery. The other bathhouses, though closed, create an eclectic display of period architecture. The Grand Promenade, built in the 1930s by the Works Progress Administration, parallels Bathhouse

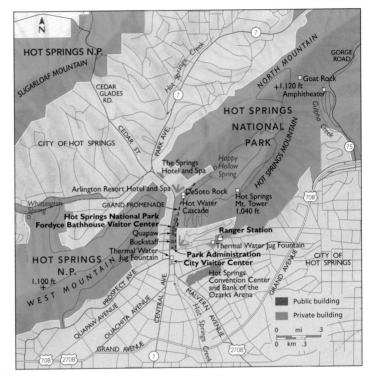

Row and looks down on the historic district, for a glimpse of what life might have been like in the spas' glory days.

Natural Wonders

Hot Springs National Park is different from most other national parks in the park system, both in its urban setting and in its lack of expansive natural areas. Nonetheless, visitors can enjoy 26 miles of attractive hiking trails through pine-oak woods on the surrounding mountains. In places, beautiful specimens of shortleaf pine more than 200 years old tower over the trail. Some of the longer trails, such as the 10-mile-long Sunset Trail, offer the chance to see deer, birds, wildflowers, and outcrops of natural novaculite.

A very hard, evenly grained, light-gray rock of almost pure silica found abundantly in the area, novaculite was valued by Indians for making tools and weapons long before Europeans arrived; it is still quarried

(though not in the park) and sold as "Arkansas stone," considered by many to be the finest whetstone in the world. (Its name comes from *novacula,* the Latin word for "razor.") Thick layers of novaculite are found throughout much of the southern Ouachita Mountains, from central Arkansas into eastern Oklahoma. Because it's so much harder than other rocks in these mountains, it often remains as rugged ridges when other materials have eroded away.

Near Bathhouse Row, the short Tufa Terrace Trail passes by a site where natural hot springs water still flows from the earth at 143°F. The springs originated as rainwater more than 4,000 years ago, sinking about a mile into the earth and resurfacing through a geologic fault. (Tufa is calcium carbonate, left as large deposits on the surface as water evaporates.) Many people still believe that the mineral-laden water here has health-giving properties, and it's common to see visitors filling jugs at public fountains throughout the park.

Hot Springs National Park may not compete with either Yellowstone or Everglades National Park in terms of its naturalness, but this hybrid city-park with a colorful history, interesting geology, and still wild places is an intriguing place to visit.

101 Reserve St.
Hot Springs, AR
501-620-6715
www.nps.gov/hosp

AT A GLANCE

West-central Arkansas, 45 miles southwest of Little Rock ▪ 5,550 acres ▪ Year-round ▪ Touring historic bathhouses, hiking

Little Rock Central High School National Historic Site

A *landmark in the American civil rights movement*

In September 1957, newspaper headlines around the world reported events taking place in Little Rock, the capital of Arkansas. Nine African-American students attempted to integrate all-white Central High School, despite opposition by Arkansas Gov. Orval Faubus and other state and local officials to court decisions ordering an end to segregated education. The threat of violence prompted President Dwight Eisenhower to order federal military troops to escort the students, and the "Little Rock Nine" eventually were allowed to attend classes.

Central High School, scene of the Crisis at Little Rock

What became known as the Crisis at Little Rock was a milestone in the decades-long struggle for civil rights in the United States. The state-federal confrontation is commemorated today at Little Rock Central High School National Historic Site, which encompasses the only still functioning high school within a national historic site.

A visitor center adjacent to the high school presents interactive exhibits on the background and importance of the desegregation crisis, as well as audiovisual programs on the events in Little Rock during the fall of 1957. Rangers conduct programs year-round, although tours of Central High School itself are available only on weekends, and with advance reservations.

2120 Daisy L. Gatson Bates Dr.
Little Rock, AR
501-374-1957
www.nps.gov/chsc

AT A GLANCE

Central Arkansas, within the city of Little Rock ▪ 18 acres ▪ Year-round ▪ Exploring the site of a seminal event in U.S. history

Pea Ridge National Military Park

The *well-preserved site of a momentous Civil War battle*

The "battle that saved Missouri for the Union" took place March 7–8, 1862, near an 1833 building known as Elkhorn Tavern, a well-known stage stop and gathering place in northwestern Arkansas just a few miles from the Missouri border. A force of 16,000 Confederate troops, heading north to capture the vital city of St. Louis, encountered a contingent of 10,000 Union soldiers. After two days of fighting, the Confederates retreated, a turn of events so significant that many historians believe Pea Ridge was the most important Civil War battle west of the Mississippi River.

The park visitor center shows

a film entitled "Thunder in the Ozarks" that explains the background and significance of the battle. And a museum here contains historic items and other exhibits. More than two dozen interpretive displays are set along the 7-mile driving tour through the battlefield.

During the fighting, Elkhorn Tavern served as a hospital and as headquarters for Confederate Gen. Earl Van Dorn. The building survived the battle (despite being hit by a cannonball) but was burned by Confederate guerrillas in 1863. The new Elkhorn Tavern was built in the 1880s in the style of that period. (In the 1960s, the tavern was rebuilt to return it to its Civil War appearance.)

Ten miles of hiking trails and 11

Elkhorn Tavern, rebuilt to resemble the original Civil War-era building

miles of horse trails wind through the fields and forests of the park, and allow for further exploration of the battlefield.

Ark. 62
Garfield, AR
479-451-8122
www.nps.gov/peri

AT A GLANCE

Northwestern Arkansas, 75 miles northeast of Fort Smith ▪ 4,300 acres ▪ Year-round ▪ Driving tour, horseback riding, hiking

---

President William Jefferson Clinton Birthplace Home
Small-town birthplace of the nation's 42nd president

William Jefferson Blythe III was born in the small town of Hope, Arkansas, on Aug. 19, 1946, just three months after his father died in an automobile accident. He, his widowed mother, Virginia, and her parents lived in a house on Hervey Street for the first four years of his life. After Billy Blythe's mother remarried he took his stepfather's name, and in 1992, as Bill Clinton, he was elected the 42nd U.S. President.

The two-and-a-half-story frame house where the future President grew up was built in a style called American Foursquare, a popular design of the early 20th century. Among his memories are learning to count from number cards his grandmother pinned to curtains in the kitchen. Although Billy moved to Hot Springs, Arkansas, with his family at age seven, he returned often to the Hope house to spend time with his grandparents.

Those touring the historic site first enter an adjacent house that serves as the park visitor center, with exhibits on President Clinton's childhood and his family. The visitor center also houses a bookstore with some of Clinton's favorite books.

Ranger-led tours of the childhood home are offered every half hour. The house had changed over the years before it was acquired by a historical foundation, but it has been restored with original details including the flooring, staircase, and paneling. Family photos, personal items, and period furnishings are on display throughout the house.

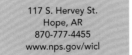

117 S. Hervey St.
Hope, AR
870-777-4455
www.nps.gov/wicl

AT A GLANCE

Southwestern Arkansas, 110 miles southwest of Little Rock ▪ 1 acre ▪ Year-round ▪ Tour the 1917 house where Bill Clinton lived as a boy

KANSAS

When pioneers on the Oregon and Santa Fe Trails traversed Kansas in the 19th century, a vast tallgrass prairie covered the eastern section of the territory. A slice of this now mostly lost habitat endures at Tallgrass Prairie National Preserve in the state's Flint Hills region. Historic sites recall the days when pro- and antislavery forces battled each other, the influx of African Americans seeking opportunity after the Civil War, and the *Brown* v. *Board of Education* court decision that helped end segregated schools in the U.S. Farms and ranches—and some oil and gas wells—blanket the state's rolling terrain.

Brown v. Board of Education National Historic Site
Honoring a watershed moment in the struggle for equality

In 1954, the Supreme Court issued a unanimous decision in *Oliver Brown et al.* v. *the Board of Education of Topeka et al.*, a case brought by more than 150 plaintiffs in several states. The court ruled that schools segregated by race violated the principle of "equal protection" as established by the Constitution's 14th Amendment. The case put in motion the dismantling of educational segregation in the United States. The decision was one of the most important landmarks in the long struggle for equality and justice by African Americans, often called the civil rights movement.

Though the case's name (usually shortened to *Brown* v. *Board of Education*) indicated the single case of an African-American girl who was barred from attending an all-white school near her home in Topeka, Kansas, it is actually a combination of five cases from Virginia; Delaware; South Carolina; Kansas; and Washington, D.C., by a legal team headed by Thurgood Marshall, who in 1967 was appointed a Supreme Court justice.

Brown v. *Board of Education* National Historic Site is located in the former Monroe Elementary School, once a school for African-American students in Topeka. Exhibits include a film entitled "Race and the American Creed" and galleries on the themes of education and justice and the legacy of the decision. Interactive displays and video help tell the story of the fight for civil rights in America.

> 1515 SE Monroe St.
> Topeka, KS
> 785-354-4273
> www.nps.gov/brvb

AT A GLANCE

Topeka, Kansas ▪ 2 acres ▪ Year-round ▪ Viewing exhibits on a historic Supreme Court civil rights decision

---

Fort Larned National Historic Site
An authentic military post set on the Santa Fe Trail

During the era of conflict with Plains Indians, traveling through the Great Plains was dangerous for pioneers, traders, and mail coaches. The U.S. Army established forts along major transportation trails to patrol routes and protect traffic as well as to provide contact points for dealing with Indian tribes. Fort Larned was sited near the well-traveled Santa Fe Trail, along the Pawnee River in today's western Kansas.

With nine of its original buildings (seven open for tours), Fort Larned ranks among the best surviving examples of these military outposts. Its structures were built of locally quarried stone, with walls up to two and a half feet thick, and date from 1866–68. Original buildings include the quartermaster's storehouse, commissary, hospital, barracks, and officers' quarters; the blockhouse is a reconstruction.

Fort Larned was typical of most military posts in the West: It never had a stockade around its grounds (contrary to Hollywood's depiction), and it never was directly attacked by Indians, who usually staged guerrilla-type raids on Army patrols and other small groups.

The fort's visitor center offers an introductory slide program and a museum with historic artifacts. During the summer and at special events, interpreters in period costume give visitors a glimpse of mid-19th-century life in the Great Plains.

| Kans. 156 Larned, KS 620-285-6911 www.nps.gov/fols | AT A GLANCE | Western Kansas, 110 miles northwest of Wichita ▪ 410 acres ▪ Year-round, though winter storms can be severe ▪ Touring restored buildings of a 19th-century U.S. Army fort |

Fort Scott National Historic Site

A U.S. Army post at the center of western expansion

The original officers' quarters at Fort Scott

From the days of Indian "removal" through the great pioneer migration to the West, continuing during the Civil War and the era when railroads spanned the continent, Fort Scott and its soldiers had a role in the country's growth, shaping the history of the United States.

Fort Scott was established in 1842 during the period when many Native American tribes were being relocated (sometimes by force) from their lands east of the Mississippi River to the American frontier. The fort's mission was to prevent conflict between Indians and white settlers and also among

the various tribes themselves. Soldiers from the fort protected travelers heading westward on the Santa Fe and other trails as well. The fort, however, never came under attack, and in fact boredom was a major problem for troops stationed here in this period.

The U.S. Army abandoned the fort in 1853. During the "bleeding Kansas" period of conflict between pro- and antislavery factions, the fort became the center of a new town called Fort Scott, where many violent confrontations occurred. Two buildings that had been sold to private owners were converted into hotels,

one pro-slavery and the other anti-slavery. Murder and intimidation were common to partisans on both sides of the issue.

During the Civil War, the fort reverted back to a military holding, with the Union Army occupying several buildings beginning in 1861. The fort served as a vital supply depot for Union forces throughout the war, as well as a military hospital and a prison. Escaped slaves, pro-Union refugees, and other people migrated to the town of Fort Scott, seeking the protection of the Union forces.

The Army again abandoned the fort in 1865, only to return in 1870, when soldiers were controversially assigned to protect railroad workers laying track in the region. At times, soldiers fought with civilians living in the area who opposed railroad expansion—one of the few times in U.S. history when the Army used its weapons against American citizens. The Army abandoned the fort for the last time in 1873.

The Fort

Visitors to Fort Scott National Historic Site see a collection of 20 buildings, 11 of them considered original and the others reconstructions. Original structures include the hospital (now the historic site's visitor center), officers' quarters, the quartermaster's storehouse, the bake house, and carriage houses. The buildings are grouped around a central parade ground, and they reflect three different architectural styles: French colonial, Greek Revival, and vernacular.

An orientation film at the infantry barracks museum provides an introduction to the fort's varied heritage, and self-guided tours are available whenever the facility is open. Guided tours are offered Memorial Day through Labor Day. The site provides other seasonal activities throughout the year, featuring, among other things, living-history demonstrations, complete with interpreters in period costume.

In addition to its historic importance, Fort Scott National Historic Site preserves a 5-acre tract of tallgrass prairie, a once common ecosystem that has nearly disappeared under the plow and other development. Head-high grasses and wildflowers grow here, aided by controlled burning and other restoration efforts. With imagination, visitors can picture the vast sea of prairie that faced pioneers heading west in the 19th century.

1 block west of U.S. 69
Fort Scott, KS
620-223-0310
www.nps.gov/fosc

AT A GLANCE

Eastern Kansas, 125 miles east of Wichita ▪ 17 acres ▪ Year-round ▪ Visiting a historic military post and restored tallgrass prairie

Nicodemus National Historic Site
A pioneer town settled by African Americans

The Emancipation Proclamation, issued by President Abraham Lincoln during the Civil War, freed African Americans from slavery, and the Reconstruction era immediately afterward seemed to offer the promise of better lives for formerly enslaved people. Some African Americans were elected to political office; and on paper, property ownership, voting, education, and other rights seemed to be guaranteed.

The reality was far different. A decade after the Civil War, many African Americans lived in conditions resembling slavery. Other than working as sharecroppers, they saw few opportunities for improving their lives in the South. Moreover, the rise of the Ku Klux Klan meant intimidation and even murder for those who resisted.

At the same time, many African Americans remembered the long, bloody struggle of those who fought to make Kansas a free state.

Nicodemus, named for a slave who bought his freedom

These favorable memories formed the foundation for some who saw Kansas as a land of opportunity, a place to start a new and better life.

Enticed by the rosy scene painted by land speculators eager to attract business, African Americans in 1877 founded the town of Nicodemus in northwestern Kansas, and farming families spread out into five surrounding townships. Many settlers came from Kentucky, where posters and fliers had sometimes exaggerated the low cost of land and ease of farming.

A decade later, Nicodemus numbered more than 200 people. Most settlers were farmers, but the town had a bank, general stores, livery stables, hotels, and pharmacies. At its height, Nicodemus had a population of 600, including some white merchants. Unfortunately a railroad line bypassed the town in 1888, dooming it to a slow decline as residents moved to towns along the rail line, the major force for development in the West.

Though much reduced in population (now 16, of whom 10 are direct descendants of original town settlers), Nicodemus endures as the only remaining African-American town west of the Mississippi River that was settled on the Great Plains by former slaves. In 1996 it became a national historic site within the National Park System, commemorating its heritage as a focal point of the hopes and dreams for self-improvement of a people seeking opportunities for education, entrepreneurship, and freedom.

The historic site encompasses five buildings: the 1939 township hall (the only structure open to the public, and home to the temporary visitor center), two churches (Old First Baptist Church and African Methodist Episcopal), the St. Francis Hotel, and the schoolhouse. The township hall offers exhibits on Nicodemus's history, audiovisual programs, a bookstore. A research library is located in the Nicodemus N.H.S. administrative offices.

Ranger-guided tours are available by appointment only.

Each year, on the last weekend in July, the Nicodemus community hosts the Emancipation/Homecoming Celebration, which attracts many descendants of original settlers and other visitors.

U.S. 24
Nicodemus, KS
785-839-4233
www.nps.gov/nico

AT A GLANCE

Northwestern Kansas, 110 miles northwest of Salina ▪ 161 acres ▪ Year-round, though winter storms can be severe ▪ Visiting historic township hall, watching interpretive programs

Tallgrass Prairie National Preserve
A vast tract of an endangered Great Plains ecosystem

When the first European explorers traveled across the prairies covering the central part of the continent, they saw a vast grassland teeming with bison, elk, deer, pronghorn, wolves, prairie dogs, and numerous species of birds. The tallgrass prairie stretched across 170 million acres from Canada to the Gulf Coast. The land—treeless, yet more fertile and with more rainfall than the mixed-grass and shortgrass prairies farther west—naturally attracted settlers looking for productive farmland. Today, less than 4 percent of the tallgrass prairie remains, much of it in fragmented and highly altered tracts.

The Flint Hills of east-central Kansas were so rocky that they were unsuitable for agriculture, being nearly impossible to plow. As a result, cattle ranching became the main livelihood, a development that protected the grassland somewhat in its original form. As conservationists looked for significant areas of tallgrass prairie to save in public ownership, they naturally looked here, only to meet resistance from local landowners opposing government acquisition of large tracts of property.

Nonetheless, Congress established the Tallgrass Prairie National Preserve in 1996, as a public-private partnership, with the area administered by the National Park Service. By its mandate, the site interprets not simply the prairie ecosystem but also the cultural heritage of ranching in the region.

A visitor center and administrative building is located south of a historic ranch complex. Exhibits and an orientation film at the visitor center help visitors understand the Flint Hills and natural and cultural resources found at the preserve. The historic ranch buildings, which are built of native limestone, include an 1881 mansion in the French Second Empire style, a three-story limestone barn and outbuildings, and the 1882 Lower Fox Creek one-room school.

Most of the tallgrass prairie land was plowed under or used for ranching.

Visitors can take a self-guided tour of the historic ranch buildings.

In warmer months, activities include bus tours of the prairie, along with living-history presentations. The historic 1882 one-room Lower Fox Creek School is open for touring daily.

Forty miles of hiking trails, ranging from easy walks to backcountry routes, offer the chance to see wildlife and prairie vegetation. Watchful hikers may see white-tailed deer, thirteen-lined ground squirrels, badgers, coyotes, or bobcats. The 500 species of plants on the preserve include tall prairie grasses such as big and little bluestem, Indian grass, and switchgrass, along with dozens of species of wildflowers. Some of the grasses can grow 8 feet in height, demonstrating the aptness of the term "tallgrass prairie."

Reintroducing Bison

In 2009, the National Park Service and the Nature Conservancy reintroduced bison (commonly called buffalo)—a signature Plains animal—into the preserve, giving visitors an even better depiction of presettlement days on the Great Plains. The herd now resides on Windmill Pasture, and is thriving in its native environment.

> 2480 Kans. 177
> Strong City, KS
> 620-273-8494
> www.nps.gov/tapr
>
> **AT A GLANCE**
>
> East-central Kansas, 85 miles northeast of Wichita ▪ 10,894 acres ▪ Year-round ▪ Hiking, wildlife-watching, bus touring, interpretive tours

LOUISIANA

South-central Louisiana is home to one of the United States' most distinct cultures: the Acadians, or "Cajuns," exiled from Canada in the 18th century, who have maintained traditions of language and music ever since. New Orleans preserves elements of Creole culture, influenced by France, Africa, the Caribbean, and other sources. Much of the nation's seafood comes from Louisiana's wetlands and the adjacent Gulf of Mexico, but oil exploration and levees threaten the environments. The vast marshland of southern Louisiana is an important wildlife habitat, home to alligators, wading birds, and waterfowl. Wetlands also help protect against storm surges that flood low-lying areas.

Cane River Creole National Historical Park

Plantation life in a culturally unique region

Along the banks of the Cane River, in northwestern Louisiana, a community developed that blended French, Spanish, Native American, European, and African cultures. Today the region features architecture and lifestyles influenced by wealthy landowners, enslaved peoples, sharecroppers of the Reconstruction era, and lingering European and Caribbean elements.

The Cane River Creole National Historical Park encompasses the grounds of Oakland and Magnolia, two 18th-century plantations that each remained in their respective families for generations. Tours explain the workings and legacy of the plantation system, which grew indigo, tobacco, and cotton; and explain details of buildings such as slave and tenant cabins, overseers' houses, a doctor's house, plantation stores, a blacksmith shop, *pigeonniers* (where pigeons were kept for food), a carpentry shop, and farm outbuildings. Unlike tours at many private plantation houses, which focus on the lives of the landowner families, tours here give attention to the entire plantation community, which included landowners, paid workers, and a large enslaved workforce. Park buildings periodically undergo preservation; visitors may see a work in progress and are likely to note archaeologists, craftspeople, carpenters, and others at work.

The historical park lies within the larger Cane River National Heritage Area *(www.canerivernha.org; www.nps.gov/crha)*, which includes picturesque Natchitoches, the oldest town in the Louisiana Territory; as well as three state historic sites, six national historic landmarks, and 24 properties that are listed on the National Register of Historic Places.

Jean Lafitte National Historical Park & Preserve
Varied sites interpreting history, culture, and nature

Spread across southern Louisiana, from the swamps of the Mississippi River Delta to the prairies to the west, the six sites comprised by Jean Lafitte National Historical Park and Preserve are as rewarding as they are varied. Visitors can tour a historic battlefield, hike through beautiful wetland forest, learn the history of New Orleans's colorful French Quarter, dance to Cajun music, learn to cook south Louisiana's famous regional dishes, and more.

Named for a notorious pirate who roamed the swamps of the Louisiana coastline and aided the United States in the War of 1812, Jean Lafitte National Historical Park and Preserve encompasses more than enough sites—from New Orleans city streets to friendly small towns to Louisiana bayous lined with bald cypresses and Spanish moss—to keep any visitor busy for several days.

The Acadian Cultural Center, in Lafayette, tells the story of the Acadian (Cajun) people who settled in southern Louisiana after being expelled from Canada in the 18th century.

The Prairie Acadian Cultural

Spanish moss, draping from a tree, thrives in the swamplands of Jean Lafitte.

Center, in Eunice, interprets the "prairie Cajuns" and presents a weekly live radio broadcast of Cajun music.

The Wetlands Acadian Cultural Center, in Thibodaux, focuses on Cajun life in the bayous. It offers ranger-guided walks and boat tours into bayou Cajun country.

Barataria Preserve, in Marrero *(6588 Barataria Blvd.)*, has a visitor center and miles of trails that wind through an extensive swath of natural forest and wetlands, offering excellent wildlife-watching opportunities.

The Chalmette Battlefield and National Cemetery, in Chalmette, commemorates the legendary 1815 Battle of New Orleans in which Gen. Andrew Jackson's army defeated the British troops.

The French Quarter Visitor Center in New Orleans offers programs of music, storytelling, dance, and cooking, as well as ranger-led walks.

New Orleans Jazz National Historical Park
Concerts and programs celebrating an American musical genre

Jazz has a long, lively history in New Orleans.

Derived from countless sources as diverse as African drumming, ragtime, and riverboat music, jazz is one of America's greatest original art forms. New Orleans played a major role in the development of jazz, as its nightclubs, concert halls, and street bands fostered the composition and performance of rhythmic tunes based on ensemble playing and individual improvisation ("taking a ride").

Jazz legends Louis "Satchmo" Armstrong, Charles "Buddy" Bolden, and Sidney Bechet, among others, got their start in New Orleans and went on to national and worldwide fame, a tradition continued by musicians such as Wynton Marsalis and the Preservation Hall Jazz Band.

Concert Venues

In recognition of the influence of jazz and the role of the city in its birth, Congress passed an act in 1994 that created New Orleans Jazz National Historical Park. The park's primary visitor center is located on Peters Street in the French Quarter, where concerts, ranger-led demonstrations, and talks are held.

Live music and concerts are also held at the Old U.S. Mint at the corner of Decatur Street and Esplanade Avenue in the southeast corner of the French Quarter. The Old Mint building also houses the Jazz Collection, which tells the story of the men and women who created New Orleans jazz and who continue its tradition, locally and globally.

The schedule of concerts and other presentations changes throughout the year; see a list of special live jazz performances and planned events on the park website. The park also offers brochures for self-guided walking tours of jazz-related neighborhoods such as Storyville and Treme.

916 N. Peters St.
New Orleans, LA
504-589-4841
www.nps.gov/jazz

AT A GLANCE

New Orleans ▪ Year-round ▪ Attending jazz concerts, watching interpretive programs, touring

Poverty Point National Monument
One of North America's most important archaeological sites

At the height of its power at about 1500 B.C., the community located at this site on Bayou Macon ranked with the largest population centers in the world, a sprawling complex of tall earthen mounds and concentric semicircular ridges, a

focal point of trade and, probably, religious activities.

There's much that archaeologists don't know about Poverty Point and the culture that created it, but they have concluded that the earthworks were built by a hunter-gatherer

society, contradicting earlier theories that an agricultural lifestyle was required to support such extensive construction activity.

Thought to have been originally 6 feet high, the massive ridges are now gentle slopes in a field once planted in cotton. The mounds, though, remain impressive; the largest measures 700 by 640 feet at its base and rises 70 feet high. Some researchers have speculated that its shape is that of a flying bird or possibly something like a tree of life.

A museum displays artifacts recovered on site, and ranger-guided tram tours are offered March through October. A 2.6-mile hiking trail winds through the ridges and past massive Mound A. Though Poverty Point is an officially designated national monument, it is administered by Louisiana as a state historic site *(www.crt.state.la.us/louisiana-state-parks/historic-sites)*.

La. 577
Epps, LA
318-926-5492
www.nps.gov/popo
www.povertypoint.us

AT A GLANCE

Northeastern Louisiana, 40 miles east of Monroe ▪ 400 acres ▪ Year-round ▪ Walking and tram tours of earthworks built by an ancient people

MISSOURI

Befitting its mid-continent location, Missouri encompasses a variety of natural habitats, from southern bottomland to eastern hardwood forest to Plains tallgrass prairie. In the Civil War era, the state split between pro-Confederate and pro-Union forces, resulting in several important battles. Missouri's most famous native son is possibly author Mark Twain, who immortalized his boyhood home of Hannibal in his novels. Set at the confluence of the Missouri and Mississippi Rivers, St. Louis became a major trade center, and its Gateway Arch commemorates its role in western expansion. Independence and Kansas City, too, were supply points for westbound wagon trains in the 19th century.

George Washington Carver National Monument
The birthplace and memorial to a famed African-American botanist

Born into slavery during the Civil War, George Washington Carver overcame countless obstacles faced by African Americans in the late 19th and early 20th centuries in education and professional advancement. His work as a scientist, especially in helping poor southern farmers find alternatives to cotton as a crop, earned him international fame. He was especially known for his promotion of the uses of the peanut, and to a lesser extent, the sweet potato.

In his work at Alabama's Tuskegee

Carver was inspired by the woods and tallgrass prairie of his childhood.

Institute, through his many public appearances, and by the force of his personality, Carver served as an inspiration for African Americans struggling to attain equal rights in the United States. Carver's admirers included Henry Ford, Presidents Franklin D. Roosevelt and Harry S. Truman, and educator Booker T. Washington.

The George Washington Carver National Monument preserves the site where he was born on a small farm owned by Moses and Susan Carver. (Carver's exact birth date is unknown.) The Carvers' 1881 house, built after a tornado destroyed many buildings on the property, is one stop on the 0.75-mile-long Carver Nature Trail, as is a statue of George as a child. Winding through tallgrass prairie and forest, the trail allows visitors to experience the natural environment that inspired Carver's life interests.

Daily guided tours of the site are offered, as are a variety of programs on subjects ranging from nature study to pioneer farm life to art (Carver was an avid and accomplished painter). The visitor center and museum honors Carver's strong belief in the ability of science to improve people's lives.

5646 Carver Rd.
Diamond, MO
417-325-4151
www.nps.gov/gwca

AT A GLANCE Southwestern Missouri, 12 miles southeast of Joplin ▪ 240 acres ▪ Year-round ▪ Visiting historic structures, hiking, exploring nature trail

Harry S Truman National Historic Site
The home and farm home of the 33rd President

Thrust into a position of power with the 1945 death of President Franklin D. Roosevelt, Harry Truman wanted to be remembered as "the people's president." His down-to-earth personality and demeanor are reflected in the relatively modest house in Independence, Missouri, where he lived with his beloved wife, Bess, from 1919 until his death in 1972. (Mrs. Truman died in 1982.) The home served as the summer White House during the 1945–1953 Truman Administration.

The house is the centerpiece of the Harry S Truman National Historic Site. It is filled with personal possessions that provide an intimate look at the Trumans' daily life. Visitors may enter the Truman Home only on a guided tour, and group size is limited. Tour tickets *(fee)* are available at the visitor center, located in a former fire station in downtown Independence, where visitors may also watch a short film on Truman's life.

The historic site also includes the 1894 Truman Farm Home in Grandview, Missouri, 19 miles southwest of Independence. The Farm Home sits on 10 acres of what was once a 600-acre farm. When he was a young man, Truman worked at the farm, which belonged to his maternal grandmother. Visitors can take a self-guided tour of the grounds and see the house, garage, chicken coop, reconstructed smokehouse, and privy. An audio tour is available at the site.

Visitor center
223 N. Main St.
Independence, MO
816-254-9929
www.nps.gov/hstr

AT A GLANCE Western Missouri, in Independence (home) and Grandview (farm) ▪ 10 acres (farm) ▪ Year-round ▪ Touring longtime home of Harry and Bess Truman (guided) and his family farm

Jefferson National Expansion Memorial
A famed city symbol commemorating the United States' westward growth

St. Louis's graceful, 630-foot-tall Gateway Arch has taken its place alongside New York's Statue of Liberty and the Washington Monument as recognizable landmarks of great American cities. Designed by architect Eero Saarinen and completed alongside the Mississippi River in 1965, the arch symbolizes St. Louis's role as an important gateway to the West during the 19th-century pioneer era. The Gateway Arch is the centerpiece of Jefferson National Expansion Memorial.

The park's Museum of Westward Expansion has closed while major landscape updates and renovations are being made to the grounds and facilities of the memorial. A new museum and visitor center are planned for completion in 2017. The arch remains open during construction, but visitors should call ahead or visit the park website or Gateway Arch website *(www.gatewayarch.com)* for updates on construction or information on interruptions to visitor access to the arch during the project.

The Jefferson National Expansion Memorial also encompasses the former St. Louis Courthouse, originally built in 1828 and remodeled through the 1850s. This historic building saw the first two trials of the famed Dred Scott case, in which the legal status of enslaved people was debated and which contributed to the outbreak of the Civil War. The Old Courthouse building remains open during construction on the park, and three exhibit galleries there tell visitors about colonial-era St. Louis; Lewis and Clark's expedition and the American period of fur trade; and the tensions that arose between emigrating pioneers and the Plains Indians of the American West.

The view of the arch from ground level is awe-inspiring, but the arch's bird's-eye view of St. Louis, the Mississippi River, and Illinois is equally amazing. Trams *(fee, 877-982-1410, www.tickets forthearch.com, or available in person at the Old Courthouse)* take visitors to a viewpoint equivalent to the top of a 63-story building, where the glassed-in observation area can hold up to 160 people. Park rangers are available to answer questions at the top, where visitors may stay as long at they like. On a clear day the view can extend up to 30 miles, but unfortunately haze usually limits visibility to a shorter distance.

Although the Gateway Arch was designed to be earthquake-proof and to sway as much as 18 inches, it is highly stable under normal conditions; a 50-mile-an-hour wind causes it to move only 1.5 inches. The stainless-steel arch is also completely insulated against lightning strikes, which are fairly common in

The Gateway Arch, signaling passage into the West

midwestern thunderstorms. The film "Monument to the Dream," shown to visitors who purchase a ticket for the arch, documents its fascinating construction.

After the completion of construction, a new park will connect downtown St. Louis to the arch and the riverfront, via a "Park Over the Highway." This landscaped greenway will extend over busy I-44 and will give visitors continuous pedestrian access from downtown to the Old Courthouse and the arch.

11 N. 4th
St. Louis, MO
314-655-1700
www.nps.gov/jeff

AT A GLANCE

Downtown St. Louis ▪ 91 acres ▪ Year-round ▪ Visiting museum, riding tram to the top of the Gateway Arch

Oregon National Historic Trail

A migration path that changed the map of the United States

When the United States bought the vast territory of the Louisiana Purchase from France in 1803, the nation's western border moved from the Mississippi River to the Rocky Mountains. Beyond lay Oregon Country (today's states of Washington, Oregon, and Idaho), which the U.S. hoped to acquire from England.

Through a series of mishaps, encounters with friendly Native Americans, and lucky choices, fur traders stumbled across South Pass, a means to cross the Rockies, in 1810. In 1836, a group of missionaries showed that wagons could make the journey across the Rockies to Oregon. Soon thereafter, in 1843, a wagon train with around a thousand travelers—called the Great Migration—set out from Independence, Missouri; most of the travelers arrived safely in Oregon. After that, a flood of people took to the trail.

Many people who looked to the West wanted land on which to start a new life, and some wanted to help the U.S. take control of the area. After the discovery of gold in California, some people went in search of riches. Between 1843 and 1869, 350,000 to 500,000 people traveled along a common corridor across the prairies and the Rockies before diverging on various trails. In 1846, as settlers poured into Oregon

Near the trail at Alcove Spring, Kansas

Country, England ceded it to the U.S.; the U.S. now controlled land from the Atlantic to the Pacific.

The completion of the first transcontinental railroad line in 1869 spelled the decline of the Oregon Trail—wagon trains would continue to travel on it for 20-some years, but in reduced numbers—but by then the route had forever changed the nation.

Following the Oregon National Historic Trail, travelers can see the path worn by the 19th-century pioneers and imagine their hardships. One in ten died along the way from diseases, winter weather, and accidents.

The trail runs 2,170 miles from Independence, Missouri, to Oregon City, Oregon, passing through Kansas, Nebraska, Wyoming, and Idaho. Dozens of related sites may be visited, and trail ruts created by the friction of countless wagon wheels can be seen in several places. The National

Frontier Trails Museum in Independence is a great place to begin exploration; exhibits tell the story of the Oregon, Santa Fe, and other western trails. Near the western end of the trail, the National Historic Oregon Trail Interpretive Center in Baker City, Oregon, is another excellent resource.

Fort Kearny State Historical Park in Kearney, Nebraska, protects a site where a U.S. military post became famous as a place to buy supplies, repair wagons, and prepare for the journey up the Platte River. Some of the most impressive wagon ruts along the route can be seen about 3 miles south of Guernsey, Wyoming. The National Oregon/California Trail Center in Montpelier, Idaho, offers interpretive displays simulating an actual wagon-train experience. Three Island Crossing State Park at Glenns Ferry, Idaho, is located at the site of a dangerous crossing of the Snake River. The End of the Oregon Trail Interpretive Center in Oregon City, Oregon, features exhibits and seasonal living-history demonstrations.

These are just a few of the numerous museums and other sites along the trail. The trail office in Salt Lake City or the Park Service website can provide more information, as can the Oregon-California Trails Association (*www .octa-trails.org*).

Park office
324 S. State St., #200
Salt Lake City, UT
801-741-1012
www.nps.gov/oreg

AT A GLANCE

Route from Missouri to the Pacific Northwest ▪ 2,170 trail miles ▪ Spring through fall ▪ Driving tour, hiking, visiting museums and historic sites

Ozark National Scenic Riverways
Two beautiful spring-fed rivers

Some of the most ruggedly beautiful landscapes in the central United States are found within the region known as the Ozark Plateau, largely located in southern Missouri and northern Arkansas. A once flat terrain, shaped by millennia of erosion, the Ozark Plateau now features forested highlands, steep-sided valleys, and—most notably, for many people—clear, cool, rocky creeks and rivers, many of them perfect for canoeing and swimming.

A number of Ozark rivers have been dammed to create expansive reservoirs, but several have been protected in their free-flowing form. Parts of two of those rivers in southern Missouri, the Current and Jacks Fork, were designated as the Ozark National Scenic Riverways in 1964, creating the United States' first national park area to protect a wild river system. Some areas within the scenic riverways were once Missouri state parks, but the entire area is now administered by the National Park Service.

Canoeing, kayaking, rafting, and other forms of boating make up the most popular activity on the Current and Jacks Fork. Many people bring their own boats and arrange for shuttles to or from their starting points. For other visitors, authorized concessionaires (the park provides a list on its website) will set up float trips ranging in length from a few hours to multiday trips with overnight camping. Canoeing is generally easy with gentle rapids; concessionaires can provide advice about sections of the rivers appropriate to skill levels. Many boaters enjoy fishing for smallmouth bass and other game fish.

There's much to see within the park apart from the rivers. Several springs feed waterways in the area. Blue Spring, on the Current River, was called Spring of the Summer Sky by Native Americans and is 310 feet deep. It displays a deep blue color, especially on days with a blue sky.

Historic structures within the park include the 1894 Alley Mill, centerpiece of a thriving late-19th-century community; and the ruins of a hospital built at Welch Spring in the early 20th century by a doctor attempting to promote the "healing" effects of clean cave air. Scenic Rocky Falls, on Rocky Creek, which flows into the Current River, is one of the most popular destinations for sightseeing within the riverways area.

Hikers enjoy the national park area as well, as several short hiking trails wind through woodlands, some leading to springs. Many old roads crisscross the area and offer additional hiking opportunities. (Hikers should note that most areas of the riverways are open to hunting. Check with park rangers for hunting-season dates.)

In summer, park rangers conduct guided walks and a wide variety of special programs at historic sites and campgrounds *(Mem. Day–Labor Day)*. Schedules are available at ranger stations and are posted at campgrounds. Rangers also lead twice-daily lantern tours *(fee)* of Round Spring Cave, a natural limestone cavern, one of more than 300 caves in the park.

Visitor center
404 Watercress Dr.
Van Buren, MO
573-323-4236
www.nps.gov/ozar

AT A GLANCE

Southeastern Missouri, 120 miles east of Springfield ▪ 80,785 acres, 134 river miles ▪ Year-round ▪ Boating, camping, swimming, hiking, horseback riding

Pony Express National Historic Trail
The legendary route of Old West mail carriers

Though it existed for only 18 months—April 1860 through late October 1861—the Pony Express occupies a prominent place among the legends of America's Old West. A business venture originally called the Leavenworth & Pike's Peak Express Company, it was established to accomplish something nearly inconceivable at the time: to deliver mail between St. Joseph, Missouri, and San Francisco, California—a distance of 1,800 miles—in only ten days. After the first pony run, the western terminus of the Pony Express was switched to Sacramento, with the mail continuing to San Francisco via ferryboat.

This feat required a line of more

than a hundred stations where fresh horses could be provided every 10 to 15 miles, and where riders (who had to weigh less than 125 pounds) could be changed every 75 to 100 miles. The Pony Express cut weeks off the time previously required to deliver a message from the eastern United States to the West Coast. But the venture never made money, and with the completion of the first transcontinental telegraph line in 1861, it ceased operations.

Pony Express National Historic Trail commemorates this renowned route and the riders who carried the mail. Although short pristine sections believed to be remnants of the original trail can be seen in Utah and California, much of the route is covered by modern roads, or its location is unknown. Nonetheless, modern

Commemorating Pony Express riders

travelers can follow the general Pony Express trail across the Great Plains and through the Rocky Mountains. The national historic trail is still under development, but eventually will link about 120 publicly accessible historic sites. Around 50 Pony Express stations still exist, either restored or as ruins.

A few of the sites related to the historic Pony Express trail include the Pony Express Museum in St. Joseph, Missouri, which preserves the original stables used by the venture; Hollenberg Station State Historic Site near Hanover, Kansas, a rare example of a Pony Express station that still stands unaltered in its original location; and the B. F. Hastings Building in Sacramento, the western terminus of the route, now part of the California State Railroad Museum. A number of other original Pony Express and stagecoach stations exist along the trail in Utah and Nevada.

For more information, contact the trail office in Salt Lake City or see its website. The National Pony Express Association *(www.xphomestation.com)* also provides information on the trail.

Park headquarters
324 S. State St., #200
Salt Lake City, UT
801-741-1012
www.nps.gov/poex

AT A GLANCE

Route from St. Joseph, Missouri, to Sacramento, California ▪ 1,800 trail miles ▪ Spring through fall ▪ Driving tour, visiting museums and historic sites

Ulysses S. Grant National Historic Site
The longtime home of a Civil War general and President

Before he led Union military forces to victory in the Civil War, before he was elected the 18th President of the United States, Ulysses S. Grant lived and worked at the family farm of his wife, Julia, in St. Louis.

Grant met Julia through her brother, Fred Dent, a classmate of his at West Point, and they married in 1848. Grant resigned his Army commission in 1854 and moved his family to the Dent farm, which he managed and where he worked alongside the

Dent family slaves. He, Julia, and their children lived for several years in the house called White Haven, a name taken from earlier Dent family residences in England and Maryland, and eventually purchased the property.

A short film at the visitor center provides an introduction to the site, its history, and its connection with the Dent and Grant families. Many visitors are surprised to learn that the Dent family and Grant himself owned slaves in the pre–Civil War period.

A quarter-mile path leads to the main house and outbuildings, including a summer kitchen, chicken house, and icehouse. Regular tours are given of the house, which dates from 1818 but was enlarged several times in later years. The stable, originally built in the 1870s for Grant's horses, now serves as the site's museum.

The adjacent commerical wildlife park called Grant's Farm was once part of the White Haven property and displays a log cabin Grant built in 1855.

7400 Grant Rd.
St. Louis, MO
314-842-1867
www.nps.gov/ulsg

AT A GLANCE

Southwest of St. Louis ▪ 9.65 acres ▪ Year-round ▪ Touring Grant home and associated outbuildings

Wilson's Creek National Battlefield
The well-preserved site of an early Civil War battle

Missouri was of great strategic importance to both sides in the Civil War; it was the site of more battles and skirmishes than any other state except Virginia and Tennessee. The first major battle fought west of the Mississippi River occurred at Wilson's Creek, near Springfield, on August 10, 1861. Brig. Gen. Nathaniel Lyon was killed in the fight, becoming the first Union general to die in battle.

At this early stage of the war, Confederate forces had gathered at Wilson's Creek in preparation for an attack on Springfield. Outnumbered Union forces under Lyon planned to retire to their supply base at Rolla, but they first attacked the Rebel army as a delaying tactic. The battle ended in a Confederate victory, but the Southerners were unable to pursue the retreating Union forces. Nonetheless, the Battle of Wilson's Creek allowed the

Confederacy to take control of southwestern Missouri for a time.

The battlefield today has been little changed from its condition in 1861, allowing visitors to see the landscape that the combatants saw. A visitor center displays many historic artifacts, and a 4.9-mile auto-tour road has eight interpretive stops at important battle locations. A trail system for hiking or horseback riding is offered, as well as five short trails for walking only.

AT A GLANCE

6424 W. Farm Road 182
Republic, MO
417-732-2662
www.nps.gov/wicr

Southwestern Missouri, 10 miles southwest of Springfield ▪ 1,926 acres ▪ Year-round ▪ Visiting museum, driving tour, hiking

---

OKLAHOMA

Oklahoma's history has been as eventful as the state is wide. In 1838 the Oklahoma Territory was the site of the forced relocation of thousands of Native Americans from their homelands in the southeastern United States. (Indians of more than 20 tribes still make up a significant part of the population.) The Chisholm Trail and other cattle-drive routes crossed the territory, and in the late 19th century a series of land rushes allowed settlers to claim land in what was virtually untouched prairie. Later, the discovery of oil turned Tulsa into a boomtown, resplendent with art deco architecture. Tragedy struck with the 1995 terrorist bombing in Oklahoma City that left 168 people dead.

Chickasaw National Recreation Area
Spring-fed streams, hiking trails, and a bison herd

Mineral springs drew crowds of health seekers to the town of Sulphur a century ago, making it a popular spa resort. Today, visitors to adjacent Chickasaw National Recreation Area can see springs, boat on Lake

of the Arbuckles, hike along trails, camp, and enjoy observing a small bison herd.

The federal Sulphur Springs Reservation was established here in 1902 to protect both mineral and freshwater springs. Later known as

Platt National Park, it was combined with the Arbuckle Recreation Area and given its current name in 1976. Rustic structures built by the Civilian Conservation Corps in the 1930s still survive, including picnic

Little Niagra on Travertine Creek in Sulphur, Oklahoma

shelters, campgrounds, and dams. The Travertine Nature Center is the best first stop for visitors, offering live animal displays, exhibits, and guided walks. Exhibits interpret the park history and the natural environment, a blend of eastern woodland and the mixed-grass prairie of the Midwest.

More than 20 miles of trails wind through the area, including one open to horseback riding and mountain biking. Among the most popular is the 1.5-mile Travertine Creek Trail, with a trailhead at the nature center.

The path follows a creek fed by springs flowing with limestone-rich water. When exposed to air, the mineral will precipitate out, forming deposits on the surface called travertine. The trail passes many waterfalls and several mineral springs along the way.

U.S. 177
Sulphur, OK
580-633-7234
www.nps.gov/chic

AT A GLANCE Southern Oklahoma, 75 miles south of Oklahoma City ▪ 9,888 acres ▪ Year-round ▪ Hiking, boating, swimming, wildlife-watching, camping, horseback riding

---

Oklahoma City National Memorial

A memorial to victims of a terrorist bombing

On April 19, 1995, the Alfred P. Murrah Federal Building in Oklahoma City was destroyed by a bomb in the deadliest act of domestic terrorism in U.S. history. Oklahoma City National Memorial honors the 168 people killed in the attack, as well as survivors, rescue workers, and "those changed forever" by the tragedy.

Dedicated in 2000 on the anniversary of the attack, the memorial consists of the Gates of Time, encapsulating the 9:02 a.m. moment of the explosion; a field of 168 empty chairs representing those who died and the loss felt by family members; a reflecting pool; a survivors' wall; and an American elm that, though severely damaged, survived the blast. Additional features are the Children's Area, with hand-painted tiles sent by children around the country; the Rescuers' Orchard, a grove of trees around the Survivor Tree; and the Memorial Fence, which displays items left by visitors.

The Oklahoma City National Memorial Museum *(fee)* stands adjacent to the outdoor memorial area and provides exhibits on the bombing, the events following the attack, and its effect on the nation.

Privately owned and operated, the memorial is an affiliated area of the National Park System. Park rangers answer questions and provide interpretive services at the outdoor symbolic memorial site.

Sixth & Harvey
Oklahoma City, OK
405-609-8855
www.nps.gov/okci

AT A GLANCE Downtown Oklahoma City ▪ 3.3 acres ▪ Year-round ▪ Viewing outdoor memorials and adjacent museum

Washita Battlefield National Historic Site

The site of a U.S. Army attack on a Cheyenne village

In 1868, conflict between Plains Indian tribes and settlers moving west, as well as increasing tension between Indian warriors and the U.S. Army, reached a tipping point. Many Indian chiefs wanted peace, but attempts to force tribes to reservations led to intertribal battles and rebellion by young warriors.

At dawn's early light on November 27, 1868, Lt. Col. George A. Custer led a surprise attack on a Southern Cheyenne village on the Washita River in what is today western Oklahoma. The exact events of that morning have been debated ever since. What some people call a battle, others have labeled a massacre, and reports on the number of Cheyenne killed have varied widely. A number of Cheyenne women and children were killed in the attack, as was the noted Peace Chief Black Kettle.

Washita Battlefield National Historic Site protects the location of the village. The visitor center features exhibits and a film entitled "Destiny at Dawn," which examines historical events leading up to the attack. Rangers give regular interpretive talks in the summer, and walking tours are available on request. The visitor center also serves the nearby 31,300-acre Black Kettle National Grassland, which encompasses several lakes and other recreation sites.

Okla. 47A
Cheyenne, OK
580-497-2742
www.nps.gov/waba

AT A GLANCE

Western Oklahoma, 150 miles west of Oklahoma City ▪ 315 acres ▪ Year-round, though winter storms can be severe ▪ Summer guided hiking, taking self-guided trail to village site

TEXAS

The second largest state, Texas has long been a synonym for everything big: wide-open spaces, big skies, vast cattle ranches, tall cowboy hats, and, big cities (three of the ten largest U.S. cities are in Texas). A broad array of historical influences have shaped Texas's image, from its proximity to Mexico to its decade-long period as an independent republic to the oil-boom days that created great fortunes. Texas's natural environment includes bottomland swamps, pine forests, Rio Grande thorn-scrub woodland, shortgrass prairie, and Chihuahuan Desert. A nature lover could spend years exploring and still only sample the Lone Star State's rich diversity of wildlife, plants, and geology.

Alibates Flint Quarries National Monument

An important site for Indian weapon and tool material

Some 13,000 years ago, Paleo-Indians began mining flint (agatized or silicified dolomite) near the stream now called the Canadian River. Excellent for making tools and weapons such as arrowheads and spear points, the material was an important trade item; it has been found hundreds of miles from its source. Native Americans continued to mine the flint into the late 19th century.

Flint is found scattered through a 10-square-mile area of today's Texas Panhandle, but the greatest concentration is located on a mesa in the center of the national monument. Indians used hand tools to excavate flint from more than 700 quarries at this site.

Visitors can take a 1-mile round-trip walk with a ranger to the ancient mining pits. Chunks of colorful flint lie on the surface, some left from mining activities. Tours of the quarries are by advance reservation only, and can be canceled at short notice in case of severe weather. Alibates is administered in conjunction with nearby Lake Meredith National Recreation Area (see p. 293), on the now dammed Canadian River.

Tex. 136 Fritch, TX 806-857-3151 www.nps.gov/alfl	**AT A GLANCE** Texas Panhandle, 30 miles north of Amarillo ▪ 1,000 acres ▪ Year-round, though winter storms can disrupt tours ▪ Visiting historic flint quarry sites

---

Amistad National Recreation Area
An expansive reservoir in Rio Grande desert terrain

Amistad means "friendship" in Spanish, and the International Amistad Reservoir, formed by a dam on the Rio Grande completed in 1969, is a joint undertaking of the United States and Mexico. Amistad National Recreation Area administers part of the reservoir and land along its northern shore. The park boundary extends 74 miles along the Rio Grande, 25 miles up the Devils River, and 14 miles up the Pecos River. Surface area of the reservoir varies greatly with water level, but at a minimum it encompasses around 25,000 acres; it can exceed twice that.

Amistad is best known for water-based activities, offering an oasis in the desert landscape of southern Texas. Boating, waterskiing, fishing (for bass and catfish), swimming, and scuba diving attract most visitors. Others come for the camping, bird-watching, or 4,000-year-old Indian pictographs (paintings on rock). Some rock-art sites are accessible only by boat, depending on lake levels, while others can be seen on guided tours at nearby Seminole Canyon State Park.

Except in the hottest summer months, the recreation area offers evening programs and guided bird walks; check with the office for schedules. Though conditions can be harsh in the surrounding terrain, occasional rains bring out a colorful variety of wildflowers. Vegetation reflects a transition zone of shrubland and Chihuahuan Desert, with a lesser influence of the Edwards Plateau to the north.

U.S. 90 Del Rio, TX 830-775-7491 www.nps.gov/amis	**AT A GLANCE** South Texas, 150 miles west of San Antonio ▪ 57,292 acres (17,820 land acres) ▪ Year-round ▪ Boating, fishing, swimming, viewing Indian rock art

---

Big Bend National Park
A vast wilderness of desert and mountains

The ecologically significant 1,250-square-mile Big Bend National Park—it's the premier preserve of Chihuahuan Desert flora and fauna—offers mountain scenery, spectacular canyons, and starkly beautiful desert vistas to impress even the casual sightseer.

Far off major travel routes in the sparsely populated badlands of West Texas, Big Bend is one of America's least known parks, with around 350,000 visitors annually. (Grand Canyon National Park can see that many visitors in a few weeks.) It's a long, long drive to reach Big Bend, but those who make the effort to visit will discover one of the most wondrous natural areas on Earth.

The list of Big Bend enthusiasts would include geologists, who consider its complicated jumble of sedimentary and igneous rocks both a delight and a challenge; bird-watchers, who rank the park as one of the handful of "must visit" sites on the continent; botanists, who know it as the foremost spot for studying the diverse plants of the Chihuahuan Desert; hikers, who delight in

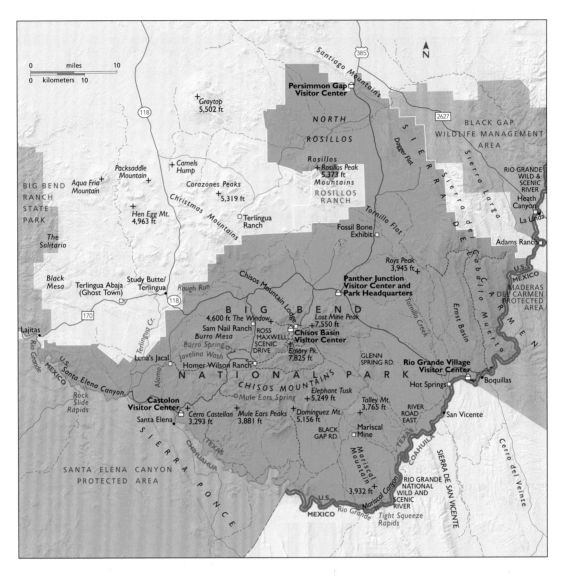

200 miles of trails ranging from short nature walks to multiday backpacking routes; and river-runners, who shoot rapids along the Rio Grande in some of the most awe-inspiring canyons anywhere (see Rio Grande National Wild and Scenic River, p. 296).

The Environment

Set where the Rio Grande makes a huge loop (a "big bend") on its course from El Paso to the Gulf of Mexico, the national park predominantly comprises Chihuahuan Desert lowlands, a place of cactuses, creosote bush, yuccas, agaves, and other arid-country vegetation. But the key to Big Bend's great appeal to naturalists is its ecological diversity. That diversity is the reason more species of birds (at least 450), bats, and cactuses have been found in Big Bend National Park than in any other national park—testimony to the richness of life in a part of the world too often considered a barren wasteland.

In the center of the park rise the Chisos Mountains, their summit 7,825-foot Emory Peak. Here, mountain lions, black bears, and white-tailed deer roam amid oaks, ponderosa pines, Douglas firs, Arizona cypresses, and even a few aspen trees—truly a world apart from the scrubby, spiny growth in the desert a mile in elevation below. The highlands of the Chisos Mountains were formed from volcanic activity about 35 million years ago and so are far

FOLLOWING PAGES: *The adobe ruins in Big Bend serve as reminders of the many families that used to live in the area.*

younger than the 500-million-year-old sandstone visible at Persimmon Gap, or the limestone of the Dead Horse Mountains and Big Bend's river canyons, about 135 million years old. In between the peaks and desert, shrub-dotted grasslands cover the mountain slopes, creating a transition zone of varying habitats.

The Rio Grande runs for 118 miles along the southern edge of the park, forming a green riparian zone just a stone's throw from the desert (and the international boundary with Mexico). Home to wetland animals and plants from frogs and beavers to willows and cottonwoods, the river adds to Big Bend's diversity, serving as a long, narrow oasis in a dry country.

Though the desert is often considered a colorless place, in years with sufficient rain the Big Bend lowlands can be a carpet of wildflowers and other blooming plants. Desert willow, skeleton-leaf goldeneye, globe mallow, cowpen daisy, desert marigold, bluebonnet, Chisos prickly poppy, desert tobacco, *ceniza,* and blackfoot daisy are just a few of the plants that brighten the desert. In addition, throughout the park various cactuses—prickly pears, chollas, claret cups, pitayas, hedgehogs, and others—blaze with colors from brilliant yellow to scarlet.

At the park visitor center (and headquarters) at Panther Junction you can learn about the area's complicated geology, study some of its plants on a short interpretive trail, buy maps and hiking guides, and find out about ranger-led walks, lectures, and other interpretive programs.

Rio Grande Village Area

From Panther Junction it's 20 desert miles to Rio Grande Village, a riverside complex with another visitor center, a campground, a store, and access to one of the three main Rio Grande canyons. The easy 0.7-mile round-trip

Rio Grande Village Nature Trail passes through spring-fed wetlands and lush riparian vegetation. A 4-mile dead-end road leads to the mouth of Boquillas Canyon, where you can walk 0.7 mile into this magnificent gorge, carved by the erosive power of the Rio Grande over millions of years. The only way to see more of the canyon is on a float trip through its entire 33-mile length.

Chisos Mountains Area

Three miles west of Panther Junction, a turn south leads up into the heart of the Chisos Mountains, the highlands that dominate the Big Bend landscape for miles in all directions. The paved, 6-mile, dead-end access road follows Green Gulch up to Panther Pass before descending slightly to Chisos Basin, a bowl surrounded by rugged rock spires that create an awe-inspiring natural setting. Here, at an elevation of 5,400 feet, you'll find a visitor center, lodge, restaurant, campground, and access to many of the park's most beautiful and rewarding hikes. All the peaks around the bowl were formed from volcanic activity when ash spewed from vents and magma rose from deep within the earth, cooling into igneous rock.

On the way up to Panther Pass, you'll go from desert lowlands into the grassland environment of the park's middle elevations. Plants such as sotol, bear grass, Torrey yucca, the imposing Havard agave, cholla, and Texas persimmon are common in the foothill belt. Higher, you'll begin seeing piñon pine, gray and Emory oaks, ash, maple, Texas madrone, and other trees dominating the slopes.

Chisos Basin lays claim to one of Big Bend's most popular hikes: the 5-mile round trip to the Window, the narrow canyon that serves as the drainage for the area. The last part of the trail runs over a waterworn creek bed to the steep drop called the Pouroff. The sunset view through the

Window is one of Big Bend's most famous scenes.

Other trails beginning in Chisos Basin range from the short Window View Trail to overnight backpacking trips into the high canyons. To stand atop 7,825-foot Emory Peak requires a 10-mile round-trip hike, rising steeply to a fine viewpoint at Pinnacles Pass and continuing west along a ridge to the summit. For an excellent day hike that samples the best of the high Chisos, head up to Laguna Meadow, circle east around Emory Peak through Boot Canyon (with its fantastic rock spire shaped like an upside-down cowboy boot), over Pinnacles Pass, and back through Boulder Meadow to the trailhead. It's 9.5 miles of great views, forested mountain canyons, and varied flora and fauna.

The montane vegetation is home to Big Bend's most sought-after bird, the rare Colima warbler, as well as zone-tailed hawks, flammulated owls, band-tailed pigeons, lucifer and blue-throated hummingbirds, acorn woodpeckers, cordilleran flycatchers, Mexican jays, Hutton's vireos, and painted redstarts. Both mountain lions and black bears haunt the Chisos forests, and, though the chances are low, both could cause problems for hikers and campers; take proper precautions to reduce the chance of encounters.

Ross Maxwell Scenic Drive

From the main east-west park road, a south turn 13 miles west of Panther Junction follows the Ross Maxwell Scenic Drive 30 miles to Santa Elena Canyon, passing through some of Big Bend's most striking landscapes along the way. The Chisos Mountains rise to the east, Burro Mesa to the west, and the road winds over and around an endless variety of rugged hills and rock formations. Interpretive signs along the road help travelers understand the region's complex geology.

Near the old Army post of Castolon, Mule Ears Peaks appear to the east. Here, volcanic lava and ash have been shaped by erosion into two pointed, definitely mule ear–shaped formations. A trail leads 1.9 miles to a spring and old ranching structures near the base of the peaks. Just before Castolon, the road passes through Tuff Canyon, where rock made of volcanic ash and other material takes a multitude of shapes and colors.

The scenic drive ends where the Rio Grande flows out of spectacular Santa Elena Canyon, one of Big Bend's three major river gorges. A fairly short trail (1.7 miles round trip) leads into the canyon, reached by crossing Terlingua Creek from the parking area. (High water may occasionally make this impossible, and at other times a little wading may be required.) The trail climbs a bit as it enters the canyon but then gradually slopes down to river level.

Limestone cliffs rise hundreds of feet overhead, and the rafts or canoes of river floaters sometimes pass by on overnight or multiday trips. The Santa Elena Canyon was formed when the Rio Grande cut down through a huge block of the earth as it was uplifted. As the land gradually rose over millions of years, the sediment-filled river eroded downward, eventually carving a canyon up to 1,500 feet deep—perhaps the most impressive sight in a park filled with awesome views. Santa Elena Canyon is the most popular float trip in the park, with 22 of the 30 miles being within the sheer canyon walls.

U.S. 385
Big Bend National Park, TX
432-477-2251
www.nps.gov/bibe

AT A GLANCE

Southwest Texas, 260 miles southeast of El Paso ▪ 801,163 acres ▪ Year-round, although summers are very hot in the desert ▪ Hiking, horseback riding, backpacking, camping, scenic driving, wildlife-watching, boating

Big Thicket National Preserve
Crossroads of ecological diversity

The tract of dense woods, wetlands, and savanna that locals have long called the Big Thicket lies at the overlapping point of several ecological zones, including longleaf pine forest, southern swamp, midwestern prairie, and southwestern desert. In combination with varying soil types, this fusion of habitats results in an extraordinary range of plants and animals found practically side by side in a relatively small area.

The beauty and richness of the Big Thicket environment led to calls for its protection as virgin forests fell to sawmills, and oil and gas firms moved in to drill in the early and mid-20th century. In 1974, after much controversy, the federal government created Big Thicket National Preserve, comprising several disjunct tracts. The National Park Service administers the area but, unlike most national parks, allows some hunting, as well as continuing oil and gas exploitation. Logging

The egret is a denizen of Big Thicket.

is prohibited, and as time passes, Big Thicket's forests will mature and come to resemble the woodlands where Alabama-Coushatta Indians hunted before European settlers arrived.

Botanists revere Big Thicket for its orchids, carnivorous plants, wildflowers, and broad range of trees and shrubs. But the preserve's attractions encompass pleasures as varied as its environment: a quiet paddle on a lake ringed by bald cypresses, the song of

a hooded warbler, the fragrant blossoms of a southern magnolia, the pied wings of a zebra swallowtail butterfly. These are just a few items from a long list of rewarding discoveries.

Exploring the Preserve
Forty miles of hiking trails provide access to the preserve's diversity, and canoeists can follow popular routes on its rivers, sloughs, and lakes. There are no developed campgrounds within the preserve, but primitive backcountry camping is allowed with a free permit.

The preserve visitor center is located on Farm-to-Market Road 420 east of U.S. 69/287, about 8 miles north of Kountze. Maps, trail guides, species lists, and advice are available here. The nearby Kirby Nature Trail threads through a woodland of beeches, southern magnolias, loblolly pines, sweet gums, and various oaks. Pileated woodpeckers frequent these large trees, and beautiful prothonotary warblers sing from swampy places along the way. The trail gradually descends to Village Creek, where you'll find some very large bald cypresses alongside red maples, swamp chestnut oaks, American hornbeams, and other wetland-loving species.

The Sandhill Loop Trail, just north of the Kirby loops, leads through drier longleaf pine woods, where water drains quickly through sandy soil and prickly pear cactus and yucca grow.

To the north, the Turkey Creek Trail provides a good look at the distinctive baygall habitat, named for sweet-bay magnolia and gallberry holly, two species commonly found in this swampy environment. Acidic water, stained dark by tannin in plant materials, collects in depressions, favoring some plants and discouraging other species. Red-bay, wild azalea, and titi (a shrub with hanging spikes of white flowers) often thrive in baygalls. Farther north, the short Pitcher Plant Trail is a must in spring, when exotic-looking, carnivorous yellow pitcher plants bloom amid a wet savanna.

Not far west of the Turkey Creek Unit is an excellent trail named for another carnivorous species. The Sundew Trail, in the Hickory Creek Savannah Unit, has a 0.3-mile disabled-accessible inner loop and a 1-mile outer loop. Sundews, which capture insects via sticky leaves, do indeed grow here, but the plants, only a few inches tall, are far less conspicuous than the foot-tall pitcher plants.

Farther west, off Farm-to-Market Road 1276, the 18-mile Big Sandy Trail in the Big Sandy Creek Unit is the only Big Thicket trail open also to horses and mountain bikes. The trail passes through beech-magnolia forest and bottomland woods.

The preserve protects nearly 80 miles of the Neches River, a popular stream for canoeing, lined with tall bluffs, dense vegetation, and sandbars. Several roads and launch areas provide access for day trips or multiday journeys. Conditions vary with the amount of water released from Steinhagen Lake, but the river is generally a lazy float. The middle part of the river, in the Neches Bottom and Jack Gore Baygall Unit, provides the best natural experience and the most solitude, with possible side trips into oxbow channels and quiet sloughs. Camping on sandbars is allowed in some places. The new Cooks Lake Paddling Trail makes a 5-mile loop from the Lower Neches Valley Authority boat ramp in Beaumont up the Neches River into Pine Island Bayou and Cooks Lake, and through a maze of bald cypress and water tupelo trees.

6102 F.M. 402
Kountze, TX
409-951-6700
www.nps.gov/bith

AT A GLANCE East Texas, 60 miles northeast of Houston ▪ 110,000 acres ▪ Year-round ▪ Hiking, camping, canoeing and rafting, bird-watching

Chamizal National Memorial

A memorial to cross-border cooperation

For around 1,000 miles, the Rio Grande forms a natural boundary between the United States and Mexico. For nearly all that distance the line is clear, but in El Paso, Texas, and the cross-border community of Juarez, Mexico, the shifting path of the river caused disputes over land ownership that lasted for decades and caused significant controversy and bad feelings.

The issue was finally resolved in 1963 with an agreement that has been called "a milestone in diplomatic relations between Mexico and the United States." Chamizal National

A mural in El Paso celebrates the cultural intersection of Mexico and the U.S.

Memorial (named for a tract of land that belonged to Mexico) endures as a cultural center where visitors learn about the shared heritage of the border region, keeping alive the spirit of cooperation that peacefully ended the international dispute.

A history museum recounts the background of the landmark Chamizal Convention, and three art galleries display changing exhibits related to the history and landscape of the border area. A mural called "Nuestra Herencia" ("Our Heritage") depicts the blending of United States and Mexican cultural elements, and represents other cultures of the borderland region. Varied music and other arts performances are held year-round. The Siglo de Oro Spanish Drama Festival, held annually at Chamizal, celebrates Spain's "golden age" by presenting theatrical groups from around the world.

El Camino Real de los Tejas National Historic Trail

The pioneer route that facilitated the settlement of Texas and Louisiana

Beginning in the late 1680s, the Spanish moved into the current territory of Texas and western Louisiana to deter French colonization. Missionaries and soldiers established a series of missions and presidios along a number of routes that shifted in response to environmental conditions and Indian threats. This network of routes is El Camino Real de los Tejas ("the royal road of the Tejas Indians"); it extended from Mexico City to Los Adaes, the first capital of the province of Texas (now located in Louisiana).

This network of roads and trails that was used to connect the missions and presidios eventually evolved into an important travel corridor that facilitated 19th-century migration to Texas. This movement shaped the border of the United States and Mexico, as settlers fought for Texas independence and eventually embraced statehood.

Designated in 2004 to commemorate this early highway, El Camino Real de los Tejas National Historic Trail covers roughly 2,600 miles. The Park Service administers the section from the southern border towns of Laredo and Eagle Pass, Texas, to the vicinity of Natchitoches, Louisiana. Maps and brochures on the trail are available, and travelers can visit many sites along its route, including the missions of San Antonio, Texas (see p. 296); the historic town of Nacogdoches, Texas; and Los Adaes State Historic Site in Louisiana. Both the Park Service website and that of the trail's association *(www.elcamino realdelostejas.org)* can provide more information.

Fort Davis National Historic Site

A well-preserved 19th-century frontier U.S. Army post

Fort Davis is among the best preserved of the many military posts that were established in the 19th century to protect traders and travelers on trails through the American West. Situated near Limpia Creek at the base of the beautiful Davis Mountains, the frontier fort provided protection to emigrants, mail coaches, and freight wagons on both the San Antonio–El Paso Road and the Chihuahua Trail.

Fort Davis was active from its founding in 1854 to 1891, except for a five-year period during and immediately following the Civil War. (The present configuration of buildings on the grounds represents the 1867 layout.) From 1867 to 1885, the post was home to contingents of African-American cavalrymen and infantrymen, including briefly 2nd Lt. Henry O. Flipper, the first black graduate of West Point. The soldiers scouted

for hostile Indians, surveyed land, built roads, and installed telegraph lines.

Visitors can see an orientation video and interactive exhibits at the visitor center, and can tour restored

stone-and-adobe buildings, including officers' quarters, barracks, and the hospital. A sound program based on an 1875 Army retreat parade is played three times a day.

Tex. 118 and 17 juncture
Fort Davis, TX
432-426-3224
www.nps.gov/foda

AT A GLANCE

West Texas, 200 miles east of El Paso ▪ 523 acres ▪ Year-round ▪ Visiting military buildings from the days of the Indian wars

Guadalupe Mountains National Park
A land of tall peaks and desert landscapes

One of the most recognizable landmarks in Texas rises in the southern part of this splendid national park set on the Texas/New Mexico state line. The massive cliff face called El Capitan has guided American Indians, western explorers, and settlers for centuries; for modern travelers, it remains one of the most impressive sights in the Southwest. Even more awe-inspiring, perhaps, is the geologic story behind this and the rest of the Guadalupe Mountains, towering over the Chihuahuan Desert lowlands to crest at 8,749-foot Guadalupe Peak, the highest point in Texas.

Natural History

These magnificent highlands—comprising not only Guadalupe Peak but the three next-highest summits in Texas also—began underwater, as the countless fossils of sea creatures found here testify. Geologists consider the rocks of the Guadalupes one of the best examples of exposed fossil reef in the world, revealing to experts' trained eyes secrets of reef formation at varying ocean depths.

In the Permian period, roughly 260–270 million years ago, a basin connected to a warm, tropical-type sea spread over this region. A

Cactus wren

horseshoe-shaped limestone reef formed around the edges of the basin, a huge structure built bit by tiny bit of the bodies of sponges, algae, bryozoans, and other sea life, augmented by minerals in the water and sand from adjacent beaches.

After the sea retreated, succeeding eons saw the reef buried by sediments eroded from distant mountains and deposited by rivers. Then, beginning about 25 million years ago, tectonic activity uplifted the reef 2 miles above its original elevation; subsequent erosion exposed it on the Earth's surface here in the Guadalupes and in the

Apache and Glass Mountains to the southeast.

Beneath the northern portion of the Guadalupe Mountains, acidic water seeping through cracks in the relatively soft limestone has eroded a series of underground chambers filled with intricate, colorful cave formations: This underground attraction is Carlsbad Caverns (see p. 344), a national park less than an hour from Guadalupe Mountains.

But it's not just geology that makes Guadalupe Mountains National Park such a fascinating place. The juxtaposition of high peaks with arid lowlands creates a superb diversity of life, from the cactuses and shrubs of the Chihuahuan Desert to hardwoods along canyon streams to ponderosa pines and Douglas firs in the mountains.

Opened to visitation in 1972, Guadalupe Mountains saw little development in the years before its protection by the National Park Service. Much of it was a goat, sheep, and cattle ranch, and part of it was owned by Wallace Pratt, an oil-company geologist who believed strongly in the preservation of this beautiful and rewarding landscape. Pratt's donation of almost 6,000 acres gave impetus to the creation of a national park here.

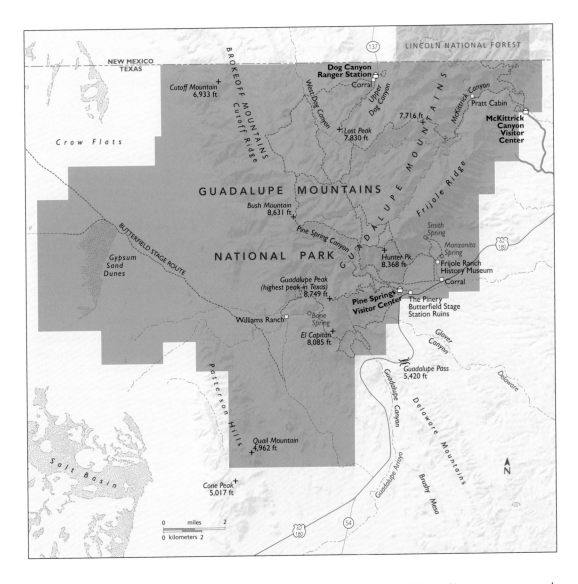

Elk, grizzly bears, bighorn sheep, and gray wolves were among the animals eliminated from the Guadalupes by overhunting (elk from a different subspecies were reintroduced in the 1920s), but the mammals, birds, reptiles, and other animals that remain make Guadalupe Mountains a rewarding place for wildlife-watching. Eighty miles of trails, from easy walks to strenuous climbs into the high country, make the area's varied habitats accessible to those ready to explore one of America's best, if least known, national parks.

Pine Springs Visitor Center Area

The visitor center offers an introductory slide show and exhibits on geology, wildlife, and plants, and information on ranger-led programs and hikes. The park's easiest trail begins at the visitor center: the 0.4-mile, disabled-accessible path to the Pinery, the ruins of an 1858 station used by the famed Butterfield Overland Mail stage route. (This was the highest station on the Butterfield route, at 5,534 feet elevation.) Interpretive signs along the paved trail identify desert plants.

The park's main campground, Pine Springs, is nearby, as well as the trailhead for hikes into the Guadalupes. To stand on the highest point in Texas, plan on a strenuous six-to-eight-hour hike to reach the 8,751-foot summit of Guadalupe Peak and return. The 8.4-mile round trip climbs 3,000 feet, with some steep stretches and exposed cliffs. Because of the danger of lightning, do not attempt this hike if bad weather is forecast or the skies threaten.

One of the park's special places is the high basin called the Bowl, where

Douglas firs and ponderosa pines create an environment reminiscent of the Rocky Mountains. The area is reached by a tough 9.1-mile round trip, gaining 2,500 feet in elevation. Bird-watchers know the high Guadalupes as the home of many species typical of more northern or mountainous climes, and they visit the Bowl and nearby woodlands to look for band-tailed pigeons, hairy woodpeckers, olive-sided flycatchers, house wrens, brown creepers, mountain chickadees, Steller's jays, and pine siskins, among others. Lucky

hikers, or backpackers spending the night in the highlands, might see or hear saw-whet or flammulated owls.

Mule deer (common in the park), elk, coyotes, ringtails, rock squirrels, and black-tailed jackrabbits are among local mammals. Look, too, for the little gray-footed chipmunk, found in Texas only here and in the Sierra Diablo Mountains to the south.

The moderately strenuous 4.2-mile round-trip Devil's Hall Trail follows Pine Springs Canyon, along the way climbing a striking series of limestone ledges called the Hiker's Staircase.

High canyon walls and varied vegetation make this an excellent route for those who don't want to climb into the mountains or deal with the crowds in popular McKittrick Canyon.

East of the visitor center area is the north turnoff to Frijole Ranch; and the trailhead for Smith Springs Trail, a 2.3-mile loop. The two springs along here provide precious water in this desert-edge habitat, attracting a wide assortment of wildlife. Mule deer and elk are found often here; an early-morning visit will turn up the greatest variety of birds. The 1876 Frijole Ranch main house is now a cultural museum.

McKittrick Canyon

Guadalupe Mountains' most popular destination is the deep chasm called McKittrick Canyon, a day-use-only area in the northeast corner of the park just a couple of miles from New Mexico. In a part of the world dominated by desert scrub and conifers, the bigtooth maples and other hardwoods here put on a brilliant show of foliage color in the fall, attracting crowds of visitors that sometimes cause park staffers to regulate entry into the area. The reds, yellows, and oranges of the maples are wonderful, to be sure, but in fall a weekday visit is a more pleasant experience.

Any time of year, McKittrick Canyon's attributes—a pretty creek, riparian vegetation, diverse birdlife, excellent scenery—repay exploration. The 0.9-mile McKittrick Canyon Nature Trail features interpretive signs explaining local geology and the ecological role of fire, as well as identifying common plants. More than 40 species of birds nest in the canyon.

To learn more about the geology of the Guadalupes, pick up a trail guide at the visitor center and hike the strenuous 4.2-mile (one way) Permian Reef Trail to the top of Wilderness

The Guadalupe Mountains' high peaks and desert lowlands offer solitude.

Ridge. Gaining 2,000 feet of elevation, the route is dotted with markers keyed to the guide, which explicates the curious origins of these rugged mountains.

The McKittrick Canyon Trail, following the main drainage up into the mountains, ranks as one of the three most popular hikes in Texas. Because it's so well used, the national park takes special care to protect the area, prohibiting off-trail hiking and entry into the waters of McKittrick Creek. Favorite picnicking destinations and easy hikes are to Pratt Cabin and the Grotto, 2.4 and 3.5 miles, respectively. On the trail the flora slowly changes from Chihuahuan Desert species to mid-level hardwoods and conifers. Prickly pear cactuses, ocotillos, chollas, agaves, and yuccas make the lower reaches of the canyon a scrubby, spiny place. Up canyon, the scene becomes lusher and greener, with ponderosa pines, alligator junipers (named for their reptile-skin-like bark), bigtooth maples, Knowlton's hop hornbeam, chinkapin and gray oaks, Texas madrones, velvet ashes, and little-leaf walnuts among the streamside trees.

Dog Canyon

To reach the park's Dog Canyon ranger station, campground, and trailhead requires a drive of about 120 miles from the main visitor center, north into New Mexico and then southwest off U.S. 285 on N. Mex. 137. You're assured of a high degree of solitude in this remote area, frequented mostly by backpackers heading south into the Guadalupes. The less intrepid can picnic or walk short sections of the trails here, of course, for day hikes of various lengths.

The Indian Meadow Nature Trail is 0.6 mile and takes less than an hour, unless you stop often to look at birds, butterflies, and wildflowers; a free trail guide provides natural- and cultural-history information on the region.

Another fine hike follows the Bush Mountain Trail to Manzanita Ridge, where you'll find a superb view down into West Dog Canyon at a stop called Marcus Overlook; retracing your steps makes a moderately difficult hike of 4.5 miles.

The isolation of Guadalupe Mountains National Park is one of its attractions, but visitors need to be aware of the extremely limited access to groceries, restaurants, gasoline, lodging (other than camping), and other services. If you've prepared accordingly, any visit will be enjoyable.

U.S. 62/180
Salt Flat, TX
915-828-3251
www.nps.gov/gumo

AT A GLANCE West Texas, 110 miles east of El Paso ▪ 86,416 acres ▪ Year-round; occasional summer and winter storms in the high country ▪ Camping, hiking, horseback riding, wildlife-watching

---

Lake Meredith National Recreation Area
A large recreational lake in the Texas Panhandle

Formed by a dam on the Canadian River and used as a water supply for several communities, Lake Meredith was designated a national recreation area in 1990. As a large reservoir in the dry, shortgrass terrain of the Texas Panhandle, it ranks among the most popular vacation and weekend getaway spots in the region.

Various water-related activities draw most of Lake Meredith's visitors, especially swimming, waterskiing, sailing, and fishing. (Anglers go after bass, catfish, and crappie, and the lake is famed for walleye.) Those who simply enjoying sailing or motorboating can explore side canyons with rock walls up to 200 feet high.

Camping is allowed both in designated campgrounds and in backcountry locations. Horseback riding is a popular activity, and the park service has set aside areas especially for off-road vehicles, as well. In proper seasons, hunters seek white-tailed and mule deer, pheasant, quail, and waterfowl. Wildlife-watchers might see porcupines, coyotes, various snakes and lizards, and scores of species of birds.

The abundant flint in the area was mined and worked by American Indians to make tools and weapons. Alibates Flint Quarries National Monument (see p. 281) is located next to Lake Meredith and is administered by the same office.

Tex. 136
Fritch, TX
806-857-3151
www.nps.gov/lamr

AT A GLANCE Texas Panhandle, 35 miles north of Amarillo ▪ 46,000 acres (lake area 10,000 acres) ▪ Year-round, although winter weather can be severe ▪ Boating, fishing, swimming, camping, horseback riding, waterskiing

Lyndon B. Johnson National Historical Park
The boyhood home and ranch of the 36th President

Though his presidential legacy includes civil rights legislation, educational initiatives, and the Vietnam War, Lyndon B. Johnson (1908–1973) always seemed to carry his Texas Hill Country home with him as part of his personality. He returned to his roots often during his political career and retired to his ranch here in 1969.

Visitors to the historical park learn about Johnson's life and career at two sites located 14 miles apart. In the small town of Johnson City, the visitor center provides information on touring the site and has exhibits on LBJ and his wife, Lady Bird. Nearby are the boyhood home, where Johnson lived from age five through high school, and the 19th-century log cabin and other farm buildings of earlier Johnson family members.

Near Stonewall, Texas, the LBJ Ranch remains a working ranch with Hereford cattle that are bloodline descendants of President Johnson's herd. The ranch encompasses a reconstruction of the house that was LBJ's birthplace as well as a private family cemetery where LBJ, Lady Bird, and many relatives are buried. Free permits for a self-guided auto tour of the ranch can be obtained from the visitor center at the adjacent Lyndon B. Johnson State Park and Historic Site.

The state park focuses on how the land influenced LBJ's life. The park's exhibits include restored buildings, a living-history farmstead, and displays of native wildlife and longhorn cattle.

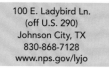

100 E. Ladybird Ln.
(off U.S. 290)
Johnson City, TX
830-868-7128
www.nps.gov/lyjo

AT A GLANCE

South-central Texas, 45 miles west of Austin ▪ 674 acres ▪ Year-round ▪ Touring restored 19th- and 20th-century buildings and cattle ranch

Padre Island National Seashore
Pristine Gulf of Mexico beaches and dunes

Padre Island National Seashore, set on the southern Texas coast just minutes from the city of Corpus Christi, protects the largest tract of undeveloped barrier island in the world. The park safeguards the great majority of this fragile and beautiful strip of beach, dunes, and grassland from permanent intrusion of vacation houses, resorts, and towns.

Visitors crowd the park's easily accessible Malaquite Beach area in the warm months for swimming and sunbathing on the Gulf of Mexico. But beyond this popular sand-and-surf spot stretch more than 60 miles of undeveloped beach,

A sea turtle makes her way inland to lay eggs.

offering solitude for swimming, camping, fishing, walking, bird-watching, and searching for seashells; most of this beachfront is accessible only via off-road vehicle.

The Park Road

The only way to enter the national seashore by land is from the north, along Tex. 22. Just past the park's entrance station, the self-guided Grasslands Nature Trail interprets the ecology of Padre Island's interior grasslands. Visitors might see a spotted ground squirrel, a black-tailed jackrabbit, or a coyote. This shadeless trail can be very hot at times, so wear a hat and sunscreen on sunny days. Mosquitoes can be ferocious throughout the inland parts of the park in summer, although the constant wind usually keeps them at bay on the beaches.

Just a mile farther down the park road, a side road leads west to Bird Island Basin on Laguna Madre, a good spot for bird-watching. A search here could turn up white pelicans, reddish egrets, roseate spoonbills, black skimmers, and a wide variety of plovers and sandpipers.

Biologists count Laguna Madre as one of the very few hypersaline lagoons in the world. Because of its physical characteristics, and because no major freshwater rivers flow into it, Laguna Madre has a salt content much higher than normal ocean water. Its complex ecosystem provides vital nursery areas for shrimp and other marine invertebrates and fish, as well as feeding grounds for waterfowl and wading birds.

Bird Island Basin, for its part, is known as one of the best windsurfing spots in the country. Warm, shallow water; the soft lagoon bed; and a steady average 18-mile-an-hour wind make it hugely popular with devotees of the sport. A concessionaire provides lessons and rentals for beginners and experienced windsurfers alike.

The main park road continues south for a couple of miles before dead-ending at the beach. The Malaquite Visitor Center, set near the end of the road, offers information, an orientation film, changing rooms and showers for swimmers, and a developed campground. Check here for ranger presentations such as beach walks and campfire programs. North of the visitor center, a 4.5-mile stretch of Malaquite Beach is off-limits to vehicles of any kind, providing a quiet retreat—as well as peace of mind for visitors with small children who might wander.

Beyond the Road

Where the road ends, visitors are permitted to drive onto the beach. The first 5 miles can be accessed by regular vehicles, and are often quite busy on summer weekends. Beyond the 5-mile marker, however, a 4WD vehicle is required to continue south—and even then, drivers should talk to a ranger about current conditions and heed warnings to avoid getting stuck in pockets of soft sand. With determination, skill, and luck, some drivers may navigate the 55 miles to the Mansfield Channel, an impassable cut separating Padre and South Padre Islands, and so the end of the road for this out-and-back adventure.

The long beach drive appeals to people looking for solitude for swimming, picnicking, or primitive camping, as well as seashell collectors looking for fresh beaches to search. (After storms is the best time to beachcomb, when waves have pushed more shells onshore—but April to June, the waves also push an abundance of seaweed ashore.) Birders look for flocks of gulls, terns, and shorebirds; and anglers surf-cast for flounder, gulf whitings, red drums, black drums, and speckled trout. The endangered Kemp's ridley turtle nests in the park, though it's seldom seen.

When wading or swimming, watch for jellyfish and Portuguese man-of-wars in the water or washed ashore. Some of these, especially Portuguese man-of-wars (or "blue jellyfish") and sea nettles, can cause painful rashes with their stinging tentacles.

Many visitors to Padre Island are simply looking for a pretty beach for swimming and relaxing. But if you're aware of the life along the shore and in the dunes—the color of tiny coquina clams and beach evening primrose, the hurried skittering of ghost crabs, the fluting song of a meadowlark—you'll get much more from a trip to this priceless preserve along the Texas Gulf Coast.

AT A GLANCE

Tex. Park Rd. 22
Corpus Christi, TX
361-949-8068
www.nps.gov/pais

East Texas coast, just south of Corpus Christi ▪ 130,434 acres, 65 miles of coastline ▪ Year-round ▪ Camping, hiking, fishing, windsurfing, shelling

---

Palo Alto Battlefield National Historical Park

The site of an important early battle of the U.S.–Mexican War

When the United States granted statehood to Texas in 1845, the action drew an angry response from the Mexican government, which had never recognized the independent Republic of Texas. The U.S. claimed ownership of territory south to the Rio Grande and built a fort on the river's north bank. In reaction, Mexico sent troops to attack in 1846.

After a series of clashes in the spring, a major engagement took place at a site called Palo Alto, 10 miles north of the Rio Grande. U.S. troops under the command of Gen. Zachary Taylor defeated a Mexican contingent with artillery power. This battle initiated a two-year war that ultimately forced Mexico to cede territory to the U.S.—area that included California and large parts of the Southwest.

Established in 1992, Palo Alto Battlefield National Historical Park preserves the site of the first battle and interprets other regional battlefields. A walking trail leads to interpretive displays at the battle site, and the visitor center offers an orientation video and exhibits. The park has a second site at the Resaca de la Palma battlefield, south of Palo Alto and within Brownsville. The only Park Service unit specifically focused on the U.S.–Mexican War, Palo Alto interprets the conflict as a whole, and presents both U.S. and Mexican perspectives on the war.

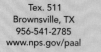

Tex. 511
Brownsville, TX
956-541-2785
www.nps.gov/paal

AT A GLANCE

South Texas, 5 miles north of Brownsville ▪ 3,400 acres ▪ Year-round ▪ Walking interpretive battlefield, viewing exhibits at visitor center

Rio Grande National Wild & Scenic River

Remote canyons of awe-inspiring beauty

As the Rio Grande flows along the western Texas border with Mexico, it passes through some of the most scenic landscapes in the Southwest. In 1978, Congress designated a 196-mile length of it as a national wild and scenic river. Big Bend National Park administers the river, working to provide recreational access while maintaining the Rio Grande's beauty, solitude, and wilderness quality.

On this part of the Rio Grande, recreation means float trips through the magnificent canyons above, in, and below the park. Rafting, canoeing, or kayaking beneath the towering walls of the river gorges can be a wonderful experience, but proper planning is imperative: Rapids can range to Class III or IV, and hazards abound. Limited road access means that help could be a very long time in arriving in an emergency.

While private trips are allowed, the easiest way to traverse the Rio Grande's canyons is by taking a float trip with an outfitter company, which will handle permits, equipment, and shuttles. Trips can range from one day to ten days or more. The Park Service controls the number of commercial outfitter trips on the river and requires permits for day use and overnight outings. In recent years, low water levels have seriously affected floating in the upper portion, especially Mariscal Canyon, at various times of the year. Contact the Big Bend National Park office for a list of approved companies.

U.S. 385
Big Bend National Park, TX
432-477-2251
www.nps.gov/rigr

AT A GLANCE

Southwest Texas, 260 miles southeast of El Paso ▪ 196 river miles ▪ Year-round, though low water levels affect boating in the upper portion at times ▪ Rafting, canoeing, kayaking

San Antonio Missions National Historical Park

18th-century missions vital to Spain's New World settlement

Beginning in 1718, Spain built five mission compounds along the San Antonio River with the goal of converting native people to Catholicism and making them Spanish citizens. France was asserting its power to the east in Louisiana, and Spain felt the need to reinforce its cultural and military presence in what is now Texas. Each mission was made up of a church, living quarters, storerooms, and other outbuildings set within defensive walls (guarding against Indian attacks). Outside the mission walls, crops were planted and animals were kept, making the sites self-sustaining communities as much as religious centers.

Perhaps the most well-known of the five missions is the Mission San Antonio de Valero, begun in 1718. Known today as the Alamo, it starred as the scene of a dramatic 13-day siege in 1836 in the Texas Revolution. Located in downtown San Antonio, it is preserved as an independent shrine of Texas history.

The other four missions, scattered along the river south of the central city, make up San Antonio Missions National Historical Park. Each site includes a church that still functions as an active Catholic parish, holding regular services. Visitors are welcome inside the churches during park hours, except during special events such as weddings and funerals.

The Missions

Mission San José, the largest of the missions and established in 1720, has been most fully restored, including its gristmill and defensive wall. Visitors with time to visit only one mission should choose San José, known as the Queen of the Missions.

The Mission Concepción church, built in 1755, is the oldest unrestored stone church in America; it still looks much as it did more than two centuries ago. Traces of its original frescoes can be seen inside since, unlike the other mission churches, it never lost its roof or walls, even when the churches were not maintained.

At the 1731 Mission San Juan Capistrano, a short trail leads to a natural section of the San Antonio River. At Mission Espada (1731), visitors can see a 270-year-old, restored *acequia* (irrigation system), including dam and aqueduct. Espada is the southernmost mission, about 11 miles from downtown San Antonio.

The period of greatest mission influence lasted from about 1745 to the 1780s, when they began a decline in population and activity. Constant raids from Apache and Comanche (enemies of the Indians who lived at the missions), as well as disease, caused challenges for the mission

Mission Concepción has the oldest unrestored stone church in the United States.

communities. Nonetheless, some of the parishioners who attend church services today are descended from the Indians who lived at the sites in the 18th century.

The park visitor center, adjacent to Mission San Jose, includes a museum with artifacts and an interpretive video shown every half hour. Rangers and docents offer regular tours of the missions, explaining their historical context and their importance to Spain's strategy for colonizing the American Southwest.

City bus routes provide transportation to two of the missions (San José and Concepción), but most visitors drive between the sites. There's also a hike-bike trail that mostly parallels the San Antonio River, offering another opportunity to visit the missions and explore the surrounding neighborhoods and countryside.

The five missions were designated a World Heritage site by UNESCO in 2015.

Visitor center
6701 San José Dr.
San Antonio, TX
210-932-1001
www.nps.gov/saan

AT A GLANCE

San Antonio ▪ 950 acres ▪ Year-round ▪ Touring historic churches and mission grounds

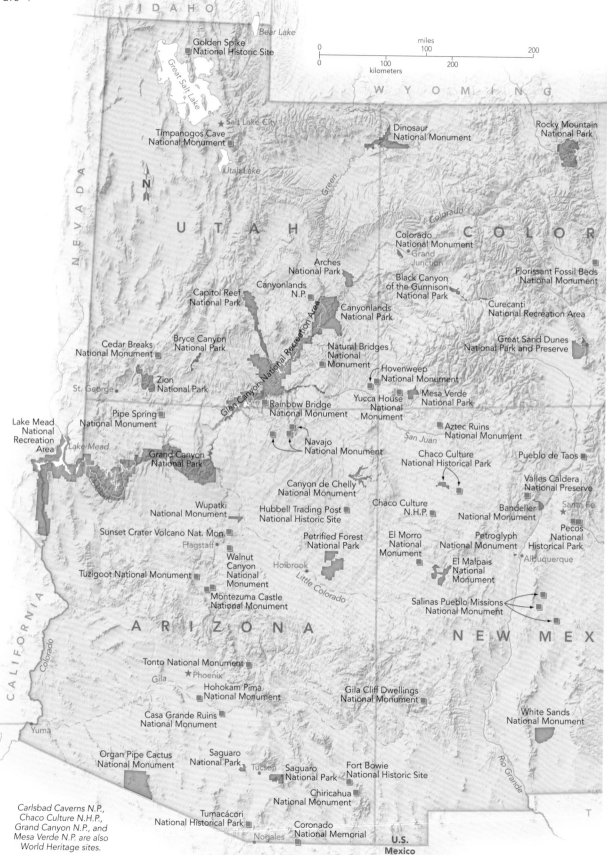

IDAHO

Bear Lake

Golden Spike
National Historic Site

Great Salt Lake

miles
0 100 200
0 100 200
kilometers

WYOMING

★ Salt Lake City

Timpanogos Cave
National Monument

Utah Lake

Dinosaur
National Monument

Rocky Mountain
National Park

N

NEVADA

U T A H

Green

Colorado

Colorado
National Monument

C O L O R

Grand
Junction

Florissant Fossil Beds
National Monument

Arches
National Park

Black Canyon
of the Gunnison
National Park

Curecanti
National Recreation Area

Capitol Reef
National Park

Canyonlands
N.P.

Canyonlands
National Park

Cedar Breaks
National Monument

Bryce Canyon
National Park

Natural Bridges
National
Monument

Great Sand Dunes
National Park and Preserve

St. George

Zion
National Park

Hovenweep
National Monument

Pipe Spring
National Monument

Rainbow Bridge
National Monument

Yucca House
National
Monument

Mesa Verde
National Park

Aztec Ruins
National Monument

Pueblo de Taos

Lake Mead
National
Recreation
Area

Lake Mead

Grand Canyon
National Park

Navajo
National Monument

San Juan

Chaco Culture
National Historical Park

Valles Caldera
National Preserve

Santa Fe ★

Wupatki
National Monument

Canyon de Chelly
National Monument

Chaco Culture
N.H.P.

Bandelier
National Monument

Pecos
National
Historical Park

Sunset Crater Volcano Nat. Mon.

Flagstaff

Hubbell Trading Post
National Historic Site

Petrified Forest
National Park

El Morro
National
Monument

Petroglyph
National Monument

Albuquerque

Tuzigoot National Monument

Walnut
Canyon
National
Monument

Holbrook

El Malpais
National
Monument

Little Colorado

Montezuma Castle
National Monument

A R I Z O N A

Salinas Pueblo Missions
National Monument

N E W   M E X

Tonto National Monument

Gila

★ Phoenix

Hohokam Pima
National Monument

Gila Cliff Dwellings
National Monument

White Sands
National Monument

Casa Grande Ruins
National Monument

Yuma

C A L I F O R N I A

Colorado

Organ Pipe Cactus
National Monument

Saguaro
National Park

Saguaro
National Park

Fort Bowie
National Historic Site

Rio Grande

Tucson

Chiricahua
National Monument

Carlsbad Caverns N.P.,
Chaco Culture N.H.P.,
Grand Canyon N.P., and
Mesa Verde N.P. are also
World Heritage sites.

Tumacácori
National Historical Park

Nogales

Coronado
National Memorial

U.S.
Mexico

Southwest

N o region boasts more renowned destinations than the four-state area of the Southwest. Famed national parks such as Carlsbad Caverns, Rocky Mountain, Zion, Bryce Canyon, Grand Canyon, and Petrified Forest hold places on every traveler's wish list. Scattered throughout the Southwest are other, lesser known parks that deserve a visit, including Sunset Crater Volcano National Monument in Arizona, Bandelier National Monument in New Mexico, and Colorado National Monument—all gems where crowds are rare and rewards abundant. Historic sites range from the spectacular cliff dwellings of Mesa Verde National Park to 17th-century Spanish missions and 19th-century trading posts and U.S. Army forts.

NEBRASKA

South Platte

★ Denver

S. Fk. Republican

A D O

K A N S A S

Colorado Springs

Sand Creek Massacre National Historic Site

Arkansas

Pueblo

Bent's Old Fort National Historic Site

Capulin Volcano National Monument

OKLA.

Canadian

Fort Union National Monument

T E X A S

I C O

Pecos

Roswell

Carlsbad Caverns National Park

E X A S

Sunrise burnishes Thor's Hammer (left) and other formations in Bryce Canyon.

ARIZONA

The Grand Canyon may be an Arizona icon and one of the world's most famous natural areas, but other sites merit attention, too. Saguaro National Park protects forests of the spectacular saguaro cactus, which grows only in the Sonoran Desert; Petrified Forest National Park comprises not only the famed fossilized trees but also the colorful landscape of the Painted Desert. History abounds, from Paleo-Indian cliff dwellings through the era of Spanish missions to Old West forts. Arizona boasts the world's most extensive ponderosa pine forest, high peaks, and lush riparian areas. The last lower 48 state admitted to the Union, Arizona maintains many aspects of frontier culture.

Canyon de Chelly National Monument

A striking canyon landscape, home to a Navajo community

Spectacular walls of red sandstone rise hundreds of feet above valley floors in Canyon de Chelly National Monument, creating scenes of stunning beauty. Ruins of ancient dwellings can be seen along ledges on the cliffs, while elsewhere in the park dozens of modern Navajo families still live and farm, part of a Native American heritage dating back 2,000 years.

In a unique management arrangement, Canyon de Chelly is administered cooperatively by the National Park Service and the Navajo Nation, within whose tribal lands it lies. Because of the proximity of a living culture to geologic features, travel within Canyon de Chelly is more limited than in most parks. Two roads wind along canyon rims, offering superb vistas, and one publicly accessible trail leads down to the canyon floor. Otherwise, visits must be accompanied by a ranger or Navajo guide, the latter available through several local firms. Vehicle tours, horseback rides, hikes, and camping trips can all be arranged, ranging from a few hours to several days.

Though named for its main canyon, the park includes another major

Native Americans have lived in Canyon de Chelly for more than 2,000 years.

canyon, Canyon del Muerto, and smaller side canyons. The two major canyons form a V shape with the park visitor center at its point. Exhibits and a film at the center offer background on both the geologic and human history of the park. Many visitors who want to see more than is available along the rim roads choose to take vehicle tours along the canyon floor. For those with time, horseback rides afford a quieter and more leisurely experience.

However you choose to explore, Canyon de Chelly's blend of enduring culture and beauty makes any visit a memorable experience.

North & South Rim Drives

The South Rim Drive at Canyon de Chelly passes some of the park's most famous scenes along its 18-mile length. Near the beginning, Junction Overlook provides a viewpoint of the confluence of the two major canyons. A few miles farther is the turn to the trailhead for the White House Trail, the only place visitors can descend into the canyon without a guide. This 2.5-mile round-trip path leads from the canyon rim 500 feet down to a ruined dwelling occupied by Puebloan people about a thousand years ago. The South Rim Drive ends at the amazing spectacle of Spider Rock, an eroded pinnacle rising 800 feet above the canyon floor.

Side roads along the 17-mile North Rim Drive lead to views of several ruins, including Mummy Cave Ruin, one of the park's largest structures, with dwellings and ceremonial buildings flanking a central tower, all beneath an overhanging bluff. Nearby is Massacre Cave, where in 1805 Spanish soldiers killed 115 Navajo who were trapped on a ledge on the canyon wall.

At several places on the drives you'll look down at the farms and traditional hogan homes of modern Navajo, with pastures and fields beside the streams that flow intermittently along the canyon floors. In fall, when the Fremont cottonwoods that line the washes turn golden yellow, the rim panoramas can be breathtaking.

Natural History

The tall cliffs of Canyon de Chelly are composed mainly of sandstone deposited as dunes in a vast desert more than 230 million years ago. The steep-sided canyons were formed as rivers cut down into sandstone rising with the uplift of the Colorado Plateau. The process began more than 60 million years ago, though the main canyon formation occurred over the past 2 million years. Canyon cutting continues today, with erosion caused by rain, ice, and wind-carried grit. In places in the upper canyons, the walls stand 1,000 feet above the streams that in part shaped them.

Dark streaks on the red cliffs are "desert varnish," created by microscopic organisms that actually take minerals from airborne dust particles and deposit them on the rocks. The minerals, primarily manganese, are then washed down the rock walls, staining them black.

U.S. 191 east of Chinle, AZ 928-674-5500 www.nps.gov/cach

AT A GLANCE — Northeastern Arizona, 150 miles northeast of Flagstaff ▪ 83,840 acres ▪ Year-round; access sometimes limited by winter snow ▪ Hiking, camping, driving scenic routes, taking guided tours of canyon and ruins, horseback riding

Casa Grande Ruins National Monument

A mysterious structure left by an ancient people

Noted and written about by explorers as long ago as the 17th century, the ruins of this *casa grande* (great house) remain a mystery to anthropologists and archaeologists. So striking is the tall structure, though, that in 1892 it became the first archaeological reserve to be given official protection by the federal government.

Casa Grande was built around the 14th century by a people who have come to be called the Hohokam (a term meaning "those who are gone" in the language of the O'odham, who claim to be descendants of the Hohokam). At the height of their culture, the Hohokam established trade routes, dug hundreds of miles of irrigation canals for their crops, created pottery and jewelry, and used a natural soil material called caliche to erect buildings like Casa Grande. By the 1400s, the Hohokam began to abandon their structures for reasons that are unclear; speculated causes include drought, invasion by other tribes, disease, floods, and intra-tribal strife.

Visitors to the national monument can take either a guided *(Dec.–April)* or self-guided tour to see the four-story, 11-room main building (whose original function is unknown), an ancient court where a type of ball game was played, and remains of walls. The visitor center shows a short introductory film and contains a museum.

1100 W. Ruins Dr. Coolidge, AZ 520-723-3172 www.nps.gov/cagr

AT A GLANCE — Southern Arizona, 55 miles southeast of Phoenix ▪ 472 acres ▪ Year-round, though summer temperatures can be very high ▪ Viewing ancient Native American ruins

Chiricahua National Monument

Fantastic rock formations in "sky island" mountains

Erosion on layers of ash, deposited some 27 million years ago, has created fantastic formations, such as the Organ Pipe.

Several mountain ranges in southern Arizona have come to be known as "sky islands": highlands that rise abruptly from the surrounding desert like islands in the ocean. Set within one of these ranges, the eponymous Chiricahua National Monument protects striking rock formations and a distinctive diversity of flora and fauna.

Massive volcanic eruptions some 27 million years ago formed the great bulk of the Chiricahuas' rocks, spewing vast amounts of ash and magma onto the surface. As the igneous material cooled it formed rhyolite, which eroded into cliffs, pillars, and other formations, making the Chiricahuas one of southern Arizona's most scenic spots. The most spectacular of these rock sculptures can be seen at Chiricahua National Monument, where a scenic drive and 17 miles of hiking trails access this dramatic landscape, including the geologic fantasyland known as Heart of Rocks. Formations such as Big Balanced Rock, Punch and Judy, and Duck on a Rock make clear why the Apache called this the "land of standing-up rocks."

The 8-mile scenic Bonita Canyon Drive leads up to 6,870-foot Massai Point, providing one of the park's best vistas. Chiricahua forests are home to ponderosa and Apache pines, alligator juniper, Arizona sycamore, Douglas fir, Arizona cypress, and several types of oak, as well as several varieties of agave and cactus. Bird-watchers make these mountains a regular stop to spot species found only in this region of the United States.

Ariz. 181
Willcox, AZ
520-824-3560
www.nps.gov/chir

AT A GLANCE

Southeastern Arizona, 120 miles east of Tucson ▪ 11,985 acres ▪ Year-round; occasional snow in winter ▪ Hiking, camping, taking scenic drive

Coronado National Memorial

A Huachuca Mountain tribute to a Spanish conquistador

In 1540, Spanish explorer Francisco Vásquez de Coronado set out from Mexico City on a journey through what is now the American Southwest and Midwest. Lured by tales about cities of gold, he and his party traveled for two years through deserts and prairies, finding villages of American Indians, but no treasure. Back in Mexico City, Coronado was called to account for the failure of his mission and the violence that sometimes accompanied it. He died in 1554 in relative obscurity.

Nonetheless, Coronado's travels revealed to Spain the extent of the lands to the north of Mexico, shaping history for centuries to come. To commemorate the expedition, the United States set aside a part of the Huachuca Mountains on the Arizona-Mexico border where visitors can learn of Coronado's journey and its influence on two countries. Coronado National Memorial overlooks the San Pedro River Valley, which historians believe was Coronado's route.

Several miles of trails allow exploration of the surrounding Huachuca Mountains, renowned among birdwatchers for their variety of species. Visitors can explore Coronado Cave, a limestone passage with stalactites, stalagmites, flowstones, and other formations (a flashlight is necessary). A 3-mile scenic road (dirt for the upper 2 miles) leads to Montezuma Pass, at 6,575 feet elevation, providing views of the valleys and peaks of Arizona's "sky island" region, where mountain ranges rise from grasslands like islands in the sea.

4101 E. Montezuma
Canyon Rd.
Hereford, AZ
520-366-5515
www.nps.gov/coro

AT A GLANCE

Southeastern Arizona, 75 miles southeast of Tucson ▪ 4,750 acres
▪ Year-round ▪ Hiking, caving, bird-watching

Fort Bowie National Historic Site

A vital military post of the Apache wars

In 1862, the U.S. Army established a fort in Apache Pass, between the Dos Cabezas and Chiricahua Mountains in southeastern Arizona, in response to a series of clashes with the Chiricahua Apache. The site chosen for Fort Bowie had two advantages: It was on a major travel route, and a nearby spring provided a dependable water source in a dry region.

Decades of conflict between the U.S. government and the Apache ended in 1886 when Apache leaders Geronimo and Naiche (son of famed Cochise) agreed to surrender.

An Apache wickiup at Fort Bowie

The Apache were forced to relocate to Florida, then to Alabama before being sent to Oklahoma. Fort Bowie was abandoned in 1894.

Visitors to today's Fort Bowie National Historic Site walk a 1.5-mile trail from the parking area to the visitor center, passing the ruins of a Butterfield stagecoach station, the post cemetery, Apache Spring, the remains of the original 1862 fort, and the ruins of the more elaborate 1868 fort. (Visitors unable to walk the path should contact the park for assistance.) Exhibits at the visitor center tell the story of the Army campaign and the efforts by the Apache to defend and remain in their mountain homeland.

3327 S. Old Fort Bowie Rd.
Bowie, AZ
520-847-2500
www.nps.gov/fobo

AT A GLANCE

Southeastern Arizona, 100 miles east of Tucson ▪ 1,000 acres ▪ Year-round
▪ Viewing historic fort ruins

Grand Canyon National Park

An awe-inspiring mile-deep chasm blending beauty and geology

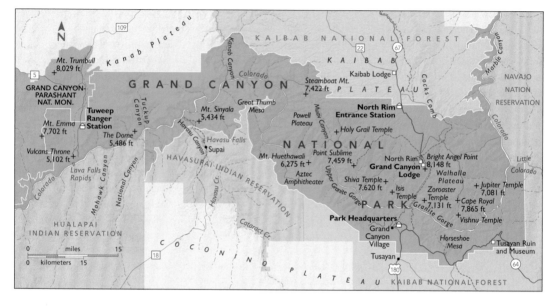

One of the natural wonders of the world, a World Heritage site, an archetypal national park—the Grand Canyon is one of the most famous, most admired, and most photographed places on Earth. It's also one of the most visited, with nearly five million people arriving annually to enjoy its awesome spectacle.

Many of those visitors simply stand at overlooks along the South Rim and gaze down into a canyon that is 18 miles across at its widest and whose floor is 4,800 feet below the rim (it's roughly 6,000 feet below if standing on the North Rim, though), exposing rocks almost two billion years old. Some people hike down into the canyon or ride the park's famed mules; other visitors take raft trips along the Colorado River, 277 miles of which flow along the canyon floor through the park.

The Colorado, which looks so small from the rim far above, carved the canyon over the course of six million years, creating one of the world's greatest displays of the power of erosion. In 1869, geologist John Wesley Powell led the first exploratory boat trip down the Colorado River; he later called it "the most sublime spectacle on the earth." In a more famous description, President Theodore Roosevelt said the Grand Canyon was "the one great sight" every American should see.

Multicolored cliffs, mesas, buttes, and spires stretch as far as the eye can see. Colors change with the sun's angle and with the season. Winter snow adds another element to the ever changing views of the Grand Canyon's expansive and multifaceted landscape.

Natural History

The Grand Canyon may be the world's most comprehensive geologic textbook, displaying material around 1.8 billion years old. Stacked at the top are shale, sandstone, and limestone created during more recent geologic eras, 546 to 270 million years ago; however, this is not a continuous geologic record, as some strata are missing, having been eroded away. These layers tell stories of deserts, seas, and swamps that have covered the land over hundreds of millions of years. At the bottom of the canyon, the strata that geologists call Vishnu basement rocks date from the Precambrian period and include both metamorphic and igneous material.

Over the past six million years the Colorado River cut down through the uplifted Colorado Plateau, giving the Grand Canyon its tremendous depth. Its width came in part from erosion of the walls caused by water running off the rims; by water seeping into cracks, expanding as ice, and splitting rock; and by the combined forces of rain and temperature on relatively soft sedimentary rock. The harder limestone and sandstone tend to form cliffs, while softer layers such as shale form slopes. The interbedding of differing materials gives the canyon its stair-stepped appearance. The Grand Canyon cuts across the south-facing slope of the Kaibab Uplift (a "bubble" sitting on the Colorado Plateau)—thus runoff from the canyon's North Rim drains into the Colorado River, resulting in a greater distance from river to rim on that side. This uplift, too, explains why the North Rim stands 1,000 feet higher than does the South.

It's hard to look away from the fantastic display of the canyon itself, but the park's wide variety of wildlife deserves attention as well. Mammals include elk, mule deer, mountain lions, bighorn sheep, coyotes, ringtails, and tassel-eared squirrels. Commonly seen birds include ravens, nuthatches, juncos, jays, chickadees, and flickers. The critically endangered California condor has been reintroduced to northern Arizona, and individuals are frequently seen in the park, especially in the summer.

Travelers planning ways to see the "sublime spectacle" should consider the park in three parts: the South Rim, the North Rim, and the Inner Canyon.

South Rim

This side of the Grand Canyon, with its hotels, restaurants, and shops clustered in Grand Canyon Village, attracts 90 percent of park visitors. Most of the canyon's famous viewpoints are here, along with the main visitor center. The rim is crowded from spring through fall; the system of free shuttle buses provides the easiest means to move around the area. The historic 7-mile-long Hermit

Road, on the South Rim between Grand Canyon Village and Hermits Rest, is closed to private vehicles most of the year *(March–Nov.)*, but it is accessible by bus, bicycle, or hiking.

Some of the renowned vistas along the South Rim are Mather Point, Yavapai Geology Museum, Maricopa Point, and Hermits Rest. The trailhead for Bright Angel Trail, the most popular route to the Inner Canyon and the Colorado River, lies a short distance west from Bright Angel Lodge. Many day hikers head for Indian Garden, 3,060 feet below the trailhead. Its side trail that leads to Plateau Point (the end point for day trips taken by mule riders) challenges even experienced hikers, especially during summer.

Desert View Drive heads east along the South Rim to popular destinations such as Yaki Point, Grandview Point, and the Desert View Watchtower.

North Rim

The canyon's North Rim is far less developed, and it hosts only about 10 percent of the park's visitors. About 1,000 feet higher than the South Rim, the North Rim receives much more snow; most facilities are open mid-May to mid-October. Day use continues into late fall, depending on weather. Accommodations are limited, and early reservations are essential. The adjoining Kaibab National Forest and its wilderness areas attract campers, hikers, and backpackers.

Higher-altitude forests on the North Rim comprise species such as Douglas fir, white fir, Engelmann spruce, and aspen—quite different from the ponderosa and piñon pines, juniper, and Gambel oak of the South Rim.

At the end of the road to the canyon's North Rim, visitors reach a visitor center and Grand Canyon Lodge. The original lodge, built by the Union Pacific Railroad, opened in 1928 but burned down in 1932; the current lodge dates from 1937. The easy Bright Angel Point Trail runs 0.25 mile to one of the finest views of any park overlook.

The Cape Royal Road winds south to the tip of the Walhalla Plateau. Along the way is the north turn to Point Imperial, a picnic area and viewpoint at just over 8,800 feet. There's a great view here of the Little Colorado River gorge, Marble Canyon, and the flattopped Marble Platform in the distance. The main road continues south to Cape Royal, where the short, easy Cape Royal Trail provides a view not only of the canyon and Colorado River below but also of Angels Window, an eroded natural arch in a wall of rock

A bighorn sheep stands near the canyon rim.
FOLLOWING PAGES: *The magnificent Grand Canyon*

sticking out from the rim. A side trail leads out to the top of the "window."

Inner Canyon

While some people are content just to marvel at the canyon, others want to reach the ribbon of water at the bottom: the Colorado River. No roads within the park reach the Inner Canyon; it is accessible only by boat or via strenuous trails. Trying to hike to the Colorado River and back in a day is very strongly discouraged. Backcountry camping requires a permit; demand is high and reservations can be made four months in advance. Rangers recommend spending at least two nights in the canyon, to avoid hiking down one day and back the next.

The only noncamping accommodation in the Inner Canyon is at Phantom Ranch, on the Colorado River at the bottom of Bright Angel, South Kaibab, and North Kaibab Trails; advance reservations are needed for rooms and meals.

A raft trip through the canyon provides perhaps the most intimate experience, including running the Colorado River's fierce rapids, camping along the river, and exploring side canyons that most visitors never see. Commercial raft trips can range in length from three days to three weeks. The park can provide a list of authorized outfitters (available on the park's website), whom you should contact as far in advance as possible for details and reservations. Private boat trips are allowed, with permits assigned by lottery. Check with the park river permit office or website for details.

Hiking in the Grand Canyon

Many visitors require help from park rangers because they underestimate the difficulty of the trails. From a rim viewpoint, the trails below look temptingly accessible—and if walking down them were all that is involved, there would be few problems. But unlike hiking up a mountain, below-rim

hikes at the Grand Canyon save the hardest part for last—returning to the rim. Many people start down a trail in late morning in pleasant temperatures, to find themselves a few hours later hiking up an extremely steep trail without water, exhausted, suffering from the effect of elevation (the South Rim averages about 7,000 feet), in the heat of midafternoon—or with darkness finding them still far below the trailhead.

It takes at least twice as long to come up a trail as it does to descend. You should turn around, no matter where you are, when you have drunk one-third of your water, unless you have confirmed that water is available along your route. Remember that when you go down into the canyon, you're traveling from a temperate woodland into a high desert. Remember, too, that park officials say that hiking from the rim to the river and back in a day is more physically demanding than running a marathon.

Ariz. 64
Grand Canyon, AZ
928-638-7888
www.nps.gov/grca

AT A GLANCE

Northern Arizona, 85 miles north of Flagstaff ▪ 1,218,375 acres ▪ South Rim year-round; North Rim road closed in winter ▪ Hiking, camping, backpacking, river running, riding mules

---

Hubbell Trading Post National Historic Site
An authentic, still operating 19th-century trading post

The Navajo (Diné) people who lived in northeastern Arizona were forced to move to a reservation in eastern New Mexico in 1864, but they were allowed to return to their homeland in 1868. Ten years later, John Lorenzo Hubbell took over an established trading post on land that would become part of the Navajo Nation, along Pueblo Colorado Wash. He provided flour, canned goods, sugar, fabrics, and similar products in trade for livestock, wool,

A pioneer wagon stands empty.

rugs, jewelry, and other items raised or made by the local residents. The Navajo had been introduced to many of the staple items offered by the post while they were in exile.

Family members ran the Hubbell Trading Post until the National Park Service acquired it in 1965. The trading post continues to operate under the management of a nonprofit organization. Visitors to the site can observe artists demonstrating the art of weaving a Navajo rug; tour the Hubbell home, with its hundreds of artifacts collected during nearly a century of Hubbell ownership; and purchase pottery, rugs, and jewelry handmade by local artisans.

The newly renovated visitor center also has interpretive exhibits.

A local group *(www.friendsofhubble .org)*, in partnership with the National Park Service, presents two Native

American art auctions each year, during which time visitors can buy contemporary and antique textiles, dolls, pottery, paintings, carvings, and baskets from Native American artists.

Ariz. 264 **Ganado, AZ** **928-755-3475** **www.nps.gov/hutr**	**AT A GLANCE** Northeastern Arizona, 120 miles northeast of Flagstaff ▪ 160 acres ▪ Year-round ▪ Visiting the oldest continuously operating Navajo Nation trading post

---

Juan Bautista de Anza National Historic Trail

The route followed by Spanish settlers of San Francisco

In the 1770s, the Spanish needed an overland route that would link the region of Sonora in New Spain (now Mexico) to Alta California (today's northern California) for two reasons. One, they were encountering problems using ships to supply the missions and military posts in Alta California; and two, they wanted to establish Spain's claim to San Francisco in an effort to deter colonization attempts by England and Russia.

Capt. Juan Bautista de Anza was chosen to lead an expedition, which in 1775–76 made its way from Tubac (near today's Nogales, Arizona) to the Pacific Ocean, near what is now Los Angeles. Having found a route, Anza returned to Culiacán (in today's Sinaloa, Mexico) and led a diverse group of 240 settlers northward to establish communities in the San Francisco Bay Area.

The Juan Bautista de Anza National Historic Trail commemorates these historic journeys. The path runs 1,200 miles from Nogales to San Francisco, guiding travelers who would like to trace the route followed by Anza

Mission San José de Tumacácori, north of Nogales, Arizona

and his companions. Along the way the trail links natural and cultural sites such as Arizona's Casa Grande Ruins National Monument (see p. 301) and Saguaro National Park (see p. 316)

and California's Anza-Borrego Desert State Park, El Presidio de Santa Barbara State Historic Park, and the Presidio of San Francisco (which was founded by Anza's settlers).

Trail office **333 Bush Street, Suite 500** **San Francisco, CA** **415-623-2344** **www.nps.gov/juba**	**AT A GLANCE** Nogales, Arizona, to San Francisco, California ▪ 1,200 miles (plus 640 miles in Mexico) ▪ Year-round ▪ Visiting national and state parks and historic sites along the trail

Montezuma Castle National Monument
The well-preserved remains of a cliff-dwelling community

Nearly a millennium ago, a Native American people built complex masonry structures on a ledge in a limestone cliff in an area now known as the Verde Valley. Archaeologists call these people Sinagua, from Spanish words meaning "without water." (The nearby San Francisco Peaks were once called Sinagua.) The local Sinagua culture encompassed thousands of people living in communities in the valley.

Sometime around the year 1425 the Sinagua abandoned their homes here for reasons unknown. Theories include disease, climate change, and prolonged drought. It is believed they moved to larger pueblos to the east and northeast.

Montezuma Castle was built some thousand years ago.

When Europeans came upon this impressive five-story cliff dwelling, they imagined it looked like a castle and named it for the Aztec leader Montezuma in the erroneous belief that its creators were somehow connected to that culture far to the south.

So important is Montezuma Castle that it was one of the first four national monuments established, signed into law by President Theodore Roosevelt in 1906. For decades visitors climbed ladders to enter the ruins, causing harm by vandalism and souvenir-taking. Public access was ended in 1951, and visitors now admire the buildings, among the best preserved cliff dwellings in the country, from

below, their appreciation enhanced by regular ranger-led programs. A 0.3-mile loop trail passes through groves of sycamores to the best vantage point of the castle; continues to another set of ruins, called Castle A; and returns along Beaver Creek.

It's not known why the Sinagua built their structures high on a cliff wall, but several factors may have contributed. The castle's location provided the Sinagua shelter from wind and rain and allowed them to live off the creek's floodplain. The structure also was cool in summer and warm in winter, and offered some relief from mosquitoes and gnats. The 19-room Montezuma Castle perhaps housed

35 to 50 people, while Castle A, excavated in 1933, had 45 to 50 rooms. The excavation of Castle A unearthed many artifacts and increased understanding of the culture.

In the flatland below, the Sinagua raised corn, beans, and squash to supplement the food they obtained by hunting. Living on the cliffs above the creek, instead of beside it, also left more room for fields.

Montezuma Well

Montezuma Well, a unit of the national monument, lies 11 miles north of the castle. A 0.5-mile loop trail here leads to where every day 1.5 million gallons of water flow out of a limestone sinkhole at a constant temperature of 74°F. People have used this water for irrigation purposes for more than a thousand years. A short spur trail heads down to the Outlet, where the water reemerges and pours into an irrigation ditch, predating the Sinagua but improved by them. Cliff dwellings (smaller than those at Montezuma Castle) stand on the bluffs above the well.

The presence of so much water in a generally dry region has created a unique ecosystem at Montezuma Well, with several small endemic invertebrate species. Ranger-led walks help visitors understand both the human and natural history of the well and its continuing importance to local residents.

Montezuma Castle Rd.
Camp Verde, AZ
928-567-3322
www.nps.gov/moca

AT A GLANCE

Central Arizona, 50 miles south of Flagstaff ▪ 1,004 acres ▪ Year-round ▪ Hiking self-guided loop trail

Navajo National Monument
Dwellings of the ancestral Puebloan people

In this region of what is now north-eastern Arizona, an ancient people that archaeologists call the ancestral Puebloan people—today's Hopi Indians, among others, consider these people their ancestors and call them the Hisatsinom—slowly changed from a nomadic lifestyle to a more settled, agriculture-based existence. They began to plant corn, beans, and squash, and around the 13th century they built cliff dwellings of stone, wood, and mud in deep canyons.

Navajo National Monument was established to protect three well-preserved examples of these masonry structures. Two can be visited on guided tours, although both require strenuous hikes. (Another ruin, called Inscription House, is closed to visitation because of its fragile condition.) Shorter, easier trails near the visitor center lead to overlooks from which beautiful sandstone Betatakin Canyon and the Betatakin cliff dwelling can be viewed from a distance. The 0.6-mile round-trip Aspen Trail takes walkers to an ancient aspen–Douglas fir forest.

The 5-mile round-trip hike to Betatakin ruin, led by a ranger, requires three to five hours and descends and ascends 700 feet. The tour is offered twice daily in summer and, staff permitting, once daily on weekends in winter. Seeing the Keet Seel dwelling requires a 17-mile round-trip hike *(permit required, available at visitor center)*. The path is primitive and several stream crossings are necessary.

Ariz. 564 (off U.S. 160)
Tonalea, AZ
928-672-2700
www.nps.gov/nava

AT A GLANCE

Northeastern Arizona, 120 miles northeast of Flagstaff ▪ 360 acres ▪ Year-round; occasional snow in winter ▪ Hiking, camping, visiting ancient cliff dwellings

Organ Pipe Cactus National Monument
A showcase of Sonoran Desert flora and fauna

Set within the volcanic terrain of the Ajo Mountains on the United States border with Mexico, Organ Pipe Cactus National Monument lies far off main tourist routes. Those individuals who make the effort to visit, though, will find a strikingly beautiful landscape and a vast protected area of the Sonoran Desert ecosystem.

So great is the national monument's environmental importance that UNESCO named it an international biosphere reserve in 1976, a distinction shared with sites such as Amazonia and the Everglades. Ninety-five percent of the park has been designated as wilderness.

The park takes its name from the organ pipe cactus, a common species farther south in Mexico, but in the United States confined to a small

area along Arizona's southern border. Named for its tall, closely spaced columns resembling the rows of sounding tubes of a pipe organ, the organ pipe cactus is just one of many notable species here, among them *senita* (another columnar cactus) and the distinctive-looking elephant tree, as well as the tall saguaro.

Natural History

There are 26 species of cactus here, and they represent just a small part of the many plants and animals that have adapted to a region of little rain, intense sun, and extreme temperatures. Some plants have hard, glossy leaves that lessen moisture loss; other plants grow leaves only when rains come, and drop them in dry conditions. Jackrabbits and kit foxes have

An organ pipe cactus

evolved huge ears that dissipate heat. The "spade" on the hind foot of a spadefoot toad helps it burrow into the cooler ground, where it stays until summer monsoon rains arrive.

Bird-watchers find many regional specialty species, including cactus wren, curve-billed thrasher, Gambel's quail, Lucy's warbler, pyrrhuloxia, black-tailed gnatcatcher, phainopepla, and verdin. Mammals are seen less often, but a lucky visitor might spot mountain lion, mule deer, desert bighorn, javelina, coyote, or kangaroo rat.

Entering the park, visitors usually note the striking peak above the ridgeline to the east. Called Montezuma's Head today, it was known to American Indians as Old Woman With a Basket. Like much of the Ajo Mountains, it's composed of rhyolite, rock formed by lava cooling on the surface of the Earth. The cliffs feature distinct bands of dark rhyolite paralleling lighter bands of tuff, volcanic ash compressed and "welded" into rock.

Visiting the Park

There's an audiovisual presentation at the visitor center introducing the Sonoran Desert ecosystem. Rangers here can provide advice and help plan a visit. Outside, a short nature trail identifies plants common to the Sonoran Desert. Drive south to the campground to hike either the Victoria Mine Trail, 4.5 miles round trip into granite hills to an abandoned gold and silver mine; or the Desert View Nature Trail, a 1.2-mile loop with vistas over the Sonoyta Basin in the southeastern part of the monument. Many other hikes are also available.

Because the monument abuts the U.S.–Mexico border, illegal activities in the area are not uncommon, though visitors are unlikely to encounter any. Nonetheless, people hiking or camping in remote areas of the monument should "exercise caution and pay attention to their surroundings."

Across Ariz. 85 from the visitor center is the start of the 21-mile Ajo Mountain Drive, an unpaved but well-graded loop around the edge of the Ajos. (Be sure to ask for the road guide at the visitor center.) Organ pipe cactuses are found in abundance near the beginning of the drive. These cold-sensitive plants live here at the northern edge of their range, and so favor sunny, south-facing slopes.

Organ pipe, saguaro, and cholla cactuses grow best in the looser, gravelly soils of *bajadas* (alluvial slopes around hills and mountains) rather than flat, low ground where the soil is more tightly packed. Creosote bush and bursage, a shrub related to ragweed, dominate the flats. Along washes grow mesquite, foothills paloverde (the Arizona state tree), and ironwood, among other more water-dependent plants.

A variety of ranger-led programs and tours are offered January through March. Birding, geology, desert plants, wildflowers, and local history are just a few of the subjects covered.

AT A GLANCE

Ariz. 85
Ajo, AZ
520-387-6849
www.nps.gov/orpi

South-central Arizona, 120 miles southwest of Tucson ▪ 330,689 acres ▪ Year-round; summer can be extremely hot ▪ Hiking, camping, driving scenic route, bird-watching

Petrified Forest National Park

A vast assemblage of petrified trees in the colorful Painted Desert

A chance combination of environmental conditions that occurred in this spot more than 200 million years ago led to the preservation of what may be the world's greatest collection of mineralized wood, as well as a significant assemblage of plant and animal fossils. Add an expanse of rocks so colorful it has come to be called the Painted Desert, and you have a national park

A cross section shows the beauty of petrified wood.

of nearly unparalleled beauty and scientific importance.

Many of Petrified Forest National Park's most striking aspects, including the huge petrified logs that are its most famous feature, can be seen quite easily from a 28-mile scenic drive through the heart of the park. Several short, easy trails just off the road reward those who take time to explore them, as do exhibits at the park visitor center and museums. For the more adventurous (and well prepared), the park allows day hikes and backpacking trips into its expansive wilderness area.

Origins of the Petrified Forest

Before the supercontinent Pangaea broke up some 200 million years ago and formed today's continents, what is now northeastern Arizona lay near the Equator. Forests here were home to, among other trees, a conifer that may be distantly related to today's Norfolk Island pine. Some trees reached 200 feet tall. Fallen trees or trees carried by streams to the Petrified Forest area were buried by mud and sand mixed with ash from volcanic eruptions. Cut off from air and protected from decay, the trunks were gradually permeated by water carrying dissolved silica, which crystallized as quartz, exactly replacing the soft plant structure with hard mineral.

The mud and sand here formed a layer of sedimentary rock, now called the Chinle formation, which was itself buried by rock layers of the Jurassic and Cretaceous periods. About 60 million years ago, this area began to rise, uplifted in some cases more than 10,000 feet above sea level. Geologists believe erosion stripped away those later layers of rock before the much younger rocks of the Bidahochi formation were laid down, creating a break in the geologic record—about a 200-million-year gap in the Petrified Forest. In many areas of the park, erosion continues to expose the Chinle formation and the petrified logs it contains.

Not only tree trunks were buried by those Triassic streams, of course. Fossils of ferns, cycads, giant horsetails, and other plants are common in the park. Many animals have been unearthed, as well, including freshwater snails, insects, fish, and amphibians.

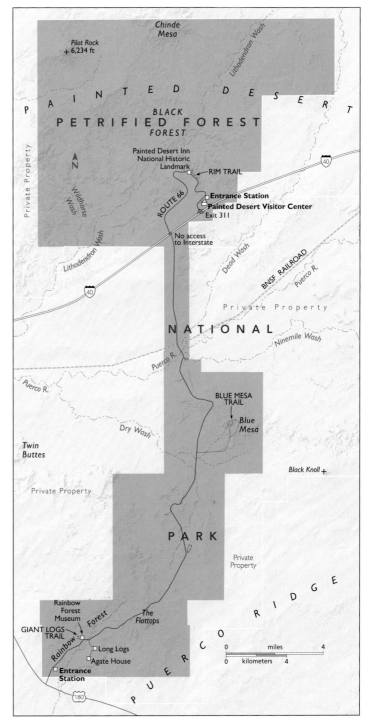

Paleontologists have discovered many types of large archosaurs, giant reptiles that were related to crocodiles, and a few early dinosaurs in the youngest layers of the Chinle formation.

The soft rocks of the Chinle formation display a wide spectrum of colors, dominated by reddish tones produced by iron oxides and including white, blue-gray, buff, and dark gray. It was this striking landscape that gave the Painted Desert its name. Such terrain covers a large expanse of northeastern Arizona, and the park encompasses a particularly brilliant portion.

Painted Desert Area

The Painted Desert Visitor Center, just off I-40, offers an orientation film. As the main road enters the park, several parking areas provide interpretive signs and views of the Painted Desert, made up of rock layers of the Chinle formation. This part of the park also contains deposits of the harder and much younger rock and lava beds of the Bidahochi formation, just a few million years old. While the Painted Desert is always beautiful, many people believe it's at its best early or late in the day, after a rain, when the light and colors are at their most profound.

At Kachina Point stands the Painted Desert Inn, built by 1924 and later operated by the famed Fred Harvey Company. Now a national historic landmark, the inn was remodeled and reopened in 2006 as a museum and bookstore, with lodging no longer offered. Inside are murals of Native American life and symbols by Hopi artist Fred Kabotie. Ask about ranger talks offered here, providing details of the inn's history.

Kachina Point is the trailhead for exploration of the north unit of the Petrified Forest National Wilderness Area, covering more than 43,000 acres in the northern part of the park. A mile-long trail begins at the inn, but after that hikers pick their own routes through the backcountry. A permit is required for camping, but none is needed for day hikes. Hikers should be aware of harsh, isolated conditions and carry plenty of water. Backpackers must hike north of Lithodendron Wash (a mile from the trailhead) before setting up camp.

Center of the Park

At Puerco Pueblo, a short loop trail leads to the remains of a hundred-room community occupied by the ancestral Puebloan people between 760 and 630 years ago. Petroglyphs can be viewed along the south end of the trail. Built of mortared sandstone and featuring a central plaza, the pueblo is located along the Puerco River, a water source used to irrigate beans, corn, and squash. Rangers lead walks regularly at Puerco Pueblo.

The park road passes through an area of cone-shaped hills in the Blue Mesa area. Formed of bentonite, a soft clay (easily eroded, and very slippery when wet), and sandstone, this terrain can be explored on the mile-long Blue Mesa Loop Trail. Of all the landscapes in the park, this is probably the most strikingly otherworldly. The bluish color derives from reduced iron in the sedimentary rock, while the rusty-maroon color comes from iron oxide.

Seeing the Petrified Logs

Three trails—all along the road and all highly recommended—access the fossil logs for which the park was

The blue-gray-and-red-striped, cone-shaped hills of the Blue Mesa area

named. The Crystal Forest Trail, a 0.8-mile loop, passes through an area that was once heavily exploited by commercial interests. Legend has it that logs were sometimes dynamited to access large crystals of amethyst, smoky quartz, and citrine.

Incredibly, in the 1890s a company proposed a business here to crush the petrified logs to make abrasive grit. At the time, many people regularly took away huge chunks to sell as souvenirs and home decor. It was such abuse, and the desire to preserve the scientific value of the site, that prompted President Theodore Roosevelt in 1906 to establish Petrified Forest as one of our first national monuments. It was designated a national park in 1962.

The petrified trees of the Long Logs Trail may have originated as a logjam in an ancient stream, resulting in the park's greatest concentration of logs, some of them well over 100 feet long. Visitors can see how organic material has been duplicated in rock: knotholes, wood texture, growth rings, and beetle borings, all in astonishingly fine detail. Every color imaginable seems to be represented in the shiny agate logs. Note how logs are broken so smoothly and evenly that they

seem to have been cut with a saw. It's believed that the logs fractured during the periods when the continents were moving apart in the Mesozoic, when the Colorado Plateau was being uplifted, as well as a settling in the softer surrounding rock.

A 0.8-mile side trail from the Long Logs area leads to Agate House, an eight-room structure built of petrified wood set in mortar, located atop a low hill. Evidence indicates this small pueblo (reconstructed in the 1930s) may have been used for only a brief period about 800 to 900 years ago.

On the Giant Logs Trail, a 0.4-mile loop, is found the most massive log in the park: "Old Faithful," about 35 feet long and almost 10 feet across at its base. This trail begins at the Rainbow Forest Museum, the park's southern visitor center, which offers geology exhibits, displays of petrified wood, and fossils and casts of some of the creatures that roamed here in Triassic times. Regular ranger programs are offered at the museum, which can include a walk on the Giant Logs Trail.

Flora & Fauna

While petrified logs, fossils, colorful rocks, and archaeological sites rate as the park's highlights, visitors should

be on the lookout for the plants and animals that share this spectacular landscape. Among the species of mammals that might be spotted along the road or on trails are mule deer, pronghorn, coyote, badger, black-tailed jackrabbit, swift fox, and bobcat. Collared lizards are sometimes seen basking on rocks. Among the many types of birds seen regularly in the park are golden eagle, prairie falcon, scaled quail, roadrunner, burrowing owl, common raven, and rock wren. Petrified Forest National Park's varied habitats—desert, grassland, and riparian—provide homes for a surprising array of wildlife for those who take time to look.

Easier to see and enjoy is the park's colorful display of wildflowers, which varies through the year with rainfall and other environmental conditions. Indian paintbrush, evening primrose, aster, yucca, and prickly pear cactus are just a few of the dozens of species that bloom seasonally.

In summer months, March, and November, cultural demonstrations are offered on many Saturdays. These presentations cover subjects that can include jewelry-making, weaving, music, and painting, and are usually held at the Painted Desert Inn.

I-40
Petrified Forest, AZ
928-524-6228
www.nps.gov/pefo

AT A GLANCE

Northeastern Arizona, 115 miles east of Flagstaff ▪ 218,533 acres
▪ Year-round ▪ Hiking, backpacking, taking scenic drives

Pipe Spring National Monument
A historic spring with diverse cultural history

The water of Pipe Spring (there are three springs, though the name is singular) has long served as an oasis for plants, animals, and people, making it possible for them to live in this dry desert environment.

Ancestral Puebloan people (aka Anasazi) and Kaibab Paiute Indians gathered grass seeds, hunted animals, and raised crops near the springs for at least a thousand years. In the 1860s, Mormon pioneers settled around

the springs, naming it Pipe Spring. By 1872 the Mormon Church had built a fort, called Winsor Castle, over the main spring and established a large cattle-ranching operation. This affected the Kaibab Paiute way of life, but they continued to live in the area; by 1907 the Kaibab Paiute Indian Reservation was established, surrounding the privately held Pipe Spring ranch. The government acquired the ranch in 1923 and set it aside as a national monument.

Visitors stop first at Pipe Spring National Monument–Kaibab Band of Paiute Indians Visitor Center and Museum, where exhibits and a video presentation interpret the heritage of local people and cultures. Guided tours are offered of Winsor Castle, and in summer there are demonstrations of Indian and pioneer life and crafts. Gardens, orchards, domestic animals (including longhorn cattle), and ranch outbuildings are also part of the national monument, as is a 0.5-mile walking trail.

Ariz. 389
Fredonia, AZ
928-643-7105
www.nps.gov/pisp

AT A GLANCE

Northwestern Arizona, 60 miles southeast of St. George, Utah ■ 40 acres ■ Year-round; occasional snow in winter ■ Visiting 19th-century ranch house, learning about Kaibab Paiute culture

Saguaro National Park
Desert and mountain landscapes protecting forests of giant cactus

Icon of the American Southwest, the instantly recognizable giant saguaro cactus stands up to 50 feet tall, displaying almost humanlike arms reaching to the sky or contorted into odd shapes. In the United States, the saguaro occurs naturally only in the Sonoran Desert ecoregion. Here in the national park named for them, an estimated 1.6 million saguaros grow, massed in vast stands that create one of the most specialized landscapes on the continent.

Weighing 8 tons or more, a mature saguaro has come a long way from its humble beginning. It begins as a seed the size of a pinhead, which kangaroo rats and birds love to eat. As a tiny seedling, the cactus is susceptible to browsing rodents, javelina hooves, and the boots of careless hikers. After 50 years, the saguaro may be taller than a person standing beside it, and as it continues to grow it exhibits marvelous adaptations to its arid surroundings.

The saguaro's roots can spread 50 feet in all directions, the better to soak up water quickly. Woody ribs support its great weight, but their flexibility and the cactus's pleated skin allow tremendous expansion in volume. A saguaro may take in 200 gallons of

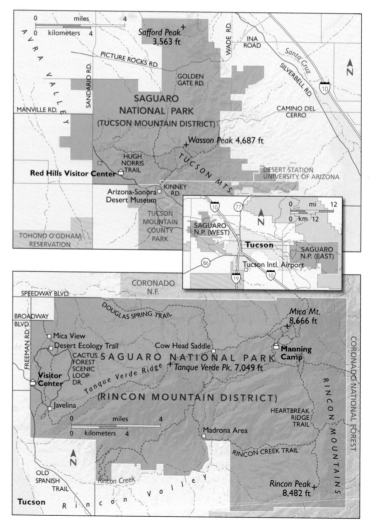

The desert landscape of Saguaro National Park takes on an otherworldly appearance at dusk.

water during one rainstorm, enough to carry it through a long period of drought.

The saguaro flower (the state flower of Arizona) offers nectar to white-winged doves, bats, bees, and moths, which in turn pollinate the cactuses. When the fruits appear in summer, all sorts of creatures relish them and the seeds they contain, from coyotes to birds to humans. During a life that may span 200 years, a saguaro can produce 40 million seeds, and though only one needs to become a mature adult to maintain the population, every adult represents a victory over very poor odds.

Many threats to the saguaro cactus have reduced its range in recent decades, from expanding subdivisions to theft (for landscaping purposes) to the introduction of exotic plants that compete for water and nutrients and increase the severity of fires. Within the national park's 142 square miles, at least, the vulnerable saguaro receives the best protection possible.

Visiting the Park

Saguaro National Park consists of two districts: the Rincon Mountain District to the east of Tucson, and the Tucson Mountain District to the west of Tucson. From desert flats with creosote bush and cholla to washes lined with mesquite and paloverde trees to *bajadas* (foothill slopes) covered by saguaros, the terrain rises in the east district to desert grassland and the peaks of the Rincons, with oak and subalpine woodlands. One trail climbs all the way to the high point of the Rincons, 8,666-foot Mica Peak. A scenic loop drive in each district provides a cross section of desert beauty, but 180 miles of hiking trails allow closer inspection.

Visitors should consider the seasons when planning a trip to the desert. After wet winters, the spring wildflower display can be breathtaking: The brilliant gold of Mexican poppy is often the first-noticed bloom, then those of penstemon, lupine, desert marigold, brittlebush,

and globe mallow. Many trees, shrubs, and cactuses also bloom, including creosote bush, paloverde, ocotillo, chollas, and hedgehog cactus. Early summer is a productive time for the saguaros, and July brings the summer monsoon rains, ushering in a "second spring" of renewed wildlife activity and flowering. In winter, flowers may be less visible, but moderate temperatures mean that hiking in the lowlands is comfortable all day.

Park rangers offer a variety of talks and guided walks, mostly during the cooler peak season *(Nov.–March)*. Check for a current schedule.

Rincon Mountain District

The visitor center in the Rincon Mountain District has exhibits and audiovisual programs on the Sonoran Desert ecology. Outside, signs identify some of the common plants. The park's Cactus Forest Drive winds through rolling desert and across several washes as it makes an 8-mile loop from the visitor center. Several trails are available along the drive.

The short, flat Desert Ecology Trail explains some of the ways plants and animals adapt to the scarcity of water in the desert. Only a quarter mile long, it winds alongside Javelina Wash. The 2.5-mile Cactus Forest Trail (open to bicycles) is accessed from either the north or south end of the drive. There are many miles of looping trails north of the drive and starting at the Mica View picnic area; several are popular with horseback riders.

The Tanque Verde Ridge Trail heads south and then east from the Javelina picnic area along Cactus Forest Drive, continuing 6.9 miles to the Juniper Basin campground. A good easier version of the hike follows the trail out 3 miles and back, allowing hikers to experience cactus desert, the grassland above, and oak-juniper forest on the ridge. Views take in Rincon Peak to the east and Tucson to the west. The grassland zone features Schott's agave, commonly known as shindagger because of its thick, sharp-tipped leaves that rise about a foot high; and sotol, which has much longer and thinner leaves, used by Native Americans to weave mats and baskets.

Tucson Mountain District

The desert plants and animals found in the park's Tucson Mountain District are much the same as in the Rincon district 30 miles east, but the landscape looks very different: Huge boulders of volcanic rhyolite form the Tucson Mountains, topped by 4,687-foot Wasson Peak—far lower than the Rincons' summits. In the western part of the district, the striking Red Hills are composed of mudstone from an ancient lake bed, given their distinctive color by iron oxide.

At the Red Hills Visitor Center (2700 N. Kinney Rd., Tucson, 520-733-5158), a video presents the American Indian perspective on the saguaro cactus. Nearby, the 100-yard, paved Cactus Garden Walk introduces desert plants; 1 mile north on Kinney Road, the Desert Discovery Nature Trail, a 0.5-mile paved loop, explores Sonoran Desert ecology in more depth. For a marvelous view of the Avra Valley to the west, take the 0.8-mile round-trip Valley View Overlook Trail, located on the park's 5-mile Bajada Loop Drive. This route passes through some of the finest stands of saguaro found anywhere, with the giant cactus growing in amazing profusion on the hillsides.

At Signal Hill Picnic Area, 5 miles from the visitor center, a 0.5-mile trail passes more than 200 ancient petroglyphs. The 4-mile (one way) Sendero Esperanza Trail is the least strenuous route to Wasson Peak, offering great long-distance views along the way; the shorter King Canyon Trail, of which the first 0.9 mile follows an old mining road, is the most strenuous.

Flora & Fauna

Animal species found in Saguaro National Park represent desert, grassland, and mountain forest ecosystems. Park reptiles include desert tortoise and Gila monster, as well as six species of rattlesnake. Mammals (some confined to the highlands of the Rincon district) include black bear, ringtail, white-nosed coati, coyote, mountain lion, black-tailed jackrabbit, collared peccary, and mule and white-tailed deer.

The park's bird list includes typical southwestern species such as Gambel's quail, red-tailed Harris hawk, Inca dove, roadrunner, elf owl, Gila woodpecker, gilded flicker, black-tailed gnatcatcher, and verdin. Every visitor to the park soon becomes accustomed to the chug-chug-chug call of the abundant cactus wren, one of the distinctive sounds of the Southwest.

The range of habitats in the park supports an equally wide array of plant life, from wildflowers and grasses to trees and shrubs such as ponderosa pine and paloverde. Desert species include ocotillo, creosote bush, and prickly pear, several varieties of cholla, and, of course, the saguaro cactuses.

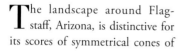

Rincon Mountain District
3693 S. Old Spanish Trail
Tucson, AZ
520-733-5153
www.nps.gov/sagu

AT A GLANCE

Southeastern Arizona, two units located both east and west of Tucson ▪ 91,440 acres ▪ Year-round, though summer is extremely hot ▪ Hiking, horseback riding, wildlife-watching, backcountry camping, scenic driving

Sunset Crater Volcano National Monument
A strikingly colorful volcanic cone and lava fields

The landscape around Flagstaff, Arizona, is distinctive for its scores of symmetrical cones of many sizes, testament to six million years of volcanic activity. The cones mark sites where the earth opened to discharge magma, gas, ash, and cinders. To the north of Flagstaff, the San Francisco Peaks, volcanic in origin, rise to Arizona's highest point: 12,643-foot Humphreys Peak. Sunset Crater Volcano, just a few miles east, though much smaller, is the best place to get a close-up look at the area's turbulent past.

Dating from the period A.D. 1040 to 1100 (the volcanic field's most recent activity), Sunset Crater Volcano is a classic example of a cinder cone. At the top, cinders that were oxidized to a reddish color caused explorer John Wesley Powell to write in the 19th century that the peak "seems to glow with a light of its own." The sunset-like colors gave the cone its name.

After stopping at the visitor center to enjoy exhibits on the geology of the San Francisco volcanic field, walk the Lava Flow Trail, which offers a choice of a paved 0.4-mile loop or a partly unpaved 1-mile loop. Many volcanic features can be seen along the trail, including lava "squeeze ups," spatter cones, and lava bubbles. No climbing is allowed on Sunset Crater Volcano itself; in the past, informal trails caused serious erosion. Visitors can climb to the top of a cinder cone on the mile-long Lenox Crater Trail, which ascends a steep slope covered with loose gravel-like cinders. The Cinder Hills Overlook, reachable by road, offers views of Sunset Crater Volcano and the surrounding area.

> Sunset Crater–Wupatki
> Loop Rd.
> Flagstaff, AZ
> 928-526-0502
> www.nps.gov/sucr

AT A GLANCE

Northern Arizona, 15 miles northeast of Flagstaff ▪ 3,040 acres ▪ Year-round; winter can bring snow and cold temperatures ▪ Hiking

Tonto National Monument
Cliff dwellings of the ancient Salado people

Set into a hillside in the Sonoran Desert are two sets of rock structures that were occupied in the 14th and 15th centuries by the Salado people. Named for the Salt (Salado, in Spanish) River, these cliff dwellers chose, for unknown reasons, to live in sites above the more populated Tonto Basin. They hunted and grew corn, beans, and squash for food.

Visitors to Tonto National Monument can see exhibits and watch an orientation film at the visitor center, and take a self-guided 0.5-mile trail to the 28-room Lower Cliff Dwelling. November through April, the park offers a ranger-led, 3-mile round-trip hike to the Upper Cliff Dwelling. *(Reservations required; not recommended for people with health problems or who have difficulty walking.)* The 40-room upper structure is set in a large cave that may have been chosen to provide protection from enemies, or simply because it offered a cool shelter from bad weather.

The Salado people produced colorful pottery and intricately woven fabrics, some of which are on display in the national monument's visitor center. At some point after A.D. 1450, the Salado people abandoned their dwellings here, as did many other peoples in the Southwest at about this same time. The reasons for this migration or disappearance are unknown, but the causes may have been prolonged drought, disease, and/or intertribal conflict.

> Ariz. 188
> Roosevelt, AZ
> 928-467-2241
> www.nps.gov/tont

AT A GLANCE

Central Arizona, 45 miles northeast of Phoenix ▪ 1,120 acres ▪ Year-round; summer can be extremely hot ▪ Viewing historic structures

Tumacácori National Historical Park
Three 18th-century Spanish mission churches

Beginning with the efforts of the renowned Padre Eusebio Kino in 1691, Spanish Jesuits established more than 20 mission complexes in the area that is now southern Arizona and northwestern Mexico. The Jesuits were expelled from the region in 1767, after which Franciscan friars operated the missions.

Three of those historic missions are preserved today in Tumacácori National Historical Park, along with a 1937 museum that serves as the visitor center and itself is a national historic landmark. Only one of the three churches, San José de Tumacácori, adjacent to the visitor center, is open for regular tours. The other two, Los Santos Ángeles de Guevavi and San Cayetano de Calabazas, must be visited on ranger-led tours on limited days January through March *(reservations required, fee)*. All three church structures date from the mid- to late 18th century, though the Tumacácori was originally founded in another location in the late 17th century and later moved to its present location.

The park is mandated to preserve the Tumacácori mission in its current state as a ruin. As a result, visitors see work that was done more than two centuries ago, without modern construction techniques or interpretation.

An attractive mission garden replicates the type of garden that was common to mission grounds during the Jesuit and Franciscan era. On winter weekends, the park hosts demonstrations of traditional arts and crafts, which include paper-flower making, basketry, leather working, and tortilla making.

Tuzigoot National Monument
A pueblo of the Sinagua culture

Sitting in a strategic position atop a 120 foot-high limestone ridge above the Verde Valley of northern Arizona, Tuzigoot National Monument centers on the ruins of a pueblo (village) built by a culture known as the Sinagua. (The name, from the Spanish words for "without water," comes from an old name for the San Francisco Peaks mountain range to the north.)

Originally composed of about 110 rooms, the pueblo is thought to have been home to some 300 inhabitants. Archaeologists have dated construction from about A.D. 1000. This is just one of many Sinaguan pueblos that once existed in the Verde Valley; another impressive

Rock walls give a sense of the pueblo's size.

Sinaguan site is protected at Montezuma Castle National Monument (see p. 310), located near Camp Verde, a distance of 25 miles.

The streams of the Verde Valley must have been a strong factor in the settlement of the area, providing water for people and crop irrigation, as well as attracting wildlife. Both pueblos, like many others throughout this part of the American Southwest, were vacated in the early 1400s for reasons that are not understood. Disease, prolonged drought, and/or conflict are the most common theories.

Workers in the 1930s performed excavation and restoration work at the pueblo and built a museum, which houses exhibits on the ruins and the Sinaguan people. Trails lead through the ruins and to an overlook at Tavasci Marsh, a wetland area as important to wildlife today as it was in prehistoric times.

Walnut Canyon National Monument

A canyon home of the ancient Sinagua people

Archaeological evidence exists for a human presence that dates back thousands of years in the area near what is now the city of Flagstaff, Arizona. It was about A.D. 1100, though, when people began to build structures of rock, mud, and wood in a beautiful canyon where walnut trees grew along the stream at the bottom.

The cliffs of Walnut Canyon provided shelter.

These people had built dwellings on the rim above, as well as in other open areas in the region. They also constructed elaborate houses on alcoves set back into near-vertical sandstone walls. While erosion and other factors have caused most dwellings built in open places to disappear, many more-protected cliff dwellings have survived to the present day.

Archaeologists call the people who built the Walnut Canyon dwellings Sinagua. The name comes from the Spanish words *sin agua* (without water); Spanish explorers felt it was noteworthy that there were so few perennial streams in the area. The Sinagua lived in what is now central Arizona; remains of their pueblos can be seen also at sites such as Montezuma Castle (see p. 310) and Tuzigoot (see opposite) National Monuments.

Building their homes into cliff walls may have had several advantages, including providing safety from attack, protection from weather, and moderation of temperature extremes. Here in Walnut Canyon, the creek at the bottom provided water for the residents and also attracted deer and wild game. The Sinagua grew corn, beans, and squash in fields on the canyon rim.

Along with similar sites in the region, Walnut Canyon was abandoned about A.D. 1250 for reasons that are unknown—possibly prolonged drought, disease, and/or conflict with other Native American tribes. In any case, the site had long been a ruin by the time European explorers and settlers arrived.

The extensive ruins here, along with their setting in a deep, strikingly attractive canyon, have long attracted tourists—some of whom took souvenirs and otherwise vandalized the dwellings. Official government protection began in 1904 as part of a "mountain reserve" (predecessor to a national forest). Walnut Canyon National Monument was established in 1915 to protect the site, first under the administration of the U.S. Forest Service, and later the National Park Service.

After getting an introduction to the ruins and the Sinagua culture in the visitor center, visitors can walk the 0.7-mile Rim Trail to look down into the canyon; the trail has two overlooks and also passes a pithouse and the remains of a pueblo. Visitors also can descend into the canyon via the 0.9-mile Island Trail to see 25 rooms of cliff dwellings, with more visible across the canyon. The steepness of the latter trail, along with the site's 6,690-foot elevation, means it is not recommended for people with health problems. The Island Trail may also be closed at times by winter snow.

Visitors with an interest in natural history will enjoy the varied flora at Walnut Canyon, which includes ponderosa pine (the region around Flagstaff is home to the most extensive forest of that species in the world), Douglas fir, piñon pine, juniper, yucca, and prickly pear cactus. Cottonwood, box elder, aspen, and Arizona walnut, the tree for which the creek and canyon were named, edge Walnut Creek at the bottom of the canyon.

Various interpretive programs are offered at the national monument in summer *(Mem. Day–Labor Day)*; check with the park for details and current schedules.

Walnut Canyon Rd.
Flagstaff, AZ
928-526-3367
www.nps.gov/waca

AT A GLANCE

North-central Arizona, 10 miles southeast of Flagstaff ▪ 3,600 acres ▪ Year-round ▪ Visiting 900-year-old cliff dwellings

Wupatki National Monument

The pueblo remains of ancestral Hopi villages

The villages—now in ruins—at Wupatki National Monument were built by people known as the Hisatsinom, ancestors of today's Hopi tribe, as well as others such as the Zuni and Havasupai tribes. They occupied the stone and mortar dwellings, built atop rock outcroppings, at Wupatki from about A.D. 1100 to 1250.

The eruption of nearby Sunset Crater Volcano (see p. 318), about A.D. 1080, forced some people to relocate temporarily, but the ash and cinders from the eruption created new, fertile soil that held water very well. Resettling in this area, the Hisatsinom built Wupatki Pueblo, eventually the largest, and possibly the richest and most influential, village in the area. Archaeologists think about 85 to 100 people lived here, with several thousand more within a day's walk. Turquoise, shell jewelry, copper items, and macaw feathers prove that Wupatki was a trade center within a network stretching hundreds of miles.

After seeing the exhibits at the Wupatki Visitor Center, walk the 0.5-mile Wupatki Pueblo Trail, a self-guided tour of the park's largest village. Other short, easy trails lead to four other pueblos: Lomaki, Wukoki, Citadel, and Nalakihu. Doney Mountain Trail climbs a half mile from the picnic area to the top of a volcanic cinder cone for excellent vistas of the Wupatki Basin and nearby San Francisco Peaks. Check with the park for a schedule of ranger-led programs.

Sunset Crater–Wupatki Loop Rd.
Flagstaff, AZ
928-679-2365
www.nps.gov/wupa

AT A GLANCE

North-central Arizona, 43 miles north of Flagstaff ▪ 35,422 acres ▪ Year-round ▪ Visiting 12th-century Native American pueblo ruins

COLORADO

With more than 50 mountain peaks topping 14,000 feet in elevation, Colorado serves as the metaphorical rooftop of North America. Its citizens are major outdoors people, with hiking, river rafting, mountaineering, and other activities within easy access. Rocky Mountain National Park protects some of the best of Colorado's terrain, but many other national and state areas also offer recreation opportunities. The Rockies draw most travelers' attention, but nearly half the state lies within the rolling shortgrass prairie of the Great Plains, in which towns and ranches are scattered across a landscape where trees grow only streamside, and pronghorn, badgers, and burrowing owls are native.

Bent's Old Fort National Historic Site

A cultural crossroads of the Old West

In 1833, William and Charles Bent, along with Ceran St. Vrain, chose a spot in the shortgrass prairie along the Arkansas River to build a fortified adobe trading post. The site, now in southeastern Colorado, was then extremely isolated, far from the cities of the United States and those to the south in Mexico (which at the time encompassed today's New Mexico).

It was the only major settlement on the Santa Fe Trail between Missouri and Mexico, and thus the only place to stock up on supplies and to repair wagons. The fort's major business was trading with Indians for valuable buffalo (bison) robes.

Until it was abandoned in 1849, the fort was a central meeting point for a wide array of people, including U.S. Army troops, Native Americans of several tribes, trappers who roamed the Rocky Mountains and other parts of the West, and traders on the Santa Fe Trail. Kit Carson, John C. Frémont, and historian Francis Parkman were among the visitors who enjoyed the fort's hospitality.

Bent's Old Fort National Historic Site centers on a 1976 furnished reconstruction of the fort, based on archaeological evidence as well as contemporary illustrations and diaries. Costumed interpreters offer demonstrations and tours seasonally; an introductory film and self-guided tours are available year-round. A 1.75-mile loop trail leads to the Arkansas River for views of the park environment.

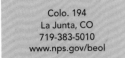

Colo. 194
La Junta, CO
719-383-5010
www.nps.gov/beol

AT A GLANCE

Southeastern Colorado, 65 miles east of Pueblo ▪ 800 acres ▪ Year-round ▪ Visiting reconstructed 1830s trading post, hiking

Black Canyon of the Gunnison National Park
A spectacular gorge in the Colorado Plateau

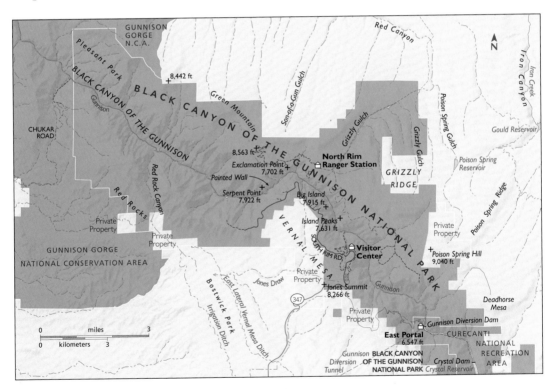

The name "black" is appropriate for this awesome gorge in western Colorado. So deep and narrow is it that in places, sunlight reaches the Gunnison River at the bottom only briefly, at midday. At its greatest depth, Black Canyon is 2,722 feet deep; its narrowest point on the rim is about 1,100 feet across, and at the river level, 40 feet. Other canyons in North America are deeper (such as Hells Canyon on the Snake River), but none combines such depth, narrow opening, and sheer walls.

One major and highly rewarding activity in the national park is simply standing at the canyon edge and taking in the sight of sheer cliffs and rock spires carved by natural processes over the course of millions of years. Sightseeing alone can take up an entire day.

Steep-sided Black Canyon was carved by the Gunnison River, trapped within in a narrow channel of its own making.

For visitors with more time, activities include camping, hiking (on easy trails at the rim and very strenuous routes down into the canyon), and various ranger-led programs and walks.

Most of the developed visitor services of Black Canyon of the Gunnison National Park lie on the South Rim, reached by Colo. 347, off U.S. 50 east of Montrose. The visitor center is here, with its exhibits on the geology and flora and fauna of the park.

Geologic Origins

The spectacular scenery found at Black Canyon of the Gunnison National Park is the result of a number of geologic forces, chief among them the Gunnison River. The Gunnison is thought to have been flowing in its present course about 10 to 15 million years ago. As the vast area of the Rocky Mountains and Colorado Plateau was uplifted, the river began to erode the material over which it ran. At first the cutting went (relatively) quickly, because the Gunnison was flowing over rocks that were deposited as ash and other materials ejected from large volcanoes in the San Juan Mountains and elsewhere; sedimentary rocks deposited at an earlier period when rivers left mud and sand along their banks; and mud and sand built up at the bottom of an ancient seafloor. Volcanic rock, sandstone, mudstone, and shale are all soft, as rocks go, and the Gunnison's water and the bits of rock it carried carved an ever deeper channel.

Then, about two million years ago, the river reached much harder rocks dating back to the Precambrian age, primarily metamorphic gneiss and schist (which make up most of the canyon walls today). Usually a river that meets such resistant rock simply changes its course, but the Gunnison was trapped in the channel it had carved in the softer rock. From that point on, the Gunnison cut through the rock at the rate of about 1 inch every hundred years, resulting in the extremely narrow, steep-sided gorge that visitors see today. (Three dams upstream from the national park mean that peak flows through the canyon are far less than they were previously.)

The national park encompasses only 14 of the 48 total miles of the Black Canyon's length. Other canyon sections are located in Curecanti National Recreation Area (see p. 327) to the east; and Gunnison Gorge National Conservation Area, west of the national park.

South Rim

On the South Rim, 7-mile-long South Rim Drive offers spectacular views of Black Canyon of the Gunnison. A short walk from the visitor center parking lot, nearby Gunnison Point is one of the drive's best lookout spots. Continuing to the west along the drive, Chasm View, Painted Wall, and Sunset View also offer don't-miss vistas. At Gunnison Point and Chasm View, the canyon is a bit more than 1,800 feet deep, or 400 feet more than the height of the Willis (formerly Sears) Tower in Chicago, the tallest building in the United States. The visitor center is open year-round, but South Rim Drive is closed to vehicles in winter (more than 8 feet of snow can fall yearly in the park), when it serves as a popular cross-country skiing trail.

The 1-mile Rim Rock Nature Trail is a moderately strenuous walk along the canyon edge near the visitor center. Winding through a woodland of oak, piñon pine, and juniper, it offers excellent views of the canyon cliffs and the Gunnison River. The adjacent Uplands Trail provides the opportunity to make a loop trip rather than an out-and-back walk.

The strenuous Oak Flat Loop Trail, a 2-mile round trip that begins near the visitor center, offers a route that descends below the rim of the canyon without the difficulties associated with trying to hike down to the river, though it is narrow and steep in places. The trail leads hikers through aspen groves to fine views of the canyon before returning through a forest of Douglas fir and Gambel oak.

The Painted Wall viewpoint offers a panorama of canyon cliffs showing colorful stripes of pink and white crystalline pegmatite, a type of granite with quartz, feldspar, and mica intermixed. At 2,250 feet high, Painted Wall is the tallest cliff in Colorado (not to be confused with the deepest part of the canyon). There's also a good view of Painted Wall from the 0.7-mile Cedar Point Nature Trail.

The South Rim Drive ends at High Point, at an elevation of 8,289 feet—the highest spot on the rim. The section of the Black Canyon near here is its deepest part, more than 2,700 feet below the rim. For good views of this part of the canyon, walk the 1.5-mile (round-trip) Warner Point Nature Trail, named for an early advocate of protecting the Black Canyon. The piñon pine and juniper growing here form a "pygmy forest" because the trees reach heights of only 20 to 25 feet.

North Rim

Though in places the South Rim and North Rim of the canyon are less than a quarter mile apart, to drive from one to the other takes at least a couple of hours. No bridge crosses the gorge in the immediate vicinity of the national park, so travelers must go east or west to find a way across. The North Rim is reached by an 11-mile gravel road off Colo. 92 east of Crawford State Park. The entrance road is closed in winter.

There's a ranger station *(staffed intermittently)* on the North Rim, as well as six designated overlooks. Because the cliffs on the north side of the canyon are nearly vertical, the views from this side are even more dizzying than those from the South Rim, and views into the inner canyon are better.

The short (0.3 mile) Chasm View Nature Trail, accessed from the North Rim campground, offers oblique views of Painted Wall and incredible scenes of the vertical monoliths; the visitors standing at the Chasm View overlook across the canyon are only 1,100 feet away. A 3-mile round-trip hike on the North Vista Trail leads to Exclamation Point, which offers one of the park's best views of the inner canyon. Continuing on the trail to Green Mountain (a strenuous 7-mile round-trip distance) brings the reward of panoramic vistas of the San Juan Mountains, the West Elks, Grand Mesa, the Uncompahgre Plateau, and an aerial perspective of the Black Canyon.

Inner Canyon & Gunnison River

East Portal Road, branching east off Colo. 347, offers the chance to drive to Gunnison River. Exhibits at the river tell the stories of a now vanished town and the Gunnison Tunnel, part of an early reclamation project. Large vehicles are not allowed on the steep road, whose grades reach 16 percent at points. *(closed late fall into spring).*

Many visitors to the park wonder about hiking from the canyon rim down to the Gunnison River below. There are no marked and maintained trails leading into the inner canyon in the park. Hikers who want to attempt such a journey should speak with a park ranger about the difficulties involved, and realize that adequate preparation (including plenty of water) is a must. Hiking back up, of course, is far more strenuous than the descent. Hikers need to obtain a permit to venture into the inner canyon.

Precautions also apply to kayaking the section of the Gunnison River through Black Canyon in the national park. Rapids are Class V, and the danger of such a trip should not be underestimated, especially during periods of high flow. Only extremely experienced and well-prepared kayakers should consider running this section of the river. Expert kayakers have died in the raging rapids here. Again, consultation with park rangers and local outfitters is imperative. Kayaking (and rafting) opportunities are less dangerous on the stretch of the Gunnison River through Gunnison Gorge National Conservation Area.

Flora & Fauna

While the park's scenery and geologic story attract the most attention, visitors should take time to enjoy its wildlife and vegetation. Several life zones linked to elevation and sunlight mean a great diversity of flora and fauna. Gambel oak, juniper, Douglas fir, quaking aspen, piñon pine, cottonwood, box elder, serviceberry, sage, and mountain mahogany are among the trees and shrubs found in the park.

Mule deer, elk, bighorn sheep, mountain lions, and bobcats might be seen, although birds are the most visible animals. Golden eagles, red-tailed hawks, and peregrine falcons are top predators; and Steller's jays, black-billed magpies, and mountain bluebirds are among the most colorful species. In the canyon, the haunting song of the canyon wren echoes off the cliffs, while white-throated swifts zoom by, and American dippers fly from rock to rock in the river.

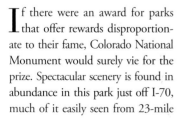

Colo. 347
Montrose, CO
970-641-2337
www.nps.gov/blca

West-central Colorado, 60 miles southeast of Grand Junction ▪ 30,750 acres ▪ South Rim: year-round; North Rim: mid-April to November ▪ Hiking, camping, driving scenic route, cross-country skiing

Colorado National Monument
Stunning rock formations and long-distance vistas

If there were an award for parks that offer rewards disproportionate to their fame, Colorado National Monument would surely vie for the prize. Spectacular scenery is found in abundance in this park just off I-70, much of it easily seen from 23-mile Rim Rock Drive. The drive has become very popular with bicyclists as well as motorists, making it imperative that travelers obey park rules on road safety.

The national monument can be entered from the east or west side; the visitor center, with exhibits and audiovisual presentations, is 4 miles from the western entrance, as is the adjacent Saddlehorn campground. Rim Rock Drive, with its many overlooks and interpretive panels, offers endless vistas of cliffs and eroded spires, and simply following its loop route is the park's most popular activity.

Trails in the monument include short walks such as 0.25-mile (one way) Window Rock, with views of Monument Canyon and 450-foot-tall Independence Monument; and 0.5-mile Otto's Trail, with similarly fine vistas. Both pass through the sparse woodland of piñon pine and juniper that's typical of the Colorado Plateau.

Among the most popular longer routes is Monument Canyon Trail, 6 miles one way; following a steep, 600-foot descent into Monument Canyon, the path reaches some of the park's major rock sculptures, such as Independence Monument, Kissing Couple, and the Coke Ovens.

Although desert bighorn sheep and soaring golden eagles are the most commonly seen wildlife in the park, visitors should keep an eye out for mule deer as well.

Colo. 340
Fruita, CO
970-858-3617
www.nps.gov/colm

AT A GLANCE

Western Colorado, 10 miles west of Grand Junction ▪ 20,534 acres ▪ Year-round ▪ Hiking, camping, taking scenic drive, bicycling, rock climbing

---

Curecanti National Recreation Area
Great boating and hiking through Gunnison River canyons

Just upstream from the awe-inspiring scenery of Black Canyon of the Gunnison National Park (see p. 323), three dams on the Gunnison River have created reservoirs that offer a wide variety of recreational opportunities. Curecanti National Recreation Area (named for a 19th-century Ute Indian) was established in 1965 as a way to protect the lands around the reservoirs and to provide ways for the public to enjoy the surroundings.

One of those reservoirs, Blue Mesa, is the largest body of water in Colorado (20 miles long, with 96 miles of shoreline), and various water-related activities are by far the most popular way to enjoy the area. Boating, waterskiing, windsurfing, and swimming attract many visitors, as does fishing for trout, kokanee salmon, and yellow perch. (Blue Mesa Reservoir is the largest kokanee salmon fishery in the United States.)

The other two reservoirs, Morrow Point and Crystal, allow only boats that can be carried by hand to their shores, which limits usage to lightweight craft such as canoes and kayaks. Even with that restriction,

Blue Mesa Lake formed behind a dam built on the Gunnison River.

Morrow Point attracts boaters for its short stretch of swift current and beautiful canyon scenery.

No matter what kind of activity a traveler plans to undertake, the first stop should be at the Elk Creek Visitor Center, located on the north shore of Blue Mesa Reservoir, about 15 miles west of Gunnison. (It is reached by way of U.S. 50.) At Elk Creek, reservations can be made for the popular Morrow Point boat tour *(Mem. Day–Labor Day; sometimes longer, depending on weather)*, a 1.5-hour, ranger-led cruise through the upper Black Canyon. Visitor centers can also provide lists of approved outfitters for fishing trips, hiking, river running, and other activities.

Landlubbers will find plenty to do at Curecanti, too. Hiking is somewhat limited by the terrain, but more than 20 miles of trails allow hikers to get away from roads and enjoy scenery and wildlife. At the eastern end of the recreation area, the easy 1.5-mile Neversink Trail passes near a heronry. Six miles west of the Elk Creek Visitor Center, the Dillon Pinnacles Trail winds through sagebrush and ponderosa pine for a view of the weirdly eroded volcanic Dillon Pinnacles.

The 2-mile Pine Creek Trail descends into the canyon and then follows an old narrow-gauge railroad bed. The strenuous 4-mile Curecanti Creek Trail rewards hikers with a view of Curecanti Needle, a 700-foot-high granite spire with a distinctive shape; it was chosen in 1882 for the logo of the Denver and Rio Grande Railroad. Three other trails in the area offer comparable views of canyons and mountains.

Flora & Fauna

Thanks to its setting, Curecanti National Recreation Area comprises a wide range of ecosystems. Riparian zones provide enough moisture for cottonwood and willow (such as along the Neversink Trail) to flourish, while drier slopes support Gambel oak, juniper, sagebrush, and rabbitbrush. Higher forests are home to ponderosa pine, Douglas fir, spruce, and aspen.

The Gunnison's prairie dog (which many visitors call "gopher") is seen often in the area, as are mule deer. Bighorn sheep and elk are present in the park, but are much less conspicuous. Among the most interesting species found here is the Gunnison sage grouse, a chickenlike bird that is found only in Colorado and Utah. Its population has declined dramatically in recent decades, and conservation efforts are being made to help it recover.

U.S. 50 & Colo. 92
Gunnison, CO
970-641-2337
www.nps.gov/cure

AT A GLANCE

West-central Colorado, 80 miles southeast of Grand Junction ▪ 41,790 acres ▪ Year-round; some facilities closed in winter ▪ Boating, swimming, fishing, hiking, waterskiing, windsurfing

---

Florissant Fossil Beds National Monument
A rich deposit of Eocene-epoch fossils

About 34 million years ago, volcanic activity deposited ash and mud in a valley in what is now central Colorado, burying huge redwood trees and other plants, as well as a variety of small insects. The conditions being right, many of them were preserved as fossils within beds of shale. Today, more than 1,700 species of plants and insects have been identified through their fossilized remains at Florissant Fossil Beds National Monument, making it one of the world's richest collections. (There are no dinosaur fossils here: The volcanic activity occurred about 30 million years after

Insects are among the most common fossils found here.

they had disappeared from Earth.)

The most visible specimens at Florissant are the stumps of redwoods up to 14 feet across, easily seen around the park visitor center and on the 1-mile Petrified Forest Walk. The most common fossils are those of small insects, spiders, snails, and other invertebrates, along with small plants such as mosses and ferns. Fossils of fish and a few birds and mammals have also been found. All the smaller specimens are best seen in visitor center displays. In summer, rangers conduct interpretive programs that touch on the park's geology, ecology, fossils, and history.

The national monument also has 14 miles of hiking trails that wind through ponderosa pine forests and meadows. The backcountry is open to horseback riding.

Cty Rd. 1 (off U.S. 24)
Florissant, CO
719-748-3253
www.nps.gov/flfo

AT A GLANCE

Central Colorado, 35 miles west of Colorado Springs ▪ 5,998 acres ▪ Year-round ▪ Seeing fossilized plants and small animals, hiking

Great Sand Dunes National Park & Preserve

Alpine peaks and the tallest sand dunes in North America

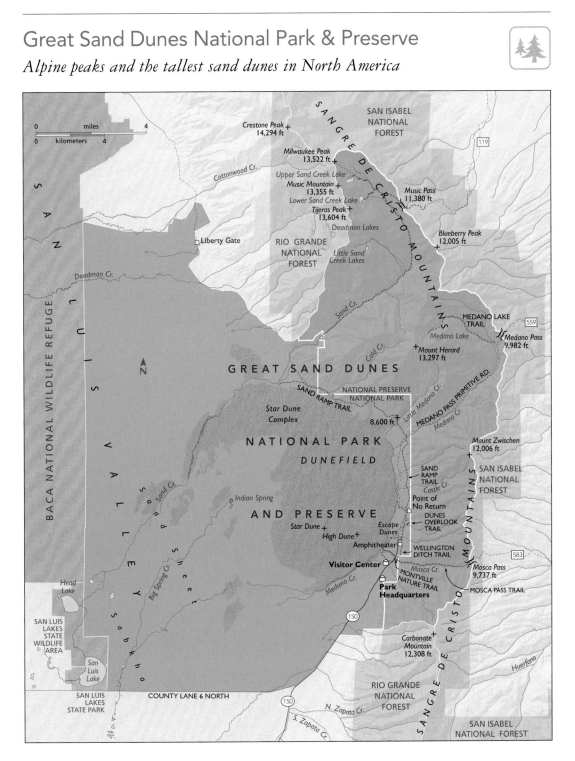

One of the country's most unusual and dramatic landscapes lies within the expansive San Luis Valley of southern Colorado. Visitors here can see a field of sand dunes covering more than 30 square miles, with the tallest of the countless sand peaks rising 750 feet from its base.

Scientists estimate the Great Sand Dunes began forming less than 440,000 years ago, when Lake Alamosa dried up.

The main field of sand dunes has been protected since 1932 as a national monument. A congressional act in 2000 allowed the creation of Great Sand Dunes National Park and Preserve, a much larger park that takes in land formerly part of a national forest, as well as additional property that helps preserve the groundwater of the San Luis Valley and the ecological integrity of the dunes. Some activities (such as hunting) are allowed in the preserve section of Great Sand Dunes that are not permitted in the national park section.

Origins of the Great Sand Dunes

Towering above the valley floor, the 13,000-foot peaks of the Sangre de Cristo Mountains lie to the east (some now lie within the national park and preserve), while the San Juan Mountains (outside the park) rise to the west; the latter are volcanic in origin, unlike the Sangre de Cristos, which were uplifted by tectonic forces.

Geologists believe that an ancient lake once filled the San Luis Valley between the two mountain ranges, eventually draining south through the Rio Grande Valley and leaving behind a vast sheet of sand on the old lake bed. Prevailing winds from the west blow the sand toward three passes in the Sangre de Cristo Mountains, countered at times by storm winds from the opposite direction, pushing up the dunes. In addition, streams continually move the sand from the mountain side of the dune field back to the valley floor, providing more sand for deposition by wind onto the dunes. The combination of these factors results in the continent's tallest sand dunes.

Exploring the Dunes

The Dunes parking lot a little way beyond the visitor center serves as the starting point for hikes into the dunes, from which it's about a 1-mile (one-way) trip to the aptly named High Dune, which towers 650 feet above the floor of the San Luis Valley. You'll find a great panorama at the top, taking in mountains, dunes, and valley. Despite its name, this is not the tallest dune in the park. To see the dune that is the tallest, continue another mile to the west to Star Dune, which measures 750 feet from base to crest. "Star" dunes are so named because they have three or more "arms," rather than the single axis of most dunes.

In summer, air temperatures at Great Sand Dune are moderate (about 85°F), but the sand can reach midday temperatures of around 140°F, so it's best to hike in the early morning or late afternoon. Good shoes or boots are necessary (no sandals), and carrying plenty of water is a must. Walking in the sand is physically tiring; when climbing a dune, hikers should zigzag up the ridges rather than head straight uphill to the top. Those exploring the dunes should also watch for any evidence of lightning nearby and retreat immediately if such a danger appears.

Some people bring snowboards or plastic sleds and enjoy sliding down the dunes, an activity that works much better when there has been recent rain and the sand is slightly wet. When dry, the sand can be too soft for sliding.

Backcountry camping is allowed in the dunes anyplace away from the main day-use areas. Night in the dunes can offer solitude and fabulous views of the night sky, but campers should be prepared for thunderstorms and occasional high winds.

No poisonous snakes or other dangerous animals dwell in the duneland, but there are more than a thousand species of arthropods (insects and spiders). Keen-eyed visitors might spot the small green-and-brown Great Sand Dunes tiger beetle, which preys on other insects. It favors sandy, lightly vegetated areas and is one of at least seven endemic insect species.

Although the dunes are constantly changing surface shape, their overall appearance has not changed significantly in historical times. Photographs from the late 19th century show that the appearance of the main dune field is much the same today, more than a century later. The vastness of the dunes and their uniformity impressed explorer Zebulon Pike, who in 1807 wrote, "Their appearance was exactly that of a sea in a storm (except as to color), not the least sign of vegetation existing thereon."

Medano Creek

Along the eastern edge of the dunes flows a shallow stream called Medano Creek. The moisture it carries is a vital part of the dune-system environment. Kids may want to build sand castles or just enjoy a shoes-off walk along the squishy streambed. At times Medano flows with enough water that small children can even raft in it. The wet sand is a good place to look for the tracks of coyotes, kangaroo rats, mule deer, or bobcats. Medano Creek usually flows only in spring, carrying snowmelt down from the mountaintops. When it contains adequate water, watch for a phenomenon called surge flow, which occurs when a small, temporary dam of sand upstream collapses, sending down a wave of water that can be up to a foot high.

Medano Pass Primitive Road

Now that the former national monument has been expanded, the current park and preserve includes desert, mountain slopes, and high Rocky Mountain forests all the way to the tundra environment, above tree line in the Sangre de Cristos. Moving up in elevation, travelers pass through a scrubby habitat of junipers and piñon pines, cross creeks lined with aspens and cottonwoods, and continue into forests of ponderosa pine and, even higher, spruce and fir. Alpine tundra tops the tallest summits above tree line, where only grasses, compact shrubs, low wildflowers, and other ground-hugging plants can survive.

Those with a four-wheel-drive, high-clearance vehicle can drive the Medano Pass Primitive Road to a 10,000-foot pass in the mountains, and on to Colo. 69 outside the park. Anyone contemplating such a trip should consult with a ranger about conditions, which include soft sand and a very rough, rocky mountain road.

Accessed from the Medano Pass road, the Medano Lake Trail begins at an elevation of 10,000 feet. It climbs 2,000 feet through meadows and forest, ending at an alpine lake just above timberline. A more strenuous hike continues from the lake up to the summit of 13,297-foot Mount Herard for a spectacular panorama of the dunes. Here at timberline, bighorn sheep scramble up rocky slopes, and Clark's nutcrackers give their raucous calls. Listen for the sharp squeaks of pikas, mammals that live among rock piles, resembling small rabbits without the long ears. More conspicuous are yellow-bellied marmots, large rodents related to woodchucks, which in their friendly inquisitiveness seem to welcome hikers to their mountain home.

Although there are no marked trails in the dune fields, several hiking routes in the uplands to the east offer the chance to explore the park away from the sand.

The easy, 0.5-mile Montville Nature Trail (named for a now defunct community of about 20 houses) loops into the foothills, where hikers might spot mule deer, least chipmunks, desert cottontails, or coyotes. Black-billed magpies, long-tailed and conspicuous, have learned to beg for food (don't feed them or other park wildlife), and friendly mountain chickadees flit from tree to tree.

Another rewarding hike, the Mosca Pass Trail follows an old overgrown toll road (used by wagons and later by a few early motor vehicles) up Mosca Creek, a tributary of the Medano. It leads past cottonwoods and aspens, ascending into a forest of Engelmann spruces, subalpine firs, and limber and bristlecone pines, reaching 9,737-foot Mosca Pass after 3.5 miles; the elevation gain is just under 1,500 feet. It provides a fine overview of the way habitats change with elevation in the Rockies. This trail is a favorite walk for bird-watchers, who enjoy the way the varied habitats provide home for an equally wide array of species. Wildflowers can provide a colorful show in areas alongside Mosca Creek.

Nearby Sights

Ask at the visitor center or speak to a park ranger about exploring areas near the park such as Alamosa National Wildlife Refuge and other wetlands in the San Luis Valley, home to thousands of migratory waterfowl and other birds. Nearby national forest areas also provide additional camping, hiking, and nature-study opportunities.

Colo. 150
Mosca, CO
719-378-6399
www.nps.gov/grsa

AT A GLANCE

South-central Colorado, 120 miles southwest of Pueblo ■ 150,000 acres ■ Year-round, though winter can be very cold and mountain areas are inaccessible ■ Hiking, backpacking, horseback riding, sand boarding

Mesa Verde National Park

Spectacularly preserved cliff dwellings of the ancestral Puebloan culture

From the 1880s, when prospectors and cowboys happened upon an astounding complex of cliff dwellings in a sandstone canyon in southwestern Colorado, the fame of the archaeological site called Mesa Verde has grown. Today, it's known worldwide as one of the most important and best preserved ruins of the pre-Columbian natives called the ancestral Puebloan people.

In 1891, Swedish scientist Gustaf Nordenskiöld explored and photographed parts of Mesa Verde; a book he published in 1893 brought attention to its significance. In 1906, President Theodore Roosevelt signed legislation establishing a national park here, the first primarily archaeological site designated a national park. In 1978, UNESCO designated Mesa Verde a cultural World Heritage site.

Cultural History

More than 4,000 archaeological sites are known to exist within Mesa

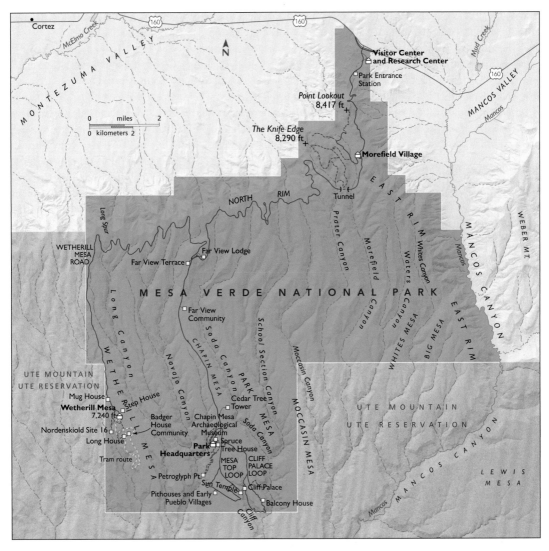

Verde National Park. Although the large and beautiful cliff dwellings are most famous, sites set into canyon walls make up only a small part of the structures within the park. Atop the mesa are found pithouses, pueblos, masonry towers, and farming structures, all part of a complex of pueblos that was occupied by thousands of people from about A.D. 550 to 1300. Though the ancestral Puebloan people lived in the area for about 700 years, it was only during the last century of occupation that they built and resided in the elaborate cliff dwellings for which

Mesa Verde National Park is famous.

Mesa Verde was abandoned in the late 13th century, going from a flourishing community to a deserted condition within just two generations or so. Many explanations have been proposed for the move away from the site, but none is known to be definitive. Warfare with other tribes or invasion is a possibility, as is prolonged drought or other climate change. Also a possible cause is the success of the pueblo itself. After a long period of occupation by a relatively large population, the surrounding area may have been

depleted of timber, food plants, game animals, and other resources. In any event, the ancestral Puebloan people moved away, and today around two dozen Native American tribes in the Southwest consider themselves descendants.

Despite a period around the beginning of the 20th century when looters and vandals caused great damage to the structures, Mesa Verde remains an evocative place, where it's possible to imagine a long-vanished culture at its height, living atop and within these canyons of the Colorado Plateau.

Visiting the Park

While parts of Mesa Verde National Park are open all year, to get the most out of your visit you should plan a trip for late spring through fall, when the road to the Wetherill Mesa sites is open.

Located at the park entrance, Mesa Verde Visitor and Research Center should be the first stop on a visit to Mesa Verde. Three of the largest and most impressive cliff dwellings—Cliff Palace, Balcony House, and Long House—can be visited only on guided tours; the tickets must be purchased at the visitor center. Exhibits here highlight the ancestral Puebloan people and their descendants, and help visitors orient themselves to the park and map out their visit.

Chapin Mesa Museum & Spruce Tree House

To get the most from a visit to any of the Mesa Verde ruins, a visit to the Chapin Mesa Archaeological Museum is a must. Here visitors can watch an orientation film, see dioramas representing daily life in an ancestral Puebloan village, and learn about Mesa Verde from other exhibits and artifacts. A quarter-mile self-guided trail begins at the museum and leads to Spruce Tree House, the best-preserved cliff dwelling in the park. (In winter, this site can be visited only on ranger-led tours.) As many as a hundred people may have lived at Spruce Tree House, which is set in an alcove in the cliff wall more than 200 feet wide. The site also features eight kivas, or underground ceremonial rooms. Although some restoration work has been done here, the stonework is 90 percent original.

Builders at Mesa Verde used sandstone blocks (shaped with harder rock into generally rectangular form); mortar made of mud, ash, and soil; and wooden beams.

The 2.4-mile self-guided Petroglyph Point Trail is adjacent to the Spruce Tree House Trail. It leads to one of the park's largest petroglyphs (figures incised in rock), a panel 12 feet wide. The path offers views of Spruce and Navajo Canyons and is the only trail in the park from which to view petroglyphs.

Chapin Mesa

At the end of the long Chapin Mesa Road, two 6-mile loop drives wind through Chapin Mesa's fire-scarred piñon-juniper woodland, offering spectacular views and access to several ancestral Puebloan dwellings.

The Mesa Top Loop Road passes

Part of the Cliff Palace, which numbers 150 rooms, 23 kivas, and several towers

several ruins with self-guided trails. At the Square Tower House overlook, a short trail leads to a dramatic viewpoint above this four-story remnant of a more extensive, multi-tiered structure *(not open to the public)*. It is the tallest site in the park.

The long D-shaped Sun Temple, set atop the canyon walls, may have been an observatory or ceremonial center; it was never thought to be inhabited. The canyon edge at the parking lot here offers a wonderful view of Cliff Palace, the largest cliff dwelling in North America.

The Cliff Palace Loop takes visitors to two of Mesa Verde's premier sites: Cliff Palace and Balcony House; both can be visited only on ranger-guided tours *(ticket required)*. Cliff Palace is reached by a 0.25-mile trail that begins at an overlook. This tour involves climbing five ladders. The one-hour, ranger-guided tour of Balcony House—well described as "adventurous"—involves climbing a 32-foot ladder, crawling through a 12-foot-long tunnel, and using ladders to climb up an open rock face.

Though not so famous as Cliff Palace, two sites on Chapin Mesa Road are well worth a visit, and both may be toured on self-guided trails. The Far View Sites Complex comprises five mesa-top villages and a dry reservoir, while the Cedar Tree Tower is a mesa-top tower and kiva complex.

Wetherill Mesa

The steep, winding Wetherill Mesa Drive *(Mem. Day weekend–Labor*

A yellow-headed collared lizard soaks up the sun.

Day; no vehicles longer than 25 feet) accesses sites on the western side of Mesa Verde. At the end of the drive, visitors can either hike or bike along the 6-mile Long House Loop (the former tram road) to see the sites atop Wetherill Mesa. The highlight of this scenic route is Long House, the park's second largest cliff dwelling. Exploring Long House, with its 150 rooms and 21 kivas, requires climbing two 15-foot ladders.

A nearby trail (which can be shortened by taking the tram) leads to Badger House Community. Set on the mesa, not within a canyon, this complex includes excavated pithouses and pueblos, different in their setting from cliff dwellings. Nearby Step House was named for its staircase; it also features petroglyphs. In the Wetherill Mesa area, as in other places around the park, visitors see evidence of wildfires that burned large areas in 2002.

Other Activities

In Spanish the name Mesa Verde means "green table," a reference to

this forested, flattopped part of the larger Colorado Plateau. And while visiting archaeological sites is by far the most noteworthy activity at the park, many visitors take time to explore other aspects of this 81-square-mile protected area.

Hiking in Mesa Verde National Park is limited to protect archaeological sites from damage, whether intentional or inadvertent. Hikers must be either on a ranger-led walk or on designated trails. Still, there are opportunities for those who'd like to see the park's more remote areas.

The 2-mile round-trip Knife Edge Trail follows a section of the old Knife Edge Road, originally built in 1914 as the main access road into the park. It runs from the Morefield Campground to an overlook with views of Montezuma Valley. The 7.8-mile round-trip Prater Ridge Trail also begins at the Morefield campground, climbing Prater Ridge and looping around the ridgetop. There are good vistas at the top, and the change of elevation along the way brings varied vegetation, from sagebrush and juniper to ponderosa pine and Gambel oak. Wildlife in the park includes mule deer, elk, porcupines, marmots, and wild turkeys.

During the summer months, park rangers nightly present free interpretive programs at the amphitheater in the Morefield campground. Subjects range from wildlife to geology to ancestral Puebloan culture. The presentations continue a tradition dating back to 1907, when Mesa Verde was the first national park to introduce campfire talks into its educational program.

Off U.S. 160
Mesa Verde, CO
970-529-4465
www.nps.gov/meve

AT A GLANCE

Southwestern Colorado, 35 miles west of Durango ▪ 52,121 acres ▪ Late spring through fall ▪ Touring cliff dwellings, hiking, camping, listening to campfire talks

Rocky Mountain National Park

A magnificent showcase of alpine scenery and wildlife

Straddling the Continental Divide, boasting some of the most spectacular high-mountain landscapes in the United States, Rocky Mountain National Park is deservedly one of the most popular destinations in the entire National Park System.

Paved roads allow access to the harsh but beautiful landscape above the tree line, as well as gorgeous alpine lakes ringed by coniferous forest and stark, glacier-sculpted cliffs. The true grandeur of the park, though, is best experienced on some of its 355 miles of trails, which wander alongside rushing mountain streams, past thundering waterfalls, below towering peaks, and through lush valleys where elk and bighorn sheep descend from mountain slopes to graze.

A few statistics give some idea of what Rocky Mountain National Park has to offer. The park encompasses more than 77 peaks above 12,000 feet in elevation, 450 miles of streams and rivers, and 150 lakes. Despite the park's popularity, it's still possible to find solitude along the trails or on the shore of a high-altitude lake where the loudest sound is the croaking call of a raven.

Natural History

Coniferous forest covers much of the park, but the most immediately compelling element of the landscape is the line of jagged mountain peaks towering above deep valleys. Much of the landscape here was given shape by glaciers over the past 18,000 years, relentless sheets of ice that left behind bare cliffs; cirques (bowl-shaped basins at the heads of mountain valleys); and the broad, U-shaped valleys characteristic of

glacial action. A few permanent cirque glaciers remain at high elevations within the park.

The great elevation difference, from 7,840 feet in the lowest valley to the top of Longs Peak at 14,259 feet, means that the park features a great diversity of habitats. Willows thrive in flat, low wetlands, and open forests of ponderosa pine and aspen blanket low slopes. Higher up on the slopes are vast forests of spruce and Douglas fir. Above the tree line is the alpine tundra, where conditions are so harsh that only low-growing herbs, mosses, and other hardy plants can survive.

Visiting the Park

Most visitors enter the park from its eastern side, from the small town of Estes Park, by way of U.S. 36 or U.S. 34. U.S. 36 joins U.S. 34 after a few miles. The latter is designated Trail Ridge Road as it crosses through the park. A smaller number of visitors enter the park on its west side from the town of Grand Lake, by way of the Kawuneeche Valley, where the Colorado River flows. There are visitor centers at all three entrances, where travelers can pick up maps and guidebooks, seek advice about trails or wildlife observation, and generally prepare for a visit.

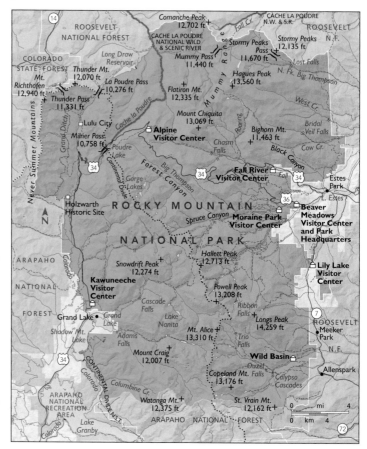

In summer, elk roam the park's high country, but in winter most move to lower elevations in and outside the park.

By far the most popular trails and destinations are on the eastern side of the Continental Divide, but the west side of the park has much to offer, including less crowded trails. The western side receives more precipitation than does the east, making the environment noticeably different. Moose, for instance, are seen on the west side of the park, grazing in the wetlands along the Colorado and other streams.

The five developed campgrounds at Rocky Mountain National Park are extremely popular; two offer advance reservations. Backpackers (who need a permit for overnight stays) can choose from over 200 sites in the park backcountry, some reachable only by lengthy hikes, but offering the pleasures of solitude in pristine wilderness far from other people.

Trail Ridge Road

Among the park's most famous attractions is the east-west Trail Ridge Road, which crosses the Continental Divide. The 48-mile route, the highest continuous paved road in the country, takes drivers from ponderosa pine forest through the zone of spruce and fir and up above tree line to the open tundra in a relatively short time, reaching a maximum elevation of 12,183 feet. Massive snowfalls close Trail Ridge Road for much of the year; depending on weather, it's usually open from about late May to late October.

As is true of the entire park, but especially here, persons with health problems or difficulty breathing should take extra care when considering a visit to high elevations, where the air is very thin. For everyone, sunburn occurs much more rapidly, as does dehydration; sunblock and lots of water are essentials for a visit.

Ascending Trail Ridge Road from the east, visitors reach several popular lookout points with stunning views, including Many Parks Curve, Rainbow Curve, and Forest Canyon Overlook. Just at tree line, note how fierce winds shape the highest trees into twisted, shrublike forms. Eleven miles of the road cross tundra, providing visitors a rare chance to experience this habitat without a long hike. In the brief summer, colorful wildflowers bloom on the seemingly barren terrain, giving incentive for visitors to leave their vehicles and walk one of the tundra trails. A short stroll at Forest Canyon Overlook is one such path; another is at the Rock Cut area. Wherever you walk in the tundra, stay on trails; alpine plants are extremely fragile, and one footstep can wipe out years of growth.

Farther up the road, the Alpine Visitor Center has exhibits and programs on the tundra environment, as well as ranger-led walks. About 4 miles west, the road crosses the Continental Divide at Milner Pass, continuing downward to the Kawuneeche Valley and the Colorado River, just beginning its long journey to Mexico. Hiking

FOLLOWING PAGES: *The smooth surface of Bear Lake reflects distant Longs Peak and Keyboard of the Winds.*

trails here include Lulu City, which visits the site of a long-abandoned mining town, and the Green Mountain Loop, passing through marshy Big Meadow and offering a good chance to see moose and elk.

An alternative route up to the Alpine Visitor Center is Old Fall River Road, constructed in 1920 as the first way for vehicles to reach the park's alpine country. Mostly gravel and featuring many switchbacks, the 9-mile, one-way road travels from Horseshoe Park to join Trail Ridge Road at Fall River Pass. With a maximum speed of 15 miles an hour, Old Fall River Road is for those who want to take time to enjoy this historic and rewarding journey.

Bear Lake Road

Rocky Mountain National Park's other famed motor route is Bear Lake Road, a dead-end road that provides access to many of the park's most popular hiking trails. To alleviate traffic problems on the road and crowding at parking lots, the park offers shuttle buses in the summer that make regular stops at campgrounds and trailheads. The route ends at Bear Lake, one of the few high-mountain lakes in Colorado reachable on a paved road, offering the opportunity for physically challenged persons to experience this environment. Just below is the extremely popular trailhead at Glacier Gorge, starting point for hikes to stunning destinations such as Alberta Falls, Mills Lake, and Loch Vale.

Other Hiking Opportunities

Rocky Mountain National Park's lowlands offer excellent scenery and rewarding hikes that present a

Pikas live in the rocky tundra area.

contrast to the high-elevation dramatic alpine peaks. In Moraine Park, near the beginning of Bear Lake Road, it's easy to note the way a massive glacier pushed up long ridges along its sides, called moraines. Nearby is the Cub Lake Trail, a relatively easy 2.3-mile (one way) hike that begins in a wetland-filled valley where elk often graze.

Easily reachable in Horseshoe Park, off the Fall River entrance road, is the alluvial fan that formed when a high-mountain reservoir broke in 1982, sending a massive wall of water down a valley and displacing tons of boulders and soil. It's fascinating to see the environment recovering after such a violent event, though the area was again damaged by 2013 floods.

The Wild Basin area in the southern part of the park, is reached off Colo. 7, south of Estes Park. Wild Basin's popular day hiking destinations include Calypso Cascades and Ouzel Falls. Parking at the trailheads can be congested, so consider hiking early or late in the day.

Also located off Colo. 7 is the

trailhead for the extremely strenuous route to Longs Peak, the park's highest point at 14,259 feet. The last 1.5 miles to the summit should be considered a climb rather than a hike. Getting started well before dawn is recommended for the 16-mile round-trip trek, for fit and experienced hikers only. Less demanding is the 8.4-mile round-trip hike to beautiful Chasm Lake, set in a dramatic site at the base of Longs Peak.

Rocky Mountains Wildlife

Wildlife-watching ranks high on the attractions in the park, with opportunities changing with the seasons. Mule deer are quite often visible along park roads, and elk can be fairly common at times as well. In fall, when the aspens turn glorious yellow, the air rings with the bugling of male elk seeking mates. Bighorn sheep are less easy to spot, although they often come to natural mineral licks in Horseshoe Park; check with a ranger for advice on seeing this impressive animal. Yellow-bellied marmots, chipmunks, chickarees (small squirrels), Abert's squirrels, porcupines, and snowshoe hares are among the smaller mammals sometimes seen along trails and around campgrounds.

Bird-watchers find endless opportunities for observation in the park's varied habitats. Black-billed magpies, Steller's jays, mountain bluebirds, mountain chickadees, western tanagers, and Williamson's sapsuckers are among the avian residents of lower elevations. In higher forests, look for gray jays, pine grosbeaks, red crossbills, and Clark's nutcrackers. American dippers frequent rocky streams, and above timberline live brown-capped rosy-finches and white-tailed ptarmigan.

Park headquarters
U.S. 36
Estes Park, CO
970-586-1206
www.nps.gov/romo

AT A GLANCE

North-central Colorado, 70 miles northwest of Denver ▪ 265,800 acres ▪ All year, though some roads and sites closed in winter ▪ Hiking, camping, backpacking, scenic driving, horseback riding, rock climbing

Sand Creek Massacre National Historic Site

Honoring Cheyenne and Arapaho killed in an unprovoked attack

On the morning of November 29, 1864, troops under the command of Col. John Chivington attacked an encampment of Cheyenne and Arapaho at Sand Creek in the plains country of eastern Colorado. Chief Black Kettle had established the winter camp and had flown an American flag to signal their desire for peace. The encampment, which consisted of about 700 Cheyenne and Arapaho, was made up of mostly women, children, and males too young or old to hunt.

In the massacre that took place (despite a white flag raised over the encampment), between 150 and 200 Cheyenne and Arapaho were killed. Attacking soldiers killed unarmed people and mutilated bodies of the dead. A later U.S. governmental committee of inquiry called the incident "a foul and dastardly massacre." Efforts to create a lasting peace between American Indians and Euro-Americans were destroyed, and, with hard-liners taking the upper hand on both sides, decades of all-out war in the West followed.

Established in 2007, Sand Creek Massacre National Historic Site aims, in part, "to enhance public understanding of the massacre and assist in minimizing the chances of similar incidents in the future." Facilities include a visitor contact station, a bookstore, and a self-guided 0.8-mile walking trail. Ranger-led programs are available *(spring–fall)*.

North off Colo. 96
Chivington, CO
719-438-5916
www.nps.gov/sand

AT A GLANCE

Eastern Colorado, 125 miles east of Colorado Springs ▪ 2,385 acres ▪ Year-round ▪ Participating in ranger-led programs, taking self-guided historical trail

NEW MEXICO

New Mexico offers travelers a wealth of historical destinations—many related to early Native American cultures and to the era when Spain controlled the Southwest and Santa Fe was a center of commerce and government. Heavily influenced by those heritages, New Mexico ranks among the most culturally distinctive states for its art and architecture. Several parks protect unique natural features, including Capulin Volcano, a cinder cone in the northeast; the vast duneland of White Sands National Monument in the south-central region; and the badlands of El Malpais National Monument in the northwest. Carlsbad Caverns is renowned for its beautiful cave formations.

Aztec Ruins National Monument

A 500-room pueblo featuring a kiva ceremonial room

The impressive ruins of this pueblo only hint at what it must have been like when three-story structures, comprising 400 to 500 rooms, provided homes and ceremonial spaces for the ancestral Puebloan people who lived here from about A.D. 1100 to 1300. The word "Aztec" was applied to the ruins in the 19th century, when it was thought, incorrectly, that the residents here were related to those people.

Builders used stone from a near distance for walls, while the wood used for roofs came from forests of ponderosa pine, aspen, and Douglas fir 30 miles away. Many original timbers used in the construction can still be seen at Aztec Ruins today; scientists using dendrochronology have examined these beams to date the site.

The visitor center features a video on Aztec Ruins; and in summer, rangers conduct interpretive talks. Other lectures and programs are scheduled as well.

A 0.5-mile self-guided trail leads through the ruins, giving close looks at construction techniques utilizing stone, wood, and adobe mortar. Interpretive signs give Native American perspectives on what visitors are seeing. A highlight of the trail is the point where it descends into the circular room called the Great Kiva, the social and religious center of Aztec Ruins. Forty-plus feet in diameter, this kiva is the oldest and largest known reconstructed building of its kind.

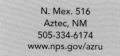

N. Mex. 516
Aztec, NM
505-334-6174
www.nps.gov/azru

AT A GLANCE

Northwestern New Mexico, 200 miles northwest of Santa Fe ▪ 320 acres ▪ Year-round ▪ Touring 900-year-old ancestral Puebloan ruins

Bandelier National Monument

A famed archaeological site amid a Rio Grande wilderness

The ancestral Puebloan culture that occupied what is now Bandelier National Monument reached its peak after the communities of Mesa Verde, in Colorado, and Chaco Canyon, farther west in New Mexico. Bandelier's occupation lasted from about A.D. 1150 to 1550, after which its inhabitants moved to pueblos along the Rio Grande.

The Bandelier ancestral Puebloan people, whose descendants live today in nearby pueblo communities, built their dwellings with different construction techniques from other contemporary villages, utilizing local materials from Frijoles Canyon.

The Pajarito Plateau, just west of the Rio Grande, is made up of volcanic ash welded into a soft rock called tuff. Over millennia, Frijoles Creek cut a deep canyon into the plateau, where a group of ancestral Puebloan people settled. They used blocks of tuff to build structures on the canyon floor, and they excavated shallow

The ancestral Puebloans carved caves in the soft tuff.

caves in the tuff to serve as back rooms for homes built along the base of the cliff. Swiss-born anthropologist Adolf Bandelier visited the ancestral Puebloan homes in Frijoles Canyon in 1880; when the national monument was designated in 1916, it was given his name.

The visitor center features a 14-minute film, as well as pottery; tools; and dioramas depicting the life of the ancient Puebloan people. On summer weekends, visitors can enjoy ranger programs and demonstrations of cultural activities such as potterymaking, drummaking, and traditional dancing, given by local Pueblo people.

The main trail to the dwellings, 0.6 mile one way, leads up the canyon from the visitor center alongside the steep and heavily eroded north wall, formed of pinkish tuff. It passes a large kiva (ceremonial room) and a series of dwellings, including the nearly circular Tyuonyi Pueblo and the impressive Long House. Ladders along the trail allow visitors to climb into *cavates* (small hand-carved caves in the tuff). The first section of this trail is accessible to wheelchairs; the rest has numerous narrow stone stairways. In winter, this is the only trail on which the snow is removed.

Visitors can continue another half mile to see Alcove House, reached by climbing a series of wooden ladders to a reconstructed kiva 140 feet up on the canyon wall.

Another popular day hike leads downstream from the visitor center 1.5 miles to Upper Falls, where Frijoles Creek splashes over a layer of hard basaltic lava that underlies the softer tuff rock.

A separate section of Bandelier National Monument, called Tsankawi, is located on N. Mex. 4, 12 miles from the main section of the park. At Tsankawi, there's a 1.5-mile walk up and around a mesa, from which cavates, petroglyphs, and an unexcavated ancestral Puebloan village can be viewed. This trail requires hikers to climb ladders in places. Tsankawi is somewhat difficult to find; ask a park ranger for directions.

About 70 percent of Bandelier has been designated as a federal wilderness area, and more than 70 miles of trails crisscross the very rugged backcountry. The huge Las Conchas Fire in 2011 caused powerful flash floods down all of Bandelier's canyons, making the landscape wilder than ever. Backpacking is allowed, but a permit must be obtained for overnight camping. Hikers planning extended treks should talk to a park ranger in advance and be prepared for strenuous routes and a lack of water on the trails.

More than 3,000 archaeological sites have been documented in the Bandelier backcountry. You can reach Yapashi Pueblo via a strenuous 6-mile (one way) hike from the visitor center. The trail passes through mid–Alamo Canyon, with an elevation change of more than 500 feet in less than a quarter mile. Except in a spring after a snowy winter, water is rarely available along this route. Another backcountry destination, Painted Cave, is known for its pictographs (ancient painted figures). Reaching it requires a round-trip hike of at least 14.5 miles.

N. Mex. 4
Los Alamos, NM
505-672-3861
www.nps.gov/band

AT A GLANCE

North-central New Mexico, 50 miles northwest of Santa Fe ▪ 33,000 acres ▪ Year-round; snow can sometimes close the park in winter ▪ Touring ancestral Puebloan sites, hiking, backpacking

Capulin Volcano National Monument
Easy access to the heart of a volcanic crater

Much of northeastern New Mexico displays evidence of volcanic activity, the result of millions of years of eruptions in what is known as the Raton-Clayton Volcanic Field. The field is believed to have last been active around 10,000 years ago.

About 60,000 years ago, a small vent opened in the ground, shooting cinders and ash into the air. When they fell to the ground they formed a ring around the vent, growing taller as more material spewed from the earth. As the resulting cone rose, cinders slipped down the sides until they found their angle of repose, creating an evenly sloped peak—although prevailing winds from the west caused the eastern rim to rise higher than the rest. At various times during the eruption, lava oozed from vents around the cone, eventually covering almost 16 square miles around the volcano. The result was Capulin Volcano, which today rises 1,300 feet above the surrounding grassland; its handsome form has been protected since 1916 as Capulin Volcano National Monument.

A 2-mile road spirals up from the visitor center, where a film and exhibits provide background on Capulin's geology and natural history. The road continues to a trailhead for two trails. The 0.2-mile Crater Vent Trail leads down into the crater; few places in the world allow such easy access into the heart of a volcano. The 1-mile Rim Trail follows the edge of the crater for wonderful views in all directions. Sierra Grande, a massive volcano, dominates the scene to the southeast. All around are smaller cones (including Baby Capulin to the northeast) and mesas formed as lava protected softer underlying rock from erosion. Capulin's own lava flows spread out from its base in all directions. On a clear day, four states can be seen from atop Capulin.

46 Volcano Road
Capulin, NM
575-278-2201
www.nps.gov/cavo

AT A GLANCE

Northeastern New Mexico, 130 miles northeast of Santa Fe ▪ 793 acres ▪ Year-round; winter weather can close park at times ▪ Hiking, viewing volcano crater

Carlsbad Caverns National Park
A *world-famous wonderland of cave formations*

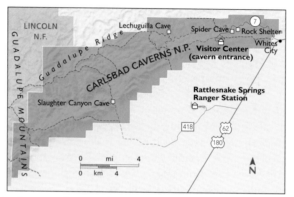

Nearly everyone has heard of Carlsbad Caverns, one of the most famous caves in the world, with room after spectacular room of stalactites, stalagmites, columns, draperies, and other speleothems (cave formations). The myriad formations have delighted visitors since famed explorer Jim White began charting its passages in 1898. (For many years, White had trouble convincing his neighbors that the cave was worth a look.)

Not everybody comes to look at the beautiful formations, though: Scientists interested in the Permian period study the fossils found in the Guadalupe Mountains to learn more about what lived here during that time. Bones from ice-age mammals, such as jaguars, camels, and giant sloths, have been found in the entrance areas of some caves in the park as well.

Geologic Origins

The story of how this underground wonder came to be formed—and how it relates to the towering peaks of nearby Guadalupe Mountains National Park (see p. 290)—begins with an ocean that covered this region in the Permian period, about 250 million years ago. Sponges, algae, bryozoans, snails, and other living things built a gigantic U-shaped reef along the shores of a broad bay. After the sea receded, the limestone reef was buried beneath sedimentary material. About 15 million years ago, tectonic forces lifted part of it above the surface,

forming the Guadalupe Mountains, under which Carlsbad Caverns lies.

Slightly acidic water seeping down through cracks began dissolving the soft limestone, a process aided by sulfuric acid formed when hydrogen sulfide gas from underlying oil and gas deposits mixed with subterranean flows. Over millions of years, the great rooms and passages of the cave were hollowed out of the limestone. Over perhaps the past half million years, water filtering through the cave roof carried with it calcite, the main constituent of limestone; this mineral, deposited on the ceiling, floor, or walls, created the formations.

More than 30 miles of passages have been mapped in Carlsbad Caverns alone, the main cave in the national park. More than 110 other caves are also known within the park boundaries, including the fabled Lechuguilla Cave *(closed to visitors)*, one of the deepest limestone caves in the United States.

Visiting the Park

Most visitors to Carlsbad Caverns National Park simply explore the major routes through the cavern, covering in total about 3 miles of paved

trails. It's possible to enter the park, ride the elevator down into the cave, see the renowned Big Room, and be on your way in just a couple of hours. But visitors will experience a more comprehensive and satisfying visit by taking a guided cave tour, attending a ranger program, and exploring the environment of the surrounding Chihuahuan Desert. Many people take time to tour nearby Slaughter Canyon Cave, and those willing to crawl and get dirty can take a guided tour to see Spider Cave. There are other special cave tours, and trained spelunkers with a permit can explore additional caves.

At the visitor center are exhibits on cave geology and natural history, registration for optional ranger-guided cave tours *(fee; prices vary by tour)*, and a listing of ranger-led programs and demonstrations. Visitors can rent an audio guide for the cave. It features illuminating commentary from geologists and cavers.

Self-guided Cave Tour

There are two options to begin a Carlsbad Caverns tour: For the most comprehensive experience, take the short walk to the Natural Entrance. Those who are less mobile or who have health problems can ride an elevator down more than 750 feet to the lunchroom area in mid-cave, from which a fairly level path loops through the famed Big Room. The route from the Natural Entrance reaches the lunchroom area after descending the same distance along a 1-mile path that usually takes about

Carlsbad Caverns' stalagmites and stalactites formed thousands of years ago when the climate was much wetter.

Swarms of Brazilian free-tailed bats exit Carlsbad Caverns at dusk.

an hour to walk. Remember that the temperature in the cave stays a constant 56°F; a light jacket and long pants are recommended.

As you descend into the cavern through the yawning limestone mouth of the Natural Entrance, leaving the sunlight behind, you'll pass Native American pictographs and Bat Cave, the side passage where hundreds of thousands of Brazilian (often called Mexican) free-taileds roost (see opposite). To prevent disturbance, no entry is allowed. Continuing down (and down and down) past Devil's Den and Natural Bridge, you'll reach Iceberg Rock, a huge hunk of cave ceiling that fell long before anyone was around to notice.

At the lunchroom area is the 1-mile Big Room Route. This trail, quite easy compared to the descent from the Natural Entrance, passes many of Carlsbad's most famous features, including Giant Dome, Bottomless Pit (not really; it's 140 feet deep), Rock of Ages, and Painted Grotto. One of the largest known cave rooms in the world, the Big Room encompasses 14 acres of varied and colorful formations.

Ranger-guided Cave Tours

The popular King's Palace Guided Tour is a 1.5-hour walk through some of the cave's most scenic rooms. Moderately strenuous (visitors must descend and climb the equivalent of eight stories), it passes through the Green Lake Room (with the famous formation called the Veiled Statue), the elaborately arrayed King's Palace, and other rooms on its 1-mile route.

For a look at cave areas off the main routes, make reservations for one of the other ranger-led tours. Attractions in the Lower Cave include the Rookery, with beautiful "cave pearls" created when layers of calcite formed around bits of foreign material. People with a fear of heights or who are uncomfortable climbing down a ladder sometimes opt out at the beginning of this three-hour tour. The two-hour Left Hand Tunnel tour isn't so intimidating, passing pretty pools of water and pausing to examine fossils more than 200 million years old.

Talk to a ranger before signing on for the Spider Cave Tour or Hall of the White Giant Tour, each four hours long. If you have even a touch of claustrophobia, these aren't for you,

since they require long belly-crawls through tight passages. Intrepid folks who don't mind getting dirty will see formations that others do not, and they'll experience something of the adventure of primitive cave exploration—in safety, with the comforting presence of an experienced ranger.

Slaughter Canyon Cave

Several miles south of the visitor center is the entrance to Slaughter Canyon Cave, accessible only on ranger-guided tours *(fee)*. Wilder than Carlsbad Cavern, this cave has no paved paths and no lights, only the lanterns of rangers and the flashlights *(required)* of participants. On the two-hour tour you may pass an 89-foot-tall column (one of the world's largest) called the Monarch; a rim-stone dam known as the Chinese Wall (formed at the edge of a cave pool); and an eerie, hooded figure called the Klansman. Though the route involves rope-assisted climbs up slick slopes, the most difficult part is the 0.5-mile walk up a steep desert slope to reach the cave entrance from the parking lot.

Chihuahuan Desert

Not all park attractions are to be found below ground: The Chihuahuan Desert overlying the cave presents opportunities for adventure, too. The Walnut Canyon Desert Drive winds through Guadalupe Mountains terrain, and 50 miles of trails beckon hikers and backpackers. More than 33,000 acres of the park have been officially designated as wilderness, where trails offer the reward of backcountry solitude and the challenge of desert travel *(permit required for overnight stay)*. The Chihuahuan Desert is the largest and wettest of the North American deserts, and the Carlsbad Caverns National Park's expanse is one of the few places where a large area of this unique ecosystem is protected.

South of the park visitor center is Rattlesnake Springs, a picnic area where tall cottonwoods grow near historic springs used by Indians, pioneer travelers, and settlers. Biologists recognize it as one of the most significant wetlands in New Mexico.

An oasis in the Chihuahuan Desert, Rattlesnake Springs provides a home for many species of snakes (including plain-bellied water snake), amphibians (including eastern barking frog and Blanchard's cricket frog), and butterflies rare or unusual elsewhere in the region. It's a special destination for bird-watchers, who search for nesting species, including yellow-billed cuckoo, Bell's vireo, eastern bluebird, summer tanager, hooded oriole, and varied and painted buntings. Amazingly, more than 350 species of birds have been found in the vicinity of this 13-acre speck of greenery in the desert.

Brazilian Free-tailed Bats

Hundreds of thousands of Brazilian (often called Mexican) free-tailed bats fly out of the cave's Natural Entrance en masse at dusk, early spring through October. Visitors may watch the spectacle from a nearby amphitheater; ask at the visitor center for the exact time, which varies according to day length. A ranger presents a program on these much misunderstood animals before the bats emerge from the cave in an immense swirling column. The bats are migratory, and they return to the cave each spring for the females to give birth and raise their pups. More than 300 bats may squeeze together to roost in a square foot of cave ceiling, each female returning unerringly to her own pup after a night of feeding on insects. (Don't be fooled by the cave swallows that nest in the Natural Entrance and continually dart in and out during the day from spring through fall. Part of what may be the largest colony of this species in the United States, they are birds, not bats; the latter, despite their flying ability, are mammals.)

U.S. 62/180
Carlsbad, NM
505-785-2232
www.nps.gov/cave

AT A GLANCE Southeastern New Mexico, 125 miles northeast of El Paso, Texas ▪ 46,766 acres ▪ Year-round ▪ Taking cave tours, hiking, backpacking

Chaco Culture National Historical Park

A major center of ancestral Puebloan culture

Fajada Butte serves as a backdrop to the numerous ancestral Puebloan sites of Chaco Canyon.

Beginning about A.D. 850 and continuing for 400 years, this high desert valley of the Colorado Plateau was the major regional center for the people known as the ancestral Puebloan. Chaco's influence extended to and beyond sites such as those known today as Aztec Ruins National Monument (see p. 341) in New Mexico and Mesa Verde National Park (see p. 332) in Colorado. In the 11th century, Chaco was the ceremonial, administrative, and economic center of the entire San Juan Basin.

For reasons that might have included prolonged drought, resource depletion, overpopulation, or social conflicts, the site's inhabitants abandoned it in the 13th century and moved to new communities. Today, about 20 Puebloan groups in New Mexico and the Hopi in Arizona claim Chaco Canyon as their ancestral homeland and are tied to it through oral traditions and clan lineages.

For Euro-American archaeologists and travelers, Chaco has always been remote, and it remains so today. Reaching it from U.S. 550 (the preferred route) involves driving 8 miles on a paved county road followed by 13 miles on a rough dirt road. A video at the visitor center helps introduce the site and its significance, while in season (May–Oct.), rangers lead tours of Pueblo Bonito and other sites and give evening programs on varied topics.

Six major archaeological sites are located around 9-mile Canyon Loop Drive. Una Vida, near the visitor center, is one of the famed Chacoan "great houses": a very large multistory public building with a large kiva (ceremonial room). The 1-mile round-trip trail to Una Vida also passes petroglyphs (figures chipped or carved into rock faces). The most important site along the drive is Pueblo Bonito, another great house, which has been the subject

of the most extensive archaeological investigation of any place in Chaco Canyon. A 0.6-mile round-trip walk leads to Pueblo Bonito, which once rose four stories high and contained more than 600 rooms and 40 kivas. This site remains a sacred place to several American Indian tribes.

The other four stops along the drive are Hungo Pavi, Chetro Ketl, Casa Rinconada (which includes the largest kiva in the park), and Pueblo del Arroyo. The 0.25-mile Petroglyph Trail runs between Pueblo Bonito and Chetro Ketl, passing many figures incised on a cliff wall. Four backcountry hiking trails lead to other great houses off the Canyon Loop Drive, including Pueblo Alto, Peñasco

Blanco, and Tsin Kletzin on South Mesa; and Wijiji, built in a single stage in the early 1100s and noted for its symmetrical layout and rooms of uniform size. Ask at the visitor center about these trails (free permit required). Backcountry camping is not allowed in the park, but there is a campground that accepts reservations.

Many of the structures at Chaco Canyon seem to have been aligned to observe astronomical events such as the summer and winter solstices. Interest in the sky and astronomy continues in today's park. The Chaco Night Sky Program (April–Oct.) presents astronomy programs, daytime solar viewing, and telescope viewing of the spectacular dark night sky.

Cty. Rd. 7900 (off U.S. 550)
Nageezi, NM
505-786-7014
www.nps.gov/chcu

AT A GLANCE

Northwestern New Mexico, 100 miles northwest of Albuquerque ▪ 34,000 acres ▪ Year-round; winter can bring snow and cold temperatures ▪ Touring ancestral Puebloan ruins, hiking, camping, observing the heavens

El Camino Real de Tierra Adentro National Historic Trail
An influential early trade and settlement route through the Southwest

Spain started exploring in earnest what is now today's southwestern United States during the late 16th century and discovered travel routes previously developed by Native Americans. One such trail became known as El Camino Real de Tierra Adentro, "the royal road through the interior lands."

Stretching for 1,600 miles, this route linked Mexico City with the Native American community now called Ohkay Owingeh (San Juan Pueblo), north of Santa Fe, New Mexico. As a result of this effort,

soldiers, missionaries, traders, and others began using travel routes that had been developed by Native Americans. Don Juan de Oñate led the first colonizing expedition in 1598. The earliest Euro-American trade route in what is now the U.S., it brought about cultural exchange among the Spanish, other European settlers, and Native American groups. Its influence extended to ranching, farming, religion, architecture, language, and government.

The route remained important until the 1880s, when railroads took

center stage. Today, a 404-mile segment of the route—established in 2000—has been designated as El Camino Real de Tierra Adentro National Historic Trail, linking El Paso, Texas; Las Cruces, Socorro, Belen, Albuquerque, and Santa Fe, New Mexico; and the historic pueblo of Ohkay Owingeh, once the Spanish capital of the region.

Travelers along the route will find many rewarding sites, from the El Paso area to Bosque del Apache National Wildlife Refuge, near Socorro; to the historic plaza of downtown Santa Fe.

National Trails–Intermountain Region, Santa Fe, NM
505-988-6098
www.nps.gov/elca
www.elcaminoreal.org/trail

AT A GLANCE

Central New Mexico, from El Paso, Texas, to San Juan Pueblo, New Mexico ▪ 404 miles ▪ Year-round ▪ Visiting sites along historic trade and settlement route

El Malpais National Monument

A stark volcanic landscape of lava flows, cinder cones, and lava tubes

Over a period of more than 100,000 years, ending only about 2,500 years ago, repeated volcanic eruptions left an expanse of cinder cones and lava flows covering hundreds of square miles of an intermountain plain in what is now northwestern New Mexico. Any visitor who ventures out into this jagged terrain will understand instantly why early explorers called it *el malpais*—the badland.

El Malpais National Monument and Conservation Area, which protects much of this volcanic area, is managed cooperatively by the National Park Service and the Bureau of Land Management. The monument and conservation area form a contiguous tract offering an array of recreational opportunities, from parking-lot sightseeing to difficult cross-country backpacking. Careful and well-prepared visitors (with a caving permit) can even venture inside lava tubes—long, narrow caves of volcanic origin.

The National Park Service operates El Malpais Information Center on N. Mex. 53 on the north side of the area. A BLM ranger station is located on N. Mex. 117, on the east side. The

Looking south from El Malpais, views take in Mount Taylor in the distance.

Northwest New Mexico Visitor Center, staffed by NPS, BLM, and Forest Service personnel, sits just off I-40. A visit to one of these centers is highly recommended before a trip venturing very far from a road. Few trails snake through El Malpais, and what routes exist are usually marked with only rock cairns; good route-finding skills are a must, as are heavy hiking boots and plenty of water. There are

occasional ranger-led hikes, and for many visitors these are the best way to explore the lava flows, cinder cones, pressure ridges, and lava tubes.

Two spots along N. Mex. 117 south of the BLM station are easily accessible by car: Sandstone Bluffs Overlook, with a panorama of the volcanic landscape; and La Ventana Natural Arch, an impressive rock span eroded from a sandstone bluff.

Northwest NM Visitor Center
1900 E. Santa Fe Avenue
Grants, NM
505-876-2783
www.nps.gov/elma

AT A GLANCE — Northwestern New Mexico, 85 miles west of Albuquerque ▪ 378,000 acres (including conservation area) ▪ Year-round ▪ Hiking, exploring lava caves

---

El Morro National Monument

A landmark site of petroglyphs and pioneer inscriptions

A small pool—the only reliable water source for many miles—attracted travelers to this tall sandstone bluff for several centuries.

Even before the days of covered wagons and Army expeditions, early Puebloan Indians had built extensive dwellings atop the bluff. The soft

sandstone enticed many of these residents and visitors to carve inscriptions in the outcropping the Spanish called *el morro*, the headland. Today there are more than 2,000 inscriptions visible at El Morro National Monument, reminders of visitors long gone.

After watching a short introductory film in the visitor center, walk the paved 0.5-mile Inscription Trail, passing hundreds of Euro-American inscriptions dating back to the 17th century (the earliest from 1605),

as well as Puebloan petroglyphs as much as a thousand years old. A spur loop off the Inscription Trail, the fairly strenuous Headland Trail ascends to the top of the bluff for great views of the Zuni Mountains and the volcanic El Malpais area. The Headland Trail also passes an ancestral Puebloan ruin called Atsinna, occupied circa A.D. 1275–1350.

Combined, the two trails amount to a 2-mile round trip.

The softness of the sandstone, which made possible these fascinating carved names and observations, also contributes to the slow erosion and loss of the inscriptions. The National Park Service continues to monitor the inscriptions and investigate ways to preserve them.

N. Mex. 53
Ramah, NM
505-783-4226
www.nps.gov/elmo

AT A GLANCE

Northwestern New Mexico, 100 miles west of Albuquerque ▪ 1,278 acres ▪ Year-round; winter snow can close Headland Trail ▪ Viewing prehistoric petroglyphs and historic inscriptions, hiking

Fort Union National Monument
Ruins of the post called the "guardian of the Santa Fe Trail"

Mexico's independence from Spain in 1821 led to the establishment of an important trade route that became known as the Santa Fe Trail (see p. 354), running from Missouri to the commercial center of Santa Fe. When the United States acquired the land that would become New Mexico in 1848, the military took on a greater role in protecting traffic along the significant route.

In 1851, a post and supply depot called Fort Union was established at the strategic intersection of the Mountain and Cimarron branches of the Santa Fe Trail. In its early years, mounted troops from the fort patrolled the trail; later, they served as escorts for mail stages. In the Civil War, soldiers from the fort faced raids by Confederate troops from Texas.

During its 40-year existence, three different forts were built (1851, 1862, and 1867), each near the site of the

Transport wagons like these were used by the U.S. Army at Fort Union.

other. The third was the largest fort in the Southwest. At its height, the soldier contingent numbered 1,666. In addition to the fort's adobe ruins, the Fort Union National Monument preserves the largest visible network of Santa Fe Trail ruts. A self-guided trail,

which can be walked in either a 0.5-mile or 1.6-mile loop, provides access to the ruins. The park visitor center shows an introductory film about Fort Union; and interpretive talks, guided tours, and living-history programs are offered in summer.

N. Mex. 161 (off I-25, exit 366)
Watrous, NM
505-425-8025
www.nps.gov/foun

AT A GLANCE

Northeastern New Mexico, 95 miles northeast of Santa Fe ▪ 721 acres ▪ Year-round ▪ Touring remains of historic 19th-century U.S. Army fort

Gila Cliff Dwellings National Monument

A Mogollon archaeological site in a beautiful national forest setting

Seven hundred years ago, people from a group that modern archaeologists call the Mogollon culture built structures of stone and wood in shallow alcoves in cliffs along the West Fork of the Gila River. Hundreds of years earlier, people who were probably their ancestors had built pithouses and aboveground dwellings in the same area. Today's Gila Cliff Dwellings National Monument focuses on the preservation and interpretation of the cliff dwellings, which were occupied for only a short time, circa A.D. 1270 to the early 1300s. No one knows why the site was abandoned or what happened to the inhabitants, though they may have moved to other pueblos in the region.

The national monument is reached from Silver City by hilly, twisting N. Mex. 15 or by the longer, less steep N. Mex. 35. A visitor center offers a short film on the Mogollon, and displays artifacts from the site along with other exhibits. Along the road to the parking lot for the ruins, watch on the east for the trailhead for the short Trail to the Past, which leads visitors to Native American pictographs.

The cliff dwellings are not visible from the road. A flat, easy walk along the canyon floor leads to a spot from which the structures can be seen high above. Reaching the dwellings requires hiking a trail that climbs 175 feet to their level. Five of the park's caves contain rock

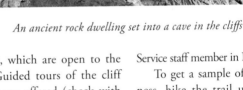

An ancient rock dwelling set into a cave in the cliffs

dwellings, which are open to the public. Guided tours of the cliff dwellings are offered (check with the park ahead of your visit for the schedule) although visitors can enter the ruins anytime the park is open.

The foundations of the cliffs were laid down beginning 28 million years ago, when three massive volcanoes erupted and molten ash filled their calderas. Several million years of subsequent volcanic activity overlaid the ash with layers of basaltic and related lavas. The capstone is Gila conglomerate, a composite of volcanic debris, representing millions of years of erosion.

Adjacent to the national monument is the Gila Wilderness, the largest wilderness in New Mexico and the world's first officially designated wilderness area. The Gila Wilderness was created in 1924 at the urging of famed conservationist Aldo Leopold, then a Forest

Service staff member in New Mexico.

To get a sample of the wilderness, hike the trail up the West Fork of the Gila River, which is a flat and easy trek for the first few miles. Beginning under high cliffs, the route passes through meadows to cross the rocky stream near beaver dams. Alligator junipers, piñon pines, willows, and cottonwoods border the trail. The endangered Gila trout, a golden-hued fish now making a comeback after near extinction, swims in the crystalline waters here. The trail soon enters a narrower, steep-sided canyon.

Another popular trail starts near the visitor center and runs up the Middle Fork of the Gila River. Just half a mile up the West Fork is a hot spring, one of many in the wilderness that remind travelers of the region's volcanic past. You must cross the stream twice in order to reach the hot spring.

N. Mex. 15
Silver City, NM
575-536-9461
www.nps.gov/gicl

AT A GLANCE

Southwestern New Mexico, 43 miles north of Silver City ▪ 533 acres ▪ Year-round; winter weather can affect accessibility ▪ Touring historic Native American structures, hiking adjacent wilderness

Old Spanish National Historic Trail

A groundbreaking trade route of the 19th-century Southwest

Traders eager to exploit new markets played a significant role in opening up today's American Southwest in the 19th century. As an end point of the Santa Fe Trail (see p. 354), the growing city of Santa Fe had a steady supply of goods for sale and trade. Far to the west, the village of Los Angeles was a potential market and source of goods and livestock, but there was no established route between the two communities, both in territory that belonged first to Spain and then after 1821, to Mexico.

In 1829, trader Antonio Armijo led the first commercial caravan from Santa Fe to Los Angeles. Others followed, using mostly pack mules to carry woolen goods west, and bringing horses and mules east. The route of the trail varied with weather conditions, relations with Indians, and when better water or other resources were found. Use of the trail declined after the United States acquired much of today's American Southwest at the end of the war with Mexico in 1848.

The Old Spanish National Historic Trail guides modern travelers along this trade route, which was highly influential in the development of the Southwest. Totaling 2,700 miles, the Old Spanish Trail includes routes in six states: New Mexico, Colorado, Utah, Arizona, Nevada, and California. The original Armijo route passes through Page, Arizona, while the North Branch winds to Grand Junction, Colorado, before heading west into Utah. The Main Route passes through Durango, Colorado, and Moab, Utah.

National Trails Intermountain Region, Santa Fe, NM
505-988-6098
www.nps.gov/olsp

AT A GLANCE
Varied routes from Santa Fe to Los Angeles ▪ 2,700 miles ▪ Year-round, though winter weather can affect travel in several areas ▪ Following historic trail, visiting diverse sites

Pecos National Historical Park

An eclectic look at southwestern heritage

One of the most eclectic historical sites in the National Park Service, Pecos National Historical Park encompasses history from pre-Columbian Native Americans, the era of Spanish missions, a Civil War battle, and 20th-century tourism and ranching.

One section of the park protects the site of an ancestral Puebloan community that became a thriving trade and cultural center in the 15th century. Later, in the 17th century, Spanish missionaries arrived and established a church at the pueblo, which was rebuilt after the original structure was destroyed in the Pueblo Revolt against the Spanish in 1680. A 1.25-mile self-guided trail leads to ruins of the pueblo and the mission church.

A self-guided 2.25-mile trail

The ruins of the Spanish mission church loom behind a kiva in the pueblo.

(sign-in required at the visitor center) brings visitors to the site of the

March 28, 1862, Battle of Glorieta Pass, in which Union forces defeated a Confederate army marching through New Mexico, intent on capturing the gold mines of Colorado and continuing to the California coast.

One other area of the park can be seen only on a guided tour *(seasonal)*. This tour visits the 1925 Forked Lightning Ranch, built by a colorful rodeo promoter, used for a time as a guesthouse, and later occupied by actress Greer Garson when she married its second owner. The ranch house has remained relatively unchanged, with original fixtures in the living and dining rooms.

N. Mex. 63
Pecos, NM
505-757-7241
www.nps.gov/peco

AT A GLANCE

Northeastern New Mexico, 25 miles east of Santa Fe ▪ 6,670 acres ▪ Year-round ▪ Touring pueblo and mission ruins, Civil War battleground, historic ranch

Petroglyph National Monument
A notable assemblage of Native American rock art

The landscape of the Southwest is peppered with examples of Native American rock art called petroglyphs. Unlike pictographs, which are images created using paint, petroglyphs are produced by carving or pecking away at the dark "desert varnish" (a mineral patina) on boulders or cliff faces to reveal lighter-colored rock underneath. Because such work is difficult to date, archaeologists are often uncertain about when such images were created. And though certain figures seem to be recognizable—handprints, snakes, birds, deer—the exact meanings can be elusive.

An extensive collection of such rock art is protected at Petroglyph National Monument, where more than 24,000 examples of petroglyphs have been located. Set in a striking volcanic landscape, including several ancient cones, the park offers an easy way for visitors to see,

Petroglyphs of hands in Piedras Marcadas Canyon

marvel at, and wonder about these ancient images.

Ancestral Puebloan people lived in the Rio Grande Valley beginning before A.D. 500, but archaeologists believe most of the petroglyphs in the park date from between 1300 and

the late 1600s. Both Indians and Spaniards created some of the petroglyphs in the period after Spain occupied the area, beginning about 1540.

Visitors to the monument should stop first at Las Imágenes Visitor Center for an introduction to the area. The monument's most popular site is Boca Negra Canyon, where three short, paved trails (all can be walked in about an hour) lead to views of about 200 petroglyphs. The natural trail at Rinconada Canyon (1.25 miles one way) passes along an escarpment of basalt, deposited in volcanic eruptions 200,000 years ago, where several hundred petroglyphs are visible, chipped into the dark patina.

At the Volcanoes Day Use Area, various loop trails wind around three volcanic cones (called JA, Black, and Vulcan), with excellent views of Albuquerque, the Rio Grande Valley, and the Sandia Mountains to the east.

Unser Blvd. (north off I-40)
Albuquerque, NM
505-899-0205
www.nps.gov/petr

AT A GLANCE

North-central New Mexico, just west of Albuquerque ▪ 7,236 acres ▪ Year-round ▪ Viewing ancient incised figures, hiking

Salinas Pueblo Missions National Monument

Three sites preserving Spanish mission churches and Native American pueblos

When 16th-century Spanish missionaries came to what is now New Mexico, they encountered thriving communities of Pueblo Indians who lived by farming, hunting, and gathering native food plants. The Spaniards established missions near many of these pueblos (as Native American villages in this area are known), to be close to the people they hoped to convert to Catholicism.

The Spaniards called this region—lying between the Manzano Mountains to the west and Mesa Jumanas to the east—Salinas, for the nearby salt lakes. The area, including missions and pueblos, was abandoned by both Spaniards and Pueblo Indians in the 1670s.

Farming was the main source of food for the pueblos (and, by extension, the associated missions), and a severe drought restricted water from snowmelt and rain that was needed for crops in this generally dry environment.

Salinas Pueblo Missions National Monument protects the sites of three 17th-century mission churches, as well as the ruins of pueblos at each location. Salinas Pueblo Missions was formed by the merging of the former Gran Quivira National Monument with two New Mexico state monuments, and it presently comprises three disjunct sites in the vicinity of Mountainair, New Mexico, where the park visitor center is located. All three sites

have visitor contact stations as well.

The Gran Quivira site, 25 miles south of Mountainair on N. Mex. 55, features a 0.5-mile trail through the remains of two churches (one later in construction date than the other) and an extensive pueblo, partially excavated. Quivira was the mythical "city of gold" sought by early Spanish conquistadores, and it's not known why the name came to be applied to this site—though its size may have led to associations of grandeur.

At Quarai, 8 miles north of Mountainair on N. Mex. 55, and Abó, 9 miles west on U.S. 60, trails lead to mission church ruins, as well as extensive walls of an unexcavated pueblo mound.

N. Mex. 55
Mountainair, NM
505-847-2585
www.nps.gov/sapu

AT A GLANCE

Central New Mexico, 50 miles southeast of Albuquerque ▪ 1,000 acres
▪ Year-round ▪ Visiting Spanish mission churches and pueblo ruins

Santa Fe National Historic Trail

A trade route that linked the Midwest and Southwest

For nearly 60 years, the Santa Fe Trail was a vital trade route, with goods moving in both directions between the United States in the east and Mexico in the southwest. When Mexico gained independence from Spain in 1821, previously banned commerce was allowed. This development started a stream of traders, military troops, gold seekers, and immigrants—in covered wagons or on horseback—between Missouri and Santa Fe, then part of Mexico. A rail line reached Santa Fe in 1880, soon

making the old route obsolete. But its heritage and romance have endured to the present day, as have scattered sections of the original trail with the ruts of wagon wheels still visible on the plains.

Santa Fe National Historic Trail was established to commemorate America's first important international thoroughfare, and to allow travelers to trace its path by using maps and road signs. Beginning in Franklin, Missouri (whence William Becknell set out on the first trip along the trail in 1821),

it heads west through Independence and Kansas City, then into Kansas though Council Grove and Larned to Dodge City.

From that point, the Santa Fe Trail splits into two main routes: the Cimarron Route, the shortest way, but considered more dangerous because of lack of water and danger of Indian attacks, and the Mountain Route to the north, longer and with more difficult terrain but generally safer. The former passed through what is now the Oklahoma Panhandle into New

The Santa Fe Trail's Mountain Route, as seen near Fort Union, was considered the safer of the trail's two routes.

Mexico, while the latter followed the Arkansas River westward into Colorado before turning south. For this reason, though a trip on the original Santa Fe Trail was a journey of about 900 miles, today's national historic trail covers about 1,200 miles.

Using the National Park Service website and available maps, travelers can explore many trail-related sites from Missouri to New Mexico. The National Frontier Trails Museum in Independence, Missouri, offers a fine introduction, with exhibits telling the story of the Santa Fe, Oregon, and other western trails.

Original wagon ruts from the trail can be seen clearly at Minor Park, in Kansas City, Missouri; at a site 9 miles west of Dodge City, Kansas; in the Kiowa National Grassland in northeastern New Mexico; at Fort Union National Monument (see p. 350) near Watrous, New Mexico; and in Santa Fe, among other places. Highlights of the trail include Fort Larned National Historic Site (see p. 266) near Larned, Kansas; Bent's Old Fort National Historic Site (see p. 322) near La Junta, Colorado; and the Santa Fe Plaza National Historic Landmark, with its associated Palace of the Governors, dating from Spanish rule in Mexico.

National Trails Intermountain Region
505-988-6098
www.nps.gov/safe
www.santafetrail.org

AT A GLANCE

Trail between central Missouri and Santa Fe, New Mexico ▪ 1,200 miles ▪ Year-round, though winter storms can impede travel ▪ Taking driving tour, visiting museums, trail segments, historic sites

Valles Caldera National Preserve

Recreation abounds on a supervolcano in the American Southwest

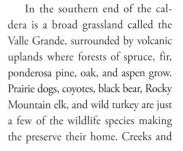

In the Jemez Mountains of New Mexico lies a caldera (a collapsed volcanic crater) nearly 12 miles across and more than 1.2 million years old. Within the circular caldera are wooded mountains, meandering streams, and broad grasslands, as well as wildlife that ranges from rainbow trout to golden eagles, and the state's second largest herd of elk.

Native Americans once hunted here, and in the 19th century this vast landscape became a private ranch. In 2000, the area's beauty and natural assets led to its acquisition by the U.S. Forest Service. In 2014, the 140-square-mile tract was transferred to the National Park Service as Valles Caldera National Preserve.

In the southern end of the caldera is a broad grassland called the Valle Grande, surrounded by volcanic uplands where forests of spruce, fir, ponderosa pine, oak, and aspen grow. Prairie dogs, coyotes, black bear, Rocky Mountain elk, and wild turkey are just a few of the wildlife species making the preserve their home. Creeks and wetlands add to the diversity of the flora and fauna.

As of this publication, facilities are limited at the preserve, but plans are under way to create additional amenities as well as increased access to trails for hiking, horseback riding, and (when the snow cover is sufficient) cross-country skiing and snowshoeing. Trails range from hiking-only paths to abandoned roads used by mountain bikes and equestrians.

39201 Hwy. 4
(mile marker 39.2)
Jemez Springs, NM
www.nps.gov/vall

AT A GLANCE Northern New Mexico, 50 miles northwest of Santa Fe ▪ 88,900 acres ▪ Year-round; winter may bring severe weather ▪ Hiking, horseback riding, cross-country skiing, mountain biking, fishing, hunting

White Sands National Monument
The world's largest expanse of gypsum sand dunes

In an intermountain basin in south-ern New Mexico, a rare series of geologic events created the right con-ditions to produce extensive dunes composed of the bright-white min-eral called gypsum. About 275 square miles of the dunes exist (the world's largest expanse of gypsum dunes), with most of them protected within White Sands National Monument.

More than 250 million years ago, repeated evaporation of a shallow sea laid down thick layers of gyp-sum, a type of calcium sulfate. After it receded permanently, the sea left behind a vast, flat expanse of land. Much later, after the region had been uplifted, a section of this expanse col-lapsed between fault lines, forming the Tularosa Basin and exposing the gypsum layers. With erosion, rain and snowmelt carry the water-soluble gypsum into the basin from sur-rounding uplands. In most regions, a river would then transport the still dissolved gypsum to the sea—but the Tularosa Basin has no outlet. Instead, the water collects in ephemeral Lake Lucero, where it evaporates and leaves behind gypsum in the form of selenite crystals. These crystals break down due to erosion, first forming small flakes. When they become small enough, prevailing winds pick up the gypsum grains, and carry them

Bleached Earless Lizard

northeast where they form dunes.

At the park visitor center, just off U.S. 70, you can learn about White Sands geology and ecology before starting on the park's 8-mile (one way) Dunes Drive. For the first couple of miles you'll have dunes on the south and Chihuahuan Desert grassland on the north.

Just as the road enters the dunes, the 1-mile Dune Life Nature Trail loops across the great waves of sand. The interpretive signs located along this trail explain how the animals survive in this harsh environment. Farther west, the wheelchair-accessible Interdune Boardwalk interpretive trail extends for a 0.33 mile through an area demonstrating the importance of the habitat between the tall dunes.

After a long period with little wind, the dunes can be covered with traces of desert dwellers, including the treadlike pattern of caterpillars, the "hieroglyphics" of darkling beetles, the X marks of roadrunners, and the paired dots of pocket mice—along with occasional tracks of larger crea-tures like coyotes, kit foxes, or badgers.

After winding through the dunes, the drive makes a short loop at the Heart of the Sands area. Here the Alkali Flat Trail leads across the dunes to the now dry bed of Lake Otero, which filled most of the Tularosa Basin in the last ice age a few thousand years ago. Long since evaporated, Lake Otero left an extensive moonscape of mineral crust to the west of White Sands. This walk follows posts across the otherwise featureless dunes for a 5-mile round trip; hikers need plenty of water and should turn back if blow-ing sand obscures visibility.

As long as you park in a desig-nated area (and there are many along the road), you're free to walk out across the sand. If you do, you may note that dunes exist in varying shapes. The first part of Dunes Drive passes through an area of parabolic dunes, where plants anchor the extremities of a formation while its middle is pushed forward by the wind, creating a U shape. Later, the road traverses barchan dunes, formed where strong winds fashion crescent shapes in areas with limited sand; and transverse dunes, created

when barchan dunes join in long ridges. Nearer Lake Lucero are dome dunes, low mounds of sand that are the first to form downwind from the gypsum deposits on the lakeshore.

Ranger-led tours visit Lake Lucero.

The park is adjacent to the White Sands Missile Range, and parts of the area are occasionally closed by military testing for brief periods.

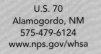

U.S. 70
Alamogordo, NM
575-479-6124
www.nps.gov/whsa

AT A GLANCE Southern New Mexico, 85 miles north of El Paso, Texas ▪ 144,000 acres ▪ Year-round ▪ Taking scenic drives, hiking, sand sledding, backpacking, picnicking

UTAH

The rocks of Utah's Colorado Plateau—colorful and relatively easily eroded—compose some of the most beautiful scenery found in North America: arches, spires, fins, hoodoos, and other formations of infinite shapes. Several national parks in southern Utah protect and offer access to much of the best of this terrain. Lake Powell, created on the state's southern border, provides a vast reservoir for boating and fishing. Rainbow Bridge, arguably the world's largest natural rock bridge, borders the lake. With large areas of sparsely populated land and the Wasatch Range, Utah offers skiing, backpacking, river rafting, and some of the country's most popular mountain-biking trails.

Arches National Park

The world's greatest concentration of rock arches

Rough Mules Ear wildflowers in bloom at Arches National Park

With more than 2,000 natural rock arches located in a relatively small site in the high desert of eastern Utah, Arches National Park boasts the world's highest density of these beautiful, graceful geologic features. A 45-mile round-trip scenic drive and hiking trails varying from easy to strenuous provide ways to see many of the most notable of the formations—including Delicate Arch, which the park, with reason, calls "the best-known arch in the world."

"Mysterious" might be another word applied to the arches. A look back at the region's geologic past, though, provides an explanation for how all these arches came to be concentrated here.

Geology Explained

About 300 million years ago, an arm of a sea covered this part of the globe, and as it repeatedly receded,

Utah's La Sal Mountains framed by Turret Arch

evaporated, and refilled, it left beds of salt that in places were thousands of feet thick. Geologists call this layer of salt the Paradox Formation. Much later, sand and other material was deposited atop the salt, eventually forming overlying layers of sandstone. At one time, the sandstone may have been more than a mile thick.

The weight of the sandstone caused the lower salt layer to flow and shift, which led to massive deformation of the sandstone above, including collapse into cavities, uplift into domes, and vertical cracks. Over millions of years, rain, ice, windblown grit, and other forces eroded the sandstone, in many cases forming thin, freestanding walls called fins. As these fins eroded, some collapsed. But when conditions were right their centers eroded away and left arches, ranging in size from 3-foot openings (the minimum size the park calls an arch) to one with an opening larger than the length of a football field. The major rock formations visible in Arches National Park today are in a layer of salmon-colored rock called Entrada sandstone. Not all formations are arches, of course. Throughout the park are tall spires, walls, and balanced rocks in an infinite variety of shapes and sizes.

The relentless force of erosion is still happening within the park, reshaping all the formations with greater or lesser effect. A large section of Skyline Arch fell in 1940, making its opening much larger; and in 1991 a part of famed Landscape Arch fell, making its fragile-looking curve look even more tenuous.

Visiting the Park

The park's visitor center is located 5 miles north of Moab, a town known among outdoors enthusiasts for its recreational opportunities, most especially mountain-biking trails. (Bicycles

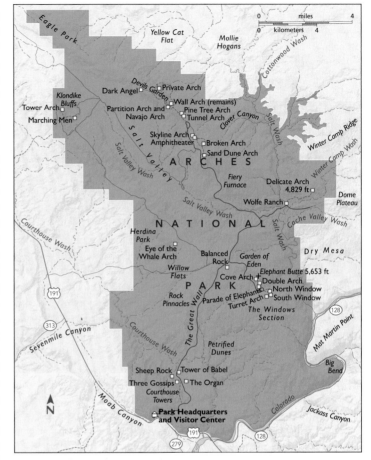

are restricted to roads within the national park.) Rangers at the visitor center can offer advice about the best way to spend your time. Tickets for the popular ranger-led tour through the rugged Fiery Furnace area can be reserved up to six months in advance online (*www.recreation.gov*) or otherwise must be bought at the visitor center. Hikers are allowed into Fiery Furnace on their own, but only after getting a permit and watching a video on safety and resource protection.

The park's 18-mile scenic drive features many roadside parking areas and overlooks. (The park asks visitors to stop only at designated areas in order to avoid erosion and to protect plant life.) Near the beginning of the road is the Courthouse Towers Viewpoint, and beyond that

point the drive passes through an area where ancient sand dunes were turned to stone. A 0.3-mile loop trail leads to Balanced Rock, which is a huge chunk of sandstone perched precariously on a pedestal that seems too small to support it. The late environmental writer Edward Abbey lived here when he was a summer park ranger; his book *Desert Solitaire* relates his experiences.

For visitors short on time, the Windows area is probably the park's highest priority site. The road passes by a collection of spires called the Garden of Eden, and several short, easy trails lead to close-up views of arches, including Double Arch, where two arches share a common base.

A side road to Wolfe Ranch offers two ways to see the park's most famous arch. The Delicate Arch Viewpoint provides a mile-distant look at the arch; an up-close look at the arch requires a fairly exposed, steep, and strenuous 3-mile round-trip hike, passing petroglyphs (incised rock art) left by the Ute Indians along the way. Such an icon is Delicate Arch that it graces the Utah license plate. Many people enjoy being here at sunset for the best photography, or just to enjoy the rich colors.

The main park road continues to an overlook at the Fiery Furnace area. A dense, amazingly varied array of spires and fins, Fiery Furnace can be disorienting to hikers and has suffered damage from careless visitors—reasons why a permit and introductory film are required for individual hikers. Ranger-led tours fill early, so popular is this site. When the setting sun tints the reddish stone, it's easy to see where the name "Fiery" came from.

The main park road ends at the Devils Garden area. The major trail here is a strenuous 7.2-mile round trip, but it's less than a mile down the trail, through towering sandstone fins, to reach the park's second most famous formation, Landscape Arch. With its delicate opening spanning 306 feet, it's one of the largest rock arches in the world. The rock that forms the arch is strikingly thin in places, and as erosion continues its work this spectacular formation inevitably will crack and fall to earth. It's another mile past Landscape Arch to 160-foot-wide Double O Arch, named because it rises above a smaller rock tunnel inside. On this part the trail follows some narrow sections with exposure to heights. Another formation along the Devils Garden

Trail, Wall Arch, collapsed in August 2008; it had been the 12th largest arch in the park.

Check with a ranger before heading down the often rough (and sometimes impassable) side road to the Klondike Bluffs. The attraction here is the 3.4-mile Tower Arch Trail. The path winds through an impressive landscape of fins, spires, and weirdly shaped hoodoos before arriving at Tower Arch, named for a rock tower beside it.

Ecology

Though not as scenic as the rock formations in Arches National Park, the dark crust that forms on the surface of the ground in many places is a vital part of the ecosystem. Called biological soil crust or cryptobiotic soil, it is composed of cyanobacteria along with lichens, mosses, algae, tiny fungi, and other organisms. Cyanobacteria, formerly called blue-green algae, are extremely ancient forms of life that, together with other living matter, bind the desert soil to lessen erosion, fix nitrogen, and make conditions more suitable for the growth of plants. One footprint can destroy this biological soil crust, which is why hikers are asked to stay on established trails or walk on bare rock or in dry washes.

Throughout the park are small basins called ephemeral pools or potholes, which collect rainwater and windblown sediment, forming tiny ecosystems where an array of plants and animals have adapted to life in the desert and found ways to survive in a harsh environment. Not only do temperatures range from well over 100°F to below freezing but also these temporary bodies of water often completely

dry up. Among the creatures that live in ephemeral pools permanently or temporarily are tadpoles, fairy shrimp, snails, and various insects.

Much more charismatic are the mammals of Arches National Park. Although many animals are nocturnal and seldom seen, visitors may spot mule deer, coyotes, porcupines, rock squirrels, and black-tailed jackrabbits, among others. The park's most notable mammal is the desert bighorn sheep, once threatened with extinction by disease, habitat loss, and hunting. In 1975, there were only an estimated thousand desert bighorns in Utah. Desert bighorns were reintroduced to Arches National Park from a native population in nearby Canyonlands National Park (see p. 364). Though there are less than 30 bighorns in Arches, and visitors are highly unlikely to see one, the Utah population has grown to several thousand.

Activities in the Park

Backpacking is allowed in Arches National Park *(free permit required),* but because sections away from roads, trails, and other developed sites are limited, the park has a relatively small area of true backcountry. Hikers should be aware that there are no designated trails, campsites, or reliable water sources away from developed areas of the park. Steep terrain, loose rock, lightning, flash floods, and dehydration are safety concerns.

Rock climbing is also allowed in the park, but there are restrictions on sites, equipment, and other factors. No climbing is allowed on any named arches, for example. Climbers should check with the park office for other conditions and constraints.

Off U.S. 191
Moab, UT
435-719-2299
www.nps.gov/arch

AT A GLANCE

Eastern Utah, 80 miles southwest of Grand Junction, Colorado ▪ 76,519 acres ▪ Year-round ▪ Taking scenic drives, hiking, camping

Bryce Canyon National Park

A wonderland of red-rock hoodoos and natural amphitheaters

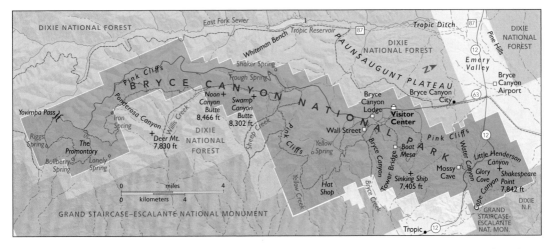

S mall compared to many national parks in the Southwest, Bryce Canyon nonetheless ranks among the most spectacular and rewarding of all America's parks. Packed into its 56 square miles are vast numbers of strikingly varied and colorful rock formations—most especially the grotesquely shaped spires called hoodoos. A Forest Service employee in 1915, upon first looking out over the landscape of Bryce Canyon, called it a scene of "indescribable beauty." One name proposed for a national monument here was "Temple of the Gods."

Geology Explained

Bryce Canyon is not a canyon—that is, it's not a valley created by a stream flowing along the bottom. Instead, the astounding rock formations and cliffs here lie at the edge of the Paunsaugunt Plateau, and are part of the geologic series of rock layers called the Grand Staircase, covering 20,000 square miles and including the Grand Canyon. The generally flat plateau lies to the west, while the terrain to the east of the escarpment drops 2,000 feet to the Paria Valley.

Because of the nature of the limestone at the cliff edge, weathering creates the particular formations displayed within the park. In winter, snowmelt enters small cracks, and when it freezes expansion splits off pieces of rock in a process called frost-wedging. (Each year there is an average of 200 days when the temperature rises above freezing and then drops below that point again at night.) Rain comes seldom to this high desert environment, but when it does the runoff causes even more erosion, especially during the summer monsoons.

Weathering forces create ridges and the thin walls that are called fins. Over time these fins erode into separate stacks or spires. Caps of resistant rock such as dolomite protect softer forms of limestone underneath. Erosion also creates narrow canyons and "windows," where a hole has been created in a fin.

On a broader scale, the edge of the Paunsaugunt Plateau erodes into horseshoe-shape or bowl-like cliff sections called amphitheaters. The most popular activity in the park is simply to stand at the edge of one of these mini-canyons and admire the formations below. Several hiking trails offer the chance to see hoodoos and other formations up close, for those who want to descend below the plateau rim.

Bryce Canyon is named for Ebenezer Bryce, a Mormon settler who, with his wife, Mary, moved to the area in 1875. Though they moved to Arizona just five years later, the name Bryce's Canyon continued to be used.

Visiting the Park

The park visitor center shows a fine introductory video every half hour, and it features exhibits on geology and the natural and cultural history of the area. Early May through early October, a shuttle bus operates in the park to help cut down on traffic congestion. (At peak times, four vehicles enter the park for every one parking space.) The shuttle makes regular stops at overlooks and campgrounds.

Come prepared for your visit to Bryce Canyon. Wear hiking boots on the steep trails. Carry water and sunscreen while outdoors. Located at 8,000 to 9,000 feet in elevation, the air at Bryce is thin; avoid overexerting yourself. In the summer watch out for lightning; in the winter expect snow and cold temperatures.

Overlooks & Trails

Just inside the park boundary, a mile-long side road leads to Fairyland Point, one of the finest panoramas in the park, with a close, eye-level look at typically varied hoodoos. The hoodoos here are geologically younger than those located farther south along the park drive. A hiking trail, one of the park's longer and more strenuous, drops down into Fairyland.

Side roads in the vicinity of the visitor center and the park lodge lead to several overlooks of famous Bryce Amphitheater, including Sunrise, Sunset, Inspiration, and Bryce (which probably compose the park's most visited sites). Sunrise and Bryce Points are highly recommended to be viewed at sunrise, Inspiration Point and Paria View at sunset. (Arrive an hour and a half before sunset to watch the colors change on the rock formations.) The panoramas at Bryce Amphitheater take in a vast number of hoodoos and other formations, which have been given fanciful names such as Alligator, Silent City, Thor's Hammer, Queen Victoria, and the Sinking Ship.

The 1.8-mile round-trip Queen's Garden Trail, beginning at Sunrise Point, is the easiest path that descends below the amphitheater rim to wind among the rock formations. It's here that the hoodoo called Queen Victoria seems to look out over the landscape. The trail links with other trails in the amphitheater area to allow the exploration of sites such as the steep-sided gorge called Wall Street.

The 5.5-mile (one way) Rim Trail runs from Bryce Point to Fairyland Point, offering countless views down across the escarpment. The section between Sunrise and Sunset Points is quite flat and easy. Also beginning at Bryce Point is the strenuous Hat Shop Trail, which descends 1,436 feet in 2 miles to a view of a cluster of hoodoos with balanced-rock caps.

All along the 18-mile (one way) Rainbow Point Drive are more viewpoints, including beautiful Natural Bridge, a rock arch 85 feet across and 125 feet high. The road reaches a turnaround spot at Rainbow Point, the park's highest elevation at 9,115 feet. The 1-mile Bristlecone Loop Trail here passes through forests of white fir, blue spruce, and Douglas fir to cliffs with expansive vistas where bristlecone pines grow. Some bristlecone pines here have lived to be more than 1,600 years old.

A favorite route for backpackers is the 22.9-mile Under-the-Rim Trail, which accesses eight backcountry campsites. Permits *(fee)* are required for overnight stays in the backcountry, and hikers should be prepared for strenuous walking and take precautions appropriate for remote areas; encounters with black bears are possible.

A private concessionaire offers horse and mule rides through Bryce Canyon *(spring–fall)*. Trips last two or four hours and wind through Bryce Amphitheater, providing a way to get close to its formations without hiking down and back. Check with the visitor center for contact information.

Flora & Fauna

The 2,000-foot difference in elevation within the park results in there being three distinct ecological zones: spruce-fir forest at higher sites, ponderosa pine forest lower, on plateau tops, and piñon pine–juniper forest at the lowest areas. There once was much more quaking aspen in the park, but past fire-suppression efforts have reduced stands of the tree, which turns brilliant yellow or orange in fall. Prescribed burns are bringing back aspen, which is a fast-growing pioneer species that colonizes areas cleared by fires and is eventually shaded out by conifers.

Elk, mule deer, pronghorn, black bear, mountain lion, golden-mantled ground squirrel, and Utah prairie dog are among the mammal residents of the park. Birds include golden eagle, peregrine falcon, Steller's jay, common raven, Clark's nutcracker, dusky grouse, black-chinned hummingbird, and pygmy nuthatch. Lucky bird-watchers might even see a California condor, a critically endangered bird that has been reintroduced in northern Arizona and occasionally soars to Bryce Canyon.

Stargazing

Far from the "light pollution" of cities, with a high elevation and clean, dry air, Bryce Canyon is renowned among stargazers for its dark night sky. On an average night, there may be 7,500 stars visible, compared to 2,500 in other rural areas in the U.S. Check at the park visitor center for a schedule of astronomy-related activities, which include solar viewing, night-sky programs, multimedia shows, and a variety of lectures from visiting professional and amateur astronomers.

Utah 63
Bryce, UT
435-834-5322
www.nps.gov/brca

AT A GLANCE

Southern Utah, 120 miles northeast of St. George ▪ 35,835 acres ▪ Year-round; winter snow can temporarily close some roads ▪ Driving scenic route, hiking, horseback riding, camping, stargazing

Bryce Canyon is studded with hoodoos (irregular spires) and fins protruding from the plateau, created by erosion.

Canyonlands National Park

A remote and pristine expanse of canyons, mesas, and river gorges

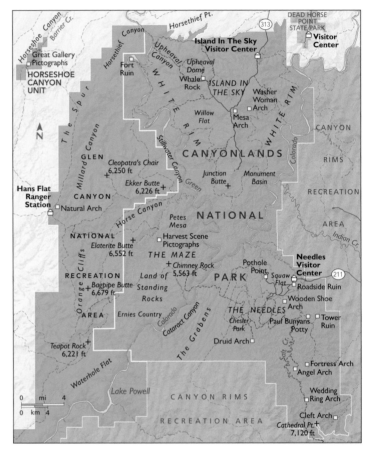

One of the most rewarding aspects of the National Park System is its near-endless diversity. Ecosystems, geology, climate, flora and fauna—all are represented in a variety that presents infinite opportunity for exploration and discovery.

Ways of experiencing parks are diverse, too: Some parks are located near cities, with miles of paved roads, abundant amenities, and attractions that are easily accessible to even casual visitors. Canyonlands National Park is different. While it has some paved roads leading to spectacular views, most of the park is accessible only to hikers, boaters, and mountain bikers, and along a network of rough unpaved roads requiring high-clearance four-wheel-drive vehicles. Of the parks in the lower 48 states, Canyonlands ranks among those with the most remote and difficult-to-reach sections.

The positive side of this remoteness, of course, is the solitude, beauty, and adventure the park offers to intrepid visitors. Canyonlands protects one of the most unspoiled areas of the vast Colorado Plateau, a high-desert region of stark rock formations, deep river-cut canyons, and sparse vegetation that receives less than 10 inches of rain in an average year.

Two of the West's iconic rivers, the Colorado and the Green, come together in the center of Canyonlands National Park. Their canyons, forming a rough Y shape, divide the park into three land sections. Between the two arms of the Y is a high mesa called Island in the Sky, 1,000 feet above the surrounding landscape and more than 2,000 feet higher than the site of the rivers' confluence. To the east is The Needles, a land of tall, colorful sandstone pinnacles. To the west is The Maze, reachable from the other sections only by a long, roundabout journey involving unpaved roads. Because of the remoteness of The Maze and time needed to reach it, most visitors spend at least three days exploring it. Park rangers, with good reason, describe the rivers themselves as a fourth section of Canyonlands.

Geology Explained

Canyonlands sits in the central part of the Colorado Plateau, a vast region that comprises many layers of sedimentary rock deposited over eons of time as coastal sands, salt left by evaporating oceans, lakeside mudflats, and other geologic features. About 15 million years ago, the entire plateau was uplifted as a relatively flat plain. What once was at sea level now averages nearly a mile above that elevation. In geologic terms the plateau has remained quite stable since, with little alteration by earthquakes, rifting, or mountain-building.

Geologically stable doesn't mean unchanged, however. For 15 million years erosive forces have eaten away the soft rock of the Colorado

Plateau: Rivers have carved deep canyons, ice has split rock walls, rain has little by little crumbled cliff edges. That erosion has created landscapes of strikingly rugged beauty, displayed especially well in the river gorges, buttes, and pinnacles of Canyonlands National Park.

Island in the Sky

The park's Island in the Sky district is the most accessible for travelers, with its visitor center just 40 minutes from the lodging and other services available in the town of Moab. Those with limited time in the park should drive directly to Grand View Point, where the panorama is, as advertised, grand. An easy 1-mile (one way) trail here leads out to the tip of Island in the Sky mesa.

Secondary priorities (all easily done in less than a day) begin with a visit to the mysterious formation called Upheaval Dome. A 0.5-mile (one way) trail leads from the parking area to an overlook of the 3-mile-wide craterlike formation, which is thought to be either an eroded salt dome or the impact crater of a meteorite that hit around 60 million years ago. Whatever it is, it's worth seeing.

Near the fork in the paved road through Island in the Sky is the short side road to Green River Overlook, where the broad vista includes a stretch of the river far below, with the wild country of The Maze on the horizon beyond. Also near the fork is an easy 0.25-mile (one way) trail to Mesa Arch, a rock arch that is set on a cliff edge. Sunrise at Mesa Arch ranks high on the special attractions at Canyonlands.

For those with ample time, the Island in the Sky district offers many other opportunities. Mountain bikers and visitors with high-clearance 4WD vehicles can explore part or all of famous White Rim Road (permits

required for overnight trips), which loops for 100 miles around the mesa. Speak to a ranger before undertaking any trip along this very rough road. No water is available, and a broken-down car may bring towing charges of more than $1,000.

The Needles

The Needles district of Canyonlands, reached via Utah 211 west from U.S. 191, takes its name from tall, narrow spires of reddish-and-tan sandstone. Past the visitor center is the Roadside Ruin Trail, which takes visitors along an easy walk to a granary used by the ancestral Puebloan people who lived in this area before European settlement; the site was abandoned more than 700 years ago.

The paved road into The Needles ends at Big Spring Canyon Overlook, where the 6.5-mile (one way) Confluence Overlook Trail leads to a cliff viewpoint down to the spot where the Colorado and Green Rivers come together. The easier nearby Slickrock Trail (1.2 miles one way) reaches several excellent viewpoints.

The 3-mile side road (unpaved but passable by two-wheel-drive

cars) to Elephant Hill provides distant views of the colorful Needles. A trailhead along this route gives access to several moderately long and strenuous hikes to see these fantastic spires up close. Many loop trips are possible by combining various trails. A good map and route-finding skills are necessary to enjoy the excellent views along the 11-mile (round trip) Elephant Canyon–Druid Arch hike, for example. The Needles derive their layered colors from different types of sandstone that were created from a dune field on the edge of a shallow sea more than 240 million years ago. Some layers of the sandstone were tinted reddish by iron-containing minerals, while others show the pale color of purer sand.

The Maze

The Maze district of Canyonlands, west of the Green and Colorado Rivers, is reached by turning south off I-70 at the town of Green River. It's two and a half hours to reach the ranger station on paved and unpaved roads. Two-wheel-drive vehicles can make it to the ranger station and a short distance beyond, but to really

A grotto shelters ancient Puebloan ruins in Canyonlands.
FOLLOWING PAGES: *Island in the Sky high country.*

explore The Maze requires a high-clearance 4WD vehicle. There is no gasoline, food, or potable water in this area of the park. Well-prepared hikers ready for primitive conditions can access steep-walled canyons for a true backcountry experience.

Horseshoe Canyon

The Horseshoe Canyon Unit of Canyonlands, a disjunct section of the national park, is best known for the Great Gallery, large ghostlike figures that were painted on a rock wall with red ocher. This collection of rock art dates back at least 2,000 years, and possibly as much as 7,000 years. A 6.5-mile round-trip hike is required to reach the site of the ancient rock art figures.

Green & Colorado Rivers

Boating on the Green and Colorado Rivers has long been a popular activity on the stretches through Canyonlands National Park. There are flat-water sections great for sea kayaks and canoes, and serious white water through Cataract Canyon after the rivers' confluence. Local outfitters are authorized by the park to provide services to boaters. In recent years, though, drought has led to very low water levels in Lake Powell downstream from the park, affecting the types of river trips that are available. Check with the park or local outfitters for conditions. Arranging put-in and take-out points and shuttles can be complicated; again, inquire about logistics and park requirements for waste disposal and other regulations.

Wildlife

While mule deer and cottontail rabbits may be the most commonly seen mammals in Canyonlands (and beavers are sometimes sighted by boaters), the park's most noteworthy mammal resident is the desert bighorn sheep. Once seriously threatened with extinction, this form of bighorn was reduced to a population of around a hundred individuals in the park and only a few thousand in total. There are now around 200 desert bighorn sheep in the park, and animals have been relocated from Canyonlands to stock other sites with suitable habitat.

Utah 313 & Utah 211
Moab, UT
435-719-2313
www.nps.gov/cany

AT A GLANCE

Southeastern Utah, 110 miles southwest of Grand Junction, Colorado
■ 337,598 acres ■ Year-round ■ Hiking, biking, boating, camping, backpacking, horseback riding, exploring in 4WD vehicles

Capitol Reef National Park
A magnificent desert textbook of geologic features

Though one of the lesser known of the Southwest's national parks, Capitol Reef offers many rewards to visitors, from strikingly scenic rock formations to fascinating human history. Much of the park is somewhat difficult to access, especially when weather conditions make unpaved roads impassable, but for most of the year a careful visitor will discover a fascinating wealth in its canyons, buttes, and washes.

Geology Explained

One geologic feature dominates the landscape of Capitol Reef: Waterpocket Fold, a nearly 100-mile-long fold in Earth's crust, exposed as a high ridge running north-south through the

A mule deer grabs a snack in Fruita.

long, narrow park. Waterpocket Fold is a classic example of a monocline: a warp or dip in a region of horizontal rock layers. The fold formed between 50 and 70 million years ago when mountains were being uplifted in western North America. Massive forces caused movement of a fault buried deep underground, and rock layers on the surface warped upward along a long line corresponding to the fault.

Erosion working on the warped rock over millions of years has created the steep-sided ridge seen in the park today. The word "reef" was applied by early prospectors to the sort of long, high ridge that was a barrier to travel; geologically speaking, it has nothing to do with coral reefs found in oceans.

"Capitol" came from the resemblance of high, white sandstone domes in the area to the domes of capitol buildings. The fold's name, "Waterpocket," was derived from the tendency of soft sandstone to be eroded into numerous small basins or potholes that retain water. In this dry climate, these pockets of water can be vital for many types of life, and they serve as miniature ecosystems in their own right.

The park visitor center on Utah 24 offers exhibits on geology, nature, and history, as well as an introductory audiovisual program. Check the schedule of ranger-led programs, offered May through September, including guided walks, talks, and evening programs at the park amphitheater.

Scenic Drive

The national park's 8-mile, paved Scenic Drive runs south from the visitor center. Travelers with limited time should make this route their first priority. Unpaved side roads lead into Grand Wash and Capitol Gorge. Though the side roads are generally accessible to regular passenger vehicles, drivers should be aware that the narrow canyons in the park are subject to sudden flash floods, and they should never enter a steep-sided gorge during stormy conditions. This can happen anytime of year but is especially prevalent July through September.

Just a little way from the start of the drive, where Sulphur Creek flows into the Fremont River, stands the now abandoned farming community of Fruita, where residents once raised livestock, grew crops, and planted fruit trees. Founded by Mormon settlers in the 1880s, Fruita was a green oasis town in a generally desert environment for nearly a century; the last resident moved away in 1969. The 200-acre Fruita Rural Historic District is listed on the National Register of Historic Places. Visitors today can

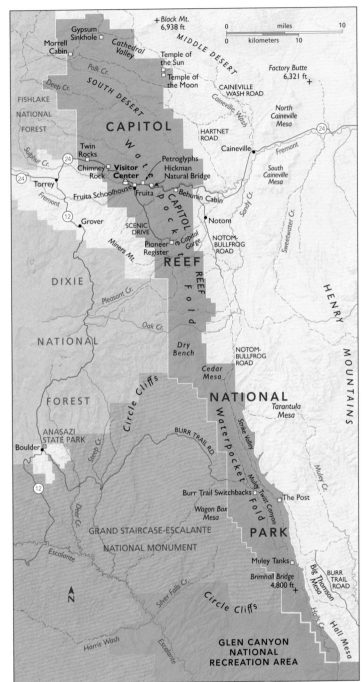

visit a blacksmith shop; a one-room schoolhouse; and the Gifford homestead, comprising a 1908 farmhouse, barn, smokehouse, garden, pasture, and rock walls.

A thriving orchard of around 2,700 fruit trees, a legacy of the farm

families who lived in Fruita, is protected and cultivated by park staff; the fruit can be harvested (fee) by visitors. The plantings are primarily of cherry, apricot, peach, pear, and apple, with a few plum, mulberry, almond, and walnut trees. The harvest season runs

Formed of Navajo sandstone, Capitol Dome, rising above the Fremont River, glows red with the setting sun.

generally from mid-June (the first cherries) to mid-October (the last apples); call the park for more information on when to visit for blossoms and harvests.

At the end of the 1-mile drive into Grand Wash, trails lead into the narrowest, most spectacular part of the canyon; a strenuous 1.7-mile trail leads up to Cassidy Arch. The rock arch was named for the notorious outlaw Butch Cassidy, who is said to have used Grand Wash as a hideout in the late 19th century.

Spectacular sandstone formations in varied colors, white domes that gave the park its name, and the remains of uranium-mining activities from decades ago line the length of Scenic Drive. Where the paved road ends, a dirt road—the main road through the area until Utah 24 was paved alongside the Fremont River in 1962—leads into narrow Capitol Gorge. The gorge features petroglyphs made by the Fremont Indians, who lived in the area circa A.D. 600–1200; and markings left by early Euro-American settlers. Capitol Gorge, like Grand Wash, can experience sudden flash floods, and caution is needed in threatening weather.

Returning to the end of the Scenic Drive, high-clearance 4WD vehicles can, in good conditions, continue on unpaved Pleasant Creek Road and South Draw Road to Utah 12, west of the park. For most vehicles, the Scenic Drive is an out-and-back route.

Cathedral Valley

To see more of the park, consider taking a 58-mile loop tour through Cathedral Valley, north of Utah 24. Though roads here are unpaved, they are passable most of the year for high-clearance vehicles *(ask at the visitor center about road conditions.)* Most visitors turn north off Utah 24 at Hartnet Road, 11 miles east of the visitor center. There is a ford of the Fremont River here that is drivable most of the time, except during high water after storms and for more extended periods during spring runoff. The road continues to reach dramatically beautiful, multicolored mesas, spires, and other rock formations with names such as Walls of Jericho and the Temple of the Moon. Quite visible in many places are black boulders that stand out from the rest of the landscape. Remnants of lava flows that capped nearby mountains about 20 million years ago, they were eroded and later moved to lower locations by various processes, including glacial melting. There are several panoramic vistas—and a primitive campground at midpoint—along the route, which returns to Utah 24 at the rural community of Caineville.

Notom-Bullfrog Road

Another driving option is the Notom-Bullfrog Road, which heads south from Utah 24 about 9 miles east of the visitor center. Paved for its first 15 miles, it then becomes dirt, though not bad for regular vehicles under good weather conditions. This road runs along the eastern side of the Waterpocket Fold into the southern section of Capitol Reef National Park, known as the Waterpocket District. There's wonderful scenery along this route, and access to the primitive Cedar Mesa campground, 21 miles south of Utah 24.

Thirty-two miles from Utah 24 is the intersection with the Burr Trail Road. A west turn here leads across the national park, into Grand Staircase–Escalante National Monument, and on to Utah 12 at the town of Boulder. A north turn on Utah 12 leads back to Utah 24 and the visitor center for a 147-mile loop. Check with park personnel before undertaking this drive, which features very steep switchbacks. Even if you don't want to make the entire loop, consider heading west for about 35 miles on Burr Trail Road to reach the turn to Strike Valley Overlook. The route to the overlook may require a high-clearance 4WD vehicle, but many people walk the 2.9 miles through a beautiful canyon to viewpoints into Muley Twist Canyon.

Utah 24

Several park attractions are accessible from Utah 24 both west and east of the visitor center. A turnoff south of the highway, west of the visitor center, leads to two short trails with excellent views: the Goosenecks Trail, looking down to winding Sulphur Creek; and the slightly longer (0.4 mile) Sunset Point Trail. The latter is renowned as a spot from which to watch the colors change on rock formations as the sun goes down.

East of the visitor center is a turnout to see petroglyphs incised into a cliff face by prehistoric Fremont Indians. A bit farther east is the 2-mile round-trip, moderately strenuous Hickman Bridge Trail, a self-guided nature hike that leads to the base of a natural rock bridge. Continuing east, you'll reach the Behunin Cabin, a one-room rock house that once was home to a pioneer family of ten. (Most of the children slept in shelters outside the house.)

Utah 24
Torrey, UT
435-425-3791
www.nps.gov/care

AT A GLANCE

South-central Utah, 200 miles south of Salt Lake City ▪ 244,601 acres ▪ Year-round ▪ Hiking, camping, backpacking, taking scenic drives, fruit picking

Cedar Breaks National Monument
A high-elevation showcase of colorful rock spires

Small compared with some of the better known National Park Service sites in southern Utah, Cedar Breaks National Monument is nevertheless a real gem—full of multicolored rock formations displaying the sculpting power of millions of years of erosion.

The story of the colorful rock formations at Cedar Breaks begins with a large lake that occupied this area more than 60 million years ago. Sediments collected in the lake bottom and over time were transformed into limestone, sandstone, and siltstone. Volcanic ash later added more material to the rock layers. Ten million years ago, movement along a fault raised the Markagunt Plateau, on which the present park now lies. Erosion along the cliff edge of the fault gradually turned the exposed limestone into fins (tall, thin walls of rock) and hoodoos (irregularly shaped pillars). Where the rocks contain traces of iron, they display shades of red, orange, and yellow; where manganese is present, the color can be almost purple.

Visiting the Park

Cedar Breaks lies at a much higher elevation than most other national parks and monuments in the Colorado Plateau region. The visitor center sits at more than 10,000 feet, and massive winter snows blanket the park late fall through spring. The visitor center and other facilities close mid-October through late May. The Cedar Breaks Scenic Drive remains open until snowdrifts make it impassable, which

The amphitheater of Cedar Breaks

happens anytime from late October to early December. Check with the park before making a trip at shoulder seasons. (Cross-country skiers, snowshoers, and snowmobilers frequent the park in winter, and in recent years a tentlike winter visitor center has been set up and staffed by volunteers.)

The centerpiece of Cedar Breaks is a large natural amphitheater where the plateau drops to adjacent lowland, full of an infinite variety of formations. Overlooks along the scenic drive offer vistas of the bowl-like canyon. For a closer look, the 4-mile Spectra Point–Ramparts Overlook Trail follows the rim for stunning views. The 2-mile Alpine Pond Nature Trail features a double loop; the lower trail offers

more views of rock formations, while the upper part passes through a forest of Englemann spruce, subalpine fir, and aspen. On summer weekends, park rangers lead interpretive hikes on both these trails; check at the visitor center for times and details.

A much longer third trail, the Rattlesnake Creek Trail, begins just outside the national monument's north entrance. It drops 2,500 feet over 4 miles to reach Ashdown Creek, where hikers then may parallel the creek upstream into the canyons of Cedar Breaks.

Ecology

Many of the park's spruce trees have been killed in recent years by an outbreak of an insect called the spruce bark beetle. Other trees, such as fir, Douglas fir, and limber pine, fill in the forest gaps left by the dead spruce, which will make a comeback when the beetle numbers return to normal. By the way, the "cedars" of Cedar Breaks are actually junipers; here, as in many places in North America, cedar has become the local common name for various species of juniper. "Breaks" is a word used across the West for rugged badland terrain where the landscape is broken, as at the edge of a mesa.

The park's most notable tree may be the bristlecone pine, some specimens of which are widely regarded as among Earth's oldest living things. One bristlecone at Cedar Breaks is believed to be more than 1,600 years old.

Utah 148
Cedar City, UT
435-586-0787
www.nps.gov/cebr

AT A GLANCE

Southwestern Utah, 65 miles northeast of St. George ▪ 6,155 acres
▪ Road open late spring through fall; accessible for winter sports
▪ Taking scenic drive, hiking

Dinosaur National Monument

A treasure trove of Jurassic-period fossils

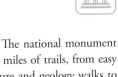

In 1909, paleontologist Earl Douglass, from Pittsburgh's Carnegie Museum, found eight vertebrae of a dinosaur called *Apatosaurus* in the arid badlands of eastern Utah. Douglass had stumbled upon one of the world's greatest collections of dinosaur fossils.

Skeleton of an allosaur, an early regional inhabitant

Douglass Quarry

During the period of intensive excavation that lasted until 1924, a tremendous number of complete skeletons, skulls, and juvenile specimens of many different kinds of dinosaurs were taken from the Douglass Quarry, as the site came to be called. Aside from those in the famed Carnegie Museum, fossils from this site are displayed at the Smithsonian Institution, the Denver Museum of Natural History, and other museums around the world. Remains of ten species of dinosaurs have been found in the area, ranging in length from less than a foot to around 76 feet.

The Douglass Quarry was given federal protection in 1915, and in 1938 it was vastly expanded into Colorado to include stretches of the Green and Yampa Rivers (an action that would have great effect on future recreational use of the park).

While many dinosaur quarries have had all their fossils removed, Dinosaur National Monument left a large wall of fossils in situ for public observation. In 1957 a structure was built to simultaneously protect the fossils and allow the public to see them up close. Unfortunately, the building was placed on unstable soil, and in 2006 it was closed for safety issues. The building went through a multiyear reconstruction effort, and was reopened in 2011. In addition to viewing the "wall of bones," as it is known, visitors can hike the 1.2-mile Fossil Discovery Trail to see fragments of fossils naturally eroding out of the rock.

Other Attractions

The famed quarry area is only a very small part of Dinosaur National Monument. Many visitors come to whitewater raft on the Green and Yampa Rivers, enjoying the scenery of river canyons and surging through rapids such as Warm Springs and Hells Half Mile. Commercial outfitters (ask the park for a list of approved firms) offer trips of various types, and private trips are allowed with a permit.

The national monument has miles of trails, from easy nature and geology walks to treks through remote back-country *(permit required for backpacking)*. Only well-prepared and experienced hikers should venture off established trails in this harsh terrain.

Though the visitor center on the Utah side of the national monument is the focal point for learning about dinosaurs, the Canyon Visitor Center, near Dinosaur, Colorado, is the gateway to much of the monument's best scenery, as well as access to the Green and Yampa Rivers. The Harpers Corner auto-tour road leads to the 2-mile Harpers Corner Trail, which offers wonderful views into three river canyons at the confluence of the Green and Yampa. The road itself features many overlooks of badlands scenery.

In addition to its other attractions, the monument is home to hundreds of examples of rock art left by the people of the Fremont culture, who lived here circa A.D. 200–1300. These Native Americans, who lived partly as hunter-gatherers and partly as farmers, left both petroglyphs (patterns chipped or carved into the rock) and pictographs (patterns painted on the rock). Rangers can provide information about viewing rock art at locations on both the Utah and Colorado sides of the park.

AT A GLANCE

Utah 149, Jensen, UT or U.S. 40, Dinosaur, CO
435-781-7700 or 970-374-3000
www.nps.gov/dino

Northwestern Colorado and northeastern Utah, 110 miles north of Grand Junction, Colorado ▪ 210,844 acres ▪ Year-round; some roads closed by winter snow ▪ Viewing dinosaur fossils and rock art, taking scenic drives, hiking, camping, white-water boating

Glen Canyon National Recreation Area

A sprawling reservoir surrounded by a vast desert backcountry

Five-hundred-foot-high Alstrom Point, in the Wahweap area, affords spectacular views of Lake Powell and its bays.

The great majority of visitors to this huge recreation area come to enjoy Lake Powell, the second largest reservoir in the United States. Fishing, waterskiing, and boating (including the very popular activity of "camping" on the water via houseboat) attract well over a million people a year to Glen Canyon. Smaller numbers enjoy drives (often requiring high-clearance 4WD vehicles) along scenic, little-traveled roads through the backcountry; or hiking trails that range from short walks into narrow canyons to strenuous backpacking trips through deserts with no marked routes.

Lake Powell was formed after the 1963 construction of the highly controversial Glen Canyon Dam on the Colorado River, which flooded one of the most scenic canyons in the Southwest, destroyed archaeological sites, and drastically altered the river's natural flow downstream through Grand Canyon National Park. A vast expanse of terrain that was once near-inaccessible desert was transformed by the presence of a reservoir with around 2,000 miles of shoreline, backing up water into countless side canyons both large and small. Lake Powell's size depends on flow of the upper Colorado River, which in turn depends on winter snowfall in the Rocky Mountains and adjacent areas. In recent years the lake has sunk to record low levels, only to rise again with increased flow.

Visiting the Area

Few roads reach the shoreline of the lake, and many of its scenic areas can be reached only by boat (many types of commercial tours are offered) or via long hikes. There are three visitor centers, including the main one, the Carl Hayden Visitor Center on U.S. 89 west of Glen Canyon Dam in Arizona. A first-time visitor should stop here and talk to rangers about the range of opportunities in this vast area. Many roads, trails, and boating possibilities depend on recent weather and lake level; knowledge of current conditions is a must. Valuable information is also available at Lake Powell's five marinas, some of which maintain ranger contact stations. Houseboats and other watercraft are available for rental at some marinas.

One of Glen Canyon's most popular activities is a visit to beautiful Rainbow Bridge, one of the largest natural rock bridges in the world (see Rainbow Bridge National Monument, p. 378), via one of the daily boat trips *(fee)* offered by the marinas. (For those interested in hiking there, a 14-mile trek begins in the Navajo Nation, but you'll need a permit). Because of the long travel distances and difficult access, most visitors use boats to reach many other places of interest, such as Hole in the Rock, where Mormon pioneers cut a road down a steep cliff; and the Defiance House archaeological site, a 13th-century ruin of the ancestral Puebloan people.

Glen Canyon National Recreation Area also includes areas along the Colorado River below Glen Canyon Dam. One of the park's most popular short hikes, the moderately strenuous 1.25-mile (one way) trail into Cathedral Wash, is reached via Lees Ferry Road, off U.S. 89A. A bit of rock scrambling is necessary, but the beauty of the canyon is worth the effort. Because of the danger of flash floods, do not enter the wash or any similar narrow gorges if storms threaten.

Driving from the recreational sites around Glen Canyon Dam to the upper part of Lake Powell, such as the popular Bullfrog Marina area, requires very long, roundabout routes. With proper planning and in good weather, many scenic drives can be made into adjacent areas such as Grand Staircase–Escalante National Monument, Dixie National Forest, and Capitol Reef National Park (see p. 368). Always inquire locally about conditions before setting out along a remote, unpaved road.

U.S. 89
Page, AZ
928-608-6200
www.nps.gov/glca

AT A GLANCE

Southern Utah and northern Arizona, 125 miles north of Flagstaff, Arizona ▪ 1.2 million acres ▪ Year-round ▪ Boating, hiking, camping, fishing, exploring in 4WD vehicles

Golden Spike National Historic Site
Where a rail line joined two oceans

On May 10, 1869, officers of the Union Pacific and Central Pacific Railroads, various government officials, and a crowd of between 300 and 1,500 spectators (estimates vary widely) met at a site called Promontory Summit, Utah, to enact a ceremony with huge significance for the United States. When the ceremony was complete, a telegraph operator sent the simple word "DONE" across the country, sparking celebrations in cities from coast to coast.

Using a silver maul (hammer) and a golden spike, participants in the ceremony symbolically completed the first transcontinental railroad line in the United States, making possible for the first time a trip by train from the Atlantic to the Pacific. The final segment of track linking the Midwest with California had taken seven years and untold amounts of human

A copy of one of the original two trains

labor, and its finish meant the end of wagon trains along the Oregon and California trails.

The visitor center at Golden Spike National Historic Site features exhibits on the historical background of the transcontinental railroad and the effort needed to bring it to reality. (The original 1869 golden spike is displayed at Stanford University in California.) Modern reproductions of the two steam locomotives that met at Promontory Summit (the originals were scrapped in the early 20th century) hold demonstration runs daily in season *(early May–Labor Day)*.

The 1.5-mile Big Fill Loop Trail leads to the Central Pacific's Big Fill, which was used to span a ravine so a gentle grade could be maintained for the trains. Two auto tour routes, one 14 miles and the other 2 miles, follow the original rail route past construction sites, hill cuts, and the Chinese Arch, a natural limestone arch dedicated to the thousands of Chinese workers who toiled on the tracks.

West off Utah 83
Corinne, UT
435-471-2209
www.nps.gov/gosp

AT A GLANCE

Northern Utah, 85 miles northwest of Salt Lake City ▪ 2,735 acres ▪ Year-round ▪ Enjoying historic reenactments and steam locomotive demonstrations, driving and walking tours

Hovenweep National Monument

Beautifully constructed buildings of the ancestral Puebloan culture

The six pueblo communities protected within Hovenweep National Monument encompass the remains of dwellings, kivas (ceremonial buildings), and, most notably, multistory towers whose function and meaning remain unknown to archaeologists. The six groups of structures are scattered across 20 miles of remote terrain, four pueblos in Colorado and two in Utah (where the park visitor center is located, near the Square Tower Group). "Hovenweep" is a Ute/Paiute word meaning "deserted valley," used for these ruins by famed Old West photographer William Henry Jackson in 1874.

Cultural History

Prehistoric Indian tribes lived in this part of the Colorado Plateau as early as 10,000 years ago, mostly by means of hunting and gathering. Beginning about A.D. 900, a people known as the ancestral Puebloan culture started to settle here permanently, farming the land to supplement wild game and native plant foods. Similar styles of construction and pottery link the Hovenweep residents to others living in the Four Corners region of the Southwest, including those at Mesa Verde (see p. 332), now a national park to the east in Colorado.

Like related tribes in the area, the Hovenweep people abandoned their pueblos in the 13th century and moved to the south; reasons for the migration could have been prolonged drought or conflict with other tribes. Today's Pueblo, Zuni, and Hopi people are descendants of the ancestral Puebloan culture.

Visiting the Park

Located in a remote part of the Southwest, Hovenweep National Monument receives relatively little visitation, especially to its more remote units. The solitude enjoyed by those who make the effort to see the ruins adds to the enjoyment and meaning of a visit, making it easier for travelers to imagine the scene when the pueblos were thriving communities of hundreds of people. The visitor center and Square Tower Group are the only unit of Hovenweep accessible by a paved road. Rangers conduct interpretive programs spring through fall.

Square Tower Group

A 2-mile loop trail (paved and wheelchair-accessible to the first lookout point) follows the rim of Little Ruin Canyon and leads to some of the dozens of ruins here, the largest collection of ancestral Puebloan structures in the national monument. The three-story Square Tower, perched at the head of the canyon, is thought, based on its prominent location and appearance, to have been a ceremonial building.

The highly skilled construction techniques exhibited at Hovenweep always impress visitors to the park. Often placed on rocky, uneven sites or canyon rims, the structures show the patience and skill of their builders, even today remaining stable and precise in the placement of the stones used to create them.

Other Hovenweep Pueblos

The other Hovenweep pueblos—Cajon in Utah; and Cutthroat Castle, Goodman Point, Holly, and Horseshoe & Hackberry in Colorado—are accessed by unpaved roads, and require hiking primitive trails to see the ruins. Visitors should inquire at the visitor center about road conditions and for additional advice on touring the sites.

Set on a canyon rim, Hovenweep Castle is part of the Square Tower Group.

West off U.S. 491, Cortez, CO or east off U.S. 191 south of Blanding, UT
970-562-4282
www.nps.gov/hove

AT A GLANCE

Southwestern Colorado and southeastern Utah, 150 miles south of Grand Junction, Colorado ▪ 785 acres ▪ Spring through fall, though summers can be very hot ▪ Touring thousand-year-old pueblo ruins, camping

Mormon Pioneer National Historic Trail

The route followed by 19th-century travelers seeking religious freedom

The Mormon Pioneer National Historic Trail runs on the north side of the Platte River across from Scotts Bluff.

Founded by Joseph Smith in New York State on April 6, 1830, the Mormon religion grew rapidly over the next decade. That growth, along with opposition to beliefs such as the sanctioning of polygamy, caused members of the Church of Jesus Christ of Latter-day Saints (commonly known as Mormons) to come under suspicion. Looking for a place where they could freely practice their religion, the main body of church members moved west, first to Ohio, then to Missouri, and then to Nauvoo, Illinois, where Smith hoped to permanently settle.

Violence followed, though, and an angry crowd killed Smith in 1844. Brigham Young assumed the leadership and began making plans to move the church to an isolated spot in the American West. Young and 3,000 Mormons set out on February 4, 1846, with little more than what they could carry. The trek across Iowa was particularly difficult, and by June they had only reached the Missouri River near present-day Omaha, Nebraska. Illness and other difficulties delayed the travelers there until April 1847. When they finally got under way, an advance pioneer party followed existing trails to to Fort Bridger, Wyoming, then they took the route blazed by the Donner party across Utah toward California.

In July, the first group of Mormons reached the Great Salt Lake Valley, where Young chose to settle. Over the next few years the trail was improved, way stations were set up to assist immigrants, and "companies" of travelers were organized to facilitate the journey. From 1847 to 1869, when the completion of the transcontinental railroad made the route obsolete, nearly 70,000 Mormons would make the journey along the Mormon Trail.

Today's Mormon Pioneer National Historic Trail follows the approximate route of the original trail from Nauvoo to Salt Lake City, a distance of around 1,300 miles. The Park Service partners with sites such as state and federal parks, museums, and historic sites to help travelers gain a better understanding of this influential migration. Maps and driving guides are being developed and are presently available on the trail website or from sites along the way.

Trail-related sites along the route include Nauvoo National Historic District in Nauvoo, Illinois; Winter Quarters Historic Site in Omaha, Nebraska; ruts left by wagons near Sutherland, Nebraska; Independence Rock State Historic Site and Fort Bridger State Historic Site in Wyoming; and of course many sites in Salt Lake City, Utah, modern headquarters for the Church of Jesus Christ of Latter-day Saints.

Development of the trail and interpretive materials is ongoing; check the trail website or call the trail office for the latest information. The Mormon Trails Association *(www.mormontrails .org)* is also a source of information.

Trail office
324 S. State St., #200
Salt Lake City, UT
801-741-1012
www.nps.gov/mopi

AT A GLANCE

Route from Nauvoo, Illinois, to Salt Lake City, Utah ▪ About 1,300 miles ▪ Late spring through fall ▪ Driving tour, hiking, visiting museums and historic sites

Natural Bridges National Monument

Massive stone bridges in a high desert landscape

Three striking rock bridges, carved by erosive forces in the sandstone of the Colorado Plateau, form the chief attraction at this small national monument east of Lake Powell.

The rock from which the bridges were formed was once the shoreline of a Permian period sea, where sand eventually compacted into a geologic formation called Cedar Mesa sandstone. Streams shaped canyon walls into thin structures known as fins, which eventually wore through, creating the natural bridges.

Overlooks along a 9-mile loop drive provide views of the park's three bridges: Sipapu, Kachina, and Owachomo. Short trails (none longer than 1.4 miles round trip) lead to the bridges for up-close appreciation. Sipapu is the second largest natural bridge in the world, after Rainbow Bridge National Monument (see below). Kachina's massive form contrasts with the more delicate shape of Owachomo. In 1992, 4,000 tons of rock fell from Kachina, the youngest

Of the three natural bridges, Owachomo is the smallest and perhaps the oldest.

of the three bridges. Erosion will eventually cause all the bridges to fall, though perhaps hundreds or thousands of years in the future.

Another short, easy trail leads to an overlook of White Canyon and the ruins of a cliff dwelling, built by the ancestral Puebloan people. Horsecollar

Ruin took its name from the unusually shaped doors of a grain-storage building, and it includes an undisturbed kiva (ceremonial building) with part of its original roof. The cliff dwelling was abandoned about 700 years ago.

The park's pristine night skies allow for outstanding stargazing.

Utah 275
Blanding, UT
435-692-1234
www.nps.gov/nabr

AT A GLANCE

Southeastern Utah, 43 miles east of Blanding, Utah ▪ 7,637 acres ▪ Year-round ▪ Hiking, camping, taking scenic drive

Rainbow Bridge National Monument

The world's largest known natural rock bridge

The Colorado Plateau region of Arizona, Utah, Colorado, and New Mexico boasts hundreds of distinctive geologic features, many of them protected in various parks and other public lands. The predominant surface rock of much of the area is sandstone, a relatively soft material that is easily eroded. Although experiencing a period of dry climate today, the plateau was once much wetter, and rivers cut deep canyons in many places—including, of course, the Grand Canyon. In addition, water was the primary erosive force in creating small hoodoos (irregularly shaped spires), buttes, arches, bridges, and other geologic formations.

Among the most stunning of these formations is Rainbow Bridge, the largest known natural bridge in the world. Measuring 290 feet from base to top, it spans 275 feet in width. The top of the bridge is 42 feet thick and 33 feet wide. The base of Rainbow Bridge is formed of Kayenta sandstone, composed of sand and mud laid down by inland seas and winds, while the upper portion is Navajo sandstone, originating as sand dunes in a dry environment. Both sandstones are around 200 million years old, though Navajo is the younger of the two. Rainbow Bridge, like all such formations, will eventually fall from continuing erosion, but studies have shown that it is currently strong and stable.

Visiting the Bridge

Though it is administered by Glen Canyon National Recreation Area (see p. 374), Rainbow Bridge National Monument is a distinct entity with its own regulations and restrictions on activities. Designated a national monument in 1910, Rainbow Bridge was very difficult to reach until the 1963 creation of Lake Powell allowed boats to approach the formation. (One early visitor was Theodore Roosevelt, who made the journey to see Rainbow Bridge in 1913.)

The formation is sacred to local Native American tribes, and visitors are asked to admire it from a designated observation area rather than approach it or stand under it. Visitors once climbed to the top of the arch, but such activity has been prohibited since the 1950s.

The great majority of visitors arrive at Rainbow Bridge by commercial boat tours from marinas on Lake Powell, or by private boat. *(For information call 800-528-6154 or visit www.lakepowell.com.)* From a dock at the site, there is a hike to the bridge itself, which varies in length depending on water level in the lake. It can be a short walk of up to 1.5 miles or more; at very high levels, water actually stands under the bridge.

Some adventurous visitors hike to Rainbow Bridge, using either the 14-mile trail or the 17-mile trail that passes through the Navajo Nation. Both trails are recommended only for experienced backpackers. Water can be very scarce at some seasons, and flash floods are a danger in some steep canyons after rain. Hikers must obtain a permit *(www.navajonationparks.org)* before setting off.

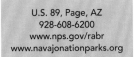

U.S. 89, Page, AZ
928-608-6200
www.nps.gov/rabr
www.navajonationparks.org

AT A GLANCE Southern Utah, 125 miles north of Flagstaff, Arizona ▪ 160 acres ▪ Year-round ▪ Viewing rock formation

---

Timpanogos Cave National Monument
Spectacular formations in a high-mountain cave

Three caverns full of beautiful formations are the main attraction at Timpanogos Cave National Monument, located high in the Wasatch Mountains of Utah. Water flowing along fault lines carved this cave system, known for its abundance of helictites—oddly shaped spiral formations, 6 to 10 inches long, created by capillary attraction and hydrostatic pressure. Rare green and yellow formations also rank as a cave highlight, tinted by the presence of nickel in the crystal structure.

Timpanogos can be visited only by guided tour *(fee)*. Each tour is limited to 16 people; tours often sell out

Colored flowstone delights visitors to Timpanogos Cave.

on weekends and in summer. Tickets can be purchased up to 30 days in advance *(www.recreation.gov)*.

To reach the cave entrance requires a fairly strenuous 1.5-mile hike that gains more than 1,000 feet in elevation, climbing to an altitude of 6,730 feet above sea level. Although the path is paved, people with difficulty breathing or other health problems should consider its difficulty before visiting. To ascend to the cave entrance, take the tour, and return usually requires about three hours.

The temperature in the cave remains about 45°F throughout the year, so a light jacket is recommended even in summer, when temperatures along the trail can reach 100 degrees. Weather closes the park in winter (*about mid-Oct.–May*).

Utah 92
American Fork, UT
801-756-5238
www.nps.gov/tica

AT A GLANCE

Northern Utah, 30 miles south of Salt Lake City ▪ 250 acres ▪ Spring through fall ▪ Taking guided cave tours

Zion National Park

Majestic, multicolored cliffs soaring above narrow canyons

For those who take time to understand the significance of the layers of rock exposed here, the spectacular cliffs of Zion Canyon, the heart of this famed national park, tell stories of life on Earth 240 million years ago. But even for travelers with no interest in geology, Zion repays a visit with dramatic scenery: walls rising more than 2,000 feet above canyon floors, fantastically eroded formations, claustrophobia-inducing gorges, one of the world's largest freestanding rock arches—the list goes on and on.

An elevation difference within Zion of nearly a mile means the park encompasses a wide array of habitats, from deserts with juniper and cactus to riparian areas with cottonwood, maple, and river birch, rising to high plateaus where Douglas fir, ponderosa pine, white fir, and quaking aspen grow tall. This diversity makes Zion an excellent destination for bird-watchers and others with an interest in natural history.

In summer, rangers lead walks and conduct programs at different locations around the park, covering topics ranging from animals to geology to history. There are early-morning walks and even night walks; check at the visitor center for a current schedule. These programs can provide a good

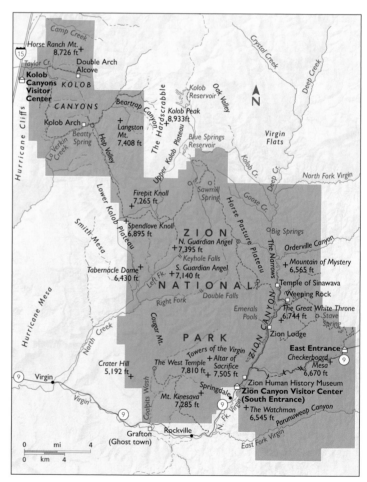

introduction to the park's diversity of life. At Zion as elsewhere, being quiet and watchful during a hike offers a better chance to see wildlife.

Zion Canyon Scenic Drive

The center of activity at Zion National Park is the 6.2-mile road through Zion Canyon, the deep chasm carved by the erosive power of the Virgin River acting on relatively soft sedimentary rock. Once, the popularity of this wonderfully scenic drive led to crowding and traffic problems that threatened the peace and quiet so important for a visit to such a beautiful place. In response, the park in 2000 banned private traffic on the road for most of the year and began a free shuttle-bus service from the visitor center to the road's end. Buses stop at eight locations along the way, providing access to nearly all the park's most popular hikes and sights, such as the Emerald Pools Area. The shuttle also stops at Zion Lodge, a concessionaire-operated hotel within the park.

It's also possible to park in the adjacent town of Springdale and catch a free shuttle to the visitor center. At times, this is the only way to see Zion Canyon, because parking lots in the park can fill to capacity by midmorning in summer and on weekends.

The park shuttle runs mid-March through October, on weekends in November, and through all of Thanksgiving Day weekend; private vehicles are allowed into Zion Canyon the remainder of the year.

Hiking Trails

The strenuous 5-mile round-trip climb to Angels Landing is not for the faint of heart. Ascending 1,488 feet, the trail rewards hikers with fabulous views of Zion Canyon, including the monolith known as the Great White Throne; however, the sometimes narrow trail has some sections exposed to very long drop-offs (there are chains to hold on to in places), and it is not recommended for those uncomfortable with heights.

The paved, short (though somewhat steep) Weeping Rock Trail passes though a side canyon where

The multicolored rock layers of Zion reveal the region's geologic history.

wetter conditions provide a home for Zion's famous hanging gardens. The trail ends at Weeping Wall, a rock alcove where dripping springs allow sufficient moisture for the growth of ferns, mosses, and varied wildflowers. This area is also the beginning of the strenuous 8-mile round-trip hike to Observation Point, a route that climbs through Echo Canyon to a lookout on the East Rim of Zion Canyon.

It's quite an effort, but the panorama from the top is worth the effort.

The Zion Canyon road ends at the striking Temple of Sinawava. Here, the easy, paved, 1-mile (one way) Riverside Walk follows the Virgin River along a narrow canyon, making for one of the park's most awe-inspiring (and popular) experiences. Adventurous, well-informed, and well-prepared hikers can continue upriver (wading is the only option much of the time) into the area called the Zion Narrows, where the surroundings are even more dramatic. Venturing into the Narrows and back as a day hike is not restricted, but hiking the entire length or making an overnight stay requires a permit *(free, determined by number of people making the hike)*.

It is vital to understand the dangers involved in hiking in the Narrows and similar confined canyons. Flash floods can occur almost without warning, and narrow gorges may offer no escape route; the park provides daily reports on conditions. Wading or swimming in cold water can lead to hypothermia, perhaps one of the greatest threats in the area.

The high cliffs that give Zion its character are part of the great geologic feature called the Grand Staircase, a series of rock layers stretching from southern Utah to the Grand Canyon in northern Arizona. Part of the Colorado Plateau, this region was relatively flat 240 million years ago, changing over time from shallow sea to intermountain basin to dune-covered desert. The resulting limestone, mudstone, shale, and sandstone were eroded after the uplift of the entire Colorado Plateau, in large part by rivers such as the Virgin. Rock strata are visible on canyon walls like differently colored cake layers.

Erosion is an ongoing process within the park, but there are sometimes major erosive events: In 1968, 5,000 tons of rock fell at the end of the Narrows Trail, while in 1995 a huge rock slide blocked the Virgin River in Zion Canyon, forming a temporary lake, washing away 200 yards of the road, and stranding

people at Zion Lodge for two days until a new road could be built.

Some visitors enter the park along the Zion–Mount Carmel Highway, a 10-mile, switchback-filled road that connects the park's east and south entrances. Along this road, the 0.5-mile (one way) Canyon Overlook Trail provides a wonderful panorama of Pine Creek Canyon. The route passes through a narrow, 1.1-mile tunnel that has size limits and travel restrictions on large vehicles; drivers of such vehicles should contact the park for more details.

Kolob Canyons

Kolob Canyons, in the northwestern section of Zion National Park, has its own visitor center located just east of I-15. Located about an hour by car from Zion's main park visitor center, and receiving far fewer visitors than Zion Canyon, Kolob Canyons features colorful cliffs and challenging hikes well worth a visit.

Kolob Canyons offers a 5-mile scenic drive where private vehicles are allowed year-round. Views improve with each turn along this route, especially beyond Lee Pass. A trail beginning here leads 7 miles (one way) to Kolob Arch, at 310 feet across possibly the largest freestanding rock arch in the world. The trail is strenuous and requires around eight hours at a minimum; many hikers obtain a backcountry permit and make an overnight stay.

Much easier is the 1-mile round-trip Timber Creek Overlook Trail, beginning at the Kolob Canyons picnic area at the end of the road. The path follows a ridge to a small peak with views of the surrounding area.

Wildlife

The park's mammalian denizens include the desert cottontail, black-tailed jackrabbit, three species of chipmunks, coyote, rock and white-tailed antelope squirrels, beaver, porcupine, ringtail, and mule deer. Desert bighorn sheep were extirpated from the park but have been reintroduced, and mountain lions are seen by a lucky few people. (Hikers should be aware of safety factors when traveling through mountain-lion country, although there has never been a recorded attack on a person or pet in Zion.)

Among the park's 291 species of birds are peregrine falcon, band-tailed pigeon, flammulated owl, spotted owl, black-chinned hummingbird, white-throated swift, willow flycatcher, gray vireo, piñon jay, American dipper, and Virginia's warbler. California condors are often seen around Angels Landing and Lava Point. Early morning and late afternoon are the best times for bird-watching; birdsong and other activity diminishes at midday, especially in hot weather.

Zion in Winter

Winters in Zion are fairly mild. The main roads through Zion Canyon and Kolob Canyons and the Zion–Mount Carmel Highway are plowed in winter, making much of the park accessible even after snows begin in late fall. Motorists should be prepared for occasional hazardous driving, though, and hikers should return to the trailhead if routes become icy or otherwise dangerous. Many of the park's trails remain snow-covered throughout winter.

Utah 9
Springdale, UT
435-772-3256
www.nps.gov/zion

AT A GLANCE

Southwestern Utah, 45 miles northeast of St. George ▪ 147,551 acres ▪ Year-round, though some roads close in winter ▪ Hiking, camping, taking scenic drive, backpacking, rock climbing, horseback riding

Within Heaps Canyon, water pours off a cliff face to fall into one of the Emerald Pools.

Far West & Pacific

The parks of the Far West and Pacific region range widely, both geographically and thematically, from urban parks and recreation areas to remote wilderness. Most parks in this region lie within the expansive state of California, land of deserts, alpine peaks, and gorgeous Pacific Ocean coastline; among them are some of the most famous protected areas in the world, including Yosemite National Park, a landmark in conservation. Nevada's Great Basin National Park shelters some of the oldest trees on Earth. Hawai'i's parks include active volcanoes as well as cultural sites important to native peoples. Parks on the Pacific islands of Guam, Saipan, and Samoa protect World War II historic sites as well as rain forests and coral reefs.

Redwood
National and
State Parks

•Eureka

Point Reyes
National Seashore

San Francisco Sites

◾ Fort Point
National Historic Site

◾ Presidio of San Francisco

◾ San Francisco Maritime
National Historical Park

*Hawai'i Volcanoes N.P.,
Redwood National and
State Parks, and Yosemite
N.P. are also World
Heritage sites.*

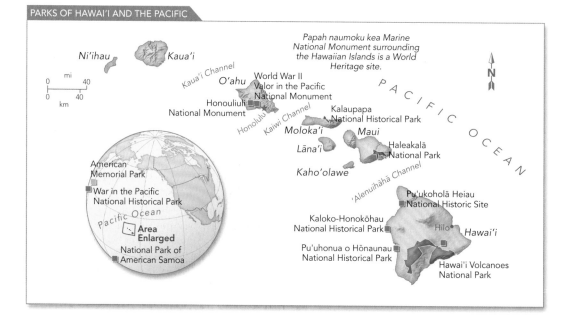

PARKS OF HAWAI'I AND THE PACIFIC

Ni'ihau   Kaua'i

Papah naumoku kea Marine National Monument surrounding the Hawaiian Islands is a World Heritage site.

Kaua'i Channel

O'ahu   World War II
Valor in the Pacific
National Monument

Honouliuli
National Monument

Kalaupapa
National Historical Park

Honolulu   Kaiwi Channel   Moloka'i   Maui

Lāna'i   Haleakalā
National Park

Kaho'olawe

'Alenuihāhā Channel

PACIFIC OCEAN

American
Memorial Park

War in the Pacific
National Historical Park

Pacific Ocean

Area
Enlarged

National Park of
American Samoa

Pu'ukoholā Heiau
National Historic Site

Kaloko-Honokōhau
National Historical Park

Hilo•   Hawai'i

Pu'uhonua o Hōnaunau
National Historical Park

Hawai'i Volcanoes
National Park

mi
0   40
0   40
km

OREGON　IDAHO

World War II Valor
in the Pacific
National Monument
(Tule Lake Unit)

*Goose
Lake*

Lava Beds
National Monument

Pit

Whiskeytown
National
Recreation
Area

Redding

Lassen Volcanic
National Park

*Honey
Lake*

Humboldt

Elko

C

*Pyramid
Lake*

Feather

*Carson
Sink*

N　E　V　A　D　A

Reno

A

*Lake
Tahoe*

Carson City

Walker

Walker Lake

Ely

Great Basin
National Park

Russian

Santa
Rosa

Muir Woods
National
Monument

Rosie the Riveter / WWII Home Front
National Historical Park

John Muir
N.H.S.

Port Chicago
Naval Magazine
National
Memorial

Eugene O'Neill
National Historic Site

San Francisco

Golden Gate
National
Recreation
Area

San Jose

Monterey Bay

L

Sacramento

I

Yosemite
National
Park

*Mono
Lake*

Devils Postpile
National Monument

Manzanar
National
Historic
Site

Kings Canyon
National Park

Death
Valley
N.P.

Tule Springs
Fossil Beds
National
Monument

F

Fresno

*San Joaquin
Slough*

Kings

Death Valley National Park

*Lake
Mead*

Pinnacles
National
Park

O

*Tulare
Lake
Bed*

Sequoia
National Park

*Owens
Lake
Bed*

Las Vegas

Lake Mead
National
Recreation
Area

R

California Aqueduct

Kern

Bakersfield

Los Angeles Aqueduct

N

César E. Chávez
National Monument

*Rogers
Lake*

Mojave

Mojave
National
Preserve

ARIZONA

Colorado

I

Santa Barbara

Santa Monica Mountains
National Recreation Area

A

San Bernardino

Bristol Lake

PACIFIC

OCEAN

Channel Islands
National Park

Los Angeles

Joshua Tree
National Park

C h a n n e l   I s l a n d s

*Gulf of
Santa Catalina*

*Salton
Sea*

San Diego

U.S.
Mexico

Cabrillo
National Monument

N

miles
0　　　50　　　100　　　150

0　　50　　100　　150
kilometers

UTAH

CALIFORNIA

Native Americans, Spanish missionaries, gold prospectors, Dust Bowl refugees, movie stars—all have contributed to the history of California, a state that claims the lowest and hottest place in the country (Death Valley) and the highest point in the lower 48 (Mount Whitney). Incredibly ecologically diverse, California has sandy beaches, rocky coasts, arid deserts, chaparrals, subalpine meadows, high peaks, volcanic landscapes, temperate rain forests, remnant wetlands, and more. Despite sprawling metropolitan areas, the state boasts some of the most famous and rewarding wild places on the continent, from spectacular Yosemite Valley to towering redwood forests to wildlife-rich Point Reyes.

Cabrillo National Monument

The first European footsteps on America's Pacific coast

In June 1542 conquistador Juan Rodríguez Cabrillo set sail from Navidad in New Spain, on what is now the west coast of Mexico, to explore north along the Pacific coast. On September 28 he sailed into a sheltered harbor he described as "very good," and landed on the east side of an enclosing peninsula. In doing so, he became the first European to set foot on what is now the United States' West Coast.

That harbor is today's San Diego Bay, the peninsula is known as Point Loma, and the historic landing site is commemorated at Cabrillo National Monument. With its elevated setting, 422 feet above sea level, the park offers wonderful views of the bay, the ocean, and the San Diego skyline. A statue of Cabrillo stands prominently located, a gift from the government of Portugal. (Though he served Spain, some historians believe he might have been Portuguese.)

Statue of Conquistador Juan Rodríguez Cabrillo

The visitor center features exhibits on Cabrillo and the age of exploration, as well as interpretive films. The monument grounds sit on land that once was part of the military reserve Fort Rosecrans. Several buildings from the early 20th century still dot the grounds. Housed in an old radio station, the exhibit "They Stood the Watch" tells the story of Fort Rosecrans. The nearby 1855 Old Point Loma Lighthouse, also within the monument, has been restored to its 1880s appearance with furnishings depicting the lives of lightkeepers and their families. It was retired from service in 1891 because fog and low clouds often obscured its beam.

Nature lovers find the monument particularly appealing. The 2-mile Bayside Trail winds through endangered coastal Mediterranean habitat with coastal sage scrub. Tide pools teem with marine life, and migrating Pacific gray whales can be seen from late December to early March from an overlook south of the lighthouse.

1800 Cabrillo Memorial Dr.
San Diego, CA
619-557-5450
www.nps.gov/cabr

AT A GLANCE

In San Diego ▪ 160 acres ▪ Year-round (winter best) ▪ Touring lighthouse, viewing historical exhibits, exploring tide pools, hiking, whale-watching, bird-watching

California National Historic Trail

Immigrants' wagon route across the Great Plains and Rocky Mountains

Until the transcontinental railroad was completed in 1869, travelers heading to the Pacific coast region packed their goods in wagons and rode or walked more than 2,000 miles of trail. Some were immigrants seeking new homes in the fertile valleys of California or Oregon, and others were seeking their fortunes in the gold rush that began in California in 1849.

Many travelers took steamboats up the Missouri River to towns such as Independence and St. Joseph, Missouri, before heading west in spring, trying to complete the difficult journey before winter. Their path generally followed rivers, which provided level paths and fresh water. The route of the California and Oregon Trails left the Missouri River to follow the Platte, then the Sweetwater, the Bear, and the Snake. At that point, the Oregon Trail (see. p. 276)

veered north to the Columbia River, while California-bound immigrants went south to the Humboldt. There was no single route but instead a multitude of somewhat parallel trails that varied slightly because of weather, flooding, water availability, and other factors, including the continual discovery of new and better trail segments.

The California National Historic Trail allows modern travelers to drive the general path of the westbound pioneers. With all its associated routes, it totals more than 5,600 miles, with about 1,100 miles of original trail still existing as ruts and other traces.

Among the scores of sites that can be visited are several National Park Service areas, such as Scotts Bluff National Monument (see p. 242) in Nebraska, Fort Laramie National Historic Site (see p. 489) in Wyoming,

and Lassen Volcanic National Park (see p. 403) in California. There are also many state and local parks that provide access to trail segments or historic sites associated with the California Trail.

The California Trail Interpretive Center in Elko, Nevada, the National Frontier Trails Museum in Independence, Missouri, and the National Historic Trails Interpretive Center in Casper, Wyoming, are three notable sites that offer historical exhibits and information on the California Trail. The Oregon-California Trails Association (*www .octa-trails.org*) is also a good source of information. The Park Service is developing auto-tour guides to each state through which the trail passes; some are already available through its trail office in Salt Lake City, Utah, and on the website.

Trail office
324 S. State St., #200
Salt Lake City, UT
801-741-1012
www.nps.gov/cali

AT A GLANCE Multiple routes across several states between Missouri and California ▪ More than 5,600 miles ▪ Spring through fall ▪ Following pioneers' travel routes, visiting historic sites and museums

César E. Chávez National Monument

Memorial to influential labor leader

Beginning in the 1960s, César Chávez became the leading figure in the fight for better pay and safer working conditions for agricultural workers in the United States. Political efforts led by Chávez resulted in the formation of a labor union that eventually became the United Farm Workers of America. He also helped promote landmark legislation that gave agricultural

workers the right to organize and negotiate for better conditions in farm fields and for insurance and pension benefits.

Chávez was a revered leader not only to his fellow Latino Americans but also for others in the civil-rights and labor movements. Sen. Robert F. Kennedy called him "one of the heroic figures of our time," and after Chávez's death in 1993 countless

schools, streets, and public buildings were renamed in his honor. A postage stamp was issued in his memory in 2003.

In 2012, César E. Chávez National Monument was established as a unit of the National Park Service. Located in Keene, California, the site— a historic property known as Nuestra Señora Reina de la Paz—is administered in partnership with the

National Chávez Center. The national monument includes a visitor center with exhibits and video presentations and Chávez's grave site, which is located in a memorial garden. A significant feature of the visitor center is Chávez's office and library, preserved just as they were at the time of his death.

AT A GLANCE Southern California, 126 miles north of Los Angeles ▪ 116 acres ▪ Year-round ▪ Touring visitor center, Chávez's preserved office, memorial garden

Channel Islands National Park

Protecting the environment of the "Galápagos of North America"

Stretching across approximately 90 miles of the Pacific Ocean off the coast of southern California, Channel Islands National Park encompasses five islands that host a world-class diversity of wildlife, vegetation, and marine life. Relatively little touched by development, these islands are sometimes called the "Galápagos of North America" in recognition of their unique and fascinating natural history, including more than 150 endemic species and the largest breeding colonies of seabirds in southern California.

In addition, the ocean within 6 nautical miles of the islands is protected as Channel Islands National Marine Sanctuary *(www.channelislands .noaa.gov),* including a vast undersea "forest" of kelp. The sanctuary is home to seals, sea lions, sea otters, more than two dozen species of whales and dolphins, seabirds, and hundreds of species of fish and invertebrates.

Opportunities for seeing these somewhat remote islands include short cruises or island visits with park-authorized boat tour companies, as well as longer trips that can involve camping on the islands for more in-depth exploration.

Two of the islands, Anacapa (actually three small islands) and Santa Barbara, were designated a national monument in 1938; and in

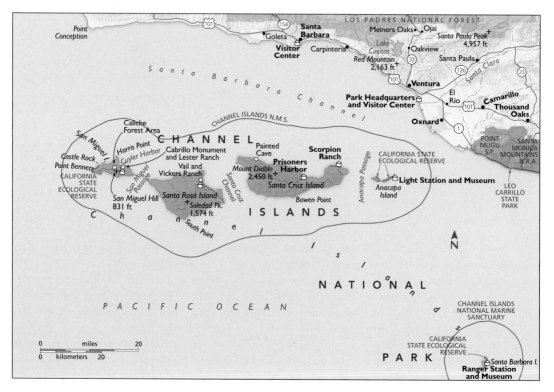

1980 Congress added San Miguel, Santa Rosa, and Santa Cruz Islands to create Channel Islands National Park.

Natural History

In the most recent ice age, the northern Channel Islands are thought to have existed as one larger island, as lower sea levels exposed more of the ocean floor. Several factors contribute to the islands' current biodiversity. They are located at the confluence of two major ocean currents in an area of oceanic upwelling. The park shows features of both the Oregonian and the Californian biogeographic provinces, which means that the Channel Islands exhibit biological diversity equivalent to nearly 2,500 miles of the west coast of North America. In the ocean around the islands, cool, nutrient-rich water rises into sunlight and mixes with warm coastal water, accelerating photosynthesis and growth rates of sea life from microscopic plankton to blue whales, Earth's largest living creatures.

Channel Islands National Park protects a significant area of the extremely endangered coastal Mediterranean ecosystem, a habitat found in only five places. In addition to its natural resources, the park also preserves archaeological sites that record nearly 13,000 years of continuous human occupation.

Chumash Indians inhabited the islands until the 19th century, sealing their boats with tar that seeped to the surface. Evidence of petroleum is present today in the large number of oil-drilling platforms in the Pacific Ocean's Santa Barbara Channel.

In 1969, an accident at an offshore oil platform allowed 200,000 gallons of crude oil to leak out over a period of 11 days. The oil created an 800-square-mile slick that polluted all the northern Channel Islands and

The red glow of a setting sun casts the Anacapa Island Light Station into sharp relief.

nearby mainland beaches and killed thousands of seabirds and marine mammals. Publicity surrounding the oil spill provided a major boost to the growing movement in the United States to enact stronger environmental safeguards.

Visiting the Park

The park's main visitor contact point, the Robert J. Lagomarsino Visitor Center, is located on the mainland in Ventura. It features exhibits on marine aquatic life and a 25-minute film called "A Treasure in the Sea." There are also interpretive exhibits examining the unique character of each park island. The Outdoors Santa Barbara Visitor Center *(113 Harbor Way, Santa Barbara, 805-884-1475)* is a partnership site that offers information about Channel Islands National Park, Los Padres National Forest, Channel Islands National Marine Sanctuary, and other recreational and natural areas.

Most visitors reach the islands via park-authorized boat tour concessionaires (check with the park for information). A few visitors travel on a short commercial airplane flight to Santa Rosa Island. Some reach the islands on private boats, but boaters should be aware of park and sanctuary regulations and must obtain landing permits for the Nature Conservancy property on Santa Cruz Island.

The transportation factor is the major reason Channel Islands is one of the least visited of the national parks, with fewer than 250,000 annual visitors. The positive side of this situation is that visitors can be assured of a certain degree of solitude when they hike and camp. The two closest islands are Anacapa and Santa Cruz, though all the islands can be visited on day trips.

Primitive camping is allowed on all five islands, but it requires a park permit, acquired in advance. A number of regulations apply to campers, to protect both temporary human residents and the permanent flora and fauna of the islands.

Anacapa

The journey to Anacapa takes about 90 minutes from Ventura. As it approaches the island the boat passes Arch Rock, one of many places where seabirds nest; passengers may also see harbor seals and California sea lions. Anacapa boasts the largest known breeding colonies of both California brown pelicans and western gulls, with additional colonies of cormorants, auklets, and murrelets.

Anacapa's 1.5-mile trail system allows close looks at birds, vegetation, and archaeological sites. There are two overlooks specifically sited for viewing seals and sea lions. The kelp forests in the ocean around the island are excellent for snorkeling and diving. In summer, park rangers dive into the Pacific with video cameras, allowing visitors on dry land to see undersea life, including sea stars, colorful fish, and the occasional mammal. Visitors can ask questions of the rangers via an interactive communications system.

Santa Cruz Island

Santa Cruz Island is far larger than Anacapa, encompassing 96 square miles and 77 miles of coastline (it's California's largest island). The Nature Conservancy owns three-quarters of the island, with the remainder owned by the National Park Service. (No camping is permitted in the Nature Conservancy area.)

Santa Cruz is noted for its biological diversity, with about 900 species of plants and animals present, including 12 found nowhere else on Earth. Ten different plant communities occur here, and among the wildlife is the island fox, much

smaller than foxes on the mainland, and subject of an intensive program to save it from extinction. Santa Cruz is famed among bird-watchers as the home of the endemic island scrub jay, a powder-blue bird that usually travels in small groups. Prisoners Harbor and Scorpion Ranch are the best places to see the jay.

In 2006, the first bald eagle chick to hatch unaided by humans on the Channel Islands in more than 50 years was raised by adult eagles on Santa Cruz. The bald eagle had been the focus of a reintroduction program in the islands since 2002; the island now is home to several dozen of the birds.

A major feature of Santa Cruz is Painted Cave, one of the largest and deepest sea caves in the world. Named for its colorful rock, lichens, and algae, it's nearly 0.25 mile long and 100 feet wide, with an entrance ceiling of 160 feet. Painted Cave is a popular destination for sea kayakers.

Santa Rosa, San Miguel, & Santa Barbara

Of the other Channel Islands, Santa Rosa is noted for its extensive archaeological sites related to the Chumash Indians. The park limits visitors here at certain times of year because of hunting and to protect wildlife. San Miguel has many archaeological sites, as well as thousands of breeding seals and sea lions. The island is the only known place in the world where four different species of seals and sea lions breed. Peregrine falcons have been reintroduced to all five of the islands, including San Miguel, and may be seen zooming along the cliffs. Santa Barbara, at 1 square mile

the smallest of the Channel Islands, is known for its nesting colony of Xantus' murrelet, a seabird that is related to the puffin.

Park Activities

Park rangers and volunteers conduct a variety of guided walks on the islands throughout the year on topics such as bird-watching, seal and sea lion viewing, and archaeology. Interpretive trips are also offered to enjoy tide pool life, during which visitors can view creatures such as anemones, sea stars, sea urchins, limpets, periwinkles, chitons, barnacles, and mussels. One of the most accessible tide pool sites is Frenchy's Cove on Anacapa Island, while the eastern end of Cuyler Harbor on San Miguel Island is known for its beautiful crescent beach.

Observers have spotted 27 species of whales, dolphins, and porpoises in the waters surrounding the Channel Islands—about a third of the species found in all the world's seas. Several commercial tour companies offer whale-watching trips from harbors on the mainland. In winter, from about mid- to late December through mid-March, gray whales migrate north-south past the islands, returning from their birthing grounds off Baja California. Blue and humpback whales may be seen during the summer.

Colorful wildflowers are often abundant on the islands, usually reaching a peak in late winter and spring. In particular, the islands bloom with brilliant yellow coreopsis flowers, with the largest numbers found on Santa Barbara, Anacapa, and San Miguel.

Robert J. Lagomarsino Visitor Center, 1901 Spinnaker Dr. Ventura, CA 805-658-5730 www.nps.gov/chis

AT A GLANCE

Off the coast of southern California ▪ 249,561 acres ▪ Year-round ▪ Hiking, camping, kayaking, snorkeling, wildlife-watching, cruising to see marine life

Death Valley National Park

A legendary name for a park with surprisingly varied rewards

Among the world's most famous geographic names, Death Valley evokes many different emotions. For some people, it seems a forbidding and even dangerous place, lacking appeal as a destination. Others are attracted by the challenge of its legendary heat, its vast empty spaces, its parched landscape.

It's true that Death Valley can be dangerous—but the same can be said about crossing a busy city street. Visitors who take proper precautions have nothing to fear from exploring this desert park, and much to enjoy in its striking scenery and fascinating history.

"Hottest, driest, lowest" is a common description of Death Valley National Park. In July 1913 a temperature of 134°F was registered at the site now called Furnace Creek Ranch. This was the hottest temperature ever recorded on Earth at the time. The average July daily high at Death Valley is 115°F.

It is the driest area in the National Park System: There have been years when no rain fell at all, and the annual average is less than 2 inches.

The elevation at Badwater Basin—282 feet below sea level—is the lowest place in North America.

Why was it called "Death" Valley? In 1849 a group of pioneers wandered into this area on their way to California, enduring a two-month ordeal of "hunger and thirst and awful silence" as they tried to find their way out of the 140-mile-long basin. One elderly man died; the others at times assumed they, too, would end their lives here. They were found and rescued, however, and as the party climbed out of the valley

Death Valley has several dunelands, including Stovepipe Wells.

over the Panamint Mountains, one of the men turned, looked back, and said, "Good-bye, Death Valley." The name stuck.

The valley is a graben, the geologic term for a sunken section of the Earth's crust. Here are rocks sculpted by erosion, colorfully hued mudstone hills and canyons, sand dunes, oases, and a 200-square-mile salt pan surrounded by mountains that rise to 11,049 feet—one of America's greatest vertical rises.

Despite its low average precipitation, there are winters and early springs when storms drop significant rain on Death Valley, leading to lavish displays of blooming wildflowers. There is wildlife here, as well, from bighorn sheep to coyotes to birds such as roadrunners, ravens, and hawks.

In the late 19th century, Death Valley saw wagons haul powdery white borax from mines long since abandoned. Over the years miners have also sought gold, silver, lead,

zinc, mercury, copper, salt, manganese, and other substances. There may be as many as 10,000 abandoned mines in the park, and visitors should pay special attention to recommended precautions about avoiding dangerous areas. Some areas are closed to visitation because of unstable ground, toxic waste, and other hazards.

Furnace Creek & Around

California Highway 190 bisects Death Valley National Park, and the main visitor contact area, Furnace Creek Visitor Center, is located along the route in the central area of the park. An interpretive audiovisual program, exhibits, and an information desk will provide answers to most questions on climate, geography, recreational opportunities, history, and wildlife. Fall through spring, rangers lead a variety of walks and programs. Nearby is a resort with restaurants and a golf course, as well as park campgrounds.

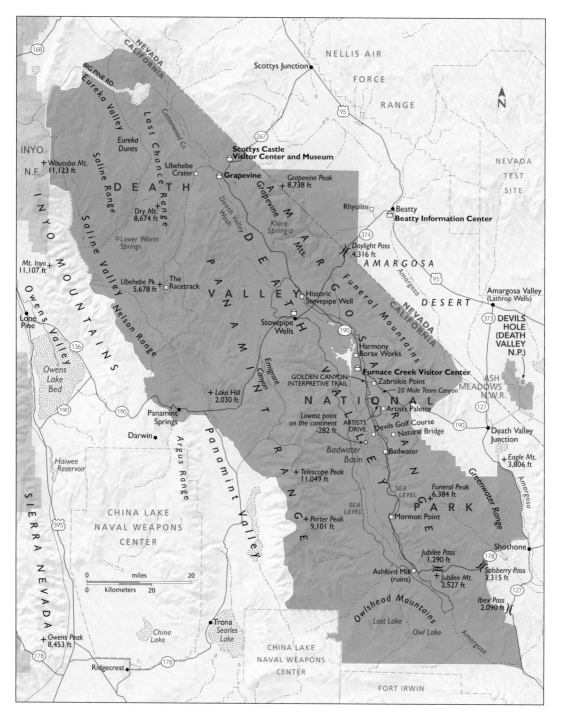

Some of the most interesting sites in the park lie south of Furnace Creek. The Golden Canyon Interpretive Trail is a 2-mile round trip through a canyon that glows gold at sunset. A 9-mile loop road passes through the Artists Palette, a rumpled terrain of volcanic ash in many colors—also especially memorable at sunset.

Farther south is a short side road to Devils Golf Course (this one only metaphorical), an odd landscape of rock salt pinnacles that form as water evaporates up through the salty crust, eroded by wind and rain. On down the road is another side road to Natural Bridge, an arch over a canyon featuring other rock formations. The arch is a 0.5-mile walk from the end of the road.

The road then reaches famed Badwater Basin, the lowest spot in North America. The road continues below sea level through the vast Death Valley Salt Pan, the residue of a fresh water lake that existed more than 20,000 years ago, but whose load of minerals concentrated into the existing salt pan as the waters evaporated.

Southeast of Furnace Creek are more don't-miss attractions. Zabriskie Point is a popular sunrise and sunset viewing spot where rain and wind have shaped rock into dramatic contours. The promontory commands a broad view of mudstone badlands. To explore them, continue to Twenty Mule Team Canyon, where a 3-mile gravel loop winds through the landscape.

Farther along is the 13-mile paved spur road to Dantes View, an overlook that ranks as Death Valley's most famous and spectacular panoramic view. The vista covers the Badwater Basin and on to the Panamint Range, with 11,049-foot Telescope Peak, the park's highest point.

Back at Furnace Creek, drive a mile north to walk the 0.25-mile paved Harmony Borax Works Interpretive Trail to the ruins of Death Valley's first successful mining venture. Farther north is a spur road to Salt Creek Interpretive Trail, where spring-fed marshy pools are home to endemic desert pupfish.

Mesquite Flat Sand Dunes can be accessed near Stovepipe Wells Village. Most of the sand is made of quartz, eroded from mountains and blown here by winds that continue to shape drifts. Visitors can walk through the dunes wherever they want, using

Scarlet Locoweed in flower

caution. A motel and restaurant are located at the resort two miles away.

Scottys Castle

One of the most famous spots within Death Valley National Park is Scottys Castle, a Mediterranean-style mansion dating from 1922. A prospector called "Death Valley Scotty," a desert rat whose name was Walter Scott, told people the place was his, built by earnings from his secret gold mine. It was actually the vacation home of a wealthy Chicago couple who allowed their friend to stay as their guest. (As further proof that truth is stranger than fiction, the man who built the house, Albert Johnson, had actually been duped by Scotty into investing in a phony gold mine. When the two met, a friendship developed that led to Johnson falling in love with Death Valley and building his winter home.) Park rangers give regular daily tours of the "castle," which features original furnishings.

Eight miles west of Scottys Castle is Ubehebe Crater, where a massive volcanic explosion around 500 years ago, caused by underground steam pressure, left a 600-foot-deep crater. A 1.5-mile loop hike leads around the crater rim, with views of smaller craters.

West Side of the Park

On the park's west side, the Panamint Springs area includes Father Crowley Vista, with views of lava flows and volcanic cinders cut by Rainbow Canyon; and Aguereberry Point, another excellent spot from which to view sunsets. The road to the point may require a high-clearance vehicle. The Wildrose charcoal kilns, built in 1876 to provide fuel to process silver-lead ore, are beehive-shaped structures that still smell of smoke today.

When to Visit

Spring is the most popular time to visit the park. During years when rains have brought a significant wildflower display, Death Valley's accommodations can be filled; advance reservations are recommended. Winter, with its moderate temperatures (December and January highs average 65°F), is also a popular time to visit the park.

Summer sees fewer visitors, but the numbers are increasing, and—thanks to air-conditioned vehicles—the trip can be made safely and enjoyably. Driving tours are just about the only activity that is recommended in summer; park rangers caution against hiking. Summertime walkers should confine their hikes to early morning and take plenty of water. Summer exertion may require up to 2 gallons of water a day to replenish body fluids. Dehydration is the second leading cause of death in Death Valley. (The first is single-vehicle auto accidents.)

The only hikes that are appealing in summer are those at high elevations, such as those to Telescope and Wildrose peaks. Summer camping at low elevation brings conditions that are uncomfortable, to say the least.

Camping & Wildlife-watching

Backcountry camping is allowed in the park, which offers more than 3 million acres of federally designated wilderness to explore. Campers should follow park rules regulating camping, which are designed to protect resources.

Wildlife viewing is best at dawn and dusk. It's a lucky visitor who catches sight of a bighorn sheep, but these animals may sometimes be spotted at Surprise Canyon, 6 miles northeast of Ballarat.

Death Valley National Park has a surprisingly long bird list (more than 300 species), thanks to habitats ranging from desert up through piñon pine–juniper woods to coniferous forests on the highest peaks. The terrain creates a natural "funnel" that leads migratory birds to pass through the park. Good places to bird-watch include the desert oasis of Saratoga Spring and riparian areas at Scottys Castle and the Wildrose campground.

Calif. 190
Death Valley, CA
760-786-3200
www.nps.gov/deva

AT A GLANCE

Eastern California, 120 miles west of Las Vegas, Nevada ▪ 3,368,000 acres ▪ Fall through spring ▪ Hiking, camping, backpacking, scenic driving

Devils Postpile National Monument
The spectacular aftermath of an ancient lake of lava

One of the world's best examples of the geologic formation called columnar basalt occurs in this national monument southeast of Yosemite National Park.

About 80,000 to 100,000 years ago, basaltic lava erupted from a vent and flowed down a valley and pooled until it was blocked by a natural dam (probably a glacial moraine), creating a lava lake up to 400 feet deep. As the lava cooled into rock it contracted, and cracks formed in a regular pattern. Later, glaciers moving down what is today's Reds Meadow Valley scraped away overlying material to expose the striking columns, which are up to 60 feet high. More than half the columns are hexagonal (six-sided), while other are three-, four-, five-, or seven-sided.

Most visitors to Devils Postpile

Erosive forces knock pieces off, creating a talus field.

National Monument must park their vehicles at the nearby Mammoth Mountain ski resort on Calif. 203 and take a shuttle bus to the park. Exceptions are made for disabled persons, those arriving very early or late in the day, and those camping in the Reds Meadow Valley or staying at the Reds Meadow Resort. From the ranger station, it's a 0.4-mile walk to Devils Postpile formation, which on close observation shows polishing and striations from the glaciers that moved over it.

The shuttle bus also stops at the trailhead for beautiful 101-foot-high Rainbow Falls on the Middle Fork San Joaquin River, reached by a 1.3-mile hike from the trailhead.

Two famed hiking trails—the 211-mile John Muir Trail, which links Yosemite National Park and Mount Whitney; and the 2,638-mile Pacific Crest Trail, which runs from Canada to Mexico—join at Devils Postpile and run through the park, providing additional hiking opportunities.

Devils Postpile National Monument receives about 400 inches of snow each winter, and its seasonal opening and closing dates depend on the weather. Generally the park is open early June through October, but visitors in spring and fall should check before planning a trip.

Calif. 203 (off U.S. 395)
Mammoth Lakes, CA
760-934-2289
www.nps.gov/depo

AT A GLANCE

Eastern California, 130 miles south of Reno, Nevada ▪ 798 acres ▪ Summer and early fall ▪ Viewing geologic formations, hiking, camping, wildlife-watching

Eugene O'Neill National Historic Site
A famed playwright's "final harbor"

One of America's most celebrated playwrights, Eugene O'Neill won four Pulitzer Prizes and, in 1936, the Nobel Prize for literature. Born in New York City in 1888, the son of an actor, O'Neill spent much of his early adult life moving from place to place. In 1937 he moved to Danville, California, east of San Francisco Bay. He and his third wife, Carlotta Monterey, helped design a home they called Tao House, which combined Spanish and Chinese influences.

O'Neill lived here for seven years, during which he wrote acclaimed plays such as *The Iceman Cometh, Long Day's Journey Into Night,* and *A Moon for the Misbegotten.* Though he loved the house and the isolation it provided for writing, O'Neill was forced by illness and World War II to leave in 1944. He never completed another play, and died in Boston in 1953.

A visit to Eugene O'Neill National Historic Site *(Wed.–Sun.)* is by guided tour and reservations must be made

in advance except on Saturdays, when self-guided tours are permitted. Visitors must take a shuttle bus from Danville, and directions are provided at the time reservations are made. Private vehicles are not allowed at the site. A commemorative sculpture of the playwright is located in Danville's park across from the library.

Plays are presented in the old barn in spring and fall by the Eugene O'Neill Foundation *(925-820-1818, www.eugeneoneill.org).*

Danville, CA
925-838-0249
www.nps.gov/euon

AT A GLANCE

Northern California, 15 miles east of Oakland ▪ 13 acres ▪ Year-round, by reservation only ▪ Touring O'Neill home, hiking

---

Fort Point National Historic Site
The imposing "Gibraltar of the West Coast"

Fort Point was built between 1853 and 1861 as part of a U.S. Army defense system to protect San Francisco Bay. It was conceived of and designed during the height of the gold rush, when the United States realized the importance of shielding California from enemy attack. Strategically sited with sight lines across the narrow Golden Gate, it was the only fortification of its formidable size and type built on the West Coast.

Fort Point readied itself for a possible Confederate attack during the Civil War, but one never occurred. In fact, the fort's guns never fired a shot

in any military conflict. When rifled artillery made brick forts obsolete, Fort Point intermittently saw other uses as barracks and a trade school. Its demolition was proposed during the construction of the Golden Gate Bridge, but chief engineer Joseph Strauss recognized its architectural value and devised a way to save it.

Today, Fort Point, standing under the Golden Gate Bridge, endures as one of the finest examples of masonry construction in the country, with arched casemates (openings for cannon) of striking design. In 1970 it was declared a national historic

site, located within San Francisco's famed Presidio, part of Golden Gate National Recreation Area (see p. 397).

Visitors to Fort Point National Historic Site can see a film on the history of Fort Point and exhibits that focus on women at war, African-American "buffalo soldiers," and the construction of the Golden Gate Bridge. Demonstrations of cannon loading are conducted regularly, showing how soldiers were taught to load and fire a Napoleon 12-pounder cannon during a Civil War artillery drill. A self-guiding tour booklet is available, and guided tours are also offered.

Marine Drive, Presidio
San Francisco, CA
415-556-1693
www.nps.gov/fopo

AT A GLANCE

San Francisco ▪ 29 acres ▪ Year-round ▪ Touring historic fort, viewing historical exhibits and films

The eponymous Golden Gate Bridge spans a mile-wide strait that connects the Pacific Ocean to San Francisco Bay.

Golden Gate National Recreation Area

A diverse collection of natural, historic, and recreational sites

A hang glider soars over the Golden Gate area.

About three dozen locations in the San Francisco Bay Area compose Golden Gate National Recreation Area (also called Golden Gate National Parks). The range of opportunities for visitors gives this collection of sites an appeal for just about every interest. Bay Area residents and travelers alike use the parks for biking, picnicking, hiking, and swimming, as well as for more specialized pursuits such as hang gliding, hawk-watching, and kite surfing.

Listed separately in this book are some Golden Gate sites, including Fort Point National Historic Site (see p. 395) and Muir Woods National Monument (see p. 409). Be aware that Golden Gate National Recreation Area, administered by the National Park Service, is not the same as Golden Gate Park, a San Francisco city park.

The Presidio & Around

Some of the most visited sites within Golden Gate National Parks are in northern San Francisco at the shore of the Golden Gate itself—the narrow strait that connects San Francisco Bay with the Pacific Ocean.

The Presidio, a former military installation at the southern end of the Golden Gate Bridge, includes restored military structures—such as artillery batteries, stables, and barracks—and a national cemetery. Crissy Field, a former airfield, features a restored coastal marsh and an education center. A former Coast Guard station now houses the visitor center for Gulf of the Farallones National Marine Sanctuary, with exhibits on Pacific Ocean marine life.

Ocean sunset views draw many people to Lands End, west of the Presidio, as do the historic Cliff House restaurant and remains of the Sutro Baths. To the south, Fort Funston has hiking trails and a combination of winds and cliffs that make it excellent for hang gliding. In between Cliff House and Fort Funston is the long expanse of Ocean Beach, the longest beach in the Bay Area. The National Park Service works here to protect a small shorebird called the snowy plover, which has suffered from disturbances to its beach habitat.

To the east of the Presidio in the Marina District is Fort Mason, a former military post that is now home to a national park information center as well as arts facilities, galleries, shops, and restaurants.

Alcatraz Island

In San Francisco Bay sits famed Alcatraz Island, once the site of a maximum-security prison where inmates included Chicago gangster Al Capone; "Machine Gun" Kelly; and Joseph Stroud, the "Birdman of Alcatraz." The island and former prison are now available for tours via a concessionaire-operated ferry. Park rangers present programs on various topics, including infamous inmates; the natural history of the island; military history; and the Native American occupation of the island in 1969–1970, which drew attention to issues of Native American rights. Alcatraz is one of San Francisco's most popular attractions, and advance reservations for the ferry ride are strongly recommended.

Marin Headlands

Across the Golden Gate Bridge lies the multifaceted recreation and historical area called Marin Headlands. Hiking and biking trails through seemingly remote hills attract many visitors, as do lookout points from which to see and photograph the Bay, the city, and the Golden Gate Bridge. Bird-watchers consider the headlands one of the area's top locations; thousands of hawks, eagles, and other raptors fly overhead in fall. Fort Cronkhite, a World War II military post; and Point Bonita Lighthouse *(limited hours)* are among other area attractions. Perhaps the most unusual site within the park is the Nike missile site *(limited hours),* built during the Cold War to defend against Soviet bombers that might attack the United States. This is the only restored Nike missile site in the nation. Other points of interest within the Marin Headlands area include the Marine Mammal Center, Bay Area Discovery Museum, and the Headlands Center for the Arts.

Tennessee Valley Area

To the north, the Tennessee Valley area offers popular hiking and biking trails. Farther north, along the coast, Muir Beach Overlook provides a good vantage for spotting migrating gray whales in winter. Nearby Stinson Beach is one of several places within the parks where swimming is possible, but visitors are cautioned here, as elsewhere, about dangers such as undertow and sharks. (Generally speaking, the area's cold-water beaches are more popular for sunbathing, picnicking, kite flying, and the like than for swimming.)

More Sites

Additional locations include Milagra Ridge in San Mateo County, managed in part to protect a rare species of butterfly; 1,232-acre Phleger Estate, also in San Mateo County, with trails through a forest of second-growth redwoods, oaks, and firs; and Bolinas Ridge, north of Marin Headlands, popular with mountain bikers. See the websites for the park and the nonprofit support group Golden Gate National Parks Conservancy *(www.parksconservancy .org)* for a complete list of sites.

Park office
Fort Mason (off Marina Blvd.)
San Francisco, CA
415-561-4700
www.nps.gov/goga

AT A GLANCE

In and around San Francisco ▪ 75,500 acres ▪ Year-round ▪ Hiking, touring historic sites, camping, swimming, wildlife-watching

---

John Muir National Historic Site

The home of one of America's greatest conservationists

Born in Scotland, John Muir came to the United States with his family as a boy. Later in life, after almost losing one eye in an accident, he decided to devote himself to nature, and went on to become one of the most influential conservationists in the country's history.

He wrote many books and magazine articles about natural history, and it was in large part through his efforts that Yosemite, Grand Canyon, Sequoia and Kings Canyon, and Mount Rainier National Parks were established. Often called the father of the National Park Service, Muir also helped found the Sierra Club and was its president until his death in 1914.

The most famous memorial to Muir is Muir Woods National Monument (see p. 409), a protected

A portrait of John Muir welcomes visitors to his home.

redwood forest north of San Francisco. John Muir National Historic Site preserves the house where he lived for the last 24 years of his life (when he wasn't away on an outdoor-oriented trip). Located in the Alhambra Valley, 2 miles south of Martinez, California, the house was built by Dr. John Strentzel, Muir's father-in-law, with whom Muir partnered in managing a fruit orchard on the property.

Visitors can take a self-guided or ranger-led tour of the 14-room Victorian-style house *(tours daily),* which includes the writing desk at which Muir wrote in the study he called his "scribble den." A 20-minute film about Muir's life called "A Glorious Journey" is shown in the visitor center. An 1849 adobe house on the property features exhibits on the Juan Bautista de Anza National Historic Trail (see p. 309).

The site also includes 325-acre Mount Wanda, named for one of Muir's daughters, which is open daily for hiking and nature study. A 1-mile path leads to the summit. Park rangers lead seasonal bird and nature walks here. Full-moon walks are also offered in summer.

4202 Alhambra Ave.
Martinez, CA
925-228-8860
www.nps.gov/jomu

AT A GLANCE

Northern California, 20 miles northeast of Oakland ▪ 344 acres ▪ Year-round ▪ Touring Muir home, taking guided nature walks

Joshua Tree National Park

The intersection of three ecosystems in a dramatic desert landscape

Stretching across more than 1,200 square miles of the southern California desert, Joshua Tree National Park encompasses large tracts of two arid ecosystems—the Colorado "low desert" and the Mojave "high desert"—and smaller areas of a third. With elevations ranging from 536 feet to more than 5,000 feet, with sand dunes, dry lakes, granite outcrops, and palm oases, and with a diversity of wildlife from bighorn sheep to songbirds, the park, established in 1994, offers endless opportunities for exploration and discovery.

Natural History

The Colorado and Mojave Deserts meet within Joshua Tree National Park, and while they are both deserts, they differ profoundly both in overall appearance and in details of vegetation and other environmental factors.

The Colorado is the western reach of the Sonoran Desert, and it is considered a subset of that larger ecosystem. It is found below 3,000 feet elevation in the eastern part of the park, which averages around 11 degrees hotter than the western part; visitors will also find it drier and less vegetated. Growing here are plants such as ocotillo, featuring whiplike branches that show red flowers after rain; cholla cactus, called "jumping" cholla because of the ease with which sections attach themselves to passing hikers; and creosote bush, which grows as isolated individuals, with shiny leaves that minimize water loss.

The most distinctive plant in the Mojave Desert of the park's western section is the Joshua tree. This striking yucca got its name (according to legend) when Mormon pioneers saw it and thought its limbs looked like the upstretched arms of the biblical Joshua leading them to the promised land. Joshua trees thrive on sandy plains studded by granite monoliths and piles of boulders.

The national park's third ecosystem is located in its westernmost part, above 4,000 feet elevation. Here, the Little San Bernardino Mountains provide habitat for a plant community dominated by juniper and piñon pine. In addition, there are five desert fan-palm oases scattered across the park, located where fault lines allow water to rise to the surface. These varying habitats mean Joshua Tree National Park is home to more than 250 species of birds, 52 of mammals, and 44 of reptiles.

Human History

The record of Joshua Tree's human history dates back to a point sometime after the most recent ice age with the arrival of people of the Pinto Culture, hunter-gatherers who may have been

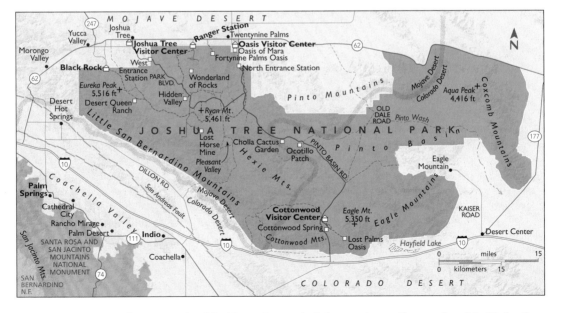

FOLLOWING PAGES: *A distinctive sight of the Mojave Desert, the Joshua tree is actually a member of the lily family.*

part of the Southwest's earliest civilizations. They lived in Pinto Basin in the eastern part of today's park, which, though inhospitably arid today, had a wetter climate and was crossed by a sluggish river some 5,000 to 7,000 years ago. Nomadic groups of natives seasonally inhabited the region when harvests of piñon nuts, mesquite beans, acorns, and cactus fruit offered sustenance. The Pinto culture was followed by other Native American groups, including the Serrano, the Chemehuevi, and the Cahuilla.

A flurry of late 19th-century gold-mining ventures left ruins in locations around the park. Visitors may come upon these old mines while hiking or driving backcountry roads. Park rangers advise caution around mine workings, and warn visitors not to enter old mine shafts.

Two species of horned lizards make their home in Joshua Tree's arid landscape.

Visiting the Park

Joshua Tree National Park has three main entrances: in the northwest in the town of Joshua Tree; in the north in the town of Twentynine Palms; and in the south off I-10, about 25 miles east of the town of Indio. Visitor centers at these entrances stay open year-round. The Black Rock Nature Center, south of the town of Yucca Valley, is open only October through May. The entrance station to the Indian Cove area is in the northern part of the park.

Visitors with limited time should drive along Park Boulevard, which loops through the northwest part of the park between the towns of Twentynine Palms and Joshua Tree. The side road to Keys View and the road through Pinto Basin are recommended for those people with a little more time, and other roads and miles of trails (including 12 self-guiding nature trails) invite those with a full day or more.

Mountain biking can be a good

way to enjoy the park, but bikers should try to avoid paved roads, which are narrow and usually lack shoulders, and stick to unpaved backcountry roads. Bikers should also note that bicycling is not permitted on trails or anywhere off roads.

Park Boulevard

The Oasis Visitor Center in Twentynine Palms offers exhibits and interpretive videos to orient visitors to the park; it also provides a schedule of ranger-led programs and tours. Nearby is the Oasis of Mara, a cluster of fan palms (the only palms native to this desert region) and mesquites watered by a seeping spring. This can be a good spot for bird-watching, as are all the park's palm oases. (Some can be reached only by hiking.)

From Twentynine Palms, Utah Trail reaches the North Entrance Station and then climbs, skirting the Pinto Mountains, which rise to the east. At the road fork, Pinto Basin Road heads east into Wilson Canyon. Along the way is Arch Rock Nature Trail, with interpretive exhibits on geology. Farther along, the road crosses the transition zone where the Mojave Desert ecosystem meets that of the Colorado Desert. The area ahead is an

ancient lake bed, now dry, dominated by creosote bush. The Cholla Cactus Garden Trail and Ocotillo Patch, both located along Pinto Basin Road, provide chances to see the Colorado Desert ecosystem up close.

Back on Park Boulevard heading west, the road passes among mammoth granite formations rising from a sandy plateau of the Mojave. Some 800 million years old, worn by eons of weather into the contours of melting ice cream, the Jumbo Rocks are one of the best examples of these formations. Joshua Tree ranks among the favorite destinations of rock climbers, with thousands of named routes. Spectators gather in parking lots to watch climbers, who may number in the hundreds on busy weekends. This many climbers can negatively affect the local environment, so learning and following park regulations is especially important in Joshua Tree.

Along Park Boulevard, aptly named Skull Rock flanks the road on the way westward to Hidden Valley, a scenic boulder area where granite has been eroded to resemble animals, human faces, and abstract forms. Those with a 4WD vehicle can head south on the unpaved Geology Tour

Road, an 18-mile round trip heading south off Park Boulevard. The route features interpretive stops keyed to a self-guiding brochure on park geology.

Farther west is the paved side road south to the spot called Keys View, which, on a clear day, offers a panorama from a 5,185-foot lookout point over the Coachella Valley and the Salton Sea into Mexico. Across the valley rises 10,804-foot Mount Jacinto, towering above Palm Springs.

North off Park Boulevard, a side road leads to Barker Dam, one of the park's best bird-watching locations. A water tank here was built by early area ranchers. This is also the way to Keys Ranch. A fascinating historic spot, the ranch can be visited only on 90-minute ranger-led guided tours *(reservations required),* which follow a 0.5-mile walking route. Here, Bill and Frances Keys lived for 60 years beginning in 1910, raising five children in this remote location. Visitors can see the ranch house, schoolhouse, store, workshop, orchard, vehicles, and mining equipment, relics that tell the story of the Desert Queen Ranch.

The 1.25-mile Hidden Valley Trail winds through a stony maze to a "hidden" bowl where it's said that rustlers once hid stolen cattle. Park Boulevard continues northwest through a forest of Joshua trees to the West Entrance Station and the town of Joshua Tree.

Cottonwood Spring

Among the attractions in the southern part of the park, around the Cottonwood Visitor Center, are trails at Cottonwood Springs. The spring, created by earthquake activity, was used for centuries by the Cahuilla Indians, and later was an important water source for prospectors searching the region for gold. Bighorn sheep sometimes appear in nearby Cottonwood Wash, and the 3-mile loop trail to Mastodon Peak offers spectacular views. The 8-mile round-trip hike to the Lost Palms Oasis rewards visitors with the largest stand of fan palms in the park.

Cottonwood Spring may be best known, though, for its excellent bird-watching. Joshua Tree National Park's desert-dwelling species include greater roadrunner, phainopepla, verdin, cactus wren, ash-throated flycatcher, Scott's oriole, Le Conte's thrasher, and Gambel's quail. In spring and fall, Cottonwood Spring and other park oases attract migrant birds such as warblers, grosbeaks, tanagers, and buntings.

The park's reptiles include the appealingly chunky-looking desert tortoise, a threatened species that spends nearly all its time underground in burrows. Once common, the tortoise has declined in population because of loss of habitat, disease, and persecution. It is strictly protected. Any visitor lucky enough to find one should observe it from a distance. Joshua Tree is also home to seven species of rattlesnakes. Hikers should follow basic rules about watching where they step and not putting hands into rocks or other places they can't see. Much more likely to be spotted are some of the park's 18 species of lizards.

Wildflowers

One of the park's most popular nature-related activities is wildflower viewing, and rangers are often asked, "When is the best time to see flowers?" The answer: It depends. Seasonal rainfall and temperatures cause dates to vary from year to year. At low elevations, such as in Pinto Basin and nearby Cottonwood Canyon, flowers may start blooming in February, while mountains higher than 5,000 feet may have plants blooming as late as June.

Calif. 62, Twentynine Palms & Joshua Tree, CA
760-367-5500
www.nps.gov/jotr
www.joshuatree.org

AT A GLANCE

Southern California, 40 miles northeast of Palm Springs ▪ 992,623 acres ▪ Fall through spring ▪ Hiking, camping, backpacking, mountain biking, rock climbing

Lassen Volcanic National Park
A land of sulphur fumes, bubbling mudpots, and hissing steam

Here in the Cascade Range in northern California, a series of volcanic events—ash eruptions, minor earthquakes, escaping gas—occurred from 1914 into 1917. The activity reached its zenith in late May 1915, when a volcanic explosion of Lassen Peak pushed lava out a new crater and sent a 20-foot-high wall of mud, ash, and melted snow down the mountainside, crushing forests. Three days later, a huge mass of ash and gas shot out of the volcano, devastating a swath of land a mile wide and 3 miles long. A cloud of volcanic steam and ash rose 30,000 feet into the air. Ash fell as far away as 200 miles to the east.

A wet, montane meadow shows little evidence of the volcanic nature of Lassen Volcanic National Park.

The explosion was the last volcanic eruption to occur in the Cascades before the 1980 eruption of Mount St. Helens in Washington. Lassen Peak is the largest of a group of more than 30 volcanic domes that have erupted over the past 300,000 years in what is today Lassen Volcanic National Park.

A Study in Volcanism

Except for a small eruption in 1921, Lassen Peak has been quiet since that series of events. But it remains an active (though temporarily dormant) volcano, the centerpiece of a vast area where volcanism displays its spectacular handiwork: devastated mountains, denuded land, bubbling cauldrons of mud, and ominously hissing steam vents smelling of sulphur. Scientists study Lassen with great interest, hoping to discover information related to other volcanoes in the Cascade Range, and—possibly someday—to be able to

predict more accurately when eruptions might occur and what they might be like.

Lassen Volcanic National Park is especially interesting because it includes four different types of volcanoes: the main peak's plug volcano (Lassen Peak may be the largest plug-dome volcano in the world); an older, layered stratovolcano (also called composite volcano); shield volcanoes, where basalt forms low, smooth domes; and cinder cones. In addition, every hydrothermal (hot water) feature found on Earth, except for geysers, appears here.

Volcanism in this area dates back millions of years in an unbroken chain of eruptions and other activity. In (relatively) more recent times, hundreds of thousands of years ago, a volcanic peak called Mount Tehama (aka Brokeoff volcano) rose here, 11,500 feet high and 11 miles across. Geologic activity caused it to collapse, leaving smaller volcanoes

around its rim. Lassen, the peak for which the park is named, rises 10,457 feet and was "born" more than 27,000 years ago.

Driving the Main Park Road

Lassen Volcanic National Park can receive 40 feet of snow in winter, which closes the 30-mile main road through the heart of the volcanic area. The road can open as early as mid-May or as late as mid-July, depending on snowfall, and can close as early as mid-October or as late as late November. Short sections of the road in the northern and southern parts of the park remain open to provide access for visitors who want to ski cross-country or snowshoe along roads or trails.

The Kohm Yah-mah-nee Visitor Center, located at the Southwest Entrance, offers exhibits, an interpretive film, and information on ranger-led programs. From here, the winding main park road leads to a first stop at the Sulphur Works, where visitors can walk by sulphur fumes and see hissing fumaroles (openings in the ground from which steam or volcanic gases are emitted), sputtering mud, and gurgling clay tinted in pastels by minerals. A visitor will agree with naturalist John Muir's description of the scene as "reeking and bubbling with hot springs." This was the heart of the ancient Mount Tehama. To the west of Sulphur Works rises 9,235-foot Brokeoff Mountain, one of the volcanic peaks left behind when the large composite volcano collapsed.

At Bumpass Hell, the road's next major stop, the large balanced rock at the edge of the parking lot is a glacial erratic: a boulder picked up by a moving sheet of ice, polished smooth, and dropped here when the glacier melted.

The 3-mile Bumpass Hell Trail (the route to walk if you have time for only one trail) takes about three hours at an easy pace. This area is named for K. V. Bumpass, a local guide who, in the 1860s, plunged his leg through the thin crust covering a hot mud pot. Though badly burned, he wisecracked about his easy descent into hell. This is the park's largest hydrothermal area, and the trail passes more fumaroles and hissing hot springs. In the springs' steamy pools float golden flakes of iron pyrite, the mineral often called fool's gold.

The park road curves around Lassen Peak. At an elevation of about 8,400 feet, it reaches the turn to the parking area for the trail to the top of the volcano. The 2.5-mile (one way) path to the summit is strenuous, but it offers the reward of excellent views of the Devastated Area, destroyed by the May 1915 eruption. The rotten-egg smell of hydrogen sulfide gas reminds hikers that Lassen is an active volcano. On a clear day Mount Shasta, 75 miles to the northwest, is visible. Don't climb Lassen if a storm is approaching, as the top is often a target of lightning strikes.

The road continues east and north of Lassen, reaching a short interpretive trail at the Devastated Area. Here visitors can see, amid the old stumps, evidence of decades of regrowth and renewal of the forest.

Ahead is a rugged landscape called Chaos Crags and Chaos Jumbles. About 300 years ago a nearby volcanic dome collapsed, perhaps because of seismic activity. Millions of tons of rock, riding a cushion of trapped air, sped across 2 miles of flat land. The horizontal avalanche smashed into a mountain and veered into a creek, damming it and creating Manzanita Lake. An easy 1.8-mile loop trail circles the lake.

At the lake is the park's Loomis Museum, with exhibits, films,

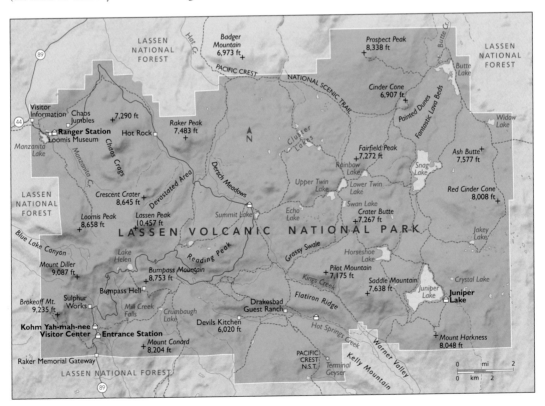

and seasonal ranger programs. The museum was named for B. F. Loomis, who documented Lassen Peak's 1914–17 eruption cycle and promoted the park's establishment. The museum displays artifacts and photographs of the eruptions and the original equipment Loomis used in his work.

Butte Lake

In the northeastern corner of the park, reached by an unpaved road off Calif. 44, is the Butte Lake campground (one of eight in the park) and the 4-mile round-trip hike to Cinder Cone. This nearly symmetrical, 755-foot-high mound of lava, surrounded by multicolored cinders, stands black and solitary above a pine forest. This kind of cone volcano ejects light lava that shatters in the air and falls back as cinders, which pile up around the vent. From the top (6,907 feet in elevation), the craters of relatively recent eruptions (the last in 1666) can be seen.

Warner Valley

Warner Valley lies in the southern part of the park. It is reached via a road that dead-ends at the Warner Valley campground and the historic Drakesbad Guest Ranch *(866-999-0914)*, which was originally built in 1890, crushed by the heavy winter snowfall of 1937–38, and rebuilt in 1938. An easy 3-mile round-trip trail leads to Boiling Springs Lake, where steam vents underneath keep the water around 125°F. The mud pots on the southeastern shore are among the best in the park.

Park Activities

Though the volcanic heritage on view is the park's most notable feature, the park offers plenty to see and do for visitors with other interests. With a free permit, backpackers can roam over much of the park's extensive wilderness area, and visitors can bring canoes or kayaks to the park in which to paddle around its scenic mountain lakes. Catch-and-release trout fishing is also popular at Manzanita Lake. Horseback riders have access to most park trails.

Flora & Fauna

Lassen Volcanic National Park is situated where three biological provinces meet. Its environment is influenced by the Cascade Range to the north, the Sierra Nevada mountains to the south, and the Great Basin desert to the east. Diversity of flora and fauna is also increased by its elevational range (5,000 to 10,457 feet) and the fact that precipitation varies from the moister western side to the drier eastern part of the park.

Areas of the park below 7,800 feet feature a mixed conifer forest of white fir and ponderosa, Jeffrey and sugar pines. Higher are found stands of western hemlock, red fir, and lodgepole pine, and above that is the subalpine zone, where vegetation is sparse.

Mammals within Lassen include black bear (campers and backpackers should follow bear-country rules about food storage), mule deer, pine marten, bobcat, mountain lion, porcupine, mountain beaver, yellow-bellied marmot, and golden-mantled ground squirrel.

Bird-watchers will find many typical species of the western mountains in Lassen, such as spotted owl, Steller's jay, Clark's nutcracker, red-breasted nuthatch, brown creeper, mountain chickadee, white-headed woodpecker, mountain bluebird, hermit warbler, and gray-crowned rosy-finch.

Calif. 89, 20 miles north of Mineral, CA
530-595-4444
www.nps.gov/lavo

AT A GLANCE

Northern California, 50 miles east of Redding ▪ 106,448 acres ▪ Year-round ▪ Hiking, camping, backpacking, horseback riding, scenic auto touring, cross-country skiing, snowshoeing

Lava Beds National Monument

A rugged landscape created by half a million years of volcanic activity

Scattered throughout this northern California park are cinder and spatter cones; lava beds; and more than 700 lava tube caves, the result of 500,000 years of eruptions from the Medicine Lake volcano. This massive shield volcano is part of the Cascade Range volcanic belt that includes Mount St. Helens, Mount Rainier (see p. 473), Lassen Peak (see p. 403), and dozens of other volcanoes of the Pacific Northwest. Eruptions as recent as 1,100 years ago spilled massive lava flows over the park area.

The park protects Native American rock art dating back at least 2,500 years. In 1872–73 Modoc Indians led by a chief known as Captain Jack used these lava fields to evade U.S. Army forces for five months.

After stopping at the visitor center,

drive first to Mammoth Crater, where a short path heads to the top, providing views of the crater responsible for much of the park's terrain. The nearby 2-mile Big Nasty Trail passes through rugged lava, and the 0.4-mile Heppe Cave Trail winds under ponderosa pine to a lava tube where water quenches the thirst of local wildlife.

More than two dozen lava caves in the park have developed trails and entrances. These and the hundreds of other caves formed when flowing lava cooled and solidified more quickly on the outside than on the inside; when the inner lava kept flowing, a hollow tube was created. Talk to a park ranger about the best way to visit the caves, and for safety tips. Free guided tours are offered in the summer.

An easy trail leads to Symbol Bridge and Big Painted Cave, where you'll find Native American pictographs (painted images); petroglyphs (carved images) can be seen at Petroglyph Point. Either the 1.5-mile outer loop trail or the 0.5-mile inner loop at Captain Jack's Stronghold snakes through the lava fortress the Modocs used to hold out against Army troops.

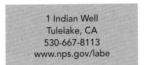

1 Indian Well
Tulelake, CA
530-667-8113
www.nps.gov/labe

AT A GLANCE

Northern California, 35 miles southeast of Klamath Falls, Oregon ▪ 46,692 acres ▪ Year-round ▪ Exploring lava caves, hiking, camping, viewing historic sites, wildlife-watching

Manzanar National Historic Site

Remembering the forced relocation of Japanese Americans in World War II

In the months following the Dec. 7, 1941, Japanese attack on Pearl Harbor, the United States government ordered more than 110,000 Japanese-American citizens and resident Japanese aliens to leave their homes and move to remote, military-style camps. Manzanar War Relocation Center was one of ten such camps set up around the country in states from California to Arkansas.

Because Manzanar was the best-preserved of the camp sites, it was designed as a park that would "stimulate and provoke a greater understanding of and dialogue on civil rights, democracy, and freedom," in the words of a monument on the site.

The historic site's visitor center presents a 22-minute film, "Remembering Manzanar," every half hour. Exhibits include a scale model of the war relocation center constructed by former internees, historic photographs

Manzanar Memorial

and audiovisual programs, and artifacts. A display includes the names of more than 10,000 Japanese Americans who spent all or part of World War II at Manzanar.

The 6,200-acre relocation center site had a history of displaced people predating World War II. The Paiute Indians who lived here were forced to relocate to California's Fort Tejon in 1863, and an agricultural town named Manzanar (Spanish for "apple

orchard") grew up. In the 20th century the Los Angeles Department of Water and Power began acquiring water rights in the valley, and by the 1930s the town was abandoned.

Today, there are two reconstructed barracks and a mess hall that houses interactive exhibits. Visitors can drive a 3.2-mile auto-tour route and see remnants of rock gardens, building foundations, and the camp cemetery as well as outdoor exhibits. All but 3 of the camp's 800 buildings were dismantled or relocated after World War II. There are still orchards at Manzanar, and visitors are allowed to pick limited amounts of fruit.

The Manzanar Committee, a nonprofit educational organization, sponsors a pilgrimage to Manzanar the last Saturday of every April. Many former internees, and a growing number of their descendants and other young people, participate in this event.

U.S. 395, 6 miles south of
Independence, CA
760-878-2194
www.nps.gov/manz

AT A GLANCE

East-central California, 170 miles north of Bakersfield ▪ 814 acres ▪ Fall through spring ▪ Viewing historical exhibits, taking auto-tour route

Mojave National Preserve

A vast desert expanse ideal for adventurous travelers

Joshua trees are found throughout Mojave National Preserve.

As varied as it is vast, Mojave National Preserve encompasses three of the four major North American deserts—Mojave, Great Basin, and Sonoran—as well as elevations ranging from 7,929 feet atop Clark Mountain to 880 feet near the town of Baker on I-15. Within the park can be found tall sand dunes; volcanic cinder cones; the world's largest forest of Joshua trees; and a variety of artifacts from a human history of mining, ranching, and military activity.

All this adds up to a place of great diversity, home to a fascinating array of wildlife and vegetation—including, after wet winters, colorful displays of desert wildflowers. Located between the metropolitan areas of Los Angeles and Las Vegas, Mojave National Preserve offers a sense of remoteness and solitude for travelers who make even a short side trip through the park, as well as tremendously varied pleasures for those who take time to explore it in greater depth.

Kelbaker Road

Along Kelbaker Road southeast of Baker, visitors will pass through a 25,600-acre area of lava flows and volcanic cinder cones, designated as Cinder Cones National Natural Landmark for its beauty and geologic value.

The Kelso Depot Visitor Center has been restored to its 1924 appearance. This attractive Spanish-style building offers a short orientation film, exhibits, a gallery with changing artworks, and a lunch counter (or "beanery," as it was traditionally called in the days when this was a working train depot).

Drive south 8 miles on Kelbaker Road to reach the side road to expansive Kelso Dunes, which rise to more than 600 feet. The dunes, the third tallest in North America, sometimes create a booming sound when they move. Visitors are encouraged to run down the slopes to try to make the dunes boom.

Exploring the Rest of Mojave

To the northeast of Kelso, Cima Road passes near the largest, densest forest of Joshua trees (a type of yucca) in the world. The 4-mile round-trip hike along Teutonia Peak Trail provides a close-up look at this remarkable habitat.

Black Canyon Road (unpaved north of Hole-in-the-Wall) passes through the Hole-in-the-Wall area, ringed in part with rhyolite cliffs. The information center (*Fri.-Sun., Oct.-April, Sat. May-Sept.*) here is near campgrounds and hiking trails, including a short nature trail with markers identifying desert plants. The park's newest trail, a 6-mile loop, encircles Barber Peak, just west of the Hole-in-the-Wall campground.

More than 1,000 miles of unpaved roads crisscross the park, inviting exploration by visitors with high-clearance 4WD vehicles. Primitive roads reach the only section of the park north of I-15, a disjunct tract containing the park's highest point, 7,929-foot Clark Mountain. The park's most famous unpaved route is Mojave Road, which traverses the preserve east to west. Dating back to an original Indian path, it was used by westbound pioneers. The U.S. Army established forts along the trail to protect travelers.

Motorists should obey the rules designed to protect natural resources before setting out on Mojave's roads. Driving in desert washes, for example, is forbidden, along with all other off-road driving.

Activities

With more than 800,000 acres of designated wilderness to explore, backpackers can roam through vast areas with nearly assured solitude. Hikers and backpackers should, however, practice "leave no trace" ethics, including camping away from water sources and packing out all trash.

Wildlife in the park ranges from tiny nocturnal rodents to mountain lions, including 1,000-plus bighorn sheep. Mule deer are the most frequently seen large mammal. Birds are the most conspicuous animals, including species such as golden eagle; greater roadrunner; raven; and cactus wren, whose *chug-chug-chug* songs are a common desert sound.

Hikers should note the presence of the Mojave rattlesnake, which possesses a venom more toxic than that of any other North American rattlesnake, potentially causing serious respiratory distress and other dangerous effects. This snake is often called the Mojave green rattlesnake because of its unique coloration. Like other desert wildlife, it usually stays hidden in the heat of the day, emerging at dusk to hunt.

Located within Mojave National Preserve is Providence Mountains State Recreation Area *(www.parks.ca .gov)*, operated by California State Parks. It includes Mitchell Caverns Natural Preserve, which offers guided tours of limestone caves. As of this publication, the park was closed for infrastructure repairs, with plans to reopen by 2016. Check the park website for updates before visiting.

Kelbaker Rd. (off I-15)
34 miles southeast of
Baker, CA
760-252-6100
www.nps.gov/moja

AT A GLANCE Southeastern California, 80 miles south of Las Vegas, Nevada ▪ 1,600,000 acres ▪ Fall through spring ▪ Hiking, backpacking, camping, horseback riding, auto touring

Muir Woods National Monument

A majestic tribute to a pioneer conservationist

Biologists estimate that more than 2 million acres of redwood forest once stood along the Pacific coast of California and Oregon. Now this magnificent ecosystem exists only in scattered stands of old-growth and more extensive second- and third-growth managed plantations.

In the early 20th century, the Redwood Creek area preserved one of the San Francisco Bay region's last uncut stands of old-growth redwoods. Congressman William Kent and his wife, Elizabeth Thacher Kent, bought land here and donated 295 acres to the federal government. In 1908 President Theodore Roosevelt declared the area a national monument. Roosevelt suggested naming the area after Kent, but Kent

The monument's trails pass massive redwoods.

wanted it named for conservationist John Muir. (To learn more about this wilderness advocate, see John Muir National Historic Site, p. 398.)

Now part of Golden Gate National Parks (see p. 397), Muir Woods National Monument contains coast redwood trees up to 260 feet in height, as well as some very tall Douglas firs. The average age of the redwoods at Muir Woods is about 600 to 800 years, with some individuals at least 1,200 years old.

Visitors can follow 6 miles of trails within the park, enjoying not just the massive trees but also exploring the entire ecosystem. The park's most famous animal resident is the spotted owl, an endangered species that breeds in the area. To protect the environment, the park does not allow picnicking, camping, or mountain biking. More than 800,000 people from all over the world come to visit each year—a lot for a relatively small park, and a visitation rate that could cause resource damage without strict regulations.

Muir Woods Rd.
(off Calif. 1 & Panoramic Hwy.)
Mill Valley, CA
415-388-2596
www.nps.gov/muwo

AT A GLANCE Northern California, 12 miles north of San Francisco ▪ 554 acres ▪ Year-round ▪ Hiking, studying nature, taking ranger-led tours

Pinnacles National Park

Remains of an ancient volcano create a stunning landscape

The spectacular rock formations called "Pinnacles" rise within the southern Gabilan Mountains of west-central California. These formations originated as material deposited by volcanic eruptions around 23 million years ago near present-day Lancaster, California—some 195 miles to the southeast. The San Andreas Fault split the volcano field in two, and tectonic movement carried half the rocks northward. They're still moving about an inch a year.

The igneous rocks of Pinnacles are dominated by feldspar and quartz.

The Pinnacles' dramatic shapes are the work of water and wind erosion in the succeeding eons, sculpting rhyolite-type rocks into spires and bluffs in countless shapes. It was the stunning scenic quality of the landscape that caused President Theodore Roosevelt to designate the site as Pinnacles National Monument in 1908. Pinnacles gained national park status in 2013.

The formations of Pinnacles National Park are extremely popular with rock climbers, and hundreds of routes have been developed and named. More than 30 miles of hiking trails wind through the rock formations, including one that reaches the highest point in the park, 3,304-foot North Chalone Peak.

The shrub community called chaparral covers much of the site, composed of plants adapted to hot, dry summers and wet winters. Park woodland is made up of oaks, pines, and buckeyes, with cottonwoods and sycamores growing along streams. The park is also famed for its wildflowers,

best seen from March through May. More than 60 percent of Pinnacles is a designated wilderness area.

Two entrance roads lead into Pinnacles. The eastern entrance is off Calif. 25 about 30 miles south of Hollister. The western entrance is reached via Calif. 146 from Soledad. The park is somewhat unusual in its access, in that no road through its interior connects its east and west sides. Though the ends of the roads in the park are less than 4 miles apart, the shortest vehicle route connecting the two developed areas is about 55 miles. The east side includes the main visitor center and the campground, while the west side (reached by a winding road that may not be suitable for large vehicles) has fewer facilities but more accessible views of rock formations.

Entering the park from the east leads to the main Pinnacles Visitor Center, with exhibits and an information desk. Ask about ranger-led programs, usually offered on spring weekends. The adjacent campground, the only one in the park, is operated

by a concessioner *(831-389-4538; www.recreation.gov)*.

Farther into the park, the Bear Gulch Nature Center is open on weekends March-September and at other times when staff is available. Some of the park's most popular hiking trails begin in the Bear Gulch area. The moderately strenuous 2.2-mile Moses Spring–Rim Trail Loop passes through woodlands to views of rock formations and Bear Gulch Reservoir. This trail also offers access to Bear Gulch Cave, one of two talus caves in the park; the other is Balconies Cave. These were formed when huge boulders fell into deep, narrow gorges and wedged in place before reaching the ground. Both caves close at times because of weather conditions or to protect nesting or wintering colonies of bats. Flashlights are required to enter either cave.

For fantastic views of Pinnacles rock formations, hike 1.7 miles up to the overlook on the Condor Peaks Trail. These spires are excellent habitat for birds of prey such as golden eagles, peregrine falcons, and prairie falcons. Pinnacles National Park is home to a small population of the critically endangered California condor, reintroduced to the park in 2003. Check a bird field guide or ask a ranger for ways to distinguish condors from similar turkey vultures.

Rock climbing attracts many adventurous visitors to the park, but regardless of a climber's level of experience, it's important to read the safety advisory. Rock in the park is volcanic rhyolite breccia (rock fragments cemented together), which is softer

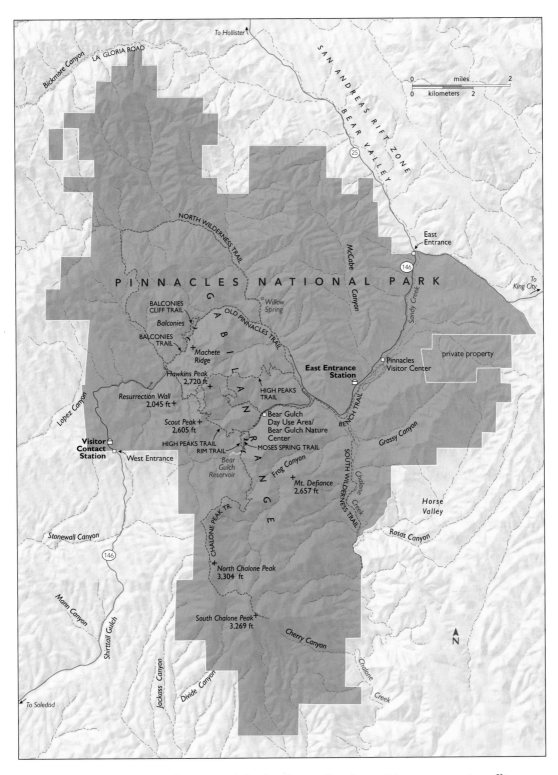

than granite and can give way without warning. Some climbing routes are closed from January through July to avoid the disturbance of nesting eagles and falcons.

On the west side of the park, a visitor contact station offers maps, exhibits, and advice from rangers. Camping is not available on the west side; this part of the park opens at 7:30 a.m. and a gate closes at 8 p.m.

Popular trails on the west side include the fairly easy 2.4-mile Balconies Cliffs–Cave Loop, which leads to the park's second talus cave. A good route to access scenic formations is the strenuous High Peaks to Balconies Cave Loop, an 8.4-mile round trip that also reaches Balconies Cave.

Those who don't plan to hike should visit the west side of Pinnacles, for views of the High Peaks rock formations from the parking area.

Spring and fall are the best seasons to visit Pinnacles National Park. Summer can be very hot; many park trails have little shade. A common problem at the park involves too much summer sun and too little water, which

can lead to dangerous dehydration for hikers. Winter days are often moderate, though temperatures can drop below freezing at night.

Parking lots and trailheads can be crowded, especially on spring weekends when many visitors arrive to enjoy the park's colorful wildflower display. A weekday visit can be more pleasant in that season.

5000 Calif. 146
Paicines, CA
831-389-4485
www.nps.gov/pinn

AT A GLANCE

Central California, 75 miles south of San Jose ▪ 27,000 acres ▪ Fall through spring ▪ Hiking, rock climbing, camping, wildflower viewing

Point Reyes National Seashore
A grand meeting place of sea and land

Not as famous as some other California national parks, Point Reyes National Seashore nonetheless ranks high as a popular destination for residents of the San Francisco Bay Area. In a part of the world becoming increasingly more developed, the beaches here, the rocky cliffs, the rolling grasslands, the woodlands … all provide opportunities to escape crowds and experience some of northern California's most beautiful scenery.

Add to that a significant diversity of wildlife, from whales to elk, from sea lions to a lengthy list of birds, and the result is a park of unending rewards for both recreation seekers and nature lovers. The area's ecological importance was recognized by the United Nations, which declared the national seashore an international biosphere reserve in 1988, known as the Central California Coast Biosphere Reserve.

The Point Reyes Lighthouse sits 300 feet below the top of the cliff.

Natural & Human History
Point Reyes National Seashore occupies a peninsula along the Pacific coast, geologically separated from the mainland by the San Andreas Fault.

The peninsula is part of the Pacific tectonic plate, which moves northwestward about 2 inches a year in relation to the adjacent North American plate to the east. Occasionally this slow movement speeds up dramatically, as in the 1906 earthquake that devastated San Francisco. The San Andreas Fault lies underground at the national seashore's southern edge. Long, narrow Tomales Bay separates the peninsula from the mainland to the north.

The Coast Miwok Indians inhabited the peninsula as long as 5,000 years ago. Sir Francis Drake landed here in 1579, the first European

explorer to do so. In the 19th and 20th centuries Point Reyes was the center of intensive dairy operations. When the park was created, many of the ranches remained in operation in what is known as the Pastoral Zone. Other ranches have been preserved as historic sites, with interpretive exhibits on the Point Reyes dairy industry.

Bear Valley Area
The park's Bear Valley Visitor Center is located in the Olema Valley, just off scenic Calif. 1. In addition to the usual information desk, exhibits, and introductory audiovisual presentation,

there's a seismograph that lets visitors see what's happening along the San Andreas Fault, deep underground.

The 0.6-mile Earthquake Trail begins nearby, featuring interpretive signs describing the geology of the area. Also here is the short walk to Kule Loklo, a re-created Coast Miwok village with trailside exhibits that describe the traditional ways of life of the first inhabitants of the Point Reyes peninsula. Nearby is the trailhead for the very popular 8.2-mile Bear Valley Trail, winding through mixed Douglas fir forest and along Bear Valley Creek to striking Arch Rock on the Pacific coast. These are just three examples of trails totaling 150 miles open to hikers, with extensive sections also open to mountain bikers and horse riders.

The Heart of the Seashore

Sir Francis Drake Boulevard, picked up north of the Bear Valley Visitor Center, leads out to Point Reyes. The road first heads north, passing the north turn to Pierce Point Ranch, where exhibits and buildings tell the history of dairy ranching in the area. Beyond lies a 2,600-acre preserve

that's home to around 400 tule elk.

The road then turns south, passing some of the national seashore's most popular beaches. Visitors heading for these beautiful sandy strands should learn regulations designed to protect both humans and wildlife. Certain areas are off-limits at times or have restrictions on activities to protect snowy plovers and seals. Beachgoers must also watch for "sneaker waves": unexpectedly large and powerful waves reaching far up the beach that can catch walkers, especially children, in rip currents and pull them out to sea.

Farther south a side road leads to the Kenneth C. Patrick Visitor Center, featuring exhibits on 16th-century maritime exploration, marine fossils, and marine environments. A minke whale skeleton is suspended from the ceiling. (Nearby Drakes Beach does not have a lifeguard.)

At the end of the road (the land's end of Point Reyes itself) is the 1870 Point Reyes Lighthouse, where park rangers lead seasonal tours *(reservations required for some tours)*. This is also a popular spot from which to watch for migrating gray whales in winter.

On the other side of Point Reyes is Chimney Rock, from which a breeding colony of elephant seals can be observed December through March. Elephant seals returned to Point Reyes in the early 1970s after an absence of more than 150 years.

Bird-watchers are among the most enthusiastic visitors to Point Reyes National Seashore. An astounding total of more than 480 species have been observed in the park and on adjacent waters. Because of the park's geographic location, it is a virtual magnet for what birders call "vagrants": birds from other geographic areas that have lost their way in migration. The park's popular bird-watching sites include Limantour, Abbotts Lagoon, Five Brooks Pond, and the rocks around the lighthouse. Cormorants, pelicans, raptors, ducks, guillemots, puffins, and oystercatchers are some of the species seen regularly.

Although the park has no developed campgrounds for car camping or RVs, backcountry camping is allowed with a permit *(fee)* in four established camping areas, accessible only on foot, by bike, or on horseback.

Bear Valley Rd. (off Calif. 1) near Olema, CA
415-564-5137
www.nps.gov/pore
www.ptreyes.org

AT A GLANCE

Northern California, 30 miles north of San Francisco ▪ 71,070 acres ▪ Year-round ▪ Hiking, biking, horseback riding, bird- and whale-watching, backpacking, kayaking

---

Port Chicago Naval Magazine National Memorial

A wartime tragedy that led to advances in civil rights

On the evening of July 17, 1944, a huge explosion occurred at the Port Chicago Naval Magazine, a U.S. Navy facility north of Oakland, California, where munitions were being loaded onto ships bound for World War II combat in the Pacific. The blast killed 320 men instantly; 202 were African Americans who were

serving in the U.S. military, which was then still enforcing racial segregation.

In the aftermath of the tragedy, surviving members of the battalion were ordered to resume work. Many refused, citing lack of safety measures and poor training. After summary courts-martial, bad-conduct discharges, and fines, 50 were singled

out by the Navy as ringleaders and were accused of mutiny. During the trial, Thurgood Marshall, chief counsel for the National Association for the Advancement of Colored People (later the first African American to serve on the Supreme Court) observed the proceedings and helped publicize racial discrimination in the military.

The men were convicted but later released from prison and given clemency, though their convictions were not overturned.

In the aftermath of the tragedy and trials, the U.S. military began ending racial discrimination, a process that included President Harry Truman's 1948 Executive Order calling for desegregation of the armed services.

Port Chicago Naval Magazine National Memorial comprises a small area with interpretive panels recalling the events. Because it is located on an active military base, visits are by guided tour only *(Thurs.–Sat.; security restrictions apply)*, with visitors transported by National Park Service shuttle. Reservations must be made one week in advance.

Marine Ocean Terminal
Concord, (off Port Chicago
Hwy.), Concord, CA
925-228-8800
www.nps.gov/poch

AT A GLANCE

Northern California, 25 miles northeast of Oakland ▪ 0.5 acre ▪ Year-round ▪ Viewing memorial

Redwood National and State Parks
A majestic land of threatened giants

The stately giants in this grove may live to be 2,000 years old, and grow to be more than 300 feet tall.

The story of North America's coast redwoods is one of nearly heedless destruction, belated appreciation, and vigorous conservation.

These magnificent trees, among the tallest on Earth, once covered 2 million acres along the Pacific coast of California and Oregon. Their valuable timber made them targets for uncontrolled logging in the 19th century—an activity that, while more regulated in the 20th century, still resulted in the loss of 96 percent of the old-growth forest that once stood as one of the most splendid and awe-inspiring ecosystems on our planet.

Much about a redwood is impressive, especially its size (up to 370 feet) and life span (up to 2,000 years—its scientific name *sempervirens* means "living forever"). A redwood cone, the size of an olive, contains 60 to 120 seeds, and one tree may produce ten million seeds.

(And what, as everyone asks, is the tallest redwood? In 2006 a new champion was discovered deep in the backcountry of Redwood National and State Parks, at 379 feet high.)

Yet redwoods can thrive only in a limited range of environmental conditions. They can't grow directly along the coast because they are vulnerable to salt spray. Yet they must be close enough to the ocean that fog can condense on them on summer nights, providing vital moisture during the dry season.

Heavy rainfall in winter washes nutrients from the soil, which means that living trees depend upon the decay of dead trees for nutrients. Logging removes dead trees, "starving" the ones that still stand. Clear-cut hillsides allow soil to erode and wash around them, smothering the shallow roots of the standing redwood trees. Removing surrounding trees makes these giants vulnerable to wind.

Saving the Redwoods
In the early 20th century conservationists became alarmed at the relentless logging that was destroying redwood forests, and a group called the Save-the-Redwoods League was formed in 1918. California protected some redwood groves in state parks, and in the 1960s Redwood National Park was established, administered by the National Park Service. Additional land has been added to the parks since

then, some of it denuded land that is being restored by replanting, as well as by recontouring hillsides to lessen erosion. The raw, clear-cut land originally had "the look of an active war zone," a park official wrote. Most of some 400 miles of logging roads are being reclaimed. It will take at least 50 years for the scars of logging to disappear, and another 250 years for the replanted redwood seedlings to grow to modest size.

In 1994 the state and national parks were administratively joined to allow for better coordination of management and conservation efforts. This joint state-federal administration is a unique arrangement in the National Park System, and the resulting entity contains about half the world's old-growth redwood forest.

Visiting the Parks

Redwood National and State Parks stretch north-south across areas covering more than 40 miles, and encompass several different units. There are five visitor centers, some open only seasonally or with limited days in winter. Spring and fall are the best times to visit the parks; summer is pleasant and visitation is moderate, while winter brings heavy rain that can impede outdoor activities. U.S. 101 runs the length of the area and provides access to park units directly or via side roads.

Lady Bird Johnson Grove & Big Tree

In the town of Orick in the southern part of the parks, the Thomas H. Kuchel Visitor Center *(707-465-7765)* features exhibits and access to some of the 37 miles of coastline protected within the parks. North of Orick, a turn east on Bald Hills Road leads to the 1.5-mile loop trail at Lady Bird Johnson Grove. This easy walk winds through woodland of old-growth redwood, Douglas fir, and tan oak. An available brochure interprets

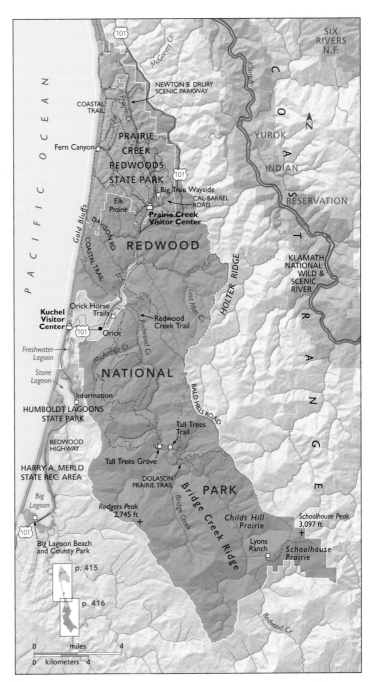

sights along the way. This is one of many places within the parks where rhododendrons make for a colorful spectacle in late spring.

Davison Road leads west off 101 to the gray sands of Gold Bluffs Beach and beautiful Fern Canyon, with its wet, fern-laden rock walls. The Trillium

Falls Trail, 2.5 miles long, passes one of the few waterfalls in the parks. It begins at the Elk Meadow day-use area, where a herd of Roosevelt elk may be seen.

It's not far north on U.S. 101 to Prairie Creek Redwoods State Park, with a campground, nature museum, and another chance to see Roosevelt elk. This is the largest subspecies of North American elk, with bulls that can weigh as much as 1,200 pounds.

The park's Newton B. Drury Scenic Parkway is a 10-mile drive through ancient redwoods. Nearby is a pullout at the Big Tree, a redwood more than 300 feet tall, 66 feet in circumference, and an estimated 1,500 years old. About 70 miles of trails branch off from trailheads in this park—up into the foothills, down into ferny canyons, and out onto the beach. One of the prettiest is a 4.5-mile ramble down James Irvine Trail to Fern Canyon, and another access point to Gold Bluffs Beach.

Although beaches along the parks' coastlines are beautiful and warm weather makes swimming enticing, park personnel strongly advise against swimming and even wading into the ocean. Unexpected "sneaker waves" can surge far up the beach with enough force to knock down people (especially children) and drag them into the cold ocean waters, where rip currents may prevent swimming back to shore. Several people drown each year while swimming or playing along northern California beaches.

Coastal Loop Drive

A side trip on Coastal Loop Drive, a partly unpaved 8-mile route, winds past wave-battered cliffs with great views of the Pacific. Rocky islands provide nesting for thousands of cormorants, murres, guillemots, gulls, and other seabirds. About 40 percent of California's seabirds breed along the 37 miles of protected coastline within Redwood National and State Parks. Trailers and RVs are prohibited on Coastal Loop Drive.

The mouth of the Klamath River can be viewed from the north end of Coastal Loop Drive or, on the opposite bank, from Requa Road. The cliffs in this area are a favored spot from which to watch for migrating gray whales in spring and fall.

Del Norte Coast & Jedediah Smith Redwoods State Parks

Farther north is Del Norte Coast Redwoods State Park, with 8 miles of coastline and great ocean views. Take Enderts Beach Road to Crescent Beach Overlook and Enderts Beach to enjoy some of these views. The 1-mile walk to Enderts Beach provides a chance to enjoy the fascinating life within tide pools at low tide.

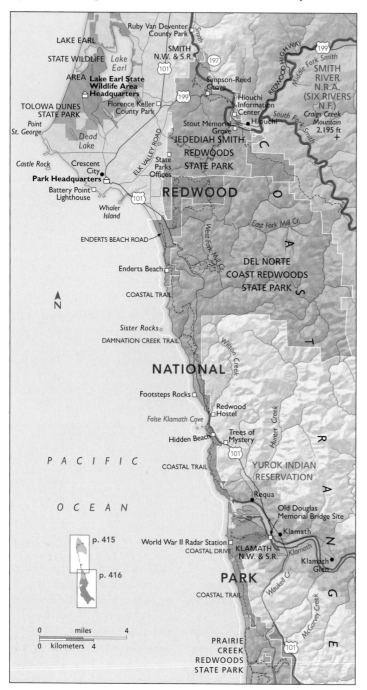

Ranger-led guided tide pool walks are offered here in summer.

The northernmost park within Redwood National and State Parks is Jedediah Smith Redwoods State Park, bisected by the Smith River. Like the park, the river was named for famed 19th-century explorer Jedediah Smith. Beginning in the Siskiyou Mountains, it is California's last major free-flowing river and is famous for salmon and steelhead. (Upstream in Six Rivers National Forest, Smith River's Class IV and V rapids challenge white-water kayakers and canoeists.)

At Crescent City, Elk Valley Road leads to Howland Hill Road, once a miners' supply road partially redwood-planked for oxcarts and horse-drawn wagons. The 6-mile road winds between redwoods that loom much closer than the ones along the highways. At Stout Grove, a mile-long trail winds among the giant trees.

Past the grove, Douglas Park Road ends at South Fork Road. Travelers should turn left onto U.S. 199 and drive west to the Hiouchi Information Center *(closed in winter)*. A short distance west on U.S. 199 is the Simpson-Reed Grove, which offers another walk among old-growth redwoods.

Wildlife

Though the coast redwoods are deservedly the main attraction here, the wildlife deserves some interest as well. Roosevelt elk, black-tailed deer, black bears, and mountain lions are among the large land mammals, while harbor seals and sea lions might be seen along the coast. Smaller mammals often seen are chickaree (a squirrel), chipmunk, ground squirrel, rabbit, beaver, porcupine, and coyote. A unique forest dweller is the Pacific giant salamander, the only salamander known to have a voice; it "barks" when agitated. It can grow to nearly a foot in length.

Bird-watchers will find many birds typical of the Pacific Northwest, including Allen's hummingbird, red-breasted sapsucker, varied thrush, Steller's jay, wrentit, and song sparrow. The endangered spotted owl lives in the forests, but the most intriguing breeding bird may be the marbled murrelet. Unlike nearly all its relatives, which nest on rocky cliffs or in burrows on seacoasts, this small seabird—no bigger than a robin—makes its nest with a single egg on large branches high in trees, sometimes as far as 30 miles inland. Logging has placed this bird on the federal list of threatened species after a population decline of more than 90 percent.

Activities

Redwood National and State Parks feature more than 200 miles of trails, from easy strolls to long-distance backpacking routes. Backpackers must obtain a permit and camp in one of eight designated sites or along gravel bars on Redwood Creek.

In summer a variety of campfire programs are presented at the campground in Jedediah Smith Redwoods State Park, Mill Creek campground in Del Norte Coast Redwoods State Park, and Elk Prairie campground in Prairie Creek Redwoods State Park.

Crescent City Information Center, 1111 Second St. Crescent City, CA 707-464-6101 www.nps.gov/redw

AT A GLANCE Northwestern California, south of Crescent City ▪ 131,983 acres (71,715 federal, 60,268 state) ▪ Spring through fall ▪ Hiking, backpacking, horseback riding, whale-watching

---

Rosie the Riveter/World War II Home Front N.H.P.

Honoring women's contribution to Allied victory

Soldiers and support personnel overseas were not the only contributors to Allied victory in World War II. On the home front, millions of Americans worked in defense plants or related jobs to provide the ships, tanks, weapons, and countless other things needed to win a war. Because so many men were on active duty, women entered the workplace in unprecedented numbers. The iconic image of Rosie the Riveter—especially on a famous poster with the slogan "We Can Do It!"—came to symbolize women's vital contributions to the cause.

The small town of Richmond, California, just north of Oakland, may have been transformed during World War II more than any similar community in the United States. Thousands of workers flooded into the town to build ships and tanks and work in war-related industries.

Rosie the Riveter/World War II Home Front National Historical Park *(www.rosietheriveter.org)*, a partnership of the National Park Service, the City of Richmond, and nonprofit groups, includes Rosie the Riveter Memorial in Marina Bay Park, based on the shape of a Liberty (World War II cargo) ship. The S.S. *Red Oak Victory,* a restored cargo ship built in the Richmond shipyards, is open for visitation; on the drive there, visitors pass the remaining buildings and dry docks of World War II Shipyard No. 3. The park also contains the Maritime Child Development Center, home to a charter school and a small exhibit on a wartime preschool classroom, and the Ford Assembly Building, one of only three World War II tank depots in the country.

Visitors should start at the Rosie the Riveter Visitor Education Center, which is open daily and features interactive exhibits as well as short films and ranger talks.

1414 Harbour Way South
Suite 3000
Richmond, CA
510-232-5050
www.nps.gov/rori

AT A GLANCE

Northern California, 9 miles north of Oakland ▪ 145 acres ▪ Year-round ▪ Touring memorial sites, historical presentations

San Francisco Maritime National Historical Park

An evocative collection of ships and maritime memorabilia

Located on San Francisco Bay in the famed Fisherman's Wharf neighborhood, San Francisco Maritime National Historical Park is dedicated to interpreting the Pacific coast's maritime heritage, especially the part of it centered on San Francisco Bay. Included within the park are vessels from rowboats to sailing ships to steamboats, five of which are listed as national historic landmarks; as well as a strikingly designed maritime museum.

The park's visitor center (conveniently located at the end of a cable car route) is in a brick cannery warehouse dating from 1908. Those entering are greeted by an impressive first-order Fresnel lighthouse lens from the Farallon Islands, gleaming brass and glass. The center features interactive exhibits and artifacts recounting the history of immigration, transportation, and industry in the San Francisco Bay Area. Park rangers can provide advice on visiting other local sites.

Park rangers and volunteers, many with considerable shipboard experience, conduct interpretive and living-history programs and guided tours.

From the visitor center it's just a short stroll to Hyde Street Pier, where the main attraction is the collection of historic ships. They include:

· *Balclutha,* an 1886 square-rigged ship

The historic schooner Alma *sailing on the San Francisco Bay*

that served as a cargo ship until 1929. Built in Scotland, with a length of 301 feet, it sailed around South Africa's Cape Horn 17 times. (A baby born during a late 19th-century voyage from Calcutta, India, to San Francisco was given the name Inda-Francis Durkee.)

· *C. A. Thayer,* a schooner built in California in 1895 to carry lumber to San Francisco from Washington, Oregon, and the northern California coast.

· *Eureka,* a 300-foot-long wooden-hulled ferryboat built in 1890.

· *Alma,* a wooden-hulled scow schooner built in 1891 to carry bulk cargo in the Sacramento/San Joaquin Delta. (The *Alma* now conducts public sailing tours around the San Francisco Bay.)

· *Hercules,* a steam-powered tugboat built in 1907.

· *Eppleton Hall,* a steam-powered sidewheeler built in 1914 in England to tow coal barges. In 1969–1970 this vessel made a six-month voyage from England to San Francisco.

· A circa 1890 houseboat, known locally as an "ark," used as a summer getaway retreat on San Francisco Bay.

The Aquatic Park Bathhouse building, constructed in the 1930s to resemble an ocean liner, houses the park's Maritime Museum. The park is also home to the Maritime Research Center, which has an extensive collection on Pacific coast maritime history.

Park rangers and volunteers, many with considerable experience aboard ships, conduct interpretive and living-history programs and guided tours through the year.

499 Jefferson St.
San Francisco, CA
415-447-5000
www.nps.gov/safr

AT A GLANCE

San Francisco ▪ 50 acres ▪ Year-round ▪ Touring historic ships, visiting museum

Santa Monica Mountains National Recreation Area

Invaluable green space in an ever growing urban area

It may give some idea of the scope of Santa Monica Mountains National Recreation Area to know that it encompasses five area codes and 26 zip codes. This being star-struck southern California, it should be pointed out that one of the latter is the famous Beverly Hills 90210.

Spanning almost 50 miles from Los Angeles westward into Ventura County, the park is a patchwork of federal, state, and local public areas that comprises 239 square miles, making this the world's largest urban national park. While recreational opportunities are excellent, the area's greatest importance may simply be the preservation of open green space in a constantly growing metropolitan area, where freeways, housing, and other development make it harder for residents to experience the renewing qualities of the outdoors.

The national recreation area's visitor center is located on the grounds of the King Gillette Ranch, south of the town of Calabasas. Maps and information are available here as well as at the six state parks located within the federal area's designated boundary.

Notable Sites

One of the park's most popular features is the Backbone Trail, a route for hikers and (in places) mountain bikers and horseback riders. The trail runs along the spine of the Santa Monica Mountains, from Will Rogers State Historic Park, just off Sunset Boulevard in Pacific Palisades; to Point Mugu. Still under development but largely completed, the Backbone Trail System will extend 65 miles, unifying parklands in Santa Monica Mountains National Recreation Area.

Other notable sites within the area include the Paramount Ranch in Agoura Hills, where many movies and television shows have been filmed (park staff lead monthly guided tours of the property's sets); 588-acre King Gillette Ranch, once owned by the shaving magnate and now combining excellent wildlife habitat with a historic mansion and other structures; the Peter Strauss Ranch along Mulholland Drive, developed by an automobile tycoon, later bought and donated to the park by actor Strauss, who wanted to preserve its natural beauty; Rancho Sierra Vista/Satwiwa in Newbury Park, where the Satwiwa Native American Indian Culture Center offers regular programs on topics related to many indigenous cultures, including the Chumash and Tongva/Gabrielino people who once lived in the area; and Cheeseboro Canyon, in the northernmost section of the national recreation area, known for its many hiking trails, its high concentration of nesting birds of prey, and its stands of the magnificent valley oak, a species found only in California.

Nature enthusiasts prize the park for preserving areas of the highly endangered Mediterranean ecosystem, which occurs in only five relatively small areas in the world: around the Mediterranean Sea, and in Chile, South Africa, Australia, and southern California. This habitat is characterized by mild, rainy winters, and warm, dry summers, and is moderated by cold ocean currents offshore. Because of the island-like isolation of these areas, they all possess many endemic species (plants and animals found nowhere else).

26876 Mulholland Hwy.
Calabasas, CA
805-370-2301
www.nps.gov/samo

AT A GLANCE

Southern California, northwest of Los Angeles ▪ 155,000 acres ▪ Year-round ▪ Hiking, biking, horseback riding, camping, picnicking, visiting historic sites

Sequoia & Kings Canyon National Parks

The home of the world's largest trees

A stream trickles down the steep mountains of the Sierra Nevada, nourishing diverse ecosystems as it descends.

Park rangers at Sequoia and Kings Canyon tell the story of Walter Fry, who moved to the Sierra Nevada in 1888 to take a job as a logger. He spent five days with a team of five men sawing through and felling a single sequoia. Fry counted the growth rings on the tree and realized that he had just helped end the life of something that had been growing for 3,266 years. The change of heart he experienced at that moment led him eventually to become a ranger at Sequoia National Park, and later park superintendent.

Visitors today may not have quite such a life-changing experience at Sequoia and Kings Canyon National Parks—two adjoining National Park Service units that are administered jointly—but few will fail to be awestruck at the sight of the giant trees that led to the 1890 establishment of Sequoia National Park, the second national park to be created in the United States. The park's famed General Sherman sequoia tree, in the area called Giant Forest, is quite simply the largest living thing on our planet. These two parks protect nearly half the remaining sequoia groves in the world.

As spectacular as the giant sequoias are, the parks offer much more to see, explore, and enjoy. There are beautiful canyons, rocky rivers, dramatic rock formations, high-mountain meadows, and hundreds of miles of trails providing access. With elevations ranging from 1,300 feet in the foothills to 14,494 feet at the top of Mount Whitney—the highest mountain in the contiguous 48 states—the parks provide habitat for a great diversity of flora and fauna. There's even a marble cave to visit via guided tour.

Visiting the Parks

No road crosses the parks from east to west because of the region's wild and rugged topography. Park roads are all on the west side of the mountain range. Travelers must go north to Tioga Pass in Yosemite National Park or south to Walker Pass or Tehachapi Pass to reach the eastern slope.

Visitors should also know that, while much can be seen from

roadsides and adjacent overlooks and short nature trails, these are primarily wilderness parks. Nearly 808,000 of the parks' acres (93.4 percent of the total area) are officially designated as wilderness. This is especially true of Kings Canyon, accessed by one dead-end road, which is open in summer only. Sequoia and Kings Canyon form the heart of the second largest contiguous roadless area in the lower 48.

Sequoia National Park: Ash Mountain Entrance to Giant Forest

Sequoia National Park is reached from the south at the Ash Mountain Entrance, where the Foothills Visitor Center is located. Exhibits here focus

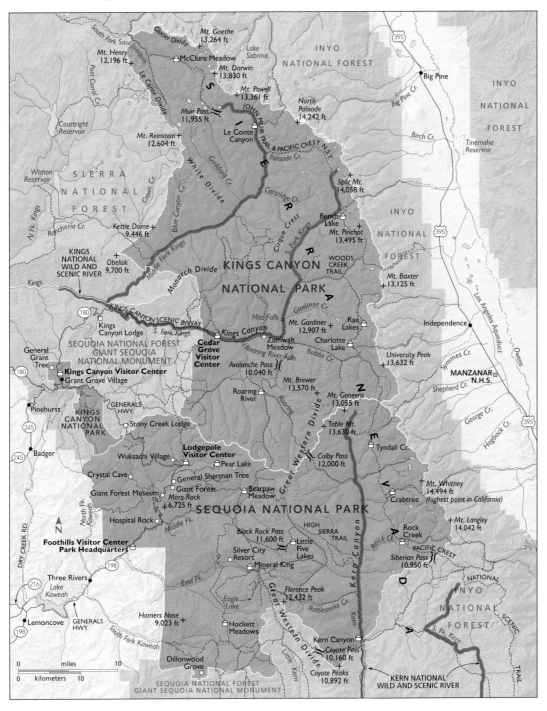

on the Sierra foothills environment, which, while not as spectacular as areas at higher elevations, is actually more biologically diverse than mountain coniferous forest. This is an area of blue oak savannas and chaparrals; some of the gnarled blue oaks may be hundreds of years old.

Generals Highway enters the park and passes Hospital Rock, where there's an exhibit on the Monache (also called Western Mono) Indians who once lived here. Still visible are hollows in the rocks where these Indians ground acorns to make flour. At the Potwisha campground on the north side of the highway, the 3.9-mile Marble Falls Trail climbs through chaparral to a beautiful cascade.

As it climbs, Generals Highway enters the mixed conifer forest that covers the lower and middle slopes of the Sierra Nevada. Unlike many other coniferous forests, which are dominated by a single species of tree, these woods are remarkably diverse, featuring a mix of ponderosa pine, incense-cedar, white fir, sugar pine, and scattered groves of giant sequoia. These trees, many of which reach tremendous heights, form some of the most extensive stands of old-growth coniferous forest that remain in the world.

The very twisting highway leads to a side road to Crystal Cave, the only one of the parks' more than 265 caves that is open to the public. The narrow 9-mile road to the cave is open in summer only. A 45-minute guided tour *(tickets available only at Foothills and Lodgepole Visitor Centers, fee)* leads through a cave full of beautiful formations created when water dissolved marble, not limestone as in most other caves elsewhere in North America.

Giant Forest Sequoia Grove

Farther up the road is one of the major attractions in the parks, the Giant Forest Sequoia Grove. Here stands the General Sherman Tree, the sequoia that is the world's largest tree. This designation recognizes volume, not height. Coast redwoods and some other species are taller but not nearly as large in circumference. General Sherman is more than 270 feet high, 102 feet in circumference, and an estimated 2,100 years old. A 13-story building would fit beneath its first large branch, and it contains enough lumber to make 1-by-12-inch boards that would stretch end to end for 119 miles. In summer, rangers conduct programs on the tree's remarkable natural history.

Learn all about sequoias at the Giant Forest Museum, one of several points of interest in the Giant Forest vicinity. A nearby road *(summer only and via shuttle on weekends)* leads to the Tunnel Log, a fallen sequoia with an opening large enough for passenger cars to drive through. This road also provides access to 6,725-foot Moro Rock, a striking granite monolith from which the views are spectacular. On a clear day the panorama stretches 100 miles west to the California coast ranges—a reward for climbing a stone stairway with almost 400 steps.

Forty miles of trails radiate out from the Giant Forest area. The easy, 2-mile Congress Trail begins at the General Sherman Tree. Sequoias of all ages line the path: young ones only a century or so old; trees scarred by fire (to which they are relatively immune because of their thick bark); and fallen sequoias, which resist rotting thanks to the tannins they contain. The tops of sequoias are often stumpy and jagged from lightning strikes, and they usually attain their full height after "only" 800 years or so. After that, they grow thicker, not taller.

Park rangers are often asked about spots from which to view Mount Whitney, the highest point in the lower 48 states. The mountain can't be seen at all from park roads because of the intervening peaks of the Sierra Nevada's Great Western Divide. (For a spot with vehicle access, Mount Whitney is most easily seen from U.S. 395 in the Owens Valley east of the parks.) For those in the Giant Forest area, the strenuous hike to 11,204-foot Alta Peak might provide a look at Whitney—if the weather cooperates.

Giant Forest to Grant Grove

Farther north on Generals Highway, a side road leads to the Lodgepole Village area, which has a visitor center (take time to see the film on black bears), shops, food stores, and cafés. Beyond, Generals Highway enters Sequoia National Forest before dead-ending at Calif. 180, near the Grant Grove Village area in Kings Canyon National Park. In this vicinity are the Kings Canyon Visitor Center, food stores, lodging, and stables at which horseback rides can be arranged.

A little ways north on Calif. 180, a 0.5-mile loop trail leads to the General Grant Tree (267 feet tall and 107 feet in circumference), the centerpiece of a 4-square-mile grove that was preserved in the late 19th century, later becoming part of Kings Canyon National Park established in 1940. Here and on nearby trails are gigantic stumps left from the logging era, including Centennial Stump, the remains of a sequoia cut down for exhibition at the 1875 Centennial in Philadelphia.

Nearby is the steep, narrow 2.3-mile road to Panoramic Point *(closed to trailers and large vehicles)*, where a 0.25-mile trail leads to a ridge top at 7,520 feet. The vista of the Sierra Nevada is breathtaking, and an interpretive display helps visitors pick out and name the distant peaks.

Kings Canyon Scenic Byway

Heading north, Calif. 180 continues back into Sequoia National Forest as the Kings Canyon Scenic Byway before reentering Kings Canyon National Park and reaching the Cedar Grove Visitor Center area. Among the attractions in this area is the Canyon View lookout point, where the vista along the canyon of the South Fork of the Kings River shows the U shape that is typical of gorges carved by glacial action. Not far away, a short paved trail leads to Roaring River Falls, an impressive waterfall rushing through a narrow granite chute. Upstream is a 1.5-mile trail through Zumwalt Meadow, a pretty place of high granite walls and lush meadows spangled with summer wildflowers.

Ahead is the end of the road, beyond which hiking trails lead into the high Sierra. A geologic note: The Sierra Nevada range is still growing today. The mountains gain height during earthquakes but are shortened by erosion almost as quickly as they grow. This erosion has deposited sediments thousands of feet thick on the floor of the San Joaquin Valley.

The Backcountry

Despite the two parks' 1,262 square miles of wilderness and more than 850 miles of wilderness trails, resource managers worry about the amount of use the backcountry receives from about 80,000 annual visitors. Permits are required for backcountry camping, and in heavily used areas a quota system is in effect late May through late September. Permits are issued for a particular trailhead; permits can be reserved in advance, though some are kept to be issued to walk-up visitors on a daily first-come, first-served basis.

It's important for all hikers and campers (and even picnickers) to be aware of the presence of black bears in the parks and to always store food in bearproof containers. Mountain lions and rattlesnakes are also present in the parks. As is the case in all national parks, though, the greatest dangers are more basic: drowning in swollen rivers, falling from cliffs, being struck by lightning, failing to carry enough water to prevent dehydration, and other perils that can be avoided with planning and care.

Calif. 198, 6 miles northeast of Three Rivers, CA
559-565-3341
www.nps.gov/seki

AT A GLANCE

Central California, 57 miles east of Fresno ▪ 865,257 acres ▪ Year-round ▪ Hiking, backpacking, camping, horseback riding, touring cave, rock climbing, taking scenic drives

Whiskeytown National Recreation Area
A popular lake, with trail access to spectacular waterfalls

Located at the site of a 19th-century gold-mining boomtown, 3,200-acre Whiskeytown Lake was created as part of a project to generate hydroelectric power and provide water for agriculture in California's Central Valley. Today it's popular with boaters, anglers (going after bass, kokanee salmon, and trout), and swimmers, as well as those who simply want to relax or picnic on its banks.

There's more to the recreation area than the lake, though, including trails to four waterfalls—three natural and one created during development of the irrigation project. The most spectacular

Whiskeytown Lake has some 36 miles of shoreline.

of them is 220-foot Whiskeytown Falls. In the 1960s staff elected to keep the existence of the falls secret while negotiations to buy the land took place, then it was forgotten until personnel

"rediscovered" it in 2004. The waterfall is reached by a moderately difficult trail of 3.4 miles round trip. Only slightly less impressive are Boulder Creek Falls and Brandy Creek Falls, both reached by less strenuous trails. Paths through the park pass through forests of canyon live oak, sugar and ponderosa pine, white fir, Douglas fir, incense cedar, and other trees.

The park's Tower House Historic District includes the 1852 home of pioneer-prospector Charles Camden and other structures from the gold-mining era. Park rangers lead seasonal tours of the house, as well as assist visitors who'd like to try their luck at panning for gold.

Whiskeytown is an ecological crossroads where the Klamath, Cascade, and California Coast mountains meet the Sacramento Valley, making it a rewarding spot for bird-watching, botanizing, and other nature study. Resident animals include black bear, mountain lion, black-tailed deer, black-tailed jackrabbit, beaver, gray fox, and three species of chipmunk. Notable bird species in the park include bald eagle, spotted owl, red-breasted sapsucker, yellow-breasted chat, yellow warbler, and olive-sided flycatcher.

Off Calif. 299 8 miles west of Redding, CA 530-246-1225 www.nps.gov/whis	**AT A GLANCE** Northern California, 8 miles west of Redding ▪ 42,503 acres ▪ Year-round ▪ Hiking, biking, boating, fishing, camping, picnicking, swimming, gold panning

Yosemite National Park
A legendary park highlighting waterfalls and granite peaks

One of the world's most famous wild places, Yosemite National Park is a historic icon of the conservation movement—not just for the United States but for all nations. The magnificent beauty of its waterfalls, massive rock formations, rushing rivers, giant sequoia trees, and alpine meadows led to calls for its protection in the mid-19th century. When President Abraham Lincoln in 1864 signed a congressional bill granting Yosemite Valley and the Mariposa Grove of Giant Sequoias to the state of California as an inalienable public trust, it marked the first time that any nation had set aside land as a wilderness preserve.

Sheep grazing and logging continued in the area, though, and in 1890 legendary conservationist John Muir was among those who led the fight to create Yosemite National Park. In 1903 Muir accompanied President Theodore Roosevelt on a camping trip to Yosemite, and three years later the federal government took back control from California of the valley and Mariposa Grove. Muir lost the battle to stop construction of a dam on the Tuolumne River in Hetch Hetchy Valley, however, and today a reservoir buries a part of the valley that he praised as among the most beautiful

Dropping off a sheer cliff, Bridalveil Fall plunges 620 feet to the valley floor.

he had ever seen. (Muir once wrote, "No temple made with hands can compare with Yosemite.")

Declared a World Heritage site in 1984 for its natural features, Yosemite National Park attracts up to 4 million visitors annually, most of whom see only the valley at its heart, a mile-wide, 7-mile-long area where the Merced River winds among waterfalls and granite monoliths. Visitors here will find lodging, camping, shopping, dining, a medical clinic, and, especially in summer, lots of other visitors. Those who get away from the park's 214 miles of paved roads to hike or

bike some of its 800 miles of trails will have a more peaceful experience.

Yosemite Valley

Entering Yosemite Valley, many visitors stop along the road to admire 620-foot-high Bridalveil Fall. A steep 0.25-mile trail leads to its base, where swirling winds often assure that visitors get wet from the spray. Rising more than 3,000 feet above the valley opposite Bridalveil, El Capitan is the largest monolith of granite in the world. It's one of many places in the park that are popular with rock climbers. (The best roadside view of El Capitan is

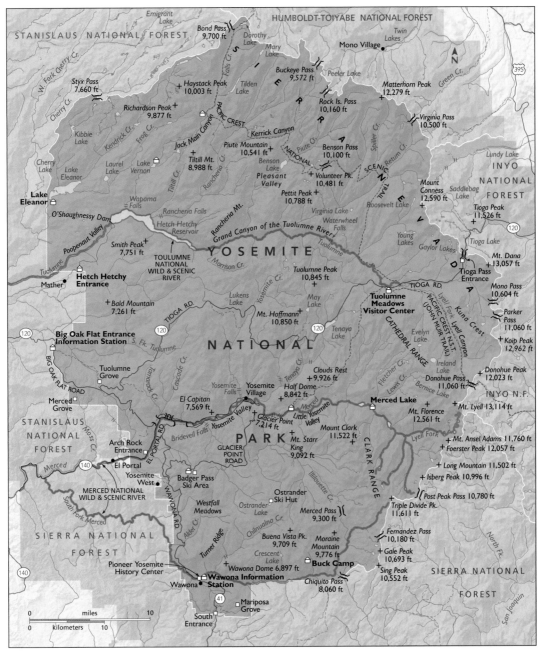

from the northern, westbound part of this divided road—i.e., leaving the valley.) To the east, 1,000-foot Horsetail Fall is famous for its fiery appearance at dusk when the sun is in the right position in mid- to late February.

There are parking lots along the valley entrance road at which shuttle buses stop; taking the bus into the valley will help lessen traffic congestion as well as eliminate the stress of driving.

The Yosemite Valley Visitor Center in Yosemite Village features an exhibit hall with displays on Yosemite's geology, human history, wildlife, and national park management. A film, the 23-minute "Spirit of Yosemite," provides an overview of the park. Next door, the Yosemite Museum interprets the cultural history of Yosemite's native Miwok and Paiute Indians, and is home to seasonal demonstrations of basket weaving, beadwork, and traditional games. The reconstructed Indian village of Ahwahnee stands behind the museum.

Mist and moonlight cast an ethereal glow over Yosemite Valley, an area of majestic cliffs and crashing waterfalls.

Many of the park's most popular hikes begin at trailheads near the visitor center or are reached by the valley shuttle bus, including the easy mile-long Cooks Meadow Loop, which offers great views of Half Dome. This glacier-carved granite peak is the park's most famous "postcard view," standing impressively above the eastern valley floor. Another popular spot from which to admire Half Dome is Mirror Lake (naturally evolving into a meadow, and sometimes more grassland than lake), reached by an easy 1-mile trail. When there's water in the lake (usually late spring) and the wind is calm, there's a classic reflection view of Half Dome on its surface.

Another magnificent waterfall, Yosemite Falls, near El Capitan, is made up of three separate drops: Upper Yosemite Fall, the middle cascades, and Lower Yosemite Fall. Taken all together, the 2,425-foot waterfall is the tallest in North America and the fifth tallest in the world. An easy 1-mile loop trail leads to the base of Lower Yosemite Fall, while a strenuous 3.6-mile hike leads to the top of Upper Yosemite Fall. Fed mostly by snowmelt, Yosemite Falls usually dries up in late summer.

At the end of Yosemite Valley, several excellent destinations are reached from a trailhead at the Nature Center at Happy Isles *(May–Sept.),* a family-oriented center that features natural-history exhibits with an emphasis on wildlife. It's 1.5 miles to striking Vernal Fall and another 2 miles to Nevada Fall; these hikes are strenuous. Only the fit should attempt the 8-mile hike-climb to the top of Half Dome, on part of which hikers use cables because of the steepness of the climb. Check with park rangers for advice and to obtain a permit before beginning this 10- to 12-hour trek.

Visitors can experience Yosemite Valley on an open-air tram tour *(fee),* a 26-mile, two-hour ride that departs several times daily from Yosemite Lodge. Moonlight tram tours are also available seasonally on the nights just prior to and after the full moon. Another excellent way to see the valley sights is by bike, along the 12 miles of paved trails winding through the area. Bike rentals are available, and bikers are reminded that bicycles are not allowed on any of the park's unpaved hiking trails. Horseback rides are offered by a valley concessionaire.

Wawona Road

Travelers who leave Yosemite Valley for points south on the Wawona Road (Calif. 41) will soon reach Wawona Tunnel, where the Tunnel View Overlook offers what has been called the most photographed vista on Earth. The panorama encompasses El Capitan, Half Dome, Bridalveil Fall, and other famed features.

Seven miles past the tunnel, an east turn on Glacier Point Road leads to the Badger Pass ski area *(the road is closed beyond this spot in winter)* and on to Glacier Point itself, another of Yosemite's dramatic viewpoints. Standing 3,200 feet above the valley, the point offers a spectacular scene of lakes, waterfalls, and rock formations.

In the southern part of the park, Wawona includes the Pioneer Yosemite History Center, a collection of historic buildings associated with the people and events that created Yosemite National Park. In summer costumed interpreters portray various historical characters such as homesteaders and cavalry troopers. Visitors can take a wagon ride or visit the studio (now a park information center) of artist Thomas Hill, visited by President Theodore Roosevelt in 1903. Hill gave T.R. a painting of Bridalveil Fall; the work hangs in the White House today. The 19th-century Wawona Hotel offers accommodations and a nine-hole golf course *(fee)*. At Wawona are also an operating blacksmith shop and a studio demonstrating old-time "wet plate" photographic methods.

Near Wawona is Mariposa Grove, Yosemite's largest stand of giant sequoias (about 500 trees). Along with Yosemite Valley, this is the attraction that inspired the original conservation efforts that led to national park status. Visitors can drive to the grove or, better, take a free shuttle from Wawona; the road is closed in winter. A small museum has exhibits on these huge trees.

The best known of the sequoias is Grizzly Giant, an estimated 1,800 years old. A trail leads past Fallen Monarch, where exposed shallow roots demonstrate why these trees are susceptible to strong winds. Another famous sight is the Wawona Tunnel Tree, which in 1881 had an opening cut through its base to create the tourist attraction of a drive-through tree, first for horse-drawn wagons and later for motor vehicles. The tree fell over in a snowstorm in 1969.

The park's two other sequoia groves are located northwest of Yosemite Valley off Calif. 120 (Big Oak Flat Road). Merced Grove is reached by a 2-mile hike, while the Tuolumne Grove is accessible by a 1-mile trail that requires a fairly strenuous uphill walk on the return trip.

Tioga Road

Bisecting the park, Tioga Road *(closed Nov.–late May/early June, depending on snowfall)* runs east-west to the north of Yosemite Valley to cross the Sierra Nevada Range via 9,945-foot Tioga Pass, at the park's eastern border. Originally a wagon road built by a mining company in 1883, this stunning route climbs into an alpine world of snowy peaks, crystal lakes, meadows bright with wildflowers, and relatively few people.

Along the road, the trails to Harden Lake or Lukens Lake, both beginning at the White Wolf campground and partly following the Tuolumne River, offer excellent experiences of the high country. Olmsted Point offers one of the finest vistas of any spot in the park, with the sheer granite walls of Tenaya Canyon and Clouds Rest framing a magnificent view of Half Dome (which has an unfamiliar shape from this angle). To the east, Tenaya Lake is a great spot for a picnic.

The Tuolumne Meadows Visitor Center can provide information on the many hiking opportunities in this alpine environment. Among the most eager travelers along Tioga Road are butterfly enthusiasts, who hope to see and photograph some of the rare species that live in this harsh climate of short summers, including Sierra Nevada Parnassian, Sierra sulphur, Sheridan's hairstreak, and the Sierra Nevada blue. (The butterflies cannot be collected. Like all the park's flora, fauna, rocks, and other natural objects, they are protected.)

Activities

Yosemite National Park offers a multifaceted schedule of seasonal ranger-led walks and programs, including children's activities, adventure hikes to waterfalls, and walks or talks focusing on subjects such as bears, insects, photography, Native American heritage, and history.

The park includes 13 campgrounds and several concessionaire-operated lodges, but visitors planning an overnight stay between April and September should make reservations in advance. Although 704,624 acres of the park (about 94 percent) are wilderness, permits for backcountry camping are limited to prevent overuse and resource damage; some of the free permits can be reserved in advance, but a few are held for walk-up hikers on the day of their visit or one day in advance.

All visitors need to beware the presence of black bears and of their propensity to break into cars, tents, and picnic baskets for food. The park has strict rules for avoiding unpleasant encounters with bears.

Calif. 120, 75 miles east of
Modesto, CA
209-372-0200
www.nps.gov/yose
www.yosemite.org

AT A GLANCE

Eastern California, 195 miles southeast of San Francisco ▪ 747,956 acres
▪ Year-round; some roads closed in winter ▪ Hiking, backpacking, camping, rock climbing, biking, scenic driving

HAWAI'I

Hawai'i, the southernmost state in the United States, is a chain of tropical islands formed as a Pacific Ocean tectonic plate moved over a volcanic hot spot, still active today. For the volcanoes Mauna Loa and Kīlauea, in Hawai'i Volcanoes National Park on the Big Island of Hawai'i, escaping steam, lava flows, and ash eruptions are nearly constant. Historic sites throughout the islands highlight the native Hawaiian culture, which flourished until European contact in the late 18th century. Hawai'i's native flora and fauna, under threat from invasive species, find safe havens in parks and refuges.

Ala Kahakai National Historic Trail

A long-distance coastal corridor on Hawai'i's "Big Island"

Established in 2000, Ala Kahakai National Historic Trail is still under development, with planning under way for management by the National Park Service. The trail corridor aims to preserve and interpret the traditional native Hawaiian culture and natural resources.

Running 175 miles along the coastline of Hawai'i, the island state's main island, the route will traverse hundreds of ancient Hawaiian settlement sites. Cultural resources along the trail include several important temples, royal centers, fishponds and fishing shrines, petroglyphs, and sacred places. Natural resources include anchialine ponds (inland ponds with underground connection to the sea), precipices, nearshore reefs, estuarine ecosystems, coastal vegetation, and sea turtle habitat.

At this writing the entire trail is not open to the public, although certain segments are available for hiking on various public lands. The trail can be accessed at four National Park Service areas on Hawai'i: Hawai'i Volcanoes National Park (see p. 432), Pu'uhonua o Hōnaunau (see p. 436) and Kaloko-Honokōhau (see p. 436) National Historical Parks, and Pu'ukoholā Heiau National Historic Site (see p. 437). Other portions can be accessed through state or county lands such as Spencer County Beach Park, off Hawaii 270; and Hapuna State Beach Park, off Hawaii 19.

Check with the National Park Service office or the state Na Ala Hele Trail and Access System (*www.hawaiitrails .org*) for future developments.

Park office
73-4786 Kanalani, #14
Kailua-Kona, HI
808-326-6012
www.nps.gov/alka

AT A GLANCE

Along the southern and western coasts of the island of Hawai'i ▪ 175 miles ▪ Year-round ▪ Hiking, viewing historic and cultural sites

Haleakalā National Park

A dramatic volcanic landscape home to rare flora and fauna

One of the world's most otherworldly landscapes lies at the top of this spectacular national park on the Hawaiian island of Maui.

The island's most visited tourist attraction, Haleakalā National Park spans an elevational range from sea level to more than 10,000 feet, and offers protection to some of the most endangered species on Earth. The park, in fact, is home to more endangered species than almost any other site administered by the National Park Service.

The remote Hawaiian Islands, created by undersea volcanoes, were colonized originally by species that arrived in only three ways: carried by wind

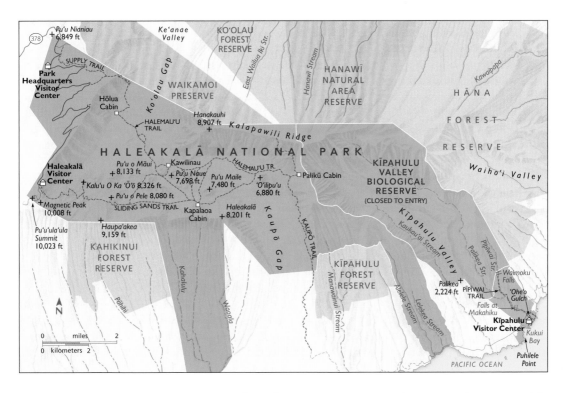

or by water or flying on their own wings. Before humans arrived in these islands (the most remote major island group on the planet) over 1,500 years ago, new species arrived at the rate of just one every several thousand years. Now, with ships and airplanes bringing people and cargo from around the world, alien species arrive in Hawai'i at the rate of dozens every year. The effect on native flora and fauna—those considered here prior to human contact—has been devastating, and places such as Haleakalā are, to biologists, like fortresses that must be defended against invaders.

The park is located on Haleakalā, a giant shield volcano that forms the eastern portion of Maui. Haleakalā means "house of the sun," and it was here, according to legend, that the demigod Māui captured the sun, releasing it when it promised to move more slowly across the sky, making days longer. The park encompasses the basin and portions of the volcano's flanks.

Visiting the Park

The park has two main visitor areas: the summit, with its expansive wilderness in a volcanic landscape; and the Kīpahulu area of rain forest on the coast to the southeast, popular for hiking to waterfalls and for swimming in freshwater pools near the coast. This means the park includes humid subtropical lowlands, aeolian desert, and several life zones in between.

The road to the summit of Haleakalā rises from near sea level to 10,000 feet in 38 miles—possibly the steepest such gradient for vehicles in the world. There is no fuel or food available in the park. Those heading for the summit should stock up at Pukalani or Makawao. At the summit the weather varies widely and can change from hot to rainy, cold, and windy within a day. Though the Kīpahulu area is always warm, it can be very rainy.

The summit roads and parking lots can be very crowded at times. Tour companies bring busloads of people to the top to see the sunrise and for general sightseeing. In addition, some commercial companies specialize in ferrying visitors to the top so they can ride down Haleakalā (outside the park) on rented bicycles. Arrive after 3 p.m. to avoid most crowds.

No road directly connects the Haleakalā summit and Kīpahulu. Roundabout connecting roads mean that those who try to visit both park areas in one day will spend most of their time looking out the windshield. It's better to choose one site and save the other for another time.

Many ranger-led programs and hikes are offered at the summit and Kīpahulu areas, ranging from half-day hikes to nature walks to programs focusing on the night sky.

Hosmer Grove

Hawaii 378 enters the park and quickly reaches the side road to Hosmer Grove, which, while attractive, interesting, and a nice place to picnic or camp, is hardly a natural feature.

In the early 20th century this was the site of an experiment to see which tree species would grow best in Hawai'i for timber harvest and watershed protection. As a result, part of Hosmer Grove features exotics such as Douglas fir, eucalyptus, redwood, deodar cedar, and many other species from around the world.

The Nature Conservancy offers tours from this spot of the adjacent Waikamoi Preserve *(808-572-7849)*, home to rare plants and animals.

Headquarters Visitor Center Area

The road continues higher to reach the Park Headquarters Visitor Center at about 7,000 feet elevation. The most striking and famous plant growing in this area is the Haleakalā silversword, with its silver-gray sphere of basal leaves topped by a stalk of flowers at maturity. A relative of sunflowers, the silversword was nearly made extinct by collecting, abuse, and grazing by non-native species. Also at the visitor center are plantings of Haleakalā geranium, another plant found only at the park.

One of the avian symbols of Hawai'i, the nēnē, may also be seen in this area. This small goose almost became extinct in the mid-20th century, the victim of overhunting and loss of eggs and goslings to introduced predators such as mongooses and cats. Intensive protection and captive-breeding efforts have rescued the nēnē from extinction, though it remains endangered. Once extirpated from Maui, the species was reintroduced in the 1960s. The birds on Haleakalā are among the fewer than 2,000 that exist in the wild.

In the woodlands of Hosmer Grove, at Waikamoi, and higher in the park, visitors may also see species of Hawaiian honeycreepers. One of the world's most striking examples of evolutionary divergence, these birds trace their ancestors back to an unknown species that reached the islands millions of years ago. More than 40 separate species evolved, with different colors and shapes, but many of them have become extinct because of habitat loss and disease (especially mosquito-borne malaria). Species around Haleakalā include *amakihi, 'alauahio, 'i'iwi, 'ākohekohe,* and *'apapane.* Some are making their last stand high on Haleakalā and other patches of remaining native habitat around the islands.

Halemau'u Trailhead to the Summit

From the Park Headquarters Visitor Center area, the park road climbs through subalpine heath where, in spring, a native shrub called *māmane* (a legume) brightens the slopes with yellow flowers. Soon there are views of the famed Haleakalā Crater, a vast depression that is actually not a volcanic crater but was formed as erosion

The mineral content of the volcanic cinder tints the desert landscape of Haleakalā Crater with a palette of colors.

ate away a ridgeline, forming a valley. This 19-square-mile wilderness area, in places nearly 3,000 feet from "crater" floor to rim, is breathtaking in its color—from black rock to silver waterfalls to green forests—and dramatic geologic forms.

Some hikers aiming to explore the crater start at the Halemau'u Trailhead, 3 miles above the Headquarters Visitor Center. The trail climbs through rolling country to the rim, then switchbacks as it drops steeply 1,000 feet down the northwest wall of the wilderness area to Hōlua Cabin and a campground. The Civilian Conservation Corps built many of the trails and structures in Haleakalā National Park in the mid-1930s. Visitors wishing to overnight in one of the three rustic cabins in the wilderness crater should make reservations well in advance. Wilderness campground permits are available on a first come, first served basis at the visitor centers.

The crater wall is broken by Ko'olau Gap, a wide, wet canyon that descends to the sea. In this area, vegetation such as the feathery *amau* fern thrives on moisture carried by clouds that float through the gap.

Motorists get views of the crater at Leleiwi Overlook and, farther along the road, at Kalahaku Overlook. Beyond is the Haleakalā Visitor Center. An exhibit shelter stands at the peak of Haleakalā volcano, at 10,023 feet. Here at Pu'u'ula'ula ("red hill"), the highest point on Maui, are fabulous views that, when the weather cooperates, take in the giant volcanoes of the Big Island of Hawai'i, as well as the islands of Lāna'i and Moloka'i. Nearby, but outside the park, are the

The nēnē is endemic to Hawai'i.

telescopes and other scientific installations of Haleakalā observatories, not open to the public.

The best way to experience the wilderness area is by hiking, either a day hike or an overnight trip. One popular two-day trip involves hiking the Sliding Sands Trail to Kapalaoa Cabin, a strenuous seven- to ten-hour trek along loose cinder.

It's also possible to hike the Sliding Sands Trail and continue across the crater to Kaupō Gap, hiking downhill to the tiny town of Kaupō, on Hawaii 31 on the south coast of Maui. This "summit to sea" trip requires advance planning and arranging for a shuttle.

Kīpahulu Rain Forest

Nearly 2 miles below the summit and 14 miles to the southeast, the park's Kīpahulu area occupies a strip of land along Pīpīwai Stream, where visitors can hike through lush rain forest and past breathtaking ocean overlooks. There are also opportunities to experience Hawai'i's cultural past, through traces of stone-walled gardens, pictographs, and temple

and shelter sites. In the coastal area, low vegetation grows thickly on dark volcanic rock.

Camping is permitted only at the Kīpahulu Campground. There is no fresh water available, and campers should be prepared for wet weather.

The most popular activity here is the 2-mile hike up Pīpīwai Trail through 'O'heo Gulch, one of the most memorable short hikes in the islands. The trail can be muddy and slippery, and hikers should be aware that heavy rain can cause the stream to rise very quickly. Hikers have died here during flash floods. The path reaches the Falls at Makahiku, 184 feet high, then enters the woods. Winding through thick stands of (non-native) bamboo, it arrives at impressive Waimoku Falls, more than 400 feet high. The trail ends just before Waimoku Falls to protect hikers from flash floods and rock falls.

Beyond this point the valley is closed to entry to protect the ecologically important Kīpahulu Valley Biological Preserve, home to an array of rare and threatened plants and animals. This is one of the last intact native rain forest ecosystems remaining in the Hawaiian Islands, with annual rainfall ranging from 120 to 400 inches.

Though the park does not recommend it, swimming is popular in the lower Kīpahulu area, in the pools and waterfalls below the highway bridge and at less crowded spots upstream. Swimmers should take responsibility for their own safety and beware flash floods and use caution on the slippery rocks. Heavy surf means there is no safe ocean entry in Kīpahulu.

Hawaii 378
20 miles southeast of Pukalani, HI
808-572-4400
www.nps.gov/hale

AT A GLANCE

Eastern part of the island of Maui, Hawai'i ■ 33,230 acres ■ Year-round ■ Hiking, camping, bird-watching, swimming

Hawai'i Volcanoes National Park

A dramatic and dynamic landscape of volcanic activity

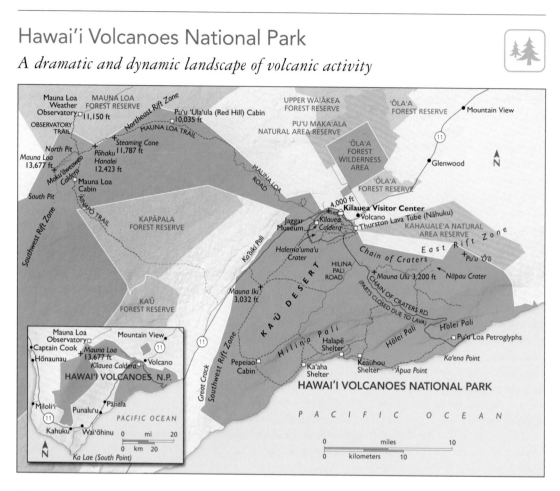

Focusing on two of the world's most active volcanoes, Hawai'i Volcanoes National Park offers visitors a chance to experience a landscape that quite literally changes by the day, and sometimes by the hour. Located on Hawai'i, the Big Island, the park encompasses Mauna Loa, which last erupted in 1984; and Kīlauea, which has been erupting continuously since 1983.

In March 2008 a new vent opened within Kīlauea's Halema'uma'u Crater, causing the indefinite closure of part of famed Crater Rim Drive, the 11-mile loop route that has long been the park's major attraction; as well as part of Crater Rim Trail, the hiking route that allowed visitors to circle the crater on foot. Trails were closed

also in the southern and eastern parts of the park. Kīlauea began emitting elevated levels of sulphur dioxide gas and an ash-laden fume cloud, which could cause a variety of health hazards for visitors. Depending on gas emissions and prevailing winds, other areas—or even the entire park—could close with little notice.

While for some travelers such developments make a visit to Hawai'i Volcanoes National Park problematic, for others the opportunity to watch volcanism reshape our planet is exciting and rewarding. Kīlauea's rumblings remind us that there are few guarantees in nature. Activity could lessen at any moment and park areas could reopen, or it could continue for many years. The volcano's 1983–1991

eruptions destroyed 181 homes, the national park's Waha'ula Visitor Center, a church, and other structures, while lava flows have added 568 acres of new land to the island of Hawai'i. At the park's coastline, fresh lava continually meets the sea amid huge clouds of steam.

The chain of Hawaiian Islands was created by undersea volcanic activity as a tectonic plate moved over a hot spot. During the past 70 million years, material erupting from this hot spot has built a succession of volcanoes that rose above the Pacific Ocean. Hawai'i is the youngest of the Hawaiian Islands. Deep beneath the sea to the southeast a submarine volcano called Loihi is active and growing, though it may not reach sea level for 250,000 years or more.

Mauna Loa rises 13,677 feet above sea level. Measured from its base 18,000 feet below the Pacific's surface, it exceeds Mount Everest in height. Mauna Loa's gently sloping bulk—some 19,000 cubic miles in volume—makes it Earth's most massive single mountain. The national park stretches from the Pacific shore to Mauna Loa's summit, encompassing extensive lava fields, cinder cones, gaping pits, and lush green rain forest that's home to rare plants and animals.

Hawai'i Volcanoes National Park also protects many cultural sites connected with the native Hawaiian culture, reminders of the Polynesian pioneers who steered their double-hulled canoes to Hawai'i beginning about 1,500 years ago.

Visiting the Park

The park can be reached on Hawaii 11 from either the Kona International Airport or the city of Hilo. The visitor center is located just off the highway. The film "Born of Fire, Born of the Sea" is shown hourly in the auditorium, and travelers can get information (especially relating to up-to-date area closures and safety-related advice) and learn of ranger-led hikes and other programs. Nearby is the Volcano House hotel, which from its back offers a fine view of the Kīlauea Caldera, a 3-mile-wide, 400-foot-deep depression at the volcano's summit.

Crater Rim Drive

Following Crater Rim Drive clockwise leads through rain forest with impressive tree ferns to a lookout point at the crater called Kīlauea Iki ("little Kīlauea"), east of the main crater. The 1959 eruption that shaped many park features filled this crater with a lava lake and produced a lava fountain that shot 1,900 feet into the air. A hiking trail leads into the still steaming crater, part of the more than 150 miles of trails within the park. A 4-mile loop can be made by walking the Kīlauea Iki Trail and joining with the Crater Rim Trail.

Nearby is one of the park's most intriguing attractions: Thurston Lava Tube. A short trail leads through a forest of tree ferns where walkers might spot native Hawaiian honeycreepers, colorful birds found only in these islands. The tube is where molten lava once ran; when the outside solidified before the inside, a tunnel was left, 450 feet long and up to 20 feet high. It is lit with electric lights to add safety and reduce claustrophobia.

Continuing on the park drive, watch for nēnē (or Hawaiian goose), a bird that neared extinction in the mid-20th century and is still endangered. The 1-mile Devastation Trail is a paved path through a forested area that was nearly destroyed by falling cinder from the lava fountains of the 1959 Kīlauea Iki eruption. Look for "Pele's hair": fine threads of volcanic material formed during eruptions when molten lava flies through the air. The "hair" is named after Pele, the Hawaiian goddess of volcanoes.

Crater Rim Drive is at this writing closed beyond this point. When it opens again, motorists (and hikers on the Crater Rim Trail) will pass through more of the Kau Desert, lying in the rain shadow of the summit and receiving half the annual rainfall of the visitor center.

Return to the Kīlauea Visitor Center, and continue the drive counterclockwise to steam vents and the trailhead to Sulphur Banks, a steamy, smelly area where the rocks are mustard yellow from sulphur carried by volcanic fumes. There are many fumaroles (steam vents) along the road.

The Jaggar Museum is a small but excellent facility featuring exhibits on volcanology, including seismographs and other equipment used by scientists to monitor volcanoes. The overlook offers spectacular views into the summit caldera and has been the best place from which to watch the eruption at Halema'uma'u Crater, which began its most recent activity in March 2008.

A "skylight" reveals molten lava flowing beneath the surface.

Chain of Craters Road

Leading off Crater Rim Drive is Chain of Craters Road, which descends 3,700 feet in 20 miles and ends where a lava flow crossed the road in 2003. The upper 4-mile section of the road follows the active East Rift Zone of Kīlauea volcano. Some geologists believe that the main vent for Kīlauea has shifted from the summit to the East Rift Zone. There are overlooks of small craters along the road.

The Nāpau Trail passes through lava flows from the eruptions of 3,200-foot Mauna Ulu, a shield volcano active from 1969 to 1974. The trail continues past Makaopuhi Crater to Nāpau Crater, where the very active vent called Puʻu ʻŌʻō can be seen steaming to the east. New vents opened here in summer 2007, pouring out lava.

Back on Chain of Craters Road, the route passes over several miles of pāhoehoe lava flows, produced by Mauna Ulu, making this some of the newest ground on Earth. Pāhoehoe flows at more than 2,000 degrees, beginning as fluid and cooling to a smooth, ropy surface. Another type of lava is called ʻaʻā: thicker, slower-moving lava that has hardened into a jumble of rough, jagged pieces. A picnic shelter, with a beautiful view of the park's coastline, is located at Kealakomo, 9.7 miles from Crater Rim Drive.

A steep, 800-foot descent marks Hōlei Pali, a cliff formed by vertical faulting; the huge coastal shelf is breaking away from the uplands and sinking into the sea, though very slowly in terms of human time. A side path leads to the Puʻu Loa Petroglyphs site, which encompasses about 24,000 images pecked into the lava by long-ago residents. There are several settlement sites of ancient Hawaiians in the area, though most are difficult to discern.

The route ends abruptly where lava has destroyed the road. Eruptions over the past decades covered parts of this road with lava up to 115 feet deep. As of this writing, this unpaved portion of the road was being developed as an emergency access route for a community in Puna (a district on the east side of the island), whose other major access routes were being threatened by lava flow that emerged from a vent in the East Rift Zone in 2014. To date, the last half-mile paved section of the Chain of Craters Road after the parking area at Hōlei Sea Arch is closed to foot traffic, but check with the park ahead of your visit for more current conditions and up-to-date information about public access to this part of the park.

Mauna Loa Road

Off Hawaii 11, the 11-mile Mauna Loa Road leads to the 6,662-foot level on the slope of the massive Mauna Loa volcano. Kīpuka Puaulu, a grove of old-growth trees, is located near the road's start; an easy, 1-mile trail loops this grove, which can be an excellent place for bird-watching.

At the end of the road, a trail leads to the crater at the 13,677-foot summit of Mauna Loa, a round trip of more than 36 miles that should not be undertaken without serious preparation and knowledge of the dangers of high-altitude hiking (free park permit required for backpacking).

The weather at and near the top can change quickly, and hypothermia is a possibility any time of year. A shorter but steeper trail leads to the top from the Mauna Loa Observatory Road, off Hawaii 200, outside the park.

Flora & Fauna

Although Hawaiʻi Volcanoes National Park is best known, of course, for volcanoes and their related landscape, it also provides a haven for native flora and fauna. Evolving in isolation over 70 million years, the plants and animals of the Hawaiian Islands branched out and now possess a high degree of endemism, with more than 90 percent of species found nowhere else on Earth. Unfortunately, many factors have caused a great loss in diversity: habitat loss as native vegetation has been cleared for development; introduced species, which have crowded out or preyed upon native species; and disease, such as avian malaria, carried by introduced mosquitoes and devastating to populations of Hawaiian birds.

Notable birds found within the park include six Hawaiian honeycreepers, Hawaiian thrush (ʻōmaʻo), monarch flycatcher (ʻelepaio), Hawaiian goose (nēnē), Hawaiian petrel (uau), and Hawaiian hawk (ʻio). The park also provides a home to the largest dragonfly in the United States and endangered sea turtles. Native plants within the park include the endangered Mauna Loa silversword (a composite, or sunflower relative) and 15 species of endangered trees. Efforts are under way to restore the park's landscape by removing invasive species and replanting endangered and native plants.

Hawaii 11, south of Volcano, HI
808-985-6000
www.nps.gov/havo

AT A GLANCE

Southeastern coast of the island of Hawaiʻi, 30 miles west of Hilo ▪ 333,086 acres ▪ Year-round ▪ Hiking, camping, viewing volcanic activity, scenic driving

Honouliuli National Monument

Site of World War II internment and prison camp

After Japan attacked the United States naval base at Pearl Harbor at the beginning of World War II, government officials began rounding up people of Japanese descent for relocation to internment camps. Most of these were U.S. citizens who had done nothing to indicate disloyalty.

Although only a small percentage of the Japanese-ancestry residents of Hawai'i were interned, they included community leaders such as teachers and priests. Many were sent to the mainland, while others spent the war at Honouliuli internment camp on the island of Oahu. Among the 400 internees were people of German or Italian descent, as well as other nationalities. Honouliuli also housed 4,000 prisoners of war from Japan, Korea, Okinawa, Taiwan, and Italy. The 160-acre camp comprised 175 buildings, 14 guard towers, and more than 400 tents.

After the war the Honouliuli camp, located in a secluded canyon, was forgotten and overgrown by vegetation; it was found in 2002.

Established in 2015, the national monument will tell the story of the camp and the effect of internment on the Japanese-American community, and it will interpret issues of civil rights during wartime.

The National Park Service is preparing a management plan for Honouliuli, with future developments dependent on funding. At present, limited public access is allowed and special events will be scheduled allowing visitation. Contact the park office for details.

Park office:
300 Ala Moana Blvd.
Honolulu, HI
808-725-6149
www.nps.gov/hono

AT A GLANCE Island of Oahu, Hawai'i, 15 miles west of Honolulu ▪ 155 acres ▪ Year-round ▪ Touring historic sites

Kalaupapa National Historical Park

A poignant reminder of a century of isolation

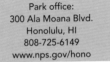

Having lived on the world's most isolated island group for hundreds of years, native Hawaiians had little resistance to diseases brought by Europeans. In the 19th century the bacterial disease leprosy (now called Hansen's disease) was spreading at a frightening rate through the islands. Lacking a cure or methods of prevention, the kingdom forced people with the disease to move to an isolated spot on the northern coast of the island of Moloka'i, cut off from the other islands by sea cliffs rising 2,000 feet high.

The first group of 12 patients arrived at Kalawao, on the Kalaupapa Peninsula, in 1866. The population peaked at 1,213, and by the time forced quarantine ended in 1969 (drugs had begun to control

St. Francis Church faces the island's historic docks.

the disease in the 1940s) some 8,000 people had been sequestered here, living apart from the rest of society.

Many people devoted themselves to caring for patients at Kalaupapa, the most famous of them Joseph De Veuster, a Belgian priest. Known as Father Damien, he spoke the Hawaiian language and, assisted by patients, built houses, organized schools, and provided medical care. His work attracted worldwide notice, bringing attention to the plight of victims of leprosy. Damien eventually contracted the disease and died in 1889. He was canonized a saint in 2009.

Kalaupapa National Historical Park serves as a reminder of a time when families were torn apart and lives changed forever. It is a place for modern visitors to learn and to contemplate how societies deal with disease and disfigurement. A few elderly patients still live at the site, voluntarily remaining apart from a world that might have difficulty accepting them. Many historic structures stand at Kalaupapa and, due to a lack of development, many important archaeological sites have been protected from destruction.

Access to the park is restricted: Those wishing to visit must pre-arrange their trip with Damien Tours *(808-567-6171)*, which will secure the required permits for entering the park.

Visit the park website for options on transport to the park. Access to the park will be denied to persons lacking authorization. No children under the age of 16 are allowed in the Kalaupapa Settlement. The park does not offer any regularly scheduled interpretive programs or activities.

Pala'au State Park, on Kalae Highway (Hawaii 47), provides a view of the Kalaupapa Peninsula and offers interpretive exhibits. Mule rides on the Kalaupapa Trail can be arranged through the park-authorized concessionaire, Moloka'i Mule Rides *(800-567-7550)*.

808-567-6802 www.nps.gov/kala	**AT A GLANCE** Northern part of the island of Moloka'i, Hawai'i ▪ 10,700 acres (authorized area) ▪ Year-round ▪ Visiting historic Hansen's-disease settlement

Kaloko-Honokōhau National Historical Park
The seaside site of a once thriving Hawaiian community

The lava-dominated landscape here along the west coast of the island of Hawai'i at first seems unlikely as a place for a settlement. Nonetheless, Hawaiians lived here for hundreds of years, finding ways to survive on a desolate landscape with abundant ocean resources. Kaloko-Honokōhau National Historical Park preserves and interprets traditional native Hawaiian activities and culture, demonstrating how people used available resources.

The site includes four different *ahupua'a*, or land divisions that stretch from the sea to the mountains, offering a variety of natural resources. The park also protects fishponds; house-site platforms; petroglyphs; stone enclosures; religious sites; and a *mauka-makai* (mountain-sea) trail network.

The Hale Ho'okipa visitor contact station provides an orientation to the park and information on guided tours and interpretive programs. Hiking trails lead to two different types of fishponds where aquaculture was practiced. In the south part of the park, an ancient *heiau* (temple) overlooks

'Ai'opio Fishtrap, a 1.7-acre fish-trap pond where reef fish were captured for food. Petroglyphs can be seen along a boardwalk a half mile south of the visitor contact station, on the way to the 'Ai'opio Fishtrap.

Animal species in the area include green sea turtle; the graceful, long-legged Hawaiian stilt; and occasionally the endangered monk seal. In winter, humpback whales sometimes can be spotted offshore.

The park is one access point for Ala Kahakai National Historic Trail (see p. 428).

Hawaii 19 3 miles north of Kailua-Kona, HI 808-326-9057 www.nps.gov/kaho	**AT A GLANCE** West coast of the island of Hawai'i, near Kailua-Kona ▪ 1,160 acres ▪ Year-round ▪ Hiking, viewing historic sites, wildlife-watching

Pu'uhonua o Hōnaunau National Historical Park
A place reserved for royalty and a refuge for the condemned

This historical park on the island of Hawai'i offers a chance to experience a part of the traditional life of Hawaiians in two very different aspects. Original and re-created

structures tell of the Royal Grounds that were a favored residence of chiefs, set on a beach that was reserved for the use of royalty. The neighboring Ki'ilae village interprets Hawaiian

history and the changes that occurred after contact with Europeans. Among the features of the park are the remains of temples; petroglyphs (carved figures); and a game stone that was used in *kōnane,* sometimes called Hawaiian checkers. Animal pens, salt vats, and church foundations date to times post-European contact.

The very impressive Great Wall, built of large rocks and 10 feet high in places, separates the Royal Grounds from the Pu'uhonua o Hōnaunau, "place of refuge." Persons who had been condemned to death for various infractions, including breaking *kapu* (sacred laws), could come here for sanctuary and be safe from their pursuers.

A reconstruction of the temple called Hale o Keawe depicts a structure, built about 1650 and later demolished, that served as the royal

mausoleum and held the remains of 23 chiefs. A son of famed King

Ki'i at Pu'uhonua o Hōnaunau

Kamehameha I was buried on these sacred grounds in 1818. The *mana* (spiritual power) of the remains was one of the factors that gave the power of sanctuary to the Pu'uhonua o Hōnaunau. *Ki'i* (carved statues) surround the Hale o Keawe, providing spiritual protection.

Demonstrations of traditional Hawaiian arts and crafts are held in the park during an annual festival held on the weekend before the park's July 1 anniversary. A 2-mile backcountry trail passes by additional historic sites as it follows parts of a route that began as a traditional path of native Hawaiians and later was used by horse-drawn wagons.

Hawaii 160
Kailua-Kona, HI
808-328-2326
www.nps.gov/puho

AT A GLANCE

West coast of the island of Hawai'i 24 miles south of Kailua-Kona
■ 420 acres ■ Year-round ■ Touring historic structures, hiking, picnicking, viewing cultural demonstrations

Pu'ukoholā Heiau National Historic Site

One of the most significant religious sites in Hawaiian history

For centuries, Hawaiian culture operated under a system of kapu, sacred laws. A heiau (temple) was a sacred place where the *kahuna* (priest) communicated with the gods and advised the *ali'i* (chief). Commoners were traditionally forbidden to enter the heiau.

Pu'ukoholā Heiau was built in 1790–91 by the leader known as Kamehameha I, who through alliances and battle eventually became the first king of the unified Hawaiian Islands. He built the large structure called Pu'ukoholā Heiau ("temple on the hill of the whale") on the island of

Hawai'i as an offering to the war god Kūkā'ilimoku. One of Kamehameha's rivals is believed to have been killed and sacrificed here, making Kamehameha ruler of the entire island.

Kamehameha was aided in his rise to power by two European sailors, John Young and Isaac Davis, who had been captured but became trusted assistants to the Hawaiian leader—in part because they taught his warriors how to use firearms. Young was given much property and was allowed to build a house near Pu'ukoholā Heiau, where he lived with his native Hawaiian wife, with whom he raised six

children. Young built three Western-style structures and several Hawaiian-style buildings.

At Pu'ukoholā Heiau National Historic Site visitors can learn about local history through exhibits at the information center and walk an interpretive trail to the remains of the temple, consisting of the stone foundation and platforms. Like most other heiau, Pu'ukoholā Heiau fell into ruins after the kapu system of beliefs lost its influence after Kamehameha I's death in 1819. Visitors can also see the remains of John Young's house nearby.

62-3601 Kawaihae Rd.
(off Hawaii 270), Waimea, HI
808-882-7218
www.nps.gov/puhe

AT A GLANCE

Northwestern coast of the island of Hawai'i, 35 miles north of Kailua-Kona
■ 86 acres ■ Year-round ■ Visiting historic temple site

World War II Valor in the Pacific National Monument

Remembering those who died on "a date which will live in infamy"

The U.S.S. Arizona *Memorial lies atop the sunken battleship.*

Relations between the United States and Japan worsened during the 1930s, and as war broke out in Europe, Japanese militarists saw a surprise attack against the U.S. Navy as the best way to achieve their nation's goals in the Pacific region. Early on the morning of December 7, 1941, Japanese airplanes and submarines launched an attack against the U.S. base in Pearl Harbor, where 130 vessels of the Pacific Fleet were docked. By 10 a.m. the attack was over. More than 20 battleships and other large vessels were sunk or seriously damaged, scores of aircraft were destroyed, and more than 2,000 people had been killed at Pearl Harbor and other bases.

At the start of the attack, a bomb fell onto the forward deck of U.S.S. *Arizona,* igniting fuel and powder below deck. The resulting explosion caused the battleship to sink in nine minutes, killing 1,177 sailors and Marines. Only 334 *Arizona* crew members survived.

In an address to the American people delivered before Congress, President Franklin D. Roosevelt called December 7 "a date which will live in infamy," and declared war on Japan. Three days later, Germany and Italy declared war on the United States, and the nation was fully engaged in World War II.

While some battleships sunk in the attack were raised, repaired, and returned to service, *Arizona* was too badly damaged and remained beneath the waters of Pearl Harbor, along with the bodies of most of her crew. (Spare parts taken from the ship were used on other ships that contributed to the ultimate U.S. victory, however.) Today's national memorial honors those who died on the battleship and elsewhere in the Japanese attack.

Those arriving at the visitor center receive a number, which will determine when they will take the short boat ride to the memorial. (The wait can be up to three hours in the busy summer season.) In the visitor center are personal items, photographs, and artifacts of the battle, as well as other exhibits interpreting the historic events of Pearl Harbor. A 23-minute documentary film on the attack is shown throughout the day. Pearl Harbor survivors are sometimes present at the visitor center to relate their memories of the day.

The 184-foot-long memorial structure lies atop the middle section of the sunken battleship and comprises three main sections: the entry and assembly rooms; a central area for ceremonies and general observation; and the shrine room, where the names of those killed on *Arizona* are engraved on a marble wall. As a special tribute to the ship and her crew, the United States flag flies from the flagpole, which is attached to the severed mainmast of *Arizona.* From the central area, visitors can see the remains of *Arizona* in the translucent water below.

On December 5, 2008, the U.S.S. *Arizona* National Memorial and Visitor Center became part of the World War II Valor in the Pacific National Monument along with four other sites in the Pearl Harbor area, three sites in Alaska's Aleutian Islands, and the Tule Lake Segregation Center National Historic Landmark, California.

---

1 *Arizona* Memorial Pl.
Honolulu, HI
808-422-3300
www.nps.gov/valr
www.arizonamemorial.org

AT A GLANCE

Hawai'i, California, Alaska ▪ 11 acres (U.S.S. *Arizona* site) ▪ Year-round ▪ Touring museum; viewing films; visiting battleship memorial, battle sites, relocation camp

NEVADA

When most people think Nevada, they think of burgeoning Las Vegas and perhaps of the Reno–Lake Tahoe area, but there's much more. The state lies mostly in the Basin and Range region of parallel mountain ranges separated by valleys. Much of Nevada is thinly populated, with towns connected by some of the loneliest roads in the country. Scarce rainfall discouraged settlers in pioneer times, though mining created some boomtowns, as recounted in Mark Twain's autobiographical *Roughing It*. The Spring Mountains are a nearby natural haven for Las Vegans. Farther afield, Great Basin National Park protects some of the world's oldest trees: bristlecone pines on 13,063-foot Wheeler Peak.

Great Basin National Park

Mountain views, alpine lakes, and a beautifully decorated cave

A glacier-carved landscape dominated by a mountain more than 13,000 feet high, some of the world's oldest living things, and a cave full of beautiful formations—all these are among the attractions of Great Basin National Park. Yet several factors combine to make a visit here a more adventurous trip than simply a casual jaunt.

The park lies in east-central Nevada in an area off typical travel routes, more than 200 miles from any major city (and not really on the way to anywhere else). There are limited services in the immediate area, so travelers must be prepared for a degree of self-sufficiency. And the park's location in a region called the Great Basin Desert may give some potential visitors pause as they imagine barren, near-lifeless terrain. The park receives about 90,000 visitors a year, while Grand Canyon National Park sees more than that in one July week.

Yet there are rewards here for those who do make the trip, including a scenic drive up the flank of 13,063-foot Wheeler Peak, hiking trails to mountain lakes, glittering stalactites

and rare "cave shields" in marble Lehman Caves, and the chance to enjoy a surprisingly diverse ecosystem in comparative solitude.

The Great Basin was given its name in the mid-19th century by explorer John C. Frémont. Including most of Nevada, half of Utah, and sections of Idaho, Wyoming, Oregon, and California, it's actually a grouping of many small basins within which water drains internally. All precipitation in the 200,000-square-mile area evaporates, sinks underground, or flows into lakes. No rivers reach the sea.

Great Basin National Park encompasses most of the South Snake mountain range. The Lehman Caves area was declared a national monument in 1922, but establishment of a national park was delayed for decades as conservationists debated with mining and ranching interests over the future of the region. The national park came into being in 1986 with the provision that traditional cattle and sheep grazing would continue. In 1999, the National Park Service acquired the permits for cattle and sheep grazing

from local ranchers, in theory ending the practice; however, sheep were seen grazing on high-elevation meadows of the park through 2008.

Great Basin Visitor Center is located just north of the town of Baker on Nev. 487. Lehman Caves Visitor Center is on Nev. 488, a half mile inside the park boundary, and offers tickets for Lehman Cave tours. Both centers feature an information desk, exhibits, bookstores, and a theater showing the park orientation film.

Wheeler Peak Scenic Drive

The paved, 12-mile Wheeler Peak Scenic Drive *(usually closed by snow Nov.–May)* climbs steeply from the park's eastern boundary to a terminus at Wheeler Peak campground at an elevation of 10,000 feet. The upper part of the road—past Upper Lehman Campground—is closed to vehicles longer than 24 feet. As the scenic drive ascends, the vegetation changes from drought-resistant sagebrush and piñon pine–juniper woodland to a forest with Engelmann spruce, limber and ponderosa pines, white fir, Douglas fir, and aspen. Mule deer are often seen along the road.

The drive passes campgrounds along Lehman Creek to reach a self-guiding trail at Osceola Ditch. Here visitors can learn about a waterway built in the 1880s to carry water for hydraulic (placer) gold mining, one of six silver and gold mining operations that once existed in the South Snake Range. The Johnson Lake Mine, inside what is now the park, operated well into the 20th century. The Osceola "ditch" here was actually a flume, a wooden tunnel through which water passed.

At Wheeler Peak Overlook there are spectacular views of Wheeler Peak on the right and Jeff Davis Peak on the left. The spire between them is called The Thumb. The north face of Wheeler drops 1,800 feet to the only glacier in the Great Basin and the southernmost glacier in the Northern Hemisphere. Snow often dusts the jagged walls of gray quartzite.

High-country Trails

Trailheads at or near the Wheeler Peak campground lead to the park's most popular hiking treks. The easy, 0.4-mile Sky Islands Forest Trail features signs interpreting the high-altitude conifer forest. The 2.8-mile Alpine Lakes Loop passes two beautiful lakes, Stella and Teresa, offering great views of Wheeler Peak in a dramatic setting with a barren sawtooth ridge rising above the smooth water surface.

The fairly strenuous 8.6-mile Wheeler Peak Summit Trail climbs 2,900 feet along ridgelines to the park's high point, offering sweeping views of the Great Basin's seemingly endless succession of mountain ranges. This hike should be started early in the day because of the risk of afternoon thunderstorms and, especially, the lightning they can bring.

The 2.8-mile Bristlecone Trail is in many ways the park's most intriguing hike, leading to a grove of bristlecone pines, with interpretive exhibits explaining the ecology of these extraordinary trees. Found in isolated groves just below tree line where conditions are harsh—cold temperatures, short growing season, and high winds—bristlecone pines grow slowly, which makes their wood very dense

and resistant to insects and disease.

Some of the bristlecones are more than 3,000 years old, twisted and gnarled in picturesque shapes. This grove is unusual in that it grows on a glacial moraine of quartzite boulders, while most bristlecones grow on limestone or dolomite. In 1964, before the creation of Great Basin National Park, a researcher cut down a bristlecone here that was later determined to be 4,900 years old, the oldest known tree.

The Glacier Trail, a continuation of the Bristlecone Trail, leads beyond the pine grove to the park's singular glacier, in the shadow of Wheeler Peak.

Lehman Caves

The human history of this region dates back more than 10,000 years to Paleo-Indians, continuing through the Fremont and Shoshone tribes to the 19th century when trappers and military expeditions entered the area, followed by ranchers and miners. In the 1870s Absalom Lehman established a ranch near today's Lehman Creek, where he grew and raised food for local miners. (Apricot trees from his orchard still survive near the Lehman

The mirrorlike surface of subalpine Stella Lake reflects the surrounding peaks of the South Snake Range.

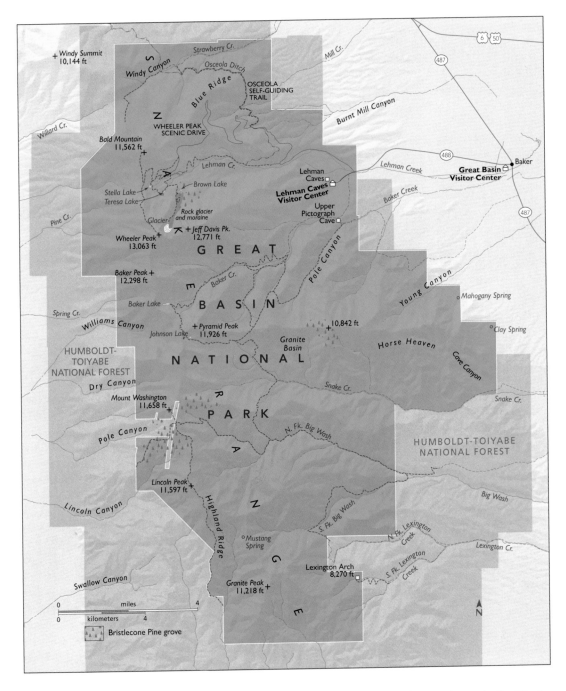

Windy Summit
10,144 ft

Strawberry Cr.

Mill Cr.

Windy Canyon

Osceola Ditch

OSCEOLA
SELF-GUIDING
TRAIL

Blue Ridge

Burnt Mill Canyon

487

WHEELER PEAK
SCENIC DRIVE

Willard Cr.

Lehman Cr.

Bald Mountain
11,562 ft

Lehman
Caves

Lehman Creek

488

Baker

Brown Lake

Lehman Caves
Visitor Center

Great Basin
Visitor Center

Stella Lake
Teresa Lake

Upper
Pictograph
Cave

Baker Creek

Pine Cr.

Rock glacier
and moraine

Glacier

Wheeler Peak
13,063 ft

Jeff Davis Pk.
12,771 ft

G R E A T

487

Pole Canyon

Baker Peak
12,298 ft

Baker Cr.

B A S I N

Young Canyon

Mahogany Spring

Baker Lake

Spring Cr.

Clay Spring

Williams Canyon

Johnson Lake

Pyramid Peak
11,926 ft

N A T I O N A L

Granite
Basin

10,842 ft

Horse Heaven

Cove Canyon

HUMBOLDT-
TOIYABE
NATIONAL FOREST

Dry Canyon

Snake Cr.

Snake Cr.

Mount Washington
11,658 ft

P A R K

N. Fk. Big Wash

HUMBOLDT-TOIYABE
NATIONAL FOREST

Pole Canyon

R

A

Lincoln Peak
11,597 ft

Big Wash

Lincoln Canyon

N

S. Fk. Big Wash

N. Fk. Lexington Creek

Lexington Cr.

Highland Ridge

Mustang
Spring

G

Lexington Arch
8,270 ft

S. Fk. Lexington Creek

Swallow Canyon

Granite Peak
11,218 ft

E

0   miles   4
0   kilometers   4

N

Bristlecone Pine grove

Caves Visitor Center.) In 1885, he discovered the cave that now bears his name, and spent the rest of his life guiding people through the cavern, now part of the national park.

Lehman Caves can be visited only on ranger-guided tours, offered daily. Tickets can be bought in advance or at the Lehman Caves Visitor Center upon arrival. Tours are limited to 20 people and often sell out in the summer. Two tours are available: a 60-minute, 0.4-mile tour; and a 90-minute, 0.5-mile tour. The former is recommended for families with young children. (Persons with limited

mobility can take just the first 30 minutes of the tour.)

Meandering into the marble and limestone of the South Snake Range, Lehman Caves (a single cavern despite the plural name) features striking formations, immediately visible in the tour's first stop, a cave

Visitors have been exploring the weird, beautiful formations of Lehman Caves since the 1880s.

room called Gothic Palace. The cave is so filled with columns, draperies, stalactites, and other formations that early explorers used sledgehammers to break through them. Because of the cave's manageable scale, visitors get close views of bizarre helictites and delicate argonite crystals.

Lehman Caves is best known for its examples of rare formations called cave shields. These large disks grow from cracks in the ceiling where seeping water deposits minerals in flat, circular forms. The walkway passes rim-stone pools and soda straws in the Lake Room and massive columns and "bacon rind" draperies in the Grand Palace, which is also home to the cave's famed Parachute Shield formation.

Baker Creek Road

Exploring the park south of Lehman Caves, Baker Creek Road in 2 miles reaches a left turn at a sign reading Grey Cliffs, by which visitors can reach Upper Pictograph Cave. The painted images here are believed to have been created by the Fremont Indians, a farming and hunting group that lived in the Snake Valley about A.D. 1000–1300. The pictographs—of human, animal, and abstract forms—have been damaged in the past by vandals, and should not be touched.

At the end of Baker Creek Road are trailheads for more of the park's hikes. Making a circuit around the flanks of 11,926-foot Pyramid Peak, the Baker Lake–Johnson Lake Loop is a challenging 13-mile day hike or a more relaxed overnight backpacking trip. *(A free permit is required for backcountry camping.)* The route starts at 8,000 feet and follows Baker Creek for a few miles before climbing switchbacks up to a glacier-cut cirque on Baker Peak, where Baker Lake lies. This alpine lake is surrounded by beautiful cliffs.

A steep and challenging primitive trail connects Baker and Johnson Lakes, in part following a ridgetop with great views in all directions. At the east end of Johnson Lake are historic structures of the old Johnson Lake Mine. Park rangers warn visitors not to enter any old mine structures or pits. Several other trails make possible various loops or out-and-back hikes in this area.

Lexington Arch

Check with park personnel about conditions on the unpaved road providing access to the Lexington Arch Trail, a 3.4-mile round-trip hike leading to a six-story-high limestone arch, believed to have once been part of a cave system. The trailhead is outside the park boundary on the South Fork of Lexington Creek, about 25 miles south of Baker.

Wildlife-watching & Stargazing

Wildlife within the park includes species such as badger, gray and kit foxes, coyote, black-tailed jackrabbit, cottontail rabbit, yellow-bellied marmot, rock squirrel, pronghorn, mule deer, and occasionally elk. Mountain lions, while seldom seen, are fairly common in the park, and hikers should know what to do in the unlikely event of an encounter with one.

Bird-watchers enjoy sightings of species such as California quail, sage grouse, golden eagle, red-naped sapsucker, western scrub-jay, Clark's nutcracker, and Townsend's solitaire. Butterfly enthusiasts hike in hopes of seeing species such as Sara orangetip, Milbert's tortoiseshell, Edith's checkerspot, Shasta blue, and chryxus arctic.

In contrast to the great number of places where the night sky is obscured by light pollution, Great Basin National Park provides exceptional visibility, and in fact it was listed by the National Park Service Night Sky Team as one of the darkest places in the United States. Astronomy buffs with telescopes and casual sky-watchers alike thrill to the sight of planets, the Milky Way, and constellations in far better conditions than elsewhere.

Nev. 488, 5 miles west of Baker, NV
775-234-7331
www.nps.gov/grba

AT A GLANCE

Eastern Nevada, 285 miles north of Las Vegas ▪ 77,180 acres ▪ Spring through fall ▪ Hiking, camping, backpacking, touring cave, stargazing

Lake Mead National Recreation Area
A water-centered park offering desert adventure as well

Located close to the nighttime playground of Las Vegas, this huge recreation area attracts throngs of boaters, swimmers, water-skiers, sunbathers, and anglers to its two reservoirs: one, Lake Mead, sprawling into countless coves; and the other, Lake Mohave, partially confined within the walls of Black Canyon.

Summers are very hot, so the lakes' waters are a cool respite from the surrounding desert, and winter temperatures are usually warm enough that water-related activities continue all year.

This fun (and electricity and drinking water provided by development) came at a price, though, as Hoover Dam (impounding Lake Mead) and Davis Dam (impounding Lake Mohave) flooded 140 miles of the Colorado River, drowning gorgeous canyons and wiping out native wildlife that depended on the free-flowing stream.

While the great majority of visitors to the park come for lake-related recreation, those more interested in nature or adventure can find it at Lake Mead. About 87 percent of the park protects areas of the eastern Mojave Desert. There are nine federally designated wilderness areas within the park, where trackless and little-visited landscapes contrast with the busy marinas and swimming areas. In the park's backcountry live mountain lions, bighorn sheep, desert tortoises, Gila monsters, and rare plants. Hikers may come across Indian petroglyphs as well.

In the eastern part of the park, the Pearce Ferry Road crosses one of the world's finest forests of the strange Joshua tree, a yucca whose branches reminded early Mormon settlers of the upstretched arms of the biblical figure Joshua.

Visiting the Park

Information on the area is available at the national recreation area's Lake Mead Visitor Center at the intersection of U.S. 93 and Nev. 146

Lake Mead is ringed by marinas, evidence of its popularity with boaters.

northeast of Boulder City. The Discovery Center here has interpretive exhibits on the Mojave Desert and its flora and fauna as well as on local geology and what the Colorado River was like before Hoover Dam was completed in 1936. Get a close look at the workings of this massive, 726-foot-high structure with tours at the nearby Hoover Dam Visitor Center *(866-730-9097)*.

National Park Service rangers lead various guided tours and programs in the fall and winter seasons on topics including nature, geology, and human history. Check with the visitor center for more details and schedules. A variety of commercial boat tours are offered on the lakes and through Black Canyon.

Hiking Trails

The Railroad Tunnel Trail, near the Lake Mead Visitor Center, follows the route of a rail line built to provide construction materials for Hoover Dam. It passes through several tunnels along the way and offers excellent views of Lake Mead and the surrounding desert. Hikers may see bighorn sheep on the slopes above the trail.

There are several short hiking trails along scenic Northshore Road, including the Wetlands Trail, good for bird-watching; the Redstone Trail, winding among red sandstone monoliths; and the Rogers Spring Trail, leading to a picnic area at a pretty oasis with a warm spring. Hikers should use caution in this hot, dry environment, drinking plenty of water, protecting themselves from the sun, and avoiding the hottest parts of the day.

Lake-related Activities

Canoeing and kayaking are popular on the Black Canyon National Water Trail, the segment of the Colorado River through Black Canyon to the upper part of Lake Mohave below Hoover Dam. A brochure is available pointing out springs, caves, and geologic formations along the way.

Fishing attracts thousands of anglers to the national recreation area throughout the year. Lake Mead is famous for its striped and largemouth bass; channel catfish, crappie, bluegill, and green sunfish are found in both Lakes Mead and Mohave. Rainbow trout are the prey of anglers at Willow Beach, Cottonwood Cove, and Katherine Landing on Lake Mohave.

Alan Bible Visitor Center
off U.S. 93, northeast of
Boulder City, NV
702-293-8990
www.nps.gov/lake

AT A GLANCE

Southeastern Nevada and northwestern Arizona, 30 miles southeast of Las Vegas ▪ 1,500,000 acres ▪ Year-round, though summer can be very hot ▪ Boating, swimming, waterskiing, fishing, hiking

Tule Springs Fossil Beds National Monument
An important trove of fossils from recent Ice Ages

Beginning in the early 1900s, scientists have been studying a vast deposit of fossils located in the desert north of Las Vegas, Nevada. Since the first fossil from the area was placed in a museum in 1919, knowledge of the Las Vegas Wash's importance has increased, leading to calls for federal park protection. In 2014, this storehouse of ancient life was added to the National Park Service as Tule Springs Fossil Beds National Monument.

Fossils found here span a range from about 250,000 to 3,000 years ago, encompassing two major ice ages and associated periods of cooling and warming. The desert wash at the center of the site was once a lush wetland, attracting grazing animals and the predators that stalked them. Paleontologists have found remains of mammoths, American lions, giant sloths, saber-toothed cats, llamas, camel relatives, dire wolves, early horses,

and bison, among other creatures.

Although thousands of specimens have been removed for study, what remains will keep scientists busy well into the future. It's known that fossil deposits at Tule Springs reach a depth of 20 feet in some areas, in addition to being scattered over the surface.

As this book goes to press, plans are in the early stages for a visitor center, exhibits, and interpretive trails at the new park.

PACIFIC

Through geopolitical events dating back to European contact and the colonial era, the United States gained possession of several islands and island groups in the western Pacific. Often, the major U.S. presence here came in the form of military bases, especially during and after World War II, when American forces used the islands as supply bases. Saipan's American Memorial Park and the War in the Pacific National Historical Park on Guam commemorate this World War II era with exhibits and artifacts. By contrast, National Park of American Samoa is a nature-oriented park where visitors can experience rain forest and coral reefs as well as traditional Samoan culture.

American Memorial Park
Honoring those who gained a vital victory in World War II

In the years before World War II, Japan developed a military presence on Saipan, a small island of the Marianas group about 1,500 miles southeast of the main Japanese islands. During World War II, U.S.

military strategists saw that taking control of the island was a critical step to advancing American forces toward Japan. Beginning in mid-June 1944, U.S. troops defeated the Japanese defenders in a three-week

effort, securing a base from which to attack Japan.

American Memorial Park honors the American and Marianas people who gave their lives during the military campaign. The Flag Circle, at the park's entrance, displays the American flag and service flags of the Army, Marine Corps, Navy, and Air Force (Army Air Corps). The Court of Honor is inscribed with more than 5,000 names and was dedicated on June 15, 1994, the 50th anniversary of the Battle of Saipan. A memorial carillon bell tower rings every half hour *(8 a.m.–8 p.m)*.

Scattered through the park and surrounding area are military artifacts from World War II, including Japanese pillboxes (fortified gun emplacements), bunkers, and a bathhouse-garden complex. Interpretive panels describe the artifacts and the events of the war.

In addition to its formal features, Memorial Park has been developed as a "living memorial" and provides a variety of recreational facilities, such as walking paths, sports fields, an amphitheater, and picnic sites.

American Memorial Park includes a 30-acre wetland and mangrove forest sanctuary consisting of mudflats and marshes, as well as the largest remaining mangrove forest on Saipan. It's home to a variety of birds and other wildlife.

The visitor center museum is staffed daily, year-round.

AT A GLANCE

Beach Rd.
Garapan, Saipan
670-234-7207
www.nps.gov/amme

Western coast of Saipan, just north of Garapan ▪ 133 acres ▪ Year-round ▪ Visiting memorials, picnicking, wildlife-watching

National Park of American Samoa
A remote island park offering adventure and discovery

A beautiful but remote and little-visited park (only a few hundred outsiders a year visit all its islands), National Park of American Samoa protects the country's finest examples of tropical rain forest and coral reef ecosystems.

American Samoa, the only United States territory south of the Equator, comprises five rugged volcanic islands and two coral atolls, located about 2,600 miles southwest of Hawai'i. Park units are located on three separate islands: Ta'u, Ofu, and Tuuila. The park headquarters and visitor center is located in the MHJ Building in Pago Pago, on Tutuila.

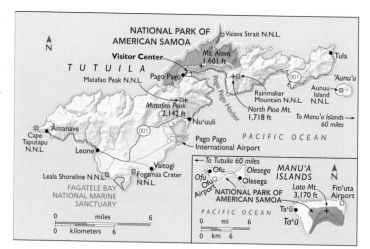

Visiting the Park
A relatively new National Park Service entity, established in 1988, the park has six trails and a ranger station on Ofu island. Adventurous visitors can find ways to explore the rain forest; beaches; and especially the nearshore waters, home to 950 of species of fish and 250 species of coral.

The island of Ofu has excellent coral reefs and the best snorkeling waters in the territory. Ofu also has what many consider the prettiest beach in American Samoa.

On Tutuila, American Samoa's largest island, a 7.4-mile round-trip trail leads to the 1,610-foot volcanic summit of Mount Alava; the trailhead is located at Fagasa Pass, a half mile west of Pago Pago. Along the way, hikers might see native birds such as white-collared kingfishers, cardinal honeyeaters, Polynesian starlings, and purple-capped fruit-doves. Quite obvious at times are huge fruit bats, sometimes called flying foxes. Walking the lovely beaches of any of the islands will bring sightings of many species of seabirds, from terns to frigatebirds to tropicbirds.

Samoan Culture
For 3,000 years Samoans have been attuned to their environment. To

show respect for the local culture, travelers should learn the simple rules of customs and proper behavior, called by the local term *fa'asamoa*, such as asking permission before taking photos, avoiding villages on Sundays, and refraining from eating or drinking while walking through a village. Ask park rangers about the Homestay program, in which visitors can stay with Samoan hosts in one of the villages.

MHJ Building
Pago Pago, AS
684-633-7082
www.nps.gov/npsa

AT A GLANCE

Tracts on four islands of American Samoa ▪ 13,500 acres ▪ Year-round ▪ Hiking, snorkeling, diving, experiencing Samoan culture

War in the Pacific National Historical Park
A memorial to those who fought in World War II's Pacific Theater

Soldiers and civilians from many nations—United States, Japan, Australia, Canada, China, France, Great Britain, New Zealand, the Netherlands, and the Soviet Union—participated in battles and support actions in the Pacific Theater during World War II. This National Park Service unit, located on the island of Guam, 1,500 miles southeast of Japan in the Marianas, is unique in honoring not just American personnel but also the bravery and sacrifices of all those who participated in the Pacific Theater.

Japanese planes attacked the U.S.-administered island of Guam on December 8, 1941, shortly after the surprise attack on Pearl Harbor. Two days later, the island surrendered, making it the first U.S. territory to be taken by the enemy. For 32 months, the islanders suffered a harsh, stringent military occupation. Guam was retaken by American troops in August 1944 and became an important command post and base from which U.S. aircraft attacked Japan. The park preserves many guns, pillboxes, and other equipment used by American and Japanese troops. They serve as the nation's

Remnants of battle on Ga'an Point

best surviving remnants of a World War II amphibious assault and battle.

The park's T. Stell Newman Visitor Center is located outside the U.S. naval base on the southwestern coast of Guam. It has a theater, exhibits, and the park's museum collection. Staff can advise about visiting units of the park, which stretch across about 9 miles.

Park units include Asan Beach, which was part of the landing area used by American troops on July 21, 1944, in the liberation of Guam; Fonte Plateau, site of a Japanese naval communications center; Piti Guns, where the Japanese placed long-range

guns intended to fire on approaching ships and landing craft (the guns were not installed in time to be used); Mount Alifan, site of intense fighting between U.S. Marines and Japanese troops, with bomb craters, foxholes, and trenches still visible; and the Agat Unit, which contains shoreline defenses as well as a sunken amtrac.

War in the Pacific National Historical Park preserves many guns, pillboxes, gun emplacements, and other equipment used by American and Japanese troops. At Asan Bay Overlook stands a Memorial Wall with 16,142 names of Chamorro (Guam native) and American casualties from the fighting on Guam, as well as bronze sculptures depicting the events during the Japanese occupation. At Asan Beach is the Liberator's Memorial, dedicated in 1994, the 50th anniversary of the American retaking of the island, honoring all U.S. forces involved.

The park also protects more than 1,000 acres of marine resources at Agat and Asan Beach, popular sites for scuba divers and snorkelers. Colorful coral and tropical fish can be seen here, and lucky visitors may spot a sea turtle.

Guam 1, 2 miles west of Agana, Guam
671-333-4050
www.nps.gov/wapa

AT A GLANCE

Southwestern Guam ▪ 1,928 acres (1,002 ocean) ▪ Year-round ▪ Visiting museum, touring battle sites, diving, snorkeling

Northwest

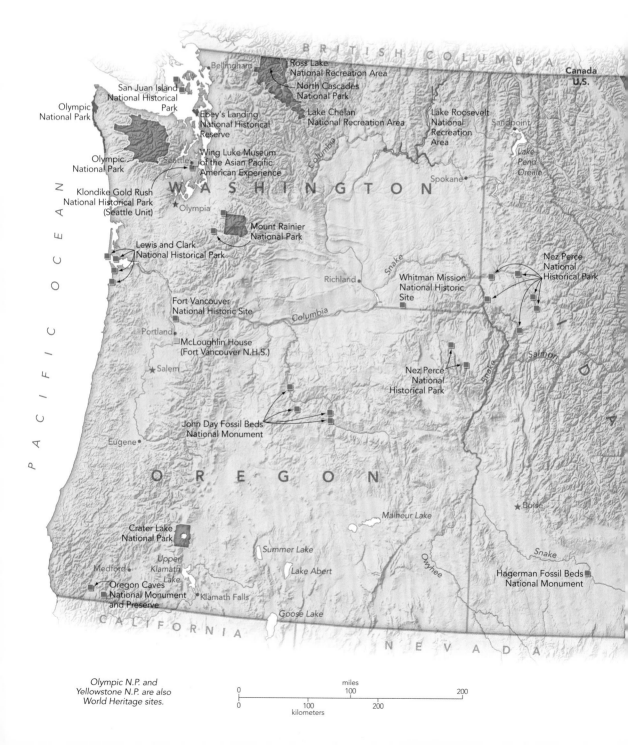

BRITISH COLUMBIA

Canada
U.S.

Bellingham

Ross Lake
National Recreation Area

North Cascades
National Park

San Juan Island
National Historical
Park

Olympic
National Park

Ebey's Landing
National Historical
Reserve

Lake Chelan
National Recreation Area

Lake Roosevelt
National
Recreation
Area

Sandpoint

Olympic
National Park

Wing Luke Museum
of the Asian Pacific
American Experience

Seattle

W A S H I N G T O N

Columbia

Spokane

Lake
Pend
Oreille

Klondike Gold Rush
National Historical Park
(Seattle Unit)

Olympia

Lewis and Clark
National Historical Park

Mount Rainier
National Park

Snake

Richland

Whitman Mission
National Historic
Site

Nez Perce
National
Historical Park

P A C I F I C   O C E A N

Fort Vancouver
National Historic Site

Columbia

Salmon

Portland

McLoughlin House
(Fort Vancouver N.H.S.)

Nez Perce
National
Historical Park

Snake

Salem

John Day Fossil Beds
National Monument

O R E G O N

Boise

Eugene

Malheur Lake

Crater Lake
National Park

Summer Lake

Snake

Upper
Klamath
Lake

Lake Abert

Owyhee

Hagerman Fossil Beds
National Monument

Medford

Oregon Caves
National Monument
and Preserve

Klamath Falls

Goose Lake

C A L I F O R N I A

N E V A D A

*Olympic N.P. and
Yellowstone N.P. are also
World Heritage sites.*

miles
0   100   200

0   100   200
kilometers

History and beauty abound in this region, where the Great Plains meet the Rockies and the volcanically active Cascade Range slopes to the Pacific. Lewis and Clark, Brigham Young, George Custer, Sitting Bull, Crazy Horse left their marks here—as did thousands of immigrants on the California, Oregon, and Mormon Trails. Here are some of our most beautiful parks, including Yellowstone, Glacier, Crater Lake, and Mount Rainier; as well as intriguing sites such as Devils Tower and Craters of the Moon National Monuments.

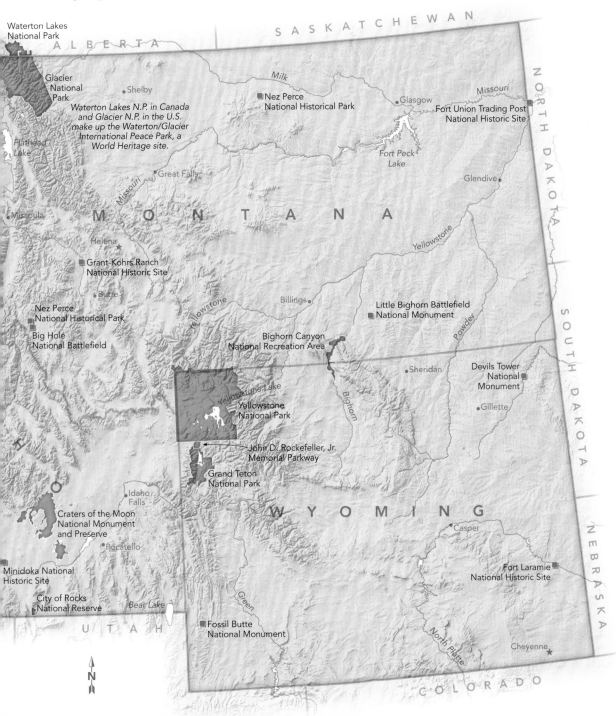

IDAHO

A topographic map of Idaho shows a central region of rugged mountains bordered on the south by the broad plain of the Snake River, where most of the state's population lives. Within those mountains lie wild places that compose one of the most remote and untouched regions in the lower 48 states. Along the Oregon border the Snake has carved Hells Canyon, the deepest gorge in North America. Craters of the Moon National Monument protects another geologic wonder—a land of craters, lava tubes, and other volcanic formations. Other protected areas in the state focus on the heritage of the Nez Perce Indians, whose descendants still live in the northern part of Idaho.

City of Rocks National Reserve

A "city" of impressive granite pinnacles

With pinnacles rising starkly from the sagebrush steppe landscape of southern Idaho, City of Rocks National Reserve has long intrigued travelers. Passing emigrant James F. Wilkins, who thought the clustered rock formations resembled the buildings of an urban area, gave the site its evocative name in 1849.

Westbound immigrants on the California Trail often stopped to make camp. Some used axle grease to write their names, which can still be seen at sites such as Register Rock and Camp Rock. At one point a "home station" for stagecoaches stood here, providing food and lodging for travelers.

Administered jointly by the National Park Service and the Idaho Department of Parks and Recreation, "the City" has gained near legendary

The view from Bath Rock takes in the "inner City."

status among rock climbers, who have developed more than 700 routes on its picturesquely eroded granite spires and domes, some of which are more than 2.5 billion years old.

More than 22 miles of trails wind through the park, offering recreation for hikers, mountain bikers, and horseback riders. Trails are

snow-covered in winter, when cross-country skiers and snowshoers enjoy the park.

The park encompasses Idaho's largest forest of piñon pines. Other plants include antelope bitterbrush, juniper, quaking aspen, sagebrush, mountain mahogany, and cottonwood.

Mammals seen often in the area include elk, moose, mule deer, black-tailed jackrabbit, yellow-bellied marmot, golden-mantled ground squirrel, and least chipmunk. Less frequently sighted are bighorn sheep, mountain lions, bobcats, and coyote. Resident birds include golden eagle, prairie falcon, sage grouse, piñon jay, Clark's nutcracker, mountain bluebird, and canyon wren.

The visitor center *(closed Sun.– Mon. late Oct.–mid-April)* provides information on ranger-led activities.

South Elba Almo Rd.
(off Idaho 77)
Almo, ID
208-824-5910
www.nps.gov/ciro

AT A GLANCE

South-central Idaho, 85 miles southeast of Twin Falls ▪ 14,407 acres ▪ Year-round ▪ Hiking, rock climbing, biking, horseback riding, camping

Craters of the Moon N.M. & Preserve

A *"weird and scenic landscape" of dramatic lava flows*

Beginning about 15,000 years ago and ending about 2,000 years ago, lava, cinders, and gas were released from fissures in the Earth's surface across an area now within south-central Idaho. Because the fluid basaltic lava flow allowed gas to escape rather than build to high pressure, there were no explosive eruptions, and no tall volcanoes formed. Rather, the result was a vast expanse of rugged lava flows that reminded some observers of the surface of the moon.

A "weird and scenic landscape peculiar to itself" is how President Calvin Coolidge described the site when Craters of the Moon National Monument was established in 1924. Since then the park has been greatly expanded in size and has been designated a national monument and preserve. (However, hunting is allowed in the preserve and BLM-managed portion of the monument.)

The park's Robert Limbert Visitor Center (named for a 1920s explorer and photographer who avocated for protection of the area) offers an interpretive film and exhibits on geology and natural history. The nearby North Crater Flow Trail (a 0.4-mile loop) leads into one of the newest (2,200 years old) lava flows in the park, with features such as pressure ridges, "squeeze ups," and both *pāhoehoe* (smooth) and *'a'ā* (jagged) lava.

Other trails along the park's 7-mile scenic drive include the ascent up Inferno Cone, a steep hike that offers panoramic views of the Snake River Plain and distant mountains; Tree Molds Trail, which leads to the edge of the Blue Dragon Flow and impressions of trees that were engulfed by lava; and Broken Top Loop Trail, which winds through almost every type of volcanic feature found in the park.

Craters of the Moon is home to many lava-tube caves, tunnels formed when the outer part of moving lava solidified while the inside part continued to flow. Ask a ranger for advice about exploring these caves safely—a permit is required. Indian Tunnel is the easiest to visit, as "skylights" allow enough sunlight to enter that safe travel is possible without a flashlight.

The park includes an extensive wilderness area—the first such designated area in the National Park System—open to hiking and backpacking. A free permit is required for overnight trips into the wilderness area.

U.S. 20/26/93
18 miles southwest of Arco, ID
208-527-1300
www.nps.gov/crmo

AT A GLANCE

South-central Idaho, 80 miles west of Idaho Falls ▪ 752,490 acres (462,880 NPS; remaining are BLM land) ▪ Year-round ▪ Hiking, exploring lava-tube caves, camping, backpacking, cross-country skiing, snowshoeing

Hagerman Fossil Beds National Monument

A *globally important site for the study of ancient horses*

Today the Hagerman Valley of Idaho is a place of agriculture and scattered towns in a landscape of springs, lava flows, and rock formations, receiving less than 10 inches of annual precipitation. Three to four million years ago, it received twice as much precipitation, creating an environment that was home to camels, sloths, saber-toothed cats, giant marmots, and waterbirds such as swans and cormorants.

Hagerman Fossil Beds National Monument protects around 600 fossil sites where more than 40,000 specimens have been found of more than 200 species of animals and plants. The most notable is the Hagerman "horse"—something of a misnomer since it is believed to be more closely related to modern zebras.

During that late Pliocene epoch, something happened one day—perhaps a sudden flood—that caused a herd of these zebra-like animals to die together. Their bones fossilized, and in the early 20th century this treasure of fossils was discovered, and scientific excavations began.

Thirty complete skeletons and portions of 200 individual horses have been found, making the Hagerman Horse Quarry one of the most important sites in the world for the study of the development of the modern horse. The quarry is designated a national natural landmark.

The best place to see fossils is the park's visitor center in Hagerman, as fossil sites are not usually open to the public. Park rangers lead seasonal walking tours that visit and interpret sites of scientific research; check for current schedules.

The park also offers a 10.5-mile self-guided auto tour, which leads to a hiking trail and scenic overlooks near the Snake River. A portion of the actual route of the 19th-century Oregon Trail (see p. 276) runs through the park; visitors can see the trail ruts dug by wagon wheels and oxen hooves.

U.S. 30
Hagerman, ID
208-933-4100
www.nps.gov/hafo

AT A GLANCE

South-central Idaho, 35 miles northwest of Twin Falls ▪ 4,351 acres ▪ Year-round ▪ Viewing visitor center exhibits, driving scenic route, hiking segment of Oregon Trail

---

Minidoka National Historic Site

A memorial to the forced relocation of Japanese Americans

In February 1942, two months after the attack on Pearl Harbor brought the United States into World War II, President Franklin Roosevelt signed an executive order that forced almost 120,000 Japanese-American citizens and resident Japanese aliens into ten isolated relocation centers located across the country.

One of those sites, Minidoka War Relocation Center, was established in south-central Idaho. (It was known locally as Hunt Camp for the Hunt post office, where internees received their mail.) Most of the 9,000 persons relocated here were from Washington, Oregon, and Alaska. Barracks, recreation areas, gardens, and

Remains of a reception building at the camp's entrance

other facilities were built, lasting until the end of the war when internees were allowed to return home. After the war, Minidoka buildings were taken away for various uses, and the land was allocated to returning U.S. soldiers.

Minidoka National Historic Site

contains the remains of a military police building and reception center, a historic barrack building, a mess hall, and a reproduction guard tower. A 1.6-mile interpretive trail takes visitors past historic structures and landscapes, and signs describe life in the camp for the people who lived here from 1942 to 1945.

There are exhibits related to Minidoka at the visitor center at Hagerman Fossil Beds National Monument (see p. 451) and the Jerome County Museum in the town of Jerome and at the Idaho Farm and Ranch Museum, southeast of Jerome. The Park Service office at Hagerman oversees Minidoka.

Hunt Rd. (off Idaho 25)
15 miles east of
Jerome, ID
208-837-4793
www.nps.gov/miin

AT A GLANCE

South-central Idaho, 20 miles northeast of Twin Falls ▪ 292 acres ▪ Year-round ▪ Visiting World War II internment camp site

---

Nez Perce National Historical Park

More than three dozen sites documenting a Native American culture

The Niimiipuu people (historically known as the Nez Perce) lived in the Pacific Northwest at the time of European contact. As was the case with other tribes, non-Indian immigration into the region in the 19th century led to a series of conflicts and treaties with the United States. Even in the wake of these conflicts, these lands remain an important part of Nez Perce culture in the 21st century.

Nez Perce War

Violence broke out between a faction of Nez Perce and whites in the Wallowa Valley of Oregon in 1877, leading to a series of battles now called the Nez Perce war. The "war" took place as a group of Nez Perce traveled from Oregon through Idaho and Wyoming into Montana, trying to cross the border into Canada while being pursued by units of the U.S. Army. The Nez Perce successfully fended off the U.S. Army for three months, but just 40 miles from the Canadian border, in today's Montana, the U.S. Army engaged the Nez Perce in a five-day battle and siege. The survivors of this encounter, the Bear Paw Battle, were forced to surrender on October 5, 1877. The Nez Perce people and culture live on in the Pacific Northwest.

Visiting the Park

Nez Perce National Historical Park is made up of 38 sites scattered across much of the traditional Nez Perce homeland. The National Park Service owns nine sites in Idaho, Montana, Oregon, and Washington, including Big Hole National Battlefield (see p. 454) in Montana. Some sites are undeveloped or located on private property; check with the park about access.

The Spalding Visitor Center (U.S. 95, Lapwai, Idaho, 208-843-7001) is the best place to begin exploring the historical park. (The visitor center at Big Hole National Battlefield can also provide information.) The Nez Perce lived at this site for thousands of years before European settlement. In 1836, Henry Spalding founded a Presbyterian mission at the site. Later the Nez Perce Indian Agency was located here, followed by the town of Spalding. Several buildings remain, including a store and Indian-agency cabin. Museum and interpretive displays introduce Nez Perce history and culture, and ranger-led programs are offered in summer.

To the east on Clearwater River is Canoe Camp, where the Lewis and Clark expedition—officially the Corps of Discovery—stopped in 1805. The nearby Heart of the Monster site includes exhibits explaining the legendary battle in which Coyote killed a monster, whose drops of blood created the Nez Perce. To the south is White Bird Battlefield, where a self-guiding trail leads across the site of the first clash of the Nez Perce war.

Both the Lewis and Clark expedition and the Nez Perce crossed the Bitterroot Mountains via 5,233-foot Lolo Pass, where the U.S. Forest Service operates a visitor center (208-942-3113, closed in winter) along U.S. 12 near the Idaho-Montana border, with exhibits on the Corps of Discovery and the Nez Perce.

On Mont. 240, south of Chinook, Montana, Bear Paw Battlefield preserves the site of the final battle of the Nez Perce war. A visitor center in the Blaine County Museum (406-357-2590) in Chinook presents a film called "40 Miles to Freedom." A self-guided 1.25-mile interpretive trail winds through the battlefield. A nonprofit organization works with the Park Service to support the various Nez Perce battlefields (www.friendsnez percebattlefields.org).

Spalding Visitor Center
U.S. 95
Lapwai, ID
208-843-7009
www.nps.gov/nepe

AT A GLANCE

Park sites located in Idaho, Montana, Oregon, and Washington
■ 2,495 acres ■ Spring through fall ■ Touring historic sites, hiking

Nez Perce National Historic Trail

Commemorating a tribe's difficult journey through the Northwest

In 1877, a group of Nez Perce Indians undertook a flight toward what they hoped would be freedom after violence broke out with white settlers near present-day Grangeville, Idaho. The Nez Perce traveled through Idaho and Wyoming into Montana, trying to cross the border into Canada while being pursued by the U.S. Army. Despite fending off the Army for three months, survivors of the five-day Bear Paw Battle and siege were forced to surrender in October 1877.

Nez Perce National Historic Trail commemorates that journey. A driving route (though there are hiking and horseback riding opportunities along the way), the trail begins at Wallowa Lake, Oregon, then traverses central Idaho and enters Montana at famed Lolo Pass, long a route across the Rocky Mountains (it was also used by the Lewis and Clark expedition). The trail heads southeast through Big Hole National Battlefield (see p. 454) and crosses Yellowstone National Park (see p. 495) before turning north into Montana to end 40 miles from the Canadian border at Bear Paw Battlefield, site of the Nez Perce surrender.

A number of the sites along the way are administered as part of

Nez Perce National Historical Park (see p. 452), which comprises 38 sites scattered across much of the traditional Nez Perce homeland. Visitor centers connected with the park are the best places to learn about the trail and the heritage of the Nez Perce (also known as Niimiipuu), who still live in the region.

MONTANA

Its name means "mountain," and indeed the Rocky Mountains cover much of the western part of Montana, where the jewel is Glacier National Park on the Canadian border, a place of superb beauty and rugged wilderness. More than half the state, though, lies within the Great Plains, rolling grassland where ranching and agriculture dominate. Little Bighorn Battlefield National Monument preserves the site of the 1876 defeat of General Custer's troops by Native American forces led by braves, including Crazy Horse and Sitting Bull. Fort Union Trading Post National Historic Site commemorates the fur-trading era when European explorers traded with Plains tribes for furs of beaver and bison.

Big Hole National Battlefield

Site of a major clash in the Nez Perce war

In 1877, five bands of Nez Perce fled the government's attempt to settle them on a small reservation in Idaho, leading to a series of battles with U.S. Army troops, collectively known as the Nez Perce war. A group of about 800 Nez Perce, chased by troops, traveled across Idaho, Wyoming, and Montana, in hope of escaping to Canada.

On August 7, the Nez Perce set up camp at Big Hole Valley, believing they were far from any pursuing troops. Army scouts found them, and soldiers and volunteers attacked on the morning of August 9. The Nez Perce, however, forced the Army troops to retreat, and held them under siege while most of the tribe escaped. Though a nominal Nez Perce victory, between 60 and 90 Indians were killed, many of them women and children. Two months later, the Nez Perce fight came to an end at Bear Paw.

Big Hole National Battlefield is a unit of Nez Perce National Historical Park (see p. 452), which numbers 38 sites related to Nez Perce heritage scattered across four states. The battlefield honors the Nez Perce, Army infantry soldiers, and civilian Bitterroot Volunteers who fought here. The visitor center offers an interpretive film, exhibits, and artifacts, including personal items of some of the battle participants. Hiking trails lead to the campsite where soldiers surprised the sleeping Nez Perce, and to the siege area where soldiers fought from trenches against the Nez Perce counterattack. Another trail leads to the Howitzer Capture Site, where Indian warriors captured and dismantled said artillery; the site has an amazing view of the battlefield. Overlooks provide views of the Big Hole Valley.

Bighorn Canyon National Recreation Area
Boating and fishing below spectacular canyon walls

Located on the border between Montana and Wyoming, Bighorn Canyon National Recreation Area was established in 1966 after the construction of a dam on the Bighorn River. The impounded waters of Bighorn Lake now stretch above the dam for 71 miles, of which more than 50 miles lie within spectacular Bighorn Canyon.

Bighorn Canyon encompasses a forest, mountains, an upland prairie, canyons, a lake, and wetlands, home to a diverse array of wildlife. In addition to native species such as black bears, bighorn sheep, mule deer, and mountain lions, the national recreation area includes part of 39,000-acre Pryor Mountain Wild Horse Range, home to about 160 wild horses. One of the few wild-horse populations in the United States with strong Spanish ancestry, these animals are protected as "living symbols of the historic and pioneer spirit of the West."

Visiting the Park

The park has two visitor centers at either end of the recreation area: one at Yellowtail Dam near Fort Smith, Montana *(Mem. Day–Labor Day)*; and the Cal S. Taggart Visitor Center in Lovell, Wyoming *(year-round)*. The only direct route between the north and south visitor centers is by water, as there are no roads connecting the two districts. Both centers have bookstores and introductory films on the area; the Cal S. Taggart Visitor Center

also has a relief map of Bighorn Canyon, and exhibits on the history and geology of the region.

Water-related recreation is the major attraction at Bighorn Canyon National Recreation Area, with excellent fishing on the lake and on the Bighorn River above and below the reservoir. The park offers many other attractions, though, including hiking, camping, and rewarding bird-watching.

The park's most enthusiastic visitors are probably anglers, who try their luck for fish, including brown, rainbow, and lake trout; walleye; sauger; smallmouth bass; crappie; and catfish. The Bighorn River below the dam is especially noted for rainbow and brown trout. Local outfitters can provide rental of pontoon

barges, canoes, and other watercraft.

Bird-watchers know the park as one of the best places in the region to spot birds of prey and wintering waterbirds, including species such as bald eagles, prairie and peregrine falcons, loons, geese, ducks, and gulls.

Bighorn Canyon National Recreation Area offers 13 hiking trails totaling 27 miles of routes, most of them in the southern section of the park. The easy 1-mile Sullivan's Knob Trail leads to the rim of Bighorn Canyon and is a good place to look for bighorn sheep and peregrine falcon. Farther north, a trail leads to Lockhart Ranch, with structures and artifacts from a late 19th- and early 20th-century ranch.

The park includes several campgrounds, some of them reached only by trail or boat.

Canyon walls rise more than 2,000 feet above Bighorn Lake in places.

Mont. 313
Fort Smith, MT
406-666-2412
www.nps.gov/bica

AT A GLANCE

Southern Montana, 90 miles southeast of Billings ▪ 120,284 acres ▪ Spring through fall ▪ Boating, hiking, camping, fishing, swimming, bird-watching

Continental Divide National Scenic Trail

A long-distance path along the "backbone of the continent"

Authorized by Congress in 1978, the Continental Divide National Scenic Trail was envisioned as a 3,100-mile route from the Canadian border to the Mexican border, roughly following the Continental Divide: the great geographic line, mostly through the Rocky Mountains, that separates streams that flow to the Pacific Ocean from those that flow to the Atlantic Ocean and the Gulf of Mexico.

Passing through five states—Montana, Idaho, Wyoming, Colorado, and New Mexico—the trail is administered by the U.S. Forest Service in partnership with the National Park Service and the Bureau of Land Management. Limited funding and issues such as trail segments through private land have prevented official completion of the project. As of 2015, the trail was about 80 percent complete, with 20 percent remaining on highways and motorized routes. Parts of the trail pass through rewarding destinations such as Glacier National Park (see p. 457) and the Bob Marshall Wilderness Area in Montana; Yellowstone National Park (see p. 495)

Bones of animals large and small litter the trail.

in Wyoming; Rocky Mountain National Park (see p. 336) in Colorado; and El Malpais National Monument (see p. 349) and Gila National Forest in New Mexico.

In some areas hikers must follow roads or highways where the trail is not complete. In many places the exact path of the trail has yet to be determined, as government agencies and trail advocacy groups debate issues such as routing and access by mountain bikes and all-terrain vehicles.

The Forest Service is the lead federal agency in charge of the trail, but the best source of information on accessing it is the Continental Divide Trail Coalition (CDTC), which assists federal agencies in trail planning and coordination of volunteer activities such as construction and maintenance. The CDTC website offers information on trailheads and updates on the trail status, and its online store sells maps and guidebooks.

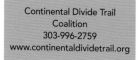

Continental Divide Trail Coalition
303-996-2759
www.continentaldividetrail.org

AT A GLANCE
Glacier National Park, Montana, to southwestern New Mexico ▪ 3,100 miles ▪ Year-round; best seasons depend on trail location ▪ Backpacking, day hiking

Fort Union Trading Post National Historic Site

A historic meeting place of many cultures

Established in 1828 by the American Fur Company, Fort Union, contrary to its name, was a place of business. Furs, including buffalo (bison) robes and the valuable pelt of the beaver, were in high demand in the early to mid-19th century. The fort was built specifically to acquire furs from Northern Plains tribes, especially the Assiniboine, in exchange for goods such as cookware, knives, beads, guns, alcohol, blankets, and cloth. The fort stayed in business until 1867, the longest life-span of any American fur-trading center along the upper Missouri River.

Located near the confluence of the Missouri and Yellowstone Rivers, Fort Union at its height had as many as 200 workers. When the fur trade came to an end, the fort was dismantled and its materials used to help expand nearby Fort Buford, a U.S. Army post active in the Indian wars. (Today Fort Buford is a North Dakota state historic site.) The wooden structure at Fort Union Trading Post National Historic Site is a reproduction based on extensive archaeological research.

The park visitor center, located in the Bourgeois House (home of the head trader), has audiovisual programs, exhibits on life at the post, and examples of the furs that were traded here. In the adjacent Trade House *(Mem. Day–Labor Day)* a ranger dressed as a fur trader presents programs on the history of the fur trade, and shelves are stocked with facsimiles of the goods exchanged with Indians.

A hiking trail leads to the lookout at which famed artist Karl Bodmer painted a view of Fort Union in the 1830s. Other notable people who visited the fort include artist George Caitlin and naturalist John James Audubon, who stayed here in 1843 and whose assistant John Graham Bell collected the first specimen of Baird's sparrow nearby.

N. Dak. 1804
Williston, ND
701-572-9083
www.nps.gov/fous

AT A GLANCE

North Dakota–Montana state line; 25 miles southwest of Williston, North Dakota or 25 miles northeast of Sidney, Montana ■ 444 acres ■ Year-round ■ Touring reconstructed fort and visitor center, hiking

Glacier National Park

"The best care-killing scenery on the continent"

Established in 1910 as America's tenth national park, Glacier encompasses more than a million acres of some of the most dramatic terrain in North America. The park was named for the evidence of massive glaciers that carved its rugged landscape—the latest ones retreated only about 10,000 years ago—as well as for the smaller mountain glaciers from the Little Ice Age, which dot the high country today.

The park is a wonderland of treeless mountain summits, alpine meadows, coniferous forests, more than 650 lakes, and dozens of waterfalls, all making up what famed conservationist John Muir called "the best care-killing scenery on the continent." Going-to-the-Sun Road crosses Glacier, allowing spectacular views for even casual visitors with limited time. An engineering marvel that still amazes visitors more than 75 years after its construction, Going-to-the-Sun Road is itself a national historic landmark.

Glacier National Park abuts the United States–Canada border and Canada's Waterton Lakes National Park. In 1932, the two countries symbolically joined the parks as Waterton-Glacier/International Peace Park, the world's first such park. While administered separately, the two parks cooperate in wildlife management, scientific research, and some visitor services. The parks are both international biosphere reserves, and were jointly named as a World Heritage site in 1995.

Flora & Fauna

The park's varied habitats include alpine, moist coniferous forest, dry coniferous forest, prairie, deciduous forest, and wet meadow. Nearly 2,000 species of vascular plants, mosses, and lichens are found here. Here in this rocky environment, the park's signature glacier lily sends its green shoots up through the snow in spring, just one of hundreds of species of wildflowers that grow from the lowland riparian zone to the alpine tundra.

More than 70 types of mammals—including notable species such as grizzly and black bears, mountain lion, wolverine, gray wolf, lynx, moose, elk, mountain goat, and bighorn sheep—can be found within Glacier, and many of them, or their traces, can be spotted by keen-eyed visitors.

Bird-watchers delight in Glacier's more than 260 species of birds. Dusky grouse, three-toed woodpecker, red-naped sapsucker, Townsend's solitaire, and pine grosbeak dwell in the forests. Rivers and lakes are home to American dipper, Barrow's goldeneye, and the beautiful harlequin duck, while the rare black swift nests on a few cliffs. Tundra species such as white-tailed ptarmigan and gray-crowned rosy-finch live high above the tree line.

Human History

Paleo-Indians inhabited this area more than 10,000 years ago. At the time of European exploration, the Blackfeet people ruled the prairies east of the mountains, while the Salish and Kootenai lived and hunted in the western valleys. One Native American description of the land now in the park was "the backbone of the world."

Around 1900, miners entered the mountains seeking gold and copper, but they had little luck. The completion of the Great Northern Railway (tracks still hug the southern border of the park) brought tourism as early as the 1890s, when visitors arriving by train took a stagecoach ride to Lake McDonald and a boat to a hotel on its shore. The railway's company, whose logo included a mountain goat, built hotels and lodges called "chalets," often reached by horseback; there were few roads in those days. Some of those lodges still offer accommodations to visitors today.

Visiting the Park

Visitor centers are located at the east and west main entrances, plus another at Logan Pass on Going-to-the-Sun Road. Most of the road is closed in winter, with opening and closing dates determined by snowfall and spring melting. Ongoing road rehabilitation is also scheduled to

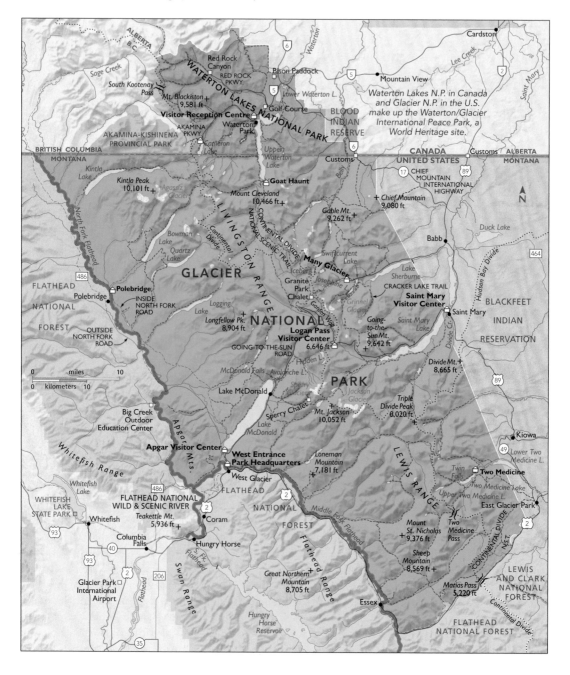

continue until 2018, so call the park or check the website for driving specifics when planning a visit. Generally, most park facilities are open late May into September.

The first priority in visiting the park is a drive along the east-west 50-mile Going-to-the-Sun Road. It offers fantastic scenic views and access to several rewarding nature trails, which, together with exhibits in the visitor centers, can provide an introductory overview of the area.

Going-to-the-Sun Road:
Lake McDonald to Logan Pass

The Apgar Visitor Center on the park's west side is located near the southern end of Lake McDonald. Glacier's largest lake, McDonald is 10 miles long and 472 feet deep, occupying a basin gouged out by a glacier estimated to have been 2,200 feet thick. (In some areas near the park, glaciers lie up to a mile thick over the earth.) Kootenai Indians called this body of water Sacred Dancing Lake, and performed ceremonies on its banks.

Going-to-the-Sun Road hugs the eastern shore of the lake to its upper end at McDonald Falls. At a viewpoint here the layered rocks demonstrate how these mountains are formed: mainly of sedimentary rock from mud and sand at the bottom of a sea that existed here for nearly a billion years. Over time, tectonic pressure uplifted, thrusted, and folded the ancient seafloors into mountains. The rock exposed at McDonald Falls is among the oldest in the park.

Not far ahead is the self-guided, 0.75-mile boardwalk Trail of the Cedars. It offers displays on the western red cedar–hemlock forest found at this elevation, and it crosses Avalanche Gorge on a footbridge. The red stone along Avalanche Creek was formed

Mountain goats live on the high peaks.

during a period when the sea retreated. Iron-rich minerals oxidized in contact with the air, forming the mineral hematite. Following the creek, the Avalanche Lake Trail climbs gently for about 2 miles to glacier-fed Avalanche Lake, with fine views of creek, lake, and waterfalls on the nearby cliffs.

Back on Going-to-the-Sun Road, the route snakes beneath the Garden Wall, a segment of the Continental Divide and a knife-edged arête, formed when two glaciers carved away opposite sides of a ridge. At the Bird Woman Falls overlook, an exhibit illustrates how glaciers dug out this U-shaped valley.

Going-to-the-Sun Road: Logan Pass

The road crests the Continental Divide at 6,646-foot Logan Pass. A visitor center offers exhibits on this subalpine and alpine world. The very popular 3-mile round-trip Hidden Lake Nature Trail climbs through subalpine fir stunted by the harsh growing conditions. Trees just a few inches in diameter can be hundreds of years old. A boardwalk protecting alpine meadow vegetation leads to views of Clements Mountain and Reynolds Mountain. Both are "horns," which form when three or

more glaciers gnaw away at a mountain from different directions, creating a sharp-pointed summit.

As the trail reaches the overlook to Hidden Lake, 750 feet below in its glacier-carved basin, mountain goats and bighorn sheep can often be seen on the mountainsides.

Going-to-the-Sun Road:
Logan Pass to Divide Creek

Heading west from Logan Pass, the road approaches Going-to-the-Sun Mountain, which gave its name to this historic byway. Soon there's a view of Jackson and Blackfoot Glaciers to the south, two of the park's few glaciers visible from a road. In 1850, the area that's now the national park had 150 glaciers; today there are 26. Looking at the effects of global climate change, some scientists predict that by 2030 there may be none. Many research projects in the park study the relationship between climate and glaciers.

At the upper end of St. Mary Lake, a 1-mile trail leads to St. Mary Falls, a double-stranded cascade that drops through a narrow chasm. A half-mile farther down the trail is 100-foot Virginia Falls. A bit farther along the road, the Sun Point Nature Trail interprets the ecology of the drier eastern part of the park. Less snowfall here means Going-to-the-Sun Road stays open longer and higher on this side in fall than it does on the western slope. The road passes through open grassland with groves of aspen and other deciduous trees to end at Divide Creek and the St. Mary Visitor Center.

Many Glacier

The Many Glacier area of the park is reached by a park road off U.S. 89, north of St. Mary. The park road skirts Lake Sherburne, created by a dam that drowned an abandoned mining

FOLLOWING PAGES: *Carved by a glacier-fed stream, narrow Avalanche Gorge is one of Glacier's premier sights for visitors.*

community. The Many Glacier Hotel near the end of the road was built in 1914–15 by the Great Northern Railway. A trail network centered in Many Glacier offers some of the park's best wildlife-watching, with chances to see grizzly and black bears, mountain goats, and bighorn sheep.

Swiftcurrent Lake lies beneath the great promontory of Grinnell Point, named for George Bird Grinnell, an early advocate for the creation of Glacier National Park. The Swiftcurrent Nature Trail makes an easy 2.6-mile loop around the lake through forests of Engelmann spruce, subalpine fir, and lodgepole pine. A more strenuous 5.5-mile trail climbs to Grinnell Glacier, one of the largest in the park.

Two Medicine Valley

One of the less visited areas of Glacier, Two Medicine Valley is reached off Mont. 49 in the southeastern part of the park. Along the entrance road is the easy, 0.5-mile round-trip boardwalk to Running Eagle Falls, a double waterfall that spills over the edge and down the face of a beautiful limestone cliff. Of the many trails in the area, the 6.2-mile round-trip hike to Scenic Point is one of the most rewarding, leading to a viewpoint of Two Medicine Valley and the plains to the east.

Two Medicine Lake is one of the spots in Glacier where the scenery can be enjoyed from a boat instead of from a vehicle or on foot. Guided boat tours are offered on Many Glacier, Two Medicine, Rising Sun, and McDonald Lakes. Some boat tours include a ranger-guided hike as well. Canoes and other small boats can be rented at several places around the park.

The Backcountry

With around 750 miles of hiking trails, the park makes it possible for everyone to experience a bit of the wilder environment. Backpackers can take multiday hikes deep into backcountry. The last two remaining historic "chalets" can be reached only by trail, offering an alternative to camping for hikers.

Hikers and backpackers should know how to avoid encounters with bears, and how to minimize the chance of attack in case of a meeting.

U.S. 2
31 miles northeast of Kalispell, MT
406-888-7800
www.nps.gov/glac

AT A GLANCE

Northwestern Montana, 31 miles northeast of Kalispell ▪ 1,013,572 acres ▪ Year-round ▪ Hiking, camping, backpacking, horseback riding, scenic driving, boating, cross-country skiing, snowshoeing

Grant-Kohrs Ranch National Historic Site
The legacy of Montana's "cattle king"

In the 1850s a French-Canadian trader named Johnny Grant established a cattle operation in the Deer Lodge Valley of western Montana, where surrounding mountains shielded animals from the worst of winter weather. He built a home in 1859 and a larger one in 1862, operating several businesses in the area.

Facing obstacles such as his poor English-language skills and the racial prejudice against his Indian wives and mixed-blood companions, Grant sold out to a businessman named Conrad Kohrs, who eventually owned 50,000 head of cattle that grazed on 10 million acres of land in four states and Canada. With reason, Kohrs was known as the "cattle king" of Montana.

Grant-Kohrs Ranch National Historic Site centers on this early cattle operation, and remains a working ranch that preserves the story of the cowboy and commemorates the role of cattlemen in American history. The park's more than 80 structures include the historic ranch and its original furnishings (it was built by Grant in 1862 and enlarged by Kohrs in 1890); the bunkhouse; the blacksmith shop; horse barns; and cattle sheds, and other outbuildings dating as far back as the 1860s. Rangers conduct tours of the main ranch house year-round, and lead a variety of other activities seasonally, among them horse-drawn wagon rides, chuckwagon talks, blacksmithing demonstrations, and programs about the real life of cowboys.

Seven miles of walking trails on the property include a nature trail that follows Cottonwood Creek to the Clark Fork River and trails that lead to the far pastures for a view of the main herd of cattle.

266 Warren Ln. (off N. Main St.)
Deer Lodge, MT
406-846-2070
www.nps.gov/grko

AT A GLANCE

Western Montana, 45 miles west of Helena ▪ 1,618 acres ▪ Spring through fall ▪ Touring historic ranch buildings, hiking

Little Bighorn Battlefield National Monument
The famed site of Custer's Last Stand

One of the most famous battles in U.S. history occurred on the plains and ridges near the Little Bighorn River on June 25–26, 1876. Twelve companies of the U.S. Army Seventh Cavalry met several thousand Lakota Sioux and Cheyenne warriors, resulting in the deaths of 263 soldiers and attached personnel, including Lt. Col. George A. Custer. The Indians, led by Crazy Horse, Gall, and White Bull, among other warriors, suffered an unknown number of casualties, but they gained one of the most decisive victories of the prolonged Plains Indian wars of the late 19th century.

The circumstances of the battle have been debated since it occurred, and the focus of the memorial has changed along with the historical perception of America's westward expansion. In 1991, the park's name was changed from Custer Battlefield National Monument to Little Bighorn Battlefield National Monument.

For decades there were no memorials to Indians who fought and died, nor was the Indian testimony significantly acknowledged. Now Indians are seen as having been displaced from their lands and fighting to maintain their traditional ways of life. Today, for instance, granite markers indicating where Indian warriors died have joined similar markers long in place honoring fallen Army soldiers. Park staff offer balanced interpretive views of the events surrounding Little Bighorn.

Custer National Cemetery covers a portion of the Little Bighorn battlefield.

Visiting the Park

A visitor center offers exhibits on the battle and a 20-minute orientation film, and ranger talks *(Mem. Day–Labor Day)* on the battle are offered.

A 5-mile self-guided auto tour allows visitors to observe battle sites marked with interpretive displays. These include the famed Last Stand Hill, the knoll where Custer and 40 to 50 men—all of whom died—were surrounded and made their final, desperate stand. The park consists of two parts connected by the tour road: the site of Custer's battle and the Reno-Benteen Battlefield, where other Army units were pinned down by fighting and unable to come to Custer's aid. These other units survived the battle.

The adjacent Custer National Cemetery was established in 1886 on a square mile of the battlefield. An earlier cemetery had protected the graves of the Army soldiers who died at Little Bighorn, but the remains of most of the soldiers were reinterred in a mass grave in 1881. (Custer was reburied at the U.S. Military Academy at West Point in 1877.) The national cemetery officially closed in 1978; it contains veterans representing wars from the Indian campaigns to Vietnam.

U.S. 212, 2 miles southeast of Crow Agency, MT
406-638-2621
www.nps.gov/libi
www.friendslittlebighorn.com

AT A GLANCE

Southeastern Montana, 60 miles east of Billings ▪ 765 acres ▪ Year-round ▪ Walking and driving tours of battlefield, participating in ranger-led programs

OREGON

Accomplishing a goal set for it by President Thomas Jefferson, the Corps of Discovery reached the Pacific Ocean in December 1805. The team wintered on the south bank of the Columbia River in what is now Oregon; a national historical park marks its camp. Later in the 19th century, thousands of pioneers came west on the Oregon Trail to the fertile Willamette Valley, between the Cascade and Coast Ranges. Today's visitors make their way to Crater Lake National Park, one of the most beautiful destinations in the West. Many others head for the coastline, where all beaches are accessible to the public. Wildlife-watching—for birds, whales, seals, and sea lions—is a popular attraction.

Crater Lake National Park

Born of a volcano, a lake of legendary beauty

One of the scenic wonders of North America, Crater Lake was known to local Indian tribes, who attributed its creation to a mythic struggle between the chiefs of the Above World and the Below World. Early Native Americans may well have witnessed the actual geologic event that formed the lake.

A volcano called Mount Mazama, part of the Cascade Range chain, exploded 7,700 years ago, sending ash miles into the air. So much pumice and ash was ejected that Mount Mazama's summit collapsed, creating a caldera up to 6 miles in diameter and 4,000 feet deep. The explosion was a hundred times as large as the 1980 blast at Mount St. Helens, also part of the Cascade Range.

No streams lead into or drain from the caldera. Over the centuries, snowmelt and rain accumulated to create a lake in the huge pit, forming a body of water more than 1,900 feet deep—the deepest lake in the United States and one of the ten deepest in the world.

The lake's depth accounts for its most famous quality—a blue

of breathtaking intensity. Another Native American legend says that the gorgeous plumage of the mountain bluebird came about when the originally gray bird flew through the lake's water.

The first European Americans to see the lake were three gold prospectors who climbed to its rim in 1853. Amazed by the color of its water, they named it Deep Blue Lake. Thanks in large part to the single-minded efforts of a man named William Gladstone Steel—he helped survey the area, provided funding for scientific studies, named several geographic features, and lobbied politicians—Crater Lake was designated as America's sixth national park in 1902.

Visiting the Park

Winters are long at Crater Lake, with an average of 44 feet of snow falling during the season. Ore. 62 and the road to the crater rim are kept open in winter, but most visitors will want to see the park during the brief summer and early fall period, when all roads and trails are open. (Depending on snowmelt

timing, the Rim Drive may not be fully open until July.) Visitors who simply drive to the crater rim and view the lake will have a memorable experience, but the national park offers much more to do, including hiking, backcountry camping, and wildlife-watching.

Visitors entering the park on Oreg. 62 will turn up to the crater rim at Mazama Village, where there are cabins, a campground, and a store *(all seasonal)*. Just up the road is the Godfrey Glen Trail, a wheelchair-accessible loop. Winding through a forest that grew on deposits of volcanic pumice and ash 250 feet thick, it offers views of deep, stream-cut Annie Creek Canyon.

It's worth a stop at Steel Information Center *(open year-round)*, farther north on the park road, to talk to rangers; pick up brochures; and see the 22-minute introductory film "Crater Lake: Into the Deep."

It's a short but twisty drive up to Rim Village, where Sinnott Memorial Overlook, a viewpoint perched on a 900-foot-tall cliff, provides one of the many postcard-quality

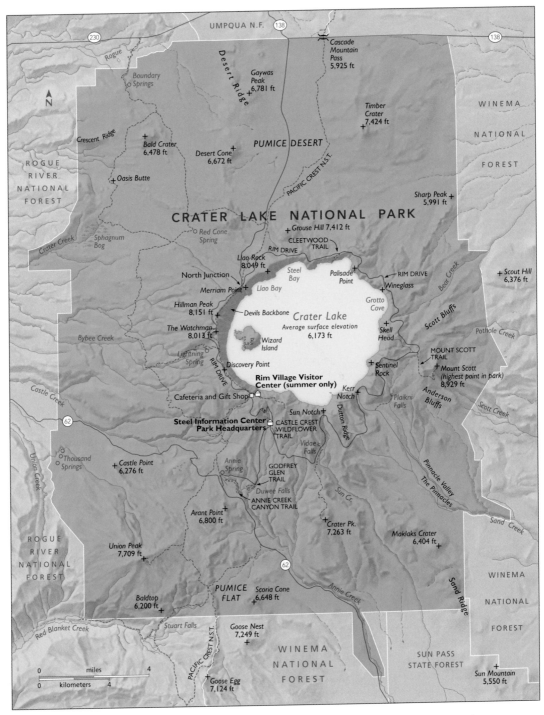

Cascade
Mountain
Pass
5,925 ft

Rogue

Boundary
Springs

Desert Ridge

Gaywas
Peak
6,781 ft

Timber
Crater
7,424 ft

WINEMA

NATIONAL

FOREST

Crescent Ridge

Bald Crater
6,478 ft

Desert Cone
6,672 ft

PUMICE DESERT

PACIFIC CREST N.S.T.

ROGUE
RIVER
NATIONAL
FOREST

Oasis Butte

Sharp Peak
5,991 ft

CRATER LAKE NATIONAL PARK

Grouse Hill 7,412 ft

Crater Creek

Sphagnum
Bog

Red Cone
Spring

CLEETWOOD
TRAIL

RIM DRIVE

Llao Rock
8,049 ft

North Junction

Steel
Bay

Palisade
Point

RIM DRIVE

Scout Hill
6,376 ft

Bear Creek

Merriam Point

Llao Bay

Wineglass

Hillman Peak
8,151 ft

Devils Backbone

Grotto
Cove

Crater Lake

Scott Bluffs

Pothole Creek

The Watchman
8,013 ft

Average surface elevation
6,173 ft

Skell
Head

Bybee Creek

Wizard
Island

Lightning
Spring

RIM DRIVE

Discovery Point

Sentinel
Rock

MOUNT SCOTT
TRAIL

Mount Scott
(highest point in park)
8,929 ft

Castle Creek

**Rim Village Visitor
Center (summer only)**

Kerr
Notch

Plaikni
Falls

Anderson
Bluffs

Scott Creek

Cafeteria and Gift Shop

**Steel Information Center
Park Headquarters**

CASTLE CREST
WILDFLOWER
TRAIL

Sun Notch

Dutton Ridge

Thousand
Springs

Castle Point
6,276 ft

Annie
Spring

GODFREY
GLEN
TRAIL

Vidae
Falls

Pinnacle Valley

The Pinnacles

Union Creek

Duwee Falls

Sun Cr.

Sand Creek

ANNIE CREEK
CANYON TRAIL

Arant Point
6,800 ft

Crater Pk.
7,263 ft

Maklaks Crater
6,404 ft

ROGUE
RIVER
NATIONAL
FOREST

Union Peak
7,709 ft

WINEMA

Baldtop
6,200 ft

PUMICE
FLAT

Scoria Cone
6,648 ft

Annie Creek

Sand Ridge

NATIONAL

Red Blanket Creek

Stuart Falls

PACIFIC CREST N.S.T.

Goose Nest
7,249 ft

WINEMA

NATIONAL

FOREST

SUN PASS
STATE FOREST

FOREST

Sun Mountain
5,550 ft

Goose Egg
7,124 ft

miles   4

kilometers   4

---

panoramas of the lake. The blue color, the dramatic cliffs rising nearly 2,000 feet above the lake surface, and cone-shaped Wizard Island—all combine to compose a vista

as splendid as those found in any other national park. Nearby are a café and gift shop *(both open year-round)* and a lodge and visitor center *(both open seasonally).*

Clear, Blue Crater Lake

In 1997 scientists conducted a standard measurement of water clarity by lowering an 8-inch disk into Crater Lake and watching to see when it

A cinder cone, Wizard Island projects above the surface of Crater Lake.

would disappear. It remained visible down to a depth of 142 feet. Scientists also found aquatic moss growing at a record 460 feet below the surface, indicating that sunlight may penetrate deeper in Crater Lake than in any other body of water in the world.

When lights passes through water, blue is the last color of the spectrum to be absorbed. At depths greater than 350 feet, shades of blue are the only illumination, which is what reflects back to the eyes of visitors looking down from viewpoints above the lake. Crater Lake's depth was first measured in 1886 with a device consisting of a weight attached to a spool of piano wire. Those first measurements showed the lake to be 1,996 feet deep,

quite close to the figure of 1,943 feet measured with sonar and other high-tech equipment in the 20th century.

Pacific Crest National Scenic Trail

The Pacific Crest National Scenic Trail (see p. 485) passes through Crater Lake National Park on its 2,650-mile path from Mexico to Canada. The 33 miles of the trail within Crater Lake make up part of the more than 100 miles of park trails.

Visitors to Rim Village can hike the Pacific Crest Trail northwest, or, to the southeast, take the strenuous 1.8-mile (one way) Garfield Peak Trail, leading to the 8,054-foot summit of the peak for which it's named. The view from the top is worth the

effort—an elevation gain of more than 1,000 feet.

Rim Drive:
Rim Village to Cleetwood Trail

The park's scenic Rim Drive winds for 33 miles around the crater rim above the lake, with more than two dozen overlooks and other points of interest along the way. Thanks to some of the cleanest air in the nation, visibility from some spots can stretch more than 100 miles.

Heading clockwise from Rim Village, the first stop is Discovery Point, from which the three gold prospectors first saw the lake in 1853. Hillman Peak, on the far left of the rim, is named for one of the trio. The peak is a 70,000-year-old volcano, one of the cluster of overlapping volcanoes that formed Mount Mazama. It was cut in half when the summit collapsed. At 1,978 feet above the lake's surface, it is the highest point on the rim and is only slightly taller over the water than the lake is deep.

A picnic site farther along offers a good view of Wizard Island, named for its resemblance to a sorcerer's hat. Rising 767 feet above the lake, the island is a classic cinder cone, built of cinders ejected from the caldera floor after Mount Mazama collapsed. A Native American legend says the island is the head of Llao, the chief of the Below World who was killed by Skell, chief of the Above World.

A little way down the Rim Drive is the steep, 0.8-mile (one way) hike to the 8,013-foot peak called The Watchman. Fire spotters watch for smoke from the fire tower at the top.

Continuing around the rim, a side road at North Junction leads away from the crater rim and into the moonscape of the Pumice Desert, a vast area covered with material ejected from Mount Mazama. The 200-foot-deep layer of volcanic pumice and other ejecta holds little water, making this a de facto desert despite substantial annual precipitation. Cones and craters dot this stark landscape.

Back on Rim Drive, the route reaches the 1.1-mile (one way) Cleetwood Trail, the only place hikers are permitted to access the shore of Crater Lake. (Rangers warn of the dangers of standing too close to the rim on unstable rock or of climbing anywhere inside the caldera.) The trail descends 700 feet to the water and the landing dock for the ranger-led boat tour *(early July–mid-Sept.)* of the lake. Interpretive talks explain Crater Lake's geology, history, and natural processes.

The boat provides access to Wizard Island, where a 1-mile (one way) trail leads to its high point. There are great views from the top, where whitebark pine trees, contorted by difficult growing conditions, rise around the cinder cone's own crater, which measures 90 feet deep.

Rim Drive:
Cleetwood Trail to Rim Village

As Rim Drive continues winding east and south, Mount Scott looms ahead—at an elevation of 8,929 feet, it's the park's highest point. The 2.2-mile (one way) hike to the top offers a great view of the east side of the park and the Klamath Basin. Not

surprisingly, this is often considered the most spectacular trail in the park.

Nearby is the side road to Cloudcap Overlook, at 7,865 feet the highest spot on Rim Drive. Phantom Ship, an island to the southwest, is composed of 400,000-year-old lava flows. The island looks small compared to surrounding cliffs, yet it stands 160 feet above Crater Lake's surface.

Back on the main route of Rim Drive, Phantom Ship Overlook at Kerr Notch offers another view of the island below. This "notch" is a U-shaped valley carved by a glacier before Mount Mazama exploded. A side road here heads southeast past the Lost Creek campground to The Pinnacles, spires of hardened volcanic ash.

Farther along Rim Drive, the short, easy Sun Notch Trail leads to a view of Chaski Bay and Phantom Ship, while the Castle Crest Wildflower Trail, an easy 0.5-mile loop, begins in a forest of mountain hemlock and red fir before entering a meadow that can be full of flowers. At this elevation, and with the winter's buildup of snow that is slow to melt, blooming season here is summer rather than spring.

Flora & Fauna

While the beauty of Crater Lake commands the full attention of visitors, the

sights, sounds, and smells of the surrounding environment provide plenty of diversions. Visitors entering the park from Oreg. 62 and driving up to the crater rim pass through life zones indicated by coniferous forest: ponderosa pine on the lower slopes, giving way to lodgepole and western white pines, then mountain hemlock and Shasta red fir, and finally whitebark pine at the park's highest elevations.

Among the mammals seen in Crater Lake National Park are black bear, pine marten, fox, yellow-bellied marmot, golden-mantled ground squirrel, Townsend's chipmunk, snowshoe hare, Roosevelt elk, and mule and black-tailed deer.

Crater Lake also offers a diversity of bird species. Bird-watchers seek out great gray owl, three-toed and black-backed woodpeckers, olive-sided and Hammond's flycatchers, gray and Steller's jays, Clark's nutcracker, mountain chickadee, Townsend's solitaire, and gray-crowned rosy-finch.

Anglers hike down the Cleetwood Cove Trail to cast for kokanee salmon and rainbow trout, stocked in the lake from 1888 to 1941. Biologists believe there were no fish in Crater Lake before 1888. Trout are also found in the park's streams, though some areas are closed to protect the threatened bull trout.

Oreg. 62
Crater Lake, OR
541-594-3000
www.nps.gov/crla

AT A GLANCE

Southwestern Oregon, 65 miles northeast of Medford ▪ 183,224 acres ▪ Year-round ▪ Hiking, camping, scenic driving, boating tours, fishing, cross-country skiing, snowshoeing

John Day Fossil Beds National Monument
A *fantastically rich record of ancient life*

In the rugged, semiarid terrain of central Oregon, paleontologists have found one of the most extensive and comprehensive records of ancient

life in North America. Comprising more than 2,200 species of plants and animals, these life-forms existed here from 54 million to 6 million

years ago, and total more than 45,000 individual specimens.

The comprehensiveness of the John Day fossil record allows scientists not simply to identify single plants and animals but also to learn about evolutionary change and the relationships among the various flora and fauna that coexisted at a particular time. Over millions of years, this area has been a semitropical forest; a cool, dry habitat; a savanna-like grassland with scattered woodlands; and a prairie, among other environments. Volcanic events often covered the land with ash, and lakes laid down sedimentary deposits.

Among the many ancient animals fossilized here are primitive horses, giant birds, crocodiles, brontotheres (large relatives of the horse and rhinoceros), camels, pigs, sloths, saber-toothed cats, and carnivorous "bear dogs."

John Day Fossil Beds National Monument comprises three units. The Sheep Rock Unit features the Thomas Condon Paleontology Center.

(Condon was a 19th-century missionary who studied fossils in the area. He became a respected self-taught paleontologist and later a professor of geology at the University of Oregon.) The Condon center acts as the park visitor center; it shows an 18-minute interpretive film and has large fossil museum exhibits. A viewing window allows visitors to watch scientists work with fossils found at some of the more than 750 known fossil sites in the national monument. The nearby Cant Ranch Museum has indoor and outdoor exhibits on the human history of the ranch and surrounding region.

The Painted Hills Unit (off U.S. 26, 9 miles northwest of Mitchell, 541-462-3961), named for colorful volcanic ash layers in the landscape, has a visitor information kiosk and more

than 2 miles of trails winding through the dramatic terrain. The Clarno Unit (Oreg. 218, 20 miles west of Fossil) also has hiking trails, but it is best known for the Palisades, tall formations created 44 million years ago by a series of volcanic mudflows called lahars. The 0.25-mile Trail of the Fossils at Clarno is the only trail in the park where visitors can easily see fossils: hundreds of plant fossils from jungle-like forests that grew here at the same time the Palisades were formed, including seeds, nuts, fruits, and leaves.

Park rangers conduct programs and lead guided walks throughout the year at John Day on topics such as geology, fossils, natural history, and the night sky. Tours and programs are also offered by the Oregon PaleoLands Institute (541-763-4480, www.oregon paleolandscenter.com), a park partner.

Sheep Rock Unit
Oreg. 19, 9 miles west of Dayville, OR
541-987-2333
www.nps.gov/joda

AT A GLANCE

Central Oregon, 160 miles east of Eugene ▪ 13,944 acres ▪ Year-round
▪ Touring museum, hiking, picnicking, taking ranger-led walks

Lewis and Clark National Historical Park
Where the Corps of Discovery reached the Pacific

Named the Corps of Discovery by President Thomas Jefferson, a group of men (as well as Lewis's dog, Seaman), led by Meriwether Lewis and William Clark, set off in May 1804 to explore the northwestern lands of the American west, fulfilling Jefferson's longtime dream. This influential undertaking made significant discoveries in geography, natural history, and climate, and it made contact with many Native American tribes in an expedition that lasted until September 1806.

A reconstruction of a building at Fort Clatsop

The Corps traveled up the Missouri River, across the Rocky Mountains, and down the Columbia River to reach the Pacific Ocean, where it

wintered over 1805–06. After two weeks on the north side of the Columbia River, the men decided to move to a site on the south bank, where they built a structure they called Fort Clatsop—named for the local Indian tribe. The spot had trees for construction and firewood, elk to hunt, a spring for fresh water, and access to the river. One soldier, Sgt. Patrick Gass, noted in an April 8, 1806, journal entry that from November 4, 1805, to March 25, 1806 (142 days), only 12 were not rainy.

Lewis and Clark National

Historical Park includes the original site of Fort Clatsop as well as 11 other park sites along a 40-mile stretch of the Pacific coast from Long Beach, Washington, to Cannon Beach, Oregon. The park encompasses both National Park Service sites and several Washington and Oregon state parks. Visitors are encouraged to stop first at one of two sites that have the most comprehensive visitor-contact and informational facilities: Fort Clatsop, just south of Astoria, Oregon; or Cape Disappointment State Park, across the Columbia River in Washington.

Fort Clatsop features a re-creation of Lewis and Clark's wooden fort, based on plans drawn in one of Clark's journals, as well as an interpretive center with exhibits and a film called "A Clatsop Winter Story." Costumed interpreters present programs in summer. Cape Disappointment State Park *(Wash. 100, off U.S. 101, 360-642-3078)* offers 27 miles of ocean beach, two lighthouses, hiking trails, camping, and the Lewis and Clark Interpretive Center. Set on a cliff 200 feet above the mouth of the Columbia, the center features exhibits telling the story of the Corps's journey, focusing on its time on the Pacific coast. This is also a great viewpoint from which to see migrating gray whales in December and March.

Other park sites include Fort Stevens, on the Oregon side of the Columbia River mouth, a popular recreation area that was once a Clatsop Indian village and later a military installation; Clark's Dismal Nitch, where the Corps spent six miserable days trapped by weather in a rocky cove on the north bank of the Columbia; Station Camp, where the Corps spent two weeks on the north bank of the river before voting to move south; the Salt Works, a spot 15 miles southwest of Fort Clatsop that was the nearest place where members of the Corps could use ocean saltwater to make salt; and Ecola State Park in Oregon, where Clark and 12 to 15 other expedition members climbed over Tillamook Head to reach a beached whale and trade with Indians for oil and blubber.

Fort Clatsop Rd.
(off U.S. 101 business route)
Astoria, OR
503-861-2471
www.nps.gov/lewi

AT A GLANCE Northwestern Oregon and southwestern Washington, 80 miles northwest of Portland, Oregon ▪ 1,583 acres ▪ Year-round ▪ Visiting historic sites, hiking, boating, whale-watching

---

McLoughlin House National Historic Site
The home of the "father of Oregon"

Canadian-born physician John McLoughlin settled on the Columbia River in 1825 and became the chief factor (trader) of the Hudson's Bay Company, a fur-trading firm whose interests stretched over a vast area of the Pacific Northwest in the United States and Canada.

McLoughlin was a very successful businessman, but he also gained a reputation as a compassionate humanitarian who aided immigrants arriving on the Oregon Trail. In 1846 he built a house on the Willamette River, eventually becoming mayor of Oregon City. He lent money that was used to found many businesses, and donated land for schools and churches. Such were his achievements that the state legislature later named him the "father of Oregon."

In 1909 the McLoughlin house was threatened with demolition, but a local group bought it, moved it from the riverbank to a nearby bluff, and turned it into a museum honoring McLoughlin. In 1941 the McLoughlin House was designated a national historic site, and in 2003 it became a unit of Fort Vancouver National Historic Site (see p. 471).

Docent-led tours of the house *(Fri.-Sat., closed in winter)* allow visitors to see historic furnishings and personal items and to learn about McLoughlin's varied career and influence on the development of the Oregon Territory. In addition to the regular tours, volunteers conduct demonstrations of Victorian-era crafts such as needlework and bonnetmaking. The site also contains the Barclay House, historic home of Dr. Forbes Barclay, who worked as a physician at Fort Vancouver in the 1840s.

713 Center St.
Oregon City, OR
503-656-5146
www.nps.gov/fova
www.mcloughlinhouse.org

AT A GLANCE Northwestern Oregon, 12 miles south of Portland ▪ 1 acre ▪ Year-round ▪ Taking guided tour of historic home

Oregon Caves National Monument & Preserve

A beautiful cave beneath a biodiversity hot spot

A tourist attraction for more than a century, this marble cavern system within the Siskiyou Mountains of Oregon was named a national monument in 1909. In 2014, it was expanded by nearly 4,000 acres into a preserve that protects the cave's entire watershed. Cave tours *(fee)* last about 90 minutes and are moderately strenuous, navigating more than 500 stairs. (Children under 42 inches in height are not permitted on tours.) The ranger-led tours pass by a series of beautiful formations such as draperies, soda straws, stalactites, stalagmites, and flowstones.

In summer, two additional tours are offered: an off-trail cave tour, providing an introduction to the sport of caving and spelunking techniques, and candlelight tours, allowing visitors

The Cliff Nature Trail begins at the cave's exit.

to experience cave exploration in the manner of the late 19th century.

As appealing as the cave is, it is not the only attraction in the national monument. The park protects an old-growth coniferous forest that can be explored on several hiking trails. One,

the Big Tree Trail, is a 3.3-mile circular loop that leads to the Douglas fir with the largest girth of any of its species in Oregon. The short, steep No Name Trail passes two waterfalls on No Name Creek. The strenuous Bigelow Lakes/Mount Elijah loop passes glacial lakes and climbs to the top of 6,391-foot Mount Elijah.

The Siskiyou Mountains are globally significant for their biodiversity, a result of the region's varied underlying rock, climate, temperatures, precipitation, and other environmental factors.

The Oregon Caves Chateau *(877-245-9022)*, a national historic landmark, is a 1930s-era lodge, offering accommodation to visitors. It is managed by a local nonprofit in cooperation with the National Park Service.

Oreg. 46, 20 miles east of Cave Junction, OR
541-592-2100
www.nps.gov/orca

AT A GLANCE

Southwestern Oregon, 50 miles southwest of Grants Pass ■ 4,554 acres ■ Late March through November ■ Taking guided cave tours, hiking, visiting historic structures

WASHINGTON

The violent 1980 eruption of Mount St. Helens was a reminder that the Cascade Range is an active volcanic area, part of the famed Pacific Ring of Fire. Washington's Mount Rainier has the potential to erupt, and it has done so time and again over the past half million years or so. The 14,410-foot volcano is just one of Washington's scenic attractions, along with the rain forests of Olympic National Park and the wilderness of North Cascades National Park. The Cascades run north-south, dividing the state; the region to the east, lying in the rain shadow, is an arid terrain of grasses and shrubs. Lake Roosevelt, formed by a dam on the Columbia, is the heart of a large national recreation area here.

Ebey's Landing National Historical Reserve

An island "paradise" that preserves a rural working landscape

"Almost a paradise of nature" is how Isaac Ebey described Whidbey Island in an 1851 letter encouraging his brother to join him by immigrating to the island in Puget Sound. Ebey was among the first to settle on Whidbey under the Donation Land Law of 1850, which offered free land in Oregon Territory (which then included present-day Washington State) to any citizen who would homestead for four years. A New England sea captain named Thomas Coupe was another early settler, claiming 320 acres that became the present-day town of Coupeville.

Ebey's Landing National Historical Reserve was established in 1978 "to preserve and protect a rural community which provides an unbroken historic record from . . . 19th century exploration and settlement in Puget Sound to the present time." Very little of the land within the reserve is federally owned. The area remains a living community, where some farmers still work fields claimed by their ancestors under the 1850 land law. The reserve is administered by a local board.

The reserve contains two state parks, Fort Ebey and Fort Casey, where camping is permitted. There

are several miles of trails, including the Bluff Trail at Ebey's Landing, with excellent views overlooking Admiralty Inlet and Ebey's Prairie. The town of Coupeville, the second oldest in Washington, features many historic structures in its downtown area.

There is no official reserve visitor center, but information and walking and driving guides are available at the Island County Historical Museum *(908 NW Alexander St., 360-678-3310, fee)* and the Coupeville Chamber of Commerce *(905 NW Alexander St., 360-678-5434)*, both located in Coupeville.

Whidbey Island
360-678-6084
www.nps.gov/ebla

AT A GLANCE

Northwestern Washington, 50 miles north of Seattle ▪ 17,572 acres ▪ Year-round ▪ Hiking, camping, visiting historic sites and museums

Fort Vancouver National Historic Site

The focal point for settlement of Oregon Territory

The British commercial enterprise called the Hudson's Bay Company operated over a vast area of North America in the 19th century, acquiring furs (especially beaver pelts) from trappers and Native Americans for use in fashions of the era. In 1825, the company built a headquarters and supply depot for its operations in the Pacific Northwest, siting it on the Columbia River near its confluence with the Willamette.

As a bustling trade center employing scores of people from many ethnic groups, Fort Vancouver had a significant influence on the cultural, political, and commercial development of Oregon Territory. The first hospital,

A Fort Vancouver observation tower

school, library, gristmill, sawmill, dairy, shipbuilding site, and orchard in the region were established at Fort Vancouver. The fort also served as the original terminus of the Oregon Trail for immigrants, and later became a U.S. Army post, the first military post in the Pacific Northwest.

Visitors to Fort Vancouver National Historic Site can tour the reconstructed trading post, which includes the palisades wall, chief factor's house, blacksmith shop, bake house, fur store, jail, and kitchen. Park rangers conduct weapons demonstrations and present living-history programs on topics ranging from cooking to gardening. The visitor center features exhibits on fort history and an interpretive film. Various guided tours are offered, or visitors can take a self-guiding audio tour of the grounds, with narration, sound effects, and period music.

Fort Vancouver National Historic Site also operates the Pearson Air Museum, which gives visitors a look at the aviation history of nearby Pearson Field, a military and civilian airfield in the first half of the 20th century and still in use as a municipal airfield today.

Fort Vancouver National Historic Site administers the McLoughlin House in Oregon City (see p. 469).

1501 E. Evergreen Blvd.
Vancouver, WA
360-816-6230
www.nps.gov/fova

AT A GLANCE Southwestern Washington, just north of Portland, Oregon ▪ 209 acres ▪ Year-round ▪ Touring re-created 19th-century trading post, viewing cultural demonstrations

Lake Chelan National Recreation Area

A pocket of recreational opportunities amid vast wilderness

Administered as part of the North Cascades National Park complex (see p. 478), Lake Chelan National Recreation Area offers a real chance to feel apart from the modern world—an adventure that begins with simply getting there. Most activities center on the small community of Stehekin, which can be reached only by boat, seaplane, or trail.

Stehekin sits on the shore of beautiful Lake Chelan in a valley gouged out by glaciers. The 50-mile-long lake is the third deepest in North America. The National Park Service–operated Golden West Visitor Center *(mid-March–mid-Oct.)* offers a short audiovisual program about the area, maps, advice, backcountry camping permits, and regular ranger-led hikes and programs. A shuttle bus operates along 11 miles of the Stehekin Road, providing easy access to campsites and trailheads. The bus makes four round trips daily.

Hikers relish the 5-mile round trip to Agnes Gorge, with wonderful views of Agnes Mountain, the gorge, and a spring-fed waterfall; while naturalists enjoy the easy 0.5-mile (one way) Imus Trail, which starts at the Golden West Visitor Center. Another trail leads through the historic Buckner Homestead and orchard, where the Buckner family lived and farmed from 1911 to 1970.

Long a tourist destination despite its remoteness, Stehekin offers lodging, food, horseback riding, mountain bike and kayak rentals, and a guided bus trip to 312-foot Rainbow Falls.

Stehekin, WA
360-854-7365
www.nps.gov/noca

AT A GLANCE North-central Washington, 150 miles northeast of Seattle ▪ 61,958 acres ▪ Spring through fall ▪ Hiking, camping, backpacking, horseback riding, biking, boating, fishing

Lake Roosevelt National Recreation Area

A vast reservoir playground for boaters and campers

During the Great Depression of the 1930s, a dam was installed on the Columbia River in eastern Washington to irrigate farmland, provide electricity, and put unemployed people back to work. The reservoir that formed behind Grand Coulee Dam, which was completed in 1941, was named Franklin D. Roosevelt Lake. It encompasses over 130 miles of the Columbia River and its tributaries and passes through a landscape that varies from arid sagebrush steppe in the south to woodlands of ponderosa pine and Douglas fir in the north.

Lake Roosevelt National Recreation Area was established to provide opportunities to enjoy this resource, and it has become popular especially for water-based activities such as fishing, sailing, houseboating, and swimming. More than two dozen campgrounds dot the shoreline, some of them accessible only by boat.

Recreation area headquarters are at Grand Coulee Dam, where

the nearby Colville Confederated Tribal Museum has exhibits on the history of the 12 tribes making up the confederation. In summer, a free laser light show is held nightly at Grand Coulee Dam *(Mem. Day weekend–Sept.)*.

A little north of the town of Kettle Falls, in the northern part of the area off U.S. 395, stands the restored 19th-century St. Paul's Mission, with a self-guiding interpretive trail nearby. At the Kettle Falls campground, a 1-mile trail winds through the town site of the community of Kettle Falls, abandoned when the reservoir was created.

The Fort Spokane Visitor Center *(off Wash. 25, summer only)* is located in the guardhouse on the grounds of Historic Fort Spokane. In 1880, the U.S. Army established a fort here, above the confluence of the Spokane and Columbia Rivers. The fort closed in 1898, and the buildings were used in later years as an Indian boarding school and then a tuberculosis hospital. Exhibits tell the story of the Army days and life in the school. The Sentinel Trail at Fort Spokane climbs 300 feet to the top of a bluff, which offers a fine view of the fort grounds and the confluence of the rivers.

There are 22 public boat ramps around Lake Roosevelt, but boaters should be aware that the water level of the lake can rise or fall significantly, affecting access to some sites. Primitive camping is allowed along the shoreline, with some restrictions. In spring the water level can rise up to 4 feet in a single day, so campers should not pitch tents too close to the water's edge.

AT A GLANCE

Wash. 155
Coulee Dam, WA
509-754-7800
www.nps.gov/laro

Northeastern Washington, 85 miles west of Spokane ▪ 100,390 acres ▪ Year-round ▪ Boating, camping, fishing, swimming, picnicking

Mount Rainier National Park

A massive volcano built by fire and shaped by ice

Dominating the landscape for hundreds of square miles, Mount Rainier rises to an elevation of 14,410 feet—the highest point in Washington State. Yet in recent geologic time it was even higher: Mount Rainier, though not literally a living thing, is nearly as changeable as the plants and animals that make it home.

An active volcano, Mount Rainier has erupted thousands of times during its relatively young life of 500,000 to one million years. Lava and ash built up its massive bulk, layer on layer, until it was at least 1,000 feet higher than its present summit at Columbia Crest. Violent explosions and landslides lowered its height, then lava from eruptions in the past 2,000 years built it back up again. Rainier will certainly come to life again—the only question is when.

Rainier is one of many active volcanoes in the Cascade Range, including Lassen Peak in California, which

Columbia lily, a Mount Rainier bloom

erupted from 1914 to 1921; and Mount St. Helens in Washington, which violently erupted in 1980 and which recently has seen substantial lava flows build up its center. Because of its history and its proximity to the heavily populated Seattle-Tacoma area, Mount Rainier is considered by geologists to be one of the most potentially hazardous volcanoes in North America, primarily because of the expected debris flows and lahars created by the sudden melting of the mountain's enormous snow/ice pack.

None of this should keep visitors away from this beautiful national park. Serious eruptions are usually preceded by increased earthquake activity, giving some warning. There are other hazards, however, including debris flows, flash floods, and rock falls, that visitors should beware.

While fire (volcanism) built Mount Rainier, ice carved it, even as it grew: Glaciers sculpted valleys and shaped peaks. The 26 named glaciers that dot Rainier's slopes today compose the greatest single-peak glacial system in the contiguous United States. Rainier has a total of around 35 square miles of snow and ice.

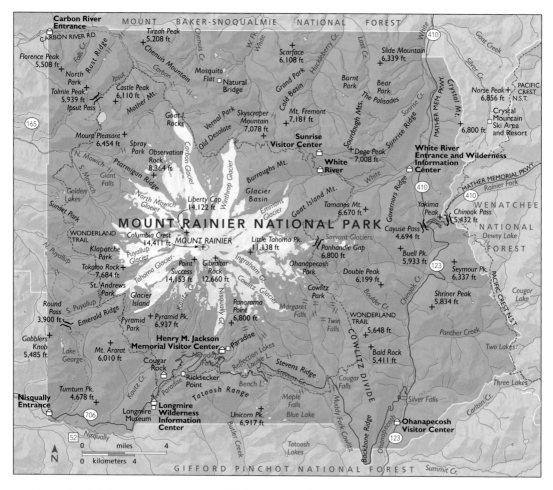

Mount Rainier's beauty, proximity to urban areas, and relatively brief summer season mean that it can be crowded at times. Summer visits will be more pleasant if they can be made on a weekday rather than a weekend, and many visitors enjoy the less crowded seasons of spring and fall. In winter, many roads and facilities close, but the Nisqually (southwest) Entrance to the park remains open, providing access for visitors who enjoy cross-country skiing, snowshoeing (including ranger-led snowshoe walks), snowboarding, and "snow play."

Nisqually Entrance to Paradise

The most popular approach to the park is through the Nisqually Entrance on Wash. 706, at an elevation of just over 2,000 feet—or 2.3 miles in elevation below Rainier's summit. The road winds through a forest of Douglas fir, western red cedar, and western hemlock to reach a nature trail at Kautz Creek. In 1947, Kautz Glacier sent a flash flood of meltwater down this valley, still evidenced today by the dead trees and debris in the area.

Six miles from the entrance is the Longmire Museum. Pioneer James Longmire homesteaded here in the 1880s, building a lodge and promoting "healing" mineral water from nearby springs. Once the park headquarters building, Longmire Museum features exhibits on the park and a bookstore offering guidebooks and park information. The Wilderness Information Center issues wilderness permits and provides hiking and backcountry camping information. The center is closed in winter, but a contact station at Longmire—open year-round—can supply information and backcountry permits to visitors. Its location and hours vary; the park website has current information.

Five miles from Longmire, Glacier Bridge offers a view of part of Nisqually Glacier up the valley. A mile farther, a side road climbs to Ricksecker Point *(summer only)*, with splendid views of Mount Rainier, Nisqually Valley and its glacier, and, to the south, the Tatoosh Range. Far older than Rainier, the Tatoosh comprises dramatic remnants of lava flows perhaps 35 million years old, carved by glaciers into pinnacles and sheer cliffs. Ahead on the main road is a small parking area for Narada Falls, where a short but steep trail leads to a viewpoint of this 168-foot cascade on the Paradise River.

Paradise

After a few more twists and turns the road reaches the Paradise area, the most popular part of the park. Here, Mount Rainier rises above rolling foothills covered in wildflowers. (The abundant wildflowers are one result of soil richly fertilized by volcanic ash.)

The Henry M. Jackson Visitor Center, the park's main visitor center *(May–mid-Oct., weekends mid-Oct.–April)*, includes a museum with exhibits on local geology and wildlife, with a section on the history of mountain climbing on Mount Rainier. Huge windows on the upper floor offer expansive views of the volcano. The nearby historic Paradise Inn is a superb example of the rustic style of architecture, for which the park was designated a national historic landmark district.

The easy, 1.2-mile Nisqually Vista Trail begins near the visitor center and loops across subalpine meadows, where as many as 40 species of wildflowers may bloom in the brief summer season. (Remain on the path, as a single misstep may destroy a plant that has survived brutal winters for decades.) Watch for rufous hummingbirds visiting the flowers in these meadows.

The more strenuous 5-mile Skyline Trail leads to spectacular views at Paradise Point. On a clear day, Oregon's Mount Hood, more than 100 miles to the south, can be seen from spots along this path.

The "snow play" area at Paradise is the only place in the park where snow tubing and sliding (plastic disks only) are allowed, conditions permitting. With an average yearly snowfall of 680 inches, it offers plenty of opportunity.

Paradise to Stevens Canyon Entrance

Continuing to the eastern part of the park, the road *(closed in winter)* passes Reflection Lakes, sitting in a hollow carved by glaciers and renowned for the mirrorlike views of Mount Rainier on calm days. A short distance farther is the fine trail to Bench and Snow Lakes, a 2.5-mile round-trip hike that offers excellent summer wildflower viewing. An overlook at Stevens Canyon faces a classic U-shaped valley that results from a glacier's slow but relentless work. Tributaries of Stevens Creek drop into the canyon as waterfalls from the "hanging valleys" left when a glacier cut into the canyon wall.

Running alongside the creek is a segment of the 93-mile-long Wonderland Trail, which circles Mount Rainier and offers a rewarding challenge for experienced backpackers. Ten to 14 days are recommended to make the entire circuit. Rangers can offer advice about trail conditions, campsites, and caching food. Long-distance hikers should be prepared for changeable weather, rugged terrain, and daily elevation gain and loss of 3,500 feet.

One of the park's most noteworthy trails can be found just west of the Stevens Canyon Entrance and the junction with Wash. 123. The easy, 1.3-mile Grove of the Patriarchs Trail leads to an island in the Ohanapecosh River full of thousand-year-old Douglas firs and western red cedars. Though park rangers describe this as a one-hour walk, visitors may well want to spend much more time simply contemplating these awe-inspiring trees. The appealing little bird called American dipper is sometimes seen along the river, perched on rocks or flying on whirring wings.

To further experience the old-growth forest, head to the Ohanapecosh Visitor Center *(June–Sept.),* a little way south on Wash. 123, where the old-growth forest is interpreted. A trail behind the center winds through the forest and past hot springs.

Sunrise

From Stevens Canyon, Wash. 123 leads north to Cayuse Pass and Wash. 410 *(both roads closed in winter),* which continues north. Three miles north of the pass, a road leads to the park's White River Entrance. This road may not open until July, depending on snow conditions. It leads west to the Sunrise Visitor Center, at 6,400 feet the highest point in the park (and the state) that can be reached by road. All around grow subalpine fir and whitebark pine, stunted and contorted by winters of frigid temperatures and harsh winds. Trees just a few inches in diameter may be 250 years old.

For an easy look at this environment, take the 1-mile Sourdough Ridge Trail, which, weather permitting, offers fabulous long-distance views of Mount Baker (130 miles north) and Mount Adams (50 miles south). The adjacent Emmons Vista Trail offers a fine view of 4.3-square-mile Emmons Glacier, the park's largest ice field.

Hikers can choose from several other hiking possibilities in the Sunrise area, including the Burroughs Mountain Trail, which passes through a true tundra landscape above tree line. (This is one of the most accessible places to explore this alpine environment in the Cascade Range.) There are wonderful views of Mount Rainier along the way as well. But check with rangers about trail conditions before setting out, as snow and ice can linger here well into summer, creating dangerous hiking conditions. As always, stay on the trails to avoid harming the fragile subalpine plants. Mountain goats are occasionally seen in these high-elevation areas,

FOLLOWING PAGES: *A variety of wildflowers bloom on the high alpine meadows of Mount Rainier in summer.*

and white-tailed ptarmigan and gray-crowned rosy-finches breed here.

Carbon River

The far-less-visited Carbon River area is in the park's northwest corner (off Wash. 165). At this writing, the road is closed to vehicular traffic by flood damage at the park entrance station, but hikers and bikers can still travel it. A ranger station *(call for hours)* is located on Carbon River Road, 5.5 miles beyond the Mowich Lake junction. The easy, 0.3-mile loop Carbon River Rain Forest Nature Trail at the entrance allows visitors to experience the state's only true inland rain forest, where Douglas fir, Sitka spruce, and western red cedar grow to enormous size. 70 to 90 inches of rain fall annually, and mosses and ferns grow in profusion.

Five miles along the Carbon River Road is the Ipsut Creek campground, where a segment of the Wonderland Trail (also called the Carbon River Glacier Trail) leads 3.5 miles (one way) to a close look at Carbon Glacier. Found at the lowest elevation of any glacier in the lower 48 states (3,500 feet), this glacier should not be closely approached because of the danger of falling rock and ice.

AT A GLANCE

Wash. 706, 8 miles east of Ashford, WA
360-569-2211
www.nps.gov/mora

Southwestern Washington, 70 miles southeast of Tacoma ▪ 235,625 acres ▪ Year-round; limited access in winter ▪ Hiking, camping, backpacking, mountain climbing, taking scenic drives, cross-country skiing, snowshoeing

---

North Cascades National Park / Ross Lake N.R.A.

Expansive wilderness and hundreds of glaciers in the "American Alps"

Stretching from British Columbia south to northern California, the Cascade Range encompasses several famous and heavily visited national parks, including Washington's Mount Rainier (see p. 473) and Oregon's Crater Lake (see p. 464).

North Cascades National Park is different from other Cascade parks in several ways, beginning with its designation as North Cascades National Park Service Complex. Established in 1968, the complex is the result of compromises made between those who wanted a national park in the area and those who feared preservation would trump recreation.

The outcome of that debate means that today's park complex comprises three units: North Cascades National Park and Ross Lake and Lake Chelan National Recreation Areas. The latter two contain hydroelectric facilities and concessionaire-operated resorts, and allow hunting. (Lake Chelan National Recreation Area is listed separately in this guide; see p. 472.) All three units are managed under one administration, and all are united by the Stephen Mather Wilderness, a contiguous unit that covers 94 percent of the park complex.

All this administrative detail slips out of mind when a visitor looks out at rugged, glacier-sculpted mountains dotted with alpine lakes, waterfalls, rocky streams, and the largest collection of glaciers in the lower 48 states. (North Cascades boasts one-third of all the glaciers present in the contiguous United States.)

Sometimes called the "American Alps" for their gorgeous scenery, jagged peaks, and snow- and ice fields, the North Cascades make up the core of more than 2 million acres of federally designated wilderness. Including adjoining land across the international border in Canada, the park complex is part of an ecosystem that includes 3 million acres of protected public land—enough that natural systems can function in ways recalling the era

Bighorn sheep inhabit the high peaks of the Cascade Range.

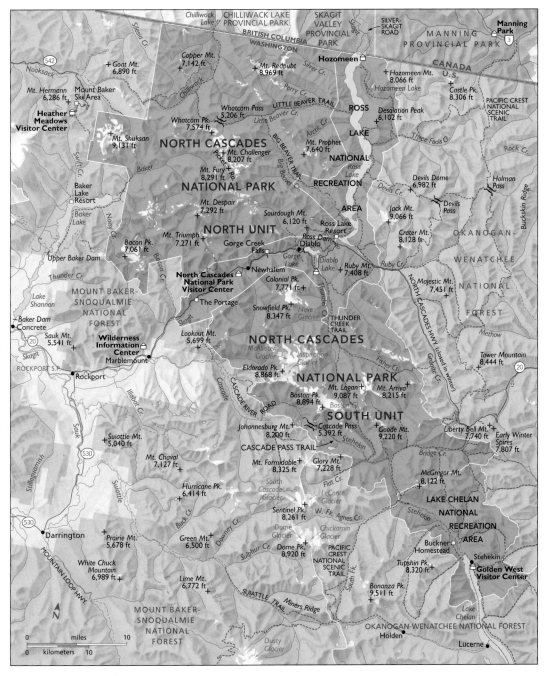

before European settlement, when animals were free to roam across large areas, and predator-prey relationships existed in balance.

North Cascades National Park

Public access to North Cascades National Park is much more challenging than in most other national parks. A single unpaved road leads into the South Unit of the park, while other areas must be reached by trail or boat.

The Cascade River Road turns south off the North Cascades Highway at Marblemount. It travels through Mount Baker–Snoqualmie National Forest for most of its 23 miles, getting narrower and steeper as it goes. The road is open as snow and road conditions permit. Normally, snow blocks all or parts of the road from October through June (or later).

Cascade River Road provides access to one of the park's most popular day hikes: the climb to 5,392-foot Cascade Pass. The route offers spectacular views of glaciers and peaks, including Eldorado, Johannesburg, Magic, and Mixup. This 3.7-mile (one way) trail provides the shortest and easiest access to the park's alpine environment. It also is the gateway to many other destinations, including Sahale Glacier and Stehekin.

This trail was used by Native Americans as a route through the Cascade Range, and in 1814 fur trader Alexander Ross passed along it. ("A more difficult route to travel never fell to man's lot," he wrote about his time in the Cascades.) After the fur trappers came prospectors, looking for gold and silver.

In rock-slide areas, watch for the little mammal called pika, looking something like a miniature rabbit with small ears. It often gives a sharp whistle when alarmed. Confined to high-elevation areas, it's being pushed out of the lower parts of its habitat as global climate change brings higher temperatures. With a seriously declining population, the pika has been proposed for endangered-species status.

More often seen are hoary marmots, looking like chubby squirrels.

Serious mountain climbers revere North Cascades National Park for its varied climbing opportunities, involving scrambling, glacier crossings, and technical rock climbing. Long approaches through wilderness make many climbs especially challenging, with the reward of unbeatable beautiful scenery and remoteness. The park's Wilderness Information Center *(360-854-7245, closed in winter)* at Marblemount is the best place to discuss climbing routes with rangers.

The glaciers that have carved—and still carve—the North Cascades landscape and provide life-giving water to the ecosystem are shrinking. As the Earth's climate ominously warms, scientists are intensively studying the park's glaciers to determine the response. Nearly all the park's glaciers are retreating, and some have disappeared. About 40 percent of the park's ice cover has been lost in the past 150 years.

Ross Lake
National Recreation Area

Ross Lake National Recreation Area, which bisects North Cascades National Park, contains three hydroelectric reservoirs and a scenic byway, providing access to campgrounds, trailheads, lodging, and commercial outfitters and tour services.

The upper portions of North Cascades Highway (Wash. 20), an officially designated scenic byway, receive heavy snowfall, and the route is closed east of Ross Dam from about mid-November to mid-April. (Exact dates depend on weather, snow depths, and avalanche hazards.)

Visitors arriving from the west on Wash. 20 can stop in Sedro Woolley at the North Cascades National Park Headquarters Information Station for maps and information. Farther east in Marblemount, the Wilderness

The mirror surface of Picture Lake reflects lovely Mount Shuksan.

Information Center issues backpacking permits for North Cascades National Park and Ross Lake and Lake Chelan National Recreation Areas. The permits are free and are required for overnight trips into the backcountry.

East of Marblemount, the North Cascades Highway enters Ross Lake National Recreation Area and parallels the Skagit River, which appears green in summer. High in the mountains, glaciers grind bedrock into fine rock "flour," which in high concentration reflects the green part of the light spectrum, giving the stream its distinctive hue. In winter, bald eagles congregate along the river to feed on salmon. Hosting one of the largest concentrations of the species in the lower 48 states, this section of the Skagit may be home to more than 300 eagles at times.

On the north side of the highway, an unpaved side road (not suitable for trailers) leads to the trailhead for Thornton Lakes. This moderately strenuous hike leads 5.2 miles, first along an old road, then through mature hemlock forest to meadows of heather and huckleberry, reaching a ridge with a spectacular view of Triumph Peak. Below is lower Thornton Lake in its cirque (a rock basin carved by glaciers).

The highway continues through Ross Lake National Recreation Area and reaches the North Cascades National Park Visitor Center, near Newhalem, which has exhibits and multimedia presentations on the park's natural and cultural history. The center displays a facsimile of one of the Native American pictographs created at Lake Chelan, as well as

examples of stone tools and a piece of ocher used to draw pictographs. Several short, easy trails begin at the visitor center or nearby, offering views up Goodell Creek to the Pickett Range, panoramas of the river, and a quick course in tree identification.

The communities ahead, Newhalem and Diablo, are company towns built by Seattle City Light, the utility that erected three dams on the Skagit River to supply electricity to the Seattle area. At the powerhouse of the Gorge Dam, the 0.4-mile loop Ladder Creek Falls Trail leads through gardens to a striking waterfall. Seattle City Light offers boat tours (206-684-3030, www.skagit tours.com, June–Sept., fee) of Diablo Lake and the Skagit River Gorge.

Past Diablo, the highway reaches Colonial Creek campground, where there's access to another fine hiking opportunity—a short, easy nature trail or a long trek, or anything in between. Behind the campground amphitheater is the trailhead for the Thunder Creek Trail. Beginning among huge old-growth western red cedar trees, it follows Thunder Arm of Diablo Lake. This trail was originally opened by 19th-century trappers and prospectors. Soon comes a turn with access to a 0.9-mile self-guiding interpretive nature trail.

The main Thunder Creek Trail offers several options. Many people enjoy a hike to the first bridge over the creek, about 2 miles from the trailhead. Beyond that is a junction, with the left fork leading to 3,501-foot Fourth of July Pass and back down to Ruby Arm of Diablo Lake. The right fork climbs to 6,059-foot Park Creek Pass (old

mining operations are visible along the way) and back down to the Stehekin Valley Road (27 miles from the trailhead), which leads into Lake Chelan National Recreation Area. Check with a ranger about trail conditions before undertaking this very strenuous backpacking trip. An ice ax might be needed at Park Creek Pass until snow and ice melts, and that could be as late as July.

Back on the highway, the route crosses Thunder Arm and reaches the Diablo Lake Overlook. To the northwest rises 6,120-foot Sourdough Mountain, site of a fire tower. Literary note: Famed Beat Generation writers Gary Snyder and Jack Kerouac worked in the North Cascades area as fire spotters in the 1950s. Snyder worked on Sourdough; and Kerouac's post was 6,102-foot Desolation Peak, east of Ross Lake.

Another lookout provides a view of Ross Lake, which cannot be reached by car from the road. (A primitive unpaved road reaches the lake's northern end, but only from British Columbia.) Ross Lake Resort (206-386-4437, www.rosslakeresort.com), accessible by only trail or boat, offers accommodations and boat rentals.

Okanogan National Forest

North Cascades Highway leaves the park and enters Okanogan National Forest, and it's worthwhile to continue about 20 miles to 5,477-foot Washington Pass Overlook, the highest point along the road. To the south is massive Liberty Bell Mountain, and south of that rise the Early Winter Spires. With binoculars, it is sometimes possible to glimpse mountain goats or climbers on the distant granite faces.

Wash. 20
Newhalem, WA
360-854-7200
www.nps.gov/noca

AT A GLANCE

North-central Washington, 110 miles northeast of Seattle ▪ 684,237 acres (park and recreation areas) ▪ Spring through fall ▪ Hiking, camping, backpacking, mountain climbing, boating, taking scenic drive, fishing

Olympic National Park

Lush rain forests, rushing rivers, and alpine glaciers

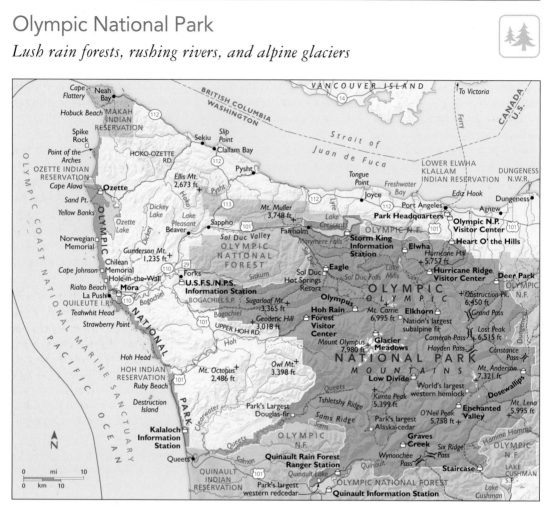

One of the last places in the lower 48 states to remain essentially a blank spot on the map, the area that is now Olympic National Park wasn't truly explored by European Americans until the late 19th century. Even then, adventurers struggled to traverse its landscape of rugged peaks, steep cliffs, dense forest, and rivers.

Today, it's easy to get acquainted with the park's highlights, but it's still a challenge to get to know its wild interior. This is not a drive-through park; no road crosses its heart, though a dozen or so lead some distance into it from various directions. Ninety-five percent of the park is officially designated wilderness.

Olympic National Park comprises three major ecosystems—high mountains with subalpine forest and alpine meadows, temperate rain forest, and 70 linear miles of sandy or rocky Pacific coastline—as well as many subhabitats from riparian zones along rivers to tide pools. All this diversity can be found in a relatively small area: From 7,980-foot Mount Olympus, overlaid with glaciers, to the Pacific Ocean surf is less than 33 miles as the raven flies.

The mountains of the Olympic Peninsula originated in the sea: Some rocks began as sedimentary deposits (marine fossils can be found on high peaks) and some as basalt from undersea lava that quickly hardened when it erupted into water. When a tectonic plate carrying the Pacific Ocean crashed (in very slow motion) against the continental plate carrying North America, these ocean materials were pushed up to become mountains. Glaciers later sculpted the peaks and rivers eroded valleys.

During the most recent ice ages, this region existed in isolation for tens of thousands of years, cut off from surrounding lands by glaciers. This led to the development of many endemic species (animals and plants found only here), such as the Olympic marmot, Olympic torrent salamander, Olympic mudminnow, Olympic grasshopper,

Flett's violet, and Piper's bellflower. The United Nations has declared Olympic National Park both a World Heritage site and an international biosphere reserve.

The main park visitor center is located in Port Angeles, just south of U.S. 101. (This highway skirts the park on three sides, and most access roads lead from it.) Exhibits and a 25-minute film interpret the park's natural and cultural history. Depending on their interests and itinerary, visitors should ask about ranger-led programs and pick up a tide table (important for exploring the coastal areas of the park). Located inside the visitor center, the Wilderness Information Center provides advice about trail conditions, issues permits for backpacking trips, and stocks animal-resistant food containers.

Hurricane Ridge

Most first-time visitors to Olympic make Hurricane Ridge, named for the force of winds that can blow here, their first destination. On a clear day, the ridge offers spectacular views of the Olympic Mountains and northward as far as the Strait of Juan de Fuca and Canada's Vancouver Island. The 17-mile road to the ridge travels from near sea level to tree line, nearly a mile in elevation. Despite staff efforts, snow may occasionally close the route in winter *(tire chains required for Hurricane Ridge in winter)*.

After the tunnels, 9 miles along the road, stop at a pullout to see "bubbles" of rock in the cliff face above the road. This pillow basalt originated when hot lava oozed into seawater, forming globules as it quickly cooled. As the road ascends Hurricane Ridge, it's of note that today's route quickly covers a distance that took explorers in 1885 about a month to traverse.

Near the road's end, the Hurricane Ridge Visitor Center features exhibits on the park's mountain habitats and signs that identify the peaks and glaciers in the distance. Mount Olympus, the park's highest mountain, received its name in 1788 when an English explorer, Capt. John Meares, saw it and decided that it was beautiful and impressive enough to be the legendary home of the gods of Greek mythology. Mount Olympus receives more than 200 inches of precipitation each year, most of it falling as snow; it features the third largest glacial system in the contiguous United States.

Several trails in the area, ranging from easy strolls of less than a mile to long-distance routes connecting with trails miles away, provide access to this mountain environment. The Hurricane Hill Trail ascends 700 feet in 1.6 miles (one way) for a great panoramic view stretching to the Pacific. Watch and listen for Olympic marmots in this area. This chubby rodent gives a variety of alarm calls. Subalpine firs here are stunted by harsh conditions and a short growing season; at tree line, a 3-foot-tall tree may be a century old.

Near the visitor center, an unpaved 7.8-mile road *(summer only, no RVs or trailers)* leads to more awe-inspiring views at Obstruction Point.

Elwha Valley

Eleven miles west of Port Angeles, Olympic Hot Springs Road leads south into the Elwha Valley, which has two campgrounds, a ranger station, and nature trails. A popular hike in this vicinity, the Boulder Creek Trail leads 2.5 miles to a hot spring. The lowland forest here includes Douglas fir, western hemlock, and western red cedar.

The Elwha River watershed is the largest in Olympic National Park, and it once was famed for its salmon. Two dams severely damaged the river's ecosystem, but in the largest dam removal project in history, the dams were removed between 2011 and 2014. The river now runs free, allowing salmon back into more than 70 miles

A tree clings to a sea stack, one of many that line Olympic's Pacific shoreline.

of river and tributaries in one of the largest ecosystem restoration projects ever undertaken in a national park.

Lake Crescent & Sol Duc Valley

Highway 101 skirts Lake Crescent as it heads west toward the coast. The Storm King Information Station stands near where Barnes Creek empties into the lake. The Marymere Falls Trail here is a 1.75-mile round trip to a striking 90-foot waterfall.

Just past Lake Crescent is the turn to the Sol Duc Valley. (The name is a Native American term meaning "sparkling water.") A concessionaire-operated resort offers lodging, dining, and mineral baths, and there are a number of enticing trails. The Sol Duc Falls Trail reaches a waterfall in less than a mile. The Ancient Groves Trail is a 0.6-mile loop through old-growth forest. The Mink Lake Trail ascends 1,500 feet in 2.6 miles to reach a beautiful subalpine lake. In fall, cohos can often be seen jumping the Salmon Cascades.

Olympic's Coastline

With over 70 miles of protected Pacific coastline, the park offers many places to explore the coastal habitat. One of the more rewarding spots is the Ozette area, reached by Wash. 113 and Wash. 112 north off U.S. 101. The popular 9-mile Ozette Loop Trail follows a boardwalk to the coast, runs 3.1 miles along the coast, and returns by another boardwalk. It's vital to know the tide schedule here, as incoming tide can force hikers up against the rocks, trapping them. Migrating gray whales are sometimes seen, and seabirds nest on offshore sea stacks. Harbor seals are the most commonly seen

marine mammal in the area.

To learn more about the coastal environment, head south to the Mora or Kalaloch areas and join a park ranger on a guided beach walk or tide pool exploration.

Hoh River Valley

The western slopes of Olympic National Park are among the rainiest places in North America, creating a temperate rain forest of almost unbelievable lushness. Ferns and mosses seem to take up every available space among the shrubs and huge trees, mostly Sitka spruce, western hemlock, and western red cedar. The Hoh River Valley, where rainfall can total 170 inches annually, is one of the finest remaining examples of temperate rain forest in the United States.

The Hoh Rain Forest Visitor Center (360-374-6925, daily in summer, limited days rest of year) is the place to learn about this environment. The old-growth forests of the Pacific Northwest produce three times the biomass (organic material) of tropical rain forests—a fact that's easy to accept during a walk along the 0.8-mile Hall of Mosses Trail or the 1.2-mile Spruce Nature Trail, both beginning at the visitor center. For a longer trek, the Hoh River Trail leads 17.3 miles to Glacier Meadows, on the shoulder of Mount Olympus; day hikers can walk the lower part of the route to enjoy more of the rain forest habitat.

Some of the birds that fly among these magnificent trees are red-breasted sapsucker, Pacific-slope flycatcher, chestnut-backed chickadee, varied thrush, Townsend's warbler, and western tanager. A lucky hiker

might spot the more elusive northern pygmy-owl (hardly bigger than a sparrow) or a sooty grouse.

Notable Wildlife

The Hoh Valley is one of the best places in the park to see Roosevelt elk, the largest subspecies of elk and one of the primary factors in the establishment of a protected area on the Olympic Peninsula. The park is home to the largest unmanaged herd of Roosevelt elk in the world, and in fact was almost named Elk National Park. The elk is named for President Theodore Roosevelt, who in 1909 designated the area Mount Olympus National Monument (it was redesignated a national park in 1938). The elk range from the high-mountain meadows to the lowland rain forest. The females and young travel in groups, while the males roam alone. In September, the males' "bugling" mating calls can be heard throughout the park.

Black bears are common here, and are sometimes in the fall seen eating ripe huckleberries. During spring and fall salmon runs, bears wade into streams and feast on the fish. It's vital that all campers store food in animal-resistant containers—which protect against not just bears but also raccoon, which can easily climb trees to get food hung from branches or lines.

Another interesting park mammal is the fisher, a weasel relative with a thick coat of fur that allows it to survive harsh winters. Wiped out throughout the state by trapping, the species was the focus of a three-year restoration program and has been reintroduced to the park. Despite its name, the fisher rarely eats fish, preferring snowshoe hares, mice, and birds.

Visitor center
3002 Mount Angeles Rd.
Port Angeles. WA
360-565-3130
www.nps.gov/olym

AT A GLANCE

Northwestern Washington, 70 miles northwest of Seattle ▪ 922,651 acres
▪ Year-round ▪ Hiking, camping, backpacking, wildlife-watching

Pacific Crest National Scenic Trail

Long-distance route across the high country of three western states

A view of Mount Rainier from the highest point on the Pacific Crest Trail.

The Pacific Crest National Scenic Trail runs 2,650 miles from the Mexican border in southern California to the Canadian border in central Washington. Authorized by Congress in 1968, it was dedicated in 1993, although route changes continue to be made to improve the hiking and riding experience. The trail is for nonmechanized travel only; hikers and horses (and other stock animals) are allowed, but mountain bikes and motor vehicles are prohibited.

The trail traverses a wide array of natural environments, from the deserts of southern California through chaparrals and scrub oaks to the high peaks of the Sierra Nevada in central California, where highlights include both Sequoia and Kings Canyon (see p. 420) and Yosemite (see p. 424) National Parks. Northward, the trail enters the volcanic Cascade Range, reaching sites such as Lassen Volcanic National Park (see p. 403), Oregon's Crater Lake National Park

(see p. 464), and Washington's Mount Rainier National Park (see p. 473) and North Cascades National Park (see p. 478). The trail actually extends a few miles into Canada to provide access to British Columbia Hwy. 3. (At the international border, the trail lies within a roadless wilderness area.)

People who attempt to hike the entire length of the trail usually start at the southern terminus in April or May to cross the passes of the Sierra Nevada when most or all snow has melted and to reach the trail's end before winter sets in.

The U.S. Forest Service administers the trail in partnership with the Bureau of Land Management, National Park Service, California State Parks, and the nonprofit Pacific Crest Trail Association (PCTA). Around 10 percent of the trail passes through private land, and conservation groups continue to acquire conservation easements to protect the route from development.

The primary source of information on the trail is the PCTA, which sells guidebooks and trail maps, issues permits, and updates trail conditions on its website.

Pacific Crest Trail Association
916-285-1846
www.pcta.org
U.S. Forest Service
www.fs.fed.us/pct

AT A GLANCE

Southern California to northern Washington ▪ 2,650 miles ▪ Best season depends on trail section ▪ Backpacking, day hiking, horseback riding

San Juan Island National Historical Park

The island where a pig almost caused a war

After years of contention over the international boundary between British and United States territories

in western North America, the two countries signed an agreement in 1846 designating the 49th parallel as

the border. The boundary remained unclear, though, when it reached the islands between the Strait of Georgia and the Strait of Juan de Fuca. England claimed San Juan Island, and the British Hudson's Bay Company set up a sheep farm on the island. American settlers moved in, though, and in 1859 the disagreement came to a head.

An American farmer shot a pig that was eating his potatoes, and later refused to pay the compensation demanded by the Hudson's Bay Company. Though the matter seemed trivial, it soon escalated. Britain dispatched warships and the U.S. sent soldiers to San Juan Island, but both sides were urged by their governments to fire only if fired upon. The crisis was defused when Lt. Gen. Winfield Scott, commander of the U.S. Army, came west to mediate. In the end, the only casualty of the war was the pig. It took 12 years to reach an agreement by which England ceded the island to the U.S. During that period both countries maintained small military posts.

Visiting the Park

Visitors to San Juan Island National Historical Park can tour both American Camp on the southern end of the island and English Camp near the northern end. A year-round visitor center at American Camp displays 19th-century artifacts and exhibits on this odd incident in British–U.S. relations. Visitors can see remains of the redoubt, an earthen defensive fortification.

The Royal Marine Barracks at English Camp, built as a privates' mess in 1860 and converted to a barracks in 1867, now serves as a visitor contact station in summer; it features historical exhibits. The lower floor of the camp blockhouse is also open to the public.

In addition to the island's intriguing history, it offers other attractions, most notably the chance to see orca whales, especially from points along the southwestern shore. San Juan Island is a favorite spot for bird-watchers, who especially enjoy the many species of raptors that frequent the American Camp prairie, one of the last of its kind in Washington State. The park is currently engaged in a project to restore the prairie to the way it appeared prior to white settlement in the 1850s.

The park protects 6.1 miles of shoreline, which can be excellent for beachcombing and enjoying the multifaceted life-forms found in tide pools. Rangers conduct guided walks that explore the tide pools, as well as wildflower walks, bird-watching walks, and history programs. There are several miles of hiking trails, including self-guiding nature trails.

The laundress quarters of the American Camp

4668 Cattle Point Rd.
Friday Harbor, WA
360-378-2240
www.nps.gov/sajh

AT A GLANCE

Northwestern Washington, 35 miles west of Bellingham ▪ 1,752 acres ▪ Spring through fall ▪ Hiking, touring historic sites, bird-watching, whale-watching, beachcombing

Whitman Mission National Historic Site

Remembering a tragic incident of the Oregon Trail era

In 1836, Marcus and Narcissa Whitman were among a small group of missionaries who traveled to what was then Oregon Country to convert Native American tribes to Christianity. The Whitmans established a mission with the Cayuse people near the Walla Walla River.

Various factors, including differing lifestyles, tension between Indians and immigrants on the Oregon Trail, and a measles outbreak that killed more than half the local Cayuse, led to an attack by the Cayuse on the mission. On November 29, 1847, the Whitmans were killed along with 11 other people, and 60 people were taken captive and held until ransomed a month later.

Settlers from the Willamette River Valley banded together to avenge the deaths, and on their way to the mission some of them burned Indian lodges. The Cayuse retaliated by burning the mission buildings. When the volunteers reached the mission site in March 1848, they reburied the victims, whose original graves had been dug up by animals.

In 1848, in response to the killings, Congress passed legislation making Oregon a United States territory. The hunt for the Cayuse attackers led to a series of Indian skirmishes in the region that ended with the surrender and trial of five Cayuse leaders, who were hanged in 1850.

At Whitman Mission National Historic Site, visitors can tour a small museum with displays that compare the cultures of the Whitmans and

Whitman Mission National Historic Site

the Cayuse. Exhibits include Native American items, archaeological artifacts, and personal items belonging to the Whitmans.

Outside, trails lead to the original

mission site; to locations of other mission structures; to a monument honoring the Whitmans; and to the Great Grave, where the bodies of the victims are buried.

328 Whitman Mission Rd.,
7 miles west of
Walla Walla, WA
509-522-6360
www.nps.gov/whmi

AT A GLANCE

Southeastern Washington, 45 miles east of Kennewick ▪ 138 acres ▪ Year-round ▪ Touring museum and historic mission site

---

Wing Luke Museum of the Asian Pacific American Experience

Community-based exhibits on Asian-American history

Asian Pacific Americans have made substantial cultural and political contributions throughout the United States, but their influence has been especially vital along the Pacific Coast. Seattle's Wing Luke Museum of the Asian Pacific American Experience (locally called "The Wing") focuses on the history, culture, and art of people from the Asian Pacific region, as well as their struggles for acceptance and civil rights.

Established in 1967, the museum was named for Wing Luke, a local

resident and World War II veteran who became the first Asian American elected to public office in the Pacific Northwest. The museum has expanded twice over the years, occupying a place in the heart of Seattle's Chinatown-International District.

Visitors will learn the history of Asian Pacific immigrants in Seattle and elsewhere through the musem's preserved historic hotel. Visitors tour a 1910 import-export store and a "family association," which helped new arrivals learn how to cope with their

adopted country. Changing exhibits include subjects such as art, the lives of Asian Pacific pioneers, and their political challenges and successes.

The museum also offers walking tours of the historic Chinatown-International District, such as "Touch of Chinatown," examining past and present life in this diverse neighborhood, and "Taste of Chinatown," which includes lunch at an Asian restaurant. Tours are conducted by local guides who relate personal and family stories as well as city history.

719 South King St.
Seattle, WA
206-623-5124
www.wingluke.org

AT A GLANCE

Downtown Seattle, Washington ▪ 0.3 acres ▪ Year-round ▪ Changing museum exhibits, walking tours of Seattle's Chinatown-International District

WYOMING

The least populous state, Wyoming is a land where mountain ranges rise from the rolling terrain of the Great Plains. Mining and ranching drive the state's economy, but a superb collection of natural areas generates substantial tourism income. Most famous of these places is Yellowstone National Park, home to half the world's geothermal features—geysers, steam vents, mud pots, and more. Just south, Grand Teton National Park encompasses some of the most ruggedly beautiful scenery in the country, and ranks among the most rewarding wildlife-watching sites. The not-so-famous-but-striking Devils Tower National Monument rises in Wyoming's northeast like a giant tree stump.

Devils Tower National Monument

An awe-inspiring landmark and America's first national monument

Rising 867 feet above the rock rubble at its base, Devils Tower has awed humans since the first Paleo-Indian travelers came upon it. Native Americans had many names for the formation, including Bear Lodge and Tree Rock. (The vertical fissures in the rock were often said to be claw marks from a bear's scratching.) It's believed that its English name came from a mistranslation of the Indian term meaning "bear's tower" as "bad god's tower," later changed to "devil's tower." So impressive is this landmark that it was designated as America's first national monument in 1906.

Though many people imagine that the tower is the core of an ancient volcano, it's actually a formation called an igneous intrusion. Around 60 million years ago, magma (molten rock) forced its way up through surrounding layers of

Many people liken Devils Tower to a tree stump.

sedimentary rock but did not reach the surface. As the magma cooled, it shrank and cracked, forming distinctive six-sided columns (a few have four, five, or seven sides). Erosion later

wore away the sedimentary rock, exposing the igneous material, a granite-like rock called phonolite porphyry.

After stopping at the visitor center, some people simply look at Devils Tower, take photos, and drive on. But it's worthwhile to walk the 1.3-mile loop trail around its base to enjoy this amazing structure from all angles.

About 4,000 people a year climb the tower—a feat that usually takes six to eight hours; the shortest ascent took less than 15 minutes—and then rappel down. Some Indian tribes consider Devils Tower a sacred place and view climbing it as a desecration. As a compromise, climbers are asked to refrain from ascending in June, when many religious ceremonies occur.

Wyo. 24 Devils Tower, WY 307-467-5283 www.nps.gov/deto	**AT A GLANCE**

Northeastern Wyoming, 100 miles northwest of Rapid City, South Dakota ▪ 1,347 acres ▪ Spring through fall ▪ Hiking, rock climbing

Fort Laramie National Historic Site

A western post that saw a colorful parade of history

In 1834, fur traders established a post near the confluence of the Laramie and North Platte Rivers to trade with American Indians, calling it Fort William. (Trading posts were often called "forts" although they were not truly military sites.) The post was later acquired by the American Fur Company, which in 1841 built an adobe fort to replace the old log structure, renaming it Fort John.

Located at a strategic site along the route of the Oregon, California, and Mormon Trails, the post was purchased by the U.S. Army in 1849 for $4,000. For more than four decades the renamed Fort Laramie served to protect travelers along these routes, to patrol the transcontinental telegraph line, and as a base of operations during conflicts with Indian tribes. In 1850, almost 50,000 immigrants passed by the fort. Over its history, the fort saw visitors such as "mountain man" Jim Bridger, Mormon leader Brigham Young, the Donner party, explorer John C. Frémont, Pony Express riders, and missionaries Marcus and Narcissa Whitman (see p. 486). The fort was abandoned by the Army in 1890, after the Indian wars had abated and the Union Pacific Railroad had bypassed it to the south.

At Fort Laramie National Historic Site, visitors can tour restored buildings, some of them furnished to reflect a particular period in its history. Included are the 1874 cavalry barracks, the 1875 surgeon's quarters, the 1866 guardhouse, and the 1849 "Old Bedlam"; the latter was designed to be bachelor-officers' quarters, but later served as post headquarters. The 1876 guardhouse displays artillery pieces and military transport vehicles, and the old commissary houses the park visitor center, which has exhibits and an 18-minute film on Fort Laramie history.

Interpretive programs are presented regularly; and an available self-guiding audio tour features narration, dramatic readings from diaries and journals, and the sounds of the fort.

Wyo. 160, 3 miles south of Fort Laramie, WY
307-837-2221
www.nps.gov/fola

AT A GLANCE

Southeastern Wyoming, 90 miles north of Cheyenne ▪ 833 acres ▪ Spring through fall ▪ Touring historic fort, hiking

Fossil Butte National Monument

One of the world's richest deposits of Eocene-epoch fossils

Southwestern Wyoming today is a high, cold desert area where sagebrush grows and winter temperatures sometimes drop to minus 30°F. Fifty-two million years ago, however, this was a warm temperate environment with large lakes. Lake sediments, now transformed into rock layers known as the Green River formation, contain millions of fossils of fish, mammals, reptiles, birds, insects, and plants. The accompanying Wasatch formation, composed of river and stream sediments, has fossilized teeth and bone fragments

Phareodus encaustus, *a toothed fish*

of many species of mammals and reptiles.

For more than a century, collectors have removed fossils for sale to museums and individuals. Fossil Butte National Monument protects a 12.8-square-mile area for scientific study and the enjoyment of visitors. The park includes less than 2 percent of the ancient Fossil Lake, which itself is the smallest of three lakes of the Green River formation. Commercial quarries outside the park allow visitors to dig fossils for a fee.

A great variety of fossils are on display at the visitor center, from crayfish, dragonflies, and tiny fish to turtles, bats, stingrays, and a 13-foot-long crocodile. Videos help interpret the scientific work that has been conducted here. Two hiking trails with interpretive panels wind through sagebrush, an aspen forest, and some fossil-bearing rock; a 5.5-mile drive provides an overview of the landscape.

In summer, the park offers ranger programs *(daily)* and a visit to the park's fossil quarry *(Fri.–Sat.)*.

U.S. 30
9 miles west of
Kemmerer, WY
307-877-4455
www.nps.gov/fobu

AT A GLANCE
Southwestern Wyoming, 120 miles northeast of Salt Lake City ▪ 8,198 acres ▪ Late spring through fall ▪ Viewing visitor center fossil exhibits, hiking, taking scenic drive

Grand Teton National Park

Where spectacular peaks rise steeply from the sagebrush valley of Jackson Hole

The Teton Range, rising sharply from the valley floor, is reflected in the waters of the morainal Jenny Lake.

There are higher mountains in North America, but none more dramatic than the Teton Range. Because of the manner of their geologic birth, these rugged mountains rise with near verticality more than 7,000 feet above the valley floor, without foothills impeding views of their rocky slopes and deep canyons.

Spectacular and easily accessible scenery combined with pristine lakes; recreational boating opportunities; and wildlife that includes grizzly and black bears, elk, moose, deer, bighorn sheep, bison, and pronghorns make Grand Teton one of America's most popular national parks—and deservedly so.

Natural & Cultural History

The Tetons are classic fault-block mountains. About nine million years ago, two huge blocks of the Earth's crust separated from each other along a fault line, one sliding upward and the other down, like horizontal swinging doors moving in opposite directions. Over time, vertical movement of the blocks relative to each other has totaled up to 30,000 feet of displacement, most of it from the eastern block moving downward.

On the western fault block, erosion has stripped away layers of sedimentary rock that once overlay what are now the mountain peaks. This has led to the seemingly contradictory facts that, while the granite and gneiss composing the core of the Teton Range are some of the oldest rocks in North America, the mountains themselves are among the youngest on the continent.

In the eons since the Tetons were elevated, they have been shaped by erosion and glaciers, especially the latter. The broad, U-shaped valleys typically created by the scouring action of glaciers are easily seen. Eroded material, deposited by receding glaciers, left behind the flat valley of Jackson Hole to the east of the Tetons and created the jewel-like lakes at their feet. Glacial action deposited varying types of soils. Sagebrush dominates on glacial outwash plains where rainfall rapidly drains through a porous, cobble-strewn rock layer, while other shrubs and trees such as lodgepole pines grow on glacial moraines at the base of the mountains.

Various Indian tribes utilized the resources of the Snake River Plain in summer, but severe winters prevented

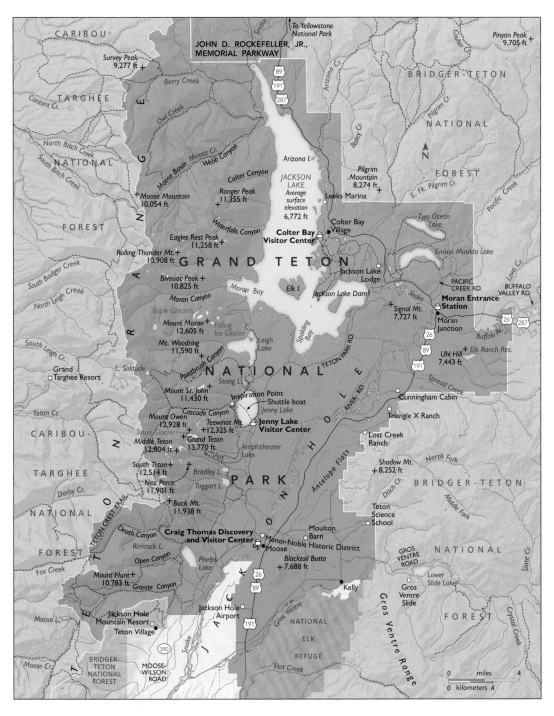

them from living in the harsh environment year-round. In the early 19th century, mountain men arrived in the Teton country. The valley acquired its name, Jackson's Hole, because of a fur trapper named Davey Jackson. (The name later lost its apostrophe and final *s.*) Following the fur trappers came the settlers, who in the 20th century opened dude ranches and started the modern era of tourism.

Teton Park Road:
Moose to Jenny Lake

From the town of Jackson, U.S. 26/89/191 leads north into the park, crossing the Gros Ventre River and arriving at Moose Junction, the intersection with Teton Park Road. Offering a scenic drive through the park, Teton Park Road first crosses the Snake River. The Craig Thomas Discovery and Visitor Center is a good first stop for general park information, to learn about ranger programs, to view exhibits on natural history, and to watch a documentary-style introductory video. Permits are available here for overnight backcountry trips or for boating on the Snake River or park lakes.

Just north of the visitor center, the Menors Ferry Historic District provides a glimpse of pioneer life in Jackson Hole. Bill Menor moved to this site beside the Snake River in 1892 and built a ferryboat that became a vital crossing for the early settlers of the valley. (The fare was 50 cents for a wagon and team, 25 cents for a horse and rider.) Visitors can see Menor's cabin and country store; a reproduction of the ferry; and a church called the Chapel of the Transfiguration, whose window frames a view of the tallest Teton peaks.

Teton Park Road ascends from the Snake River as the impressive Teton peaks rise ahead, punctuated by the Grand Teton, the park's high point at 13,770 feet above sea level.

The mountain is flanked to the south by Middle Teton and South Teton, and to the north by Mount Owen. About 12 peaks in the park tower more than 12,000 feet in elevation.

Some of the park's most charismatic wildlife might be seen almost anywhere, so it pays to look to the side of the road and not just ahead. Elk, mule deer, bison, and pronghorn (often called antelope, though this mammal is not a true antelope) are commonly seen from roads, and moose can be seen in wetland areas. Not quite as large but seen with some regularity are coyotes and badgers. Predators such as gray wolves, mountain lions, and black and grizzly bears are far more elusive, and more often seen by hikers in the backcountry.

Farther up the road is the trailhead for the 3.2-mile round-trip hike to Taggart Lake, which reveals the ways a forest regenerates itself after a fire, in this case a blaze that occurred in 1985. Shortly beyond is the Teton Glacier Turnout, with postcard-quality views of the three Tetons and neighbors such as Nez Perce and Teewinot Mountain. In the steep, glacier-carved gulch on Grand Teton's northeast face lies Teton Glacier, one of about a dozen relatively small glaciers remaining in the park.

The road soon reaches Jenny Lake, named for the wife of 19th-century fur trapper Dick Leigh. (Leigh Lake, to the north, is named for "Beaver Dick" himself.) The Jenny Lake Visitor Center *(summer only)* features geology exhibits, and rangers conduct a variety of programs and walks. This is also the starting point for one of Grand Teton National Park's most popular hikes, following a trail up Cascade Canyon, across Jenny Lake from the visitor center.

The Jenny Lake area is extremely popular. The parking lot can fill early during summer. Arrive as early as possible to avoid the peak of visitors.

A renewal project for the Jenny Lake area may also affect trails and parking until 2017—check ahead of your visit.

Cascade Canyon Trail

There are two ways to reach the canyon mouth: Hike the trail around the southern end of Jenny Lake, or take a shuttle boat *(fee)* across the lake, which cuts 2 miles off the route (one way). Once on the west side of the lake it's a fairly easy 0.6-mile ascending walk to a view of 200-foot Hidden Falls, tumbling down a ramp of boulders and rock ledges. The appealing songbird called American dipper is often seen along Cascade Creek here. Another 0.4 mile of steep switchbacks leads to Inspiration Point, a knob of bare rock with great views of Jenny Lake and the terminal moraine (rocks carried forward by a moving glacier) that is its natural dam. Beyond the valley to the east rise the Gros Ventre Mountains.

From Inspiration Point the trail climbs gradually into the mountains along one of the park's least strenuous canyon ascents, traversing meadows with sheer rock walls rising more than 3,500 feet on either side. Some hikers continue to Lake Solitude, 7.5 miles from Jenny Lake. It's a strenuous day hike: estimated eight hours round-trip time if using the lake shuttle, ten hours if walking all the way. Black bears are sometimes seen in Cascade Canyon, though it's more likely hikers will spot a yellow-bellied marmot, occasionally a snowshoe hare, or, among the rocks, the small rabbit relative called pika.

Teton Park Road:
Jenny Lake to Jackson Lake Dam

Teton Park Road continues north to the junction with Jenny Lake Scenic Drive, which leads southwest to a trailhead for walks to String Lake and Leigh Lake. From the latter lake there are great views of 12,605-foot Mount Moran. There's a great view of the mountains

Hikers on a trail in Death Canyon in Grand Teton National Park

Elk often graze in the meadows along the Snake River.

along Jenny Lake Scenic Drive at the Cathedral Group Turnout. Falling Ice Glacier can be seen just southeast of Mount Moran's summit, and above it a line of dark rock called the Black Dike. Here, long before the Teton Range rose, an intrusion of magma flowed into a crack in older rock; the harder intrusion stands out where the surrounding rock has been eroded away. There's a thin layer of sandstone atop Mount Moran, a remnant of the sedimentary rocks that once covered this entire area. A corresponding layer of sandstone lies more than 20,000 feet below the surface of Jackson Hole. Millions of years of movement along the Teton Fault has separated the once horizontal layers by up to 30,000 vertical feet.

Teton Park Road now swings around the south end of Jackson Lake, the park's largest body of water. A natural lake created by an ancient vast glacial ice sheet, it was enlarged by a dam built at its outlet before the national park was established.

A dead-end side road leads off to the east to Signal Mountain. Though only 7,727 feet tall, its location gives it one of the park's finest panoramic vistas—and it's one of the easiest to reach: The road goes right to the top *(large vehicles and trailers are prohibited).* The view takes in the jagged peaks of the Tetons, Jackson Lake, the meandering Snake River, and the length and breadth of Jackson Hole. From here, it's easy to see why early trappers used the word "hole" to refer to mountain-ringed valleys like this one.

The East Side of Jackson Lake

Teton Park Road crosses the dam over the Snake River and joins U.S. 89/191/287, which leads along the eastern shore of Jackson Lake toward the John D. Rockefeller, Jr. Memorial Parkway (see opposite) and Yellowstone National Park (see opposite). There are several roadside overlooks along this route that are excellent for spotting moose, bald eagles, ospreys, sandhill cranes, white pelicans, and trumpeter swans. The Colter Bay Visitor Center includes the Indian Arts Museum, which displays

some pieces of the David T. Vernon Collection, Native American artifacts donated by the Rockefeller family.

Snake River

One of the park's most popular activities is canoeing, rafting, or kayaking along the Snake River from Moran Junction down to Moose Landing. It's important to check with park rangers for the necessary permits and advice about natural hazards along the river's course. This is especially true on the section below Deadman's Bar. Though the Snake appears to be a quietly meandering stream in places, its cold water, tangled channels, and logjams can create problems, especially for inexperienced paddlers. For those unsure of their skills, several outfitters operate guided float trips as authorized park concessionaires.

Whether by individual kayak or by a group rafting trip, a journey down the Snake River can be a true highlight of a visit to Grand Teton National Park. In addition to moose, which like to browse streamside willows, wildlife might include otters, muskrats, beavers, bison, elk, herons, swans, and bald eagles.

The Tetons in Winter

Winter brings deep snow and frigid temperatures to the park, but cross-country skiing and snowshoeing are popular activities. The Jackson Hole Visitor Center *(532 N. Cache St.)* is the best place to get advice about winter trails. The park authorizes some concessionaires to offer winter tours, and from late December through March, rangers offer guided snowshoe hikes beginning at the Taggart-Bradley trailhead.

U.S. 26/89/191
12 miles north of
Jackson, WY
307-739-3300
www.nps.gov/grte

AT A GLANCE

Northwestern Wyoming, 12 miles north of Jackson ▪ 310,000 acres ▪ Late spring through fall ▪ Hiking, camping, backpacking, horseback riding, climbing, boating, fishing

John D. Rockefeller, Jr. Memorial Parkway

A scenic drive honoring a national park benefactor

In the long and sometimes contentious effort to create Grand Teton National Park and expand its boundary into the valley called Jackson Hole, noted philanthropist John D. Rockefeller, Jr., played a major behind-the-scenes role. The heir to an oil-company fortune, he also helped create other national parks, including Acadia, Great Smoky Mountains, and Virgin Islands.

Established in 1972, John D. Rockefeller, Jr. Memorial Parkway comprises 23,777 acres linking Grand Teton National Park (see p. 490), which administers the parkway, with Yellowstone National Park (see below). The Rockefeller Parkway name also applies to the length of the highway from the south boundary of Grand Teton to West Thumb in Yellowstone, a distance of 82 miles.

Just south of the Yellowstone boundary is the Flagg Ranch Information Station *(307-543-2372),* which has exhibits on the parkway. The 8-mile section of parkway, which is also U.S. 89/191/287, is kept open in winter to this point, making it a popular access spot for cross-country skiers and snowshoers.

Grassy Lake Road leads west from the main parkway road, providing a less crowded drive through the lands within the park boundary. It's also a popular winter-sports route. Grassy Lake Road is closed to motor vehicles for a period in spring because of grizzly bear activity.

A concessionaire at Flagg Ranch offers lodging, dining, horseback riding, and Snake River float trips.

U.S. 89/191/287
45 miles north of
Jackson, WY
307-739-3300
www.nps.gov/grte

AT A GLANCE

Connects Grand Teton and Yellowstone National Parks ▪ 23,777 acres; 82 miles ▪ Year-round, weather permitting ▪ Driving scenic route, boating, cross-country skiing, snowshoeing, camping

Yellowstone National Park

Abundant wildlife in a global geothermal hot spot

The iconic image of Old Faithful geyser comes to mind when most people think of Yellowstone National Park, and with good reason. Not only is it one of the most spectacular sights and most popular attractions in America's parks, but it also nicely symbolizes an amazing geologic fact: Yellowstone's 10,000-plus hydrothermal features include more than 300 active geysers, about half of the world's total, and the largest concentration on Earth.

Yet there is much more in Yellowstone than spouting geysers, steaming thermal pools, and burbling mud pots. The park ranks among the continent's greatest areas for wildlife-watching, with a diverse array of fauna from songbirds to huge bull bison. Here,

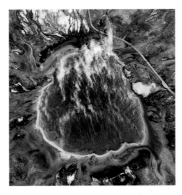

Grand Prismatic Spring

it's possible to observe herds of grazing animals and stalking predators in scenes bringing to mind what North America was like before European settlement altered the environment. In addition, the landscape itself offers scenes of stunning beauty, including canyons, waterfalls, lakes, and rugged mountain peaks.

In recognition of its geologic features, beauty, and wildlife, Yellowstone was designated as the world's first national park in 1872. So venerable is Yellowstone that some of the park buildings are themselves valued for their historical and architectural significance.

The geysers and boiling hot springs within Yellowstone National Park are indicators of ongoing activity in the Yellowstone volcano. Some 640,000 years ago, a catastrophic eruption occurred—an explosion a thousand times the size of the 1980 eruption of Mount St. Helens in Washington State—and ash from the event has been found across the continent.

The magma chamber underlying the volcano then collapsed, forming a caldera 28 by 47 miles in area, which was later partially filled by lava flows. Part of this caldera is the 136-square-mile basin of Yellowstone Lake. Today, there is evidence of two rising resurgent domes, which began to form hundreds of thousands of years after the cataclysmic eruption. The Sour Creek resurgent dome, just north and east of Fishing Bridge, is causing Yellowstone Lake to "tilt" southward, creating larger sandy beaches along the north shore and more flooded areas in the southern part. This, along with 1,000 to 3,000 earthquakes per year and the 10,000 thermal features, shows that Yellowstone is still an active volcanic site—though geologists say the odds of another massive explosive eruption occurring soon are small.

Yellowstone has served as a kind of laboratory for many issues facing parks everywhere. There have been intense debates about management of the

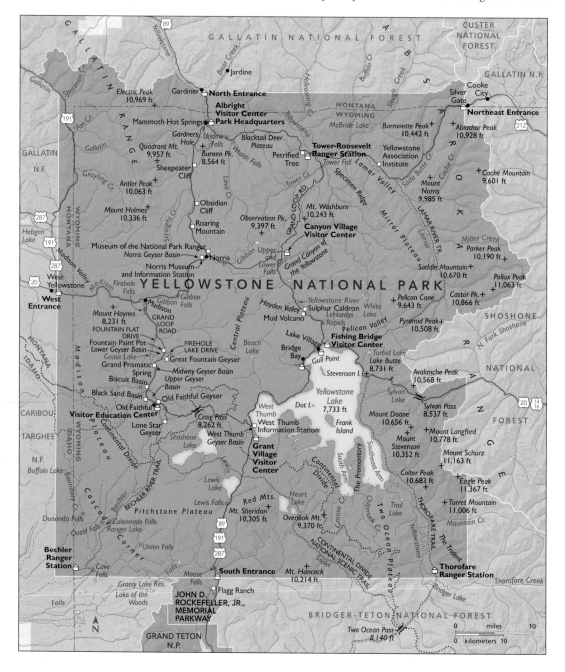

park's bison and elk herds, about the reintroduction of wolves, about snowmobile use, and other topics. In 1988 fires burned 36 percent of the park, giving impetus to discussions about fire prevention, controlled burning, and other aspects of fire management in parks. Though the 1988 fires were widely considered a huge tragedy at the time, in fact the park's major features were relatively unaffected by the blazes. The ecosystem is quickly renewing itself, providing an opportunity to observe the resilience of nature.

Visiting the Park

There are five entrances to Yellowstone, all leading inward to the 142-mile, figure-eight-shaped Grand Loop Road. While it's possible to drive through the park and see highlights such as the Upper Geyser Basin and the Mammoth Hot Springs area in a day, two or three days will allow a more relaxed and complete Yellowstone experience.

More than half the park's annual visitors arrive in July and August. Fall is an excellent time to visit, with good weather and smaller crowds. All park roads are closed by snow in winter, with the exception of the road between the North and Northeast Entrances (between Gardiner and Cooke City, Montana). Many people enjoy touring the park in winter, traveling by snow coach or snowmobile; some lodging remains open. When spring arrives in May and June, newborn animals can be seen, but the weather can be cold, rainy, or even snowy.

The park features more than 1,100 miles of trails for day hiking and backpacking, from flat, easy strolls to multiday treks. A permit is required for backcountry camping, and all hikers should learn and follow rules about safety in bear country. Some trails may occasionally be closed because of bear activity or conditions such as fire, high

Grizzly bear, denizen of Yellowstone

water, or snow. Current conditions and permits can be obtained at most visitor centers.

Concessionaires within the park offer a wide variety of activities, from lodging and dining to horseback rides, fishing expeditions, guided bike rides, photography workshops, and snowmobile tours.

Cautionary note: When touring Yellowstone's thermal areas, remain on boardwalks and marked trails. Stepping off the trail onto seemingly solid ground could result in a fall through the thin crust into scalding water, leading to serious injury or death.

Geyser Basins:
Upper Geyser to Norris

Every park visitor wants to see a geyser erupt. Park staffers issue predictions on the anticipated eruptions of six geysers. Five of them—including famed Old Faithful—are in Upper Geyser Basin. Geyser predictions are available at the Old Faithful Visitor Center, which also features a fine film on geothermal activity. Old Faithful (named for its regular activity rather than for any exact predictability) can be viewed from benches built to accommodate spectators or from a trail encircling it.

The 1 square mile of Upper Geyser Basin contains at least 150 of these geothermal features, visible from trails winding through the area. In addition to geysers, there are dozens of colorful boiling springs and delicate formations of geyserite, a silicate mineral deposited by hot water. Morning Glory Pool, named for its resemblance to the flower, lies near the north end of the basin.

From the Old Faithful area the park road leads north past several areas of interest, including Midway Geyser Basin. Here, a boardwalk leads past the huge Excelsior Geyser, a crater 200 by 300 feet that discharges more than 4,000 gallons of water a minute into the Firehole River. The path continues across the delicate terraces of Grand Prismatic Spring, 200 to 330 feet in diameter and more than 121 feet in depth. The largest and most beautiful hot spring in the park, Grand Prismatic features bright colors caused by algae and bacteria, different types of which thrive in different water temperatures.

To the north, the one-way Firehole Lake Drive leads into Lower Geyser Basin, site of the Great Fountain Geyser, one of the six geysers for which eruptions may be regularly predicted. This geyser is one of the park's most spectacular—jets of water bursting 75 to 220 feet into the air for 45 minutes to an hour while waves cascade down rings of raised terraces—and it erupts every 9 to 15 hours; however, the predicted schedule is accurate only to within two hours.

Back on the main road, the Artist Paint Pot area is well worth a visit for its multicolored springs and mud pots, named for the hues of an artist's palette. Burned in the 1988 fires, this area is a good place to see the subsequent vigorous regrowth of lodgepole pine, a species whose cones require fire to release their seeds.

Great Fountain Geyser, in Lower Geyser Basin, sits in the middle of terraced, concentric, reflective pools.

Farther north, Firehole Canyon Drive parallels Firehole River for a short distance, leading past pretty Firehole Falls. Early explorers saw steam in this region and thought it came from fires, and an old name for a mountain-ringed valley was "hole" (as in Jackson Hole to the south), hence the river's name. The pool below the falls is a popular swimming area, and the river is famed among anglers for its trout.

At the Norris area is a museum dedicated to the work of park rangers; retired rangers are often present to talk with visitors. Nearby Steamboat Geyser is the world's tallest geyser; it erupts very infrequently.

Mammoth Hot Springs

Near the park's northern boundary, the Mammoth area is the hub of many park activities, with lodging, camping, a medical clinic, and other services also available. The stone, red-roofed buildings here were built by the U.S. Cavalry when this was Fort Yellowstone, an Army post dedicated to protecting the national park before the creation of the National Park Service. The visitor center (housed in the former Army bachelor-officers' quarters) features a museum on the area's human history.

The Mammoth Hot Springs thermal area wows visitors with its colorful steaming pools surrounded by terraces of travertine (calcium carbonate), which the water brings to the surface from underground limestone. Trails wind through the area.

Bighorn sheep are sometimes seen on the road leading to the park's northern entrance, where pronghorns often graze. The cornerstone of the rock arch here was laid by President Theodore Roosevelt.

Grand Canyon of the Yellowstone

In the heart of the park, the Grand Canyon of the Yellowstone is best known for the Lower Falls and Upper Falls of the Yellowstone River, subject of countless photographs and paintings, especially by 19th-century landscape painter Thomas Moran. From the Canyon Village Visitor Center, follow the one-way Canyon Rim Drive to lookout points for great views of the canyon and 308-foot Lower Falls, almost twice as high as Niagara. The bright yellow, orange, and red of the canyon walls are caused by the oxidation of iron compounds in the gray and brown rhyolite rock.

Walk the rim trail from Inspiration Point to Grandview Point for the best look at the canyon's grandeur. Also consider the paved but strenuous Brink of the Lower Falls Trail, which descends several hundred feet to a lookout near where the river drops into space.

Back on the main road, a turnoff reaches a short trail leading to a viewpoint of 109-foot Upper Falls. Farther south, a side road crosses the river to Artist Point, the best overall view of the canyon.

Hayden Valley & Yellowstone Lake

Continuing south, the main road crosses the expanse of Hayden Valley, one of the best places in the park to observe wildlife. From roadside parking areas, visitors may see bison and elk, and in spring grizzly bears and wolves may appear to feed on the calves of both species. Coyotes trot across the sagebrush-dotted plain, and birds such as white pelicans and trumpeter swans swim in wetlands. Bald eagles sometimes soar

overhead, and sandhill cranes nest in the valley.

At LeHardys Rapids, cutthroat trout can be seen on their way to spawning grounds in June. Trout can also be seen at Fishing Bridge (where no fishing is allowed), located where the Yellowstone River flows out of Yellowstone Lake. This is the largest lake in North America above 7,000 feet elevation. The loop road follows the shore of the lake for 21 miles.

West Thumb, almost a separate lake, is a water-filled caldera created by an eruption about 150,000 years ago, a smaller version of the great Yellowstone caldera. A boardwalk leads around the West Thumb Geyser Basin, a small grouping of geothermal features.

Northern Yellowstone

The northern section of Yellowstone National Park, between Mammoth and Cooke City, Montana, is warmer and drier than the interior, characterized by sagebrush and grassy valleys. The Blacktail Plateau Drive, between the Mammoth and Tower-Roosevelt areas, is a good place to look for wildlife, as is the Lamar Valley in the park's northeastern corner. Bison, pronghorns, elk, coyotes, grizzly and black bears, and sometimes wolves can be spotted from this road. Dawn and dusk are best for wildlife-watching. Remember: It is against the law to approach on foot within 100 yards of bears or wolves or within 25 yards of other wildlife.

Lamar Valley streams are popular fly-fishing destinations. Anglers should study park fishing regulations before a trip, especially the rules pertaining to the threatened cutthroat trout, which must be released unharmed.

North Entrance
U.S. 89
5 miles south of Gardiner, MT
307-344-7381
www.nps.gov/yell

AT A GLANCE

Northwestern Wyoming, southern Montana, eastern Idaho, 65 miles north of Jackson, Wyoming ▪ 2,221,766 acres ▪ Late spring through fall and late winter ▪ Hiking, camping, backpacking, wildlife-watching, fishing, cross-country skiing, snowmobiling, snowshoeing

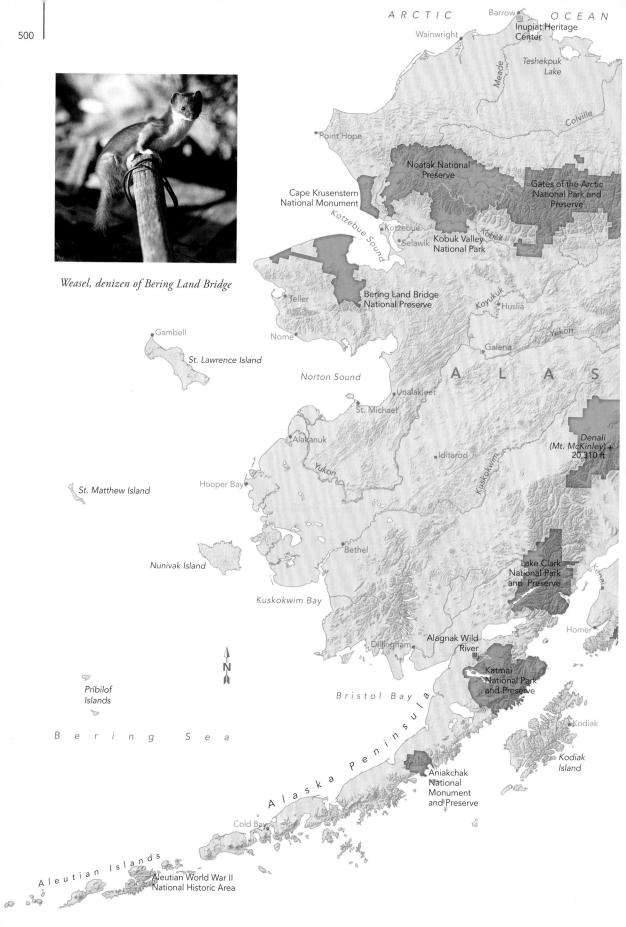

ARCTIC OCEAN

Barrow
Inupiat Heritage Center
Wainwright
Meade
Teshekpuk Lake
Colville

Point Hope

Noatak National Preserve
Gates of the Arctic National Park and Preserve
Cape Krusenstern National Monument
Kotzebue Sound
Kotzebue
Kobuk
Selawik
Kobuk Valley National Park
Koyukuk
Huslia
Bering Land Bridge National Preserve
Teller
Yukon
Nome
Galena

Gambell
St. Lawrence Island
Norton Sound
A L A S
Unalakleet
St. Michael
Alakanuk
Denali (Mt. McKinley) + 20,310 ft
St. Matthew Island
Hooper Bay
Yukon
Iditarod
Kuskokwim

Nunivak Island

Bethel

Kuskokwim Bay
Lake Clark National Park and Preserve
Kenai
Homer

Alagnak Wild River
Dillingham
Pribilof Islands
Katmai National Park and Preserve
B e r i n g   S e a
Bristol Bay
Kodiak
Alaska Peninsula
Kodiak Island

Aniakchak National Monument and Preserve

Cold Bay

Aleutian Islands
Aleutian World War II National Historic Area

Weasel, denizen of Bering Land Bridge

N

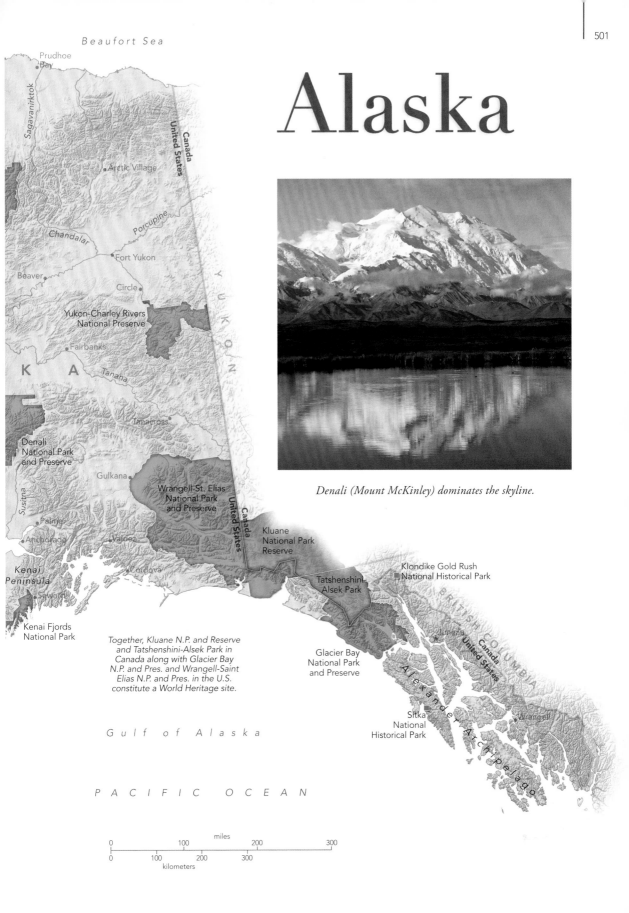

Alaska

Beaufort Sea

Prudhoe Bay

Sagavanirktok

Arctic Village

Porcupine

Chandalar

Fort Yukon

Beaver

Circle

Yukon-Charley Rivers National Preserve

Fairbanks

Tanana

K   A

Tanacross

Denali National Park and Preserve

Gulkana

Wrangell-St. Elias National Park and Preserve

Susitna

Palmer

Anchorage

Valdez

Cordova

Kenai Peninsula

Seward

Kenai Fjords National Park

Kluane National Park Reserve

Tatshenshini-Alsek Park

Klondike Gold Rush National Historical Park

Denali (Mount McKinley) dominates the skyline.

YUKON

Canada / United States

Canada / United States

BRITISH COLUMBIA

Canada / United States

Juneau

Alexander Archipelago

Glacier Bay National Park and Preserve

Sitka National Historical Park

Wrangell

Together, Kluane N.P. and Reserve and Tatshenshini-Alsek Park in Canada along with Glacier Bay N.P. and Pres. and Wrangell-Saint Elias N.P. and Pres. in the U.S. constitute a World Heritage site.

Gulf   of   Alaska

P A C I F I C   O C E A N

miles
0   100   200   300

0   100   200   300
kilometers

ALASKA

Ask someone to picture Alaska, and a number of scenes come to mind: huge brown bears fishing for salmon in a rushing river; a rugged coastline where glaciers calve icebergs into the sea; Denali, the highest peak in North America; herds of caribou migrating across tundra; broad rivers where rafters float for days, far from signs of civilization. Alaska's parks encompass all of that and more, including historic gold-rush towns, dogsled trails, and even a field of sand dunes north of the Arctic Circle. In Alaska, travelers experience the biggest state, with the largest national park, the highest mountain, and the most expansive wilderness areas in the country.

Alagnak Wild River

World-class fishing and abundant wildlife

Flowing out of Kukaklek Lake in Katmai National Park and Preserve (see p. 516), the Alagnak River has become one of the most popular destinations in southwestern Alaska for anglers. With populations of five species of Pacific salmon, as well as rainbow trout, arctic char, arctic grayling, and northern pike, the Alagnak offers great recreational opportunities for those who make the journey. The river is not accessible by vehicle; most visitors arrive by floatplane.

The upper 67 miles of the stream have been designated as Alagnak Wild River, administered by Katmai National Park and Preserve. Headquarters are in the town of King Salmon, where many visitors begin their journey. The Park Service manages about 83 percent of the river within the Alagnak Wild River corridor; the rest is private property. There are several fly-in lodges that offer accommodations, meals, and guided fishing trips. The park has no visitor facilities along the river.

Most of the river is a gently flowing braided stream. The word *alagnak* means "making mistakes" or "going the wrong way," a reference to the constantly changing channels. One section, though, features rapids up to Class III, providing thrills for rafters and other boaters. Local outfitters can arrange rafting trips, including equipment and transportation.

Wildlife seen often along the Alagnak River includes brown bears (attracted to the abundant salmon), moose, caribou, beavers, river otters, bald eagles, ospreys, harlequin ducks, and occasionally gray wolves. As is the case across much of Alaska, it's vital here that visitors know rules for avoiding confrontations in bear country. The river provides critical habitat for brown bears in summer.

Headquarters
King Salmon, AK
907-246-3305
www.nps.gov/alag

AT A GLANCE

Southwestern Alaska, 290 miles southwest of Anchorage ▪ 28,400 acres ▪ Summer and early fall ▪ Fishing, boating, wildlife-watching

Aleutian World War II National Historic Area

A fort built to protect the "back door to America"

The volcanic Aleutian Islands arc more than 1,000 miles across the northern Pacific Ocean from Alaska toward Asia, and are home to the Unangan (Aleut) people. In June 1942, as World War II raged, the Japanese bombed the U.S. military complex at Dutch Harbor on Amaknak Island and invaded the islands of Attu and Kiska.

These islands could have served as stepping-stones for an invasion of the North American mainland. (This was the first time that an enemy had occupied U.S. soil since the War of 1812.) Fort Schwatka on Amaknak Island's Mount Ballyhoo was one of four defense posts built to protect Dutch Harbor, which served as a staging ground in the 15-month-long effort to push the Japanese off the islands.

The U.S. government forced more than 800 Unangan people from nine villages to leave their homes and live for two years in internment camps in southeastern Alaska, where conditions were poor, food was scarce, and medical care almost nonexistent. Their homes were burned to prevent the Japanese from using them for shelter.

Aleutian World War II National Historic Area was established to tell the little-known stories of the war's Aleutian Islands campaign and the hardships suffered by the Unangan people during their internment. It is managed by a local organization, the Ounalashka Corporation, in partnership with the Park Service. The visitor center is at the Unalaska airport on Amaknak, in a historic 1943 Navy building. Features include exhibits on the war and the Unangan people, a reconstructed radio room, and regular showings of World War II–era films.

With permits, visitors can tour the site of Fort Schwatka, which still has intact bunkers. Visitors should take care while walking in the area and remain on trails because of possibly unsafe conditions in tunnels and deteriorating buildings.

Amaknak Island, AK
907-581-9944
www.nps.gov/aleu

AT A GLANCE

Aleutian Islands, 800 miles southwest of Anchorage ▪ Less than 1 acre ▪ Summer ▪ Visiting historic military post, viewing museum exhibits

---

Aniakchak National Monument & Preserve
A *volcanic landmark within a little-visited wilderness*

In a massive eruption 3,500 years ago, the summit of a 7,000-foot volcano on the Alaska Peninsula collapsed, leaving a caldera 6 miles wide and 2,500 feet deep. Later, this depression was filled by a deep lake similar to that in Oregon's Crater Lake National Park (see p. 464). At some point a section of the caldera rim gave way, and the outflow of lake water cut through 1,500 feet of rock to create a formation called "the Gates," through which the Aniakchak River now runs. Surprise Lake, 2.5 miles long, is a remnant of the much larger ancient lake.

Located in a remote section of the thinly populated Alaska Peninsula, with long stretches of bad weather and inaccessible by vehicle, Aniakchak

Caribou visiting Aniakchak

National Monument and Preserve ranks as one of the least visited areas within the National Park System. (There are no visitor services.) Adventurous boaters land on Surprise Lake in floatplanes, taking rafts through "the Gates" and continuing the three- or four-day trip to the Pacific Ocean.

Alaska outfitters offer trips on the Aniakchak, combining rafting with fishing for salmon and char.

Aniakchak is administered by Katmai National Park and Preserve (see p. 516), with headquarters in the town of King Salmon. Anyone thinking of visiting the park without a local guide should check with rangers about conditions and make extensive preparations for a wilderness sojourn, bearing in mind that weather may delay air transportation for days.

Those who do make a trip to Aniakchak will find solitude; the otherworldly landscape of the caldera with its cinder cones and explosion pits (it's still volcanically active); and wildlife, including brown bears, moose, caribou, and bald eagles.

Headquarters
King Salmon, AK
907-246-3305
www.nps.gov/ania

AT A GLANCE

Alaska Peninsula, 450 miles southwest of Anchorage ▪ 577,000 acres ▪ Summer ▪ Rafting, fishing, hiking

Bering Land Bridge National Preserve
The "bridge" that once connected Asia and the Americas

More than 13,000 years ago, when sea levels were lower, a "bridge" of exposed ground up to 1,000 miles wide connected Asia with North America. Many scientists believe that humans—and animals—migrated to North America via this connector. A remnant of this bridge has been set aside as Bering Land Bridge National Preserve on Seward Peninsula in order to provide opportunities for study.

Paleontological and archaeological resources abound; large populations of migratory birds nest here. Ash explosion craters and lava flow, which are rare in the Arctic, mark the landscape. Tundra features, such as polygons and pingos, are prevalent in many areas of the preserve.

Bering Land Bridge National Preserve is difficult to visit: No roads reach it. One must fly (small, fixed-wing aircraft), boat, snowmobile (in winter), or hike in. Activities within the preserve include hiking, primitive camping, and sport hunting. (Traditional subsistence activities such as hunting and trapping are also permitted.) Some visitors base themselves at Serpentine Hot Springs, where a bunkhouse provides shelter. Check the park website for a list of air taxis and current conditions at Serpentine Hot Springs.

Wildlife species in the region include grizzly bear, reindeer, gray wolf, wolverine, muskox, and fox. Seabirds, shorebirds, and waterfowl are abundant in summer in the preserve, and because of its proximity to Asia it is often home to species rare or unknown elsewhere in North America.

The park office and visitor center in Nome (a town reached only by air, as no highways connect the Seward Peninsula with the rest of Alaska) features exhibits on Beringia and the natural and cultural history of the area. Ranger programs and cultural workshops are offered in the Nome area and at the visitor center.

AT A GLANCE

Visitor center
214 Front St.
Nome, AK
907-443-2522
www.nps.gov/bela

Western Alaska, 95 miles north of Nome ▪ 2,698,919 acres ▪ Summer and winter ▪ Hiking, backpacking, bird-watching

Cape Krusenstern National Monument
A wild, remote land of tundra, coastline, and lagoons

Located north of the Arctic Circle and accessed through the community of Kotzebue, Cape Krusenstern National Monument was established primarily to protect archaeological resources. More than a hundred beach ridges along the Chukchi Sea and Kotzebue Sound preserve 5,000 years of Inupiaq Eskimo culture in the Arctic, while nearby sites may date back to 9,000 years before the present.

The national monument is usually reached by chartered aircraft, though visitors who own boats can

Some Alaska natives still live above the Arctic Circle.

also reach it by water, or in the winter, with a snowmobile. It is not a place for inexperienced or casual visitors: There are no facilities or formal trails within the park, and even in summer

the weather can quickly turn cold, rainy, and windy.

Visitors are generally free to hike and camp anywhere in the park except on the private property that lies within the area. At this latitude, summer daylight lasts around the clock, and in June and July the mosquitoes can be fierce. Hikers may well see caribou (part of the Western Arctic herd, with as many as a half million individuals), brown bears, muskoxen, moose, or gray wolves. The tundra and lagoons host significant numbers of waterfowl and shorebirds. Some of the park's most enthusiastic visitors are bird-watchers, who are always alert for rare strays from Asia as well as breeding birds such as arctic warbler, bluethroat, yellow wagtail, red-throated pipit, snow bunting, and hoary redpoll.

The Northwest Arctic Heritage Center in Kotzebue is open year-round and provides information on federal lands in the area, including Noatak National Preserve (see p. 530) and national wildlife refuges. Park rangers can provide information on companies licensed to provide transportation and guide services.

Kotzebue, AK
907-442-3890
www.nps.gov/cakr

AT A GLANCE

Arctic Circle, 175 miles north of Nome ▪ 675,840 acres ▪ Summer and early fall ▪ Hiking, backpacking, kayaking, wildlife-watching

Denali National Park & Preserve

An expansive wilderness surrounding North America's highest peak

This vast park—at 9,492 square miles, it's larger than the state of New Hampshire—beckons travelers for a variety of reasons, beginning with one very large one: the tallest mountain in North America. The 20,310-foot peak was given the name Mount McKinley in the late 19th century, but it is now called by its native

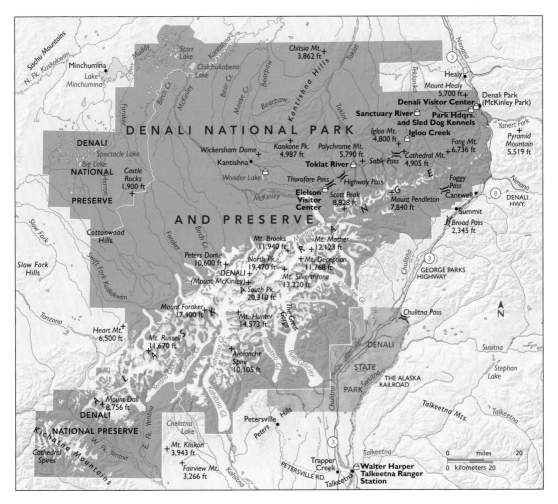

The majestic snowcapped peaks of the Alaska Range dwarf a Dall sheep in Denali National Park and Preserve.

Athabaskan name of Denali, "the high one." On any given summer day the odds are less than even that clouds will lift to reveal the rugged, snow-covered summit, but when it happens the sight is unforgettable.

All visitors, too, want to see the park's legendary wildlife—grizzly and black bears, moose, gray wolves, caribou, Dall sheep, lynx, and wolverines, as well as birds such as golden eagles, gyrfalcons, trumpeter swans, and all three North American species of ptarmigan. Many of these can be seen from the park road, while others require some searching—and luck.

Some visitors want to experience the park's expansive wilderness, to shoulder a pack and trek through a landscape little changed over thousands of years, where trails are few and hikers plot their own routes along glacier-fed rivers and across tundra.

A few adventurous visitors set out to climb "the high one," an arduous ascent for experienced and well-prepared mountaineers only, usually requiring two weeks or more. Fewer than a thousand climbers reach the summit annually.

Establishing Denali National Park

Denali takes center stage as the park's most famous feature, but the national park actually was established to protect the wildlife rather than to preserve Denali and other mountains in the Alaska Range.

A hunter and naturalist named Charles Sheldon, a friend of Theodore Roosevelt, spent the 1907–08 winter in a cabin on the Toklat River, and years later wrote a fine account of that stay in his book *The Wilderness of Denali*. Gold had been discovered in the area in 1903, and hunters were slaughtering wildlife to provide food to the influx of miners. Inspired partly by the area's beauty and partly by his desire to see game managed in a sustainable way, Sheldon spent years working for the creation of a national park, an effort that was rewarded when Mount McKinley National Park was established in 1917.

In 1980 the park was renamed Denali, though the mountain continues to be officially called McKinley (at least according to the federal government until 2015: The state of Alaska always called the mountain Denali).

Visiting the Park

Only one road goes into Denali National Park, a 92-mile, mostly unpaved route that leads from the intersection with Alaska 3 (George Parks Highway) to the historic Kantishna mining district. The park's entrance campus, just west of Alaska 3, includes an airstrip, a post office, a campground, and the depot for the Alaska Railroad (an option for traveling to the park from Anchorage or Fairbanks). The park's main visitor center *(mid-May–mid-Sept.)* is located here, with exhibits; information on ranger-led programs; and an interpretive film, "Heartbeats of Denali." The Wilderness Access Center, operated by a park concessionaire, shows "Across Time and Tundra," a film on the story of early tourism in the park.

To protect wildlife and the environment, private vehicles are restricted from all but the first 15 miles of the park road. Visitors wishing to travel beyond that point must purchase a ticket for one of the several types of buses that run back and forth along the road. While this setup limits access to a degree, it eases traffic on the narrow, winding road. The buses stop frequently for wildlife observation and photography.

Courtesy shuttle buses operate in the park entrance area. The Savage River shuttle runs out to the day-use area at mile 15 of the park road, providing a brief ride into the park; the Riley Creek shuttle links all the major facilities in the entrance area; and the sled-dog shuttle ferries people to the kennel where rangers keep sled dogs, used to patrol the park in winter. In summer, rangers hold daily sled-dog demonstrations at the kennel.

Bus Options

The park offers two basic types of bus trips along the park road in summer: the shuttle bus and the tour bus. There is a fee for all bus trips beyond the entrance area.

The shuttle bus system runs the entire length of the road, and it allows riders to hop off wherever they like, catching a ride with a later bus (on a space-available basis) to continue on the road or return to the entrance area. There is no food provided, and drivers answer questions and point out wildlife but do not give a formal tour presentation. A subset of the shuttle bus system is the camper bus, with space for backpacks and bicycles. This type of bus is available only to those staying at campgrounds or possessing backcountry permits.

The tour bus is operated by a driver-naturalist who provides narration during the trip. Food and beverages are included. Four interpretive trips are offered: a 4-hour trip that goes to mile 17 on the road, a 5- to 6-hour trip that goes to mile 30, a 7- to 8-hour trip that goes to approximately mile 53, and an 11- to 12-hour trip that goes to the historic mining district of Kantishna at the end of the road.

The Road Through Denali

From the entrance area, the road climbs through boreal forest into tundra, and views open to the Alaska Range to the southwest. On a clear day, Denali can be seen 70 miles away. While 20,310-foot Denali stands some 9,000 feet lower than 29,035-foot Mount Everest, the world's highest mountain, it's actually taller in its visual aspect: Everest rises only 12,000 feet above its surrounding plateau, while Denali has a vertical relief of 18,000 feet above its surroundings.

The road winds below Primrose Ridge before dropping into a marshy flat where spruce trees lean haphazardly. This "drunken forest" forms as permafrost thaws and the land slumps gradually downhill, tilting the trees. Beyond Igloo campground, the road cuts between Igloo Mountain and Cathedral Mountain, home of Dall sheep. Grizzly bears are sometimes seen from the road at Sable Pass, and lucky bus riders might spot gray wolves. Moose are most often seen along streams where willows grow, and caribou might be seen almost anywhere.

Near Polychrome Mountain the road takes a white-knuckle route along cliff edges. Great views of the Alaska Range and the occasional golden eagle help distract riders from the steep drops. The road reaches its highest elevation at 3,980-foot Highway Pass and continues to the Eielson Visitor Center. Constructed with state-of-the-art environmental features and energy efficiency, the center offers indoor and outdoor viewing areas, exhibits, and space for interpretive programs. On good-weather days Denali rises to the southwest in a spectacular panorama. There's about a one-in-three chance the summit will be visible.

The road runs along the braided McKinley River to reach Wonder Lake campground. This is the closest (27 miles) that the road comes to Denali. The moderately strenuous 4.5-mile (round trip) McKinley Bar Trail

heads through spruce forest and across tundra to the river.

The road ends at Kantishna, an area that became part of the national park and preserve in 1980, when the park's boundaries were expanded. Private lodges here offer an alternative to camping for people who want to stay in the park's interior.

Hiking

Day hikers are free to wander almost anywhere in the park, though some areas may close temporarily for reasons such as recent prey kills or resource protection. Backpackers and day hikers alike are cautioned not to overestimate how much ground can be covered in a day. While walking along river gravel bars and tundra can be relatively easy, traveling through brushy areas can make for very slow progress. Bad weather can come up suddenly at any time in Denali, and snow has been recorded in every month.

There are nearly 20 trails in the interior of the park. A few are located deep within the park, but most begin near the visitor center. The 0.9-mile (one way) Taiga Trail travels through subarctic boreal forest and provides access to other trails. The more strenuous Mount Healy Overlook Trail (4.5 miles round trip from the visitor center) ascends 1,700 feet through several habitats to a ridge with splendid views of the Nenana River Valley and alpine ridges, where Dall sheep sometimes appear. The most popular trail is the 1.4-mile Horseshoe Lake Trail. Winding past various wetlands and providing views of the Nenana River, this path is a good one for seeing wildlife, possibly moose and waterfowl. (Park rangers lead hikes on

the Horseshoe Lake Trail in summer.)

Backpackers must first obtain a free permit at the park's Backcountry Information Center (this must be done in person), establishing their trip itinerary. Denali is divided into backcountry units, each thousands of acres in size; the system is set up to allow solitude in the backcountry, in many cases limiting the number of campers per night per unit. Backpackers must attend a safety program and are required to use approved bear-resistant food containers. It's vital that all hikers know rules for keeping safe around bears, moose, and wolves, and what to do in case of an encounter with these potentially dangerous animals.

An excellent way to learn more about Denali and see off-road areas is to join one of the seasonal Discovery Hikes, which vary in destination and difficulty. Check at a visitor center for weekly schedules. Limited to 11 participants, these hikes last three to five hours and are for hikers who don't mind crossing streams (bring extra shoes and socks), pushing through brush, climbing hills, and generally bushwhacking off-trail. Sometimes the ranger him- or herself is discovering the area for the first time, so routes and other details may have to be improvised. Participants must sign up one to two days in advance at the Denali Visitor Center for these hikes.

The number of avid travelers arriving at Denali National Park has led to the development on the park's outskirts of a thriving business catering to adventure seekers. For a price, visitors can take an airplane or helicopter tour of the area, go boating, or take an off-road-vehicle tour outside the park, among other activities.

Mile 237, Alaska 3
Denali Park, AK
907-683-2294
www.nps.gov/dena

AT A GLANCE

South-central Alaska, 125 miles south of Fairbanks ■ 6,075,030 acres ■ Year-round; limited access in winter ■ Hiking, backpacking, wildlife-watching, mountaineering, taking scenic bus tours

Gates of the Arctic National Park & Preserve

The vast wild heart of the mighty Brooks Range

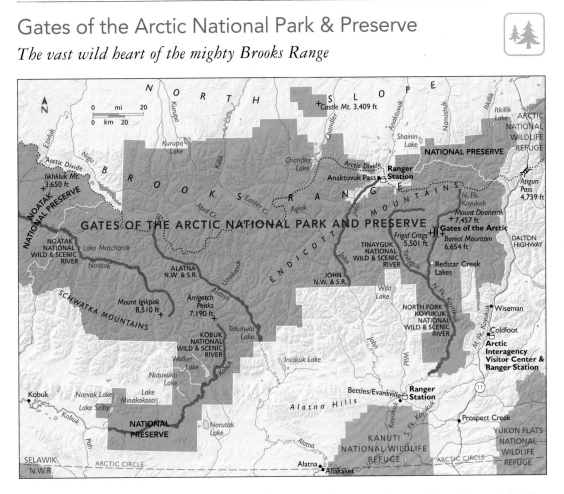

Gates of the Arctic National Park and Preserve, more than any other National Park System unit in Alaska, offers wilderness adventure and the opportunity for solitary self-reliance. With boreal forests, near-endless expanses of tundra, glacier-carved peaks, and broad rivers that rush though rocky canyons and wind lazily through valleys, the park—larger than Massachusetts and Rhode Island combined—lies entirely north of the Arctic Circle.

Gates of the Arctic's Beginnings

Three legendary American conservationists—Bob Marshall, Olas Murie, and Mardy Murie—had a hand in the creation of Gates of the Arctic National Park and Preserve.

Wilderness advocate and forester Bob Marshall first visited Alaska's Brooks Range in 1929, exploring this arc of northern mountains while looking for what he called "blank spaces on maps." He returned three more times in the 1930s, living for periods in the Koyukuk River area and writing about his experiences. "No sight or sound or smell or feeling even remotely hinted at men or their creations," Marshall wrote of a view from a prominent point in what is now the park. "It seemed as if time had dropped away a million years and we were back in a primordial world." His 1933 book *Arctic Village* told of his adventures in the Koyukuk area and the people who became his friends. When Marshall came upon two summits, Frigid Crags and Boreal Mountain, flanking one stretch of the North Fork Koyukuk, he called them "the Gates of the Arctic"—a name later applied to the park. His enthusiastic advocacy of the need to protect the pristine quality of the Brooks Range gave impetus to conservation efforts in the region.

In the 1950s, writer and naturalist Olaus Murie and his wife, Mardy, made expeditions into the eastern part of the Brooks Range and became concerned about the ways in which future development could affect Alaska natives and their traditional lifestyles. Their subsequent efforts eventually led to the creation of the vast Arctic National Wildlife Refuge. The work of Marshall, the Muries, and others encouraged the National

The aurora borealis shimmers above the Brooks Range in Gates of the Arctic.

Park Service to identify a large part of the central Brooks Range as a possible new park. Designated as Gates of the Arctic National Monument in 1978, it became a park and preserve in 1980.

Today, Gates of the Arctic National Park and Preserve stretches nearly 200 miles from the upper reaches of the Kobuk and Noatak Rivers in the west to the area around the North Fork Koyukuk in the east. The trio of this park, Noatak National Preserve (see p. 530), and the Arctic National Wildlife Refuge protect a nearly 800-mile-long region of wild Alaska.

Visiting the Park

There are no roads, campgrounds, maintained trails, ranger stations, or other visitor amenities in Gates of the Arctic. While it's possible for determined hikers to walk into the park—from the Dalton Highway, which runs within a few miles of the park's eastern boundary, or from the community of Anaktuvuk Pass—most people fly in on floatplanes that land on lakes or bush planes that land on gravel bars along rivers.

Before traveling, it's important to check with rangers for information about current conditions in the park. Wildlife-watching is among the highlights of a visit—moose, Dall sheep, gray wolves, caribou, and muskoxen all live here—but visitors must be aware that they are in bear country and should take necessary precautions. River crossings can be extremely dangerous, and hikers should be prepared to search for safe crossing locations or wait a day or more for water to recede. Less life-threatening but highly distressing are the abundant mosquitoes and other flying insects of summer. Head nets, long-sleeved shirts, long pants, and plenty of repellent are recommended.

Information about Gates of the Arctic National Park and Preserve is available at several locations. The main ranger station and visitor center *(907-678-5494, closed weekends fall–spring)* is located in the town of Bettles *(accessible only by air)*. It is staffed year-round to provide trip planning information to visitors. Another ranger station *(907-678-4227, closed weekends)* and the federal Arctic Interagency Visitor Center *(907-678-5209, summer only)* are located in the community of Coldfoot on the Dalton Highway, which

runs north from Fairbanks to Prudhoe Bay. (Coldfoot got its name from gold miners who got "cold feet" and left the region when they faced the difficulties of prospecting in northern Alaska.) The Anaktuvuk Pass Ranger Station *(907-661-3520),* on the north side of the park, is open at irregular times depending on staff availability. This community, too, is accessible only by air.

While an independent trip to Gates of the Arctic is feasible for experienced backpackers and river runners, many visitors will find it most convenient to enjoy the park (at least the first time) on a guided trip.

For a park so vast and remote, a relatively large number of outfitters, guide services, and charter air companies offer access to the interior. Backpackers can arrange to be dropped off for a specified period and picked up at a different location, although the changeable weather means that travelers should always be prepared for delays in transportation. It can drop below freezing and can snow during any month of the year, so wilderness skills, proper clothing and equipment, and preparation are vital.

Wild & Scenic Rivers

Gates of the Arctic National Park and Preserve is home to six national wild and scenic rivers: Alatna, Noatak, North Fork Koyukuk, Kobuk, John, and Tinayguk. Floating these rivers is probably the park's most popular recreational activity. Scheduling extra days beyond those required for a float trip allows time for hiking, seeing wildlife, and simply relaxing around camp and enjoying the feeling of being in one of the most untouched wilderness areas in North America.

Even in this remote place, travelers are beginning to have an effect on the land. At popular put-in spots, campsites and trails have caused destruction of vegetation. Visitors are encouraged to use existing sites and not expand camp areas, to avoid creating new trails across tundra; and to use camp stoves and not wood fires for cooking. Gravel bars make the best campsites, though campers should be aware that rivers can rise quickly, so campers should select high sites away from the water's edge. Away from gravel bars, camps should be set up on grasses and sedges where possible, not on more-fragile mosses and lichens.

The Alatna makes a fine float of from four to seven days depending on put-in location. Most floats end at the village of Allakaket, at the Alatna's confluence with the Koyukuk. The river is part of the migration route for one of the region's caribou herds.

The North Fork Koyukuk features some rapids in its upper reaches, depending on water levels, but is mostly Class II or less. It passes through Marshall's "Gates of the

Arctic," and there are remains of old gold-mining operations along the way.

The Noatak River is known for running through the largest watershed in North America essentially undisturbed by human activity—though places along its path are areas of concern due to overuse and resource damage. The upper 65 miles of the river lie within Gates of the Arctic, with another 265 miles in Noatak National Preserve. Floating the entire river can take three weeks or more. While there are few technical issues relating to rapids or tricky river-running, the length of a Noatak trip and its remoteness from assistance require careful planning and preparation.

The Kobuk features a few short stretches of rapids up to Class V within canyons on its upper reaches (portaging or lining boats is usually necessary) before reaching lowlands and becoming one of the broad, meandering, sometimes-braided rivers

so common to Alaska. The Kobuk traverses one of the largest contiguous areas of spruce forest in the Brooks Range. The river runs 110 miles through Gates of the Arctic; downstream it passes through Kobuk Valley National Park (see p. 525). Like the Koyukuk, the Kobuk saw a gold rush, after the famed Klondike gold rush of 1897. Most of the gold proved difficult to extract, however, and the booms faded as quickly as they started, though a few miners settled permanently in the area, scraping out a living with prospecting, trapping, fishing, and hunting.

The 52 miles of the John River within the park feature rapids up to Class III+ on the upper sections and gentler floating downstream.

The Tinayguk River is the largest tributary of the North Fork Koyukuk, and is the least visited of the six wild and scenic rivers within Gates of the Arctic.

Visitor center
Bettles, AK
907-692-5494
www.nps.gov/gaar

AT A GLANCE

North of Arctic Circle, 200 miles north of Fairbanks ▪ 8,472,506 acres
▪ Summer ▪ Backpacking, boating, wildlife-watching

Glacier Bay National Park & Preserve

A newly exposed landscape around a bay of incomparable scenery

Glacier Bay National Park and Preserve, although accessible only by boat or airplane, receives more than 400,000 visitors a year. This visitation number is made possible by the massive cruise ships that motor into this narrow, many-armed bay on the Alaska Panhandle, carrying thousands of passengers a day, who stand at railings and enjoy one of the most spectacularly scenic experiences available from a ship anywhere on the planet. Lucky passengers might, in a single day, see a glacier loudly calve an

iceberg into the bay, watch a humpback whale breach the water's surface, spot a brown bear walking along the shore, and admire a bald eagle soaring overhead. All the same sights, and more, are available to kayakers, who paddle Glacier Bay in solitude and quiet, and can camp around its shores for an even more personal experience.

In combination with its neighbors —Wrangell–St. Elias National Park and Preserve (see p. 532) and Canada's Kluane National Park Reserve and Tatshenshini-Alsek Provincial

Park—Glacier Bay National Park and Preserve has been designated a World Heritage site, and the four parks together compose the world's largest international protected wilderness.

Natural History

Sixty-five-mile-long Glacier Bay didn't even exist 250 years ago. When Capt. James Cook, the British navigator who explored much of the Pacific Ocean, sailed along this part of the coast in 1778 he found glacial ice several miles wide, filling what is now the bay.

When Capt. George Vancouver arrived in 1794, the ice had shrunk back to create a bay 5 miles long. Pioneer conservationist John Muir paddled a canoe into the bay in 1879 and found it to be 48 miles long. The Little Ice Age was ending, and the glaciers of Glacier Bay have continued to shrink since, with a few exceptions.

At the mouth of the bay, where melting ice first exposed land around 250 years ago, a mature temperate rain forest of Sitka spruce and western hemlock has established itself. Moving into the bay, the land becomes progressively "newer." Ground from which glaciers retreated only decades ago hosts thickets of alder, cottonwood, and willow. On even newer land grow mosses, avens, horsetail, and the ubiquitous fireweed. Finally, lichens exist on the most recently exposed rock, getting nutrients from the air where there is no soil, and secreting acid that dissolves rock to create soil.

The relatively recent and rapid glacial retreat in Glacier Bay makes it a living laboratory for studying plant succession. In fact, it was the enthusiasm of plant ecologists and other scientists who came here to study the postglacial environment that led to the establishment of the original Glacier Bay National Monument in 1925.

As an adjunct to the retreat of glaciers, the land around Glacier Bay is actually rising. With the weight of uncountable tons of ice removed from the land, the Earth's surface is rising as much as an inch a year, a rate that's among the highest in the world.

Visiting the Park

Apart from cruise-ship passengers, most visitors to Glacier Bay National Park and Preserve arrive via the Alaska capital city of Juneau, from which there are seasonal daily commercial airline flights and year-round daily small-plane flights to the small town of Gustavus. There is also regular ferry service from Juneau to Gustavus *(www.dot.state.ak.us/amhs)*. A 10-mile road links Gustavus to Bartlett Cove, the hub of park activity, on the eastern shore of Glacier Bay. There are also commercial boat tours in the bay, and some visitors arrive in their own boats.

The only commercial lodging within the park is Glacier Bay Lodge *(866-761-6634, www.visitglacierbay .com)*, which stands amid the temperate rain forest at Bartlett Cove. Apart from rooms and a restaurant, the lodge offers a guided boat trip tour. (There are other lodging options in Gustavus.)

The park's visitor center is located on the second floor of Glacier Bay Lodge, with exhibits, information on ranger-led walks and evening programs, and regular showings of several interpretive films in the auditorium. A huge humpback whale skeleton is on display in Bartlett Cove, just a short walk from the lodge. The park's only developed campground lies along the shore of the bay south of the main boat dock and is walk-in tenting only.

Bartlett Cove

While many visitors are eager to get out on the bay and see glaciers and

Icebergs clog a new inlet created by the receding McBride Glacier.

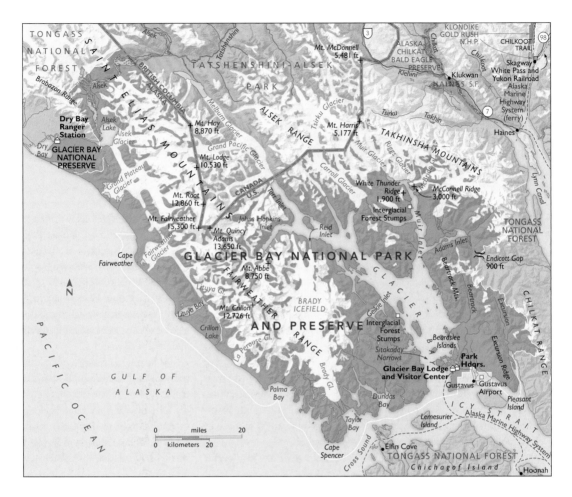

look for wildlife, there are interesting things to do on dry land at Bartlett Cove. The newly opened Huna Tribal House there is a reproduction 18th-century plank Tlingit house that educates visitors on Tlingit culture and the history of Huna clans in Glacier Bay.

The park offers four maintained hiking trails, all located at Bartlett Cove. The easy 1-mile loop Forest Trail passes through both the temperate rain forest and beach environments of Glacier Bay. Park rangers lead guided walks along this trail every afternoon. Songbirds that might be spotted along the trail include ruby-crowned kinglet, varied thrush, hermit thrush, winter wren, and yellow-rumped warbler.

The 4-mile round-trip Bartlett River Trail leads through the forest to the estuary where the river meets the bay. This can be a good spot for wildlife, including harbor seals that congregate to feed on salmon in late summer. The 8-mile Bartlett Lake Trail branches off the river trail to climb a moraine (a ridge of rock pushed up by a moving glacier) and reach the lake, where loons nest.

The Beach Trail runs along the shore of the bay for a mile south of the boat dock, and is excellent for observing the life of tide pools. This hike can be extended to a 6-mile (one way) trek along the shore to Point Gustavus. Here, as elsewhere in the park, hikers must sometimes fight their way through thickets of alder, a tedious experience. Low tide is the best time for the walk. Harbor porpoises, humpback whales, and sea otters are sometimes spotted from the point.

Hikers are free to wander the park's backcountry; a free backcountry permit is required before setting out. Permits and backcountry orientation are available from the visitor information station. All hikers and backpackers need to beware the presence of bears and moose and know how to avoid potentially dangerous encounters. (Moose are recent immigrants to the park: The first one was seen here only in 1966.) Backcountry camping is not allowed within a mile of Bartlett Cove.

Glacier Bay Boat Tour

For those staying at Gustavus or Bartlett Cove, the easiest (and, at least in some ways, the best) way to explore

Glacier Bay is via the daily tour boat *(fee)*. This eight-hour trip departs each morning in summer from the Bartlett Cove dock and makes a trip of 130 miles around the bay. A park ranger helps spot and identify wildlife and provides information on natural history and geology. Binoculars, rain gear, and warm layers of clothing are imperative for this superb trip.

The wildlife spectacle starts quickly, as the boat stops off South Marble Island, where as many as 300 Steller's sea lions may be loafing on the rocks. Bird-watchers enjoy sightings of seabirds such as tufted and horned puffins, common murres, pelagic cormorants, and black-legged kittiwakes (a small gull). This island emerged from its glacier blanket around 1835.

The boat continues deeper into the bay, where humpback whales may be present, having returned from their wintering grounds off Hawai'i. Having many pairs of eyes on board helps in spotting animals such as gray wolves, moose, and black and brown bears along the shoreline. Harbor seals

and sea otters might also be seen; the former has suffered mysterious population declines, while the latter is thriving after having been reintroduced to the park region in the 1960s. High up on cliffs, mountain goats walk along slopes that seem impossibly sheer. To the northwest rise the snowy peaks of the Fairweather Range, topped by 15,320-foot Mount Fairweather, one of the snowiest places on Earth.

Toward the head of the bay, icebergs appear—chunks of ice that have broken off the feet of tidewater glaciers. These glaciers, which once numbered many more than the current seven, extend from high up in intermountain valleys to the bay, where they calve icebergs into the water. Most of the glaciers have retreated and now end before they reach salt water. There are 50 named glaciers in the park, and more than a quarter of the park's total land area is covered in permanent ice. Three glaciers—Grand Pacific, Brady, and Carroll—each cover more than 200 square miles.

The boat tour passes several

tidewater glaciers, pausing so that passengers have a chance to see an iceberg calving—an event that begins with a sound like a rifle shot, followed (in the case of a large iceberg) by a huge splash. Margerie Glacier, in the bay's Tarr Inlet, is a stable tidewater glacier and often the site of iceberg calving. It's one of the few glaciers in the park that is not retreating.

Sea Kayaking

Paddling a sea kayak allows a more intimate experience of Glacier Bay. Kayaks can be rented at Bartlett Cove, and the park authorizes some commercial concessionaires to offer guided kayak trips. One popular trip heads north to the area called Beardslee Entrance, a maze of small islands and narrow channels.

As another alternative, the park's tour boat will also drop off kayakers (and campers) at a few select spots during its daily cruise, allowing paddling in areas far from Bartlett Cove. In all, the park offers kayakers more than 700 miles of coastline to explore.

Bartlett Cove 10 miles northwest of Gustavus, AK 907-697-2230 www.nps.gov/glba	AT A GLANCE	Alaska Panhandle, 50 miles west of Juneau ▪ 3,283,000 acres ▪ Late spring through early fall ▪ Kayaking, boating, hiking, camping, backpacking, wildlife-watching, watching glaciers calve

Iditarod National Historic Trail
A wilderness path that became a world-famous mushing route

The name Iditarod has become synonymous with a world-famous annual dogsled race across central Alaska, a stringent winter test of "mushers" and dog teams. It first garnered attention in 1908, though, as a shorter route across the then territory of Alaska than the existing path from Valdez through Fairbanks to Nome. A gold strike on the Haiditarod River gave impetus to the route, with more

than 65 tons of gold eventually being shipped out of the area, much of it by dogsled to the port of Seward. Further fame arrived in 1925 when diphtheria struck Nome in midwinter, and teams of mushers carried serum 674 miles to the town in five and a half days.

The Iditarod (modified from the river's spelling of Haiditarod) Trail fell into disuse until the 1970s, when Alaskans wishing to draw attention to

its historic significance began a long-distance dogsled race from Anchorage to Nome. The race revived dogsledding and has gone on to become a celebrated sporting event, using much of the original trail route.

Today's Iditarod National Historic Trail generally follows the original 1908 route, with side roads and trails leading to points of interest, bringing the length of the entire system to around

2,400 miles. The trail can be accessed at many points, including parks, nature centers, developed recreational trails, and similar sites. Because of the nature of the terrain and factors such as insects, it's not a route that should be considered a long-distance summer hiking trail. Shorter segments, though, are suitable for day hikes, backpacking, or mountain biking, and in winter it's available for cross-country skiing, snowmobiling, and of course dogsledding. Some sections are paved and suitable for bicycling or family outings.

Among the trail's highlights are the scenic Seward Highway between Seward and Anchorage; the Alaska Railroad through the Chugach National Forest; Girdwood, which features some of the most accessible segments of the original trail; the Eagle

The Siberian husky is one of the breeds used in the Iditarod Sled Dog Race.

River Nature Center in Chugach State Park; and the Iditarod Sled Dog Race headquarters in Wasilla.

The trail is a partnership of several different agencies and organizations and is administered by the Bureau of Land Management. Information is also available from the Iditarod National Historic Trail Alliance *(www .iditarod100.org)*.

BLM Anchorage field office
907-267-1246
www.blm.gov/ak/iditarod

AT A GLANCE

Central Alaska, from Seward to Nome ▪ 2,400 miles ▪ Year-round ▪ Hiking, dogsledding, backpacking, biking, mountain biking, cross-country skiing

Inupiat Heritage Center
Commemorating Inupiat Eskimo contributions to the whaling industry

In the late 19th and early 20th centuries hundreds of whaling ships traveled to the Arctic Ocean off the coast of northern Alaska to seek bowhead whales. Inupiat Eskimos were among the native peoples who worked on ships and cooperated and traded with whalers, making significant contributions to the industry.

The Inupiat Heritage Center in Barrow (the northernmost community in the United States) was established in 1999 to tell the story of the Inupiat people and their part in the commercial whaling heritage of the area. It features exhibits on subjects such as migratory birds, historical photos of life in an Inupiat village, and local artifacts, as well as a gift shop and a traditional room that allows local artists and people to continue their traditions. The center works with local schools and elder groups to share history and traditional knowledge.

The North Slope Borough Department of Inupiat History, Language, and Culture manages the Inupiat Heritage Center, which is affiliated with the New Bedford Whaling National Historical Park (see p. 33) in New Bedford, Massachusetts. New Bedford was the center of the whaling industry not just in the United States but also worldwide. Its ships traveled more than 20,000 miles south through the Atlantic Ocean, around Cape Horn, and north through the Pacific to reach the rich whaling areas of the Arctic and hunt bowhead whales.

5421 N. Star St.
Barrow, AK
907-852-0422
www.nps.gov/inup

AT A GLANCE

Northern Alaska, in Barrow (500 miles north of Fairbanks) ▪ 1 acre ▪ Summer and fall ▪ Viewing exhibits

Katmai National Park & Preserve

Bears galore and a volcanic moonscape

This immense wilderness park—nearly half again as large as Connecticut—is best known for a mammal of proportionately awesome size: the brown bear. During the summer viewing season, visitors can see these huge creatures at close range as they feed on migrating salmon, in a scene as spectacular as any wildlife-watching opportunity in North America. The bears, however, are not the reason Katmai National Park and Preserve exists: The area was set aside originally as a national monument in 1918 to protect the site of one of the largest volcanic eruptions of the 20th century.

A Volcano Erupts

On June 6, 1912, a new vent opened up near Mount Katmai with an explosive force that could be heard in Juneau, 750 miles away. Ten times as powerful as the 1980 eruption of Mount St. Helens in Washington, the eruption lasted for 60 hours; the resulting ash cloud darkened the sky over Kodiak Island, to the south, for three days. More than 6 cubic miles of ash were ejected, covering more than 40 square miles of a nearby mountain valley to depths of up to 700 feet.

Botanist Robert Griggs, during one of a series of expeditions sponsored by the National Geographic Society, discovered an amazing scene as he crossed a mountain pass. "The whole valley as far as the eye could see was full of hundreds, no thousands—literally tens of thousands—of smokes curling up from its fissured floor," he later wrote. The smoking fumaroles inspired Griggs to name the area the Valley of Ten Thousand Smokes.

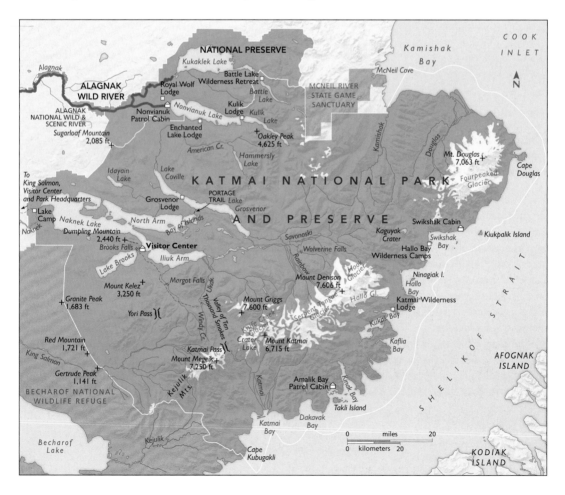

Believing he had found a natural feature as significant as Yellowstone (see p. 495), Griggs spearheaded a campaign for federal protection of the area, and in 1918 President Woodrow Wilson designated it as Katmai National Monument. In 1980 the site was redesignated as Katmai National Park and Preserve, and it has grown to 4.1 million acres in size. Though the Valley of Ten Thousand Smokes no longer displays the number of geothermal features that Griggs saw, it's still a staggeringly stark scene, a moonscape demonstrating the power of volcanism to reshape Earth's surface.

Decades later, geologists determined that the eruption had not occurred from Mount Katmai, as Griggs had thought, but instead from a new vent called Novarupta—"new eruption." Massive amounts of magma were released from the chamber beneath Mount Katmai, causing its summit to collapse and form a caldera, now filled by Crater Lake. The Katmai area remains an active volcanic landscape today, with more than a dozen volcanoes. Further activity is inevitable—though at what future levels no one can predict with certainty.

Visiting the Park

In addition to bears and scenery, the park offers backpacking, kayaking and canoeing, and some of the best fishing in Alaska. Venturing outside the developed areas requires preparation and wilderness experience—especially in regard to precautions necessary in bear country—but adventurous travelers will find unlimited opportunities to explore a little-visited wilderness.

No roads lead from the outside world into Katmai. Most park visitors fly to the community of King

Mount Steller, Kukak Volcano, and Devils Desk, as seen from the Hallo Bay area

Salmon, where the park headquarters and visitor center are located. The Katmai offices also serve as the headquarters for Alagnak Wild River (see p. 502) and Aniakchak National Monument and Preserve (see p. 503). From there, it's a trip by floatplane or boat to Brooks Camp, located where the Brooks River flows into Naknek Lake (the largest lake contained within any unit of the National Park System).

Tour operators can also arrange visits to coastal areas such as Hallo Bay and Geographic Harbor, where brown bears congregate at seasons when they are not common at Brooks Camp. Lodging is available at some coastal locations.

Brooks Camp

Brooks Camp, open early June through mid-September, is the center of most park activity. Floatplane trips can be arranged from other Alaska locations to Brooks Camp. (More than a hundred park-authorized companies operate fishing, hunting, bear-watching, scenic flights,

and other trips in the Katmai area.)

Lodging at Brooks Camp includes both a park-operated campground and a concessionaire-run lodge *(reservations required)*. There are special camp rules regarding food storage and cooking because of the high level of bear activity at the site. On arrival, all visitors attend a program on bear safety. Park rangers work hard to keep bears from associating humans with food—a situation that would lead to potential dangers. The campground is surrounded by an electric fence, which, while not "bearproof," discourages bears from approaching campers.

Park rangers present nightly programs at the Brooks Camp auditorium on topics ranging from wildlife to history to geology. Rangers also lead a short walk around the camp area, explaining why it is also known as the Brooks River Archaeological District and National Historic Landmark. The easy 0.25-mile walk provides information about local archaeological investigations and about the way native peoples used local resources. There is evidence in the area of human

FOLLOWING PAGES: *One of Katmai's some-2,000 brown bears ambles toward the shoreline of Nonvianuk Lake.*

presence dating back 5,000 years, and more than 900 ancient homesites have been found.

The popular Dumpling Mountain Trail is one of the few maintained trails in the park and ascends 800 feet over 1.5 miles (one way) to an overlook with a great vista of Naknek Lake and distant mountains. Visitors may continue another 2.5 miles on the trail, through forest and meadows good for wildlife-spotting, to the top of the mountain.

Bear-watching

A very large percentage of visitors to Brooks Camp arrive specifically to view and photograph browns from a platform that stands beside falls on the Brooks River, about a mile from the lodge and campground. (At times the number of telephoto lenses makes the platform look like an artillery emplacement.) Park rules limit the number of people on the platform; when people are waiting to take a place on the platform, there's a one-hour limit on viewing time. Two other riverside platforms, though not as popular as the falls location, offer alternative viewing sites.

Brown and grizzly bears are the same species (Ursus arctos). Bears that live near the coast are called browns, while inland bears are known as grizzlies. Browns gather in large numbers on the Brooks River for the annual run of sockeye salmon, reaching their peak numbers in July and September. There may be few or no bears present around Brooks Camp in June and August. The park is home to as many as 2,000 brown bears, and up to 100 have been individually spotted in July along the Brooks River.

The presence of these very large (sometimes over 1,000 pounds), fast, and powerful animals means all park visitors need to follow rules designed to minimize the chances of bear encounters. This includes anglers who come to fish for rainbow trout and salmon. Bears that learn to steal fish from anglers present serious problems and, in worst-case situations, might have to be killed. Proper storage of food, avoiding taking odorous substances into the field, and ceasing fishing when a bear approaches can help keep bears wild—and alive.

Valley of Ten Thousand Smokes

Aside from bear-watching, the other must-do activity at Brooks Camp is the seven- to eight-hour ranger-led bus trip (fee) over a 23-mile unpaved road to the Valley of Ten Thousand Smokes. The tour stops for lunch at Three Forks, an overlook with a spectacular view of the valley. Visitors can take an optional ranger-led hike down into the valley. The 3-mile round-trip hike, with an elevation change of 800 feet, provides a chance to see the moonscape-like terrain created by the mammoth 1912 Novarupta eruption. The Ukak River has cut a deep canyon, and its tributaries have carved gorges into the packed ash from the eruption.

Backcountry Camping

Experienced backpackers with the requisite wilderness hiking skills and proper equipment can set out to explore almost anywhere within the vast park, as long as they have done the preparation. In addition to precautions concerning bears, hikers need to be aware of Katmai's notoriously

changeable weather, which can bring cold and rain any time of year. Stream crossings can be dangerous, and hikers should be prepared at times to wait a day or more for safe conditions. No permit is required for backpacking at Katmai, but backcountry hikers are encouraged to inform park rangers of their plans and route.

In the Valley of Ten Thousand Smokes, backpackers can depart from the Three Forks Overlook for multiday trips to sites such as Katmai Pass, from which Robert Griggs first viewed the valley; Novarupta, the 200-foot-high dome of solidified magma that was the extrusion plug of the 1912 eruption; and the caldera lake of 6,715-foot Mount Katmai, crossing the Knife Creek Glaciers.

Savonoski Loop

Another popular adventure at Brooks Camp is the 80-mile Savonoski Loop, a wilderness water trail for canoeists and kayakers. (Canoes and kayaks can be rented at Brooks Camp.) Traveling across Naknek Lake to Grosvenor Lake, along the Grosvenor and Savonoski Rivers to the Iliuk Arm of Naknek Lake and back to Brooks Camp, the journey requires a 1.5-mile portage.

While hard-core paddlers intent on racking up miles might make the trip in four days, most people take up to ten days to enjoy the scenery and wildlife. In addition to brown bears, Katmai is home to moose, caribou, gray wolves, wolverines, lynx, river otters, pine martens, and porcupines. Nesting birds include tundra swans, bald eagles, gyrfalcons, arctic terns, and white-winged crossbills.

King Salmon, AK
907-246-3305
www.nps.gov/katm

AT A GLANCE

Southwestern Alaska, 290 miles southwest of Anchorage ▪ 4,021,384 acres ▪ Summer ▪ Wildlife-watching, hiking, camping, backpacking, fishing, canoeing, kayaking

Kenai Fjords National Park

A massive icefield rising above a stunning coast

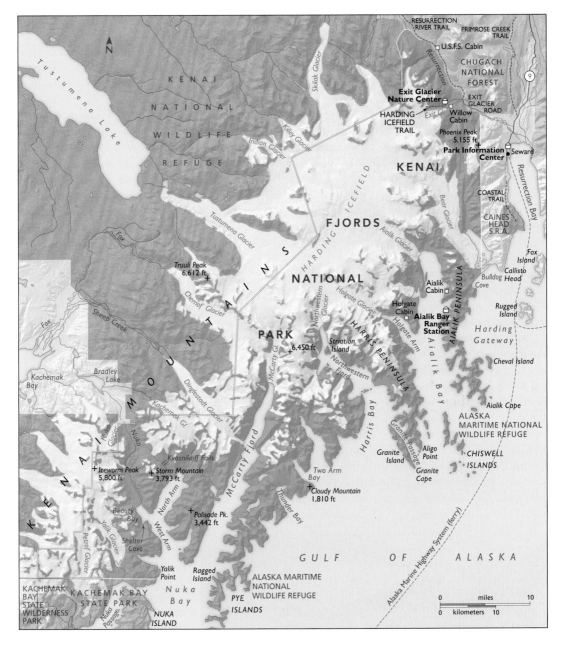

Alaska's smallest national park—yet 20 percent larger than Great Smoky Mountains National Park—Kenai Fjords encompasses a spectacular meeting of land and sea. Rocky headlands jut out into Resurrection Bay and the Gulf of Alaska in terrain that's the very definition of "rugged coastline." The fjords that gave the park its name bring fingers of sea into the Kenai Peninsula along glacier-carved U-shaped valleys.

The crown, literally, of the park is the Harding Icefield. The largest icefield lying entirely within the United

States, it covers more than 700 square miles and is in places thousands of feet thick. Harding Icefield is the parent of nearly 40 glaciers, a few of them reaching downward all the way to the sea.

Between 400 and 800 inches of snow accumulate on the Harding Icefield annually, and new glacier material continues to form. (It can take up to 50 years for snow to compress into glacial ice.) Yet when the rate of melting at the foot of a glacier exceeds the rate of formation, it retreats, and such is the case throughout Kenai Fjords. When ice retreats, land is exposed that may have been locked under ice for thousands of years. Scientists can learn valuable lessons about ecology by studying which plants colonize newly exposed land and which species succeed as time passes. After lichens help create new soil, fireweed is one of the first plants to grow, followed by shrubs such as alder and later by forests of spruce and hemlock.

A massive earthquake that shook this region in 1964 caused the land to drop 7 feet. Vestiges of the event can be seen in the "ghost forests" that formed when the newly lowered coastline was swamped by salt water, killing expanses of spruce and other trees. The relatively narrow fringe of temperate rain forest along the park's convoluted coast provides a home for many animals, and coastal and island cliffs are home to thousands of seabirds.

Visiting the Park

The heart of the park is the Harding Icefield, a beautiful place but one whose environment makes extensive exploration difficult except for experienced mountaineers. Unpredictable weather means those touring the coast by boat should also be well prepared. Many visitors use guides and outfitters to facilitate a trip to Kenai Fjords, leaving the planning and preparation to others who know this country well.

The Kenai Fjords National Park visitor center is located near the small-boat harbor in Seward; it provides maps and advice and shows interpretive films. Lists are available here of companies authorized to provide services such as guided hikes, dogsled tours, flightseeing tours, and fishing trips.

Exit Glacier

Exit Glacier, at the head of the Resurrection River Valley, is the only feature of the national park accessible by road. The 8.6-mile road (3 miles north of Seward, on the Seward Highway) is usually open to vehicles between mid-May and mid-November; it is open for cross-country skiing, dogsledding, and snowmobiling in winter. For those visitors without their own vehicle, a shuttle service and bus tours do run to Exit Glacier. In summer, park rangers are present at a small nature center and offer interpretive programs *(Mem. Day weekend–Labor Day)*.

In the 19th century, Exit Glacier stretched down to the Resurrection River, more than a mile below its present terminal point. Signs along the entrance road indicate where the glacier stood at various years in the past.

From the nature center, visitors can often walk to the foot of Exit Glacier, and see the way glaciers sculpt the landscape, and see plant succession. Approaching the glacier is in a way like going back in time, as the visitor crosses "newer" terrain nearer the ice.

The first 0.25-mile of the trail, passing though a cottonwood forest, is fully wheelchair accessible to a vista called Glacier View, where Exit Glacier can be seen reaching down from Harding Icefield. From Glacier View, the accessible trail loops back to the nature center, or at the trail intersection visitors can head left to cross the outwash plain to the foot of the glacier, or take a moderately strenuous hike to the Edge of the Glacier viewpoint. Park rangers warn about getting too close to overhanging ice: Glaciers constantly reshape themselves, and heavy chunks of ice can fall at any time. (A tourist was killed here in 1987 by an ice ledge that broke away.) Rangers lead nature walks three times a day in summer, and there's a walk-in campground in the area.

For a more adventurous hike, the 8.2-mile round-trip Harding Icefield Trail offers spectacular views as a reward for strenuous exertion. (The trail gains more than 3,000 feet in elevation, and a round trip takes six to eight hours.) Ascending beside Exit Glacier's flank, it passes through alder and cottonwood forests and meadows to reach a point above tree line, where there's a memorable panorama of the Harding Icefield. The expanse of snow and ice reaches to the horizon, the sheet of white broken here and there by a *nunatak* (isolated peak), the exposed summit of a mountain

Kenai Fjords' harbor seal population has severely declined in the past 20 years.

that is completely surrounded by ice.

Bad weather can adversely affect the Harding Icefield Trail at times, and hikers should be aware of the presence of black bears. Attracted by trailside salmonberries, bears are spotted from the trail almost every day, and should be approached no closer than 100 yards. Be especially cautious of females with cubs. Rangers lead hikes on the trail each Saturday in July and August.

Resurrection Bay

Apart from a visit to Exit Glacier, by far the most popular activity at Kenai Fjords National Park is a boat tour south through Resurrection Bay to explore the fjords, experience tidewater glaciers (sheets of ice that extend to meet the sea), and see wildlife. Tours leave from Seward harbor and are offered to match interests (and pocketbooks). Some ships feature heated cabins, onboard restaurants and bars, multiple viewing decks, and national park rangers to provide narration and spot and identify wildlife. All-day trips (six hours or more) make a cruise of more than 100 miles to Aialik Bay to see a tidewater glacier, where there's a chance of seeing a large chunk of ice calve (break) off the snout of the glacier and crash into the water. Some tours also cruise past the Chiswell Islands, part of Alaska Maritime National Wildlife Refuge.

Marine mammals often seen on cruises include humpback whales, orcas (also called killer whales, though they are dolphins), harbor seals, Steller's sea lions, Dall's porpoises, and sea otters. As winter approaches, humpbacks generally migrate to the waters around Hawai'i and birth their young;

they return to the subarctic seas in summer, when plankton is abundant. Three groups of orcas are found in the waters near the park: residents that eat fish; transients that eat marine mammals such as seals; and offshore orcas that stay in open water and eat fish.

While everyone enjoys the sight of a bald eagle or puffin, avid birdwatchers thrill at the notable array of species a Kenai Fjords cruise affords. A partial list of possible birds includes red-faced and pelagic cormorants, harlequin duck, black oystercatcher, mew gull, black-legged kittiwake, common murre, pigeon guillemot, and horned and tufted puffins. Some of these species, such as murres and cormorants, nest on sea cliffs in enormous colonies, creating an amazing spectacle during the height of breeding season when the sky is filled with birds arriving and leaving their nests.

Visitors who opt for a boat tour should dress in layers, including a wind- and waterproof top layer, and wear a hat, gloves, and sunglasses. Even if a tour advertises a heated cabin for comfortable viewing, the panorama is better from an open deck, and the wind can create very chilly conditions even on a sunny summer day.

Sea Kayaking

Paddling a sea kayak around the coastline for close-up views of cliffs and glaciers can be a memorable adventure for park visitors. But it is not without its risks. Sea kayakers without extensive experience, including paddling in high wind and rough seas, should take a guided kayak trip. Many outfitters in the Seward area offer kayak tours that range from half a day to a week or more.

Kayakers need to know that Resurrection Bay on a calm day might not present problems, but heading farther south can lead to potential danger. Kayaking around Aialik Cape, for example, is not recommended because of treacherous waters and long stretches of coastline with no landing spots. Water taxi and floatplanes can drop kayakers off in a bay for a camping-paddling trip.

It's best to check with park rangers about campsites in the park's bays, as some are closed at times for resource protection and others may present issues of high surf or bear visitation. It's also important to be aware of private property within the park boundary owned by the native village corporation of Port Graham. Permits may be required for visits to these areas.

Hiking & Flightseeing

The routes in the Exit Glacier area are the park's only maintained trails, and traveling in the backcountry is discouraged for casual hikers. Experienced local outfitters offer guided trips that allow visits to the Harding Icefield area. In this extreme climate, backpackers should be prepared for sudden spells of high winds, rain, and cold that can cause delays of a day or more even in summer.

The ultimate grand-scale view of the park comes on a flightseeing trip, which gives passengers a panorama of the expanse of the Harding Icefield and the fjords of the coast. Because flightseeing trips do not land in the park, the National Park Service does not authorize concessionaires, but the Seward Chamber of Commerce (www.sewardak.org) can provide a list of companies that offer flights.

1212 4th Ave.
Seward, AK
907-422-0500
www.nps.gov/kefj

AT A GLANCE

South-central Alaska, 125 miles south of Anchorage ▪ 670,000 acres ▪ Year-round ▪ Hiking, boat tours, kayaking, camping, mountaineering, flightseeing, snowshoeing, dogsledding, cross-country skiing, snowmobiling

Klondike Gold Rush National Historical Park
Reliving the great Yukon gold rush of 1897–98

In 1896, a small group out looking for salmon found gold in a tributary of the Klondike River in Canada's Yukon Territory. When word made it to the outside world, their discovery set off one of the most famous gold rushes in history.

In 1897, thousands of fortune seekers boarded ships in Seattle and other West Coast cities for the trip to Alaska, first stop on their road to riches (at least in their dreams). Skagway and Dyea sprang up almost overnight into boomtowns where would-be prospectors prepared themselves for the arduous 600-mile trip to the Yukon. Few of those headed for the goldfields knew that most of the good claims had already been staked, and only a tiny fraction of them struck it rich. The boom was essentially finished after three years. Although Skagway survived, Dyea—home at its peak to 48 hotels and 39 taverns—dwindled to a ghost town.

Klondike Gold Rush National Historical Park tells the story of the great Yukon gold rush. The park visitor center *(May–Sept.)* and museum *(year-round),* located in the restored White Pass & Yukon Route rail depot, has maps and historical exhibits, and shows a film, "Gold Fever: Race to the Klondike," several times a day. Park rangers present programs on various topics in the auditorium. Rangers also lead guided tours of Skagway. Within Skagway's historic downtown are several other park sites, including the 1904 Mascot Saloon and the Moore House and Cabin, which relate the experience of early homesteaders.

A modern passenger train on the historic White Pass & Yukon Route Railroad.

Just a few miles northwest of Skagway stand the remains of Dyea, the boomtown that was the starting point for the Chilkoot Trail, one of the two routes that prospectors took over the mountains to Bennett Lake, where they built boats for the trip downriver to the goldfields. When a railroad was completed up the Skagway River Valley, travel ceased on the Chilkoot Trail. (The *White Pass & Yukon Route* is now a popular tourist train.)

Today there is a primitive campground at Dyea, and rangers lead seasonal tours of the old town site. Many people make the strenuous 33-mile, three- to five-day hike up the Chilkoot Trail, which was originally a trade route of the Tlingit Indians. Visitors are required to check with rangers before beginning this challenging trek to learn about trail conditions and about customs requirements for entering Canada. Local outfitters can help with planning a hike and arranging a shuttle back to Dyea or Skagway. The Chilkoot Trail takes hikers from sea level to alpine tundra in just 16 miles.

Seattle Unit

A separate unit of the park is located in Seattle, Washington, in the historic Cadillac Hotel at the corner of Jackson Street and Second Avenue *(206-220-4240, www.nps.gov/klse).* Exhibits tell the story of the gold rush of 1897–98, focusing on the role Seattle played as the major outfitting and transportation link for those heading to Alaska and on to the Yukon. Interactive exhibits allow visitors to experience the gold rush through the stories of would-be prospectors, using journals and personal accounts. Seasonal programs include gold-panning demonstrations and ranger-led walking tours of nearby

Pioneer Square Historic District. The park partners with two Canadian sites, Chilkoot Trail National

Historic Site and Dawson Historical Complex National Historic Sites, in interpreting the Yukon gold-rush days.

2nd Ave. & Broadway St.
Skagway, AK
907-983-9200
www.nps.gov/klgo

AT A GLANCE

Southeastern Alaska, 96 miles north of Juneau ▪ 13,191 acres ▪ Year-round ▪ Visiting historic sites, hiking, camping, riding historic train

Kobuk Valley National Park
The geologic curiosity of sand dunes in the Arctic

The Western Arctic caribou herd, numbering close to 235,000 animals, annually migrates through the Kobuk Valley.

The name Kobuk is said to come from an Inupiaq Eskimo word meaning "big river," and in places in this park the Kobuk River is indeed big—at least in width. Originating in the mountains of Gates of the Arctic National Park and Preserve (see p. 509), it churns through canyons in Class V white-water rapids. By the time it reaches the lowlands of Kobuk Valley National Park, however, the river flows tranquilly in braided channels—wide, but

for most of the year not very deep.

For millennia, vast herds of caribou have used this valley as a migration route, moving north in spring, south in fall. For at least 9,000 years, humans have met them here to harvest meat to eat in the arctic winters. Today, Kobuk Valley National Park in northwestern Alaska, 35 miles north of the Arctic Circle, sees about half a million migrant caribou twice annually, and hunters wait for the animals, the largest caribou herd in Alaska.

Kobuk Valley is best known for a geologic oddity dating back to the Pleistocene. At least five times, vast glacier fields moved across northwestern Alaska during cold periods, and retreated with planetary warming. Between two early glaciation periods, probably around 33,000 years ago, retreating ice left pulverized rock in its wake. This material was blown by prevailing easterly winds into an expansive tract of sand dunes, some 200 feet high or more. Covering an area of

The following labels appear on the map:

NOATAK NATIONAL WILD & SCENIC RIVER

Kanaktok Mountain 3,320 ft

Noatak

+ 948 ft

NOATAK NATIONAL PRESERVE

Kunyanak Cr.

Kangyat Cr.

Saburi Cr.

Kanaktok Cr.

Salmon

Namielik Creek

Cutler

Imelyok

Mt. Angayukaqsraq 4,760 ft +

Natmotirok Cr.

Nokolikurok Cr.

Anaktok Cr.

B A I R D

Sheep Cr.

+ 3,928 ft

M O U N

4,040 ft +

N

Cutler

+ 3,310 ft

SALMON NATIONAL WILD & SCENIC RIVER

Tutuksuk

Hunt

Akiak Mountains

+ 4,056 ft

2,678 ft +

+ 3,699 ft

Akiak Cr.

3,383 ft +

T A I N S

+ 3,550 ft

Kikok

Salmon

+ 3,370 ft

Akillik

+ 3,446 ft

K O B U K   V A L L E Y   N A T I O N A L   P A R K

Nekakte Cr.

3,490 ft +

2,905 ft +

Kitlik

Kallarichuk

Klery Cr.

K a l l a r i c h u k   H i l l s

Tutuksuk

295 ft +

Kaligurncheak

Hunt

Nuna Cr.

+ 3,333 ft

Miluet Cr.

+ 471 ft

Jade Mountains

3,485 ft +

Kallarichuk

Salmon

231 ft +

Kobuk

Akillik

Ambler

Onion Portage Ranger Station (summer only)

334 ft + Ambler

Nigeruk Cr.

Kallarichuk Ranger Station (summer only)

2,261 ft

Great Kobuk Sand Dunes

Natuakik Cr.

Nakochelik Cr.

Tununuk Cr.

Kobuk

Kovet Creek

Squirrel Cr.

166 ft • Kiana

WINTER TRAIL

Kobuk

+ 1,364 ft

W A R I N G   M O U N T A I N S

2,102 ft +

Little Kobuk Sand Dunes

SELAWIK NATIONAL WILDLIFE REFUGE

0   miles   20
0   kilometers   20

---

25 square miles, these barchan dunes (crescent shaped, with tips pointing downwind) make up the largest area of sand dunes north of the Arctic Circle in North America. A combination of the terrain's topography and winds keep the dunes in motion.

The Northwest Arctic Heritage Center in Kotzebue is open year-round and provides information on Kobuk Valley and other federal lands in the area, including Cape Krusenstern National Monument (see p. 504), Noatak National Preserve (see p. 530), and nearby national wildlife refuges.

Kobuk Valley National Park has no maintained trails or campsites. Access is by airplane or boat (or, for extremely hardy winter travelers with their own equipment, by dogsled or snowmobile).

Kobuk is one of the least visited units within the entire National Park System. Many of its visitors—only 1,000 to 2,000 annually—fly to the village of Ambler, east of the park boundary, and float the Kobuk River downstream to the village of Kiana, west of the park. It usually takes five to seven days to float

the 61 miles of slow-moving river through the park.

Floating the Kobuk River

The floating season on the Kobuk is short. Ice can remain on the river into June, and the water can start to freeze again as early as late September. Late August is in some ways the best time to visit, coinciding with the great caribou migration. At this time, local Inupiaq hunters, the only people allowed to hunt in the park, gather at favored spots to harvest caribou as many generations of their ancestors have done.

In August and September the mosquitoes are usually less abundant than in June and July—an important consideration for Alaska travelers.

Within the park, boaters can stop along the river (about 1 mile east of Kavet Creek is a good spot) and hike south into the dune field to explore this geologic anomaly, where—despite being north of the Arctic Circle—temperatures occasionally top 100 degrees in summer. A plant called Kobuk locoweed *(Oxytropis kobukensis)* is endemic to these dunes.

The boreal forest reaches its northern limit in the park area, so woodland consists mainly of an open growth of small spruce and birch trees dotting an expanse of thick tundra. On the western edge of the sand dunes, vegetation is moving onto the dunes, with the tops of spruces sticking up above the dunes. Even though Kobuk Valley gets only 20 inches of rain and snow a year, much of the lowland tundra is perpetually soggy because subsurface permafrost keeps water from draining away. For this reason, cross-country hiking is much easier along drier ridgelines than across the squishy tundra.

Boaters on the Kobuk River should be aware that private property exists within the boundaries of the national park. Privately owned structures and camps should be avoided.

Those exploring Kobuk Valley National Park may well come upon evidence of human activities, recent and very ancient. As is true in all national parks, such historical artifacts are protected, and archaeological sites should not be disturbed in any way. At Onion Portage, archaeologists have excavated evidence of nine cultural complexes, ranging from the Akmak Complex (about 8,000–6,500 B.C.) to the Arctic Woodland Eskimo (about A.D. 1000–1700). All these peoples depended on caribou as a major food source, hunting them as they crossed the river at this spot. The stratigraphic sequence found at Onion Portage is used as the model for a cultural chronology for this region.

Anglers fishing within the Kobuk River drainage find abundant grayling, chum salmon, and sheefish, the last a type of whitefish that can grow to 40 pounds or more.

Kobuk Valley is grizzly-bear country, and bear-resistant food containers are a necessity. Campers should store and cook food at least 100 yards from their campsite to minimize the chance of bear visits.

The park can provide a list of outfitters authorized to offer air-taxi service, guided fishing or backpacking trips, and other services.

Kotzebue, AK
907-442-3890
www.nps.gov/kova

AT A GLANCE

Northwestern Alaska, 200 miles northeast of Nome ▪ 1,795,280 acres ▪ Year-round ▪ Boating, hiking, backpacking, fishing, snowmobiling, dogsledding

Lake Clark National Park & Preserve
Wild rivers and glacial lakes amid a volcanic landscape

Lake Clark National Park and Preserve offers visitors a microcosm of vast Alaska: alpine tundra, coastal rain forest, spectacularly rugged mountains, three designated National Wild Rivers, glacier-carved lakes (including Alaska's sixth largest), and an array of wildlife for which the state is famed.

Volcanoes are part of Alaska, and they, too, compose part of Lake Clark, adding their earth-altering actions to the ancient work of glaciers. In late March 2009, Redoubt volcano provided unquestionable proof that southern Alaska constitutes one of the most tectonically active places in the world. Redoubt, one of two active volcanoes in Lake Clark National Park and Preserve (two others lie just outside the park boundary) began an eruption cycle that included earthquakes, steam and gas emissions, debris flows (lahars), and ash clouds rising to heights of more than 60,000 feet. After multiple explosive events, an enormous lava dome formed, filling the north side summit vent.

Seismic activity has since subsided and according to the latest report (as of press time for this book), Redoubt is in a "typical background, noneruptive state."

Visiting the Park
Situated relatively close (by Alaska standards) to Anchorage, Lake Clark ranks among the least visited national parks. It is a wilderness park. No roads provide access. Boats can enter the park via Cook Inlet, but most people arrive either by floatplane, which lands on lakes; or wheeled plane, which lands on unpaved airstrips, beaches, or riverside gravel bars. Visitors commonly arrange to be dropped off and picked up, either at the same spot or, in the case of river trips, at a spot downstream.

With few exceptions, no

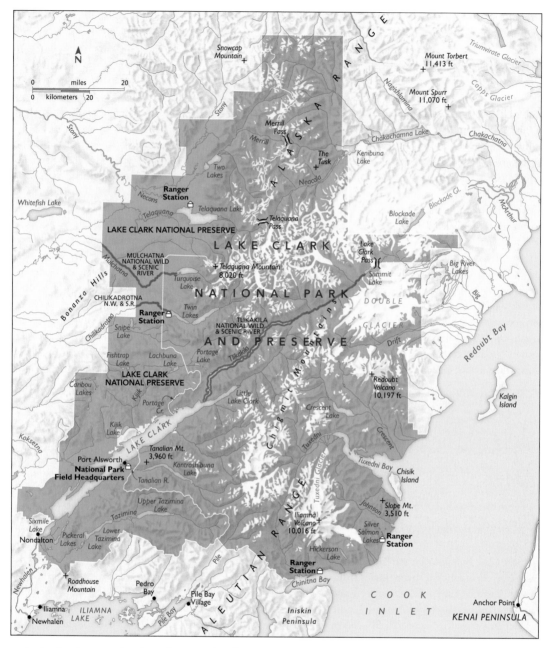

maintained trails exist within the park; neither are there developed campgrounds. The park's remoteness—lack of facilities, healthy population of bears, and unpredictable weather—means that travelers heading to the backcountry should either be self-sufficient and experienced in wilderness skills or use a guide service.

All this is not to discourage travelers from going to Lake Clark. On the contrary, adventurous visitors will find an expanse of superb terrain that can be enjoyed in solitude, and many local outfitters offer guided trips for backpacking, fishing, bear viewing, or river running. In addition, several lodges located in the area provide comfortable places to stay with easy access to park lakes and rivers.

June through September is by far the most popular time for visits.

The park's Field Headquarters is located in Port Alsworth on the shore of Lake Clark, and features a small visitor center (907-781-2117). The center offers exhibits on nature and history, a gift shop, and occasional programs. Most important, it's home to park rangers who can provide up-to-date information on travel conditions and advice about activities and safety. Port Alsworth has two private airstrips, lodging, and a post office.

The park also has a field office *(907-235-7903)* in Homer, on the Kenai Peninsula, and during the summer months rangers provide programs at the Alaska Islands and Ocean Visitor Center and the Pratt Museum, both in Homer. Homer is one of several towns in the Lake Clark region where air taxis and guides can be hired.

Hiking Routes

The park's only developed hiking routes, the Tanalian Falls Trail System, begin at a trailhead in Port Alsworth. The 2.4-mile (one way) hike to the falls ascends through a forest of black and white spruce and white birch, with thickets of alder—the bane of cross-country hikers in much

of Alaska—here and there. Fireweed, dwarf dogwood, and Labrador tea, ubiquitous in the north country, grow along the trail, as do salmonberries, blueberries, cranberries, and crowberries. When these treats ripen they attract hungry bears, so hikers on this trail (as everywhere in the park) should talk, sing, clap hands, or shout occasionally to encourage bears to move away.

The trail parallels the Tanalian River, which flows from Kontrashibuna Lake to Lake Clark, to reach the pretty falls, foaming between large boulders. It's only a half mile farther to reach Kontrashibuna Lake, one of the many park lakes offering excellent fishing for species such as arctic char and lake trout.

Before reaching the falls, an often marshy side trail leads to a beaver pond where moose and waterfowl might be seen. Another route, splitting off the Beaver Pond Loop, reaches the western

slope of Tanalian Mountain and continues to the 3,960-foot summit, gaining a total of 3,600 feet (from Lake Clark) in about 4.1 miles. There's no marked trail to the top, and hikers are encouraged to spread out across the tundra rather than walk in single file to minimize damage to fragile vegetation.

The park's most notable long-distance backpacking route is the 50-mile Telaquana Trail, a historic native Dena'ina Athabaskan route from Telaquana Lake to Lake Clark. Unmarked and unmaintained, it calls for backcountry experience, good preparation, and wilderness hiking skills. The route fords rivers, ascends to high mountain passes, and crosses tundra. Interested hikers should contact a field office for advice. Most hikers are dropped by air taxi at Telaquana Lake and walk to Lake Clark, although beginning at different lakes offers opportunities for shorter hikes.

The forest-clad slopes of Tanalian Mountain are reflected on the surface of Lake Clark, Alaska's sixth largest lake.

Rafting the Rivers

Other than hunting (allowed in the preserve section in season) and fishing, the most popular activity in the area is rafting the park's rivers. Three of the rivers—Mulchatna, Chilikadrotna, and Tlikakila—are designated National Wild Rivers. Several outfitters offer rafting trips, which simplifies the logistics of arranging for transportation, food, and camping gear for a trip of several days or longer.

The Mulchatna offers trips of 100 to 230 miles, and is suitable for small rafts and kayaks, with rapids up to Class III. The Chilikadrotna (the "Chilly") is narrow and twisting with limited Class III rapids; trips vary from 70 to 200 miles when combined with the Mulchatna. Beginning at Twin Lakes (where there is a seasonally staffed patrol cabin), the Chilly is popular with fly-in anglers as well as boaters. The Tlikakila, fed by 150 glaciers, runs through the park; it has white water to Class IV, with a usual trip length of 70 miles. (Airplanes buzz through the valley regularly, following the main air route between Anchorage and southwestern Alaska.)

Raft or kayak river trips intersperse river running with relaxing on gravel bars, observing wildlife, taking short hikes, and fishing. (Tlikakila, has poor fishing due to the glacial silt in the water.) Even more freedom is available to those who bring canoes or kayaks to one of the many splendid lakes in the park, taking several days to paddle leisurely around and camp. (Those who'd like to try such a trip must transport watercraft in small planes, so inflatable kayaks are a good solution.) Park rangers urge caution even on calm-looking inland lakes. Rain and high winds can blow in quickly, causing a dangerous situation for paddlers caught in significant waves. Lakes such as Telaquana, Turquoise, Upper and Lower Tazimina, Clark, and Kontrashibuna are all popular with boaters.

Wildlife

Some regional outfitters specialize in trips to see and photograph the park's brown bears, but these predators are only one species among many found within Lake Clark National Park and Preserve. Black bears, caribou, moose, gray wolves, red foxes, lynx, wolverines, river otters, and beavers all make the park home. White Dall sheep might be spotted along the western slopes of the Chigmit Mountains on the west side of the park or on the slopes of Tanalian Mountain.

Birds within the park include raptors such as bald eagles, ospreys, peregrine falcons, gyrfalcons, and merlins. Both tundra and trumpeter swans might be seen here, and more than two dozen species of ducks have been seen in the park. Montane-nesting shorebirds breed in the tundra along the west side of the mountains.

Kijik National Historic Landmark

Situated on the north shore of Lake Clark, Kijik National Historic Landmark contains the world's largest concentration of prehistoric and historic Dena'ina Athabaskan houses. The Kijik area, which includes Kijik Lake and the Kijik River between the lake and Lake Clark, possesses a large number of archaeological sites, including a village possibly dating from the 18th century and abandoned at the beginning of the 20th century. The Dena'ina Athabaskan people continue to live throughout the region and are just part of the human history of the area, which encompasses continuous occupation for at least 10,000 years.

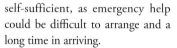

AT A GLANCE	
Field headquarters Port Alsworth, AK 907-781-2218 www.nps.gov/lacl	South-central Alaska, 160 miles southwest of Anchorage ▪ 4,030,025 acres ▪ Summer ▪ Backpacking, hiking, rafting, kayaking, wildlife-watching, fishing

Noatak National Preserve
The largest wilderness watershed in North America

The huge, remote Noatak National Preserve—lying entirely north of the Arctic Circle—was established to protect the largest undisturbed watershed in North America, the region drained by the Noatak River. The upper reaches of the river lie within Gates of the Arctic National Park and Preserve (see p. 509). The preserve is generally reached only by airplane; it has no roads, trails, campgrounds, or regularly staffed ranger stations. Visitors must be prepared to be entirely self-sufficient, as emergency help could be difficult to arrange and a long time in arriving.

Most visitors to the park (other than native people) are hunters on guided trips or boaters rafting or kayaking down the Noatak, designated a national wild river for 330 miles of its 400-mile length. The park can provide a list of authorized outfitters and guide services. While the river does not present many technical challenges in terms of white water, the trip—which may last two to three weeks—involves dealing with weather, bears, food, and logistical issues related to access.

The Western Arctic caribou herd, about 235,000 animals, travels through Noatak National Preserve twice a year, migrating between its southern wintering areas and northern calving grounds. Within the preserve runs the northern tree line, where the boreal coniferous forest gives way to tundra. Grizzly bears, gray wolves, moose, arctic foxes, snowy owls, gyrfalcons, and many species of water-fowl make the area home.

The Northwest Arctic Heritage Center in Kotzebue is open year-round and provides information on Noatak and other federal lands in the area, including Cape Krusenstern National Monument (see p. 504), Kobuk Valley National Park (see p. 525), and nearby national wildlife refuges.

see p. 504 ... see p. 525

AT A GLANCE

Kotzebue, AK
907-442-3890
www.nps.gov/noat

Northwestern Alaska, 250 miles northeast of Nome ▪ 6,721,280 acres ▪ Summer ▪ River rafting, backpacking

---

Sitka National Historical Park

A battle site that interprets Tlingit culture

In 1804, a battle took place near today's city of Sitka, Alaska, between native Tlingits and Russian fur traders and military forces. The site of this last major clash between Europeans and northwestern native people, on what is now called Baranof Island, is commemorated as Sitka National Historical Park, designated as Alaska's first federal park in 1890. A district governor later collected totem poles from villages in southeastern Alaska, and more than a dozen Tlingit and Haida poles were placed along the park's trails in the early 1900s.

Sitka National Historical Park is located along both banks of the mouth of the Indian River on the east side of Sitka. It includes a visitor center featuring exhibits on traditional Tlingit life and interactions with Russian colonists. A 12-minute film entitled "The Voices of Sitka" is shown regularly. Within the center is

A smiling bear figure on a totem pole

the Southeast Alaska Indian Cultural Center, where world-renowned local artists keep traditional Tlingit art forms alive.

Two miles of trails wind through a temperate rain forest of Sitka spruce

and western hemlock and past totem poles, some of them re-creations of those poles that had suffered weathering. (The originals stand in the visitor center's Totem Hall.) Only a clearing remains at the site of the Tlingit fort, which was bombarded by Russian navy ships in the 1804 battle.

A separate unit of the park, the Russian Bishop's House, stands 0.4 mile away in downtown Sitka. The restored 1843 log building was once the center of Russian Orthodox Church regional authority. Exhibits interpret the 125-year period when Russia was the dominant colonial power along the northwestern coast of North America, an era lasting until the United States bought Alaska in 1867. The structure is one of four surviving examples of Russian colonial architecture in North America, and it houses 19th-century Russian furniture and Orthodox icons.

AT A GLANCE

106 Metlakatla St.
Sitka, AK
907-747-0110
www.nps.gov/sitk

Alaska Panhandle, 90 miles south of Juneau ▪ 112 acres ▪ Summer and fall ▪ Viewing historic sites and totem poles, watching cultural demonstrations, hiking

Wrangell–St. Elias National Park & Preserve
The vast wilderness of America's largest national park

Just as it is impossible to talk about Alaska without acknowledging its size (more than twice as large as the second biggest state, Texas), it would be folly to introduce Wrangell–St. Elias National Park and Preserve and not state immediately its rank as the largest national park in the United States—six times the size of Yellowstone National Park (see p. 495), and twice as big as the state of Maryland. Wrangell–St. Elias has a wilderness area as large as Massachusetts and Connecticut combined.

Much else about Wrangell–St. Elias can serve as symbolic of Alaska as well. The great majority of its area is difficult to access, with only two roads penetrating relatively short distances into its interior. There's a brief peak season for visitation, from around mid-May to mid-September, though hardy travelers can extend that period. Visitors often must deal with fickle weather, poor road conditions, and plagues of insects, and need always to be aware that wildlife in Alaska is truly wild and can be dangerous.

There have been controversies in the park's history over public versus private land, preservation versus development, and hunting areas versus wildlife refuges. Yet despite its remoteness, lack of typical tourism amenities, and past land-use disputes, the essential fact remains that Wrangell–St. Elias National Park and Preserve—just like Alaska—is a vast area of spectacular scenery, exciting recreational opportunities, and abundant wildlife, offering endless chances for adventure, solitude, and challenge. It encompasses awe-inspiring mountains, rushing rivers, massive glaciers, expansive tundra, and rugged coast. And no one, no matter how dedicated, could ever hope to explore more than a part of it.

Four major mountain ranges extend into the park: Wrangell, St. Elias, Chugach, and the eastern part of the Alaska Range. The St. Elias Mountains are the world's tallest coastal range, and Mount St. Elias, at 18,008 feet, is the second highest peak in the United States. Wrangell–St. Elias includes 9 of the 16 highest mountains in the country.

Steam vents and the occasional earthquake demonstrate that the earth beneath these mountains is seismically and volcanically active, as the Pacific and North American Continental plates push against each other deep beneath the surface. On clear, calm days, steam can be seen coming from Mount Wrangell—at 14,163 feet, the largest active volcano in Alaska. (It last erupted in 1900.)

Perpetual ice and snow cover as much as one-fourth of Wrangell–St. Elias, bringing another set of superlatives: Malaspina Glacier, larger than the state of Rhode Island, is the largest nonpolar piedmont glacier on the continent; Nabesna Glacier, at around 76 miles, is the longest nonpolar valley glacier; and 92-mile-long Hubbard Glacier is one of the largest and most active tidewater glaciers.

In combination with its neighbors—Glacier Bay National Park and Preserve (see p. 511) and Canada's Kluane National Park Reserve and Tatshenshini-Alsek Provincial Park—Wrangell–St. Elias has been designated a World Heritage site, and the four parks together compose the world's largest international protected wilderness.

The process of designating parks in Alaska has sometimes brought contention, as conservationists square off against logging, mining, and hunting interests. Many compromises have

been made to accommodate the needs and desires of differing viewpoints, including those of Alaska natives wishing to continue traditional subsistence activities. The "preserve" part of the Wrangell–St. Elias designation, as is the case with many Alaska parks, means that sport hunting is allowed. The park's wilderness allows airplanes, all-terrain vehicles, snowmobiles, and cabins. Nonetheless, human activities affect only a tiny fraction of the park area, and anyone who wants to be alone in the natural world will find unlimited opportunities here.

Visiting the Park

The park's attractive visitor center is located in the community of Copper Center on the Richardson Highway. A three-dimensional map there provides a good overview of the park's mountains, rivers, and glaciers, and there's an interpretive film on the area. The easy Boreal Forest Trail, a 0.5-mile loop, passes among white

Beautiful 18,008-foot Mount St. Elias, on the U.S.-Canadian border, is the second highest peak in the United States.

and black spruce, aspen, and willow to a view of the Wrangell Mountains to the east, dominated by 12,010-foot Mount Drum. The Copper River, an important salmon stream, flows below. Birds such as gray jay, varied thrush, pine grosbeak, and common redpoll flit through the trees, and a lucky visitor might spot a black bear or red fox.

Many outfitters and concessionaires offer tours into Wrangell–St. Elias National Park and Preserve, from river rafting and sea kayaking to scenic flights and guided hikes across glaciers. Considering the park's size and the logistical problems involved in arranging transportation and supplies, using an outfitter makes sense for many adventure seekers. The park provides a list of authorized guide companies, many of which are based in small towns around the park perimeter.

Those who wish to explore the park on their own can (with care and depending on weather) enter the park on two mostly unpaved roads, which provide access to trailheads, campsites, and historic sites.

McCarthy Road

The McCarthy Road begins in the community of Chitina, the end of the Edgerton Highway, and runs 59 miles through boreal forest to the towns of McCarthy and Kennicott. Located in part on an old railroad right-of-way, the road can take up to three hours to navigate, and drivers should check with the park office for conditions before starting. Some rental-car companies do not allow their vehicles on this road. A good spare tire and a jack are necessities.

There's a park ranger station (907-823-2205) at Chitina. Nearby, the McCarthy Road crosses the Copper River, where local residents can often be seen fishing for salmon.

After crossing two more rivers (Kuskulana, on an old railroad bridge; and Gilahina), the road arrives at the Kennicott River, where there's a park information station, open in summer. Just a mile farther, the road effectively ends for visitors. To continue on to the town of McCarthy, visitors must park, cross a footbridge, then either walk or take a shuttle bus to the town, where a store, lodging, dining, guide services, an airstrip, and a museum can be found.

The abandoned town and mill site of the Kennecott copper mine, a national historic landmark, lie 5 miles farther up the road from McCarthy. (The two different spellings result from the company's mistaking the name of an early explorer.) Between 1911 and 1938, almost $200 million in copper was extracted from the mines here. While anyone can walk around the ghost town, some of the buildings' interiors can be toured only with a guide. Visitors can reach Kennecott by bus, bicycle, foot, or guided tour. The Kennecott Visitor Center is open Memorial Day to Labor Day.

The popular 4-mile round-trip Root Glacier Trail leaves from Kennecott. It allows an up-close look at one of the park's numerous glaciers. Several other trails begin in the McCarthy-Kennecott area, including strenuous hikes to old mine sites at Bonanza and Jumbo.

Nabesna Road

The other vehicle access route into the park's interior is the Nabesna Road, which begins on the Tok Cutoff–Glenn Highway. The Slana Ranger Station (907-822-7401) can provide information on the 42-mile unpaved road, which is usually passable by regular passenger cars—although high-clearance 4WD vehicles are sometimes needed past mile 29.

At mile 4, a side road leads to the Slana settlement, one of the last places in the U.S. opened to homesteading. Although 800 claims were filed, most were eventually abandoned when homesteaders faced the reality of Alaska winters and lack of employment opportunities. Beginning at about mile 15, there are fabulous views of the Wrangell Mountains to the south. Mount Sanford, at 16,237 feet, is the sixth highest mountain in the U.S.

Trailheads along the road provide access to the park's environment. The easy, 6-mile round-trip Caribou Creek Trail at mile 19.5 can be good for spotting not just caribou but moose, grizzly (brown) and black bears, gray wolves, red foxes, and porcupines—or at least the signs of these mammals. More likely to be seen are red squirrels, arctic ground squirrels, and snowshoe hares, as well as birds such as black-billed magpies, hermit thrushes, Wilson's warblers, and white-crowned sparrows. Hikers should be aware that trails in this area are used by all-terrain vehicles and can be very muddy at times.

The Kendesnii Campground at mile 27.8 is one of several spots offering primitive campsites, and one of several places with good fishing for trout, grayling, and other species. At mile 36.8, the Skookum Volcano Trail ascends 2.5 miles to a beautiful mountain pass through a landscape of volcanic features where Dall sheep may graze. Wrangell–St. Elias contains one of the largest concentrations of Dall sheep in North America.

The last few miles of the road offer wonderful mountain views and additional chances to spot Dall sheep. The road ends at the former mining town of Nabesna, where there is an airstrip. Private property should be avoided, especially mine sites that are occasionally still worked. Hikers should stay clear of piles of highly acidic mine tailings, the waste left after minerals have been extracted.

The Backcountry

Few places in the U.S. offer such opportunities for wildness and solitude as Wrangell–St. Elias. No permit is required for backpacking, but hikers are encouraged to fill out a backcountry itinerary at a park visitor center. Hikers in remote areas should be aware of the presence of bears and moose and take proper precautions. Good map-reading skills are a must, since the park has very few marked trails, and cross-country route finding is necessary. Extra food should always be taken in the event that high water makes streams unfordable or bad weather delays the arrival of air taxis scheduled to pick up hikers.

Mile 106, Richardson Hwy.
Copper Center, AK
907-822-5234
www.nps.gov/wrst

AT A GLANCE

Southeastern Alaska, 150 miles east of Anchorage ▪ 13,170,000 acres ▪ Mid-May through mid-September ▪ Hiking, camping, backpacking, wildlife-watching, rafting, kayaking, fishing, scenic driving, touring historic sites

Yukon-Charley Rivers National Preserve

Floating adventures on two very different rivers

Bordered on the east by Canada's Yukon Territory, Yukon-Charley Rivers National Preserve is best known for the boating opportunities on its two title rivers. The streams offer adventures in contrast.

The mighty Yukon River runs through the preserve for 128 of its 2,300 miles. Here the river is broad, gently flowing, and bordered by tall bluffs and forested hills. Many visitors travel (by canoe, kayak, raft, or jet boat) between the towns of Eagle and Circle, a trip that takes a minimum of five days for nonmotorized boats (longer if travelers stop to explore their surroundings). Most boaters camp on riverside gravel bars, but a few primitive cabins are available on a first-come, first-served basis.

The Charley River, protected within the preserve for all of its 108 miles, features white-water rapids rated Class II and III (occasionally Class IV during high-water periods). The most common float trip, the 75 miles from Gelvin's airstrip to the Yukon River, takes about six days,

The Kandik River is a tributary of the Yukon River.

with two more days on the Yukon to reach Circle. Rafts, not kayaks or canoes, are the recommended craft on the Charley.

On either river, boaters should be prepared for unexpected bad weather and remoteness from emergency help, and they should take precautions appropriate to the presence of bears and moose. As is the case in much of Alaska, dealing with the logistical aspect of access is the first step in visiting the preserve. A vehicle shuttle is possible on the Yukon, but air travel is a necessity to reach the upper Charley.

There are several historic structures along the Yukon, including relics from the gold-mining era and a former roadhouse.

Eagle Visitor Center
Eagle, AK
907-547-2233
www.nps.gov/yuch

AT A GLANCE

Eastern Alaska, 150 miles east of Fairbanks ▪ 2,500,000 acres ▪ Summer ▪ Boating, backpacking

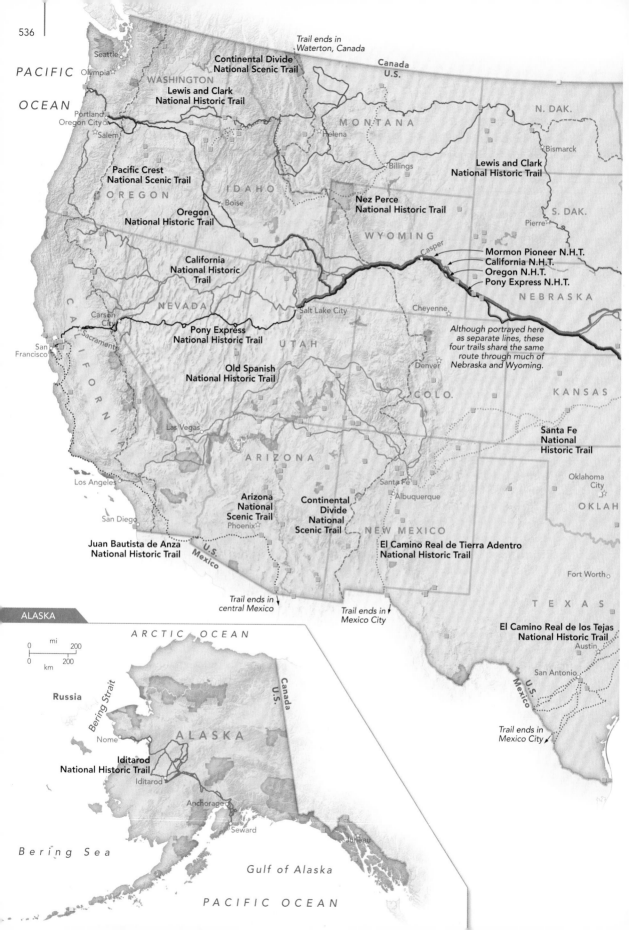

536

PACIFIC
OCEAN

*Trail ends in
Waterton, Canada*

Canada
U.S.

**Continental Divide
National Scenic Trail**

**Lewis and Clark
National Historic Trail**

WASHINGTON

Seattle

Olympia

Portland
Oregon City
Salem

OREGON

**Pacific Crest
National Scenic Trail**

**Oregon
National Historic Trail**

IDAHO

Boise

MONTANA

Helena

Billings

**Lewis and Clark
National Historic Trail**

N. DAK.

Bismarck

S. DAK.

Pierre

WYOMING

Casper

**Nez Perce
National Historic Trail**

**California
National Historic
Trail**

NEVADA

Carson
City
Sacramento

San
Francisco

CALIFORNIA

Los Angeles

San Diego

**Juan Bautista de Anza
National Historic Trail**

**Pony Express
National Historic Trail**

Salt Lake City

UTAH

**Old Spanish
National Historic Trail**

Las Vegas

ARIZONA

Phoenix

**Arizona
National
Scenic Trail**

**Mormon Pioneer N.H.T.
California N.H.T.
Oregon N.H.T.
Pony Express N.H.T.**

Cheyenne

NEBRASKA

*Although portrayed here
as separate lines, these
four trails share the same
route through much of
Nebraska and Wyoming.*

Denver

COLO.

KANSAS

**Santa Fe
National
Historic Trail**

Oklahoma
City

OKLAH

**Continental
Divide
National
Scenic Trail**

NEW MEXICO

Santa Fe
Albuquerque

**El Camino Real de Tierra Adentro
National Historic Trail**

U.S.
Mexico

*Trail ends in
central Mexico*

*Trail ends in
Mexico City*

Fort Worth

TEXAS

**El Camino Real de los Tejas
National Historic Trail**

Austin

San Antonio

U.S.
Mexico

*Trail ends in
Mexico City*

ALASKA

ARCTIC OCEAN

mi
0   200
0   200
km

Russia

Bering Strait

Nome

ALASKA

Canada
U.S.

**Iditarod
National Historic Trail**

Iditarod

Anchorage

Seward

Juneau

Bering Sea

Gulf of Alaska

PACIFIC OCEAN

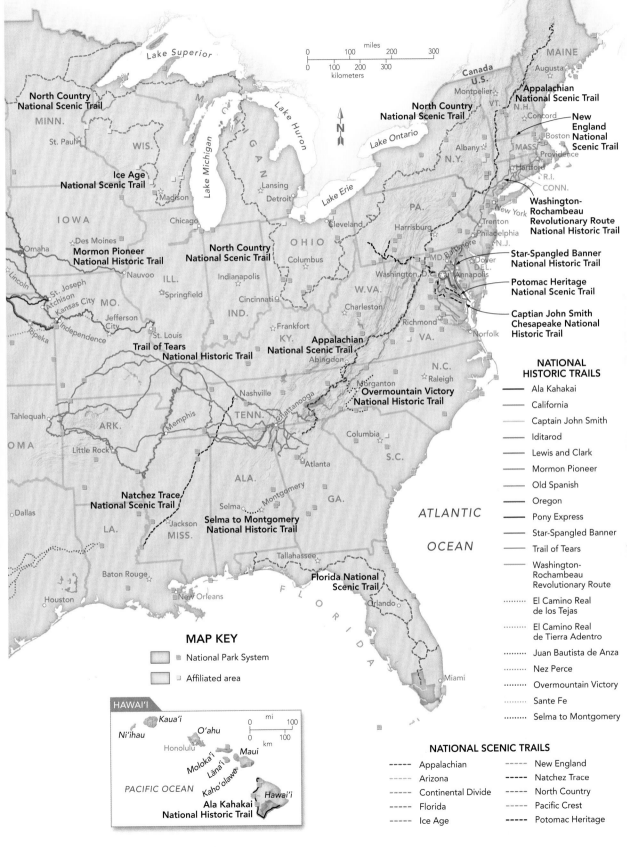

THE NATIONAL TRAILS SYSTEM

537

INDEX

ABOUT THE AUTHOR

Mel White is an Arkansas-based freelance writer specializing in travel and natural history. He has worked on National Geographic Society publications since 1990 and has written more than 100 magazine articles and books covering destinations including Australia, Borneo, the Swiss Alps, the Amazon River, and Madagascar, as well as North American sites from Alaska to the Everglades.

ACKNOWLEDGMENTS

National Geographic Books wishes to thank the National Park Service for all of its assistance on this book, especially for the National Trails map data; for the overall guidance from the Office of Public Affairs, National Park Service; and to staffs of the individual parks for their review of this material and the individual photographs provided.

PHOTO CREDITS

Shutterstock; 237, David Muench/Corbis; 238, ::IntraClique:: LLC/Shutterstock; 239, James P. Blair/National Geographic Creative; 240, NPS; 242, Philip Eckerberg/Shutterstock; 244, iStock.com/ericfoltz; 246-7, NPS; 250-251, Phil Schermeister; 253, NPS; 254, iStock.com/step2626; 256, Jim Pisarowicz/NPS; 258, Tom Bean/Corbis; 260, Terry Smith Images Arkansas Picture Library/Alamy; 261, Randy Olson/National Geographic Creative; 262, Buddy Mays/Corbis; 263, Jose Gil/Shutterstock; 264, Don Smetzer/Alamy; 265, NPS; 267, NPS; 268, Kevin Stewart/Getty Images; 269, Jim Richardson/NGS/Getty Images; 271, Jill Tarchala/ShutterPoint Photography; 272, NPS; 273, AP/The Joplin Globe/Vince Rosati; 275, Rick Grainger/Shutterstock; 276, NPS; 278, Chuck Milliken/NPS; 279, Ulysses S. Grant National Historic Site; 280, NPS; 284-5, Carr Clifton; 287, Tim Thompson; 288, Andre Jenny/Alamy; 290, Michael J. Thompson/Shutterstock; 292, Mike Norton/Shutterstock; 294, NPS; 297, Mike Norton/Shutterstock; 299, iStock.com/ltphoto; 300, urosr/Shutterstock; 302, Nathan Chor/Shutterstock; 303, NPS; 305, Michael J. Thompson/Shutterstock; 306-307, Michael Nichols/National Geographic Creative; 308, Jeffrey M. Frank/Shutterstock; 309, Rich Reid/National Geographic Creative; 310, iStock.com/luchschen; 311, NPS; 312, Robert F. Sisson/National Geographic Creative; 314, iStock.com/ericfoltz; 317, iStock.com/ericfoltz; 320, iStock.com/randymir; 321, NPS; 324, Dean Pennala/Dreamstime.com; 327, Sharon Day/Shutterstock; 328, Wendy Shattil/Bob Rozinski; 330, Mellow/Dreamstime.com; 334, Gary Yim/Shutterstock; 335, iStock.com/HDCineman; 337, iStock.

com/sherwoodimagery; 338-9, iStock.com/David Parsons; 340, iStock.com/David Parsons; 342, 7505811966/Shutterstock; 345, Altrendo Travel/Getty Images; 346, Walter M. Edwards/National Geographic Creative; 347, iStock.com/P_Wei; 349, U.S. Geological Survey; 350, NPS; 351, NPS; 352, Zack Frank/Shutterstock; 353, NPS, Petroglyph National Monument; 355, George H.H. Huey/Corbis; 356, NPS; 357, NPS Photo/Neal Herbert; 358, NPS Photo/Jacob W. Frank; 361, BenC/Shutterstock; 363, Rebecca Roth; 365, Walter M. Edwards/National Geographic Creative; 366-7, Bruce Dale/National Geographic Creative; 368, iStock.com/ericfoltz; 370, Frank Jensen/Utah Office of Tourism; 372, Dean Pennala/Shutterstock; 373, U.S. Geological Survey; 374, Natalia Bratslavsky/Shutterstock; 376, Allen Livingston/ShutterPoint Photography; 377, Don Smetzer/Alamy; 378, Inc/Shutterstock; 379, NPS; 381, kavram/Shutterstock; 383, Stephen Vecchiotti/Dreamstime.com; 386, NPS; 389, Rich Reid/National Geographic Creative; 391, Doug Lemke/Shutterstock; 393, NPS; 394, Phil Schermeister; 396, Phil Schermeister; 397, Phil Schermeister; 398, Phil Schermeister; 400-401, David M. Schrader/Shutterstock; 402, Eugene Buchko/Shutterstock; 404, Michael J. Thompson/Shutterstock; 407, James Feliciano/123RF; 408, Benjamin Chemel/NPS; 409, NPS Photo/Alison Taggart-Barone; 410, Phil Schermeister; 412, iStock.com/ejs9; 414, iStock.com/ericfoltz; 418, NPS; 420, kavram/123RF; 423, Zack Frank/Shutterstock; 424, Phil Schermeister; 426, Phil Hawkins/National Geographic Your Shot; 430, Stephen Vecchiotti/ShutterPoint Photography; 431, Wunson/Shutterstock; 433, Amy Nichole

Harris/Shutterstock; 435, Dan Leeth/Alamy; 437, Tose/Dreamstime.com; 438, Vacclav/Shutterstock; 440, Bcbounders/Dreamstime.com; 442, iStock.com/frontpoint; 444, iStock.com/c_sorvillo; 447, Wikimedia Commons/Daderot (https://creativecommons.org/publicdomain/zero/1.0/legalcode); 450, NPS; 452, AP Photo/Chris Smith; 455, Linda Johnsonbaugh/Shutterstock; 456, Paul Chesley/National Geographic Creative; 459, iStock.com/Zeiss4Me; 460-461, Carr Clifton; 463, Michael S. Lewis/National Geographic Creative; 466, Mike Norton/Shutterstock; 468, Connie Ricca/Corbis; 470, NPS; 471, Zack Frank/Shutterstock; 473, iStock.com/aimintang; 476-7, zschnepf/Shutterstock; 478, iStock.com/Charles Schug; 480, iStock.com/davelogan; 483, Phil Schermeister; 485, Tim Nair/Shutterstock; 486, Mike Vouri/NPS; 487, NPS; 488, iStock.com/Mike Norton; 489, Bob and Bonnie Finney/NPS; 490, iStock.com/Steinthor; 493, NPS; 494, iStock.com/cjmckendry; 495, David Maisel Photography/Getty Images; 497, iStock.com/JudiLen; 498, Michael Melford/National Geographic Creative; 500, Chris Russoniello/NPS; 501, iStock.com/dagsjo; 503, Troy Hamon/NPS; 504, Pat O'Hara/Corbis; 506, Mark Newman/LPI/Getty Images; 510, Hugh Rose/Danita Delimont Agency/Alamy; 512, Tim Rains/NPS; 515, Alaska Stock Images/National Geographic Creative; 517, Roy Wood/NPS; 518-19, George F. Mobley/National Geographic Creative; 522, iStock.com/Dougfir; 524, Lee Prince/Shutterstock.com; 525, Tom Walker/Getty Images; 529, Michael J. Thompson/Shutterstock; 531, iStock.com/Nancy Nehring; 533, NPS; 535, Brian Heaphy/NPS.

Editor's Note: There are several sites that have been designated to become part the National Park Service list of properties. As of press time for this book these locales await further action, acquisition of additional land, or have no visitor facilities. These sites include: Adams Memorial, DC; Blackstone River Valley NHP, RI/MA; Coltsville NHP, CT; Dwight D. Eisenhower Memorial, DC; Harriet Tubman NHP, NY; Manhattan Project NHP, WA/NM/TN; National Desert Storm/Desert Shield Memorial, DC; Ronald Reagan Boyhood Home NHS, IL; Waco Mammoth NM, TX.

The information in this book has been carefully checked and to the best of our knowledge is accurate. However, details are subject to change, and the publisher cannot be responsible for such changes, or for errors or omissions.

COMPLETE
National Parks
OF THE UNITED STATES

Mel White

Published by the National Geographic Society

Gary E. Knell, *President and Chief Executive Officer*

John M. Fahey, *Chairman of the Board*

Declan Moore, *Chief Media Officer*

Chris Johns, *Chief Content Officer*

Prepared by the Book Division

Hector Sierra, *Senior Vice President &*
General Manager

Lisa Thomas, *Senior Vice President &*
Editorial Director

Jonathan Halling, *Creative Director*

Marianne R. Koszorus, *Design Director*

Barbara A. Noe, *Senior Editor*

R. Gary Colbert, *Production Director*

Jennifer A. Thornton, *Director of Managing Editoral*

Susan S. Blair, *Director of Photography*

Meredith C. Wilcox, *Director, Administration*
& Rights Clearance

Staff for 2016 Edition

Caroline Hickey, *Project Editor*

Olivia Garnett, *Text Editor & Researcher*

Sanaa Akkach, Elisa Gibson *Art Directors*

Kay Hankins, *Designer & Illustrations Editor*

Debbie Gibbons, *Director of Intracompany Cartography*

Matthew Chwastyk, *Map Research & Production*

Nicholas P. Rosenbach, *Map Editor*

Allie Fahey, Mark Jenkins, *Contributors*

Marshall Kiker, *Associate Managing Editor*

Judith Klein, *Senior Production Editor*

Will Cline, *Production Project Manager*

Katie Olsen, *Design Production Specialist*

Nicole Miller, *Design Production Assistant*

Darrick McRae, *Manager, Production Services*

The National Geographic Society is one of the world's largest nonprofit scientific and educational organizations. Its mission is to inspire people to care about the planet. Founded in 1888, the Society is member supported and offers a community for members to get closer to explorers, connect with other members, and help make a difference. The Society reaches more than 450 million people worldwide each month through *National Geographic* and other magazines; National Geographic Channel; television documentaries; music; radio; films; books; DVDs; maps; exhibitions; live events; school publishing programs; interactive media; and merchandise. National Geographic has funded more than 10,000 scientific research, conservation, and exploration projects and supports an education program promoting geographic literacy. For more information, visit www.nationalgeographic.com.

For more information, please call 1-800-NGS LINE (647-5463) or write to the following address:

National Geographic Society
1145 17th Street N.W.
Washington, D.C. 20036-4688 U.S.A.

Your purchase supports our nonprofit work and makes you part of our global community. Thank you for sharing our belief in the power of science, exploration, and storytelling to change the world. To activate your member benefits, complete your free membership profile at natgeo.com/joinnow.

For information about special discounts for bulk purchases, please contact National Geographic Books Special Sales: ngspecsales@ngs.org

For rights or permissions inquiries, please contact National Geographic Books Subsidiary Rights: ngbookrights@ngs.org

The Library of Congress has cataloged the the first edition as:

White, Mel, 1950-
  Complete national parks of the United States : featuring 400+ parks, monuments, battlefields, historic sites, scenic trails, recreation areas, and seashores / Mel White.
    p. cm.
  Includes index.
  ISBN 978-1-4262-0527-9 (hardcover) -- ISBN 978-1-4262-0528-6 (deluxe)
  1. National parks and reserves--United States--Guidebooks. 2. National monuments--United States--Guidebooks. 3. Battlefields--United States--Guidebooks. 4. Historic sites--United States--Guidebooks. 5. Coasts--United States--Guidebooks. 6. Recreation areas--United States--Guidebooks. 7. Wild and scenic rivers--United States--Guidebooks. 8. United States--Guidebooks. I. Title.
  E160.W47 2009
  917.3--dc22

                    2009026852

ISBN: 978-1-4262-1692-3 (hardcover)
ISBN: 978-1-4262-1729-6 (deluxe)

Printed in China

15/RRDS/1